KU-256-707

Marsilius of Padua

THE DEFENDER OF PEACE

VOLUME I · MARSILIUS OF PADUA AND MEDIEVAL POLITICAL PHILOSOPHY

Number XLVI of the

RECORDS OF CIVILIZATION, SOURCES AND STUDIES

Austin P. Evans, Editor

Marsilius of Padua

THE DEFENDER OF PEACE

Volume I: Marsilius of Padua and Medieval Political Philosophy

by ALAN GEWIRTH

ASSOCIATE PROFESSOR OF PHILOSOPHY

UNIVERSITY OF CHICAGO

COLUMBIA UNIVERSITY PRESS

New York and London

The American Council of Learned Societies

AND THE

Department of Philosophy of Columbia University

HAVE GENEROUSLY PROVIDED FUNDS

TO ASSIST IN THE PUBLICATION OF THIS VOLUME

First printing 1951
Third printing 1964

MANUFACTURED IN THE UNITED STATES OF AMERICA

Records of Civilization, Sources and Studies

To My Parents

PREFACE

THIS is the first of two volumes on the political philosophy of Marsilius of Padua. The second volume, which is to appear shortly, will contain a complete translation of Marsilius' *Defensor pacis,* together with an introduction and notes.

The justification for presenting this work on the famous fourteenth-century political thinker is perhaps too obvious to require elaboration. Yet it is only as peripheral to that justification that I would mention the lack of any adequate study of Marsilius in English, the vital part played by his treatise and his ideas in the crises which convulsed western civilization from the fourteenth to the sixteenth centuries and which produced the modern world, and the vigorous interest in him which, renewed about a century ago, has grown increasingly strong in recent years. Apart from strictly antiquarian concerns, the study of the great political philosophies of the past has as its chief justification the aid it can give in the philosophic task of understanding ourselves and the bases of our society, both as dynamic outgrowths of past eras and as bearers of an at least partially permanent structure. In this task, the doctrine of Marsilius has, I believe, a profound contribution to make. He is one of the few truly revolutionary figures in the history of political philosophy; and the effects and the problems of the revolution he propounded are still with us. The Marsilian revolution consisted not only in the radical change in the theory of the relations of "church" and "state," religion and politics, which culminated in the Protestant Reformation and other central developments of the modern era, but, even more importantly, in the whole conception of man, his nature, acts, values, and socio-political relations, on which the advocacy of that change was at least partly based. To elucidate the perennial issues raised by Marsilianism in this latter form has been the ultimate aim of the present study. The execution of this aim has involved not only the analysis of Marsilius' basic concepts and doctrines but also the concomitant examination of the whole panorama of medieval political philosophy, particularly in its later stages. Despite the labors of such scholars as Gierke and Carlyle, much can still be learned concerning this crucial period in the history of political ideas through its confrontation with the challenging figure of whom one of his sixteenth-century critics said: *homo fuit magis Aristotelicus quam Christianus.*

The intensely controversial character of Marsilius' ideas has continued to the present day; concerning no other medieval thinker do partisan attitudes persist with such vehemence. Consequently, the ideal of objectivity, so difficult of achievement in any discussion concerned with politics, is perhaps unattainable in dealing with the Paduan. Nevertheless, I have endeavored to avoid the approach, common in much of the Marsilian literature, of identifying him unqualifiedly with the forces of good or of evil, or labelling him with various encomia or epithets according to preconceived simple standards of social truth or value. With respect to one especially popular mode of such labelling, I have eschewed the temptation to classify him outright either as a liberal democrat opposed to the papal and monarchic authoritarians of his age, or as a left-wing totalitarian opposed, according to the individual commentator's predilections, to the right-wing totalitarianism or the divinely inspired justice of the papalist adherents. The political and axiological components of the medieval and modern worlds, as well as of Marsilius' political philosophy, are too complex to be reduced to a few general formulae on which complete approval or rejection should follow automatically. If this study should succeed in exhibiting and clarifying some of this complexity at the level of conceptual analysis, it will have fulfilled one of its chief aims; and thereby too, it is hoped, it will have forestalled a too facile identification of the present writer with any one side of his subject matter.

I am profoundly grateful to Professor Richard P. McKeon for the help he has given me in many ways over many years, and especially for furnishing me with a model of philosophizing which, reflected all too inadequately in the present work, has yet been a source of constant inspiration. I have benefited from the kindly guidance of Professor Herbert W. Schneider, both with respect to the general plan of this work and in particular connection with the religious aspects of Marsilianism. To Professor Dino Bigongiari I owe some valuable clues to the institutional background of Marsilius' doctrines; his aid with respect to the translation of the *Defensor pacis* will be acknowledged more fully in the second volume. Professor Austin P. Evans clarified my understanding of a number of historical matters. For helpful suggestions on particular points, I am also indebted to Professors John H. Randall, Jr., James Gutmann, Paul O. Kristeller, and Ernest A. Moody. Among my predecessors in the field of Marsilian studies, I have profited most from the work of Lagarde, McIlwain, Battaglia, and Previté-Orton; I should not wish my various criticisms of the first two of these scholars to obscure this indebtedness.

The aid of the following institutions is hereby gratefully acknowledged: the Rockefeller Foundation, for the award of a Post-War Fellowship in the Humanities which enabled me to finish this work in 1947; Columbia University, and especially its Department of Philosophy, for awarding me the Woodbridge Prize; the American Council of Learned Societies, for a subvention toward the cost of publication.

This volume is dedicated to my parents.

A. G.

Chicago, Illinois
February, 1951

NOTE ON REFERENCES

The *Defensor pacis* is referred to in the footnotes without explicit mention of its title, except when it would otherwise be doubtful which work was being cited. Thus, such a reference as "I. xii. 3" means: *Defensor pacis,* Dictio I, cap. xii, par. 3. The division of each chapter into numbered paragraphs renders unnecessary any reference to page numbers in the editions; but citations have uniformly been taken from the edition of C. W. Previté-Orton, Cambridge, 1928.

Other works are referred to in the editions listed in the Bibliography. For the sake of brevity, such references have uniformly omitted all data save those required for identification of the passage being cited; thus, the reader should consult the Bibliography for full titles, editions, volume numbers where relevant, and other information. For example, "Albert the Great *In Eth.* Lib. x. Tr. I. cap. xi (p. 620)" refers to page 620 of Volume VII of Albert's *Opera omnia,* edited by A. Borgnet, Paris, 1890–99; since Albert's *In Ethicorum libros* is listed in the Bibliography as being contained in Volume VII of Borgnet's edition, it has been deemed unnecessary to give the volume number as well as the page number with each reference to this work. On the other hand, where a work is contained in several volumes of the edition listed, the volume number as well as the page number has been given; thus, in such a reference as "*Corp. jur. can., Decretal. Greg. IX* Lib. I. Tit. 6. cap. 56 (II, 95)," the numbers in parentheses refer to Volume II, column 95 of E. Friedberg's edition of the *Corpus juris canonici,* Leipzig, 1879–81.

In quotations of primary sources, italics for emphasis are mine.

The following standard abbreviations have been employed:

MGH = *Monumenta Germaniae historica.*

PL = *Patrologiae cursus completus,* series Latina, ed. J. P. Migne, Paris, 1844–64.

CONTENTS

Marsilius of Padua

THE DEFENDER OF PEACE

VOLUME I · MARSILIUS OF PADUA AND MEDIEVAL POLITICAL PHILOSOPHY

CHAPTER I

THE HISTORICAL BACKGROUND

1. THE APPROACH TO MARSILIUS

EVERY POLITICAL PHILOSOPHY is involved in many different dimensions of meaning. To the extent that it is philosophic, it deals with general problems of human society and political authority, problems which transcend its time; it propounds solutions of permanent relevance, and bases them upon premises which the philosopher usually claims to have attained by intellectual methods. But his view of these problems is conditioned by the historical context which generated them in the particular form in which they presented themselves to him; and since in this form they are usually subjects of intense partisanship, the philosophy itself assumes a polemical, non-cognitive character. For an adequate interpretation of the philosophy, therefore, it is at once necessary and difficult to do justice to all these aspects: the historically particular as well as the philosophically general, the polemical as well as the cognitive. An interpretation which treats the philosophy solely as a piece of propaganda or rationalization, or as exhaustively confined by its historical context, leaves unexplained the important lessons which it has for later ages and ignores the conceptual framework upon which it is based. On the other hand, if the particular circumstances and problems which give concrete meaning to its concepts are overlooked, the result is an excessive generality and an anachronism frequently involving claims of prophetic anticipation which ignore important differences both in institutions and in doctrines.

The political philosophy of Marsilius of Padua, contained in his one great work, the *Defensor pacis,* provides a supreme example of these difficulties of interpretation. He has frequently been acclaimed as the most important and most original political thinker of the middle ages,[1] and this for reasons not medieval but modern. For he has been hailed as the great

[1] E. Emerton, *The Defensor Pacis of Marsiglio of Padua,* p. 1: "His book has often been called the most remarkable literary product of the Middle Ages, and I am inclined to accept that verdict." H. B. Workman, *Christian Thought to the Reformation* (London, 1911), p. 218: "the most original political treatise of the middle ages." R. G. Gettell, *History of Political Thought* (New York, 1924), p. 120: "the greatest and most original political treatise of the middle ages was the work of Marsiglio of Padua." H. J. Laski, "Political Theory in the Later Middle Ages," *Cambridge Medieval History,* VIII (1936), p. 650: "it is difficult, in the long range of medieval philosophy, to find any thinker with a deeper insight into the conditions of human association."

prophet of modern times[2] and the precursor of nearly every significant modern political theorist, doctrine, and development: Machiavelli and the divorce of morals and politics,[3] Luther and the Protestant Reformation,[4] the ecclesiastic polity of Hooker and other Elizabethans,[5] Bodin's doctrine of legislative sovereignty,[6] the omnipotent state of Hobbes,[7] Locke's religious toleration,[8] Montesquieu's separation of powers,[9] the democratic

[2] E. Friedberg, *Die mittelalterlichen Lehren über das Verhältnis von Staat und Kirche,* p. 49: "Fast wird man veranlasst, einen Anachronismus anzunehmen, und für ein Werk des sechzehnten Jahrhunderts anzusehen, was der kühnste Denker des vierzehnten construirt hat." R. L. Poole, *Illustrations of the History of Medieval Thought,* p. 240: "The two books of the *Defensor Pacis* thus comprise . . . the whole essence of the political and religious theory which separates modern times from the middle ages. . . Marsiglio belongs to that rarest class of doctrinaires whom future ages may rightly look back upon as prophets." C. W. Previté-Orton, "Marsiglio of Padua, Doctrines," *English Historical Review,* XXXVIII (1923), 2: "he is the prophet of succeeding times, the promulgator of new theories which have only received a general acquiescence since the French Revolution." R. H. Murray, *History of Political Science* (Cambridge, 1929), p. 81: "he not merely divined the Europe of his own day, but he also divined the Europe of ages unborn." Laski, *op. cit.,* p. 629: "The conceptions they [Marsilius' theses] involve foreshadow almost every point of modern political philosophy."

[3] A. Dempf, *Sacrum Imperium,* p. 432: "er ist philosophisch tieferer und feinerer Machiavellismus als der des Machiavell selbst." See also C. Benoist, *Le Machiavélisme* (Paris, 1907), p. 335; A. Solmi, *Il pensiero politico di Dante* (Florence, 1922), p. 67; G. de Lagarde, *Marsile de Padoue ou le premier théoricien de l'état laïque,* pp. 91–92, 246; P. Mesnard, *L'Essor de la philosophie politique au XVIe siècle* (Paris, 1936), p. 79; A. P. d'Entrèves, *The Medieval Contribution to Political Thought,* pp. 18, 83; F. Battaglia, "Sul *Defensor Pacis* di Marsilio da Padova," *Nuovi studi di diritto, economia e politica,* II (1929), 145–46.

[4] O. von Gierke, *Political Theories of the Middle Age,* trans. F. W. Maitland (Cambridge, 1900), p. 5: "many of the ideas of the Reformation, and even many of the ideas of the French Revolution were proclaimed, though in scholastic garb, by such men as Marsilius of Padua. . . ." See F. Laurent, *L'Eglise et l'état* (Brussels, 1858), p. 132; B. Labanca, "Marsilio da Padova e Martino Lutero," *Nuova antologia,* XLI (1883), 210 ff.; Laski, *op. cit.,* p. 628.

[5] See the parallels between Marsilius and Hooker listed by Previté-Orton, "Marsilius of Padua," *Proceedings of the British Academy,* XXI (1935), 165–66. See also R. Scholz, "Marsilius von Padua und die Idee der Demokratie," *Zeitschrift für Politik,* I (1908), 91; d'Entrèves, *Medieval Contribution,* pp. 112–13, 140; F. L. Baumer, "Thomas Starkey and Marsilius of Padua," *Politica,* II (1936), 188–205. See also below, p. 303, n. 7; p. 304, n. 9.

[6] F. Battaglia, *Marsilio da Padova e la filosofia politica del medio evo,* p. 96: "In questa costruzione legislativa Marsilio si distacca dal medio evo. . . Si ricongiunge a Bodin, e prima di lui afferma come derivazione necessaria della sovranità il diritto di far leggi." Previté-Orton, "Marsilius of Padua," p. 153: "He may be said to discover sovereignty in the Austinian sense long before Jean Bodin. . . ." See also C. E. Osborne, *Christian Ideas in Political History* (London, 1929), pp. 157–58.

[7] A. P. d'Entrèves, "La Fortuna di Marsilio da Padova in Inghilterra," *Giornale degli economisti e annali di economia,* n.s., II (1940), 151: "Le immagini possenti create dall' Hobbes sembrano tradurre in un linguaggio nuovo le vecchie idee marsiliane." See *ibid.,* p. 152, and also Battaglia, *Marsilio,* p. 58; Osborne, *op. cit.,* p. 158; J. Beneyto Perez, *Historia de las doctrinas politicas* (Madrid, 1948), p. 206.

[8] J. MacKinnon, *A History of Modern Liberty* (London, 1906), I, 383: "Marsilius of Padua advocated a thoroughgoing toleration three and a half centuries before John Locke." See also P. Janet, *Histoire de la science politique dans ses rapports avec la morale,* 3d ed. (Paris, 1887), I, 461; F. Ruffini, *La libertà religiosa* (Turin, 1901), p. 47; A. Matagrin, *Histoire de la tolérance religieuse* (Paris, 1905), p. 133; Scholz, *op. cit.,* p. 91; Murray, *op. cit.,* p. 87; H. Kohler, *Studien aus dem Strafrecht* (Mannheim, 1897), pp. 732 ff.; A. S. Turberville, *Medieval Heresy and the Inquisition* (London, 1920), p. 83.

[9] F. Pollock, *History of the Science of Politics* (London, 1883), p. 17: "Marsilius likewise

theories of Rousseau and the French Revolution,[10] nineteenth-century doctrines of socialism,[11] and Marx's materialist interpretation of ideologies.[12] This diversity in the descendants attributed to Marsilius is startling enough to indicate something of the complexity and the fecund suggestiveness of his ideas. In recent years, however, there has been a reaction against some of the earlier panegyric approaches: scholars have asserted that Marsilius' specifically political conceptions contain nothing new,[13] that the modern doctrines which had been acclaimed in his thought are not even there,[14] and particularly that his popular sovereignty or democracy is more apparent than real.[15] Indeed, so far has the pendulum swung in the opposite direction (although with the same predilection for modern terminology)

---

distinctly marked the separation of the executive power (which he calls by its modern name) from the legislative." See also A. Franck, *Réformateurs et publicistes de l'Europe: moyen âge,* p. 144; G. Vadalà-Papale, "Le leggi nella dottrina di Dante Alighieri e di Marsilio da Padova," in *Studi giuridici a F. Schupfer,* p. 82; Scholz, *op. cit.,* pp. 74–75; A. Cappa-Legora, *La politica di Dante e di Marsilio da Padova,* p. 84; E. Ruffini-Avondo, *"Il Defensor Pacis* di Marsilio da Padova," *Rivista storica italiana,* XLI (1924), 134.

[10] F. Atger, *Essai sur l'histoire des doctrines du contrat social,* p. 71: "Il est le créateur de ce radicalisme politique qui compte Althusius et Rousseau parmi ses illustres représentants." F. von Bezold, "Die Lehre von der Volksouveranität während des Mittelalters," *Historische Zeitschrift,* XXXVI (1876), 346: Marsilius upholds unrestricted sovereignty of the people, "wie im heutigen Amerika." Comparison to the United States of America is also made by F. Scaduto, *Stato e chiesa negli scritti politici dalla fine della lotta per le investiture sino alla morte di Ludovico il Bavaro,* p. 122. Scholz, *op. cit.,* p. 92: "Beide [i.e., Marsilius and Rousseau] sind revolutionär, beide Verkünder einer neuen Weltanschauung, einer neuen sozialen Ordnung." See Franck, *op. cit.,* p. 143; Labanca, *Marsilio,* p. 174; d'Entrèves, *Medieval Contribution,* p. 63; and above, nn. 2, 4.

[11] Labanca, *Marsilio,* pp. 223–24: "Il nostro Marsilio è profeta dell' avvenire, o ch' è lo stesso, padre della storia, anche per aver presentiti nella sua opera alcuni principii del contemporaneo Socialismo." See *ibid.,* p. 174.

[12] P. Sorokin, *Contemporary Sociological Theories* (New York, 1928), p. 544: The Marxian theory of ideologies "was expressed, and more clearly, many centuries before Marx. . . A sufficient example is furnished in the *Defensor Pacis* of Marsilius of Padua, where we find quite a 'materialistic' interpretation of the role of religion, and of the discrepancy between the objective reality and its disfigured reflection in beliefs and ideologies."

[13] Cf. R. W. and A. J. Carlyle, *A History of Mediaeval Political Theory in the West* (Edinburgh, 1903–1936), VI, 9: "He is not, as appears to be thought by some writers who are not very well acquainted with mediaeval political literature, setting out some new and revolutionary democratic doctrine, but is rather expressing, even if in rather drastic and unqualified terms, the normal judgment and practice of the Middle Ages: he represents not the beginning of some modern and revolutionary doctrine, but the assertion of traditional principles." M. de Wulf, *Histoire de la philosophie médiévale,* 5th ed. (Paris, 1925), II, 210: "Marsile de Padoue ne fait que donner des interprétations plus larges de principes empruntés à ses prédécesseurs."

[14] C. H. McIlwain, *The Growth of Political Thought in the West,* p. 307: "Most of the mistakes made in interpreting this interesting political treatise are the result of reading into it a meaning which was never there. There is nothing in it of democracy, nothing of majority rule, no 'separation of powers'. . . ."

[15] J. Rivière, "Marsile de Padoue," *Dictionnaire de théologie catholique,* X, 160: "Rien, en tout cas, ne permet de voir en lui un précurseur de l'idéal révolutionnaire à la manière de J.-J. Rousseau." Cf. G. Piovano, "Il *Defensor Pacis* di Marsilio Patavino," *Scuola cattolica,* 5th series, XXII (1922), 167; Lagarde, *Marsile,* p. 198; N. Valois, "Jean de Jandun et Marsile de Padoue, auteurs du *Defensor Pacis,"* p. 587.

that Marsilius, while being called an opponent of totalitarianism,[16] is now also himself declared to be a totalitarian.[17]

Whatever else may be indicated by the sequence of these comments, they emphasize both the continuing relevance of Marsilius' ideas for the broad problems of political philosophy, and the extreme caution which must be exercised in tracing that relevance. It is not difficult to find in the variation of critical interpretations the influence not only of improved scholarship but also of recent political developments which Marsilius could not have foreseen. And in some interpretations it is also easy to see clear traces of that same polemical partisanship in which he himself was engaged, for while much of the acclamation of his prophetic brilliance has come from Protestants, Catholics have castigated his work as an "infernal machine" [18] which undermined all that was good in medieval institutions. The very setting which Marsilius provides for his enterprise, however, seems to invite such interpretations which generalize the significance of his doctrines beyond their particular historical context. For on the one hand, he emphasizes in his opening chapter the uniqueness of the historical problem to which his treatise is addressed: it is a problem which arose long after Aristotle's time, and neither he nor any other ancient philosopher could have foreseen its specific character or scope.[19] Yet Marsilius then goes on to base his solution of the problem on Aristotle's *Politics,* and on general principles concerning the nature of the state and of political authority.

This ambivalence is in no sense a contradiction. The Marsilian politics is whole-heartedly involved in a great historical polemic; and yet its significance reaches far beyond that polemic, both because of the nature of the problem out of which it arose and because of Marsilius' approach to it. The immediate purpose to which the *Defensor pacis* is dedicated is the refutation of what he calls the "perverted opinion . . . pernicious to the human race" [20] that the pope of the Roman Catholic Church is endowed

[16] See F. Gavin, *Seven Centuries of the Problem of Church and State* (Princeton, 1938), p. 106: "Marsiglio of Padua in his *Defensor Pacis* in 1324 made the ground ready for not only an implicit but an explicit recognition of another principle as a corrective to the papal totalitarianism."

[17] P. Mesnard, *L'Essor de la philosophie politique au XVIe siècle* (Paris, 1936), p. 9: "Le *Defensor Pacis,* le *Defensor Minor,* nous donnent pour la première fois une théorie radicale de l'Etat totalitaire." E. F. Jacob, *Essays in the Conciliar Epoch* (Manchester, 1943), p. 93: "Marsilius, the totalitarian, has scarcely any conception of the church as a self-governing body. . . ." See also D. J. B. Hawkins, *A Sketch of Medieval Philosophy* (New York, 1947), p. 141; J. Bowle, *Western Political Thought* (New York, 1948), p. 240; J. Beneyto Perez, *Historia de las doctrinas politicas* (Madrid, 1948), p. 206. See also below, pp. 304–5 and n. 10.

[18] See Piovano, *op. cit.,* p. 164.

[19] I. i. 3, 7. See I. xix. 3.

[20] I. i. 3; see I. xix. 13: "perniciosa pestis haec, humanae quieti atque felicitati suae omni adversans penitus. . . ." See also the resolve to carry the polemic into "external execution," I. xix. 13; II. iv. 13.

with "plenitude of power." Marsilius' work thus belongs directly to that long tradition known as the church-state controversy, which, having grown out of the historical drama whereby a persecuted religious sect was made the established church of the Roman Empire, came to generate a degree of bitterness and a range of doctrinal discussion unparalleled in antecedent political thought.[21] In one sense, therefore, it is quite true, as he himself points out, that this was a problem unknown to ancient philosophers. One looks in vain in Plato, Aristotle, or Cicero for a situation in which the central issue concerns the relation of a "temporal power" to a visible and distinct "spiritual power." Yet not only did this problem occupy the bulk of political thinkers from the eleventh to the sixteenth centuries, but it was also of important concern to such later philosophers as Hobbes, Locke, and Rousseau; and its ramifications have still not entirely disappeared from the political scene.

From a broader point of view, moreover, the church-state conflict not only fits into the tradition of political philosophy as a whole, but it exhibits certain fundamental aspects of that tradition with exceptional sharpness. The proof of this statement cannot, indeed, be given with complete unambiguity at this point; for the determination of what constitutes the object of political philosophy has itself traditionally been involved in many of the same kinds of disagreements as have affected the discussion of particular political problems. Whether the basic subject matter and categories of politics are moral, theological, psychological, economic, or of some other kind is a question which has divided the tradition of political thinkers no less sharply than have the more immediate issues with which they have dealt; and the answer to the former problem has frequently been an important factor conditioning the position taken on those issues themselves. Moreover, in specific reference to the present question, the very meanings of the central concepts entering into the controversy were themselves among the main objects of dispute. The various parties differed strongly on the definitions to be given to such terms as "church," "state," "spiritual," and "temporal,"[22] so that a completely neutral indication of the relation of the conflict to traditional political thought is for this further reason difficult of attainment.

It is possible, however, to indicate at least a significant initial aspect of

[21] For the development of the controversy, particular reference may be made to the excellent accounts and bibliographies in the *Cambridge Medieval History,* especially Volumes IV, V, and VI; and, for the doctrinal information, to Carlyle, *op. cit.,* Vol. IV and Vol. V, Part II.

[22] On the relation of these points to Marsilius and the church-state controversy, see below, pp. 46 ff., 93 ff., 101 ff., 261 ff., 292 ff. On the general question of the subject matter and categories of politics, see A. Gewirth, "Political Power and Democratic Psychiatry," *Ethics,* LIX (1949), pp. 136–42; and "The Psychological Approach to Politics," *ibid.,* pp. 211–20.

the church-state controversy which will emphasize, in a manner directly recognizable to modern readers, the continuity of that controversy with basic phases of political thought as a whole. For the disputants on both sides held that the conflict was over *power:* long indeed would be the list of works written on both sides of the controversy and bearing some such word as *potestas* in their titles.[23] In Marsilius' direct doctrinal opponents, who upheld the "church" side of the conflict at the end of the thirteenth century and the early years of the fourteenth—such largely forgotten men as Egidius of Rome, James of Viterbo, Henry of Cremona, Augustinus Triumphus, Alexander of St. Elpidius—the claims and arguments in behalf of the papal plenitude of power brought the whole conception of political power to an unparalleled degree of development. To the pope, as vicar of Christ, was attributed supreme rulership and jurisdiction over all men in both spiritual and temporal affairs.[24] The papal power is full (*plenum*) in the sense that no greater political power can possibly belong to a human being in this life; it is above all other power; it contains all power, temporal as well as spiritual; it acts upon all other power, so that no other power is legitimate unless subjected to it; and no other power can in turn react upon it.[25] Hence the temporal government is at most the "executive" or "minister" of the pope;[26] it must be established and judged by him;[27] its laws must serve and conform to those of the pope and undergo his examination and approval.[28] It follows, therefore, that the pope can depose the temporal ruler when in his judgment the ruler's crime or injustice requires it.[29]

The defense of these far-reaching claims involved the papalist writers

[23] See the treatises entitled *De ecclesiastica potestate* of Egidius of Rome, Alexander of St. Elpidius, Augustinus Triumphus; the *De potestate papae* of Henry of Cremona; the *De potestate regia et papali* of John of Paris; the *De imperatorum et pontificum potestate* of William of Ockham.

[24] See Egidius of Rome *De ecclesiastica potestate* I. ii; III. iv (pp. 9, 50) and *passim*. James of Viterbo *De regimine Christiano* II. v, ix (pp. 208, 273). Augustinus Triumphus *Summa de ecclesiastica potestate* qu.1. aa.3, 4. Ptolemy of Lucca *De regimine principum* III. x, xix (pp. 59–60, 73). Henry of Cremona *De potestate papae,* p. 465. Alexander of St. Elpidius *Tractatus de ecclesiastica potestate* Tr. II. cap. iv–ix (pp. 18–27).

[25] Egidius *De eccl. pot.* III. x (pp. 196–99). See the similar list of the attributes of plenitude of power given by James of Viterbo *De reg. Christ.* II. ix (p. 273).

[26] Egidius *De eccl. pot.* III. iv (p. 163). Augustinus Triumphus *S. de eccl. pot.* qu.1. a.1.

[27] The papalists here cite the statement of Hugh of St. Victor *De sacramentis* II. ii. 4 (PL 176, 418): "Nam spiritualis potestas terrenam potestatem et instituere habet ut sit et judicare si bona non fuerit." See Egidius *De eccl. pot.* I. iv, v (pp. 11–12, 17). James of Viterbo *De reg. Christ.* II. vii, x (pp. 234, 295). Augustinus Triumphus *S. de eccl. pot.* qu.1. a.1; qu.44. a.4.

[28] Egidius *De eccl. pot.* III. viii (p. 188). James of Viterbo *De reg. Christ.* II. vii, viii (pp. 234, 260–61). Augustinus Triumphus *S. de eccl. pot.* qu.1. a.3.

[29] James of Viterbo *De reg. Christ.* II. vii (pp. 234–35). Augustinus Triumphus *S. de eccl. pot.* qu.46. a.2.

in a detailed consideration of almost every conceivable question bearing upon political power: its nature, kinds, sources, locus, justification, conditions, limits. And in opposing these claims, Marsilius had to deal with the same questions. It is for this reason that his work constitutes not merely a polemic but a political philosophy, which continues to be of intense interest long after the disappearance of the particular controversy with which he was directly concerned.

Amid the many disagreements of commentators as to the precise nature of this interest which they uniformly attribute to Marsilius' treatise, they agree at least that he propounded a revolutionary solution to the historic conflict between the temporal and spiritual powers. Where the extreme papalists asserted a thoroughgoing control of the spiritual power over the temporal, and where the moderates on both sides argued for a parallelism of the two powers, Marsilius set up a thoroughgoing control of the temporal power over the spiritual. There were, to be sure, precedents for this position in the law books of Justinian, where the *jus sacrum* was part of the *jus publicum*,[30] and in such documents of the investiture controversy, written early in the twelfth century, as the anonymous *York Tracts* and Gregory of Catino's *Orthodoxa defensio imperialis*.[31] But in none of these sources was the position propounded with the scope and detail, nor defended with the breadth of principles and arguments, found in the *Defensor pacis*.

It is, indeed, in these principles and arguments that the basic intelligibility of Marsilius' admittedly revolutionary conclusions is to be sought. The mere assertion of a position is never important in itself. The permanent significance of Marsilius' ideas is to be found not merely in his opposition to the papal and ecclesiastic institutions of medieval Christendom, but in the entire doctrinal structure which he adduces in support of such opposition. That structure is concerned with the basic problems of political power which have already been cited, so that Marsilius' novel ecclesiastic politics is from this point of view less important than the general political ideas from which the former was deduced. Moreover, since whatever is in the conclusion must in some way be in the premises, the force of Marsilius' ecclesiastic ideas is to be found equally in his solution of the problems of political power as such: those problems receive at his hands a consistent and striking treatment from a fresh point of view.

The question of "novelty" and "modernity" is almost inevitably introduced into any discussion of Marsilius' achievement. Philosophically, whether a doctrine is "new" or "old," "modern" or "medieval," has nothing

[30] See *Corp. jur. civ.*, *Digestum* I. i. 2; *Codex passim*.

[31] On these works see Carlyle, *op. cit.*, III, 122 ff.; IV, 107–8, 272–83.

to do with either its meaning or its value. Yet a doctrine is best understood when one grasps not only its continuity with antecedent doctrines but also what distinctive contribution, if any, it makes to the discussion of the problems with which it deals. From this perspective, it is important to recognize that in opposing the theory of papal plenitude of power, which in many ways represented the culmination of medieval theologico-political ideas, Marsilius both used the materials common to all the political thinkers of his time and gave them some drastically different interpretations. Historically, therefore, his doctrine presents both the vestiges of medieval political ideas and the germs of modern ideas, in such fashion that their interrelations, their aspects of continuity and discontinuity, are brought out with great clarity. The significance of this combination is not that Marsilius is to be congratulated on the one and commiserated on the other, according to the predilections of the individual commentator, but that a study of his work can help to make clear the basic premises and assumptions of many of the political attitudes and ideas we call "modern," by examining them in a strategic juncture with the ideas they superseded. And philosophically, even apart from this historical perspective, Marsilius presents an analysis of basic human political problems from a point of view which is permanently significant. Indeed, while he could not have foreseen the occurrence of the recent institutional developments which have been a partial factor in the conflicting interpretations passed upon his work, his analysis provides lessons which are themselves suited to explain the nature of many of those same developments.

It is in these historical and philosophic factors—the profound importance of Marsilius' work for the understanding not only of a crucial period in medieval thought but also of the nature of the human political situation as such—that the justification for the present study lies. The fact that there does not yet exist an adequate study of Marsilius' ideas in English is merely a supplementary consideration; for the studies in other languages have too frequently obscured the essential content and contribution of the Marsilian politics by entering into the same polemic in which he himself engaged, or by an overeagerness to find in his work anticipations of favored modern developments.

The approach of the present study to the political philosophy of Marsilius is determined by the above considerations. Three main aspects will characterize this approach: the systematic, the comparative, and the institutional-biographical.

First, the attempt will be made to analyze the content and method of Marsilius' own doctrines, by examining their essential rationale and by making clear the nature of their premises and the meaning and scope of the conclusions which follow from them. The doctrines will here be viewed, as Marsilius himself viewed them, as constituting a systematic and coherent political philosophy which, whether ultimately true or false, good or bad, deals with the perennial issues of human politics.

Secondly, the Marsilian ideas will be studied in relation to those of his predecessors, who comprise what we shall call "the medieval tradition." This tradition was itself composed of various elements: institutionally, the devices and concepts of feudalism and of Roman and canon law; philosophically, the doctrines of Augustinianism, which were dominant throughout the greater part of the middle ages, and of Aristotelianism, which became an important influence from the middle of the thirteenth century onward. Writing in 1324, Marsilius inherited this tradition; but his manner of dealing with its elements marked a decided change from the traditional combinations erected by such philosophers as Thomas Aquinas and Egidius of Rome. For a full understanding of Marsilius' contribution to political philosophy, therefore, it is necessary to view his ideas in the context of this antecedent tradition which constituted his point of departure and by comparison with which the specific character and scope of his contribution can be measured.

Thirdly, Marsilius' ideas will be studied against the background of his own life and institutional setting. This background supplies the particular context for the two factors previously indicated; for it was through Marsilius' experience and education that he came to grapple in his own peculiar manner with the historical problems that agitated his time. Hence, while this context is by no means a sufficient explanation of all phases of the Marsilian doctrine, it can help to illuminate many of those phases by indicating the particular occasions and circumstances out of which they arose.

These three aspects of the approach to Marsilius involve a conspicuous omission. We shall study him in relation to his own past and present; but what of his relation to the future? The comparison of Marsilius' ideas with those of subsequent thinkers has, indeed, been the aspect most emphasized by the bulk of Marsilian commentators. Apart from its intrinsic interest and importance, such comparison has a clear justification in Marsilius' own convictions; for he regarded himself not only as a destroyer of past doctrines and institutions but also as a creator of new ones, and in many respects he was right on both counts. But the comparison of Marsilius with subsequent developments, to the end of ascertaining the former's anticipations of the latter, logically requires, if it is to be done adequately, a careful prior consideration of the three aspects listed above as characterizing the approach of the present study. Unless one knows what the Marsilian doctrines are, in their relevant content and systematization, and what are their relations to antecedent doctrines, one cannot know what is "new" and what is "old" in Marsilius, how far he "anticipates" later developments, and to what extent such anticipations are common to other writers in the tradition. Indeed, many of the earlier studies of Marsilius have been vitiated by acclaiming in his thought departures from the medieval tradition, and anticipations of subsequent developments, which a closer study of Marsilius and of his predecessors would have shown not to be such departures or anticipations. Moreover, the approach to Marsilius in terms of his anticipation of later developments requires, if it is to be adequate, a far more careful examination of the nature of those developments themselves than most past Marsilian commentators have undertaken.

The present study, then, will consider specific modern doctrines only at points where such consideration is particularly relevant to establishing important historical interrelations. Primary attention, however, will be centered upon the immanent characteristics of Marsilius' doctrines, and upon the tradition of medieval political philosophy from which he took his point of departure and in relation to which his novelties and anticipations, insofar as they are such, are to be understood.

With respect to the first aspect of our approach to Marsilius, one further point must be made. The *Defensor pacis* is divided into three "discourses" (*dictiones*), of which the third is a brief summary of conclusions. It is usual among commentators to view the first two discourses as dealing respectively with the "state" and the "church," and to divide their own studies of the work accordingly. The fact that Discourse I, after its introductory chapter, begins with definitions of the term "state" (*regnum*),[32] and Discourse II, after its introductory chapter, begins with definitions of the term "church" (*ecclesia*),[33] might seem to constitute strong supporting evidence for this procedure. Yet Marsilius himself, far from viewing the two discourses as having such distinct subject matters, regards them as having essentially the same subject matter. It is in two other, complementary ways that he conceives the relation between Discourses I and II. First, and mainly, the two discourses treat the same subject matter by different *methods,* reason and revelation:

In the first discourse I shall demonstrate my views by sure methods discovered by the human intellect, based upon propositions self-evident to every mind not corrupted by nature, custom, or perverted emotion. In the second discourse,

[32] I. ii. 2.

[33] II. ii. 2–3.

the things which I shall believe myself to have demonstrated I shall confirm by established testimonies of the eternal truth, and by the authorities of its saintly interpreters and of other approved teachers of the Christian faith. . . .[34]

Secondly, the two discourses treat the same subject matter by its general and its singular *causes,* respectively. For both discourses are concerned with civil "peace" and "strife"; but whereas the first discourse presents their general causes, the second discourse deals at length with one "singular" cause of peace and strife, the pretensions and acts of the papacy.[35]

These two relations between Discourses I and II, as Marsilius conceives them, are complementary to one another. For the demonstration of the general causes of civil peace and strife is the work of reason; while the papacy as the singular cause of civil strife can be understood and evaluated only if its pretended theological sanction is contrasted with the truths of Christian revelation and history. Reason sets forth general causes, nature operating according to its "usual" course; [36] revelation presents the precepts and counsels whereby the claims of the papacy, the singular cause, can be properly assayed. But since the singular cause is also an instance of the general causes, as such, the doctrine of Discourse I concerning the general conditions of civil peace and strife applies also to the papacy. The papacy, indeed, is convicted of being the cause of civil strife both on the general grounds ascertained by reason and on the special ground ascertained through Scripture. Thus, Discourse II considers from the standpoint of revelation or Scripture the peculiar conditions emerging from the rise of Christianity which constitute a special case of the general problems of peace discussed in Discourse I.

From these relations between the two discourses there follow important consequences. On the one hand, Marsilius' discussion of general causes in Discourse I is undoubtedly tendentious, being oriented toward the special polemical problems of Discourse II. Yet the first discourse also constitutes, in explicit intention as well as in effect, a discussion of general political principles which might conceivably be followed, in a different age, by a quite different second discourse, that is, by one concerned with a different "singular cause" of civil strife. The proper balancing of these various aspects—the polemical and the philosophic, the employment of reason and of revelation, the treatment of general causes and of the singular cause—constitutes some of the chief problems of the interpreter of Marsilius. But in any case, it is clear that for Marsilius the subject matters of Discourses I and II are not so disparate as the traditional dichotomy of "state" and

[34] I. i. 8.
[35] See I. i. 3; I. xix. 3; III. i; III. iii.
[36] See I. i. 3.

"church" would indicate. Hence the present study will treat the two discourses together throughout the major issues with which they are jointly concerned. The fact that our final chapter is entitled "The People's Church" must not mislead the reader into thinking that Discourse II is treated only in that chapter. Rather, Discourse II is dealt with explicitly in all the intermediate chapters as well, from the standpoint of the two complementary aspects whereby Marsilius conceives it to be related to Discourse I. Thus the particular consequences for the church-state controversy which Marsilius draws in Discourse II from the general political doctrines established in Discourse I will be treated at each stage where those doctrines themselves are examined. In this way it is hoped to do justice concomitantly to both phases of the Marsilian enterprise, while reserving for the final chapter those unique aspects of the singular cause—the internal structure of the church, as against the relation between the state and the papacy—which do not follow directly from the general political causes of the state and its peace dealt with in Discourse I.

2. THE PROBLEM

In the doctrine of plenitude of power, as it was upheld by Marsilius' papalist opponents—not only in the dispute between Pope John XXII and Ludwig of Bavaria with which he was immediately concerned in 1324, but also in the earlier controversy between Boniface VIII and Philip the Fair at the end of the thirteenth and the beginning of the fourteenth century—a long development extending throughout the greater portion of the middle ages achieved its mature outcome. Entering into the doctrine's formulation were important elements of medieval philosophic, legal, and social thought; and at the hands of its chief expositors, who were philosophers and theologians as well as publicists, it received a strikingly systematic elaboration. These were writers conscious of metaphysical principles and sensitive to dialectical methods; and it was their use of both of these which provided Marsilius at once with his problem and his point of departure.

The common conception underlying the arguments and procedures of the papalists consisted in a universalized theologico-political interpretation of the traditional ideas of "unity" and "order." The universe was an organic unity in the sense that all objects within it were interrelated and possessed a common structure. These objects formed an axiological order, in that they fell into a hierarchy of higher and lower, better and worse. And finally, this was a *divine* order in the sense that it was controlled by and ordered to God, so that the ultimate criterion of the "higher" and the "better," and hence of moral and intellectual evaluation, was a theological one.[1]

A definite mode of approach to the state and to political affairs generally was entailed by this conception. Since the order of political power did not differ essentially from any other order of powers, it followed that physical, biological, psychological, moral, theological, aesthetic, intellectual analogies could be employed indiscriminately in the analysis of political phenomena.[2] But ultimately all these concerns, including the political, were controlled by the theological. For the claim to the attainment of any values, and specifically of justice, could be justified only through God, so that human law was subordinated to divine law, and nature to grace.

It was by fitting all political phenomena into such a theological order that the papalists proved the necessity of the papal plenitude of power. They repeated St. Augustine's rhetorical question, "If justice be removed, what are kingdoms but great bands of thieves?"; [3] but where Augustine had identified justice with theological virtue and subjection to God,[4] the

[1] This entire conception is well illustrated in the use made of a text from the Pseudo-Dionysius the Areopagite *De coelesti hierarchia* iv. 3 (PG 3, 503–4). E.g., Egidius of Rome *De eccl. pot.* I. iv (pp. 12–13): "Possumus enim ex ordine universi hoc liquido declarare, quod super gentes et regna sit ecclesia constituta. Nam 'secundum Dionysium in *De Angelica Ierarchia* lex divinitatis est infima in suprema per media reducere. Hoc ergo requirit ordo universi, ut infima in suprema per media reducantur. Si enim eque immediate infima reducerentur in suprema, sicut et media, non esset universum recte ordinatum, quod est inconveniens dicere et potissime in istis potestatibus et auctoritatibus . . . Gladius ergo temporalis tamquam inferior reducendus est per spiritualem tamquam per superiorem, et unus ordinandus est sub alio tamquam inferior sub superiori." The same text and argument are found in the famous bull of Pope Boniface VIII, *Unam sanctam,* and in the commentary on that bull attributed to Egidius (both ed. P. de Lapparent, in *Archives d'histoire littéraire et doctrinale du moyen âge,* XVIII [1940–42], 127, 145); also in Augustinus Triumphus *S. de eccl. pot.* qu.44. a.1; Alexander of St. Elpidius *Tract. de eccl. pot.* II. vi. 4 (p. 21); Francis of Mayron *Quaestio de subjectione* I. 10 (p. 83); and a closely related one in James of Viterbo *De reg. princ.* II. ii, v (p. 164–65, 204). See also Ptolemy of Lucca *Determinatio compendiosa* cap. xix, xx (pp. 39–42).

[2] The fullest catalogue of such organic interplay of political with other concepts is found in Egidius of Rome. See *De eccl. pot.* II. vi (pp. 61–62), where he points out a common structure in "quattuor genera potestatum": "virtutes naturales . . . artes . . . scientiae . . . principatus et gubernationes hominum . . *Prout videbimus in potestatibus aliis, poterimus de principibus et gubernationibus hominum aliqua declarare.*" See also Francis of Mayron *Tract. de principatu temporali* VI (pp. 69–70): "Quod autem principatus temporalium sit melior si est spiritualibus subjectus quam si ponatur sui gratia, tantum declaratur: Primo in naturalibus . . . Secundo in moralibus . . . Tertio de virtutibus intellectualibus . . . Quarto in supernaturalibus. . . ." See Francis' *Quaestio de subjectione* I. 3 (p. 78); *Tract. de princ. regni Sicilae* I, III (pp. 98–99, 106). See also James of Viterbo *De reg. Christ.* II. iii, vii (pp. 173, 234).

[3] *De civ. Dei* IV. iv: "Remota ita justitia quid sunt regna nisi magna latrocinia?" See Egidius of Rome *De eccl. pot.* I. v; II. vii; III. ii, x (pp. 15, 73, 149, 153–4, 198, 201). James of Viterbo *De reg. Christ.* III. x (p. 302). Ptolemy of Lucca *De reg. princ.* II. v (p. 52); *Determinatio compendiosa* cap. xxii (p. 44). Alexander of St. Elpidius *Tract. de eccl. pot.* II. iii (p. 16). Augustinus Triumphus *S. de eccl. pot.* qu.46. a.2. Alvarus Pelagius *De planctu ecclesiae* I. xxxvii (p. 44).

[4] *De civ. Dei* XIX. xxi, xxiii, xxv.

papalists' analogical method went on to identify the latter with subjection to the pope: "no men are under the rule of Christ unless they are under the supreme pontiff, who is Christ's general vicar"; [5] hence to appeal from the pope to God would be "ridiculous and frivolous," because "the sentence of the pope and the sentence of God are one sentence." [6] The *ordinatio ad unum,* the ordering of all the parts of the universe to God, was mirrored in the ordering of all men to the papacy.[7]

This whole conception had its obvious source in the philosophy of Augustine, who found a common, divinely controlled pattern of "peace" and "order" in the body, in the soul, in man, and in the state.[8] But apart from its specifically Christian aspects, this conception was also that of the teleological orientation of Aristotle. Several of the papalists assimilated the Augustinian "order" to the passage of the *Politics* where Aristotle points out a common pattern of a relation between ruler and ruled in all composite wholes, ranging from the inanimate to human associations; [9] and other Aristotelian ideas were similarly repeated,[10] including even the doctrine of the naturalness of the state and of political authority.[11] While they were frequently not interpreted in a sense consonant with that which they have in Aristotle himself, these ideas formed an important part of the mature papalist philosophy.[12]

[5] Egidius of Rome *De eccl. pot.* III. x (p. 198). See James of Viterbo *De reg. Christ.* II. x (p. 283). Alvarus Pelagius *De planctu ecclesiae* I. xxiv (p. 33).

[6] Augustinus Triumphus *S. de eccl. pot.* qu.6. a.1.

[7] See Egidius *De eccl. pot.* III. ii (p. 152). James of Viterbo *De reg. Christ.* I. iii (pp. 117–18). Augustinus Triumphus *S. de eccl. pot.* qu.22. a.3.

[8] *De civ. Dei* XIX. xiii. See below, pp. 95 ff.

[9] *Pol.* I. 5. 1254a 28 ff. See *ibid.* VII. 14. 1333a 22, where the principle that the worse is always for the sake of the better is found exemplified "in both artificial and natural things." See the combination of Aristotle and Augustine in Ptolemy of Lucca *De reg. princ.* III. ix: "In his autem quae sunt ad invicem ordinata, oportet semper aliquid esse principale et dirigens primum, ut tradit Philosophus in I *Polit.* Hoc etiam ostendit ipsa ratio ordinis, sive natura, quia ut per Augustinum scribitur in praedicto libro [i.e., *De civ. Dei*], ordo est parium dispariumque rerum sua cuique tribuens dispositio." See also Ptolemy's *Determinatio compendiosa* cap. xvii (p. 36). The same assimilation is also made by Alvarus Pelagius *De planctu eccl.* I. xli (p. 69). See also Alexander of St. Elpidius *Tract. de eccl. pot.* I. i (p. 3).

[10] See the use of the distinction between potentiality and actuality in Egidius *De eccl. pot.* I. vi (p. 19 ff.) (Scholz's index to this work lists 26 citations of texts of Aristotle, and 38 of Augustine); and the distinction between matter and form in James of Viterbo *De reg. Christ.* II. vii (p. 232).

[11] Ptolemy of Lucca *De reg. princ.* III. ix (p. 58). James of Viterbo *De reg. Christ.* II. iii, vii (pp. 176–77, 232). Augustinus Triumphus *S. de eccl. pot.* qu.23. a.3. Alexander of St. Elpidius *Tract. de eccl. pot.* II. viii (p. 24). Alvarus Pelagius *De planctu eccl.* I. xli (p. 69).

[12] M. Grabmann, who attempts to correlate the proponents of the "direct power" of the pope in temporal affairs with Augustinianism, and the proponents of the "indirect power" with Thomist Aristotelianism, admits that this correlation can be made "nur mit einer gewissen Einschränkung und Zurückhaltung und nur in grossen Linien. . . ." See his "Studien über den Einfluss der aristotelischen Philosophie auf die mittelalterlichen Theorien über das Verhältnis von Kirche und Staat," *Sitzungsberichte der bayerischen Akademie der Wissenschaften,* Phil.-hist. Abt. (1934), Heft 2, p. 7.

The writers who, before Marsilius, opposed the papal plenitude of power did not form so homogeneous a group as the papalists themselves. They ranged from philosophers like Thomas Aquinas and John of Paris who provided, although in different degrees, for the intervention of the pope in the authority of temporal rulers where these depart from the Christian faith, to Pierre Dubois who proposed that the king of France confiscate church property to effect "peace" and help pay for a crusade.[13] Intermediate between these positions were writers who argued simply for a parallelism of the spiritual and temporal powers without any intervention of either in the other's affairs; this group, which itself exhibited varying emphases, included Dante Alighieri and the anonymous authors of the *Disputatio inter militem et clericum,* the *Quaestio in utramque partem,* and *Quaestio de potestate papae,* all dating from the quarrel between Boniface VIII and Philip the Fair.

The point on which all these writers agreed was in emphasizing distinctions which resulted in a normal dualism of authority as against the analogies whereby the papalists had reduced the political realm to the theological.[14] Obstacles were thus interposed against indiscriminate argument from one kind of order to another, for example, from the superiority of grace over nature,[15] or of spiritual ends over temporal ends,[16] to the political jurisdiction of the spiritual over the temporal power. The papalist arguments from "order" were answered by emphasizing that the situation is more complex than is indicated in their simple analogies: an order of dignity does not necessarily involve an order of power or jurisdiction;[17] temporal and spiritual affairs are "of diverse order or genus," so that one must not be placed under the other.[18] The papalist arguments from "unity," with their assimilation of the pope to God, were similarly answered by emphasizing the distinctions between the divine and the human,[19] between

[13] For Thomas and John, see below, pp. 18–19. For Pierre, see *De recuperatione sancte terre* par. 40 ff. (pp. 33 ff.).

[14] This difference is epitomized in the titles of the works written on each side: the papalists write *De ecclesiastica potestate* (Egidius of Rome, Augustinus Triumphus, Alexander of St. Elpidius), or *De potestate papae* (Henry of Cremona); whereas their moderate opponents write *De potestate regia et papali* (John of Paris), *De imperatorum et pontificum potestate* (William of Ockham).

[15] See Thomas *S. theol.* II. II. qu.10. a.10. Resp.

[16] See John of Paris *De pot. reg. et pap.* cap. iv, xvii (pp. 113, 131). Dante *De mon.* III. xvi (pp. 375–76).

[17] John of Paris *De pot. reg. et pap.* cap. v (p. 113).

[18] *Ibid.* cap. xvii (p. 131). Dante *De mon.* III. xvi (pp. 375–76). *Quaestio in utramque partem* a.5 (p. 107). *Quaestio de potestate papae,* pp. 670 ff., 678.

[19] John of Paris *De pot. reg. et pap.* cap. xix (p. 134). *Quaestio in utramque partem* a.5 (p. 103). Dante *De mon.* III. xii (p. 373).

[20] John of Paris *De pot. reg. et pap.* cap. viii, ix (pp. 116–18). *Disputatio inter militem et clericum,* pp. 13–14. *Quaestio in utramque partem* a.5 (p. 104). *Quaestio de potestate papae,* pp. 668–69. These writers use the distinction between Christ *qua* God and *qua* man to argue that the pope has only the powers which Christ had when he was a man in this world; these

Christ's powers *qua* God and *qua* man,[20] between a chief and his vicar.[21]

These replies were not, however, able to effect the complete reversal which was necessary to refute the papal claims. For so long as politics was viewed in axiological terms, and the theological was conceived to be superior to all other values, a similar superiority of the pope over secular rulers had to be admitted. It is instructive to see here the dialectical working out of the papalists' assimilation of politics and theology, with its corollary that justice requires obedience to God, and hence to the pope. The reply given not only by the anti-papalists, but also by several papalists, following the lead of Thomas Aquinas, asserted a distinction between moral and theological virtue, natural and divine law, nature and grace. Men and states can be just even if they are not Christian, because the moral virtues, which include justice, derive from the very nature of man, which is not abolished by grace; similarly, the state is not merely a result of sin but arises from men's natural inclinations.[22] Yet this reply still leaves the state in a moral context in which the moral, while not entirely identified with the theological, is nevertheless subordinate to it, and hence to the papacy. Thus Thomas Aquinas, James of Viterbo, Augustinus Triumphus, and Alexander of St. Elpidius have no sooner declared that the state is based upon natural law or natural inclination, than they go on to assert that the church, or the pope, *can* remove political authority from infidels,[23] that political power *does* require "ratification" by the pope.[24] Nor is this a contradiction: it is based upon the interpretation given to the dictum that "grace does not abolish nature, but *forms and perfects it*"; for this is taken to mean that human nature needs grace to will or do any good,[25] that nature is imperfect unless formed by grace,[26] that "grace *has* to perfect and form nature." [27] John of Paris alone declares that the moral virtues

---

included not temporal jurisdiction but humble submission. The papalists, on the other hand, while also recognizing the distinction, interpret it only as denying to the pope such superhuman powers over all of creation as belong only to God. See Egidius of Rome *De eccl. pot.* III. ix (p. 193). James of Viterbo *De reg. Christ.* II. ii, ix (pp. 163 ff., 268 ff.). Alexander of St. Elpidius *Tract. de eccl. pot.* Tr. I. cap. iv (pp. 5–6). Ptolemy of Lucca *De reg. princ.* III. x, xv (pp. 59, 68).

[21] Dante *De mon.* III. vii (p. 368). See *Quaestio de potestate papae,* p. 676.

[22] Thomas Aquinas *S. theol.* I. qu.96. a.4; II. II. qu.10. a.10. Resp.; qu.12. a.2. Resp. John of Paris *De pot. reg. et pap.* cap. xix (p. 134). For the extreme papalists who embraced this naturalism, see above, p. 16, n. 11.

[23] Thomas *S. theol.* II. II. qu.10. a.10. Resp.: "Potest tamen juste per sententiam vel ordinationem Ecclesiae auctoritatem Dei habentis tale jus dominii vel praelationis tolli. . . ." See James of Viterbo *De reg. Christ.* II. x (p. 286). Augustinus Triumphus *S. de eccl. pot.* qu.24. a.6.

[24] James *De reg. Christ.* II. vii (p. 232). Alexander *Tract. de eccl. pot.* II. viii (p. 24).

[25] Thomas *S. theol.* II. I. qu.109. a.2. Resp.

[26] James *De reg. Christ.* II. vii (p. 232).

[27] Alexander *Tract. de eccl. pot.* II. viii (p. 24): "gratia enim habet perficere et formare naturam."

can be "perfect" without the theological virtues, so that states can be just without obedience to God or to the pope.[28] Yet even he provides that if a ruler is heretical or otherwise "delinquent in spiritual things," the pope may excommunicate him and incite the people to depose him.[29]

A similar fate befell the anti-papalists' general emphasis upon diversity and multiplicity. To their argument that the spiritual power should be superior in spirituals only, and the temporal power in temporals, the papalists replied with renewed insistence upon the requirement of "order." As Egidius of Rome put it with condescending clarity:

Those who speak thus do not grasp the force of the argument. For if kings and princes were under the church only spiritually, there would not be a sword under a sword, nor would temporals be under spirituals, *nor would there be an order in the powers,* nor would the lowest things be reduced to the highest through intermediaries. If, therefore, these are ordered, the temporal sword must be under the spiritual, kingdoms must be under the vicar of Christ. . . .[30]

James of Viterbo made a similar reply:

As for what they argue concerning the double order of powers, it must be said that *these are not such diverse orders, since one is reduced to the other,* just as the order of corporeals is other than the order of spirituals, and yet the order of corporeals is under the order of spirituals.[31]

These replies made it clear that in an all-encompassing monistic hierarchy, the approach in terms of distinctions and diversity could not succeed without further, and far more fundamental, doctrinal alterations.

It was this background of failure to provide a definitive refutation of the papalists' reduction of all things, all concepts, and all values to the

[28] John of Paris *De pot. reg. et pap.* cap. xix (p. 134): "virtutes morales acquisitae possunt esse perfectae sine theologicis, nec ab ipsis perficiuntur, nisi quadam accidentali perfectione. . . ." The *Quaestio de potestate papae,* on the other hand, accepts it as "certainly true" that "vera iustitia non est in Republica, cuius Christus non est rector," but replies that Christ has *two* vicars, one in spirituals, the other in temporals (p. 680).

[29] John, cap. xiv (p. 127). Dante's denial that the ruler "in aliquo Romano Pontifici non subiaceat," and his affirmation that "Caesar" owes "Peter" the reverence which a son owes to his father (*De mon.* III. xvi [p. 376]) could be turned in the same direction. So too could his statement that "regnum temporale . . . ab eo [spirituali] recipit, ut virtuosius operetur per lucem gratiae" (*ibid.* III. iv [p. 367]). See below, p. 78, n. 2.

[30] *De eccl. pot.* I. iv (p. 13). *Ibid.* I. v (p. 17): "isti sic dicentes vim racionis non capiunt. . . ." The quoted passage is repeated in almost identical terms by Alexander of St. Elpidius *Tract. de eccl. pot.* II. vi (p. 21), who begins by saying of the anti-papalist reply to the argument from order: "talis responsio non evacuat virtutem rationis factae."

[31] *De reg. Christ.* II. x (p. 286). See also Francis of Mayron *Tract. de principatu temporali* IV (pp. 62 ff.), who refutes at length through the four Aristotelian causes the argument, attributed to the "legists," that "ordo rerum temporalium ab ordine rerum spiritualium est totaliter disparatus." The same point is found in Francis' *Tract. de principatu regni Siciliae* III (p. 107), and in other papalists: Ptolemy of Lucca *De reg. princ.* III. x (p. 60). Augustinus Triumphus *S. de eccl. pot.* qu.I. aa.I, 6. Alvarus Pelagius *De planctu eccl.* I. xxxvii, xl (pp. 49, 60–62).

theological which provided the specific challenge for the work of Marsilius of Padua.

3. THE LIFE OF MARSILIUS

The life of Marsilius contains few facts on which we have sure information.[1] He was born Marsilio dei Mainardini, son of Bonmatteo dei Mainardini, notary to the University of Padua; the year of his birth was probably between 1275 and 1280. That he was educated at the University of Padua is likely; [2] he was rector of the University of Paris on March 12, 1313,[3] probably occupying this position from December, 1312, to March 1313. Our main source of information about Marsilius' life before writing the *Defensor pacis* is a metrical epistle composed by the Paduan civic leader and writer Albertino Mussato, addressed "To Marsilius of Padua, Master, Naturalist, reproaching him for his inconstancy." [4] In this epistle Mussato relates that Marsilius had once asked his advice on whether to study law or medicine, and had been directed to the latter; but then, after a period devoted to medical studies, Marsilius had joined the forces of Can Grande della Scala,[5] ruler of Verona, and Matteo Visconti of Milan. Subsequently, he had returned to his studies of "nature" (*physis*) with an "egregious teacher" who has been variously identified as William of Brescia,[6] John of Jandun,[7] and Peter of Abano.[8] Once more, however, he had turned "from the path of sacred study to the unspeakable acts of men," girding himself with the "German sword"; and it is at this period that Mussato reproves him for his fickle changes of vocation, and reminds him that "sublime philosophy" had given him "everything that was knowable."

[1] For Marsilius' life, see especially Valois, *op. cit.*, pp. 560 ff.; C. K. Brampton, "Marsiglio of Padua, Life," *Eng. Hist. Rev.*, XXXVII (1922), 501–15; J. Haller, "Zur Lebensgeschichte des Marsilius von Padua," *Zeitschrift für Kirchengeschichte*, XLVIII (1929), 166 ff.; Battaglia, *Marsilio da Padova e la filosofia politica*, pp. 22–50, 180–95; Lagarde, *Marsile*, pp. 14–39.

[2] Among the relatively few names of students of whom there is some record of their having attended the University in the thirteenth and early fourteenth centuries, Marsilius' is not included. See A. Gloria, "Monumenti della Università di Padova, 1222–1318," *Memorie del R. istituto veneto di scienze, lettere, ed arti*, XXII (1882), 624 ff. That Marsilius studied law at the University of Orleans, as held by Brampton, *op. cit.*, p. 505, is not supported by the passage of the *Defensor*, II. xviii. 6 (p. 308), on which this hypothesis is based. See Valois, *op. cit.*, p. 566; Battaglia, *Marsilio da Padova e la filosofia politica*, pp. 33–35.

[3] See *Chartularium Universitatis Parisiensis*, ed. H. Denifle and A. Chatelain (Paris, 1891), II, 158.

[4] *Ad Magistrum Marsilium Physicum Paduanum eius inconstantiam arguens.* The epistle is printed in J. G. Graevius, *Thesaurus historiae Italicae* (Venice, 1636), Vol. VI, Suppl. II, col. 48; in Labanca, *Marsilio*, pp. 227–29; and in Haller, *op. cit.*, pp. 195–97.

[5] "Calle quidem primo demulsus ab ore Canino. . . ." Note the imitation of "Arma virumque cano, Trojae qui primus ab oris. . . ." (Virgil *Aeneid* I. 1).

[6] Haller, *op. cit.*, p. 179.

[7] Scholz, ed., *Def. pac.*, p. lvi, n. 1.

[8] G. Gentile, "La filosofia," in *Storia dei generi letterarii italiani*, fasc. 41 (Milan, n.d.), p. 151; Lagarde, *Marsile*, p. 27.

When did all these tergiversations occur? We cannot be sure. There are, however, several other events in this period of Marsilius' life for which we have documentary evidence. On May 24, 1315, he was a witness to the profession of faith made by Peter of Abano.[9] On October 14, 1316, Marsilius was promised a canonry in Padua by Pope John XXII; [10] and on April 15, 1318, the pope reserved for him the first vacant benefice in Padua.[11] It would appear to be during this period that Marsilius had returned to the "sacred study" of natural philosophy with an "egregious teacher." But in 1319, by a transition as abrupt as that described in Mussato's epistle, Marsilius is found mentioned in a letter of Pope John XXII, dated April 29 of that year, as having been sent by Can Grande della Scala and Matteo Visconti to Count Charles of La Marche, offering the latter the captaincy of the Ghibelline League.[12] It would appear to be this period that witnessed his return to "the unspeakable acts of men."

Marsilius' mission failed, however, and again he resumed scholarly pursuits, settling in Paris where he gave lectures on natural philosophy and engaged in medical research and practice. It was probably here, too, that he became acquainted with the persons and doctrines of Ubertino da Casale, Michael of Cesena, and the other Spiritual Franciscans who upheld evangelical poverty. When he began work on the *Defensor pacis* we do not know, but it was finished on June 24, 1324.[13] Meanwhile he continued his studies and teaching, and was also preparing to give a course in theology when his authorship of the *Defensor* became known in 1326. Thus he was forced to flee with John of Jandun, whose assistance had caused him to be regarded as co-author of the work; [14] they made their way to the court of Ludwig of Bavaria in Nuremberg, and were accepted as members of his entourage. The following year Marsilius and John were condemned as heretics.[15]

The interest of Marsilius' career with Ludwig lies in the light it throws upon the former's practical interpretation of the meaning of his treatise. In 1322 Ludwig had won an eight-year struggle against Frederick of

[9] The document is printed in C. Ronzoni, "Della vita e delle opere di Pietro d'Abano," *Real. accad. dei Lincei, Atti, Mem. stor. fil.*, 3d series, II (1877–78), 330. The relation of this document to the author of the *Defensor pacis* was first pointed out by Lagarde, *Marsile*, p. 20.

[10] *Vatikanische Akten zur deutschen Geschichte in der Zeit Kaiser Ludwigs des Bayern*, ed. S. Riezler (Innsbruck, 1891), p. 5, n. 6.

[11] *Ibid.*, p. 66, n. 100.

[12] The letter is printed in *Régistres de Jean XXII. Lettres sécrètes*, ed. G. Mollat (Paris, 1908), n. 860; the relevant passage is also printed in C. W. Previté-Orton, "Marsilius of Padua and the Visconti," *Eng. Hist. Rev.*, XLIV (1929), pp. 278–79.

[13] See *Def. pac.* III. iii (p. 501), i.e., the concluding words.

[14] For a statement of the reasons why Marsilius must be regarded as the sole author, see A. Gewirth, "John of Jandun and the *Defensor Pacis*," *Speculum*, XXIII (1948), 267–72.

[15] Bull *Licet iuxta*, in MGH, *Constitutiones*, Vol. VI, Part I, n. 361, pp. 265 ff.

Austria over the crown of the Empire, following which his accession to the throne was acknowledged by the seven prince-electors. But Pope John XXII insisted that Ludwig must have papal confirmation before his accession could be valid. In this repetition of an old pattern Ludwig was able to make use of the antipapal doctrines of Marsilius, just as the latter saw in Ludwig their effective embodiment. There ensued in 1327 Ludwig's expedition to Italy to seize the imperial crown, a chain of events in which Marsilius played a leading role. First they marched on Milan, where Marsilius not only preached [16] but found time to indulge his scientific interests; [17] then to Rome, where there occurred the fabulous spectacles in which Marsilius' doctrines were put into practice. On the people's invitation Ludwig entered Rome in January 1328; there he was crowned by Sciarra Colonna as delegate of the people; next, acting "by our authority together with the entire clergy and Roman people," [18] he deposed John XXII and named a new pope. That Marsilius, who had been appointed spiritual vicar of the city, helped write Ludwig's pronouncements and was otherwise his intellectual guide, there can be no question.[19] In his role of spiritual official actively aiding the elected ruler of the "people," Marsilius was presumably following the model set forth in the *Defensor pacis* for the functioning of the priesthood as a "part" of the state. That he energetically persecuted the clergy who maintained allegiance to John [20] is a further aspect of the same role.

Following the débâcle of Ludwig's enforced departure from Rome owing to the people's displeasure, Marsilius passed the rest of his life at the court of Ludwig in Bavaria, together with William of Ockham and other Franciscans.[21] In 1342 Marsilius composed a brief resumé of his one great work, fittingly entitled *Defensor minor,* part of which is a *Tractatus de jurisdictione imperatoris in causis matrimonialibus* written to aid the marriage of

[16] O. Raynald, *Annales ecclesiasticae* (Lucca, 1750), V, 533; see Brampton, *op. cit.,* p. 510.

[17] L. Thorndike, *A History of Magic and Experimental Science* (New York, 1934), III, 260, cites the following "note at the close of what seems to be one of John of Linerius' canons on astronomical tables": "Explicit canon super tabula magistri Johannis acta Parisius anno Christi 1321 et communicata Mediolan. per magistrum Marxilium de Padua magistro Symoni de Moronis 1327 die 17° novembris." This note has not previously, to my knowledge, figured in biographies of Marsilius.

[18] MGH, *Constitutiones,* Vol. VI, Part I, p. 366.

[19] See K. Müller, *Der Kampf Ludwigs des Baiern mit der römischen Kurie* (Tübingen, 1879–80), I, 179 ff.; Lagarde, *Marsile,* p. 312 ff.; and, for a fuller study of the relations of Marsilius and Ludwig, O. Bornhak, *Staatskirchliche Anschauungen und Handlungen am Hofe Kaiser Ludwigs des Bayern* (Weimar, 1933).

[20] See Valois, *op. cit.,* p. 596.

[21] On the relation between Marsilius and Ockham, see especially J. Sullivan, "Marsiglio of Padua and William of Ockham," and G. de Lagarde, "Marsile de Padoue et Guillaume d' Ockham." Both articles show the untenability of the long-held belief that Ockham influenced Marsilius in the writing of the *Defensor pacis.*

Ludwig's son to Margaret Maultasch. William of Ockham also produced a tract to this end. Marsilius died shortly thereafter.[22]

4. THE INSTITUTIONAL SETTING

Padua and Paris: these were the chief milieux of Marsilius' life prior to his composition of the *Defensor pacis.* The former, however, made by far the more profound contribution to his book: it supplied the particular circumstances which were the main sources in Marsilius' experience of the general doctrines set forth in the *Defensor pacis.* The character of those circumstances is thus of some importance for the understanding of the doctrines.[1]

The Padua in which Marsilius was born, and in which he probably spent the first twenty-five or thirty years of his life, was a prosperous trading and manufacturing city. Like the other cities of Lombardy, it had won what amounted to actual independence from the Empire through the treaty of Constance in 1183. The subsequent development of its political institutions, despite several serious vicissitudes in the thirteenth century, had been in a predominantly republican direction, to which the structure of the *civitas sive regnum* elaborated in the *Defensor pacis* bears obvious and yet fundamental resemblances. In Padua the legislative body was the "greater council" (*concilium majus*), which had grown in size from four hundred to six hundred and then in 1277 to a thousand members, chosen from all the citizens of the commune by a property qualification.[2] In the *Defensor pacis,* similarly, the legislator is the general assembly of the citizens or its *pars valentior,* determined by both quantitative and qualitative standards.[3] The chief administrative officer of Padua was the *podestà,* elected by the greater council;[4] his primary function was described as the "execution" of the statutes enacted by the council, and he was himself required to observe those same statutes, being subject to clearly stated penalties for transgressing them, and having to undergo a "syndicate" of inquiry into his administration at its close.[5] The ruler or *pars principans* of Marsilius' state

[22] A statement of Pope Clement VI on April 10, 1343, refers to Marsilius as being dead. See Valois, *op. cit.*, p. 603.

[1] The similarities of the institutions of the Padua of Marsilius' time to those set forth in the *Defensor pacis* have long been recognized by scholars, but for the most part only in general terms which have not brought out the specific features most relevant to the understanding of the interrelations between the city and the doctrines. Some of these features are treated in Labanca. *Marsilio.* Ch. 4, and in C. W. Previté-Orton, "Marsiglio of Padua, Doctrines," *Eng. Hist. Rev.*, XXXVIII (1923), 1 ff.

[2] *Statuti del comune di Padova dal secolo XII all' anno 1285* nn. 16, 16.I, 1182.I (pp. 13–14, 361).

[3] I. xii. 3. Cf. Battaglia, *Marsilio,* pp. 88, 98.

[4] *Stat. com. Pad.* n. 1.I (p. 7).

[5] *Ibid.* n. 52 (p. 25): "Potestas padue teneatur et debeat omnes refformationes maioris conscilii observare et eas executioni mandare usque ad proxime quindecim dies venturos post-

is likewise elected by the whole body of citizens;[6] his function is described as "execution" of the laws,[7] which he must observe and for whose transgression he is subject to deposition and punishment.[8] The Padua *podestà*, moreover, functioned as a judge, handing down sentences in accordance with the statutes on persons accused of crimes, and following the "common laws" or his own discretion in those cases not determined by the statutes.[9] The *pars principans* of Marsilius is likewise a judge,[10] and Marsilius tells us in almost exactly the same words as are used in the Padua statute, that where the law does not determine, or where it does not fit a particular case, the ruler must follow his own discretion in prudence, or use equity.[11]

Behind these resemblances there are others even more fundamental, reaching down to the very basis of the city's life. Like other medieval cities, Padua had developed as a "commune" out of almost untraceable beginnings, through a consolidation and growth of originally small trading and manufacturing outposts.[12] With its economic development came the need for a corresponding political development, for law and government which would regulate the manifold relations among its various parts. Such regulation had not only the negative task of settling the disputes which inevitably arose among the burghers, but also the positive function of bringing all the persons within and about the commune under a common order of justice which would effect an equal apportionment of necessary burdens and other responsibilities. It therefore provided the conditions whereby the commercial industrial life of the city could go on without interruption, and with increasing growth. Such regulation, in its fullest content, was given the name of "peace." The peace of medieval cities thus meant not only the absence of war—although it certainly did mean this too—but also the

---

quam fuit refformatum, et si poterit ante dictum terminum executioni mandare eas. Teneatur sub pena librarum centum pro qualibet refformatione non observata." For other references to penalties to be paid by the *podestà* for non-observance of statutes, see nn. 1.I, 2.I, 16.I, 30, 35, 54, etc. (pp. 6, 7, 14, 18, 20, 25). For the "syndicate" of inquiry, see n. 94 (p. 37).

[6] *Def. pac.* I. xv. 2. [7] *Ibid.* I. xv. 4. [8] *Ibid.* I. xviii. 2–7.

[9] *Stat. com. Pad.* n. 35 (p. 20): "Et fiant dicte condemnationes et absolutiones secundum statuta et ordinamenta comunis padue in illis casibus qui determinati sunt per statuta et ordinamenta comunis padue. *In illis vero casibus qui non sunt determinati per dicta statuta et ordinamenta dicte condemnationes et absolutiones fiant secundum jura comunia.*" See *ibid.* n. 37 (p. 21): "In aliis factis in quibus certa banna non sunt statuta liceat potestati punire delinquentes suo arbitrio. . . ."

[10] *Def. pac.* I. v. 7.

[11] *Ibid.* I. xiv. 3: *"In quibus namque humanis actibus civilibus actus ipse vel modus non determinatur a lege, per prudentiam dirigitur principans in judicando et etiam exequendo. . . ."* I. xiv. 6: "non facile aut non possible simul omnia determinare legibus, sed aliqua committi oportere principantis arbitrio. . . ." See I. xiv. 7.

[12] See A. Bonardi, "Le origini del comune di Padova," *R. accad. di scienze, lettere, ed arti in Padova: Atti e memorie,* n.s., XIV (1897), 209–54; XV (1898), 11–48; N. Tamassia, "Le origini del comune di Padova," *Atti del R. istituto veneto di scienze, lettere, ed arti,* LVIII (1899); M. Roberti, "Nuove ricerche sopra l'antica costituzione del comune di Padova," *Nuovo archivio veneto,* n.s., III (1899), 77–97.

punitive laws whose application removed war, the political order which resulted from those laws, and the consequent economic stability whereby every man could fruitfully go about his daily business.[13] And it was to the effecting of such all-inclusive peace that the *podestà* and other officials of Padua had to dedicate themselves.[14]

The kinship of the *Defensor pacis* to this orientation of the cities is too obvious to require emphasis. The very title of the work is reminiscent of the oaths of the *podesti* and other officials to "conserve and defend the commune in peaceful status." [15] The "captain of the people" who ruled Florence at the time when Marsilius was writing had as part of his title *Defensor artium et artificum et Conservator pacis;* [16] in Verdun the magistrates were called "warders of the peace"; [17] in Siena they were later called *defensores status pacifici.*[18] The "peace" which Marsilius' ruler defends [19] is also the peace of these cities: not only the absence of strife but "the good disposition of the city or state whereby each of its parts can perfectly perform the operations appropriate to it." [20] The entire social and economic order and the juridical unity of the Marsilian state are evolved out of this definition of peace.[21]

[13] See H. Pirenne, *Medieval Cities* (Princeton, 1925), p. 208: "The burghers were essentially *homines pacis*—men of the peace. The peace of the city (*pax villae*) was at the same time the law of the city (*lex villae*). . . By virtue of the peace with which it was endowed, the city formed a distinct legal district." J. Luchaire, *Les Démocraties italiennes* (Paris, 1915), p. 77: "L'opinion publique admettait alors qu'un des droits fondamentaux du citoyen était de vaquer *en paix* et fructueusement à son industrie ou à son commerce; c'était une des premières garanties que la Commune doit assurer à tous" (my italics). F. Schevill, *Siena—The Story of a Medieval Commune* (London, 1909), p. 212: "peace was their lodestar, a commercial peace which would enable every man to go about his daily business."

[14] *Stat. com. Pad.* n. 85 (p. 33): "Ad paces hujus terre faciendas et discordias sedendas potestas et anciani toto posse laborent." See *ibid.* nn. 147, 423 (pp. 56, 136).

[15] See *Statuto dell' unione delle arti Padovane,* in M. Roberti, "Le corporazioni padovane d'arti e mestieri; Studio storico-giuridico con documenti e statuti inediti," *Memorie del R. istituto veneto di scienze, lettere, ed arti,* Vol. XXVI, No. 8 (1902), p. 71: "Et tunc inter gastaldiones fratalearum populi paduani fiat proposicio . . . ut civitas Padue semper conservetur in statu pacifico et tranquillo." See also *Le Statut des Nove* n. 1; in "Le Statut des neuf gouverneurs et défenseurs de la commune de Sienne, 1310," ed. J. Luchaire, *Mélanges d'archéologie et d'histoire,* XXI (1901), 245: "Giuro io podestà del comune et del popolo di Siena tenere et mantenere et difendere el comune et lo popolo di Siena in buono et pacifico stato." With these statements compare *Def. pac.* III. iii: "salvabitur regnum . . . in esse pacifico seu tranquillo"; II. v. 7: "causa tranquillitatis factiva et conservativa est actio principantis."

[16] *Statuti della repubblica Fiorentina,* ed. R. Caggese (Florence, 1910), Lib. I. n. I.

[17] See Pirenne, *op. cit.*, p. 209.

[18] *Siena statuto* 31; in *Documenti per la storia dei rivolgimenti politici del comune di Siena dal 1354 al 1369,* ed. J. Luchaire (Lyons, 1906), p. 16.

[19] Several commentators (Labanca, *Marsilio*, p. 121; Valois, *op. cit.*, p. 574) have held that by the title *Defensor pacis* Marsilius intends to refer to himself. That he means by it the ruler, however, is shown in his initial dedication of the book to "Ludovice, Romanorum Imperator," as one whose aim is "pacem seu tranquillitatem ubique diffundere ac nutrire" (I. i. 6); and also in his later statement that the ruler is "causa efficiens et conservans" of peace (I. xix. 3). See also II. v. 7, quoted above, n. 15.

[20] I. ii. 3.

[21] See below, pp. 96 ff., 118 ff.

It was in the context of the cities that the "church-state" problem made itself felt with that peculiar force which motivates so much of Marsilius' enterprise. For the clergy were one of the chief obstacles to the achievement of the structure of peace as the cities conceived it. This peace required for its fulfillment that all the inhabitants of the city and district be subject to one legal order; but it was precisely this to which the clergy would not agree. There was, indeed, a historical basis for their recalcitrance in the "immunities" which successive emperors had given to bishops and other church prelates. Such an immunity had been granted to the bishop of Padua by Ludwig II in 855.[22] But the result, from the standpoint of the burghers, was that the clergy not only derived all the material benefits of the city—roads, bridges, protection—without sharing any of its burdens,[23] but they could commit almost any crime with impunity, for the ecclesiastic courts were notoriously lenient with clerical offenders, and the latter were correspondingly numerous and extreme. The chronicles of Padua contain bitter protests against "the many and enormous crimes committed by clergymen, about which no justice was done by the bishop of Padua." [24]

The reaction of the Paduan burghers to this situation was equally violent. It took four closely related forms: (1) all ecclesiastic jurisdiction over laymen in both civil and criminal cases was abolished, even if one of the parties involved was a clergyman; [25] (2) the city's jurisdiction over the clergy in both civil and criminal cases was insisted upon; [26] (3) the clergy

[22] *Codice diplomatico padovano* n. 13 (ed. A. Gloria, in *R. deputazione di storia patria* [Venice, 1877], II, 27). See *Corp. jur. can., Decret. Gratiani* Pars II. can. 47. C. XI. qu.1 (I, 641); *Decretal. Greg. IX* Lib. II. Tit. 2. cap. 2 (II, 248–9). See also Imbart de la Tour, "Des immunités commerciales accordées aux églises du VIIe au IXe siècle," *Etudes d'histoire du moyen âge dédiées à Gabriel Monod* (Paris, 1896), pp. 71–87; G. Le Bras, *L'Immunité réelle* (Paris, 1920).

[23] See *Stat. com. Pad.* n. 459 (p. 147).

[24] *Liber regiminum Paduae* an. 1282 (ed. A. Bonardi, in *Miscellanea di storia veneta,* 2d series, VI, 125). See *ibid.* an. 1301 (p. 183), where it is reported that a certain "clericus . . . circa XX peccata inter homicidia et furta et violationes mulierum, quas postea interficiebat etiam pregnantes, commiserat, propter quod dignus erat morte pro uno quoque eorum, sed occidi non poterat, quia clericus erat."

[25] *Stat. com. Pad.* nn. 481–82 (p. 158): Excommunication of a layman for failing to appear in an ecclesiastic court is to be disregarded, and enforced taxation or punishment of laymen by the bishop of Padua is forbidden; a tax exacted from a citizen under force is to be repaid doubly.

[26] *Ibid.* nn. 236, 248, 1132 (pp. 83, 85, 361): Those who do not pay taxes or "help bear the burdens and operations of the commune" are not allowed to vote, or to hold any civil office or emolument, or to enjoy any of the benefits of the statutes, or to engage in any commercial transaction in Padua or the Paduan district. The last provision is found in a statute of 1280, in L. A. Botteghi, "Clero e comune in Padova nel secolo XIII": Documenti, *Nuovo archivio veneto,* n.s., IX (1905), 270–71. *Stat. com. Pad.* nn. 455, 470 (pp. 145, 152–3): crimes committed by clergymen against laymen are to be punished by the *podestà* and his judges "prout tenentur punire quemlibet laycum sue jurisdictioni subjectum, vel quamlibet aliam personam aliquod maleficium committentem in padua vel paduano districtu." Exceptions or privileges claimed by clergymen against such decisions are not to be admitted, and if

was placed, in effect, outside the protection of the city's laws,[27] a point dramatically illustrated in the famous provision that the penalty for killing a clergyman was to consist "only in one Venetian grosso";[28] and (4) further restrictions were placed upon the clergy, even its specifically spiritual and ecclesiastic functions being made subject to the communal jurisdiction.[29] The declared purpose of all these provisions was to abolish the exemptions which had led to the clergy being called *privilegiati*—an epithet which epitomized the basic complaint of the burghers against the ecclesiastic institution.[30]

These relations of Padua to the clergy, which were closely paralleled not only in most of the other north Italian cities but also in many parts of southern France and elsewhere, provided the fundamental background of the *Defensor pacis.* The latter declares that the clergy constitute the primary "impediment" to the realization of peace in the state,[31] and it expresses the same insistence as the Padua statutes, in almost the same words, that those who enjoy the "peace" and protection of the state must not be exempt from its burdens and jurisdiction.[32] Similarly the *Defensor* abolishes all

---

the judge or judges who handed down the sentence are excommunicated as a consequence, "ille vel illi tractetur et tractentur ac si excommunicatus seu excommunicati non essent seu fuissent."

[27] *Ibid.* nn. 475, 507, 812 (pp. 156, 164, 267): Laymen are not to be punished for nonpayment of debts to clergymen; the latter, where they do not help bear the burdens of the commune, or seek exemption from its jurisdiction, are to receive no legal consideration in either civil or criminal affairs.

[28] *Liber regiminum Paduae* an. 1282 (p. 125): "Et multi presbiteri, clerici et religiosi fuerunt occisi in Padua et paduano districtu; quoniam tunc fuerat per commune Paduae stabilitum, et scriptum in quodam parvo volumine, quod vocabatur Donatellus, in quo continebatur, ut pro homicidio commisso in personam alicujus ecclesiasticae personae condemnari debeat homicida solummodo in uno denario veneto grosso. . . ." See also G. Gennari, *Annali della città di Padova* (Bassano, 1804), III, 36. The fixing of a monetary fine for homicide was not, however, peculiar to Padua; even Gratian took over a chapter of the *Capitularies* (v.xxv) which set a sliding scale for killing clergymen from 300 *solidi* for a subdeacon to 900 for a bishop: *Corp. jur. can., Decret. Gratiani* Pars II. can.27. C.XVII. qu.4.

[29] *Stat. com. Pad.* nn. 577, 586 (pp. 186, 190): Monks cannot possess more than 200 lire; and those who desert a religious life after entering upon it can inherit nothing from their parents. *Stat.* an. 1299, in Botteghi, *op. cit.*, pp. 268–69: priests must administer penance to those designated by the commune to receive it, and are to be paid by the commune.

[30] See *Stat. com. Pad.* n. 470 (p. 152–53), where it is provided that no attention is to be paid to "exceptions" and "objections" raised against decisions of the *podestà* with respect to "aliquos qui dicerent vel dixissent se clericos vel alio modo privilegiatos." This statute also brings out clearly the tactic of the clergy in excommunicating officials of the commune who brought proceedings of any kind "contra aliquem occasione alicujus clerici vel alterius privilegiati." See also *ibid.* n. 236 (p. 83).

[31] *Def. pac.* I. xix. 3 ff. See below, p. 59.

[32] *Def. pac.* II. viii. 9: "Qui enim gaudet honoribus et civilibus commodis, ut pace et tutela legislatoris humani, ab oneribus et jurisdictione non debet eximi absque determinatione legislatoris eiusdem." See *Stat. com. Pad.* n. 1182 (p. 361): "Nullus gaudeat beneficiis statutorum comunis padue nisi sit in dacya comunis padue, et nisi faciat et attendat onera et factiones comunis." See *ibid.* n. 475 (p. 156); and *Stat.* an. 1280, in Botteghi, *op. cit.*, pp. 270–71.

coercive jurisdiction of the clergy over laymen,[33] and makes excommunication devoid of effect unless the "faithful legislator" has sanctioned it.[34] And finally, even the spiritual functions of the clergy are subjected to the state's jurisdiction: as in Padua, the state can force priests to administer the sacraments.[35]

In respect both of their republicanism and of their anti-clericalism, then, the *Defensor pacis* is the authentic spokesman of the north Italian cities. There had, indeed, been earlier works based upon the institutions of those cities,[36] but in none was the treatment so thoroughly concerned with the controversial problems which were agitating the cities, nor did they present so complete a doctrinal development of its institutions.

In seeking to establish the relation of Marsilius to the political milieu of Padua and other Italian cities, we must recognize also that he omits three vital "impediments" to their peace: the violent class struggle between the *magnati* and *popolani,* the strife between cities, and their departure from republicanism.

The first was in many respects similar to the strife between the clergy and the burghers, for just as the clergy had been called *privilegiati,* so the *magnati,* comprising feudal lords and other extremely wealthy men, were called *maleablati* ("the wrongly withdrawn"), since they too tried to remain outside the city's jurisdiction.[37] The result was the same lawlessness

[33] *Def. pac.* II. iv–v. [34] II. vi. 12–13; II. xxi. 8. [35] II. xvii. 8, 12, 15.

[36] See *Oculus pastoralis,* written ca. 1222; printed in L. A. Muratori, *Antiquitates Italicae medii aevi* (Arrezzo, 1776), Dissertatio 46; Vol. IX, cols. 791–856. The anonymous author of this work has been called "the first writer who attempted to present a theory of the communal state" (by P. S. Leicht, "Un principio politico medievale," *Rendiconti della R. accad. dei Lincei,* Cl. sci. mor. stor. e filol., 5th series, XXIX [1920], 240). See also John of Viterbo, *Liber de regimine civitatum,* ed. G. Salvemini, in *Bibliotheca juridica medii aevi,* III, 215–80; the section called "Del gouvernement des cités," in Brunetto Latini, *Livres dou tresor* III. ii, in *Collection de documents inédits sur l'histoire de France* (Paris, 1863), V, 575–620; Orfinus of Lodi, *Poema de regimine et sapientia potestatis,* ed. A. Ceruti, in *Miscellanea di storia patria edita per cura della Regia deputazione di storia patria,* VII (1869), 27–94. For a discussion of these works, see F. Hertter, *Die Podestàliteratur italiens im 12. und 13. Jahrhundert* (Leipzig and Berlin, 1910). Two more famous works also explicitly discuss the "cities of Italy" at some points: Egidius of Rome *De reg. princ.* Lib. III. Pars II. cap. ii; Ptolemy of Lucca *De reg. princ.* II. viii, x; III. xx; IV. i, viii, xviii, xxvi (pp. 33, 36, 74, 79, 90, 103, 112).

[37] See *Stat. com. Pad.* nn. 10, 418, 457, 631, 636–40, incl. (pp. 10, 135, 147, 205–8). On the strife between *magnati* and *popolani* in Padua, see M. Roberti, "Le corporazioni padovane d'arti e mestieri; Studio storico-giuridico, con documenti e statuti inediti," *Memorie del Reale istituto veneto di scienze, lettere, ed arti,* Vol. XXVI, no. 8 (1902), pp. 52–53; R. Cessi, "Le Corporazioni dei mercanti di panni e della lana in Padova fino a tutto il secolo XIV," *ibid.,* Vol. XXVIII, no. 2 (1908), pp. 13–14. For the similar struggles in other Italian cities, see J. Luchaire, *Les Démocraties italiennes* (Paris, 1915), pp. 108 ff., 145 ff.; L. Zdekauer, ed., *Il costituto del comune di Siena dell' anno 1262* (Milan, 1897), pp. xxxii ff., lxiii ff., lxxvii–lxxviii; G. Salvemini, *Magnati e popolani in Firenze dal 1280 al 1295* (Florence, 1899); J. Luchaire, ed., *Le Statut des neuf gouverneurs . . . Sienne,* p. 28; F. Ercole, *Dal comune al principato* (Florence, 1929), Ch. I, "La Lotta dèlle classi alla fine del medio evo," esp. pp. 26 ff.

and "infinite quarrels" as we saw above with respect to the clergy; [38] and the reaction of the burghers, the *popolani,* was almost equally violent.[39]

It is possible to find various reminiscences of this class struggle in the *Defensor pacis,*[40] but Marsilius does not deal with it in the direct sense in which he treats the problem of the clergy. His plea is, in effect, for a "popular front" of all elements of the laity, including the *magnati,* against the clergy.[41] His lineage would put him on the side of the most influential *popolani,* who had perhaps the biggest stake in combatting the *magnati;* for he was the son of a notary, and the notaries were in many respects supreme among the *arti* or guilds of Padua.[42] But his actions seem to place him on the side of the anti-republican *magnati,* for, as we have seen, he served as ambassador of Can Grande and Matteo Visconti in 1319, one year after Padua's capitulation to the latter and the consequent demise of its republicanism.[43]

As for the strife between cities,[44] the "peace" of Marsilius' treatise is entirely internal to the state.[45] He does indeed refer at several points to the division from which the *Italicum regnum* suffers,[46] but only as a consequence of the loss of peace for which he blames the papacy, not as itself a cause of that loss. In this respect, then, his blaming of all the loss of peace in Italy upon the papal pretensions to plenitude of power is a falsification of the history of Padua and of almost all the other cities of Italy. His position preserves some validity only if his own definition of "peace" is main-

[38] See *Liber regiminum Paduae* an. 1282 (p. 124): "Eo tempore multae et infinitae querellae, ac petitiones datae fuerunt contra magnates Paduae per populares, vigore statuti de male ablatis, quae his temporibus fuere confirmata; pro quibus querellis, et petitionibus condemnati fuerunt dicti magnates, et maximum scandalum in civitate Paduae est exortum."

[39] See *Stat. com. Pad.* nn. 10, 86, 418, 424, 628, 636–38, 640 (pp. 10, 33, 135, 137, 204, 206–8).

[40] The whole argument of the chapters in behalf of the *populus* as legislator (I. xii–xiii), with their defense of the "pluralitas civium," the "minus docti," the "homines humiloris ingenii," against the "pauciores," constitutes a rejoinder against the claims of the *magnati.* See also the provision that "studiosi pauperes" must be eligible for election to office (I. xiv. 8). More generally, the entire "peace" and "unity" of the Marsilian state involve the subjection of the *magnati* to the jurisdiction of the whole state. See below, Ch. III, Secs. 2 and 3.

[41] This is epitomized in Marsilius' use of the term *populus* for the "whole body of citizens," as against the more particularistic use of the term *popolani* or *populares* in Padua and other Italian cities to mean not all the citizens but those from whom the *magnati* were distinguished. See below, pp. 180–82.

[42] Roberti, "Le corporazioni padovane," p. 14: "Fino dai primi tempi si nota una certa disugualianza fra le diverse corporazioni: quella dei notai, ad esempio, ha sempre maggiori diritta ed una certa supremazia sopra tutte le altre."

[43] See above, pp. 20–21.

[44] For a succinct history of Padua's strife with Vicenza, Bassano, Verona, Trevisa, and Venice in the thirteenth and early fourteenth centuries, see G. Cappelletti, *Storia di Padova dalla sua origine sino al presente* (Padua, 1874).

[45] See I. ii. 3; and below, p. 97.

[46] I. i. 2; I. xix. 4, 12; II. xxvi. 19, 20.

tained—but then it does not have the applicability to the plight of contemporary Italy which he indicates in many parts of his book.

The third important hiatus between Marsilius' doctrine and the actual historical career of Padua consists in the fact that at the same time as Marsilius was depicting a state with strictly republican institutions in the *Defensor pacis,* Padua, and indeed most Italian cities, had left republicanism for the *signoria* or absolutism of one man.[47] There are, to be sure, aspects of his doctrine which remove from it the anachronism which this relation would appear to indicate. In particular, his emphasis upon the unity of the government, whereby all rival jurisdictions are either subordinated to it or abolished, reflects the motivation which led to the institution of the *signoria.* However, where the latter was almost always embodied in one man, Marsilius declares that his unified government can consist in one or many citizens; [48] and where the *signoria* involved complete legislative, executive, and judicial power for the *signor,* Marsilius insists that his government, although unified and brooking no rival jurisdiction, must be under the control of the "legislator," consisting in the whole people.

The picture which emerges from our examination of Marsilius in the context of his Padua background is thus compounded of paradoxes. His doctrine reflects faithfully the republicanism and anticlericalism of thirteenth and early fourteenth century Padua; but it omits the wars between cities almost completely, and the class conflict between *magnati* and *popolani* to a marked extent; while in Discourse I the contemporary fact of the departure from republicanism is simply ignored. His familial affiliations would appear to put him on the side of republicanism, but his actual conduct in 1319, and even earlier, is on the side of the anti-republican *signori.*

What, now, of Paris, the other chief milieu of Marsilius' life prior to the composition of the *Defensor?* There is an obvious difference between it and republican Padua. Paris was the capital of a France becoming constantly more centralized and of a hereditary monarchy becoming increasingly absolute, a fact not contradicted by the calling of *états généraux* in 1302, 1308, and 1314.[49] Yet—and this point is of central importance for the understanding of the *Defensor pacis*—Marsilius brings the French king,

[47] "When Bologna accepted Taddeo di Pepoli as its *signor* in 1337 no city east of the Appenines (except Venice) retained its republican constitution": M. V. Clarke, *The Medieval City State* (London, 1926), p. 107. Jacopo da Carrara became absolute lord of Padua in 1318, under the modest title of "captain of the people." He was given "plenary jurisdiction" over the city, including all the authority, previously exercised by the greater council, to make, interpret, or abolish statutes at will; all the officials of the city were to derive their authority from him and to swear obedience to him. Jacopo in turn swore to "defend the city in peaceful status" (G. Gennari, *Annali della città di Padova* [Bassano, 1804], III, 213–14). This *signoria carrarese* lasted until 1405.

[48] I. xvii. 2.

[49] See *Cambridge Medieval History,* VII, 326–27.

as well as the head of the Empire, under the same general rubric of his doctrine as the *pars principans* who, as we saw, was the faithful image of the *podestà* of Padua and other Italian cities. When, in Discourse II of the *Defensor,* the *princeps* is referred to, the illustration given is sometimes Philip the Fair of France [50] or Emperor Henry VII; [51] and Marsilius also goes back to earlier emperors. Can he mean that these are the equivalents of the *pars principans,* popularly elected, rigorously controlled by the people and by the laws made by the people, subject to correction and removal by the people? This is a point which we shall discuss at greater length in subsequent contexts.[52] It suffices to point out here that the differences of the historical milieux in which Marsilius formed his doctrine are reflected in corresponding oppositions in the doctrine itself. Throughout these differences, however, one fixed point remains: opposition to the papal claims. And it is on that point that Marsilius fastens all the otherwise disparate elements of the several contexts. The oppositions between Philip the Fair and Boniface VIII, between Henry VII and Clement V, and finally between Ludwig of Bavaria and John XXII are all exploited in the *Defensor;* but they are all assimilated, also, to that relation between the *pars principans* and the *sacerdotium,* as two "parts" of the state, which Discourse I propounds.

[50] I. xix. 10; II. xx. 9; II. xxi. 9.

[51] I. xix. 10; II. xxiii. 12; II. xxv. 17.

[52] See below, pp. 253 ff.

CHAPTER II

THE PRINCIPLES OF MARSILIUS' POLITICS

1. THE PHILOSOPHIC SOURCES

THE POLITICAL PHILOSOPHY of Marsilius achieves its far-reaching conclusions by means of principles which diverge in basic ways from the antecedent medieval tradition. It is in these principles that are to be found the doctrinal roots not only of Marsilius' reversal of the historic conception of the relation between the spiritual and temporal powers, but also of his theory of the state as such, from which that reversal is explicitly deduced. The direct stimulus came from the failure of earlier attempts to frame a philosophy which would successfully cope with the metaphysical, methodological, and axiological premises of the doctrine of the papal plenitude of power.[1] The papalists' theologizing of politics and their analogical assimilation to it of the evaluative criteria found in all other orders forced Marsilius to deal with such basic questions as the method and subject matter of politics as a science or philosophy, the relation of that subject matter to those of other sciences and of political to other kinds of values, the nature of man as involved in political action, and, underlying all these, the general problem of the relation between the natural, human, and divine orders. It was the answers to these questions which determined the character of much of medieval political philosophy, as well as of philosophy as a whole; and Marsilius' answers must be made explicit if his own doctrine is to be understood.

Our examination of Marsilius' principles will follow several different routes. The initial indication of their character and content is to be obtained by considering the way in which he treated the philosophic sources common to the political thinkers of his time. Those sources were political Aristotelianism, as found in the *Politics,* and political Augustinianism, as found in the *De civitate Dei* and in the Bishop of Hippo's commentaries on the New Testament. An additional source, peculiar to Marsilius among the major political thinkers of the period, was political Averroism, which represented his mode of relating the other two sources viewed as political doctrines based upon reason and revelation, respectively. Marsilius' Aristotelianism and Augustinianism also correspond in general to the procedures

[1] See above, Ch. I, Sec. 2, esp. pp. 18–19.

of Discourses I and II; for the first Discourse is almost a commentary on certain aspects of the *Politics,* while the second presents a large-scale exegesis of the New Testament from a point of view strikingly similar to that which Marsilius himself lengthily quotes in support from St. Augustine. His treatment of these sources, even apart from his Averroism, was profoundly different from the way in which they were used by his predecessors and contemporaries; and this difference had as its result a drastic change in the whole orientation of political philosophy.

(1) *Aristotelianism and efficient causality.* The obvious reliance of Discourse I of the *Defensor pacis* upon the *Politics* of Aristotle follows a systematic pattern based upon a selection from the materials presented in that treatise. According to Aristotle, a complete political science must deal with four general questions: *(a)* what is the *absolutely* best constitution, *(b)* what constitution is best suited to *what different kinds of people, (c)* what constitution is best suited to *most people,* and *(d)* what are the means of *generating* constitutions and *preserving* them from destruction through revolution.[2] These four questions, which have been correlated, respectively, with the final, material, formal, and efficient causes analyzed in Aristotle's physical and metaphysical works,[3] are treated extensively in different portions of the *Politics;* [4] but a different selection was made from them by Marsilius and by the other medieval Aristotelians.[5] The latter all centered their discussion upon that portion of the *Politics* in which the finalistic orientation of the absolutely best constitution is developed. The reason for this selection is to be found in the ethico-theological predilections of these writers. Whether they were partisans of the papal or of the temporal power,

[2] *Pol.* IV. 1. 1288b 10 ff.

[3] *Phys.* II. 3. 194b 22 ff.; *Metaphys.* I. 3. 983a 25 ff. See R. McKeon, "Aristotle's Conception of Moral and Political Philosophy," *Ethics,* LI (1941), 282–85.

[4] For the first question, see Books VII–VIII and also the discussion of ideal kingship: Pol. III. 13. 1284a 3 ff. For the second question, see especially *Pol.* IV. 12. 1296b 13: "What constitution is beneficial for what persons . . . must next be discussed. . . ." For the third question, see especially *Pol.* IV. 11. 1295a 25: "What is the best constitution and what is the best life for most cities and for most men. . . ." These two questions are also discussed throughout many other portions of Books IV and VI, respectively. For the fourth question, see Book V. The numbering of the books of the *Politics* which is followed in this study is the traditional one found in the edition of I. Bekker and in the Oxford translation.

[5] The term "Aristotelians" as it is used throughout this study means nothing more than those writers who used any of the concepts or doctrines of Aristotle. It is thus an inclusive term, and does not imply any judgment as to the correctness or authenticity of the interpretation of Aristotle made by any of the writers so designated. On the general medieval use of the *Politics,* see G. von Hertling, "Zur Geschichte der aristotelischen Politik im Mittelalter," in *Historische Beiträge zur Geschichte der Philosophie* (Kempten and Munich, 1914), pp. 20–32; M. Grabmann, "Studien über den Einfluss der aristotelischen Philosophie auf die mittelalterlichen Theorien über das Verhältnis von Kirche und Staat," *Sitzungsberichte der Bayerischen Akad. der Wissenschaften,* Phil.-hist. Abt. (1934), Heft 2; *Idem,* "Die mittelalterlichen Kommentare zur Politik des Aristoteles," *ibid.* (1941), Band II, Heft 10.

or were comparatively neutral, they all viewed the state as dedicated to the moral end of aiding men to achieve the best possible life in this world, and to the theological end of preparing men for salvation in the next world. It is not accidental, therefore, that all these writers make kingship the preferred form of government and view the state from the standpoint of those lofty virtues which the ideal king or emperor should enable men to attain, and which he perhaps embodies in his own person.[6]

Marsilius is the first of the medieval Aristotelians to adopt the orientation of that portion of the *Politics* which is at the opposite pole from the finalistic: the book on revolutions. In the opening chapter of the *Defensor* he points out that Aristotle had treated all the "usual" efficient causes of the strife which leads to the destruction of states, but that a new cause, the papal claim to plenitude of power, has arisen since Aristotle's day.[7] Marsilius proposes, therefore, to expose this new cause; [8] and it is from this point of view that he develops his analysis of the state in Discourse I. This orientation at once provides a profound change from the antecedent tradition. For the basic problem is no longer one of ideal ends but rather of proximate means; the setting is no longer that of a perfect moral and intellectual community but rather that of a state hovering precariously on the brink of destruction and hence requiring that attention be completely directed to its preservation.[9] As a consequence, the central emphasis no longer falls upon final causes but rather upon efficient causes, since the preservation of the state is accomplished by concentrating not upon ultimate goals but upon explicit agencies which control political institutions and are hence capable of effecting immediate results therein.

The specific characteristics and consequences of this reorientation from final to efficient causes will be dealt with at many points below. It is important, however, to understand here the general manner in which this concentration proceeds, for it involves not only the basic structure of Marsilius' arguments but also the relation which he sets up between morals and politics. The distinction between final and efficient causes is in general the same as that between ends and means; hence it can be said that just as means are always relative to the ends toward which they are instruments,

[6] See Thomas Aquinas *De reg. princ.* I, *passim*. Ptolemy of Lucca *De reg. princ.* III. ii (p. 61). Engelbert of Admont *De ortu* cap. ii, xiv, xv. (pp. 363–64, 369–71). John of Paris *De potestate regia et papali* cap. i, xviii (pp. 109–10, 131). Dante *De monarchia* I. ii-v (pp. 342–44). Egidius of Rome *De reg. princ.* Lib. I. Pars. I. cap. iii; Pars II. cap. vii; Pars III. cap. iv. James of Viterbo *De reg. Christ.* II. ii, vi, viii (pp. 165–66, 169, 224, 258). Augustinus Triumphus *S. de eccl. pot.* qu.44. a.I. John of Jandun *Quaestiones in duodecim libros metaphysicae* I. qu.I, 18; II. qu.II (fols. 2A, 14M, 35G).

[7] *Def. pac.* I. i. 3. See I. xix. 3.

[8] I. i. 7.

[9] For detailed references on this point see below, pp. 106–7.

so there is no treatment of efficient causes without an at least implicit concern with final causes. Nevertheless, varying degrees of emphasis are possible, such that ends or means become the primary consideration. When the emphasis is on final causes, the sole or chief concern is to propound what are the highest values or best ends to which men and states are to be dedicated. The question of specific means or efficient causes for achieving these ends relatively to existing conditions is considered either not at all or else with great brevity; moreover, the means, when they are designated at all, are espoused because what they provide is directly constitutive of the ends in question. Such was the approach, in varying degrees, of the pre-Marsilian tradition, with its concentration upon the theological end of eternal life, its explanation and evaluation of political institutions by reference to that end, and, in one of its main phases, its insistence upon the political hegemony of the priesthood as providing the basic condition for the achievement of the end. On the other hand, when the emphasis is on efficient causes, the sole or chief concern is to propound the agencies, processes, and mechanisms of law and government. The question of the ends which these political means are to achieve, other than the direct end of the smooth functioning of government, is considered either not at all or else with great brevity; moreover, these ends are so designated not because they are conceived to embody maximal normative values, moral, theological, or other, but simply because they are in fact attained, projected, desired. The most famous example of this type of doctrine is, of course, Machiavelli's *Prince,* where the dominant preoccupation is with the means of achieving and retaining political power, the ends, where they are mentioned at all, being the power and glory of the prince himself. The fifth book of Aristotle's *Politics,* which is the ancestor of Machiavellianism, is similarly concerned with the means of generating and preserving constitutions, partial abstraction being made from the moral values by which, in the finalistic orientation, they are assayed.

The sense in which Marsilius' doctrine is oriented in efficient causality may be best understood as involving a reinterpretation of all the other elements of the Aristotelian analysis in the light of the primary concern with the preservation of the state. Discourse I of the *Defensor* explicitly treats all four causes of the state and its institutions; [10] moreover, those institutions are initially deduced from the final cause, which Marsilius calls the "sufficient life." [11] That deduction involves a moral commitment in a sense in which Machiavelli's discussion of political means for the end of princely power and glory does not, because Marsilius views the sufficient life as be-

[10] See below, p. 48.

[11] See I. iv, *passim.*

ing desired and attainable by all, or almost all, men, as against the egocentric, self-aggrandizing end of Machiavelli's prince. Hence, Marsilius is concerned, as Machiavelli was not, with avoiding those efficient causes which may lead only to the "private advantage" of one or a few men as against the "common benefit" of all.[12] Nevertheless, the Marsilian final cause no longer has the pervasive role which it played in the antecedent tradition. The sufficient life as the end of man, which becomes the "common benefit" of the state, is not justified by specifically moral or theological criteria, but is posited without argument simply on the basis of its being "naturally" desired by all men;[13] and most of the remainder of the work is concerned not with evaluating political institutions in the light of the characteristics which uniquely constitute that final cause, but rather with the means of achieving its minimally necessary political preconditions: the preservation of the state and its institutions of law and government. Hence, Marsilius' doctrine, viewed as a whole, is not amoral in the manner of Machiavellianism; but neither is it integrally tied to ultimate ethical ends in the manner of the medieval tradition. Where the dominant position in antecedent political doctrines had been held by ultimate final causes specified in a "higher law," natural and divine, the dominant position in Marsilius' doctrine is held by an efficient cause called the "legislator." Consequently, it is in those sections of the *Defensor* which set forth the efficient causes of the law, of the government, of the other parts of the state, and of peace, that Marsilius' decisive doctrine is found; and the basic characteristics of the state—its peace, order, unity—are similarly elaborated in terms not of final causes, as in the previous tradition, but of efficient causes.[14] Thus where in the antecedent tradition—as found in Thomas Aquinas, for instance—the central concern had been to set forth the goals and limits of political institutions, but comparatively little stress had been laid upon who controls those institutions or who enforces the adherence to those goals and limits, Marsilius' procedure is precisely the reverse. Hence, at exactly the points where Thomas is vague, Marsilius is definite; but also, where Thomas had carefully indicated the moral limits beyond which political power cannot go, Marsilius, having indicated that such power belongs to the people, sets no limits to it.

[12] See esp. I. xii. 5, 8; I. xiii. 5. The egocentric orientation of Machiavelli's *Prince* must, of course, be distinguished from his *Discourses on the First Ten Books of Titus Livius*, where the orientation is specifically republican and hence much closer to that of Marsilius.

[13] I. iv. 2. See I. i. 7, and below, p. 60.

[14] See, for the efficient cause of law, I. xii–xiii; of government, I. xv. 2; of the other parts of the state, I. vii. 3, I. xv. 4 ff.; of peace, I. xix. 3. On the reorientation of the basic characteristics of the state from final to efficient causality, see below, pp. 98 ff., 111, 118 ff.

In this reorientation from final to efficient causes consists a basic aspect of Marsilius' "modernity,"[15] of that practicality and concreteness which commentators have felt to contrast so sharply with the idealistic utopianism of the previous tradition. Yet the doctrinal source of the change is the fact that Marsilius, like Machiavelli after him, derives his principles from Aristotle's book on the preservation of constitutions.[16] And it is this specific derivation, too, rather than the use of Aristotle's *Politics* as such, which in large part underlies Marsilius' radical departures from the tradition with respect to the church-state problem.

(2) *Augustinianism and positivism*. The importance of Augustinianism for Marsilius' political thought has received almost no recognition,[17] despite the fact that Augustine is the chief interpreter of the profusion of Biblical citations in the Discourse II of the *Defensor*.[18] The selection which Marsilius makes from that interpretation is determined by the central dualism which permeates the entire political philosophy of St. Augustine, between the city of God and the city of man. The basis of the dualism is in the ends which men set before themselves, the objects of their "love," and these objects are themselves viewed as a strict dualism: either God or man.[19] It is in terms of this dualism that Augustine draws his famous consequence from Cicero's definition of a "commonwealth" (*res publica*) as comprising a people associated by consent to justice.[20] For since justice, as well as all other moral virtues, can be had only where God is loved, it follows that there never was a Roman commonwealth, for the Romans did not love God.[21] Yet this is not Augustine's final word on the subject. For the dualism between love of God and of man has as its context a world created and ordered by God; and in that world even perverted men are

[15] See J. N. Figgis, *From Gerson to Grotius*, 2d ed. (Cambridge, 1931), pp. 12–13: "There has been a revolution in political thought, not dissimilar to the substitution of efficient for final causes as an account of natural phenomena." See also McKeon, *op. cit.*, p. 290: "in politics as in physics all four of the Aristotelian causes have been reduced to efficient causes. . . ." Neither of these writers was referring to Marsilius in these statements, but only to the orientation characteristic of modern political thought.

[16] Only one commentator that I have found has noted that Marsilius' kinship with Machiavelli rests upon his taking his point of departure from Book v of the *Politics*: E. Barker, *The Political Thought of Plato and Aristotle* (London, 1906), p. 511.

[17] Thus Lagarde, in his chapter on "Marsile et la théologie," *Marsile*, pp. 70–77, does not consider the question of Augustine's influence at all, contenting himself with mentioning the saint among other commentators used by Marsilius (p. 76).

[18] After Aristotle and the Bible itself, Augustine is cited more frequently than any other author by Marsilius—55 times, followed by Ambrose with 42 citations and Jerome with 38. This does not mean, of course, that Marsilius was well read in any of these three authors; he obtained these citations from various "helps to Bible students," especially the *Collectanea* of Peter Lombard and the *Catena aurea* of Thomas Aquinas. See C. W. Previté-Orton, "The Authors Cited in the *Defensor Pacis*," pp. 407 ff.

[19] *De civitate Dei* XIV. i ff.

[20] *De re publica* I. XXXIX.

[21] *De civ. Dei* XIX, xxi, xxiii, xxv. Cf. above, p. 15.

subject to the "peace" and order of God's natural laws.[22] Hence even the city or state which is not dedicated to God, or "eternal peace," as its ultimate end, has a divine function, that of fostering the "temporal peace" whereby men attain the economic and political security necessary for the sustenance of their mortal life.[23] On this ground, then, the normative requirement of justice and of the theological virtues generally can be omitted, and the definition of the "commonwealth" is now given in purely positivist terms: any group of human beings associated in some common object of "love," that is, some common end, is a "people" and comprises a "commonwealth." In place of the initial normative dualism, a sliding scale is introduced, whereby the value of commonwealths is proportional to the value of their ends.[24]

In the subsequent development of medieval political thought the normative orientation of Augustine's doctrine received thorough exploitation.[25] The papalists, in particular, by identifying subjection to God with subjection to the pope,[26] made the papal plenitude of power an inevitable consequence of the Augustinian norm.

In Marsilius, on the other hand, it is the positivist orientation of Augustine's politics which becomes the center of attention. The Marsilian state is more like Augustine's "city of man" than is any other state propounded by a medieval thinker; Augustine's description of the earthly city and its

[22] *Ibid.* xix. xii: "Quod autem perversum est, *etiam hoc* necesse est ut in aliqua et ex aliqua et cum aliqua rerum parte pacatum sit, in quibus est vel ex quibus constat; alioquin nihil esset omnino . . . *Nullo modo tamen inde aliquid legibus summi illius creatoris ordinatorisque subtrahitur,* a quo pax universitatis administratur. . . ."

[23] *Ibid.* xix. xiii (*fin.*), xvii, xxvi.

[24] *Ibid.* xix. xxiv. McIlwain, *op. cit.*, pp. 157–58, contends that the subsequent positive definition of *res publica* is advanced by Augustine not as his own view but simply to show the untenability of heathenism; this interpretation is concurred in by Sabine, *A History of Political Theory,* p. 192. But this seems not to take account of Augustine's references to the positive definition as "Secundum *probabiliores* autem definitiones" (*De civ. Dei* ii. xxi) and "Secundum istam definitionem *nostram*" (*ibid.* xix. xxiv); and it ignores the broader context indicated in the text above. It also requires a distinction between *res publica* and *regnum* (McIlwain, *op. cit.*, pp. 154–55) which is not made by Augustine himself. It should be noted that in another fundamental text (*De libero arbitrio* i. vi. 14 [PL 32, 1229]), Augustine treats the closely related term *populus* from the same positive point of view as he does *res publica* in the *De civ. Dei.* The interpretation of Augustine's definitions followed here is that held also by J. N. Figgis, *The Political Aspects of St. Augustine's "City of God"* (London, 1921), pp. 61–63; G. Combès, *La Doctrine politique de saint Augustin* (Paris, 1927), pp. 110–12; H. X. Arquillière, *L'Augustinisme politique* (Paris, 1934), pp. 6 ff., 17 ff. The fact that subsequent medieval writers do not repeat Augustine's positive definition of *res publica* is no indication of his own thought; most of them also make an identification, denied by him, of the *civitas Dei* with the visible church.

[25] See the evidence collected in C. Mirbt, *Die Stellung Augustins in der Publizistik des gregorianischen Kirchenstreits* (Leipzig, 1888), esp. pp. 88 ff.; also Combès, *op. cit.*, pp. 428 ff.; E. Bernheim, "Politische Begriffe des Mittelalters im Lichte der Anschauung Augustins," *Deutsche Zeitschrift für Geschichtswissenschaft,* n.s., I (1896), 1–23; Arquillière, *op. cit.*

[26] See above, pp. 15–16.

peace[27] is closely matched by the orientation of "civil happiness" and socio-economic "peace" into which Marsilius fits his state.[28] Moreover, not only does he fail to make obedience to God the condition of the legitimacy of political power, but he cites from Augustine texts which go to the opposite extreme: even bad rulers—no matter how bad—must be obeyed by divine commandment.[29] These texts are not from the *City of God* but rather from Augustine's commentaries on the New Testament; but they are logical applications of Augustine's positivist definition whereby a true commonwealth does not require justice. It is in keeping with this same positivist orientation that Marsilius removes justice from the essence of law.[30]

Marsilius' combination of Aristotelianism and Augustinianism gives rise to serious stresses in his doctrine between naturalism and supernaturalism, and between republicanism and absolutism.[31] But both orientations have a basic homogeneity in their common emphasis upon preservation of the state in "peace" and their concomitant withdrawal of the state from a concern with ultimate ethical ends. The positivist orientation which Marsilius takes over from Augustine enables him to make the same concentration upon specifically political means geared to minimal values as had the orientation in terms of efficient causes which he derives from Aristotle's book on revolutions.

(3) *Averroism and secularism*. The philosophic movement known as Latin Averroism was based upon a complete acceptance of the Aristotelian philosophy even where it was in opposition to the Christian faith. Although the University of Padua in the period when Marsilius presumably studied there was not the stronghold of Averroism which it became shortly thereafter,[32] his association with the movement has long been recognized,[33]

[27] *De civ. Dei* XIX. xvii.

[28] See I. i. 7; I. xix. 2. See below, pp. 64–65, 78, 97.

[29] *Def. pac.* II. v. 4. This entire "paragraph," covering five pages, should be read to grasp the complete opposition of Marsilius' Augustinianism to that of the papalists. See also below, pp. 250–51.

[30] I. x. 5. See below, pp. 134–35.

[31] See below, pp. 253 ff., 299.

[32] See *Monumenti della Università di Padova, 1222–1318,* pp. 389–91. For the four "professors of philosophy and logic" of whom alone there is any record as having taught at Padua during the thirteenth and early fourteenth centuries, see *ibid.*, pp. 598–99. No evidence is presented by T. Greenwood in support of his statement that "C'est à Padoue qu'elles [i.e., doctrines averroïstes] s'installèrent le plus fortement, *vers la fin du xiiie siècle,* dès le début de la fondation de cette illustre université" ("L'Humanisme averroïste en France et les sources du rationalisme," *Revue de l'Université d'Ottawa,* XVI [1946], 189; my italics). The University of Padua was founded in 1222.

[33] P. Mandonnet, *Siger de Brabant et l'averroïsme latin au XIIIe siècle,* 2d ed. (Louvain, 1911), I, 188: "Jean de Jandun et Marsile de Padoue, les défenseurs des prétentions royales, étaient des averroïstes notoires." See E. Renan, *Averroes et l'averroïsme,* 3d ed. (Paris, 1882), p. 340.

and is attested by his membership in the arts faculty at Paris, where Averroism flourished, his friendship with and possible medical studentship under Peter of Abano, the leading physician and astrologist of his day,[34] and his close relations with John of Jandun, the outstanding Averroist of Paris. Indeed, together with Peter, Marsilius is considered one of the co-founders of Padua Averroism,[35] and he has been declared to have effected the liaison between the Paris Averroism of John and the Padua Averroism of Peter.[36] This liaison is well symbolized by the fact that it was through Marsilius that John became the first of the philosophers at Paris to obtain a copy of Peter's commentary on the *Problems* of Aristotle.[37] The *Defensor pacis* is itself viewed as the leading, and even the first, exponent of "political Averroism."[38]

With respect to internal doctrinal evidence, however, the establishment of the precise meaning and grounds of Marsilius' Averroism is less simple. For "Averroism" itself did not constitute a single doctrine or group of doctrines in the thirteenth and early fourteenth centuries, so that it has been possible both to affirm and to deny Averroism not only of Peter of Abano[39] but also of Dante,[40] and to declare that while John of Jandun

[34] See above, pp. 20, 21.

[35] E. Troilo, "L'averroismo padovano," *Atti della Società italiana per il progresso delle scienze,* XXVI Riunione (Rome, 1938), III, 260.

[36] M. M. Gorce, "Averroïsme," *Dictionnaire d'histoire et de géographie ecclésiastiques,* V, 1075: "Cette liaison entre l'averroïsme parisien de Jean de Jandun et l'averroïsme padouan, qui allait avoir de si longues et si extraordinaires destinées, avait été operée par Marsile de Padoue."

[37] See the ms. quoted by Renan (*op. cit.,* p. 340): "Et ego Joannes de Genduno qui, Deo gratias, credo esse primus inter Parisius regentes in philosophia ad quem praedicta expositio pervenit per dilectissimum meum magistrum Marcilium de Padua, illorum expositionem manibus propriis mihi scribere dignum duxi. . . ."

[38] E. Gilson, *La Philosophie au moyen âge,* 2d ed. (Paris, 1944), p. 692: "*le Defensor Pacis* est un exemple d'averroïsme politique aussi parfait qu'on le peut souhaiter." See also M. de Wulf, *Histoire de la philosophie médiévale,* 5th ed. (Paris, 1925), II, 217; B. Nardi, *Saggi di filosofia dantesca* (Milan, 1930), p. 284; Lagarde, *Marsile,* pp. 89 ff.; Grabmann, "Studien," pp. 41 ff.; Sabine, *op. cit.,* p. 291; d'Entrèves, *Medieval Contribution,* pp. 48, 86; Gentile, *op. cit.,* pp. 150–51; E. Troilo, "L'averroismo di Marsilio da Padova," in A. Checchini and N. Bobbio, eds., *Marsilio da Padova: Studi raccolti nel VI centenario della morte* (Padua, 1942), pp. 47–77. With respect to Marsilius as the first "political Averroist," it may be pointed out here that, even if it remains forever impossible to find Siger of Brabant's lectures on Aristotle's *Politics* (which Pierre Dubois reported hearing; see *De recup. terre sancte* par. 132 [p. 121]), we have extensive political writings by John of Jandun which show the explicit influence of Averroes himself. See John's *Quaestiones in duodecim libros Metaphysicae,* especially Lib. I. qu.18 (fols. 14E–15M); also Lib. I, qus. 1, 17, 21, 22; Lib. II, qus. 4, 11; Lib. XII, qu. 22. John's political discussions appear to have been completely overlooked by scholars. For a brief examination of them, see A. Gewirth, "John of Jandun and the *Defensor Pacis,*" *Speculum,* XXIII (1948), 267–72.

[39] For affirmation of Peter's Averroism, see Renan, *op. cit.,* p. 326; Sante Ferrari, *I tempi, la vita, le dottrine di Pietro d'Abano* (Genoa, 1900); Lagarde, *Marsile,* p. 81; Troilo, *op. cit.,* p. 260. On the other hand, that Peter is an Averroist is denied by B. Nardi, "La teoria dell'-anima e la generazione delle forme secondo Pietro d'Abano," *Rivista di filosofia neo-scolastica.*

was an Averroist, he was not one in the manner of Siger of Brabant but is rather closer to Albert the Great.[41] The fact that the charge of Averroism was brought in the thirteenth century against Christian Aristotelians like Albert and Thomas Aquinas, and against an Augustinian like Roger Bacon,[42] emphasizes further the difficulty of presenting a precise meaning for this concept.

The problem of identifying particular Averroists arises largely from the fact that between the Christian and the Averroist Aristotelians there were similarities as well as differences, to the extent of their common acceptance of Aristotelianism and their formal distinction of it, and of reason generally, from faith. For while the Thomists, unlike the Averroists, held that reason and faith could not be in contradiction to one another, one of the essential conditions of this Thomist harmony was a careful allocation of the respective spheres and objects of reason and faith. Consequently, there is need for great caution in identifying the Averroism of Marsilius. Some attempts at such identification have adduced criteria which apply equally to Marsilius, to Thomas Aquinas, and to Albert the Great, such as the separation of reason and faith [43] and the reliance for certainty upon self-evident principles, necessary demonstrations, and sense experience.[44]

IV (1912), 723 ff.; "Intorno alle dottrine filosofiche di Pietro d'Abano," *Nuova rivista storica,* IV (1920), 81 ff.; L. Thorndike, *A History of Magic and Experimental Science* (New York, 1923), II, 888; C. Giacon, "Pietro d'Abano e l'averroismo padovano," *Atti della Società italiana per il progresso delle scienze,* XXVI Riunione (Rome, 1938), III, 334–39.

[40] Dante's Averroism is denied by Mandonnet, *op. cit.,* pp. 301–2; and by M. M. Gorce, *L'Essor de la pensée au moyen âge* (Paris, 1934), p. 178. It is affirmed by Nardi, *Saggi di filosofia dantesca,* p. 266; and by E. Gilson, *Reason and Revelation in the Middle Ages* (New York, 1938), p. 108. However, in *Dante et la philosophie* (Paris, 1939) Gilson strongly qualifies this affirmation; see pp. 123–24, note; 157, 169 ff., 210 ff.

[41] Gorce, "Averroïsme," col. 1074.

[42] See Mandonnet, *op. cit.,* I, 231 ff., 238 ff.

[43] See Lagarde, *Marsile,* p. 86; d'Entrèves, *Medieval Contribution,* p. 49. Phrases of Marsilius like "simplici credulitate absque rationem tenemus" (I. ix. 2) and "quod tamen sola fide tenemus" (II. xxx. 4) are matched by such statements of Thomas Aquinas as "Respondeo dicendum quod mundum non semper fuisse *sola fide tenetur,* et demonstrative probari non potest" (*S. theol.* I. qu.46. a.2. See *ibid.* I. qu.1. a.1. ad 1; qu.32. a.1. Resp.; qu.99. a.1. ad 1; II. II. qu.1. a.8. ad 1; *Cont. gent.* I. v). See also Albert the Great *De generatione et corruptione* I. Tr. I. cap. xxii (*Opera,* ed Borgnet, IV, 363): "nihil ad me de Dei miraculis, cum ego de naturalibus disseram." This phrase is quoted, with explicit reference to Albert, by Peter of Abano *Conciliator differentiarum* Diff. IX. Prop. 3 (fol. 14G) and by John of Jandun *Quaestiones in duodecim libros Metaphysicae* Lib. I. qu.16; Lib. II. qu.4 (fols. 13A, 25O). It is significant that this phrase is almost identical with one of Siger of Brabant which has often been taken as the epitome of Averroism; see *Quaestiones de anima intellectiva* III (p. 154): "nihil ad nos nunc de Dei miraculis, cum de naturalibus naturaliter disseramus." See Mandonnet, *op. cit.,* I, 150–51. A similar phrase is also used by Albert *In Eth.* Lib I. Tr. VII. cap. v (p. 114).

[44] See Lagarde, *Marsile,* pp. 87–89. Phrases of Marsilius like "non potuit philosophorum universitas per demonstrationem convincere, nec fuit de rebus manifestis per se" (I. iv. 3) are matched by such passages of Thomas as "quae tamen non sufficiunt ad hoc quod praedicta veritas quasi demonstrative vel per se intellecta comprehendatur" (*Cont. gent.* I. viii).

Similarly, the view which attributes to Averroism Marsilius' "anti-metaphysical" separation of politics from morals [45] runs into the serious difficulty that the recognized Averroists are far closer to Thomas Aquinas than they are to Marsilius with respect both to this-worldly values [46] and to the relation between morals and politics.[47] Moreover, it is not the case that Marsilius has a sharp Averroist "demarcation" amounting to a complete lack of agreement between reason and faith.[48] His fundamental program, as he sets it forth in his opening chapter, provides that while Discourse I will proceed by rational demonstration, Discourse II will *"confirm"* these demonstrations "by the testimonies of the eternal truth," that is, by faith and revelation.[49] And in the second discourse, accordingly, there is a frequent emphasis that faith and reason, Scripture and demonstration, go hand in hand to establish the same conclusions.[50]

The fact is that there are three different relations which, in respect of different classes of objects, Marsilius upholds between reason and faith: separation, agreement, and opposition.[51] This last, which is based upon his naturalistic ethics, constitutes one of the strongest genuine indications of his Averroism.[52] Other such indications are found in his apotheosis of Aristotle [53] and in his determinism,[54] with its attendant view that the modality of political science is necessary, not merely contingent.[55]

[45] See Lagarde, *Marsile*, pp. 91–92.

[46] See below, p. 64.

[47] The political ideas of John of Jandun, particularly as found in his *Quaestiones in lib. Metaphys.*, are the fullest proof of this statement (see above, n. 38). See also the definitions of politics given by Peter of Abano and John of Jandun, cited below, p. 103, n. 78.

[48] D'Entrèves, *Medieval Contribution*, p. 49: "Where Thomas Aquinas had proposed to conciliate the spheres of reason and faith . . . Marsilius draws a clearcut and impassable line of demarcation . . . Marsilius does not believe that a study of *philosophica documenta* might well agree with the acceptance of religious dogma. . . This radical opposition between rational truth and religious convictions has been rightly compared to the averroistic doctrine of a twofold truth." See also Sabine, *op. cit.*, p. 292.

[49] I. i. 8: "In prima quarum demonstrabo intenta viis certis humano ingenio adinventis, constantibus ex propositionibus per se notis. . . In secunda vero, quae demonstrasse credidero, *confirmabo* testimoniis veritatis in aeternum fundatis, auctoritatibus quoque sanctorum illius interpretum, necnon et aliorum approbatorum doctorum fidei Christianae. . . ." See above, pp. 12–13.

[50] See II. vi. 9: "Sicut ex dictis apostolorum Petri et Pauli et aliorum sanctorum evidenter apparuit, et ratione demonstrativa convinci potest ex hiis quae dicta sunt xv° et xvii° Primae. . . ." II. xvii. 3: "Haec autem videntur *Scripturae et rationi consona.*" To the same effect, see II. i. 4; II. xvii. 9; II. xviii. 7, 8; II. xxi. 1, 11; II. xxiii. 4. Lagarde, who cites many of these same passages (*Marsile*, p. 48), does not establish their relation to what he calls Marsilius' effort to "séparer le domaine des vérités rationelles de celui de la révélation" (*ibid.*, p. 86; see *ibid.*, p. 47).

[51] See below, pp. 68 ff.

[52] See below, pp. 77 ff.

[53] E.g., I. xi. 2: "sententia divini Aristotelis." See Peter of Abano *Expositio in libros Problematum Aristotelis* (s.l., 1482), Proem. (fol. a 2r): "Aristoteles . . . secundum Averroem magis dignius mereretur dici divinus quam humanus." See also Mandonnet, *op. cit.*, I, 153; Lagarde, *Marsile*, p. 85.

[54] See below, pp. 57 ff.

[55] See below, pp. 48 ff.

The specifically political feature of Marsilius' Averroism consists in his completely secular approach to all aspects of the state, including those connected with religion, theology, and the church. The Averroist method meant that problems could be investigated by rational procedures alone in complete independence of faith and of the theological tradition founded upon faith. Marsilius attains this result by setting up a politics based upon reason alone in Discourse I, omitting the consideration of eternal life and divine causation on the plea that they are not amenable to reason.[56] To be sure, as was pointed out above, he proceeds in the second Discourse to "confirm" by revelation the rationally established conclusions of the first. But the salient point of this procedure is that it permits the establishment of the central doctrines of a political philosophy in complete disregard of the supernatural order. Hence when revelation is invoked in the second Discourse to "confirm" the first, a complete rational, non-supernatural political system lies already at hand, and the texts of Scripture can be so selected and interpreted as to support that system.

What is of particular importance in this connection is that even the ecclesiastic authority is given its political status by means of the same exclusively rational method. The nature and function of the priesthood, and its political subordination to the secular government, are consequences which Marsilius establishes in Discourse I solely from rational and empirical consideration of the necessary requirements of a well-functioning state.[57] This procedure thus differs sharply from that of Thomas Aquinas, John of Paris, and Dante, all of whom view the nature and function of the priesthood and papacy from the standpoint of the Christian faith alone.[58] Moreover, Thomas provides for the political hegemony of the pope over the secular ruler on the ground of his superior end,[59] while John not only accepts the exemption of the clergy from the secular judiciary but also provides, through excommunication, means whereby the pope can procure the deposition of a heretical ruler.[60] Marsilius' non-theological approach to the political aspects of the priesthood is the precise analogue of the Averroist procedure in discussing theologically important questions like the eternity of the world by rational methods alone. That Marsilius is able to show in Discourse II that the status assigned to the priesthood

[56] I. iv. 3; I. v. 10; I. ix. 2; I. xii. 1.

[57] I. v. 10–13; I. xv. 6–11. See below, pp. 83 ff., 108 ff., 119 ff.

[58] Thomas Aquinas *De reg. princ.* I. xiv (p. 21). John of Paris *De pot. reg. et. pap.* cap. ii, iii (pp. 110–11). Dante *De mon.* III. iii (p. 364). Dante also fits his whole discussion of the Roman Empire into a combined theological-Aristotelian context; see *ibid.* II. i ff. (pp. 350 ff.). See also above, p. 19, n. 29.

[59] *De reg. princ.* I. xiv, xv (pp. 21–22).

[60] *De pot. reg. et pap.* cap. xiv (pp. 127–28). See above, p. 19.

by reason is confirmed by revelation, is simply a consequence of the fact that the Scriptural texts could be made to support a rationally established political conclusion far more readily than they could a rational conclusion of metaphysics or physics or psychology.

The homogeneity of Marsilius' Averroism with his Aristotelianism of efficient causality and his positivistic Augustinianism will receive many illustrations in our subsequent discussions. Suffice it to say here that this Averroist secularism results in a politics which is free from domination by theological ends, and his biological determinism supplies the basis for an analysis of human nature, acts, and values which fits politics into a context quite different from the traditional ethico-theological one. It was by his thoroughgoing and effective use of this unique combination of philosophic sources that Marsilius overturned the arguments of the papalists.

2. THE METHOD AND CONTEXT OF REASON

We are now ready to consider the specific ways in which Marsilius reoriented the principles of political philosophy. That reorientation proceeds on many levels and touches on many different aspects of politics. In most general terms, it involves two different fields of application, one in the sphere ascertainable by reason, the other in the sphere dealt with by faith and revelation. In each sphere, in turn, the fundamental question concerns what may be called the "context" of politics, that is, the scene and the essential character of human political activity; for it is the answer to this question of context which determines Marsilius' conceptions of human nature and values, and of human society itself. Our analysis of each sphere will begin with a consideration of Marsilius' method. This consideration should clarify his explicit procedures in his use both of rational arguments and of the materials of faith. But even more, since every method implies a metaphysics, the methodological consideration is directly revelatory of the metaphysical context which Marsilius substitutes for the divine order into which the papalists had fitted the state.

Marsilius exhibits throughout his work an extraordinary sensitiveness to the problems of the method of political argument. Indeed, he presents his entire polemic against the papalists in methodological terms, as the "unmasking" of a "sophism." [1] The doctrine that the pope is entitled to pleni-

[1] See I. i. 4: "Quodque communis utilitas non parva foret, quinimo necessitas . . . reserare sophisma." I. i. 8: "desuper mihi datum est nosse sophisma et reserandi potestas." II. xxiv. 17: "reserato sophismate. . . ."

tude of power is but a "sophistic line of argument," [2] a "sophistic opinion," arising from a "sophistic cause," [3] using "equivocally sophistic language," [4] propounded by a "sophist and abuser of words," [5] professing "sophistic piety," [6] and allied with "sophistic and false teachers." [7] This unusually extensive emphasis upon sophistry refers in part, of course, to the insincerity and drive for self-aggrandizement which Marsilius holds to be the primary characteristic and motivation of the papalist position.[8] But he also views the "sophistic art" in the setting of the whole Aristotelian method and logic, as concerned with the analysis of fallacies arising from the use and construction of terms, propositions, and arguments.[9] His correction of the papalists' sophistry involves a fundamental reorientation of the Aristotelian method in its political application.

Where the papalists had effected a complete assimilation of political concepts with all other kinds of concepts, under the ultimate aegis of the theological, Aristotle maintains a sharp distinction between "theoretic" and "practical" sciences, the latter comprising ethics, economics, and politics. The theoretic sciences are concerned with objects having unchanging essential characteristics; hence they proceed by way of exact uni-

[2] II. xxiii. 2: "non modicum elementum fuerit, extet, futurusque sit eis *locus ille sophisticus,* quem sibi videlicet ascribunt titulum 'plenitudo potestatis'. . . ." The term *locus* is William of Moerbeke's translation of Aristotle's *τόπος*, which in the *Topics* and *Rhetoric* means a general "topic" used in argument.

[3] I. i. 3: "Est enim haec et fuit opinio perversa . . . *sophistica,* honesti atque conferentis faciem gerens." III. i: "Supradicta pestis eiusque *sophistica* causa. . . ."

[4] II. xxv. 17: "Quo siquidem execrabili titulo et oratione *sophistica* secundum aequivocum . . . paralogizant." See II. i. 1: "ad talium *sophisticorum* tam dictorum quam scriptorum observationem." II. xxiv. 8: "sub hujusmodi verborum *sophismate." Def. min.* XVI. iii: "Hic enim sermo rhetoricus apparens sive *sophisticus* est. . . ."

[5] II. xxix. 7: "Dicat enim quaeso *sophista* et vocabulorum abusor. . . ."

[6] II. XXVI. 2: "quamquam *sophistica* pietas haec derisibilis sit." See II. xxiv. 16: "honestatis *sophisticae*. . . ."

[7] II. xxvi. 13: "*sophistici* et falsi doctores . . . quales sunt hii persecutores Romani principis."

[8] For Aristotle, from whom Marsilius derives his conception of sophistry, it is this factor of deceitful purpose which differentiates sophistic from dialectic and rhetoric. See *Rhetoric* I. 1. 1355b 17–22; *Sophistical Refutations* 1. 164a 19 ff.; *Metaphysics* IV. 2. 1004b 17–27. See also Aristotle's discussion of *σοφίσματα* in the sense of deceptive political devices set up by a ruling class to diminish the power of its opponents (*Pol.* IV. 13. 1297a 14 ff.; see *ibid.* V. 8, 1308a 1).

[9] See II. xiv. 18, where Marsilius corrects a fallacy which he ascribes to his opponents: "Unde similis est paralogismus ei quem format Aristoteles II Elenchorum juxta *locum sophisticum* qui dicitur 'figura dictionis'. . . Verumtamen ut amplius satisfiat quaestioni, quoniam quaerentis sophisma dissolutum est, et propter minus doctos in *arte sophistica,* dico. . . ." In counterbalance to Marsilius' charges of sophistry, it may be noted that he was himself similarly accused by Albertus Pighius *Hierarchia ecclesiastica* V. i (p. 122): "nec ab initio ingenue et simpliciter proponit id quod conatur demonstrare, sed plane dissimulat, sensim ad hoc veniens, et alias quasdam sententiolas subdole adstruens ratiunculis quibusdam dialecticis et Aristotelicis."

vocal definitions, "unshakable" principles, and necessary demonstrations, whose norms are set forth in the *Posterior Analytics*. The practical sciences, on the other hand, deal with human actions and institutions, which are capable of being other than they are, for they are contingent upon habits, ideals, and external circumstances. Consequently, the definitions in the practical sciences will be only rough approximations; their principles will be only generally true, and, far from being "unshakable," the extent to which they are admitted will depend upon prior habituation; their arguments and conclusions will be only probable and dialectical, not necessary demonstrations.[10]

This conception of the contingency of political doctrines was explicitly accepted by many of the medieval Aristotelians, including even some who otherwise assimilated politics and theology.[11] On the other hand, Marsilius opposed this assimilation, and thus achieved in politics a particularity of reference similar to that which Aristotle had obtained by distinguishing the sciences according to the unique distinctive traits of their respective subject matters. Yet in so doing, Marsilius also departed at basic points from the characteristics which Aristotle had propounded for political science.

With respect to *terms,* Marsilius criticizes the papalists for their "equivocations" and insists upon univocal definitions. An important part of his entire enterprise thus consists in drawing sharp distinctions between the various meanings of key terms, such as "law" and "judge," where the papalists had run these meanings together.[12]

Were what is involved here simply a question of equivocation or even a disagreement as to the meaning to be given to words, the issue would be simple enough. It is complicated, however, by the opposed assumptions which underlie this dispute over words. The papalists, as we have seen, were committed by their theological-organismic conception of the universe to an analogical use of terms, such that their meaning is stretched from one context to another. Marsilius' emphasis upon fixed and distinct meanings, on the other hand, means that where his adversaries had emphasized

[10] See *N. Eth.* I. 3. 1094b 12 ff.; I. 7. 1098a 26 ff.; II. 1. 1103a 14 ff., esp. 1104a 1 ff.; V. 10. 1137b 18 ff.; VI. 5. 1140a 32 ff.

[11] See Thomas Aquinas *S. theol.* II. I. qu.91. a.3; qu.94. aa.4, 5; qu.105. a.2. ad 8; II. II. qu.57. a.2. ad 1. In these texts Aquinas holds that while the "common principles" of the practical reason are necessarily true and self-evident, in their application to particulars they are only true "ut in pluribus," because "ratio practica negotiatur circa contingentia." See also Egidius of Rome *De reg. princ.* Lib I. Pars I. cap. i. Ptolemy of Lucca *De reg. princ.* IV. viii, xiii (pp. 90, 97). Dante *De mon.* II. ii, v; III. i, v (pp. 352, 354, 363, 366). Pierre Dubois *De recup. terre sancte* par. 109 (pp. 96–97); *Summaria brevis,* p. 47.

[12] See the many definitory paragraphs and chapters: I. ii. 2; I. x. 3, 4; II. ii. 2–8; II. xii. 3–33; II. xxii. 1–6; II. xxiii. 3.

the continuity and coalescence of political with moral and theological criteria, he brings out instead their discontinuity and separateness. Law is no longer defined by its justice, its relation to the eternal standard of God or the rational structure of natural law; instead, it is sharply differentiated from all of these and is defined simply as a coercive command.[13] Political judgment is no longer defined by analogy to moral and intellectual judgments; instead, it too is sharply discriminated from these and is defined simply as the "sentence" made by the ruler having coercive authority.[14] The whole range of political concepts is thus given what may be called a "specifically political" orientation, and it is removed from the broader range of concepts to which the antecedent tradition had assimilated it. The consequence is that the papalist method of solving political problems by appeal to moral and theological criteria is decisively halted at some of the most crucial phases of the political structure.

This Marsilian resolution of his opponents' approach to politics is not, however, so facile or conclusive as it may at first appear. For it raises fundamental questions: What are "specifically political" concepts? Are they indeed such as are essentially distinct from the moral, the intellectual, the theological, and all the other spheres to which the papalists had assimilated them? What warrant is there for assigning "coerciveness," rather than "justice," as the "most proper" meaning of such a term as "law"? The answers to these questions are not simply that a study of existing political institutions, "laws" and "governments," has convinced Marsilius of their frequently non-moral, non-theological character; for the question insisted on by his predecessors would still remain—the question of what justification there is, in that case, for regarding them as entitled to these appellations. It is rather that he has a different conception of the nature of political entities as such, and of their place in the nature of things. What this is will emerge most clearly after we have examined the other phases of his method.

With respect to *propositions and principles,* Marsilius calls those of the papalists "quasi-political,"[15] as if to imply that they are not proper to politics at all, whereas he calls his own "political" without qualification because they are "proper" to politics.[16] Hence too he bases his doctrine upon "essential" rather than "accidental" characteristics, upon the "precise

[13] I. x. 4. See below, p. 134.

[14] II. ii. 8. See below, p. 227. For other such specifically political definitions, see the concepts of "peace," "order," "unity," "natural law" (below, pp. 96 ff., 111, 118 ff., 149 ff.).

[15] II. i. 3, 5; II. iii. 10.

[16] II. i. 4: "politicae demonstrationes quarum *principia propria* XII° Primae, XV°, et XVII° continentur." On the difference between "proper" and "common" principles, see Aristotle *Posterior Analytics* I. 7. 75a 38 ff.; I. 9. 75b 37 ff.; I. 10. 76a 36 ff. *Rhetoric* I. 2. 1358a 10 ff.

or primary essential causes" of political phenomena.[17] His principles are thus universal, applying to "all men"; [18] and they are "self-evident" [19] or "almost self-evident," [20] on the basis of intuitive apprehension, or induction, or definition.

With respect to *arguments,* finally, Marsilius accuses the papalists of constantly "misreasoning" [21] on the basis of their equivocal terms, whereas he regards his own arguments not only as formally valid but as constituting "demonstrations" in the strict Aristotelian sense, proving "necessary" truths through their causes. The terminology of causes is found throughout the *Defensor.* The bulk of the first discourse, indeed, consists simply in a presentation of the material, formal, final, and efficient causes of the state,[22] of its parts,[23] of the government,[24] of law,[25] and of peace.[26] The general efficient causes of peace and strife, inferred at the end of Discourse I from the preceding causal demonstrations, are then used in Discourse II, to "expose" in full detail the "singular cause" of strife in Marsilius' own day, the papal claim to plenitude of power.[27] Thus the first discourse is related to the second, among other ways, as general to singular causal analysis. This analysis, moreover, proceeds through "demonstrations" which are "necessary" and "certain," [28] as against the merely

[17] See II. viii. 6: "Non enim tollitur id quod est per se neque variatur per id quod accidit. . . ." II. x. 7: "est per se prima causa, quae in philosophia secundum quod ipsa dici solet, quoniam ipsa posita ponitur et remota removetur effectus. . . ." See also II. xxix. 7. On the Aristotelian meanings of "primary" (*primum*), "essential" (*per se*), and "as such" (*secundum quod ipsum*), see *Posterior Analytics* I. 2. 72a 6; I. 4. 73a 33 ff.; 73b 27 ff. These three expressions are William of Moerbeke's translations of πρῶτον, καθ' αὑτὸ, and ᾗ αὐτὸ, respectively. Moerbeke's translation is given in Thomas Aquinas *In Post. anal. expositio* Lib. I. Lects. 10, 11 (*Opera omnia,* ed. Leonine [Rome, 1882], I, 175, 179).

[18] I. iv. 2; I. xiii. 2.

[19] I. i. 8; I. iv. 2; I. v. 2; I. x. 2; II. xiii. 3, 5; III. i, iii.

[20] I. xi. 1; I. xii. 5, 6, 7; I. xiv. 5.

[21] II. xxv. 17: "paralogizaverant hactenus, paralogizant, et amplius paralogizare nituntur." See I. xix. 9; II. i. 1; II. x. 11; II. xiv. 18; II. xxvi. 5; II. xxviii. 7, and the sustained and detailed refutation of papalist arguments at II. xxx. 1–3.

[22] I. iv. 1; I. xv. 6; I. xvii. 11, 12; I. xix. 2.

[23] I. iv. 3–I. vii, incl.; I. xv. 4, 6.

[24] I. iv. 4; I. v. 7; I. ix, xiv–xvi.

[25] I. x–xiv. The overlapping with the texts relating to the government, in the preceding note, is owing to the fact that the law is the formal cause of the government, which in turn is the material cause of the law. See I. x. 1, 2; I. xiv. 10.

[26] I. ii. 3; I. xix. 2, 3. Peace has no formal cause, "cum forma seu dispositio quaedam sit civitatis aut regni" (I. xix. 2).

[27] I. i. 7: "Est ergo propositum meum, auxiliante Deo, singularem hanc litis causam solummodo pandere." See I. i. 3; I. xix. 3, 12; II. xxvi. 19; III. i. See above, p. 13.

[28] This claim to necessity of demonstration is made so consistently throughout the *Defensor* that an exhaustive listing of passages would be unduly long. See the statement of method at I. i. 8: "In prima dictione *demonstrabo* intenta viis *certis* humano ingenio adinventis, constantibus ex propositionibus *per se notis.* . . ." Some other typical passages are found at I. xiii. 2: "per demonstrationem conclusimus . . . per necessitatem sequitur. . . Unde satis evidenter per necessitatem infertur. . . ." See II. xviii. 8: "per necessitatem inferemus . . . ostendam per certitudinem."

"probable."[29] Based upon self-evident principles, Marsilius' conclusions are drawn "by sure (*certis*) methods,"[30] and follow in an ever-growing chain from the initial principle which is itself "naturally had and freely granted by all."[31] And this necessity is confirmed by "everyone's sense experience."[32]

This apodictic character of the Marsilian politics provides culminating evidence that, with respect to subject matter and method, Marsilius conceives his doctrine on the model of an Aristotelian theoretic rather than practical science. It states what is and must be as well as what ought to be; it is concerned with self-subsistent entities having essential natures and necessarily connected attributes, rather than with habits, actions, and institutions which are capable of being other than they are. On this specific point there is a possible Averroist influence, for Averroes also had demanded necessary demonstrations for politics, while rejecting what was merely "probable."[33] Indeed, Marsilius' conception of his relation to the "sophistic" papalists is strongly reminiscent of Averroes' scornful classification, also made in Aristotelian terms, of the doctrines of theologians as based upon merely "dialectical" arguments as against the "demonstrations" of the philosophers.[34]

Underlying these methodological divergences of Marsilius is a different view of the subject matter and context of politics. Like Aristotle, he begins from the biological source of human political actions. But Aristotle at once proceeds to show that ethical factors of habit and deliberation supervene on that source, and that men not only aim at biological ends but also act from considerations of the just and the beneficial.[35] It is the indeterminacy of such sources and values of human action that makes contingency in-

[29] See I. xv. 3: "Est autem et hoc cum sua veritate probabile valde, si necessarium probabile liceat dicere." See also II. xvii. 11, 15.

[30] I. i. 8; III. i.

[31] I. iv. 2.

[32] I. xvii. 9: "Cum dictis autem rationibus est hoc videre, verum expediens et necessarium experientia cunctis sensata. . . ." See also I. xi. 3; II. xxiii. 11.

[33] *Paraphrasis in libros de Republica Platonis* Tr. I (fol. 491B): "Praesentis operis propositum est summatim excerpere ea quae Plato *sub demonstrandi ratione* in libro de Republica explicavit: his tamen praetermissis, quae *probabilia* videntur." See *ibid.* Tr. III (fol. 519E). In his commentary on the *Nicomachean Ethics*, however, Averroes accepts Aristotle's ascription of contingency to the practical sciences: *Commentarius in Moralia Nicomachia* I. iii (in *Aristotelis opera* [Venice, 1560], Vol. III, fol. 181F). See also below, p. 57. Neither the *Paraphrasis* nor the treatise of Averroes cited in the next note had been translated in Marsilius' time, so that the influence of the conceptions referred to would have had to come to Marsilius indirectly, perhaps through other treatises of Averroes.

[34] See *Traité décisif sur l'accord de la religion et de la philosophie*, trans. L. Gauthier (Algiers, 1942), pp. 8, 26. The Aristotelian terminology is less obvious in the English translation of this work: *A Decisive Discourse on the Delineation of the Relation between Religion and Philosophy*, trans. Mohammad Jamil-Ur-Rehmann (in *The Philosophy and Theology of Averroes* [Baroda, 1921], pp. 25, 55 ff.). See also *Paraphrasis in libros de Republica* Tr. I (fols. 491F, 493F).

[35] *Pol.* I. 2. 1253a 16 ff.

herent in politics, "the nature of the thing itself," "the very matter of practical affairs."[36] Marsilius is so far from being unfamiliar with this Aristotelian position that he quotes a passage in which it is presented, in order to prove the need for prudence in the ruler to supplement the laws, which cannot determine all the circumstances in which human acts are involved "because they vary and differ with time and place."[37] At other points, he also recurs to the variations found in human political affairs.[38] But amid such recognitions of variation, Marsilius' repeated insistence upon the invariability of the social and political arrangements whose "necessity" he "demonstrates" is all the more striking. Thus, while admitting that the method of establishing or electing governments "varies perhaps according to the variety of provinces," he at once goes on to emphasize that "in whatever ways it may be diversified, *this must be observed in each case,* that such election or establishment is always to be made by the authority of the legislator,"[39] that is, the whole body of the citizens. Similarly, while recognizing that there is more than one legitimate form of government, he insists upon the "necessity" that the government be unified.[40] This apodictic character attaches to all the major theses of Marsilius.

What enables Marsilius to propound such necessities in politics is the fact that he not only begins from the biological source of human actions but bases his central political doctrines entirely upon that source. The fundamental context of the state is the physico-biological "nature" studied by "natural science."[41] Not only does human life depend upon nature,[42] but nature is also the source of the inclinations and aptitudes which are the material causes of the various functional parts of the state,[43] as well as of the wills and desires which are the efficient causes of all the major political institutions of the state.[44] The ineluctable sequences of this "nature" account for Marsilius' constant invocation of "necessity" at each stage of his analysis. For Aristotle, the "necessary" comprises only the material preconditions which are indispensable to, but not constituent "parts" of, the state. Contrasted with these necessaries is the "noble" (τὸ καλόν), comprising the moral and intellectual ends for which the state

[36] *N. Eth.* I. 3. 1094b 25; V. 10. 1137b 18.

[37] I. xiv. 4. The passage quoted is from *N. Eth.* I. 3. 1094b 14.

[38] See I. ix. 10; I. xvi. 11.

[39] I. xv. 2.

[40] I. xvii. 2.

[41] For references to "natural science," see I. v. 2; I. xiii. 2; I. xvii. 8. These passages show that by "nature" and "natural science" Marsilius means the subject matter and doctrines of Aristotle's physical and biological treatises. See also below, p. 55.

[42] I. v. 2. It is significant that Marsilius here bases his analysis of the state upon an analysis of "living" (*vivere*) taken from the biological sections of Aristotle's *De anima* rather than from the *Nicomachean Ethics* or *Politics*.

[43] I. vii. 1. See I. xv. 8.

[44] I. xiii. 2. See I. iv. 2. See below, pp. 56 ff., 208 ff.

at its best exists, and the degree of whose realization is a supreme measure of the state's value and justice.[45] For Marsilius, on the other hand, the "necessary" is the sole explanatory principle of the state. For although he invokes both "living" and "living well" as the state's final cause,[46] he bases his doctrine upon the biological and economic needs which are the indispensable prerequisites, the necessary rather than sufficient conditions, of the good life. His whole discussion turns not upon the values in which "living well" essentially consists, but rather upon the political instrumentalities for achieving its various preconditions. Thus Marsilius does not, like Aristotle and Thomas Aquinas, balance one interpretation of the good life or of the ultimate end of man against another, and derive his political structure from this consideration;[47] rather, having indicated that living well is the end which "men who live a civil life" (*viventes civiliter*) attain, he goes on to concern himself with the means of preserving such *civil* life. The "just" and the "beneficial," consequently, are given an instrumental status, not for the realization of moral or theological ends above them, but for the preservation of the "civil" communities, the essentially biological and economic groupings below them. The Marsilian politics thus has its full basis not in ethics or theology but in biology: it is grounded in naturalistic necessity, the uniquely determinable economic and political conditions required for the fulfillment of biological needs.

This does not mean that Marsilius regards the state itself as a biological organism, in the manner of some of the more extreme interpretations of the organic analogy. To be sure, whenever Marsilius uses analogies, they are characteristically to physical and biological phenomena, not to moral and theological ones.[48] Yet he also recognizes that the state is a product of reason and art which advance beyond nature.[49] In a fundamental sense, however, his position on the biological basis of politics effects a far closer liaison of biology and politics than had the traditional organic doctrines; for where they had moralized biology, Marsilius biologizes morals and politics. For it is biological nature which is the source both of the physical and appetitive factors whence the need for law and government arises and of the further desires which guide the political work of reason in satisfying this need. The biological, therefore, is not merely the initial mainspring of the political realm, soon surmounted by ethical and theological values; it is

[45] For this distinction, see *Pol.* III. 5. 1278a 3 ff.; IV. 4. 1291a 18 ff.; VII. 8. 1328a 22 ff.

[46] I. iv. I.

[47] See Aristotle *Pol.* III. 9. 1280a 25 ff.; VII *passim* 1323a 14 ff. Thomas Aquinas *De reg. princ.* I. xiv, xv (pp. 21–22).

[48] See I. ii. 3; I. xv. 5, 6, 7; I. xvii. 8, 9.

[49] See I. v. 2, 3, 5. See also I. xvii. 8 and below, p. 89.

rather the sufficient context which sets all the problems to whose solution politics is directly addressed, and which, moreover, also provides the essential criteria for the functioning and evaluation of political institutions.

It is by this reorientation of the subject matter of politics that Marsilius solves the problem presented by the papalists' theologizing of politics. Where the papalists had begun their arguments from God and had set up a divine order in which the whole emphasis was axiological, in terms of better and worse, higher and lower, Marsilius begins from physical nature and sets up a biological realm in which the central concern is with the satisfying of natural desires and the political consequences directly entailed thereby. Theological standards, consequently, are no longer relevant to the determination of political relations. Nor is there any danger that moral standards of political evaluation will be forced upward into the theological sphere for their ultimate validation, as was the case with some of those who tried to preserve an Aristotelian moral naturalism. Instead, the agencies of political control are now determined by the specifically political exigencies of preserving a state based upon the common biological needs of its members.

The source of these changes in the method and subject matter of politics —from a probable science cognate with ethics or theology to a necessary science centered in biology—may be found in such aspects of Marsilius' intellectual biography as his medical background and his Averroist associations.[50] In terms of the philosophic structure of his enterprise, however, a further explanation of these changes is his shift in orientation from the portion of Aristotle's *Politics* concerned with ideal ends to the portion of the same treatise concerned with the means of preserving constitutions. Marsilius' Aristotelian predecessors—philosophers like Aquinas, Egidius of Rome, James of Viterbo, John of Paris, Dante, and the rest—were as well acquainted as he was with the corpus of the Aristotelian philosophy, including its physical and biological treatises. But because they centered their political philosophies in the finalistic orientation of the best possible state dedicated to the highest possible ends, they preserved both the fundamental ethical allegiance of politics and the contingency which such ideals (apart from theological dogma) introduce into human actions. And it is because Marsilius is concerned rather with the efficient causes which preserve and control the state, and with the minimal biological-economic

[50] The Averroist influence on this point is, however, not decisive, for Peter of Abano and John of Jandun classify politics among the practical sciences dealing with inner moral acts in the same manner as does Thomas Aquinas. See below, p. 103, n. 78.

needs guaranteed thereby, that his politics becomes biological in basis and necessary in modality. Between Marsilius' biologism and his emphasis upon efficient rather than final causes there is thus an intimate connection.

Formally, therefore, Marsilius' relation to his predecessors has two different aspects. On the one hand, it involves an emphasis upon distinctions and diversity similar to that seen above in the moderate anti-papalists.[51] Thus Marsilius takes over many of his predecessors' arguments for the distinctions between the temporal and the spiritual, Christ and pope, priest and ruler. But on the other hand, it involves a unification of all phases of human life, spiritual as well as temporal, through their coming under the control of a naturalistic politics. For Marsilius' doctrine, the "political" is defined by the biologically-based requirements of the preservation and control of the state, and it is for this reason that Marsilius can provide "specifically political" definitions which involve no reference to moral standards at the same time that he uses principles which assimilate biological and even mathematical considerations to political ones.

It is this reductive, unificatory side of Marsilius' method which is ultimately decisive in his doctrine. Not only does his assimilation of politics to biology explain his distinction of politics from morals and theology, but it results in an all-inclusive unity, a naturalistic biological-economic-political context, whose requirements are such that it comes to assimilate to itself and to control even moral and theological concerns. In this respect, the Marsilian context is at once parallel and opposite to that of the papalists, for the naturalistic order has the same status and function in his doctrine as the divine order had in theirs. This point deserves emphasis, because it has very often been held that Marsilius merely "separates" the divine and the human, faith and reason, spirituals and temporals. Such separation is but part of his total method and doctrine; by itself, it would not account for the fact that Marsilius not only separates the priesthood from the secular government, but also subjects the former to the latter and to the whole people of which both are but parts. It is by the unificatory side of his method, involving in its full development the concepts of "peace," "unity," and "the whole," that this latter result is obtained. The outcome is that, although he begins from the opposite premises, the Marsilian people or *universitas* with its church-state is at least as all-embracing in its power as is the papacy in its conception of *plenitudo potestatis*.

The bridge between this general naturalistic context and the institutions of the state is found in human nature and its values.

[51] See above, pp. 17 ff.

3. NATURAL DESIRE AND THE SUFFICIENT LIFE

In keeping with his methodological approach, Marsilius sets forth near the outset of his treatise a "self-evident" first principle: "All men not deformed or otherwise impeded naturally desire a sufficient life, and flee and avoid what is harmful thereto; which has been admitted not only concerning man but concerning every genus of animals." [1] This principle exercises a pervasive influence throughout Marsilius' entire politics: his naturalism, his voluntarism, his conception of values, his republicanism, his view of the function of law and government are all bound up with the development he gives to it. This development can be best understood by examining the three main concepts of which the principle is composed: "nature," "desire," "sufficient life."

(1) *Nature.* In the Aristotelian philosophy, the context of "the natural" is primarily that of change, motion, growth; and "the nature" may refer to either the beginning or the end of the process, to the material cause which is the potentiality underlying the process and persisting throughout, or to the formal and final cause in which the process eventuates and which is therefore the actuality, the full development, of the thing involved therein.[2] Now in the *Politics,* among the four different approaches which Aristotle follows in that work,[3] the concept of nature is initially applied in the finalistic approach, that concerned with the absolutely best state. For it is by its full development or end that the "nature" of the state, and the distinctive traits of political associations, can most adequately be differentiated from other forms of association. Hence, the "natural" in the opening chapters of the *Politics* means primarily the highest ends or values which the political process, and men living in the state, can achieve. The famous Aristotelian conceptions of the state as "natural" and of man as having a "natural impulse" toward the state and as being "by nature" a political animal,[4] are all explicitly based upon a conception of nature as final cause: "the nature of a thing is its end; for what each thing is when fully developed, we call its nature." [5] It is in this sense, also, that Thomas Aquinas distinguishes between the nature common to man with other substances and animals, and the nature proper to man, and derives from the latter the "natural law" which leads men to live in society.[6]

[1] I. iv. 2 (reading, with Scholz, *huic* instead of *hinc*). See I. v. 2, where this principle is called *per se notum;* and III. iii, where it is called *per se manifestum.*

[2] See Aristotle *Physics* II. 1. 192b 8 ff.

[3] See above, p. 33.

[4] *Pol.* I. 2. 1252b 31 ff., 1253a 30.

[5] *Ibid.* I. 2. 1252b 32.

[6] *S. theol.* II. I. qu.94. a.2. Resp. See Egidius of Rome *De reg. princ.* Lib. III. Pars I. cap. iv. See also Aristotle's doctrine of "natural justice," which is found in the "best" constitution, which is itself "according to nature" (*N. Eth.* V. 7. 1134b 18 ff.).

Marsilius departs completely from this view of human nature. As was to be expected from the biological context in which he places his politics, the "natural" as he conceives it is always the primitive, not the perfected; it consists in man's material endowment, physical and biological, not in his rational powers or virtues. Thus man's "natural" desire for the sufficient life is a desire which man shares with "every genus of animals." [7] Whereas for the other Aristotelians reason is "natural" to man *qua* man, for Marsilius the use of reason always means going "beyond natural causes." [8] Natural causes, like natural science, are those pertaining to "plants and animals"; [9] they are "separate from cognition." [10]

Marsilius was not, to be sure, the first of the Aristotelians to view "nature" in this biological, non-rational sense.[11] But when the state is itself based upon "natural desire" in the sense of an exclusively biological desire, the norms which were integral to the preceding doctrines suffer a corresponding reduction. The standard of reference and evaluation no longer consists in ideal ends, as with the other Aristotelians, but rather in original potentialities and desires. Thus where "natural" law in the sense of a standard of justice equivalent to or deduced from reason had been of controlling importance in the antecedent tradition, Marsilius' interpretation of the "natural" enables him to deny the existence or political relevance of such law.[12] Instead, he refers to a primitive "quasi-natural law" which is below rather than above positive enactments.[13] Similarly, where the distinction between "natural" slaves and "natural" rulers had been a keystone of the Aristotelian politics,[14] it finds no place in Marsilius.[15] The finalistic conception of nature had, indeed, been one of the sources of the aristocratic aspects of Aristotelianism, since most men were deemed incapable of attaining the heights of virtue indicated in the norm of "nature" as complete development of man's rational powers. Marsilius' view of the natural, on the other hand, emphasizes the characteristics common to all men in terms of their native endowments. His doctrine of popular sovereignty will

[7] I. iv. 2. [8] I. v. 3. [9] I. v. 2. See I. xvii. 8.

[10] I. v. 4. This view of the "natural" distinguishes Marsilius from St. Augustine as well as from the Aristotelians. For Augustine too the "natural" is the primitive, but the primitive, on the other hand, is the perfected: man's original nature, before it became vitiated through sin, was perfectly good, social, and rational. See *De civ. Dei* VIII. x; XI. xvii; XII. v, xxiii, xxvii.

[11] When Aristotle considers the efficient causes of the virtues, he contrasts nature to habit and instruction (*N. Eth.* II. I. 1103a 19 ff.), and to habit and reason (*Pol.* VII. 13. 1332a 40). See also Thomas Aquinas *De reg. princ.* I. i (p. 2); Egidius of Rome *De reg. princ.* Lib. III. Pars II. cap. xxv. On the relation between the concepts of nature in Aristotle's *Ethics* and *Politics,* cf. R. McKeon, "Aristotle's Conception of Moral and Political Philosophy," *Ethics,* LI (1941), 280–81.

[12] II. xii. 7–8. See below, Ch. IV, Sec. 3. [13] I. iii. 4; I. xix. 13.

[14] *Pol.* I. 2. 1254a 14 ff. For the medieval Aristotelians' continuation of this distinction, see below, pp. 177–78. [15] See below, pp. 178–79.

hence appeal to "nature"[16] as had the doctrine of natural slavery; but the difference in the natures leads to a similar difference in the conclusions.

The relation of nature to grace and the divine order in general undergoes a corresponding divergence. Far from regarding nature as being "formed" and "perfected" by grace, in the manner of his predecessors,[17] Marsilius maintains a sharp discontinuity between the two realms. To be sure, he indicates at one point, in an Augustinian passage, that man's natural predicament of biological weakness is a consequence of the original sin stemming from Adam.[18] But between the ends for which nature and grace respectively operate on the basis of man's natural condition, no affirmative relation is set up. Whereas the Thomist interpretation of human nature could readily lend itself to a finalistic culmination in grace, the primitivist biological nature of Marsilius leads to desires, values, and acts which are diametrically opposed to those produced by grace.[19] From this opposition, which is one of the basic aspects of his Averroism,[20] results some of the most characteristic doctrines of Marsilius: the denial that divine law is really a law in the present world,[21] the subordination of the priesthood to the secular government,[22] and, in general, the complete autonomy of the secular sphere in relation to the religious.[23]

(2) *Desire.* The concept of natural desire plays a prominent part in Aristotle's philosophy,[24] but the medieval Aristotelians adopted conflicting interpretations of it. Thomas Aquinas upheld what was at least in principle a rationalist determinism: each thing has a "natural desire" for the good or operation consequent upon its own substantial or natural form; since the natural form proper to man is reason, whose perfection is happiness, all men "naturally and necessarily" desire happiness and its essential preconditions.[25] Duns Scotus agreed as to the necessity of man's "natural desire" for happiness, but argued that in addition to this desire man has a "free will" (*velle liberum*); however good be an object, this will can suspend itself from willing it.[26]

Marsilius follows neither of these variants. Since the "natural" is biologi-

[16] I. xiii. 2. See also the discussion of the senses in which the state is "natural" and man has a "natural impulse" toward political association; below, pp. 89 ff.

[17] See above, pp. 17 ff.

[18] I. vi. 2.

[19] See below, pp. 61 ff., 80 ff.

[20] See above, p. 42.

[21] II. ix. 3. See below, pp. 154 ff.

[22] See below, pp. 108 ff.

[23] See below, p. 70.

[24] See *N. Eth.* III. 5. 1114a 30 ff.; *Physics* I. 9. 192a 18; *Metaphysics* I. 1. 980a 22; *Pol.* I. 2. 1253a 30.

[25] *S. theol.* I. qu.26. a.2. Resp.; qu.80. aa.1, 2; q.82. aa.1, 2; qu.83. a.1 ad 5; II. I. qu.10. a.2; II. I. q.94. a.3. Resp. Thomas also holds, however, that this desire is not specified as to its precise object in the present life; see *ibid.* I. qu.82. a.2. Resp.

[26] *Opus Oxon.* Lib. IV. dist. 49. qu.10. nn. 2–10.

cal, man's natural desire will be neither rational nor free. Although he twice refers to freedom of the will, in neither case does he indicate unambiguously that this is his own doctrine.[27] On the other hand, he not only says that all men who are "not deformed" naturally desire a sufficient life, but repeatedly insists that it is "impossible" for them not to desire also all the objects which are necessary for such life. The determinism of the will is, indeed, a basic corollary of Marsilius' view of politics as a theoretic science composed of necessary demonstrations. The "necessary" chain which he traces from antecedents to consequents is in two parallel series: one in the objective conditions necessary for sufficiency of life as he views it, the other in the desires for each of these conditions.[28] And guaranteeing the coalescence of the desires with the conditions is not reason but the "nature" studied by "natural science."[29] The human will, for Marsilius as for the other Averroists, is thus part of the whole context of physico-biological nature, and exhibits the same necessity.[30]

Marsilius' entire politics is pervaded by this natural necessity of desire, will, election, consent (he does not distinguish among these terms). It is this determinism which is the basis of his insistence upon the inevitable justice of the people's will, and which thus gives to his doctrine of popular sovereignty a dogmatic fixity unparalleled in antecedent political thought. Given the self-evident principle that all men naturally desire a sufficient life, it necessarily follows that "all or most men wish a law appropriate to

[27] See II. viii. 3, where the doctrine of free will is said to be true "secundum christianam religionem"; and II. xii. 6, where it is qualified by "*dicitur* homo . . . suorum actuum habere dominium. . . ." With the latter statement, compare Thomas Aquinas *De veritate* qu.22. a.5. ad 7 *in contrarium:* "hoc enim est proprium voluntati . . . quod sit domina suorum actuum."

[28] For the necessity of the objective conditions, see I. iv. 3 ff. For the necessity of the desires for the conditions, see I. xiii. 2. See also I. vii. 1, and texts cited below, nn. 31–34. This parallelism of necessities is akin to the double mode of necessity analyzed by Aristotle in his theoretic sciences. The sequence of desires is itself necessary in the mathematical sense, from antecedent to consequent: the sequence begins from "that which is," a desire which is an actually existing fact and upon which other desires actually and necessarily follow. On the other hand, the sequence from the sufficient life to the various conditions necessary for its attainment is necessary in the physical sense, from consequent to antecedent: like the modality which Aristotle assigns to "natural science," this is a sequence which begins from "that which is to be," a projected end, and moves from it to the means progressively required for its realization. See Aristotle *Physics* II. 9. 199b 34 ff.; *Parts of Animals* I. 1. 639b 21 ff.

[29] I. xiii. 2.

[30] On the Averroist determinism, see Albert the Great *De quindecim problematibus* (ed. Mandonnet, *op. cit.*, II, 29–30); and "Condemned Propositions of 1277," nos. 152–56, 159–61 (*ibid.*, II, 187). The identity of the "masters" who upheld this determinism is, however, still in doubt. Mandonnet (*ibid.*, I, 186, 219) attributes it to Siger of Brabant, but this is not borne out by Siger's text: *Impossibilia* v. ad 4 (*ibid.*, II, 89); see Gorce, *L'Essor de la pensée,* p. 156. John of Jandun declared that "coelum non necessitat intellectum et voluntatem, tamen inclinat aliqualiter et facit multas inclinationes in humano appetitu" (*Quaestiones super libros Aristotelis de coelo et mundo* I. qu.1 [Venice, 1614], fol. 2*v*). See, to the same effect, John's *Quaestiones de physico auditu* Lib. VIII. qu.6 (Venice, 1506), fol. 104*v*.

the common benefit of the citizens"; [31] "by the election of the human legislator [i.e., the whole body of citizens] the common benefit of the citizens is almost always aimed at and attained, rarely failing"; [32] "election is always done for the common benefit, which the human legislator almost always wishes and attains"; [33] "the legislator aims in most cases at what is just." [34]

In these quotations, it will have been noted that Marsilius qualifies his strict universality by alternative or exceptive phrases: "all or most men"; "almost always"; "in most cases." These exceptives were already apparent in his first principle, which attributed a natural desire for the sufficient life to "all men *not deformed or otherwise impeded.*" It is the concepts of "deformity" and "impediment" here referred to which explain the exceptions, and they also reveal more fully the profoundly biological basis of Marsilius' doctrine of the will and of his whole politics. The concept of "deformity" (*orbatio*) occurs frequently in Aristotle's biological works, where it means an abnormality in some organism, an incompleteness which is contrary to the nature of the species.[35] A "deformity" is thus something unusual; it does not occur "in most cases." [36] Marsilius' use of the term in relation to natural desire thus assimilates his politics to Aristotle's biology: [37] men will desire a sufficient life and whatever is necessary thereto so long as their "natures" are not deformed; if all or most men did not

[31] I. xii. 8. [32] I. xvi. 11. [33] I. xvi. 19.

[34] I. xvi. 21. For other similar statements, see I. xii. 5; I. xiii. 2, 3, 5, 6; II. xxi. 3. Compare J.-J. Rousseau *Contrat social* II. iii: "La volonté générale est toujours droite et tend toujours à l'utilité publique." Marsilius does not, however, distinguish like Rousseau between the "general will" and the "will of all." See below, p. 215. A possible source of Marsilius' specific exaltation of "election" is the Aristotelian doctrine that "choice" (προαίρεσις, translated *electio* by William of Moerbeke) is that desire for means to an end which is based upon previous deliberation (*N. Eth.* III. 2. 1112a 15). See Peter of Auvergne *In Pol.* Lib. III. Lect. 14: "Electio est appetitus ratione determinatus." However, the determinist fixity of the Marsilian "election" is quite contrary to Aristotle's doctrine of choice; moreover, the election in question is that of the whole people, not that of one or a few individuals; and Marsilius emphasizes the volitional aspect of election far more than the rational. See below, p. 170.

[35] The term used in Greek is variously πήρωσις, πήρωμα, ἀναπηρία, all of which William of Moerbeke translates *orbatio*. For the full list of occurrences of these terms, see H. Bonitz, *Index Aristotelicus* (Berlin, 1870), s.v.

[36] See Aristotle *Generation of Animals* I. 18. 724b 32: "Semen is not contrary to nature, nor a deformity [πήρωμα], *for it is present in all animals. . . .*" See A. L. Peck's introduction to his translation of this work (London, Loeb Classical Library, 1943), p. xiv.

[37] The term also occurs six times in the *Nicomachean Ethics,* including three times in relation to the "bestiality" which leads to "unnatural" pleasures (VII. 1. 1145a 32; VII. 5. 1148b 18; VII. 6. 1149b 30), and once in relation to the non-acquisition of happiness: "happiness can be attained by all those who are not deformed (πεπηρωμένοις, *orbatis*) with respect to virtue" (I. 9. 1099b 18). Thomas Aquinas explains *orbatis* in this passage as follows: "habentibus aliquod impedimentum ad operandum opera virtutis, vel per defectum naturae sicut qui sunt naturaliter stulti, aut per malam consuetudinem quae imitatur naturam" (*In Eth.* Lib. I. Lect. 14, n. 170.). See also Albert the Great *In Eth.* Lib. I. Tr. VII. cap. vii, and John of Jandun, *Quaest. in Metaphys.* Lib. II. qu.4 (fol. 25J). The term occurs only once in the *Politics* (VII. 16. 1335b 21), in the provision that no "deformed" child shall be reared.

desire good laws, "there would be deformity (*orbatio*) in nature and art in most cases."[38] This same concept is at the basis of Marsilius' famous term *pars valentior:* what makes it necessary to have laws established by the "weightier part" of the citizen-body rather than by all the citizens is the fact that unanimity is difficult or impossible to obtain, because "some men have a deformed (*orbatam*) nature, disagreeing with the common judgment through singular malice or ignorance."[39]

The frequent characterizations of Marsilius' doctrine as "voluntarist"[40] must hence take account not only of the biological necessity under which he subsumes the will but also of the statistical-majoritarian interpretation he gives of its uniformities. It is not to anyone's will that he allows political control; on the contrary, he opposes the papal voluntarism which claims plenitude of power "following every impulse of the will."[41] It is rather the will of "all or most" of the citizens which is sovereign.[42]

The concept of "impediment" shows still further how Marsilius has assimilated the subject matter of politics to the uniformities of the "nature" analyzed in the physical and biological treatises of Aristotle. In the *Physics,* Aristotle points out that natural sequences proceed "always" to the "same" end—that is, they are uniform and invariable—*"if there is no impediment."*[43] It is this concept of "impediment" which Marsilius uses to explain that break in the necessary sequence from which his problem arises. His technical charge against the papacy is initially not a moral one but rather that it has interjected an "impediment" to the smooth functioning of the government.[44] For this reason, the papacy is the efficient cause of civil strife,[45] for tranquillity and intranquillity are themselves defined as the "unimpeded" and "impeded" functioning, respectively, of the parts of the state;[46] and the efficient cause of peace is the "unimpeded" functioning of the government.[47]

[38] I. xiii. 2.

[39] I. xii. 5. See below, pp. 185 ff.

[40] See Capograssi, *op. cit.*, p. 580; d'Entrèves, *Medieval Contribution,* pp. 47, 86.

[41] II. xxiii. 2: "secundum tamen omnem impetum voluntatis." See *Disputatio inter militem et clericum,* p. 13: "C. *Jus* voco decreta patrum, et statuta Romanorum pontificum . . . M. Nihil ergo aliud erit ius habere, quam *velle:* non habet ergo, nisi ut scribat: hoc *volo* ius esse, cum *voluerit* castrum meum. . . ."

[42] See below, p. 170.

[43] Aristotle *Physics* II. 8. 199b 15–26. The last phrase of this passage—*ἐν δὲ τοῖς φυσικοῖς ἀεὶ οὕτως ἂν μή τι ἐμποδίσῃ*—is translated by William of Moerbeke: *in physicis autem semper sic est, nisi aliquid impediat.* See also *ibid.* 199a 10–11.

[44] I. xix. 4: "Haec autem dudum hactenus et nunc amplius continuo actionem debitam principantis *impediens* in Italico regno. . . ." See II. xxiv. 15.

[45] I. xix. 3: "Quod vero hujus partis actionem per se *impediverit,* ab eo civitatis intranquillitas seu discordia proveniet tanquam causa factiva."

[46] I. ii. 3; I. v. 1; III. iii.

[47] II. v. 7. The limitation upon necessity and universality in Marsilius' politics indicated by the concepts of "deformity" and "impediment" differs from the practical contingency of

Since, then, the will as Marsilius conceives it is so thoroughly a part of the natural, biological order, what is its relation to reason? Marsilius follows Aristotle in holding that "the human race lives by art and reason," and that natural causes "receive their fulfillment" from these.[48] It is by such rational "fulfillments" or completions of natural inclinations that the state and its parts are established.[49] But in these and all other functions reason is only instrumental; the goal of the fulfillment is set, and its attainment controlled, by natural desire. Reason does not, as for Thomas, fix objective final causes which the will must desire. Rather, it is the fact of being naturally desired that itself constitutes goods and ends; reason then serves as a secondary efficient cause for the attainment of the objects so desired.[50]

This difference has decisive consequences for political doctrine. It means that the supreme political authority no longer belongs to the most rational or most prudent men in the state, as in the antecedent Aristotelian tradition, but rather to those whose wills are most trustworthy because least subject to unnatural deformity or impediment. Hence, not the few "experts" but the whole people constitute the legislator.[51] The basic criterion for Marsilius' evaluation of political institutions thus comes to consist not in objective final causes but rather in the people's will. Where the antecedent tradition had held that the tests of valid human laws and of just governments are to be found in their conformity to the rational criteria of natural law and their being directed to the common benefit, Marsilius makes the people's "consent," "election," or "will" the decisive factor.[52] His substitutions of volitional for rational criteria and of a republican for an aristocratic or monarchic constitution are thus parallel to his replacement of the antecedent concern with final causes or ideal ends by an emphasis upon efficient causes. It is these differences which underlie the fact that the people's will

Aristotle in that the latter arises from the *habituation* which supervenes upon nature, whereas the Marsilian arises within nature itself. For Aristotle the very matter (ὕλη) of practical affairs is contingent and variable, but for Marsilius that matter is necessary and deformities within it are accidental.

[48] I. v. 2. See Aristotle *Metaphysics* I. I. 980b 27; *Pol.* VII. 13. 1332b 5.

[49] See I. ii. 3; I. iii. 5; I. v. 3, 5.

[50] For reason as instrumental, see especially I. v. 3. For the relation of desire to goods and ends, see I. iv. 2, and also such texts as the following: I. i. 7: "civili felicitate frui, quae in hoc saeculo possibilium homini *desideratorum* optimum videtur. . ." I. iv. 5: "diversa sunt necessaria *volentibus* sufficienter vivere. . ." I. v. 2: "Ex quibus siquidem vivendi modis, *desideratis* homini velut finibus. . ." II. ix. 13: "propter finem quem *volunt* homines et licite in vita mundana." III. iii: "Quas tamen velut fines et optima *desideratorum* humanorum. . ." Compare Thomas Aquinas *S. theol.* II. I. qu.9. a.I. Resp.; *De veritate* qu.22. a.11. ad 5; a.12. Resp.

[51] I. xii. 3, 5 ff. See below, p. 170.

[52] I. ix. 5–9; I. xii. 3. See below, pp. 143, 170, 223, 241.

is the supreme efficient cause of all the institutions of the Marsilian state.

The first principle that all men naturally desire a sufficient life is also turned by Marsilius in a different direction from the preceding. When the "all" is viewed collectively, the principle eventuates, as we have seen, in the inevitable desire of "all or most men" for the *common* benefit. But when the "all" is viewed distributively, it means that each man pursues his own *private* advantage,[53] whether he be a priest[54] or a professor.[55] And this pursuit inevitably results in clashes of man against man, that is, in "harmful" acts of the kind which Marsilius calls "transient" because they affect other persons, as contrasted with "immanent" acts which remain within the agent.[56]

This theme of strife and conflict pervades the whole of the *Defensor pacis*. "Contentions," "injuries," "disputes," "crimes," "scandals" appear as the dominant trait of the Marsilian society, occurring wherever men are gathered together.[57] Even in the original human family there already appeared "injuries," acts which, Marsilius says, "we shall henceforth call 'civil.'"[58] The use of the term "civil," or as Marsilius also calls them, "political," for these acts is an emphatic indication of their essential connection with "civil" life, the life of men living in association with one another.[59] And the occurrence of such acts has the same necessity as Marsilius attributes to his entire politics; thus he repeats approvingly the statement in Matthew (18:7) that "it is *necessary* that scandals arise," and

[53] II. viii. 9: "Est enim quilibet pronus ad commodum proprium prosequendum et incommodum fugiendum."

[54] See II. ii. 3: "ipsorum quaedam congregatio, *propter proprium et temporale commodum* et aliorum incommodum fraudulenter adipiscendum. . . ."

[55] See II. xxi. 15: "Nolentes enim aut dubitantes viri literati suorum magisteriorum titulos perdere, *appetitu commodi et gloriae consequentis*. . . ."

[56] For the distinction of immanent and transient acts, see I. v. 4, 11; II. ii. 4, 5; II. viii. 3; II. ix. 11; II. xvii. 8. Thomas Aquinas' distinction between *actus manentes* and *transeuntes* is not precisely the same as Marsilius', for by the latter Thomas means acts of producing or making (*factivi*), not acts which affect *other persons*, so that Thomas' distinction is identical with that of Aristotle between action and production. See Aristotle *N. Eth.* VI. 4. 1140a 1 ff., and Thomas *In Eth.* Lib. VI. Lect. 3. n. 1151; also *ibid.* Lib. I. Lect. 1, n. 13; Lib. II. Lect. 4. n. 282; Lib. VI. Lect. 2. n. 1135; *S. theol.* I. qu.18. a.3. ad 1; qu.23. a.2. ad 1.

[57] See I. iv. 4: "inter homines sic congregatos eveniunt *contentiones et rixae*. . . ." I. v. 11: "in communitatibus *multae contentiones et iniuriae*. . . ." I. xi. 3: "subortam litem seu civilem causam. . ." I. xv. 6: "Haec autem sunt contentiones atque iniuriae hominum invicem. . . ." I. xv. 11: "si patiatur aut agat iniuriam. . . ." I. xix. 12: "iniuriae ac contentiones eveniunt facile." II. ii. 7: "ceteraque committere scelera, crimina, et contentiones. . . ." See also I. xvii. 3; II. iv. 8; II. v. 2; II. viii. 6, 7, 8; II. ix. 12, 13, and *passim;* also the references to *lites* and *pugna* in the texts cited below, p. 106, nn. 94–96.

[58] I. iii. 4.

[59] See I. ix. 7: "principans . . . debet regulare *actus civiles* omnium aliorum." See I. x. 2: "haec est pars principans, cuius est secundum legem regulare *politicos seu civiles hominum actus*." For other references to "civil acts," see I. x. 1; I. xi. 3; I. xii. 2; I. xv. 3, 4.

at once adds: "these are men's contentions and injuries toward one another." [60] No political philosopher before Marsilius had evinced so great a preoccupation with this theme of men's inevitable conflict with one another; none was to do so again until Hobbes.[61]

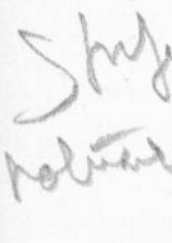

The necessity of such strife is a direct consequence of the biological context into which Marsilius fits the human will. Where the antecedent tradition had adduced moral, rationalist, or theological considerations of "pride," "lust," "ignorance," "unrestraint" to explain why men cease to follow God or reason or the good, Marsilius' biological voluntarism puts the explanation in terms of nature itself. All human acts, he points out, by their very nature emerge in "excesses," that is, they are always involved in an unstable equilibrium because of the imbalances constantly effected in the operations of the organism and in its relations with the physical environment. This holds true not only of man's nutritive and sensitive functions,[62] but also of his cognitive and appetitive acts: [63] the latter belong to the same necessary order of nature as do the former. Hence, the "transient" impingement of one man upon another, in which cognitive-appetitive acts partly consist, by its very nature incurs imbalance. Men can no more avoid strife with one another than they can avoid becoming hungry.[64]

The contrast between the individual and collective results of men's natural desires generates the basic features of Marsilius' politics, just as that contrast is itself a result of his fundamental biological orientation. The people's will is accepted, and the individual will is rejected, as the

[60] I. xv. 6. Marsilius' complete acceptance of the "necessity" indicated in this statement is in sharp contrast with Thomas Aquinas' efforts to mitigate it, for if the occurrence of scandals were "necessary" they would not be sins. See *S. theol.* II. II. qu.43. a.2. ad 1: "hoc quod dicitur, 'Necesse est ut veniant scandala,' non est intelligendum de necessitate absoluta, sed de necessitate conditionali, qua scilicet necesse est praescita vel praenuntiata a Deo evenire; si tamen conjunctim accipiatur, ut dictum est. Vel necesse est evenire scandala necessitate finis, quia utilia sunt ad hoc ut 'qui probati sunt, manifesti fiant.' Vel necesse est evenire scandala secundum conditionem hominum, qui sibi a peccatis non cavent. . . ."

[61] Augustine and his tradition, dwelling on the depravity of man, had discussed the "works of the flesh" which result therefrom; thus he had presented from St. Paul a list of such "works" which includes many of Marsilius' "harmful" acts: "adultery, fornication . . . contentions, emulations, animosities, dissensions" (*De civ. Dei* XIV. ii. See Galatians 5:19). But the cast of the doctrine was theological and moral, not biological and political as in Marsilius. The Marsilian "transient acts" are the same as those called "transactions between man and man" (συναλλάγματα) by Aristotle (*N. Eth.* v. 2. 1131a 1 ff.) and "operationes quae sunt ad alterum" by Aquinas (*S. theol.* II. I. qu.60. a.2. Resp.; II. II. qu.61. a.3. Resp.). But these philosophers center attention primarily upon the "immanent" bases of the acts, not upon their external effects. See below, pp. 102–4.

[62] See I. iv. 3; I. v. 3–6.

[63] I. v. 4, 7.

[64] This conception of the basis of human conflicts is similar to that of Hobbes in its acceptance of their necessity, but differs from it in the same way that a biological explanation differs from a mechanical one based upon an abstraction from existing conditions.

repository of political authority because the former aims at the common benefit with the same necessity as the latter aims at its private benefit. Even more, the very problems of human conflict which necessitate in the first place that there be political authority controlled by the people's will, are the results of the inevitable clash of individual wills. From this contrast emerges the characteristic exaltation of the many and disparagement of the few which Marsilius uses so effectively in his doctrines both of the church and of the state. The combination of the several elements entering into the contrast, moreover, forms a unique variant in the history of voluntarism.

(3) *Sufficient life.* What, then, is the "sufficient life" which is the object of these natural desires of men? The concept itself was derived from Aristotle, who made "self-sufficiency" (αὐταρκεία) one of the chief characteristics of happiness,[65] and also defined the state, which enables men to "live well," in terms of its self-sufficiency.[66] But Marsilius' interpretation of the concept contains important variants from the Aristotelian tradition, as a result not only of his differences with respect to natural desire but of his whole change in political orientation. The shift in emphasis from final to efficient causes means directly that politics will no longer be centered in ultimate ends; it will deal with only such ends as are commensurate with the control and preservation of the state. Thus its ends will be specifically political, not ethical or theological; these latter, insofar as they affect the functioning of the state, will be absorbed into the political. There will thus be a levelling of values, not a hierarchy of better and worse.

Aristotle's doctrine of the specific content of the good life, or happiness, is based upon an analysis of the specific nature of man and the objects of his acts. That analysis proceeds by a series of axiologically graduated distinctions: between nutritive and sensitive functions, on the one hand, and on the other, the activity which is "proper" (ἴδιον) to man, the use of reason;[67] between the moral and the intellectual virtues, which pertain to the appetitive and the rational part of the soul, respectively;[68] and, within the intellectual virtues, between the "practical" and the "theoretic."[69] It is the theoretic intellectual virtues which are the habits of the "best" in man's soul, because they are concerned with the highest objects, unchanging essences and the constituents of the cosmos. Accordingly,

[65] *N. Eth.* I. 7. 1097b 7. William of Moerbeke translates αὐταρκεία as *per se sufficientia.*

[66] *Pol.* I. I. 1252b 29. Marsilius uses "sufficient life" interchangeably with "good life" (*bene vivere*) and also with "happiness" (*felicitas*); see I. i. 7; I. iv. 2, 3, and *passim.* It should be noted that Egidius of Rome distinguishes *sufficienter vivere* from *bene et virtuose vivere,* the former being economic, the latter moral (*De reg. princ.* Lib. III. Pars I. cap. ii).

[67] *N. Eth.* I. 7. 1097b 34 ff.

[68] *Ibid.* I. 13. 1103a 4 ff.

[69] *Ibid.* VI. 3. 1139b 20 ff.

man's happiness will consist primarily in theoretic activity, for it is this which assimilates him most closely to the gods.[70]

Although the Thomist Aristotelians were unable to grant the ultimacy of this-worldly happiness in the manner of Aristotle, both they and the Averroists repeated his position so far as the hierarchy of the values of the present life was concerned. The summit of the hierarchy was expressed in many instances as the superiority of "theoretic happiness" over "practical" or "political happiness." [71]

For Marsilius, on the other hand, since the sufficient life is constituted by being the object of man's biological desire rather than by what fulfills his rational nature, that life does not have the lofty normative qualities assigned to it by the other Aristotelians. In contrast to their exaltations of the theoretic, Marsilius declares that it is "civil happiness" (*civilis felicitas*) which constitutes "the best of the objects of desire possible to man in this world, and the ultimate aim of human acts." [72] This civil happiness is not viewed as excluding theoretic activity, as with the other Aristotelians; [73] rather, it includes both. "Those who live a civil life not only live, which beasts or slaves do, but they live well, having leisure for the liberal functions which derive from the virtues of both the theoretic and the practical soul." [74] Thus theoretic and practical activities are placed on the same level. Even more, despite his differentiation of the mere living of beasts from the living well of men, Marsilius places *all* "human actions and passions" on the same level, and includes "natural" or nutritive acts among these, with no attempt to make them inferior.[75] All appear as equally "necessary" to the sufficient life. It is significant also, in view of his emphasis upon the will, that he makes no attempt to differentiate the cognitive from the appetitive powers, but always lists them together.[76] In this he follows not the "exoteric" moral distinctions of Aristotle's *Ethics*,[77] but rather the "scientific" biological approach of the *De anima*.[78]

[70] *Ibid.* vi. 7. 1141a 20 ff.; x. 7. 1177a 12 ff. *Pol.* vii. 3. 1325b 14 ff. The summary here given does not, of course, adequately represent the complex scope and detail of the discussions of the virtues and happiness in the *Ethics*. It does, however, indicate the basic distinctions developed both in those discussions and in the medieval Aristotelian tradition.

[71] Thomas Aquinas *S. theol.* II. i. qu.3. a.5. Resp.; II. ii. qu.152. a.2. Resp.; qu.182. aa.1–4; *Cont. gent.* iii. lxiii. Peter of Auvergne *In Pol.* Lib. vii. Lect. 2 (p. 436). Siger of Brabant *Quaestiones morales* IV (p. 175); *Quaestiones de anima intellectiva* III (p. 156). Boethius of Dacia *De summo bono*, p. 213. Dante *De monarchia* i. iii (pp. 342–43). John of Jandun *Quaest. in Metaphys.* Lib. i. qu.1 (fol. 1F); *Quaest. de anima* Proem. (fol. 2*r*). Albert the Great *De anima* Lib. iii. Tr. iv. cap. iv (*Opera*, ed. Borgnet, V, 400).

[72] i. i. 7.

[73] See Albert the Great *In Eth.* Lib. x. Tr. i. cap. xi (p. 620): "*felicitas civilis* ultima operatio est practici [intellectus]; felicitas autem contemplativa . . . est operatio speculativi."

[74] i. iv. 2.

[75] See i. v. 4.

[76] See i. v. 4: "Aliae vero sunt actiones et passiones a nobis vel in nobis per virtutes nostras cognoscentes et appetentes. . . ." See also i. v. 7; i. vi. 1, 9; ii. viii. 2, 3; ii. xxx. 1.

[77] See *N. Eth.* i. 13. 1102b 13 ff.

[78] See *De anima* iii. 9. 432b 5.

The sufficient life, then, consists in all the values which men naturally desire, and which they derive by living in the state resulting from that desire. Whatever moral, intellectual, and theological aspects that life may achieve are outgrowths of the initial biological impulse, and have evolved from it in the same way as the state evolved out of the simple biological unit of the family.[79] As a consequence, Marsilius' conception of the sufficient life not only tends to level the values which the antecedent tradition had arranged in hierarchically ascending order, but it even reverses that order; for he is so far from regarding theoretic activity as an end in itself, in the manner of Aristotle, that he rather treats it in the same fashion as the practical, as instrumental to all the needs of life, both of body and of soul.[80]

It is inevitable, as a result of this approach, that when Marsilius gives more specific indications of values, these will be practical rather than theoretic. An important example is provided in his discussion of the final cause of peace. For Dante, the value of peace is that it permits the human race "always to actuate the whole power of the possible intellect"; [81] for Engelbert of Admont, following St. Augustine, it is eternal concord with God; [82] and even the tough-minded Pierre Dubois declares that the purpose of peace is to enable men "to have leisure for acquiring the virtues and the sciences." [83] For Marsilius, on the other hand, the values to be derived from peace consist in various aspects of social and economic cooperation: "the mutual intercourse of the citizens, their communication of their functions to one another, their mutual aid and assistance, and in general the power, unimpeded from without, of exercising their proper and common functions, also the sharing of common benefits and burdens according to the measure appropriate to each . . ." [84]

In Marsilius' practical approach there is possibly an influence of his medical training.[85] Even more obviously, it is closely related to his whole socio-political background; for his conception of the sufficient life, with its avoidance of the lofty heights of intellectual and moral virtue pro-

[79] See I. iii. 5, and below, pp. 86 ff., 91, 92.

[80] See the couplings of "virtutibus et artibus *tam practicis quam speculativis,*" "disciplinae *tam speculativae quam activae,*" "*operativorum et speculativorum habituum*" (I. v. 3; I. vi. 9; I. vii. 1), as furnishing the means "quibus compleatur efficientia et conservatio suarum actionum et passionum secundum corpus et animam."

[81] *De mon.* I. iv (p. 343).

[82] *De ortu* cap. xiv (p. 370C); see Augustine *De civ. Dei* XIX. xiii.

[83] *De recup. sanctae terrae* par. 2 (p. 4); *Summaria brevis*, p. 5.

[84] I. xix. 2. See also the statement which Marsilius quotes from Cassiodorus, at I. i. 1.

[85] Note that he refers to "medicinalis *practica*" as one of the functions to be carried on in the state (I. v. 6), and to the "medicus" as "doctor *operativus*" (II. xxx. 1). The question whether medicine is a theoretic or a practical science was frequently debated; see Peter of Abano *Conciliator differentiarum* Diff. 4 (fol. 8r–9r): "Utrum medicina sit theorica necne"; Duns Scotus *Opus Oxon.* Prologus, qu.4, nn. 10, 44 (VIII, 220, 289–90).

pounded by the other Aristotelians, was such as the burghers and guildsmen of the *arti* and *mestieri* of Padua would readily recognize. Doctrinally, however, it is a consequence of his whole orientation in efficient causes and in a biological voluntarism. To center a political philosophy in the agencies which establish, control, and preserve political institutions rather than in the highest final causes which those institutions may achieve, involves that ends not only will receive subordinate emphasis but will be of such kind as are directly commensurate with the workings of such agencies. When men seek to preserve the state they are concerned with the minimal rather than maximal values which the state enables them to achieve, and they regard all other values from the standpoint of what contribution they can make to that preservation.

These contrasts with respect to ends have further decisive political consequences. For on the principle of distributive justice whereby men's contributions toward the end determine their political, economic, and social power and status, the hierarchies of values require corresponding hierarchies in the state. Thus in Aristotle's absolutely best state only those men are citizens who can attain and contribute to the heights of virtue constituting that best life which is the end of the state; those who can contribute only to nutritive and sensitive needs, farmers and artisans, will be slaves.[86] A similar principle was used by the papalists to make the "spiritual power" superior to the "temporal power," because the end which the former enables men to attain is higher than that of the latter.[87] In Marsilius' departure from these procedures of discriminating higher and lower ends lies one of the main bases both for his republicanism and for his overturning of the papalist claims. For the sufficient life as he conceives it is both attainable and directly controllable by far larger numbers of men than are the aristocratic ends specified by the other Aristotelians. It is, indeed, by appealing to the concern of all the people with the "sufficient life" that he establishes his doctrine of popular sovereignty;[88] and republicanism in all ages has involved a similar view of ends as inclusive or moderate rather than as exclusive or extreme.[89] It is this, too, which

[86] *Pol.* VII. 8. 1328b 39 ff. [87] See below, pp. 104–5.

[88] See I. xii. 7.

[89] This point is well illustrated in the contrast found in Aristotle's *Politics* between the values of the "absolutely best" state and those of the state which is "best for most men"; for the former is dedicated to the best possible life viewed as consisting in theoretic activity (*Pol.* VII. 3. 1325b 14–22), whereas the latter is concerned rather with the best life for most men, consisting in the activity of the virtues viewed now not as heights of excellence but rather as means between extremes, with emphasis upon socio-economic moderation (*ibid.* IV. 11. 1295a 25 ff.). Consequently, the former state is an aristocracy with highly limited suffrage, whereas the latter is a middle-class republic. The contrast is analogous to that between most of the other Aristotelians and Marsilius.

makes intelligible the fact that while Marsilius still retains some of the medieval conceptions of hierarchy and status,[90] his arguments for the people as legislator are taken up largely with a defense of the intellectual and moral competence of the *vulgus*.[91]

4. THE METHOD AND CONTEXT OF FAITH

The theologizing approach of the papalists was integrally interwoven with an extensive use of the authorities of the Christian faith. For the primacy of the theological over all other orders, upon which the doctrine of the papal plenitude of power was based, involved a similar primacy of faith over reason. The materials of faith as such, therefore, supplied the primary arguments for the papalist position, and it was as derivative from those materials that cogency was also attributed to the rational arguments which invoked analogies from the divine order of the universe and of all its parts. Consequently, Marsilius had to consider the arguments based upon religious faith as well as those based upon reason and experience. He had to show that faith no less than reason supported the political doctrine he was advancing in opposition to that of the papalists.

The consideration of the materials of faith comes in Discourse II of the *Defensor pacis,* not in Discourse I, which presents rational "demonstrations"; so that Marsilius' order of argument is precisely the reverse of that of the papalists. Yet he states at the outset of his treatise that he will "confirm" his rational arguments by the authorities of the Christian faith,[1] and the second discourse consists largely in a detailed attempt at such confirmation. It is important, therefore, to examine the principles upon which this second enterprise of Marsilius is based; for in his doctrine, as well as in that of his predecessors and contemporaries, serious political consequences hinge upon the answers given to the questions of what constitutes the object or content of faith, how that content is to be interpreted, and what is its relation to reason. Such an examination is indeed of particular importance for an understanding of Marsilius' doctrine; for his explicit acceptance of the materials of religious faith confronted him anew with the problem of safeguarding the biological, naturalistic basis of his politics from the papalists' reduction of politics to theology.

While Marsilius does not give a formal definition of faith, he indicates that it involves "firm belief" in the "irrevocable truth" of statements, and that the belief is necessary in order to obtain eternal salvation.[2] Statements of this kind are found in the holy Scriptures, especially the articles of

[90] See below, pp. 190 ff.
[91] See I. xii–xiii *passim,* and below, pp. 193 ff., 208 ff.
[1] I. i. 8.
[2] See II. xix. 1, 2.

faith.[3] What, however, is the basis of such belief? It is that these statements have come from God, who alone can never err.[4] But what is the proof either that God is their source, or that such a source means infallible truth? Here Marsilius is at an impasse. He says on the one hand that the necessity of having faith in the Scriptures is "self-evident to all Christians," and can be proved only through the Scriptures themselves.[5] But he also points out that belief in the divine origin of the Scriptures, and in their truth, may come either from human testimony, on the one hand, or from faith, miracle, or other sensible sign, on the other.[6] Yet human testimony has at best only derivative dependability, while the warrant of faith is precisely what is at issue; and as for miracles, they are quite infrequent: the truth and divine origin of the Scriptures "are believed by many who have not seen Christ, have not known him by any external sense, and have never perceived a miracle or sensible sign concerning him." [7]

Marsilius was not alone in these difficulties regarding the basis of faith.[8] But they raise the question of what support reason can give to faith; and on this question Marsilius' position presents significant divergences from the doctrines of his predecessors.

In general, there are three possible relations between reason and faith, which may be designated as "separation," "agreement," and "opposition." There is separation when a proposition held by faith or by reason is not held by the other faculty at all, as to either its truth or its falsity. There are agreement and opposition when a proposition held as true by one faculty is held, respectively, as true or as false by the other. All three of these relations may be found in the doctrine of Marsilius; and the various objects to which each extends are revealing as to his further attitude toward the relations between the natural, human, and divine orders.

(1) *The separation of faith and reason.* This is initially a consequence of the accusation with which Marsilius begins Discourse II, that the papalists "have enveloped divine and human doctrines concerning human acts, both individual and civil, in a motley entanglement very difficult to unravel." [9] His own procedure, in contrast, consists in "*separating* divine from human writings, which the Roman pontiffs had confused." [10] Can

[3] *Ibid.*

[4] II. xix. 4, 7.

[5] II. xix. 2. See Thomas Aquinas *S. theol.* II. I. qu.100. a.4. ad I: "Hoc quod est credere in Deum est primum et per se notum ei qui habet fidem."

[6] II. xix. 9.

[7] *Ibid.*

[8] See Thomas Aquinas *S. theol.* II. II. qu.6. a.I. Resp., where it is pointed out that "external causes" of faith, such as miracles or human persuasion, are insufficient to induce faith without the "interior cause," grace, for of men who see the same miracle and hear the same preaching, some believe and some do not.

[9] II. i. I. See II. xxvi. 19: "Propter divinarum et humanarum scripturarum involucrum. . . ."

[10] II. xxvi. 18.

human reason, then, establish any of the doctrines of religious faith? Marsilius' specific answers are instructive when compared with those of Thomas Aquinas. Although Thomas, like Marsilius, declares that the basis of faith is not human reason but divine authority,[11] and separates the spheres of rational knowledge and faith,[12] he points out that some propositions which are objects or "preambles" of faith can be demonstrated by reason, such as the existence and unity of God.[13] Faith, consequently, is not entirely devoid of rational foundation. Marsilius' naturalistic metaphysics, on the other hand, with its view of nature as the realm of necessary uniformities which includes even the human will, has done away with the axiological hierarchy of "ordered natures," involving the dependence of the imperfect upon the perfect, upon which Thomas' demonstrations had reposed.[14] Hence Marsilius declares indemonstrable those objects of faith with respect to which Aquinas finds demonstrations possible. While he does not explicitly deal with the question of whether God's existence is demonstrable, he seems to imply that it is not.[15] In any case, however, he explicitly declares that the causal action of God in establishing human governments and laws is impossible of rational proof; [16] he does not follow the procedure whereby Aquinas, although holding divine providence to be indemonstrable,[17] nevertheless infers the divine governance of the world from the observed order of things.[18] For Marsilius, again, the fact of eternal life [19] and the consequent "true and primary necessity of the priesthood" [20] cannot be proved by reason, whereas Aquinas, while making eternal life an article of faith,[21] yet demonstrates the immortality of the soul [22] and presents "evident reasons" in support of resurrection of the flesh.[23] The situation is similar when it comes to adducing rational grounds for the superiority of Christianity over other religions, which Marsilius frequently affirms in declaring that Christianity is the only religion which contains the "truth." [24] Where Aquinas points out the contrasts between Mohammedanism and Christianity, in the former's appeal to carnal pleasures, its shallow truths mixed with falsehoods, its recourse to armed force, its initial lack of support among wise men,[25] Marsilius can find nothing more to say for the superiority of Christianity than that

[11] *S. theol.* II. II. qu.2. a.10.
[12] *Ibid.* II. II. qu.1. aa.4, 5.
[13] *Ibid.* I. qu.2. a.2. ad 1; II. II. qu.1. a.5. ad 3.
[14] See *ibid.* I. qu.2. a.3. Resp.; II. II. qu.2. a.3. Resp.
[15] See I. ix. 2.
[16] I. ix. 2; I. xii. 1.
[17] *S. theol.* II. II. qu.1. a.8. ad 1.
[18] *Ibid.* I. qu.103. a.1.
[19] I. iv. 3.
[20] I. v. 10.
[21] *S. theol.* II. II. qu.1. a.8. Resp.
[22] *Ibid.* I. qu.75. a.6; *Cont. gent.* II. lxxix.
[23] *Cont. gent.* IV. lxxix.
[24] I. v. 13; I. x. 3; II. viii. 4.
[25] *Cont. gent.* I. vi.

"we hold it by faith alone." [26] This point is particularly significant in view of the fact that he elsewhere presents a discussion of religions which were "invented" by "philosophers" solely for this-worldly political ends.[27] It would seem, then, that only "false" religions can have a rational or philosophic basis, and the rationality in such cases is rhetorical rather than demonstrative.

For Marsilius, consequently, as for the other Averroists, the separation between faith and reason is far more extensive than it had been for Thomas.[28] The divine creation, governance, and end of the world and of man are no longer in any sense susceptible of rational proof, and consequently the entire divine order exercises no control whatsoever upon a political doctrine established by rational demonstration. Conversely, the natural realm of necessary sequences has no intelligible relation to the divine order of providence and miracles. Marsilius nowhere suggests that nature is itself a "work of God," [29] and hence the traditional political problems which emerged from this conception—the relation of nature and grace, the derivation of human law from divine or eternal law—play no part in his doctrine.[30] The metaphysical basis of his naturalistic politics thus preserves its autonomy from the theological emphasis of the papalists.

(2) *The agreement of faith and reason.* Nevertheless, as we have seen, Marsilius undertakes to "confirm" by the authorities of faith the conclusions which he had established by reason. In a preceding section we cited a long list of passages in which he, unlike the Averroists, asserts an "agreement" between reason and Scripture; [31] these are epitomized in his statement that he has presented a "harmony of divine and human writings." [32]

[26] II. xxx. 4: "Non enim actio sacerdotum in aliis legibus nobilior est actione principantis . . . sed in sola lege Christianorum actio sacerdotum est aliarum perfectissima; quod tamen sola fide tenemus." Although this passage refers primarily to the relative "nobility" of the priesthood and the government as "parts" of a single state, it indicates also Marsilius' view that the superiority of the Christian priesthood to that of other "laws" cannot be proved by reason. The use of *lex* as meaning "religion" or "religious law" should be kept in mind in interpreting this passage. See also below, p. 84, n. 45. There is an interesting contrast on this point between Marsilius and John of Jandun. See John's *Quaest. in Metaphys.* XII. qu.22 (fol. 144 C-D).

[27] I. v. 11. For a discussion of this point, see below, pp. 83–84.

[28] The Averroists were not, however, the only philosophers who widened the gap between faith and reason; Duns Scotus also denies the demonstrability of many propositions which are demonstrable for Thomas. See *De primo principio* cap. iv, conclus. 10, fin. (ed. E. Roche [St. Bonaventure, N.Y., 1949], pp. 146–48).

[29] See Thomas *S. theol.* I. qu.44. a.3. Resp.: "Manifestum est autem quod ea quae naturaliter fiunt, determinatas formas consequuntur. Haec autem formarum determinatio oportet quod reducatur, sicut in primum principium, in divinam sapientiam. . . ." James of Viterbo *De reg. Christ.* II. iii (p. 173): "opus naturae est opus Dei."

[30] See above, p. 18; below, pp. 91, 133.

[31] See above, p. 42, n. 50.

[32] II. xxvi. 19: "ad veritatis callem, praeco veritatis existens, *per divinarum et humanarum scripturarum concordiam* temptavi reducere. . ." See III. iii: "Per ipsum librum [i.e., the

What is the relation of this "harmony" to the "separation" which we have just been examining? The separation had referred to the necessity of not giving the same credence to human as to divine writings, and had referred also to the disparateness of the respective objects of reason and faith. Now those objects, as we have seen, were all in the cosmological or superhuman sphere of eternal life and divine causation, which constituted the metaphysical bases of the papalist position. The harmony or agreement of reason and faith, on the other hand, refers to a different kind of object: human government, both in the state and in the church. The scriptural texts which Marsilius adduces as being in "agreement" with reason pertain primarily to the acts of the apostles and to their assertions of the divine sanction of government, with the consequent necessity that all, including priests, be obedient thereto.

Now the agreement in this political sphere might take one of two opposed forms. It could mean either the rational confirmation of previously stated theological doctrines of politics, or the scriptural confirmation of previously stated naturalistic doctrines. The former is the approach of the papalists; the latter is the approach of Marsilius. Hence where the papalists begin with the divine order and bring all matters to the test of axiological criteria based upon God, Marsilius brings in God only as an *a posteriori* "confirmation" of a system set up in total independence of theological considerations. This confirmation thus involves no fundamental concessions from the naturalistic orientation of the Marsilian state; the resulting "agreement" of reason and faith does not entail a parallelism of the priesthood and the secular government, or of religious considerations and political power. On the contrary, it serves to reinforce the positions which Discourse I had established by holding reason separate from faith: the separation of the priesthood from the government and its subordination to the government and the whole community. What this means is that, as Pighius was later to complain, Marsilius does not admit that the coming of Christ and the establishment of the church have made any essential political difference whatsoever: "He imagines (as always) that political communities, kingdoms, empires, are among us as they were among the pagans: he cannot understand that the Christian church is that kingdom of Christ which all nations and kingdoms, kings and emperors, are to serve. . . ."[33]

Fully to understand how Marsilius' incursion into the theological aspects

Defensor pacis] enim scitur auctoritas, causa, et *concordantia divinarum et humanarum legum*. . ."

[33] Albertus Pighius *Hierarchia ecclesiastica* v. viii (p. 154).

of politics attains this result which Pighius characterized so aptly, we must examine what Marsilius means by the content or object of faith, and how he interprets it. Essentially, it involves a divisive method basically similar to that seen above in his rational use of terms; for the content of faith is sharply narrowed down from its traditional amplitude by a series of distinctions: not only between Christianity and other religions, but also between the Old and New Testaments, human and divine writings, analogical and literal interpretations. It is because of these distinctions that Marsilius' "harmony" of reason and faith can fully achieve the confirmation of his secularized political doctrine.

(a) *The distinction between the Old and New Testaments.* To begin with, Marsilius declares the Old Testament to be devoid of all binding authority over Christians. Although its original source was God,[34] it is now obsolete: not only is observance of the ceremonial commands of the Mosaic law forbidden to Christians, but its legal commands are not obligatory.[35] For this reason, Marsilius refuses in Discourse II to concern himself, as had virtually all his predecessors, with the Old Testament.[36] The same refusal had been effected in Discourse I through his announced determination to deal only with what is self-evident or demonstrable; hence in discussing the efficient cause of governments and laws, their establishment by God as recounted in the Mosaic law can be removed from consideration.[37]

The motivation of this removal is to be found in the fact that the Old Testament was an outstanding source not only of the papal "decretals" [38] but also of papalist arguments: the exercise of judicial functions by Moses, Melchisedech, Samuel, and others was frequently cited as proof that priests were, and should be, kings or superior to kings, by direct appointment of God.[39] In refusing to deal with the Old Testament, Marsilius is thus deny-

[34] I. vi. 3.

[35] II. ix. 10. See *Def. min.* iii. 8: "Mosaica legalia aut ceremonalia ad observationem non obligant Christi fideles. . . ."

[36] II. iii. 9: "De Veteri autem Scriptura seu Testamento ad propositam conclusionem et illius oppositam, probationes omittemus inducere. . . ."

[37] I. ix. 2; I. xii. 1.

[38] See Duns Scotus *Opus Oxon.* IV. d.15. qu.3. n. 4 (XVIII, 365): "multa talia in Decretalibus sumuntur ex judicialibus legis Mosaicae. . . ."

[39] See Egidius of Rome *De eccl. pot.* I. v; II. v (pp. 14–15, 55); James of Viterbo *De reg. Christ.* II. x (p. 283); Alexander of St. Elpidius *Tract. de eccl. pot.* II. iii. 8 (p. 17), all of whom cite the following text from Hugh of St. Victor *De sacramentis* II. ii. 4 (PL 176, 418): "Quod autem spiritualis potestas major sit dignitate et potestate terrena in illo antiquo *Veteris Testamenti* populo manifeste declaratur, ubi primum a Deo sacerdotium institutum est, postea vero per sacerdotium jubente Deo regalis potestas est ordinata." For other citations of the Old Testament to the same effect, see Ptolemy of Lucca *Determinatio compendiosa* cap. v, xxxi (pp. 12, 62 ff.). Henry of Cremona *De pot. papae,* p. 62. Augustinus Triumphus *S. de eccl. pot.* qu.1. a.7. ad 2; qu.45. a.1. Scholz's Index IV to his edition of Egidius' *De eccl. pot.* lists 105 citations of the Old Testament and 103 of the New. See also the criticism of

ing the relevance of one of the primary foundations of the papalist position.[40]

(*b*) *The distinction between human and divine writings.* Within the Christian tradition, Marsilius takes the further step of separating out all "writings based upon the human discovery of an individual person or a partial group." [41] For all human writings are susceptible of error,[42] and hence are not entitled to that unquestioning belief which is the peculiar prerogative of the canonic scriptures. This point is aimed specifically at the whole body of "canon law" which, as Dante pointed out,[43] had long provided one of the strongest weapons in the papalist arsenal, and which nevertheless even the moderate antipapalists, including Dante, used and respected.[44] But for Marsilius it is neither "canon" nor "law," but merely human "stories or documents," and oligarchic ones at that,[45] designed only to abet the papal claims to power.[46]

A similar approach is applied by Marsilius to the entire patristic tradition and all the other standard authorities of medieval Christendom. Where Dante declares that the traditional doctors, "Augustine and the others," had been "aided by the Holy Spirit," [47] Marsilius says only that the statements which they make "on their own authority" he will accept or reject depending upon whether or not they are in accord with the Scripture.[48] On this ground, he repudiates statements of Ambrose, Jerome, Bernard, Theophylact, and Chrysostom,[49] discards glosses of Jerome and Augustine in favor of those by Origen and Gregory,[50] and points out that even Peter fell into error.[51] This fallibility of the saints is further emphasized by the fact that they sometimes contradicted themselves—for example, Jerome and Bernard [52]—as well as one another.[53]

Marsilius in Albertus Pighius *Hierarchia ecclesiastica* v. viii (p. 155): "Deinde, quod dicit leges divinas non exigere a sui transgressoribus poenas in hac vita, aeque falsum esse demonstrat *lex vetus Mosaica.*" This background makes clear that Marsilius' rejection of the Old Testament requires no recourse to a supposed influence of the Waldensians, as Lagarde suggests (*Marsile*, pp. 127–28). See also C. W. Previté-Orton, "Marsilius of Padua," *Proc. Brit. Acad.*, XXI, 171, n. 15; and R. Scholz, "Marsilius von Padua und die Genesis des modernen Staatsbewusstseins," *Historische Zeitschrift*, CLVI (1937), 97–98.

[40] For a further aspect of Marsilius' rejection of the Old Testament, see below, pp. 152–53.

[41] II. xix. 4.

[42] II. xix. 4, 6.

[43] *De monarchia* III. iii.

[44] *Ibid.*: "Decretales . . . *etsi auctoritate Apostolica sint venerandae.* . . ." See John of Paris *De pot. reg. et pap.* cap. v, vi, xxiv (pp. 113, 115, 144–46). *Quaestio in utramque partem* Proem. and *passim*. *Quaestio de pot. papae*, pp. 666 ff.

[45] II. xxviii. 29. See II. v. 5. For the reason why the decretals are not human "laws," see below, p. 143.

[46] II. xxiii. 13.

[47] *De mon.* III. iii (p. 365).

[48] II. xxviii. 1.

[49] II. xxviii. 17, 20, 22, 25.

[50] II. iv. 11; II. v. 2.

[51] II. xxviii. 5.

[52] II. xxviii. 10, 23, 24.

[53] II. xxviii. 1: "Quoniam et ipsi quandoque circa Scripturam et praeter Scripturam sententiis ad invicem dissident, ut Hieronymus et Augustinus super illud II[1] *ad Galatas* . . . et rursum Ambrosius cum Hieronymo de virginitate Joseph. . . ." See II. xxviii. 6.

The calling attention to such contradictions was an old procedure before Marsilius' time: it had been practiced by Gratian in the *Decretum,* by Peter Abelard in the *Sic et non,* by Peter Lombard, and was the basis of the scholastic method.[54] But where the motivation of these earlier writers was to harmonize what were interpreted as only apparent contradictions, to provide a "concordance of discordant canons," as Gratian expressed it, or else to point out that the church through the pope provides authoritative resolutions of such contradictions,[55] Marsilius' aim is rather to emphasize that no human mind, as contrasted with the canonic Scriptures, is free from error and deserves to have its products regarded as completely authoritative.

This emphasis upon human fallibility raises the question of its relation to the certainty attributed by Marsilius to his own demonstrations, which he says are obtained "through sure (*certis*) methods discovered by the human intellect."[56] The two positions may be reconciled by the distinction between the human mind viewed generically, and its specific rational powers of intellectual intuition and demonstration. Marsilius himself, however, does not adduce this distinction, nor does he, like Thomas Aquinas, distinguish between the "absolutely" greater certainty of faith (since its cause is God rather than human reason, "which can err"), and the greater certainty of the intellectual virtues "relatively to us" (since their objects are more proportioned to the dimensions of the human intellect than is God, the supra-rational object of faith).[57] Rather, Marsilius insists upon a simple dualism of God and man, the infallible and the fallible.[58] In an important sense, however, this insistence upon accepting only the certainties of the divine Scriptures is in keeping with the modality of necessity and certainty which Marsilius demands for his rational politics. Thomas Aquinas could hold that "sacred doctrine" employs not only the "proper" and "necessary" arguments taken directly from the canonic Scripture, but also the "extraneous" and "probable" arguments of the philosophers based upon natural reason, as well as the "proper" and "probable" arguments of the doctors of the church other than apostles and prophets.[59] But Marsilius is as much opposed to such a sliding scale of acceptable modalities and sources in the sphere of faith as in that of reason.

This difference between Marsilius and his predecessors has two further aspects. In the first place, while his dualism of the divine and the human

[54] See M. Grabmann, *Die Geschichte der scholastischen Methode* (Freiburg, 1911), I, 234 ff.

[55] See Thomas Aquinas *S. theol.* II. II. qu.11. a.2. ad 3.

[56] I. i. 8; see III. i. See above, p. 48.

[57] *S. theol.* II. II. qu.4. a.8; see *ibid.* I. qu.1. a.5.

[58] See William of Ockham's lengthy critique of Marsilius on this point: *Dialogus* Pars III. Tr. I. Lib. III. cap. xxiii (pp. 840–41).

[59] *S. theol.* I. qu.1. a.8.

enables him to reject the traditional authorities with a devout air, it also rejects what had been regarded as the continuing influence of the divine upon the human. In the medieval view, the "sacred doctrine" was a continuum carried on successively from the original divine revelation through the mass of gloss, commentary, canon, and systematic theology in which its meaning was gradually amplified and applied to all human concerns. It is this continuum of tradition, with its implied approval of the papal institution as having a divine basis, which Marsilius' flouting of tradition disrupts. Instead, he asks: "Why should anyone believe in human tradition, whether of a saint or a non-saint, rather than in the very clear statements of Christ?" [60]

In the second place, Marsilius' frequent rejection of the traditional authorities on the ground of their being at variance with Scripture betokens a self-conscious insistence upon independent interpretation. Thus he does not hesitate to attribute infallibility to his own interpretation of Scripture [61] and to say that he understands Scripture better than does St. Bernard: "Do you ask how I prove this? From the word of the Lord more evidently than he does." [62] In this resolve not to accept the traditional authorities merely as authorities but rather to start fresh and to undertake a new critical scrutiny of scriptural texts, Marsilius is clearly a precursor of the individualism of the Reformation.[63]

(*c*) *The distinction between analogical and literal interpretations.* Having removed all merely "human" doctrines from the ranks of "divine" writings, and having declared the Old Testament to be obsolete, Marsilius is left with the New Testament itself. This was given by immediate inspiration of God, and is hence infallible.[64] There at once arises, however, the question of the method by which it is to be interpreted. A long tradition, going back to St. Augustine, held that beside their "historical" or literal sense, scriptural statements also have other meanings, "etiological," "analogical," "allegorical," inasmuch as God, their author, can make not only words signify things, but also things signify other things.[65] To be sure, as Thomas Aquinas points out, these latter meanings, which he calls

[60] II. xvi. 11. See II. xxviii. 6: "Et est mirandum si magis credere debeamus auctoritati Glossatorum quam Christi, quicumque fuerit ille Glossator etiam sanctus. . . ."

[61] II. xix. 2: "Quod etiam ex Scriptura et in ipsa *infallibili deductione* firmata ostendere possumus. . . ." II. xix. 3: "Hoc etiam *deductione infallibili* ex Scriptura vim sumente patere potest. . . ." II. xxviii. 1: "*infallibilem rationem* in Scriptura firmatam. . . ." II. xxviii. 6: "Significat autem *infallibiliter* nos verum dicere sequens Evangelii series. . . ."

[62] II. xxviii. 22.

[63] Cf. Emerton, *op. cit.*, p. 70. Marsilius' conciliar doctrine, however, does not maintain this individualism; see below, pp. 284 ff.

[64] II. xix. 4.

[65] Augustine *De utilitate credendi* III. v (PL 42, 68). For other instances of such classifications, see R. McKeon, "Rhetoric in the Middle Ages," *Speculum,* XVII (1942), 20, n. 2.

by the common term "spiritual," are all based upon the literal, and anything necessary to faith which Scripture presents in a spiritual sense is also presented elsewhere in Scripture in a literal sense.[66] Nevertheless, these spiritual senses are of central importance because they indicate the manifold extensions and applications which the scriptural statements were conceived to have: far from constituting merely a historical record of a group of particular and local events, they were fraught with implications for the whole life of man in all ages and in all spheres. The spiritual interpretation of Scripture was thus one with the organismic metaphysics and analogical method followed by the papalists, and permitted the same assimilation of the human and divine, including the apotheosis of the pope and the claim of a divine sanction for the hierarchic institutions of the visible church.

It is not surprising, therefore, that Marsilius insists upon as close confinement to the literal interpretation of Scripture as possible. With the same dialectical sensitiveness which motivated his charges of "sophistry," he declares that the papalist position is "based upon metaphorical expositions of Scripture contrary to its literal sense." [67] He is acutely aware that such interpretations, which he usually refers to as "mystical," [68] permit flights of fancy which go far afield from what can be ascertained in the text itself,[69] and that these "wandering expositions" have furnished the papalists with support for their "corrupt opinion." [70] Thus he reproaches the "glosses of the saints" for turning to the "allegorical or mystical" sense because they assume the literal sense to be clear; [71] he himself instead emphasizes frequently that the literal sense is so clear that it requires no gloss or other interpretation.[72]

[66] *S. theol.* I. qu.1. a.10. Resp. ad 1.

[67] II. xxii. 20. Cf. Lagarde, *Marsile,* pp. 74–76; Previté-Orton, "Marsilius," *Proc. Brit. Acad.,* XXI (1935), 145–46.

[68] II. iv. 1, 6; II. xxviii. 1, 24. See II. iv. 8: "allegoricum seu mysticum." It should be noted that Thomas Aquinas distinguishes between the "metaphorical" and the "spiritual" senses of Scripture (see *S. theol.* I. qu.1. aa.9–10). Only Scripture can be said to have "spiritual" senses in the strict meaning of the term, i.e., wherein things signify other things; hence, on the division of senses into "literal" and "spiritual," all human writings, including even the metaphorical fancies of poets, are literal, not spiritual. See Thomas Aquinas *Quaestiones quodlibetales* VII. qu.6. a.16.

[69] See II. i. 3, where he refers to the papalists' use of "sacri canonis auctoritates, cum quibusdam fictis et alienis quorundam interpretationibus. . . ." This point had been made earlier by anti-papalists, using a frequently quoted statement of Pseudo-Dionysius: "mystica theologia non est argumentativa" (*De mystica theologia* I. i; PG 3, 997). See *Quaestio de potestate papae* ad 2 (pp. 676–77); John of Paris *De pot. reg. et pap.* cap. XV (p. 128).

[70] II. xxviii. 24: "Verum qui ad usurpandos principatus sacerdotes anhelant . . . *peregrinas expositiones* Scripturae, quae ipsorum opinionem corruptam et affectionem perversam sapere videantur, libenter recipiunt."

[71] II. iv. 8.

[72] II. xxviii. 6: "Series enim Scripturae tam manifesta est quod glossatore non eget in hoc." See II. xvi. 6, 10; II. xxviii. 16, 26.

This preference for literal interpretation rests upon the same methodological and metaphysical basis as Marsilius' insistence upon literal definitions of terms. The literal is restrictive and exclusive; it prevents those assimilations of divine and human, moral and political, which analogical approaches to concepts and statements render possible. The specific effect of Marsilius' literal interpretation of Scripture lends special force to this consideration. For the primary question whose answer he seeks therein is what authority Christ "in fact" (*de facto*) bestowed upon the priesthood; and this will be only "such authority as we can prove to have been given to them *through the words of Scripture, no other.*" [73] Thereupon Marsilius quotes and expounds such passages as Christ's encounter with Pontius Pilate and the Pauline declaration that the powers that be are ordained of God—all of which, in their literal statement, emphasize Christ's lack of temporal authority and the duty of submission to such authority.[74] The crux of Marsilius' literalism is thus that it insists upon viewing the story of Christ and the apostles in its specific historical context. He hence enjoins all the political disabilities of the "primitive church" upon the pretenders to plenitude of power.

This very preoccupation, however, forces Marsilius to recognize the need for "mystical" rather than literal expositions of certain texts, such as the passage concerning the "two swords." [75] His general method, then, is to follow completely the "manifest literal sense" wherever possible; but when "mystical exposition" is necessary, "I shall adhere to the more probable view of the saints." [76] We have already seen with what independence Marsilius constitutes himself the judge of the weights of probability here referred to.

(3) *The opposition of faith and reason.* In addition to the separation between reason and faith on questions of divine causality, and the agreement between them on political questions made possible by the literal, anti-traditional interpretation of Scripture, Marsilius also upholds a third relation between reason and faith: opposition. This opposition is found in the general sphere of ethical and religious values. For although the political arrangements deriving from a naturalistic and a theological approach could be made to agree, the ethos underlying the respective approaches could not be harmonized so readily. It is in this sphere of fundamental axiological principles, involving the whole question of the relation between the "city of God" and the "city of man," that Marsilius' Averroism achieves some of its most striking results.

[73] II. iv. 2. [74] II. iv. 4 ff. [75] Luke 22:38; see II. xxviii. 24.
[76] II. xxviii. 1.

5. RELIGIOUS AND SECULAR VALUES

Augustine set the pattern for subsequent medieval philosophy in his insistence that the temporal goods of this world must be regarded not as good in themselves but only as instrumental to the spiritual goods of eternal life; men should "use" (*uti*) the former only in order to "enjoy" (*frui*) the latter.[1] The Christian Aristotelians, on the other hand, while they also held that the goods of this life are inferior to and must be ordered toward those of the future life,[2] did not disparage the former as did the Augustinians: there can be happiness in the present life, although some held that it is imperfect.[3] Marsilius' position differs from both these. In a few scattered contexts, to be sure, he affirms the superior value of the future life; [4] but at no point does he indicate that the goods of the present life must be ordered to or perfected by other-worldly goods. His usual procedure, rather, is to set temporal and eternal happiness side by side as two kinds of "sufficient life" or "ends desired by man," [5] as if they were of equal value deriving from the same kind of natural desire. Indeed, he does not hesitate to say, in opposition to Augustine, that men should "enjoy (*frui*) civil happiness, which seems the best object of desire possible to man in this world, and the ultimate aim of human acts." [6] That it is the last statement which represents Marsilius' own conception of values is obvious from his entire political doctrine where ends, when mentioned, are usually the this-worldly "sufficient life." [7] In this secularism he is in agreement with the other Averroists.[8]

[1] *De civ. Dei* XI. XXV. See *ibid.* V. XXV; X. i; XIV. i, XXV.

[2] See Thomas Aquinas *S. theol.* II. I. qu.3. a.8; *De reg. princ.* I. ix, xiv (pp. 12, 20–21). Egidius of Rome *De reg. princ.* Lib. I. Pars I. cap. xii. John of Paris *De pot. reg. et pap.* cap. ii, v (pp. 110, 113). Dante *De mon.* III. xvi (p. 376). Some question has been raised as to the bearing in this connection of Dante's statement (*loc. cit.*) that "mortalis ista felicitas quodammodo ad immortalem felicitatem ordinetur." See E. Gilson, *Dante et la philosophie* (Paris, 1939), pp. 196–99. See also above, p. 19, n. 29.

[3] Thomas *S. theol.* II. I. qu.3. a.2. ad 4.

[4] See I. vi. 2: "privata quoque propter delictum suo *finali optimo* ad quod fuerat ordinata." II. xvii. 12: "eternal death" is "graver" than "temporal death." See also II. xxvi. 16, 19.

[5] See I. iv. 3; I. v. 2; III. iii. See also I. vi. 9.

[6] I. i. 7.

[7] See below, p. 108. See also I. xvi. 14: "Hic [i.e. the ruler] agens . . . propter finem optimum in hoc saeculo, virtutis opus scilicet, ac propter extrinsecum consequenter honorem et famam. . ." Marsilius thus differs from the Christian Aristotelians, who insist that this-worldly goods are inadequate ends for the ruler, who must consider God alone as his reward. See Thomas Aquinas *De reg. princ.* I. vii–ix (pp. 10 ff.). Egidius of Rome *De reg. princ.* Lib. I. Pars I. cap. iv, xii, xiii. Compare Dante *De mon.* I. xi; III. xvi (pp. 346, 375–76).

[8] See Boethius of Dacia *De sompniis* (in M. Grabmann, *Mittelalterliches Geistesleben* [Munich, 1936], II, 217): "Summum bonum quod est homini possibile ex actionibus moralibus est felicitas politica." See also texts of Siger of Brabant, Boethius of Dacia, John of Jandun, cited above, p. 64, n. 71. Although these Averroists here differ from Marsilius in viewing happiness as theoretic contemplation rather than as all aspects of "civil" life, and declare

The most salient aspect of Marsilius' position, however, is the further relation it indicates between this-worldly and other-worldly values. The Augustinians had held that only the latter are "true"; the former when pursued for their own sakes, in separation from the theological virtues, are "false."[9] Augustine expressed this position by a dualism between the virtue of humility and the vice of pride, which arise, respectively, when men spurn and pursue this-worldly goods and their self-gratification in those goods.[10] The Christian Aristotelians, on the other hand, undertook to establish a continuity and harmony rather than an opposition between secular and religious values. This is epitomized in the manner in which Thomas Aquinas removes the contrariety between the Christian virtue of humility, which "respects man's subjection to God,"[11] and the Aristotelian virtue of magnanimity or "highmindedness," which "aims at great honors"[12] (and which might therefore have been confused with the Augustinian "pride"),[13] by pointing out the homogeneity of the evaluative principles involved in each: both virtues are in accordance with right reason, but they proceed by diverse considerations, humility making a man think little of himself by the consideration of his own deficiencies, magnanimity making him think highly of himself by the consideration of the gifts which he possesses from God.[14]

In contrast to both these approaches, Marsilius sets secular and religious values in stark opposition, not by holding that only the latter are "true," like the Augustinians, but rather by concomitantly affirming both their validity and their contrariety. He thus establishes what amounts to a "two-

that the highest object of contemplation is God, they regard such contemplation in the Aristotelian manner as entirely this-worldly *θεωρία*, not as the beatific vision (*visio Dei*) in the future life, like Thomas Aquinas (*S. theol.* II. II. qu.4. a.8). See also "Condemned Propositions of 1277," no. 170 (in Mandonnet, *op. cit.*, II, 188), and M. Grabmann, "Der lateinische Averroismus des 13. Jahrhunderts und seine Stellung zur christlichen Weltanschauung," *Sitzungsberichte der bayerischen Akad. der Wissenschaften*, Phil.-hist. Abt. (1931), Heft 2, pp. 73–75. As this book was going to press I found some important confirmations of the points made in this note and in other parts of the present section, in an article by R. A. Gauthier, "Trois commentaires 'averroïstes' sur l'Ethique à Nicomaque," *Archives d'histoire doctrinale et littéraire du moyen âge*, XVI (1947–48), 187–336. On the present point, see especially pp. 278–81, 288–93 of Gauthier's article.

[9] See Augustine *De civ. Dei* XIX. XXV. See also Egidius of Rome *De eccl. pot.* II. iv, vii (pp. 49, 74). Guido Vernani *De reprob. Monarchiae* I (p. 126). Alvarus Pelagius *De planctu eccl.* I. xl (p. 63).

[10] *De civ. Dei* XIV. xiii; see XIX. XXV.

[11] *S. theol.* II. II. qu.161. a.1. ad 5.

[12] *Ibid.* II. II. qu.129. a.2. ad 3. See Aristotle *N. Eth.* IV. 3. 1123a 34 ff.

[13] See *S. theol.* II. II. qu.162. a.1 ad 3.

[14] See *ibid.* II. II. qu.129. a.3. ad 4; qu.161. a.1. Resp. and ad 3; a.2. ad 3. See also Albert the Great *In Eth.* Lib. IV. Tr. II. cap. ii (pp. 296–97); Egidius of Rome *De reg. princ.* Lib. I. Pars II. cap. XXV. Subsequently, Thomas assimilates humility to the Aristotelian virtue of temperance: *S. theol.* II. II. qu.161. a.4. Cf. Aristotle *N. Eth.* IV. 3. 1123b 5. See also Gauthier, *op. cit.*, pp. 294–333.

fold truth" in the realm of the practical, analogous to the other Averroists' contrariety between reason and faith in theoretic philosophy.[15]

This opposition between secular and religious values runs throughout the *Defensor pacis*. Its basis is the double context in which Marsilius develops his doctrine. On the one hand, he accepts, and in Discourse I almost exclusively so, the secular "middle-class" values deriving from his biological view of natural desire. But on the other hand, when he comes in Discourse II to discuss the state in relation to the church with the whole theological context entailed thereby, he propounds the Augustinian religious conceptions, together with the even more ascetic doctrines of the upholders of "evangelical poverty." Hence, where Marsilius' secular values envisage men energetically pursuing their natural desires for this-wordly goods on a biological and economic plane, and ceaselessly clashing with one another as a result of that pursuit, his religious values envisage those same men as interested only in the future world and as maintaining, for that purpose, an ascetic, quietistic mode of life.

The polemical basis of this opposition is, of course, the fact that Marsilius insists upon the latter orientation as alone proper to the priesthood, because it serves to remove the priesthood from all influence upon, let alone control over, secular life and government. But in declaring that the priests, like Christ, must be concerned only with the "eternal kingdom" and the "theological virtues" by which it is attained,[16] Marsilius also has to insist that the priests should enjoin that concern upon all others also; and he has to defend those religious values himself. The priest "must urge upon others contempt for the world . . . he teaches those whom he addresses to spurn riches and governmental office." [17] This-worldly goods are now called "vanities and carnal pleasures"; temporal possessions "by their very nature move inordinately the emotions of their possessors," [18] and men "who desire them for their own benefit" are "weak." [19] There is an obvious contradiction between this attitude and that of Marsilius' secularism in

[15] Other Averroists before Marsilius seem also to have extended this contrariety to the realm of the practical, to judge from the remarks of their opponents. See Godfrey of Fontaines *Quodlib.* X. qu.6 (IV, 325), who declares that on the question of whether a man must love his own good more than anything else "male assignatur differentia inter Aristotelem et peripateticum et quemcumque doctorem theologicum. . . ." See the discussion by G. de Lagarde, *La Naissance de l'esprit laïque au fin du moyen âge,* III (Paris, 1942), 64, 255. See also Durand of St. Pourçain *De origine et usu jurisdictionum* qu.3 (p. 130 F-G): "virtus non opponitur virtuti secundum morales *philosophos* et secundum *veritatem*. . . ." The relation of reason to faith was expressed by the Averroists as that of "philosophy" to "truth"; e.g., Siger of Brabant *Quaest. de anima intellectiva* III. See also E. Gilson, "La Doctrine de la double vérité," in *Etudes de philosophie médiévale* (Strasbourg, 1921), pp. 51–75. For other examples of this contrariety in the sphere of the practical, see Gauthier, *op. cit.,* pp. 278 ff.

[16] II. iv. 5. [17] II. xi. 3. [18] II. xi. 3; II. xiii. 23, 24.

[19] II. xiii. 38.

which "riches" are defended as being "in their own nature determined more toward the good and sufficiency of the life of this world than toward the opposite."[20] Similarly he upholds on the one hand the Christian "humility" which eschews secular rulership, obeys the ruler in all things not contrary to *divine* law, and "pays even unjust tribute rather than fight over such things."[21] But on the other hand he defends as "appropriate" the Aristotelian highmindedness or "magnanimity" which seeks rulership and other honors and "justly" engages in sedition if these are undeservedly withheld,[22] and he urges strict supervision of the ruler to see that he conforms to *human* law.[23] Marsilius does not attempt, like Thomas, to conciliate humility with magnanimity.[24]

These oppositions occur not only between the secularism of Discourse I and the ascetic chapters of Discourse II, but also within the second discourse itself; they are not mere inadvertent contradictions but a basic aspect of Marsilius' axiology. Thus he points out the "contrariety" between Christ's afflicting with sorrows even good men in this world in order to lead them to their eternal reward, and the justice of secular rulers who apportion rewards and punishments in this world to those who observe and transgress the laws.[25] Augustine had also dwelt upon the contrariety between the secular and the theological orders of justice, but only to disparage the former except as ordered to the latter, which alone is fully valid.[26] Marsilius, on the other hand, equally defends both orders. Similarly, he points out the utter incompatibility of the Sermon on the Mount with the requirements and assumptions of secular rulership;[27] yet he insists that the priesthood must literally observe the former, and urge their flocks to observe it. Thus, on the one hand, unless the secular rulers carry on their regulation and adjudication of men's secular acts, there will result an

[20] I. xvi. 15. See I. iv. 4; I. v. 9. This difference is epitomized in the manner in which both the state and groups of men practising evangelical poverty are called *perfecta communitas* (I. iv. I; II. xiii. 28), the former because of its self-sufficiency in temporal goods, the latter because of their complete lack of such goods.

[21] II. iv. 9–13. See II. xxv. 13.

[22] I. xvi. 21.

[23] I. xviii. 4.

[24] The disparagement with which Marsilius, from his secular point of view, regards humility as against magnanimity is explicit in Siger of Brabant; see *Quaestiones morales* I (p. 173): "perfectior virtus est magnanimitas quam humilitas. . . ." See also "Condemned Propositions of 1277," no. 211 (in Mandonnet, *op. cit.*, II, 190): "Quod humilitas . . . non est virtus." The "Averroist" position on the relation between magnanimity and humility, as found in Siger, in Egidius of Orleans, and in two anonymous writers, is discussed in detail by Gauthier, *op. cit.*, pp. 319–28. His summation is that "On ne pouvait être plus méprisant pour l'humilité" (p. 328). Note that Machiavelli follows the same position in contrasting the ancient pagan religions with the Christian religion (*Discorsi sopra . . . Livio* II. ii).

[25] II. iv. 6.

[26] See *De civ. Dei* I. viii–x; XIX. xx, xxii; XX. ii. See also Augustinus Triumphus *S. de eccl. pot.* qu.6. a.I.

[27] II. xi. 7.

"insufficiency of human *worldly life,* which almost all men shun in accordance with nature." [28] But on the other hand, "the way to deserve eternal salvation" is to practice "humility and *contempt for this world.*" [29] In contrast, Marsilius' predecessors had attempted to conciliate the Sermon with the requirements of actual moral and political conditions by indicating the common values involved in both, and by stressing that it applies to mental preparation rather than to overt conduct.[30]

Marsilius thus sets up two contrary orders of values without indicating any definitive choice or conciliation between them. The impulses of nature and the conditions which reason shows to be necessary to their fulfillment are contrary to the determinations of grace which are objects of faith or revelation. In effect, Marsilius is saying that men cannot be both secular citizens and Christians; the two are incompatible. Nor is the incompatibility removed by the distinction he draws between counsel and command in the case of poverty,[31] for he still insists that the priesthood should observe the counsels of perfection and urge them upon others.[32] It is significant that Thomas Aquinas' conception of Christian "perfection" is far less austere than Marsilius', consisting primarily in love of God and of one's neighbor, so that it is a command, not merely a counsel.[33] Hence, whereas for Thomas a perfect Christian can also be a secular citizen, for Marsilius this is impossible.[34]

[28] II. ix. 12.

[29] II. xi. 2.

[30] See Thomas Aquinas *S. theol.* II. I. qu.108. a.4. ad 4; II. II. qu.40. a.1. ad 2; qu.43. a.8. ad 2; qu.73. a.3. Resp.; qu.108. a.1. ad 4; qu.124. a.1. ad 3. Egidius of Rome *De eccl. pot.* II. vi. Augustinus Triumphus *S. de eccl. pot.* qu.44. a.7.

[31] II. xiii. 37.

[32] The same contrariety between religious and secular values is found in Marsilius' discussions of the virtues of rulers and priests. From the standpoint of reason he declares that the secular ruler must be the "best man in the state" (I. ix. 7), "nobler and more perfect" than the other parts of the state (I. xv. 7). But from the standpoint of faith the function of the priest is "nobler" and "more perfect" than that of the ruler (II. xxx. 4; see II. xvi. 14; II. xxii. 8). This antithesis may be partly resolved by the distinction between moral and theological virtue (see I. xv. 7: "virtute moris"; II. xvi. 14: "sanctis moribus"); but it is significant that Marsilius does not attempt any such resolution. For the political consequences of this antithesis, see below, pp. 108–9.

[33] *S. theol.* II. II. qu.184. a.3. Thomas also distinguishes, as Marsilius does not, between being "perfect" and having the "status of perfection" (*ibid.* II. II. qu.184. a.4).

[34] It would go beyond the limits of this study to examine the relation of the axiological opposition here indicated to other such oppositions in the history of thought and culture. In particular, however, it would be worth examining the bearing of this opposition on the development of the "Protestant ethic" discussed by Max Weber (see especially *The Protestant Ethic and the Spirit of Capitalism,* trans. T. Parsons [London, 1930]) and R. H. Tawney (*Religion and the Rise of Capitalism* [New York, 1926]). The "worldly asceticism" which Weber conceives as the dominant characteristic of the Protestant ethic appears to combine the religious and secular values separated by Marsilius in such fashion that the untrammeled pursuit of economic goods is given the sanction of the religious values from which Marsilius divorced it, yet without the restraining effect which morals and religion (natural and divine law) were to exercise upon that pursuit according to Thomas Aquinas and other medievals.

From this contrariety of values there results a similar opposition with respect to the nature and function of religion itself. From the standpoint of reason, Marsilius views religion as having been "invented" by "philosophers" only because it serves a "quasi-necessary" function in the state. Although the "inventors" of religions "did not believe in the resurrection of men and in that life which is called eternal, they nevertheless feigned and persuaded men that it exists." For the promises which a religion makes of eternal rewards for good behavior, and its threats of eternal punishment for the bad in a hereafter, can serve as powerful deterrents to wrongdoing and as incentives for good deeds in this world, thereby helping to stabilize the social order.[35]

This naturalistic conception of religion is not, indeed, so revolutionary as some commentators have thought;[36] the same reference to the "invention" of religion for its this-worldly social utility is found not only in Aristotle[37] and Averroes,[38] but also in Augustine (who describes it as the "civil theology" expounded by Varro),[39] Albert the Great,[40] and Thomas Aquinas.[41] But whereas all these thinkers except Averroes treat this conception of religion with disparagement or indignation, Marsilius' lengthy exposition of the idea is integrally connected with his naturalistic politics as a whole. Apart from saying that such "gentile" religion is false,[42]

Both Weber and Tawney recognized the incompleteness of their researches with respect to the medieval background; it is here suggested that a study of the Averroist ethic of Marsilius and others might throw further light on the history of modern conceptions of the relation between religious and economic values.

[35] I. v. 11.

[36] See J. W. Allen, "Marsilio of Padua and Mediaeval Secularism," in *The Social and Political Ideas of Some Great Mediaeval Thinkers*, ed. F. J. C. Hearnshaw (London, 1923), p. 180; Lagarde, *Marsile*, p. 46; d'Entrèves, *Medieval Contribution*, p. 68; E. Gilson, *Dante et la philosophie* (Paris, 1939), p. 215, n. 1.

[37] *Metaphysics* XII. 8. 1074b 4–8.

[38] *Metaphysicorum expositio media* II. iii (in *Aristotelis opera* [Venice, 1560], VIII, fol. 55D); *Destructio destructionum*, Disp. in Physicis, IV (X, fol. 352A).

[39] *De civitate Dei* IV. xxxii: "Sicut enim daemones nisi eos, quos fallendo deceperint, possidere non possunt, sic et homines principes, non sane justi, sed daemonum similes, ea, quae vana esse noverant, religionis nomine populis tamquam vera suadebant, hoc modo eos civili societati velut aptius alligantes, quo similiter subditos possiderent." See *ibid.* VI. v ff.

[40] *In lib. de Anima* I. Tr. II. cap. vii (*Opera*, ed. Borgnet, V, 160): "Et ideo videntur quidam loqui de anima . . . ac si ipsi arbitrentur fabulas Pythagorae in legibus suis dictas esse veras. Volens enim Pythagoras facere cives colere pietatem et justitiam, fabulatus est animas malorum civium exire de uno corpore in aliud dexterioris conditionis, ita quod anima hominis ingrediebatur corpus leonis vel asini." Marsilius makes the same reference to Pythagoras (I. v. 11). The text on which Albert is here commenting (Aristotle *De anima* I. 3. 407b 22) does not ascribe to Pythagoras the aim of "making the citizens cultivate piety and justice."

[41] *S. theol.* II. I. qu.99. a.3. Resp.: "leges humanae non curaverunt aliquid instituere de cultu divino, nisi in ordine ad bonum commune hominum: et propter hoc etiam multa confinxerunt circa res divinas, secundum quod videbatur eis expediens ad informandos mores hominum, sicut patet in ritu gentilium."

[42] I. v. 13.

he is so far from condemning the "philosophers" who "invented" it that he rather praises them as "wise," their results as valuable,[43] their practices as "fitting,"[44] and the whole idea as "quasi-necessary" for the well-being of the state.[45] Religion is, in effect, the opium of the people, but Marsilius readily admits the utility of such opium. From the necessities of biology to the socio-political necessity of religion is but a short step for the Marsilian politics, a step which Machiavelli and Hobbes were later to take with equal facility.

Marsilius does not, however, apply this naturalism to the Christian religion and priesthood. The other religions, he declares, are "false" while only Christianity is "true,"[46] so that the eternal happiness which the latter promises is a fact. The Christian religion, therefore, is not a mere human invention as in the case of all other religions, but rather a divine revelation, and its function is not a rhetorical political one but rather the teaching of the truth which leads men to God. However, both the truth and the consequent superiority of Christianity cannot be proved by reason, but are held "by faith alone."[47] Once again, therefore, Marsilius sets up an Averroist "two-fold truth": what the reason of the "philosophers" can establish about the nature and function of religion is contradictory to the deliverances of faith. According to reason, God and the future life are fictions having only a socio-political utility; according to faith, they are eternal truths. A rational politics will hence make religion at most a subordinate instrument to be used by the state, not the highest end.

[43] I. v. 11.

[44] I. v. 13.

[45] I. v. 11. This acceptance that the "falsity" of religion does not militate against its social utility is strongly in the Averroist tradition. See Averroes *Metaphysicorum expositio media* II. iii (*Aristotelis opera* [Venice, 1560], VIII, 55D): "Enumerantur plures opiniones, quae sunt veluti radices et fundamenta legum, ut quod Deus sit, quod sit intelligens, et volens, et mundi causa, et summum bonum, et optimum, et Gubernator, ac mundi rector, et reliqua, quae ponuntur in legibus, non ut homines, qui vivunt sub illis, sciant, sed ut boni fiant. Lex enim non est ut sciamus, sed ut boni fiamus. Et causa est, quoniam perfectio hominis non acquiritur nisi per congregationes hominum in civitatibus, et congregatio, id est Civitas, non erit perfecta nisi propter bonitatem, et non propter scientiam. Quare, ut homines sint boni necessarium est lex, non ut sciant." The last phrase of the penultimate sentence ("congregatio, id est Civitas . . . scientiam") is quoted four times by John of Jandun *Quaest. in Metaphys.* I. qu.1; I. qu.17; I. qu.18; I. qu.21 (fols. 1C, 13C, 14E-F, 17P). John develops this point in great detail, but refutes it by distinguishing the *lex Christianorum*, as alone true, from all other *leges*. See *ibid.* II. qu.11 (fol. 34O ff.). See also Siger of Brabant *Quaestiones in Metaphysicam* Lib. II. qu.16 (ed. C. O. Graiff [Louvain, 1948], p. 74): "legislator non ponit de primis principiis secundum quod opinatur, sed secundum quod magis conferens est hominibus, et secundum quod magis potest instruere bonis; aliquando autem per falsa et frivola possunt homines fieri boni." Compare the far milder statements of Thomas Aquinas in his brief commentary on the same passage of Aristotle's *Metaphysics* (II. 3. 995a 4) on which Averroes and Siger were commenting (*In Metaphysicam Aristotelis commentaria*, ed. M. R. Cathala [Turin, 1935], Lib. II. Lect. 5. n. 333). On the other hand, Albert the Great's lengthy commentary on this passage shows the detailed influence of Averroes, even as to terminology (*Metaphysicorum libri XIII* Lib. II. Tr. unic. cap. xi; in *Opera*, ed. Borgnet, VI, 129).

[46] See above, p. 69.

[47] I. v. 10; II. xxx. 4. See above, pp. 69–70.

CHAPTER III

THE STATE AND ITS PEACE

I. THE PERFECTION OF THE STATE

THE INCORPORATION of Aristotle's *Politics* into Western thought, some three-quarters of a century before the writing of the *Defensor pacis,* provided an alternative to the antecedent Augustinian tradition, which held an exclusively theological conception of the state. Rather than as a result of sin, the state was now viewed as "natural," that is, based upon fundamental traits of the integral human nature which existed even before the corruption of sin; and rather than regarded as justified only by its advancement of men toward a divine goal, the state was now conceived to have a moral mission as well, the perfection of man's "natural" powers. This new conception was epitomized in Aristotle's definition of the state as "the perfect community having almost the limit of self-sufficiency, which originated for the sake of life but exists for the sake of the good life." [1] This definition was repeated by Marsilius [2] and was common in one form or another to most of the medieval Aristotelians.[3] It meant that the state was the complete society, rather than, as in the Augustinian conception, sharing the vitiating incompleteness of all temporal institutions,[4] or, as in the modern view, with its distinction of "state" from "society," embodying merely the political organization of society.

Nevertheless, in defining the state as the "perfect community" Marsilius differs considerably from the other Aristotelians, because of his frequent departures with respect to principles which have been examined above. These differences lead him to a conception of the state in which, while the other Aristotelians had shifted the emphasis from theological to ethical ends, the emphasis now falls not upon ends at all but upon political means. He thus develops a legalistic or specifically political view of the state. But in view of the state's "perfection," these political means come to absorb the whole content of men's social life.

[1] *Pol.* I. 2. 1252b 27. For the Augustinian doctrine, see *De civ. Dei* XIX. XV.

[2] I. iv. I.

[3] See Thomas Aquinas *De reg. princ.* I. i (p. 3). Engelbert of Admont *De ortu* cap. xiii (p. 369B). Egidius of Rome *De reg. princ.* Lib. III. Pars I. cap. i. James of Viterbo *De reg. Christ.* I. i (p. 92). Dante *De mon.* I. v (p. 344). John of Paris *De pot. reg. et pap.* cap. i (p. 109). Augustinus Triumphus *S. de eccl. pot.* qu.I. a.6. William of Ockham *Dialogus* Pars III. Tr. II. Lib. II. cap. v (p. 794). Ptolemy of Lucca *De reg. princ.* IV. ii (p. 82).

[4] See *De civ. Dei* XIX. v.

When Aristotle defines the state as the "perfect" community, he is viewing the "perfect" (τέλειος) as the "end" (τέλος). The state is perfect in two senses: first, because it is the "end" or culmination of the process of development leading from the lesser "communities," the family and the village, to the state; and second, because in it man can achieve his "end" in the sense of his chief good, which is a full or "self-sufficient" life.[5] In each of these respects, Marsilius treats the perfection of the state differently from the other Aristotelians.

For Aristotle the state is a growth or development out of lesser natural communities. The fact that it is a development, however, rather than a retrogression or vitiation, means that it attains an end superior to that of more primitive forms of association; consequently, Aristotle traces this development by centering attention upon the progressively higher end achieved by each association over the preceding one. The end of the pairing of male and female is procreation; that of the master-slave relation, security; of the household or family composed of these, the satisfaction of everyday needs; of the village, more than daily needs; and finally of the state, self-sufficiency, the good life.[6] Aristotle's discussion is thus primarily analytical and only incidentally historical: it indicates the ends or final causes achieved by each form of association at any time, and not merely the fact that at some time in the past the quantitatively larger community grew out of a smaller one. The same emphasis upon final causes is repeated by the medieval Aristotelians in their account of the state in relation to lesser communities.[7]

Marsilius, with his orientation in efficient rather than final causes, has a quite different view of the state's development. His discussion is primarily historical and only incidentally analytical: he considers the historical growth from family to state in such fashion that the difference he finds between the various kinds of community is unique to the epoch when each was respectively the largest unit of human association. By thus making his differentiations historical, he avoids that determination by permanent, specified ends which the other Aristotelians make the basis of their political analyses. The significance of this change emerges when we see what aspect of the development Marsilius singles out for attention. The sequence from family to state as he traces it is no longer in terms of *ends* but rather in terms of specifically political *means:* the coercive regulation of transient

[5] *Pol.* I. 2. 1252b 31 ff.

[6] *Ibid.* I. 2. 1252a 27 ff.

[7] Thomas Aquinas *De reg. princ.* I. i (p. 3). Egidius of Rome *De reg. princ.* Lib. III. Pars I. cap. i. John of Paris *De pot. reg. et pap.* cap. i (p. 109). Engelbert of Admont *De ortu* cap. xv (p. 370G). James of Viterbo *De reg. Christ.* I. i (p. 92). Dante *De mon.* I. iii, v (pp. 342–44).

acts. He points out that when the family was the largest social unit,[8] all the acts of its members, "especially those acts which we shall henceforth call 'civil,'" were regulated by the eldest member "apart from any law or custom." But when the village came into existence, there had to be some kind of "quasi-natural law" based upon a sense of "equity apart from lengthy research," because "injuries" among the villagers were no longer a private matter affecting only the head of one family but touched others as well. Without some systematic provision for punishing injurious conduct, the village itself would have been destroyed.[9] Already at this stage there emerges Marsilius' concern with the preservation of the community. As villages increased in size, they were ruled by constantly "less imperfect ordinances," until finally the state with its full "rules for living" was reached.[10] Only after he has discussed this question of coercive regulation at some length does Marsilius mention, almost incidentally, that "more perfect arts and modes of living" were also gradually discovered.

As Marsilius views it, then, the development from family to state is primarily marked not by a *differentia finis* but rather by a *differentia regiminis*.[11] This kind of "political" emphasis is the hallmark of the Marsilian approach. In a sense its materials are derived from Aristotle, who also discusses the relations between the various groups in the family —husband-wife, master-slave, parent-child, brother-sibling—by analogy to the various political relations under different kinds of constitutions.[12] But he does not make this the crux of the development leading to the state as does Marsilius; and, even more important, Aristotle views the respective kinds of "political" relations in the family as depending upon the ends subserved by each relation. Marsilius, on the other hand, makes the coercive political emphasis central, without reference to unique ethical ends. Thus from the very outset his doctrine of the state exhibits his "specifically political" concern with the efficient causes which control acts and institutions— a concern which such thinkers as Machiavelli and Hobbes were to make the distinguishing feature of modern "scientific" politics.

This tracing of the state's development in terms of political means has important consequences. What Marsilius is pointing out is that only in the state are law and government, properly so called, to be found. There is no law at all in the family, only a "quasi-natural law" in the village,

[8] I. iii. 4: "quamdiu fuerunt homines in unica domo. . . ."
[9] *Ibid.*: "contigisset vel contingeret inde pugna et vicinorum separatio."
[10] I. iii. 4, 5.
[11] See I. iii. 4: "Hujus autem *differentiae* causa *regiminis* in domo unica et vicinia est. . . ."
[12] See *N. Eth.* v. 6. 1134b 9–18; VIII. 10. 1160b 23 ff.; *Pol.* I. 12. 1259a 39 ff.

but fully developed law in the state; and the case is the same with government, which is correlative to law. Hence Marsilius will be able to reject a continuum of kinds of coercive powers, and to set up instead a simple dualism in which coerciveness belongs only to the state's law and government but not to divine law, nor the priesthood, nor any other group or part of the state.[13] Moreover, where the papalists had viewed governmental power as a family inheritance the "ownership" of which is valid only if its possessor has been spiritually regenerated by the church,[14] Marsilius obviates this argument by emphasizing that political power arises not in the family but only in the state, a point made explicit by his subsequent chapter refuting the arguments for hereditary succession.[15] Similarly, the very fact that political power grows "naturally," like the state itself, out of more elementary communities, removes the need for any transcendental "justification" of it in such fashion as Augustine's normative insistence that true justice, and hence a true commonwealth, can exist only where God is loved.[16] Finally, and most important of all, the state itself comes to be viewed in terms of political power rather than of moral values: its "peace," its "order," its "unity," like its perfection, will be defined by reference to its possession of the means whereby coercive authority is effectively exerted.

What, then, is the relation of the state as "perfect" to human ends? For Aristotle, this relation is a direct one: the state is the proximate condition of man's achieving his highest good, self-sufficiency. The relation of this good to the state is indicated by the famous phrases that "the state exists by nature" and "man is by nature a political animal." [17] As we have seen, "nature" is here used in the sense of end or final cause, so that it means man's highest development of his specific powers.[18] The state is natural because only in it can man attain such development. For the "property" of man, his distinctive trait in comparison with other animals, is that he has a "sense" of good and bad, justice and injustice; and to enable him to set forth these qualities to other men, nature has endowed him with speech as against the mere expression of pain and pleasure which is all that the other animals have. The naturalness of the state is shown by the fact that it provides the direct field for the exercise of this sense;

[13] See below, pp. 118 ff., 154 ff.

[14] See Egidius of Rome *De eccl. pot.* II. viii (p. 79). For the papalist claim that inheritances are subject to papal approval, see James of Viterbo *De reg. Christ.* II. viii (p. 254). Egidius of Rome *De eccl. pot.* III. v (pp. 170–71). Alvarus Pelagius *De planctu eccl.* I. lxvi (p. 159). See also Ptolemy of Lucca *Determinatio compendiosa* cap. iii (pp. 8–9), who makes election of the emperor contingent upon papal approval because the pope is to the emperor "as father to son."

[15] I. xvi.

[16] See above, p. 37; also below, p. 91.

[17] *Pol.* I. 2. 1252b 31, 1253a 2.

[18] See above, p. 54.

indeed, man's possession of speech proves him to be a political animal in greater degree than the bees and other animals.[19] The medieval Aristotelians all emphasize this relation of speech and of man's rational and social nature to the state.[20]

Marsilius' doctrine repeats many aspects of this Aristotelianism. Men have a "natural impulse" or "inclination" toward political association;[21] hence they "came together in the beginning (*a principio*) . . . under the persuasion or exhortation of prudent and able men," and out of this beginning they progressed "to the form of the perfect community."[22] In this conception of Marsilius and the other Aristotelians, there is no idea of a social contract in any sense which would imply either that the political association is contrary to human nature, or that men did not always find themselves in some community proximately related to the state. For Marsilius, as for the other Aristotelians, this rational establishment of the state is a "fulfillment" (*complementum*) of natural tendencies.[23]

Beneath these similarities, however, there are far-reaching differences, based upon Marsilius' biological view of "nature," including human nature.[24] Thus he does not declare, like the other Aristotelians, that the state is "natural" or exists "by nature." The nearest he comes to it is when he says that the state is "like (*velut*) an animal or animate nature."[25] But this is only an analogy; the state is not in fact natural because only physical and biological objects are natural,[26] whereas the state is a product of human reason and art.[27] This difference in itself would not be decisive, for the other Aristotelians also regard the state as a product of rational construction as well as of historical development out of lesser communities. But from it results a further difference, as to the respect in which the state fulfills man's "natural inclination." It is significant that Marsilius does not

[19] *Pol.* I. 2. 1253a 10 ff.

[20] Thomas *De reg. princ.* I. I (p. 2): "est proprium hominis locutione uti, per quam unus homo aliis suum conceptum totaliter potest exprimere. . . Magis igitur homo est communicativus alteri quam quodcumque aliud animal." See Egidius *De reg. princ.* Lib. II. Pars I. cap. i; Lib. III. Pars I. cap. iv. Ptolemy of Lucca *De reg. princ.* IV. iii (pp. 83–84). John of Paris *De pot. reg. et pap.* cap. i (p. 109). See G. de Lagarde, "Une Adaptation de la *Politique* d'Aristote au XIVe siècle," *Revue historique de droit français et étranger,* 4th series, XI (1932), 236–37.

[21] I. iv. 3; I. xiii. 2.

[22] II. xxii. 15.

[23] I. v. 2, 3, 5. The doctrine of social contract is erroneously attributed to Marsilius by O. von Gierke, *Political Theories of the Middle Age,* trans. F. W. Maitland (Cambridge, 1900), nn. 137, 308; G. del Vecchio, *Su la teoria del contratto sociale* (Bologna, 1906), p. 76; E. Barker, *The Political Thought of Plato and Aristotle* (London, 1906), p. 514; Atger, *op. cit.*, pp. 70 ff. Cf. Battaglia, *Marsilio,* p. 72.

[24] See above, p. 55.

[25] I. ii. 3. See I. xv. 5, 6; I. xvii. 8.

[26] See I. xvii. 8, where Marsilius analogizes unity "in composito animali . . . bene formato secundum naturam" and "in civitate convenienter ordinata." After a brief statement, he continues: "Haec autem praetermittantur, quoniam ad *naturale* pertinent negotium magis."

[27] I. v. 2.

repeat Aristotle's phrase that "man is by nature a political animal," as do most of the other Aristotelians.[28] For there is nothing in man's "nature" which *directly* corresponds to, and evokes, a life of political association. The state is a result of man's natural desire for a sufficient life; but since that desire is biological rather than moral or intellectual, its immediate object is the food and shelter without which men cannot live.[29] These, however, are strictly localized in each individual, and are not, like justice or the desire for friendship, essentially social because relative to other men. In order to satisfy their biological needs, men must associate with one another in agricultural and mechanical pursuits; and it is only in this sense that men have a "natural impulse" toward association. But the sense of justice and the other social qualities attributed by the Aristotelians to human nature are not in fact natural to men.

From the point of view of Marsilius, then, the other Aristotelians have reversed the order of antecedents and consequents. Justice and other political values are the consequent or derivative rather than the antecedent of human association; it is only because men associate with one another in farming and mechanical arts, and as a result engage in transient acts impinging upon other men, that standards of right and wrong are evoked.[30] Marsilius' theory of law, consequently, will be based not upon a subsistent justice found in "natural" law but solely upon the responses of men's wills to the exigencies of preserving their association. This Marsilian reversal is similar to that which modern physical theories worked on the "Aristotelian" qualitative physics: instead of using specific kinds of qualities to explain the phenomena in which they were manifested, those qualities were themselves explained as consequences of more elementary quantitative particles. Similarly, rather than explaining the state by man's specific "sense of justice," that sense is itself explained by Marsilius as a consequence of elementary biological needs forcing men into economic association with one another. In Aristotelian terms, this is a substitution of explanation by material causes for explanation by formal causes, parallel to Marsilius' substitution of efficient for final causes as the determining factors in politics.

[28] Thomas Aquinas *De reg. princ.* I. i (p. 2): "Naturale autem est homini ut sit animal sociale et politicum." Egidius of Rome *De reg. princ.* Lib. III. Pars I. cap. iv: "homo est naturaliter animal politicum et civile." Ptolemy of Lucca *De reg. princ.* IV. ii (p. 81): "homo . . . secundum naturam est animal sociale sive politicum." Dante *Il convivio* IV. 4 (p. 298): "l'uomo naturalmente è compagnevole animale." John of Paris *De pot. reg. et pap.* cap. i (p. 110): "homo est naturaliter animal civile seu politicum et sociale." James of Viterbo *De reg. Christ.* I. i (p. 91): "Homo enim naturaliter est animal sociale."

[29] See I. iv. 3; I. v. 5, 6.

[30] See I. iv. 4; I. v. 7.

Marsilius' approach to the state is thus entirely economic and individualistic. There is no indication that men desire the company of other men for its own sake,[31] or that, apart from economic necessity, men are incomplete without the society of others. In this difference between Marsilius and Aristotle there is a paradox which further emphasizes the position of the state in their respective schemes of values. For Aristotle, man is by nature social, but nevertheless, as we have seen, the ideally best life is the non-social one of theoretic contemplation;[32] for Marsilius, on the other hand, man is by nature individualistic, but the best life he is in fact capable of leading is one involving the social relations and "peace" which enable his individual desires to be satisfied.

This reversal of the Aristotelians' justification of the state as natural is reinforced by the seeming paradox that Marsilius accepts, or at least propounds, the orthodox Augustinian version of the genesis of the state. If man had not fallen from grace, "the establishment of civil offices would not have been necessary to him or to his posterity."[33] The motivation of this Augustinian interpolation is clear: since Marsilius wishes to include the Christian priesthood within the state and to subject it to the state's jurisdiction, he has to account for its existence and fit its function into the general framework of the state.[34] But this view of the state as a result of sin does not entail any of the theological justificatory consequences which the traditional Augustinianism made so important. For it is not with respect to justice or any other moral qualities that Marsilius discusses the fall, but only with respect to biological and economic sufficiencies. The reason why the state would not have been necessary if man had not sinned is that "nature would have produced for him the advantages and pleasures of the sufficiency of this life in the earthly or pleasurable paradise, without any punishment or suffering on his part."[35] It is only because man's fall forced him to earn his living by the sweat of his brow that the state became necessary. Thus the Augustinian context is simply fitted into the individualistic biologico-economic framework of the Marsilian state.

[31] See Aristotle *Pol.* III. 6. 1278b 20: "man is by nature a political animal, and therefore even when they do not need one another's help men nonetheless desire to live together." It is significant that while Marsilius quotes from Cicero (*De officiis* I. vii. 22) the Stoic dictum "homines hominum causa generatos esse" (I. i. 4; cf. also I. xix. 13), he applies it only to his own practical enterprise and not to his doctrine of man and the state as such.

[32] See above, pp. 63–64.

[33] I. vi. I. For the Augustinian source, see above, p. 85, n. I; also *De civ. Dei* XIII–XV, XIX, *passim*. This Augustinian doctrine is also repeated by Dante *De mon.* III. v (p. 366).

[34] By emphasizing its non-rational aspect, however, he avoids discussion of the various papalist arguments which would have interfered with his rationally constructed politics in Discourse I. See above, pp. 43, 69.

[35] I. vi. I.

2. THE PEACE OF THE STATE

The state as it emerges from Marsilius' intial analysis is thus a group of men forced into association with one another by biological necessity, and attaining through that association a "sufficient life" in the generalized biological-social-practical-theoretic sense in which Marsilius understands such life.[1] Hence, while the most salient aspect of the state's "perfection" as he had traced its historical development had been its possession of full-fledged government and law, the state as "perfect" also contains all the other functions needed for sufficiency of life.[2] In conformity with medieval terminology, Marsilius calls the men who exercise these several functions the "orders" and "offices" of the state; [3] thus, insofar as they are "of" the state, they all have a quasi-public or "official" status. But he also follows Aristotle in calling them the "parts" of the state and in listing the six principal parts: farmers, mechanic artisans, bankers, judges or rulers, soldiers, and priests.[4] We have already noted the different ways in which the priesthood is a part of the state from the standpoints of reason and of faith.[5] The "true" or Christian priesthood is a part of the state in the same way that man's natural desire has for its object the sufficient life of the future world as well as of the present one; for the parts of the state are defined by their contribution to the sufficient life.

The question which immediately arises, however, is: What is the structure or order of these parts of the state in relation to one another and to the whole? How are they organized as parts, and who controls that organization? The importance of this question can be seen from the fact that the answer will also show what is the order and controlling agency of the state as a whole, and what is the political position of the priesthood in relation to the state and to the other parts.

Some commentators have held that the basis of Marsilius' revolutionary reversal of the dominant position which the papalists had claimed for the "church" in relation to the "state" consists in the very fact that Marsilius has made the "church" a part of the "state." [6] To begin with, however, it is necessary to be more precise with regard to terminology. Marsilius' approach was an unusual one in that he discusses the "church-state" problem not as the relation of "church" and "state" at all, or of spiritual

[1] See above, pp. 64–65.

[2] See I. iii. 5; I. iv. 5.

[3] I. iv. 5; I. v. 1, 5.

[4] I. v. 1. See Aristotle *Pol.* VII. 8. 1328b 3 ff.

[5] See above, pp. 83–84.

[6] See McIlwain, *op. cit.*, p. 313: "By the extremer papalists the State for some time had been treated as a subordinate department of the Church. The *Defensor* is the first book which reverses the process and regards the Church as a department of the State in all matters of earthly concern." See also d'Entrèves, *Medieval Contribution*, p. 46.

and temporal "powers," but simply of two "parts" of the state. The government is no longer the "royal" or "temporal power" but simply the "ruling part" (*pars principans*) of the state;[7] the priesthood is no longer the "papal" or "spiritual power" but rather the "priestly part" (*pars sacerdotalis*) of the state;[8] so that both government and priesthood are fitted into a context, a "whole," which is greater than either of them separately or together. Significantly, too, Marsilius was the first of the medieval Aristotelians to use Aristotle's classification of the six "parts" of the state, with its inclusion of the priesthood among those parts, as a springboard for the discussion of the "church-state" problem.[9]

Yet these points do not provide a sufficient explanation of Marsilius' overthrow of the papal supremacy. Although the papalists from the time of the investiture controversy had made the *regnum* a part of the *ecclesia*,[10] the name of the latter must not mislead; for this inclusion of the *regnum* within the *ecclesia* could in fact lead to a thoroughgoing subordination of the pope to the emperor, as in the "York Tracts"[11] and Gregory of Catino.[12] Moreover, Marsilius was not the first to make the priesthood a part of the state; John of Salisbury, for example, had made rulers and priests two of the many "offices" (*officia*) of the political body which he calls the *res publica;*[13] and yet he had asserted that the priests, not the rulers, preside over that body.[14] Similarly, such a papalist as James of Viterbo makes the secular and the spiritual powers parts of one *regnum,* which he defines as the Aristotelian state and equates with *ecclesia* because it enables men to achieve salvation, the highest "good life."[15] And in the years immediately following the publication of the *Defensor pacis,* two papalist writers who sought to refute Marsilius took over the same six-fold

[7] I. v. 7.

[8] I. v. 10.

[9] Ptolemy of Lucca uses a five-fold list of "parts" which he derives from Aristotle's review of Plato's *Laws* (*Pol.* II. 3. 1264b 33), but this list does not include the priesthood and is not used to discuss the church-state problem; see *De reg. princ.* IV. xxiv (p. 110). John of Jandun presents the same six-fold list as does Marsilius, but he does not use it to discuss the church-state problem; see *Quaest. in Metaphys.* Lib. I. qu.18 (fols. 14G-H, 15J). Peter of Auvergne and Albert the Great do not discuss the problem in their commentaries on the passage of the *Politics* where the six parts are listed.

[10] See Cardinal Humbert *Adversus simoniacos* III. xxi (MGH, *Libelli de lite,* I, 225); Honorius of Autun *Summa gloria* cap. xxvi (*ibid.,* III, 75).

[11] See *Tract. Eborac.* IV, V (pp. 663, 684–85).

[12] *Orthodoxa defensio imperialis* cap. iii (p. 536): "Habet etiam sancta eadem *ecclesia* singula membra propriis officiis deputata, habet levam, habet dextram . . . et per levam *regnum,* per dextram vero intelligitur *sacerdotium.*" Similarly, the late thirteenth-century imperialist Jordan of Osnabruck includes within the *ecclesia* not only the *imperium* and the *sacerdotium* but also the *studium;* see *De praerogativa Romani imperii* cap. v (ed. G. Waitz [Göttingen, 1868], p. 70).

[13] *Policraticus* v. ii (I, 282–4).

[14] *Ibid.* See also *ibid.* IV. iii (I, 239).

[15] James of Viterbo *De reg. Christ.* I. i (pp. 94 ff.). Cf. *ibid.* I. iv (p. 128) on *res publica.*

classification of the parts of the state which he had used, making them parts now of the *politia Christiana* and arguing that since the ruler-judges must be the best men in the state, they must be identical with the priests.[16]

Now it may be argued that these papalists were not, like Marsilius, making the priesthood part of the "state," but were rather making the secular government a part of the "church," whatever the term they used to describe the latter. But this is itself the very question: since terms like *regnum, res publica,* and *politia* can be used to describe the church as well as the state, or rather a unitary church-state, then what is the criterion of a "state" properly so called? By what means does Marsilius make the priesthood a part of the "state" and thereby overturn the doctrine of those who, like James of Viterbo, made it a part of the *regnum?* If it be replied that the difference is that in James' *regnum* the spiritual power is supreme, this of course begs the question; for by precisely what doctrinal means does making both the priesthood and the government parts of one *regnum* lead to the superiority in authority of one over the other? If it be replied further that the crucial difference consists in whether the *regnum* in question is dedicated primarily to the future life (in which case it would be a "church" state) or only to the present life (which would make it a "secular" state), this advances us closer to an understanding of what Marsilius has effected. But it is not a sufficient reply; for, as we have seen, Marsilius also admits that the future life is better than the present,[17] and he too declares that the state is dedicated to both lives.[18] Indeed, it is precisely because the state is concerned with the future life that the priesthood is one of its parts.

It is in a different direction, therefore, that the answer must be sought to the question of the organization and control of the Marsilian state and its parts, and to the concomitant question of the political position of the priesthood. The answer which Marsilius gives can be summed up in one word: *peace.* For peace is the formal cause of the state, that is, the principle of the state's order or organization; and its definition, which Marsilius presents by an organic analogy, shows why peace is such a cause: peace is to the state as health is to the animal; it is "the good disposition of the city or state whereby each of its parts can perfectly perform the operations belonging to it according to reason and its establishment." [19]

Nothing appears more surprising, at first glance, than that this concept of peace should be the proximate basis of Marsilius' radical conclusions.

[16] Anon. *De potestate papae,* in R. Scholz, *Unbekannte kirchenpolitische Streitschriften aus der Zeit Ludwigs des Bayern* (Rome, 1911), I, 253; Alvarus Pelagius *De planctu eccl.* I. xl (p. 61). See also Guido Vernani *De reprobatione Monarchiae* Lib. I (p. 128).

[17] See above, p. 78.

[18] I. v. 2.

[19] I. ii. 3; I. xix. 2.

For it was obviously a very traditional concept. That the state is composed of parts, that each of these parts has a specific function, and that the well-being of the state consists in each part's doing its own function without interfering with the others—these ideas go back at least to the "justice" of Plato's *Republic,* as does the use of an organic analogy to describe them. The same factors are found in the familiar treatment of John of Salisbury,[20] as well as in many of Marsilius' immediate predecessors.[21] Moreover, ever since St. Augustine the medieval tradition had frequently described these ideas by the same term as Marsilius now uses—"peace."[22] Nevertheless, it is precisely because Marsilius gives a radically different interpretation to the common materials which he takes over as the concept of peace that his doctrine of the organization and control of the state achieves its basic departures from the antecedent tradition.

From St. Augustine's *City of God* to the writings of Marsilius' contemporaries, the main lines of the interpretation of peace had involved two central features. First, peace is the universal order which subsists in all things and reflects the divine law governing their relations. For "the peace of all things is the tranquillity of order," and "order is the disposition of equal and unequal things attributing to each its place"; but that attribution is made in accordance with the laws which God has established for the universe.[23] Consequently, in the second place, peace as it is found among men is not merely an external relation but rather a "concord,"[24] a rapport of their hearts, based upon their common ordering by and to God. This internal, theological aspect of peace was emphasized in subsequent definitions of it as an effect of the principal act of charity, which is love;[25] a union of intellectual desires;[26] a uniform motion of

[20] *Policraticus* v. ii ff. (I, 282 ff.).

[21] See Thomas Aquinas *In Eth.* Lib. iii. Lect. 8. n. 474 (p. 162): "pacem quae se habet ad civitatem sicut sanitas ad corpus hominum. . . ." See also Thomas *S. theol.* II. ii. qu.183. a.2. ad 3; *De reg. princ.* i. xii (p. 18). Egidius of Rome *De reg. princ.* Lib. i. Pars ii. cap. xi. Ptolemy of Lucca *De reg. princ.* iv. xxiii (p. 109).

[22] On the medieval use of Augustine's concept of peace, see E. Bernheim, "Politische Begriffe des Mittelalters im Lichte der Anschauung Augustins," *Deutsche Zeitschrift für Geschichtswissenschaft,* n.s., I (1896), 1–23. See also above, p. 38, n. 25; below, p. 96, nn. 31, 32.

[23] Augustine *De civ. Dei* xix. xiii, xiv. See Thomas Aquinas *S. theol.* II. ii. qu.29. a.2. Engelbert of Admont *De ortu* cap. xiv (p. 370B). James of Viterbo *De reg. Christ.* i. iv (p. 120). Ptolemy of Lucca *De reg. princ.* iii. ix; iv. xxiii (pp. 58, 109). Alvarus Pelagius *De planctu eccl.* i. xli (p. 67).

[24] Whereas Augustine defines lesser "peaces" in terms of *temperatura, requies, consensio,* and *vita,* when he comes to the *pax hominum* he introduces the new term *concordia;* and each of the *paces* from that point on—of the *domus,* the *civitas,* and the *civitas caelestis*—similarly involves *concordia. De civ. Dei* xix. xiii.

[25] Thomas Aquinas *S. theol.* II. ii. qu.29. a.3. James of Viterbo *De reg. Christ.* i. iii (p. 120). Egidius of Rome *De eccl. pot.* iii. vi (pp. 175, 177).

[26] Thomas *S. theol.* II. ii. qu.29. a.1. Resp.

many wills;[27] a spiritual bond.[28] The state itself is "nothing other than a concordant multitude of men,"[29] and the peace of the state (*pax civitatis*) is "the ordered concord of the citizens in commanding and obeying."[30] Such an order can be had only by conformity to the order established by God. Otherwise, it is only a temporal peace, "false" and "imperfect," not "true" and "perfect."[31]

Peace, therefore, meant for the medieval tradition the whole metaphysical context which was at the basis of the papalists' analogical method and theological interpretation of politics. The universality of peace meant that no true values, hence no justice, could be achieved without membership in the visible church. The equivalence of peace to the order of divine law became for the papalists the necessity of obeying the pope as vicar of Christ. The spiritual aspects of peace—the sense in which it is a concord, a spiritual bond—meant that anything affecting peace came under the jurisdiction of the spiritual power.[32] To be sure, there were some writers, like Engelbert and Dante, who used the concept of peace to exalt the empire rather than the papacy. But their emphasis upon universalist ethical considerations left an easy opening for those papalist emphases upon axiological order which meant the hegemony of the spirtual power.

Now Marsilius' definition of peace as the "good disposition" of the state with respect to its parts preserves the generic principle of an "order" or "disposition" of parts within a whole which was of the essence of the traditional concept of peace. Like the tradition, also, he uses "peace" and "tranquillity" interchangeably. But apart from this, Marsilius' concept involves three important differences from the antecedent doctrines. First, it is entirely a secular political concept, a "civil peace,"[33] having no cosmo-

[27] Dante *De mon.* I. xv (p. 349).

[28] James of Viterbo *De reg. Christ.* II. viii (p. 254).

[29] Augustine *De civ. Dei* I. xv: "cum aliud civitas non sit quam concors hominum multitudo." This definition is repeated by Ptolemy of Lucca *De reg. princ.* IV. ii, xviii, xxiii (pp. 82, 103, 108). James of Viterbo *De reg. Christ.* I. i (p. 90). Guido Vernani *De reprobatione Monarchiae* Lib. I (p. 125).

[30] Augustine *De civ. Dei* XIX. xiii.

[31] *Ibid.* XIX. iv ff. For subsequent repetitions of this distinction between true and false peace, see Sedulius Scotus *De rectoribus Christianis* cap. iii, ix, xii, xvi (PL 103, cols. 297, 307, 313, 323). Hincmar of Rheims *De regis persona et regio ministerio* cap. x (PL 125, 842). Hugh of St. Victor *De claustro animae* III. ix; IV. xxi (PL 176, cols. 1102, 1160). Thomas Aquinas *S. theol.* II. II. qu.29. a.2. ad 3, 4. James of Viterbo *De reg. Christ.* I. ii (p. 104). See also above, pp. 15–16, 37–38.

[32] An early instance of such papalist use of the concept of peace is found in Sedulius Scotus, *loc. cit.* See also Egidius of Rome *De eccl. pot.* III. vi (pp. 175, 177). James of Viterbo *De reg. Christ.* II. viii (p. 254). See the discussion of this point in H. X. Arquillière, *Le Plus Ancien Traité de l'église* (Paris, 1926), pp. 34–42; and "Sur la formation de la théocratie pontificale," in *Mélanges d'histoire du moyen âge offerts à M. F. Lot* (Paris, 1926), pp. 16–24.

[33] III. iii: "*civilis pax sive tranquillitas. . . .*"

logical, theological, or other extra-political reference whatsoever. To be sure, in the opening paragraph of his book he quotes some passages of the Gospels where peace is invoked, as in Jesus' "Peace be with you." [34] But even the peace of these rhetorical quotations is interpreted as occurring only in the state.[35] Peace is treated almost solely as the prerequisite of "*civil* happiness" [36] without any reference of it to eternal life; it is hence equivalent only to that "temporal peace" which Augustine considers "false." Secondly, Marsilius' peace is entirely internal to individual states; it is not a "universal peace" involving a world-state, in the manner of Engelbert [37] and Dante,[38] and it does not refer even to relations between particular states. For a state to be "at peace" in Marsilius' sense means only that its parts are functioning properly and interacting smoothly; it does not mean necessarily that the state is "at peace" with other states. Thus he can write that "when the inhabitants of Italy lived peacefully together (*convixerunt pacifice*) . . . they brought the entire habitable world under their sway." [39] Thirdly, Marsilius' peace is entirely on the level of external functional interrelations among the various parts of the state. It involves none of the psychological, moral, or spiritual "concords" upon which his predecessors had insisted; in his terminology, it consists only in transient acts, not in immanent acts.[40]

With this last point Marsilius departs from the finalistic orientation of Aristotle as well as from the Augustinian tradition. For the other Aristotelians, as for Aristotle himself, the state is a "community" in the ideal sense that men "commune" with one another morally and intellectually; it is a friendly sharing of distinctively human values, of "good living." [41] At the opposite extreme is a mere trade association or military alliance which is not a state at all.[42] For Marsilius, on the other hand, the state is an

[34] John 20:19; quoted I. i. I.

[35] See I. i. 2: "ex opposita tranquillitati discordia provenient *civili regimini seu regno.* . . ."

[36] I. i. 7. Cf., however, II. xxvi. 13; III. iii.

[37] *De ortu* cap. xix ff. (p. 375 ff.).

[38] *De monarchia* I. iv (p. 343).

[39] I. i. 2. At only one point does Marsilius depart from this intra-state view of peace, when he is discussing the "financial part" of the state; see I. v. 9: "civitas quandoque pacifice disponitur *ad vicinas.* . . ." See Engelbert *De ortu* cap. xiv (p. 370D): "Pax igitur uniuscuiusque gentis et regni consistit in duobus, scilicet in habendo concordiam inter se *et in non habendo discordiam cum extraneis.*" See also James of Viterbo *De reg. Christ.* II. iv. (p. 191).

[40] See the "necessary consequences" of peace listed at I. xix. 2. See also above, p. 65.

[41] Aristotle *Pol.* III. 9. 1280b 39. See Thomas Aquinas *De Reg. princ.* I. xiv (p. 21): "hi soli partes sint multitudinis congregatae, qui *sibi invicem communicant* in bene vivendo." Peter of Auvergne *In Pol.* Lib. III. Lect. 7 (p. 231): "communicatio politica consistit in communicatione bonarum actionum. . . ." See Egidius of Rome *De reg. princ.* Lib. III. Pars II. cap. xxxii. Ptolemy of Lucca *De reg. princ.* IV. iii (p. 83).

[42] *Pol.* III. 9. 1280a 34 ff. The difference between the finalistic orientation of the *Politics* and its orientations with respect to other causes (see above, p. 33) is graphically illustrated by this point; for in some of his more positive discussions of actually existing states, Aristotle

individualistic and economic community, its members "being able to seek out *for themselves* the various necessaries, and exchanging (*communicantes*) them with one another."[43] This "exchange," when it proceeds "without impediment," is identical with peace,[44] which is therefore primarily a division of labor, a network of external relations among men.

It is obvious, therefore, that when Marsilius makes "peace" the basic principle of the state's order or organization, it will have a meaning and outcome quite different from that of the antecedent tradition. His three restrictions make peace a specifically political concept, cut down to the precise dimensions of politics as he conceives it, and involving none of the universalist spiritual factors which the papalists had exploited. He thus renders untenable those arguments which are based upon the view that peace is a "spiritual bond," or which place "civil peace" within a cosmological order of universal peace in which a common spiritually controlled structure leads to the earthly hegemony of the spiritual power. The precise character of these restrictions can be seen from the fact that Marsilius identifies peace with the opposite of the civil strife or revolutions analyzed by Aristotle in the fifth book of the *Politics*.[45] Consequently, the "good disposition of the state" by which Marsilius defines peace will primarily mean the stable equilibrium in which the state endures. This identification is typical of his entire approach, for it reduces the final causes involved in the traditional idea of peace to the efficient causes involved in the generation, preservation, and destruction of states. The Marsilian peace thus refers to political statics and dynamics, not to a theological cosmology; it is the peace of Padua's burghers, not that of her clergy.[46]

Precisely how, then, is the organization of the state determined by its peace? It will be recalled that peace involved the performance by each part of the state of "the operations belonging to it according to reason *and its establishment*." The various parts, then, must be "established" in their respective functions, and there must be an explicit agency which controls that establishment. Who is this agency? Marsilius gives two answers. Since peace pertains to the whole state, the primary controlling

---

recognizes and even urges that too much "communion" may be a bad thing; thus the best kind of democracy is that of farmers who are too busy working to take part in political affairs or to come together for social intercourse, while the worst kind is that in which all men share (i.e., "commune," κοινωνεῖν) in government (*ibid.* VI. 4. 1318b 12–1319b 2). Thomas Aquinas repeats this point (*De reg. princ.* II. iii [p. 27]) without noting its inconsistency with his previous emphasis upon association "in living well" (see preceding note).

[43] I. iv. 5.

[44] See I. v. I: "de partibus civitatis, in quarum actione et communicatione perfecta invicem, nec extrinsecus impedita, tranquillitatem civitatis consistere diximus. . . ." See also above, pp. 59, 65.

[45] See I. i. 3, 7; I. xix. I, 3. See above, pp. 34–35.

[46] See above, pp. 24 ff.

authority will belong to the whole people, since "the whole is greater than any of its parts."[47] We shall examine what this answer involves in subsequent chapters.[48] The people cannot, however, exercise this authority directly by itself, both because it is more economical to have such supervision carried on by a few rather than by all, and because the various parts of the community would be diverted from the performance of their respective functions.[49] The authority must thus be delegated to one of the parts of the state, and this, since it controls the "establishment" of the other parts, will itself be the "first part" of the state. Marsilius makes the government this first part, and thereby subordinates the priesthood to it. This subordination is entailed by the very nature and background of the peace of the state, in a sequence precisely opposed at every point to the papalists' peace, which had made the priesthood rather than the secular government the "primary part" of the political organism. In the understanding of the various arguments by which the primacy of the government over the priesthood is successively established lies the key to the understanding of one of the crucial phases of the Marsilian politics. These arguments all involve in various ways the application of peace to the principles of Marsilius' politics examined in the preceding chapter.

(1) *Differentiation*. Peace requires that each part of the state perform its proper function "without impediment." If, therefore, the priests attempt to exercise governmental authority, or call themselves "kings,"[50] they will be impeding the function of another part of the state, so that strife, the opposite of peace, will result.[51] In this respect the peace of the state is a consequence of its perfection, for the state is distinguished from lesser communities by its increased differentiation of functions.[52]

This insistence upon differentiation does not, however, of itself remove the papal supremacy. The papalists could also agree upon the desirability of differentiation, holding that the pope needs separate "ministers," who include secular rulers, and indeed that the pope will not normally interfere in the functions of these subordinates.[53] The question is, what is the rela-

[47] I. xv. 4. See I. xii. 5; I. xiii. 2, 4.

[48] See below, pp. 167 ff., 236 ff.

[49] I. xv. 4.

[50] See James of Viterbo *De reg. Christ.* II. iii (p. 180). See also texts cited above, p. 94, n. 16.

[51] See I. xix. 3.

[52] I. iii. 4. See the reiterated emphasis upon *diversi* in I. iv. 5. In view of Marsilius' insistence upon this point, it is noteworthy that while Aristotle in some contexts upholds such differentiation of "one man, one job" (see *Pol.* II. 11. 1273b 10), in others he is indifferent to it (*ibid.* IV. 4. 1291a 29, 1291b 3). A large state should have more differentiation than a small one (*ibid.* IV. 15. 1299a 35 ff.); democracies and oligarchies are distinguished by the fact that non-differentiation is a principle of the former, differentiation of the latter (*ibid.* VII. 9. 1328b 24–33).

[53] See Egidius of Rome *De eccl. pot.* I. vii (p. 26). See also Thomas Aquinas *De reg. princ.* I. xiv (p. 21).

tion between the respective functions of the government and the priesthood? It is to the specification of this relation, so essential to "peace," that the further arguments are directed.

(2) *Soul and body.* The traditional papalist method of allocating the spheres of the spiritual and temporal powers was by apportioning them to respective "parts" of man. Although the most famous such method was the organic analogy, another approach was used much more frequently, which may be called the suppletive method. This was the approach whereby the priesthood was described as the "spiritual power" or "sword" and the secular government as the "material," "carnal," or "corporeal power" or "sword," because the former supplies the needs of man's spirit or soul, and the latter those of his flesh or body. The argument ran that since the body is inferior in dignity to the soul and must subserve the soul, the government must similarly subserve the priesthood.[54]

Marsilius uses a similar suppletive method, describing the function of the various parts of the state as that of "tempering" or "moderating" the various parts of man, and thereby "fulfilling" his actions and passions "in that to which nature cannot lead." [55] It is characteristic of him to take Aristotle's moral terminology, oriented inward toward the virtues which "moderate" human acts, and to turn it outward so that the parts of the state assume the place of the virtues.[56] The papalists' allocation is refuted, moreover, by removing their simple Augustinian dualism of body and soul and substituting therefor the Aristotelian biological doctrine that the soul is the form of the living body and hence the principle of all its functions: nutritive, sensitive, cognitive, locomotive.[57] Consequently, *all* the parts of the state are concerned with man's soul. Thus the farmers moderate the "acts of the nutritive part of the soul," [58] the mechanical arts moderate the various "senses," [59] and the government and priesthood both moderate,

[54] See Egidius of Rome *De eccl. pot.* I. vii; II. v (pp. 23, 57–8). Henry of Cremona *De pot. pap.*, p. 465. Ptolemy of Lucca *De reg. princ.* III. x (p. 60). Even Dante, despite his dedication of the "temporal monarchy" to intellectual activity (*De mon.* I. iii–v [pp. 342–45]), also finally apportions the papal function to caring for man's incorruptible soul, and the temporal imperial function to man's corruptible body (*ibid.* III. xvi [pp. 375–76]).

[55] I. v. 5–7; I. vi. 1, 9.

[56] See *N. Eth.* II. 6. 1106a 27 ff., on virtue as mean; and *ibid.* III. 10. 1117b 25 ff., on temperance. Marsilius specifically refers to the governmental function as "ad moderandos *excessus* actuum" (I. v. 7).

[57] See *De anima* II. 2. 413b 12. In the less "scientific" context of the *Politics*, however, Aristotle himself uses the body-soul dualism to establish the naturalness of slavery (I. 2. 1254a 4) and to set the "noble" parts of the state above the merely "necessary" parts (IV. 4. 1291a 24).

[58] I. v. 5. See II. xxx. 1, where in discussing the papalist argument, Marsilius restates its premise as follows: "Anima rationalis et appetitiva nobilior est *corpore, id est, animato secundum nutritivam*. . . ." See also II. xxii. 4, where he refers to the *anima vegetans* of plants.

[59] I. v. 6.

although in different ways, the acts of man's cognitive and appetitive powers.[60] Hence, in reply to the papalist argument that as the body is to the soul, so is the ruler of the body to the ruler of the soul,[61] Marsilius can say that "although the soul is distinguished from the body inasmuch as the soul is not the body, nevertheless there is no ruler of the body who is not also in some way the ruler of the soul, and conversely."[62] Peace, therefore, requires not a subordination of body to soul, as in the Augustinian conception, but the moderating by each part of the state of that power or act of the soul to which its function is adapted.

(3) *Inner and outer.* What, however, is the relation between the cognitive-appetitive acts of the soul moderated by the government and by the priesthood? The government moderates transient acts alone,[63] while the priesthood moderates immanent acts as well—it is concerned not only with overt acts affecting other men but even more with the thoughts and desires which underlie these.[64]

On this point, the papalist doctrine took a further step which led still more decisively to the hegemony of the priesthood. Building on the preceding allocation of the objects of the two "powers" as soul and body, it in effect reduces the latter to the former. For, as Egidius of Rome puts it, "although body cannot become spirit, yet a corporeal thing, and the body itself, can be called spiritual because of some spiritual conditions in which it can participate."[65] This participation is conceived by a method which, in common with other idealisms from Plato to Hegel, emphasizes the "spiritual" or "ideal" aspects of all seemingly "material" or "corporeal" acts and objects. Egidius presents an elaborate analysis of "all those modes in which temporal things can be called spiritual," under three general rubrics, each having at least three subdivisions.[66] For example, "all crimes

[60] I. v. 7; I. vi. 1, 9. The functions of the "military" and "financial" parts of the state are discussed without reference to parts of the soul, but this is because their functions are auxiliary to those of the other parts.

[61] II. iii. 10, 11.

[62] II. xxx. 1 (p. 480). Marsilius was not, however, the first to deny the soul-body allocation. See *Tract. Eborac.* IV (p. 663); John of Paris *De pot. reg. et pap.* cap. xviii (p. 132); and the papalist treatises of James of Viterbo *De reg. Christ.* II. vi (pp. 224–25) and Alexander of St. Elpidius *Tract. de eccl. pot.* II. iv (pp. 17–18). None of these, however, bases the denial upon exclusively biological grounds as does Marsilius, but rather upon ethical or theological premises. See also *Quaest. de pot. papae,* p. 680; and Hobbes *Leviathan* ch. xxxix (p. 252).

[63] I. v. 7.

[64] I. vi. 1, 9. On the distinction of immanent and transient acts, see above, p. 61.

[65] *De eccl. pot.* III. v (p. 168).

[66] *Ibid.* III. v–viii (pp. 169–89). The initial statement is at III. v: "Advertendum ergo, quod ipsa temporalia tripliciter possunt considerari: primo quantum ad ipsas res; secundo quantum ad potestatem temporalem sub qua sunt; tertio quantum ad potestatem summi pontificis. *Omnibus autem istis modis temporalia possunt dici spiritualia;* ideo per comparationem ad omnia ista ipsa temporalia sub iurisdictione potestatis spiritualis poterunt collocari."

and mortal sins can be called spiritual, because they kill our spirit or soul." [67] War or strife of any kind is a "spiritual vacuum" because it is a discontinuation of souls; [68] and peace is a "spiritual bond." [69] Hence, although the temporal power had been viewed as guardian of "temporal" affairs, that is, of men's physical and economic security through the prevention of strife, this function is now subsumed under the spiritual power because of the "spiritual" aspects of the acts in which those affairs are involved. The superior jurisdiction of the spiritual power is consequently without limit; as Egidius puts it in a very revealing statement, *"this condition through which the church can intervene concerning temporal things is so broad and ample that it includes all questions of any temporal things,* because a question can always be connected with crime." [70] The general upshot is, in the words of James of Viterbo, that "the temporal is reduced to the spiritual." [71]

Marsilius' reply is to insist upon sharp, irreducible distinctions between the "temporal" and the "spiritual." He indicates three valid forms of such distinctions. The temporal may mean the corporeal, in which case the spiritual is the incorporeal; or, again, the temporal may refer to an act done for the sake of the present life, in which case the spiritual is whatever orders men to eternal life; and finally, the temporal may mean transient acts, in which case the spiritual refers to immanent acts.[72] It will be noted that Marsilius does not, like the papalists, indicate any bridge or continuity between the respective sides of each of these distinctions. What of the fact that such "transient" acts as crimes have "immanent" bases, which led the papalists to call them "spiritual" evils? His reply is to insist that such extensions of the term "spiritual" are "very improper" [73] and "abuse the term"; [74] he dwells upon the *prima facie* character of the transient acts of which priests are capable, and points out that, as such, they are utterly different from "spiritual" acts.

For not all their acts are or should be called "spiritual;" on the contrary, many of them are civil, contentious, and carnal or temporal. For they can lend at

[67] *Ibid.* III. v (p. 171). [68] *Ibid.* III. vi (p. 177).

[69] James of Viterbo *De reg. Christ.* II. viii (p. 254).

[70] *De eccl. pot.* III. v (p. 172). [71] James of Viterbo *De reg. Christ.* II. viii (p. 254).

[72] II. ii. 4–5. See William of Ockham *Dialogus* Pars III. Tr. II. Lib. II. cap. iii (pp. 903–4), where eleven different distinctions between "spiritual" and "temporal" are listed, many of which (e.g., where ecclesiastic property, judges, cases, crimes, are called "spiritual") are rejected by Marsilius as "improper" and "abuses" of the term "spiritual." See text quoted below. In his following chapter (p. 904), Ockham reduces these distinctions to one between the rule of men "in solis naturalibus" and "divina revelatione."

[73] II. ii. 5.

[74] II. ii. 6. See II. xxix. 7: "Dicat enim quaeso sophista et vocabulorum abusor, qui spirituale vocat quod est simpliciter saeculare. . . ."

interest, deposit, buy, sell, strike, kill, steal, commit adultery, rob with violence, betray, deceive, bear false witness, fall into heresy, and commit other outrages, crimes, and contentions, such as are also perpetrated by non-priests. Hence it is appropriate to ask them whether such acts as these, of which we have said they are capable, are "spiritual" or should be so called by anyone of sound mind. And it is clear that the answer is *no,* but rather carnal and temporal.[75]

This passage is directly aimed at the tradition of the canon law which insisted upon separate "ecclesiastic" courts for the trial of all "spiritual" cases, which included all cases in any way involving clergymen.[76] But it is also a reply to the whole spiritualizing method of the papalists; transient acts affecting the welfare of other persons than the agent are *toto caelo* different from the immanent thoughts and desires which are their sources. Hence the papalist argument which reserved the former acts to the "spiritual power" because of their "spiritual" aspects is turned aside. Peace and strife involve transient, not immanent, acts; they are temporal, not spiritual.

This point reveals a distinctive and basic aspect of the Marsilian politics. When Aristotle dedicates the best possible state to the life of virtue, this involves a "spiritualizing" of politics similar to that of the Augustinians; for the ultimate concern of the law and government of the state becomes moral and intellectual, to "make the citizens good," and this not merely in the sense of regulating their external, overt acts, but rather in the sense of moulding their internal characters, educating them to the virtues.[77] This concern is taken over by the medieval Aristotelians. They define politics as one of the "moral sciences," dealing with internal "manent" acts rather than with "transient" acts.[78] And they declare that the end of human

[75] II. ii. 7. See II. viii. 8. See above, p. 26 and n. 24.

[76] See *Corp. jur. can., Decret. Gratiani* Pars II. can. 31–47. C. XI. qu.I. (I, 635–41); *Decretal. Greg. IX* Lib. II. Tit. 2. cap. 1–3 (II, 248–49). See above, p. 26; also below, p. 120.

[77] See *Pol.* III. 9. 1280b 1 ff.; VII. 13. 1332a 4 ff. See also *N. Eth.* II. 4. 1105a 29 ff., where the moral goodness of an act is shown to depend not upon its external characteristics or consequences, but rather upon the internal conditions of the agent: knowledge, choice, and fixed habit of character. This applies even in the case of the externally oriented virtue of justice; see *ibid.* V. 6. 1134a 17–23; 8. 1135a 16 ff.; VI. 12. 1144a 14.

[78] See Thomas Aquinas *In Pol.* Prologus (p. 90): "cum ratio quaedam operetur per modum factionis operatione in exteriorem materiam *transeunte* quod proprie ad artes pertinet, quae mechanicae vocantur, utpote fabrilis et navifactiva et similes: quaedam vero operetur per modum actionis operatione *manente* in eo qui operatur, sicut est consiliari, eligere, velle, et huiusmodi quae ad moralem pertinent: manifestum est politicam scientiam, quae de hominum considerat ordinatione, non contineri sub factivis scientiis, quae sunt artes mechanicae, sed sub activis quae sunt scientiae morales." As this text shows, Thomas interprets "transient" acts as acts of *production* or *making,* not, like Marsilius, as acts affecting other persons. The same view of politics as dealing with "manent acts" is found in such an Averroist as John of Jandun, *Quaest. in Metaphys.* Lib. I. qu.18 (fol. 14R): "quidam sunt habitus factivi et quidam activi . . . Habitus activi sunt quorum operationes *immanent* et non *transeunt* in rem extra: sicut sunt actus prudentiae, qui sunt tres: et unus est actus prudentiae monasticae, alius est actus prudentiae economicae, tertius est actus prudentiae politicae." See also Peter of Abano *Conciliator differentiarum* Diff. 57. Prop. 1 (fol. 83, col. 4F), for whom ethics, eco-

law and government is "to lead men to virtue" in the internal sense.[79]

Marsilius, on the other hand, almost completely excludes immanent acts from politics. It is with transient acts, he says, that "the makers of human laws are mostly concerned." [80] This may appear surprising in view of his emphasis upon the will, for he classifies volitions and desires as immanent acts.[81] But as was already suggested by the biological context in which he places the will, he does not treat the will in itself, from the side of its own "subjective" or immanent acts, but rather—and this is an important difference between Marsilius' voluntarism and that of the whole medieval tradition from Augustine to Duns Scotus—as externalized in overt conduct. For transient acts are themselves "*pursuits* of things desired." [82] The pursuits alone, not the desires themselves, are relevant to government. Thus the Marsilian politics is what would now be called "behavioristic," as against the predominant internalism of the antecedent traditions.

(4) *Ends and means.* The problem of peace is thus reworked once again into a further relation between the government and the priesthood. Both, as we saw above, moderate transient acts, while the priesthood in addition moderates immanent acts; but there is an important difference in the ends of these moderations, for the government is concerned with acts only as they bear upon "the status of the present world," [83] whereas the priesthood deals with acts "according as the human race is ordered through them to the best life of the future world." [84]

On the basis of this difference, the papalists erected their most decisive argument. It is succinctly stated by James of Viterbo: "Since from the end is taken the judgment of those things which are means to the end, the spiritual power, which intends the ultimate and highest end of man, has to judge and correct the temporal power, which intends a lower end ordered to the end of the spiritual power." [85] The secular values of the

---

nomics and politics are three species of that "activa virtus" which "operatur intra seipsam," as against "ars" which "in exteriorem incipit materiam."

[79] Thomas Aquinas *S. theol.* II. I. qu.96. a.3. ad 2: "alio modo dicitur actus virtutis, quia aliquis operatur virtuosa eo modo quo virtuosus operatur; et talis actus . . . est finis ad quem legislator ducere intendit." See *ibid.* II. I. qu.96. a.2; qu.100. a.9; *De reg. princ.* I. xiv, xv (pp. 21–23). Godfrey of Fontaines *Quodlib.* I. qu.6 (II, 17–18). Ptolemy of Lucca *De reg. princ.* III. iii; IV. xxiv (pp. 48, 110). John of Paris *De pot. reg. et pap.* cap. xviii (p. 132). James of Viterbo *De reg. Christ.* II. iv (p. 190). Engelbert of Admont *De ortu* cap. vii, viii (p. 366). Durand of St. Pourçain *De origine et usu jurisdictionum* qu.2 (p. 129). Alexander of St. Elpidius *Tract de eccl. pot.* II. iii. 7 (p. 17). John of Jandun *Quaest. in Metaphys.* Lib. I. qus. 1, 18; Lib. II. qu.11 (fols. 2A, 14O, 35G).

[80] II. ii. 4.

[81] I. v. 4; II. ii. 5; II. viii. 3.

[82] II. viii. 3: "Transeuntes autem sunt et dicuntur omnes prosecutiones desideratorum. . . ."

[83] I. v. 7.

[84] I. vi. 1.

[85] *De reg. Christ.* II. vii (p. 234). See Thomas Aquinas *De reg. princ.* I. xiv (pp. 20–21). Egidius of Rome *De eccl. pot.* I. ix; II. vi (pp. 33, 63). Augustinus Triumphus *De duplici pot.*

present life aimed at by the temporal power are but means to the eternal values of the future life aimed at by the spiritual power, and consequently the temporal power must itself be subject to the spiritual.

Besides its Augustinian source, this argument also has a close affinity to the finalistic orientation of Aristotle. The opening paragraph of the *Nicomachean Ethics* distinguishes arts, sciences, or actions in the same way as the papalists distinguish "powers," in terms of the order among their respective ends: where the end of one art is but a means to the end of another art, the latter, the "architectonic" art, is itself "more desirable" than the former art.[86] One of the illustrations which Aristotle uses in this connection—that the art of bridlemaking is subordinate to the military art because the former's end is pursued for the sake of the latter's [87]—is explicitly repeated by a large number of the papalists in proof of the subordination of the temporal to the spiritual power.[88]

Before Marsilius the few criticisms which were made of this argument from ends were all based upon the Gelasian differentiation and parallelism of the temporal and spiritual powers. But just as Gelasius himself had held that "the weight of the priests is heavier" than that of the secular rulers,[89] so these criticisms left the core of the argument intact.[90] It could not be refuted by professed Christians so long as the approach to the state and the temporal government was made in terms of ultimate ends or final causes, because the papalists could always point to the loftiest and most ultimate end of all.

The basis and the force of Marsilius' doctrine derive from the fact that he completely overturns this axiological orientation of ideal ends. We have seen above that the good life in this world as he conceives it is less lofty than that of the other Aristotelians,[91] and also that unlike the whole medi-

---

praelatorum et laicorum, pp. 498–99. Alvarus Pelagius *De planctu eccl.* I. xxxvii (pp. 48–49). See also below, n. 88.

86 *N. Eth.* I. I. 1094a 7–18.

87 *Ibid.* 1094a 11.

88 See Egidius of Rome *De eccl. pot.* II. vi (p. 68): "Hoc ergo potissime faciunt principes terreni, quod disponunt et praeparant materiam principi ecclesiastico. . . Sicut ergo frenifactiva, imponens frenum equo, praeparat equum militi, ut ei liberius famuletur, sic potestas terrena, imponens frenum laicis, ne forefaciant in ecclesiam nec in se ipsos, disponit eos, ut potestati ecclesiasticae liberius sint subiecti." The same illustration of the subordination of *frenifactiva* to *militaris* is found in James of Viterbo *De reg. Christ.* II. vii (p. 231). Augustinus Triumphus *S. de eccl. pot.* qu.35. a.1. Francis of Mayron *Tract. de princ. temp.* IV (p. 65); *Idem, Quaestio de subiectione* I. 8 (p. 81). Alexander of St. Elpidius *De eccl. pot.* II. iii. 10 (p. 17). Durand of St. Pourçain *De origine et usu jurisdictionum* qu.3 (p. 133E).

89 Epist. xii. 2 (quoted in Carlyle, *op. cit.*, I, 191).

90 John of Paris twice restates the argument among his objections *a contrario: De pot. reg. et pap.* cap. xi (pp. 122, 123); his replies are given in cap. xviii, xx (pp. 132–33, 136). See also Dante *De mon.* III. xvi (pp. 375–76) and the criticism of Dante on this point by Guido Vernani *De reprobatione Monarchiae* Lib. III (p. 146).

91 See above, pp. 64 ff.

eval tradition he does not regard that life as existing for the sake of eternal life.[92] But these views concerning ends attain their complete political effect in the utter absorption of the Marsilian politics in the efficient causes or means required for the preservation and endurance of the state. The primary function of government is no longer, as with the other Aristotelians, the moral and educational one of "leading men to virtue"; Marsilius at no point repeats this doctrine. Government exists rather "to moderate the excesses of men's transient acts" by "reducing them to equality or due proportion." [93] The Marsilian ruler, in other words, is a coercive judge, dispensing what Aristotle calls "rectificatory justice." [94] Hence he is not concerned with educating men to a moral end, but solely with correcting their injurious conduct and adjudicating their disputes.

This is, of course, an immediate consequence of the biological basis of Marsilius' politics, its immersion in transient acts, its emphasis upon the inevitability of strife. But even more important is the fundamental motivation of this governmental function. Is it, as the Aristotelians and papalists insisted it should be, only a means to the end that men may live a life of virtue and prepare themselves for the future life? On the contrary, the purpose of the governmental function is simply the preservation of the state: "Because among men thus gathered together there arise disputes and quarrels, which if not regulated by the norm of justice would cause battles and the separation of men *and thus finally the destruction of the state,* there had to be established in this association a standard of things just and a guardian or maker thereof." [95] The overwhelming emphasis upon this one aim—preventing the destruction of the state—fixes a standard pattern of Marsilius' arguments. A typical example is the argument against a plurality of governments in a single state: if there were such a plurality, "the judgment, command, and execution of things beneficial and just would fail; and hence, men's injuries being unavenged, there would follow fighting, separation, *and finally the destruction of the city or state. But this consequence is the evil which is most to be avoided.*" [96] It is this *maximum inconveniens* of the destruction of the state which is similarly invoked to prove the necessity of all the other main theses of Marsilius: that the

[92] See above, p. 78.

[93] I. v. 7.

[94] See II. iv. 8: "per judicium scilicet lites civiles dirimere; quod tamen nulli dubium est *opus propriissimum principantium saeculi.*" See I. xv. 6. See Aristotle *N. Eth.* v. 2. 1131a 1; v. 3. 1131b 25 ff., esp. 1132a 20.

[95] I. iv. 4. See also I. v. 7: "aliter namque causaretur ex hiis pugna et inde civium separatio, *demum civitatis corruptio. . . .*" I. xv. 6: "contingeret inde congregatorum hominum pugna et separatio, *et demum corruptio civitatis. . . .*" I. xix. 12: "pugnas causant, unde civium separationes demumque Italicarum politiarum seu civilitatum *solutiones* contigerunt. . . ."

[96] I. xvii. 3. See I. xvii. 5: "Rursum, contingeret ex hoc civium sectio et oppositio, pugna et separatio, demumque *civitatis corruptio. . . .*"

state have laws,[97] that these laws be made by the whole body of citizens,[98] that the ruler or government use prudence to supplement the laws,[99] that the government designate the members of the other parts of the state,[100] that the ruler be chosen by election rather than by hereditary succession,[101] that he be corrected for grave offenses,[102] that the papal drive toward plenitude of power be checked,[103] and that the government exercise coercive jurisdiction over the membership and acts of the priesthood [104] as well as over the distribution of benefices.[105]

In this emphasis upon preventing the destruction of the state there is a manifest conviction of the concomitant extreme instability of, and grave urgency for, civil association, such as political philosophy had never before known. It is the same dominant concern as subsequently motivated Hobbes, and exhibits the same preoccupation with the deleterious consequences to which the civil strife of his time had led. But it follows from Marsilius' own premises concerning the biological basis of human nature, and it is the direct result of basing a political philosophy upon that book of Aristotle's *Politics* where the central concern is with the prevention of revolutions, that is, the preservation of constitutions.[106] Methodologically, the ubiquitous appeal to the destruction of the state is simply the *reductio ad impossibile* which establishes the necessity of Marsilius' various demonstrations.[107] It brings out clearly his conception of politics as a theoretic science which sets forth the necessary conditions for the preservation of any state.

This emphasis is of decisive importance with respect to the papalist argument from ends. Where that argument, and indeed the whole political philosophy of the middle ages, is oriented in ultimate ends or final

[97] I. xi. 5: "minus patiuntur seditiones, et per consequens suorum principatuum *solutiones*. . . ."

[98] I. xii. 7: "ex quibus tandem contingit *solvere* politiam."

[99] I. xiv. 3: "exorta foret inde verismiliter civilis pugna politiae *solutiva* propter seditionem. . . ."

[100] I. xv. 10: "ne propter ipsarum excessum invicem immoderatum contingat politiam *solvi*. . . ."

[101] I. xvi. 21: "unde illis *seditionis* movendae datur occasio . . . iuste *seditionem* movebunt. . . ."

[102] I. xviii. 4: "Ex ipso enim non vindicato possibilis esset in populo concitatio, et politiae turbatio atque *solutio*."

[103] II. xvii. 13: "vinculum et nexum cuiuscumque civilitatis et regni *dissolvi*." II. xxviii. 29: "et consequenter per necessitatem ad *solutionem* cuiuslibet politiae perducens."

[104] II. viii. 9: "quod est gravissimum inconveniens, et politiae *corruptivum*." *Ibid.*: "ne principatuum etiam pluralitate inordinata politiam *solvi* contingat. . . ." II. xvii. 14: "quod est inconvenientium et impossibilium, si debeat *manere* civitas. . . ."

[105] II. xxi. 12: "omnia regna et omnes politiae maiores et minores *solutionis* exponuntur periculo." II. xxi. 13: "regna et politiae omnes *solutionis* aut immensae perturbationis periculo subiacent. . . ."

[106] See above, pp. 34 ff.

[107] See above, pp. 48 ff.

causes and views the dominant political authority (whether spiritual or temporal) as either embodying or directly providing for the factors constitutive of those ends, Marsilius' doctrine is oriented in proximate means or efficient causes, and it views government as employing those means to attain the specifically political factors necessary for the state to endure. The politics of the antecedent medieval tradition was based upon a moral and theological *summum bonum;* that of Marsilius is based upon a specifically political *summum malum*. To be sure, he also mentions at several points that the "sufficient life" will be lost if the state is destroyed.[108] Since the sufficient life is the highest this-worldly good for Marsilius, a factor of moral ends remains in the background of his whole doctrine. But it is kept in the background: the constitutive factors which give the sufficient life its value are not invoked in any of the discussions. Having posited that life as the end of the state, Marsilius goes on neither to separate out those of its features which uniquely characterize it and make it the highest good, nor to dedicate the state to the achievement of those unique features. Rather, his concern is with the specifically political efficient causes for establishing and preserving the state and its institutions as the indispensable means for achieving the sufficient life. Hence, where the argument from ends had held that because the priesthood subserves a higher end than does the government, therefore it must have higher political authority, Marsilius declares instead that because the government performs the function which is "most necessary" for the preservation of the state, it must have superior political authority. He freely admits that the priesthood is "nobler" and "more perfect" than the government because of the former's higher end, the higher law it uses to help men attain that end, and its superior "legislator."[109] But this is irrelevant to the problem of political authority, for political "necessity" rather than moral "nobility" is the decisive consideration in the allocation of political power. The government is the "most necessary" of all the parts of the state, because

the sufficiency which is had through the other parts or offices of the state, if they did not exist, could be had sufficiently from some other source, such as through shipping and other kinds of commerce, although not so easily. But *without the existence of the government the civil community cannot endure or long endure,* for "it is necessary that scandals arise," as it is said in Matthew. These scandals are men's contentions and injuries toward one another, and if they were not avenged or measured by a standard of justice, i.e., the law, and by the ruler

[108] See I. v. 7: "demum civitatis corruptio *et vitae sufficientis privatio.*" See also I. xv. 6; II. ix. 12; II. xxvi. 13; III. iii.

[109] II. xxx. 3, 4. See the arguments *a contrario:* II. iii. 12, 13.

whose function it is to measure such things in accordance with the law, there would result the fighting and separation of the assembled men, *and finally the destruction of the state* and loss of the sufficient life.[110]

It will be noted that the priesthood is not mentioned in this striking passage. Yet in what sense can it be true to say that the "sufficiency" which is had through the priesthood "could be had sufficiently from some other source"? Marsilius is not a believer in the priesthood of every Christian; to be a priest, one must have the "character" imprinted by God.[111] The most obvious explanation of Marsilius' meaning is that since his doctrine is centered in the proximate means of preserving the state rather than in the ultimate ends to which the state might lead, the priesthood becomes from this point of view a luxury rather than a necessity: of the government alone can it be said that its "action can never cease without harm." [112] The priesthood is reduced to an agency whose function is "merely" other-worldly. It is thus far removed from influence, let alone control, over the practical political exigencies involved in regulating men's this-worldly pursuits and conflicts.

It is this orientation which explains Marsilius' exclusive concern with transient acts, as against the whole antecedent tradition's concentration upon immanent acts.[113] For only transient acts can affect the preservation of the state, since they alone involve that impingement of man upon man which gives rise to strife. Immanent acts, on the other hand, not only affect no one besides their agent, but cannot even be known by anyone else, except God.[114] This latter factor of knowledge is at least in part the explanation of the former, for acts which cannot be perceived by others cannot affect the endurance of the state, since strife cannot result from them. The concentration upon transient acts is thus based upon the possibility of proof: if someone commits a transient act, he "can be *proved* to have done it, even if he denies it." [115]

Marsilius was not the first to note the political relevance of this distinction between immanent and transient acts. The same considerations are found in Thomas Aquinas, for whom one of the reasons why divine law is required in addition to human law is that

man can make law about those things about which he can judge. But the judgment of man cannot be about interior acts, which are hidden, but only about exterior movements, which are apparent; and yet for the perfection of virtue it

[110] I. xv. 6. [111] II. xv. 2. See below, pp. 268–69. [112] I. xv. 13.
[113] See above, pp. 103–4. [114] I. v. 11; II. ix. 11.
[115] II. xvii. 8: "quod sibi *probari* potest inesse, id etiam ipso negante. . . ." See also the emphasis upon *probari* in the texts cited in the preceding note.

is required that man be right in both kinds of acts. Hence, human law could not sufficiently control and order interior acts, but it was necessary that for this, divine law supervene.[116]

Moreover, since for Thomas as for Marsilius human law and government are ordered toward men's association with one another, it follows that the law prohibits only those vices "without whose prohibition human society could not be conserved," such as homicide and theft.[117] Other political philosophers had also emphasized the human unknowability of "interior" acts or thoughts,[118] the function of human law and government as regulating men's exterior acts and punishing their crimes,[119] and the importance of the preservation of the state.[120]

In no case, however, had these considerations been given the predominant position which they occupy in the Marsilian doctrine. Despite the unknowability of "interior" acts, it is still in them that the antecedent tradition is centered, as was seen above in the papalists' emphasis upon the "spiritual" bases of human acts and the Aristotelians' concentration upon internal "virtue" as the end of human government and law.[121] Similarly, the discussion of the coercive functions of government in punishing crimes and regulating disputes is placed in a larger axiological context in which the value of those functions, as such, is sharply restricted, and they are shown to be only means to the complete values which the state and its government, or the church and its priesthood, are designed to realize. It was this point which the papalists exploited in the argument from ends; the general tenor is indicated in John of Salisbury's statement that "that is inferior which is exercised in the punishment of crimes and seems to represent an image of the hangman." [122] More generally, the view which was upheld was that expressed by Aristotle when he insisted that a community concerned merely with preventing men from harming one another, and not concerned with "virtue," is not a state at all.[123] In the normative

[116] *S. theol.* II. I. qu.91. a.4. Resp. See *ibid.* qu.100. a.2. Resp.; a.9. Resp.

[117] *Ibid.* II. I. qu.96. a.2. Resp. See *ibid.* qu.98. a.1. Resp.

[118] See Aristotle *N. Eth.* v. I. 1129b 32–1130a 2; x. 8. 1178a 29 ff. Augustine *De civ. Dei* I. xxvi; v. xiv; xix. v, vi. Egidius of Rome *De reg. princ.* Lib. I. Pars II. cap. xii. Gilbert of Tournai *Eruditio regum et principum,* II. iv (ed. A. de Poorter [Louvain, 1914], pp. 46–47). James of Viterbo *De reg. Christ.* II. ix (p. 272).

[119] See Aristotle *Pol.* IV. 4. 1291a 23 ff.; VI. 8. 1321b 40 ff.; VII. 13. 1332a 13. John of Salisbury *Policraticus* IV. iii (I, 239). Ptol. of Lucca *De reg. princ.* IV. xxiv (p. 110). Egidius of Rome *De reg. princ.* Lib. III. Pars I. cap. iv, v. James of Viterbo *De reg. Christ.* II. x (pp. 287–88, 303). Dante *De mon.* I. x (p. 345). John of Paris *De pot. reg. et pap.* cap. iii, vii (pp. 111, 116).

[120] See Aristotle *Pol.* III. 4. 1276b 28; v, *passim.* Thomas Aquinas *De reg. princ.* I. i, xiii, xv (pp. 2, 20, 22–23). Egidius of Rome *De reg. princ.* Lib. I. Pars II. cap. xi; Lib. III. Pars I. cap. ii. Dante *De mon.* I. v (p. 344). John of Paris *De pot reg. et pap.* cap. i (p. 109). Ptolemy of Lucca *De reg. princ.* III. xix; IV. viii, ix (pp. 73, 90, 92).

[121] See above, pp. 101 ff.

[122] *Policraticus* IV. iii (I, 239).

[123] *Pol.* III. 9. 1280b 3 ff.

context of the absolutely best state Aristotle also distinguished sharply between the merely "necessary" function of government, consisting in the punishment of crimes, and the "noble" function, aiming at what is honorable in itself. The former is "only the choice of a lesser evil," whereas the latter is "the foundation and generation of the good." [124] The preservation of the "state," in the same way, meant not merely the preservation of the association of men with one another as the minimal condition for the attainment of any other values, but rather the preservation of all the values for which the state at its best exists.[125]

The consequence of these differences is that the Marsilian government comes to control all the other parts of the state, including the priesthood, and this not for moral or theological reasons but for specifically political ones. The central argument is that since the governmental function is supremely necessary for the preservation of the state, anything which threatens that preservation must likewise come under governmental control. Now if everyone in the state were free to choose whatever functional occupation he liked, then "the immoderate excess of some parts of the state in relation to others" would cause the state to be destroyed.[126] It follows, therefore, that it is the government which must "establish" and "distinguish" the other parts of the state.[127] From this, in turn, it follows that the government is the "first part" of the state and the principle of the "order" of all the other parts.[128] The order of the Marsilian state, like its peace, is thus a juridical rather than a moral or theological one; it is determined not by contribution toward ultimate ends but rather by the governmental exercise of rectificatory justice as the efficient cause of the state's preservation. But since, moreover, the peace of the state consists in the order whereby each part of the state performs its proper function in accordance with its "establishment," the government is the efficient cause of peace.[129]

Such, then, is the outcome of the peace of the Marsilian state. It is apparent how the initial differences in the definition of peace, based as they were upon the first principles of Marsilius' politics, result in a totally different conception of the structure and control of the state. They thereby overturn the doctrine of the papalists, but they also provide an extensive

[124] *Ibid.* VII. 13. 1332a 12 ff.

[125] See texts cited above, p. 110, n. 120.

[126] I. xv. 10. See I. xvii. 7: "eliget enim sibi quod quisque volet officium, unum aut plura, nullo regulante nec talia separante. Tot quoque sequerentur ad hoc inconvenientia ut ea non facile aut non possibile sit dinumerare."

[127] I. xv. 6, 10.

[128] I. xv. 14.

[129] II. v. 7: "causa tranquillitatis factiva et conservativa est actio principantis debita non impedita." See I. xix. 3.

analysis of the scope of political power required for the preservation of the state.

The governmental "establishment" of the other parts of the state is conceived by Marsilius not primarily as the historical process by which the state was originally formed,[130] but rather as the continuing control by the government of the other parts of the state, as to who shall exercise what functions, and in what manner. There is to be no free choice of occupations by each individual.[131] This conception of a tightly regimented socio-economic order was fully in accord with the facts of medieval economic life, and criticism of it in terms of a *laisser-faire* system[132] is quite unhistorical. Marsilius himself quotes in support Aristotle's description of politics as the architectonic science which "ordains what disciplines there must be in states, and which ones each person must learn, and to what extent."[133] The same description and concomitant conception of distributive justice were taken over by the other medieval Aristotelians to show that the ruler "distributes" to all the persons in the state their respective functions and regulates them therein.[134] The pervasive employment of the suppletive method and the organic analogy had a similar outcome.

The difference between Marsilius and his predecessors on this point lies

[130] See II. xxii. 15, where the historical origin of the state is described as a far more gradual and informal process than the schematic "establishment" indicated by the organic analogy. See above, p. 89.

[131] I. xv. 10. See, however, below, pp. 122 ff., 312 ff.

[132] See L. Pastor, *The History of the Popes* (London, 1899), I, 77: "The jurisdiction of the civil power extends even to the determination of the number of men to be employed in every trade or profession. Individual liberty has no more place in Marsiglio's state than it had in Sparta." Cf. A. P. Evans, "The Problem of Control in Medieval Industry," *Political Science Quarterly,* XXXVI (1921), 605: "One is struck at the outset by the freedom with which group authority—be it that of the state, of the municipality, or of the gild—in the Middle Ages could interfere with the enterprise of the individual through the imposition of minute rules."

[133] *N. Eth.* I. 2. 1094a 30; quoted I. xv. 8.

[134] Albert the Great *In Eth.* Lib. VIII. Tr. II. cap. ii (p. 540): "Rex enim distribuit omni officio et omni dignitati et omni negotio finem proprium, ad quem contendat, legem qua reguletur in operationibus quibus devenitur ad finem, ordinem quo ad commune bonum respiciens ad reipublicae conservationem ordinetur." Thomas Aquinas *In Sent.* Lib. IV. dist. 25. qu.1. a.1: "Politica autem, ut dicitur in I *Ethic.,* ponit legem inferioribus artibus, scilicet quis quam debeat exercere, et quantum et qualiter . . . officia saecularia in civitatibus distribuuntur ab eo qui habet excellentiorem potestatem, sicut a Rege." See also *S. theol.* II. 1. qu.1. a.2. ad 3; *De reg. princ.* I. xiii, xv (pp. 20, 22). James of Viterbo *De reg. Christ.* II. iv (p. 191): "Pertinet autem ad eos [reges] verisimiliter distributio . . . laborum et onerum, sive officiorum, que ad ordinem et perfectionem rei publice requiruntur. Unde regis est disponere et ordinare per omnia multitudinem cui preest." See also Egidius of Rome *De reg. princ.* Lib. I. Pars II. cap. xi. Ptolemy of Lucca *De reg. princ.* IV. xxiii (pp. 108–9). John of Paris *De pot. reg. et pap.* cap. xviii (p. 132). John of Jandun *Quaest. in Metaphys.* Lib. I. qus. 18, 21, 22 (fols. 14P ff., 18A, 19A). In this connection, compare "the Liberty . . . to choose . . . their own trade of life" which Hobbes holds to pertain to the subjects because it has been "praetermitted" by the sovereign (*Leviathan* ch. xxi [Everyman's ed., p. 112]).

precisely in the reasons which they respectively advance for this governmental control. The ground on which Aristotle makes politics the architectonic science is that "its *end* embraces the *ends* of all the other sciences."[135] The hegemony of the ruler thus extends only so far as his end or final cause is superior to, or more inclusive than, that of other parts of the state. For the medieval Aristotelians, consequently, the ruler's control extends only to secular or temporal functions, not to religious or spiritual ones.[136] But since the ground on which Marsilius makes the government the first part of the state is not its higher end but rather the supreme necessity of its function as efficient cause of the preservation of the state, it follows that the limitation of ends which for the other Aristotelians removed the priesthood from governmental control does not exist for Marsilius. Consequently, the priesthood is "established" by the government just as are the other parts of the state. For the same threat to the endurance of the state arises from uncontrolled entry into the priesthood as into the other parts of the state.[137] Indeed, the threat as Marsilius saw it in his own day was even greater, for the papacy was seeking to enroll large numbers of men in the priesthood in order to build up its own power; hence "the jurisdiction and coercive power of rulers will be invalidated, and there will be almost no one to bear the public burdens; which is the gravest evil, and destructive of the state."[138] For the same reason, the government must also control all the temporal possessions or benefices of churches; for otherwise the wealth of the clergy may be built up to a point where they can challenge the jurisdiction of the government, so that "all kingdoms and all polities, large and small, will be exposed to the danger of destruction."[139]

As was suggested earlier, this appeal to the exigencies of the preservation of the state, made in the name of "peace," is so sweeping that it enables Marsilius to effect the same subjection of all human concerns to the government as his opponents had accomplished for the papacy by their appeal to ultimate theological ends and the spiritual aspects of human acts. Marsilius thus goes far beyond the moderate Aristotelians' position. Thomas Aquinas, followed by John of Jandun, had insisted upon two sharp restrictions of the "architectonic" character of politics in relation to the theoretic sciences: politics in no sense controls the subject matter or the conclusions of those sciences; and it will in no sense use them for its

[135] *N. Eth.* I. 2. 1094b 6. See also *Pol.* I. I. 1252a 4–7.

[136] See Thomas Aquinas *De reg. princ.* I. xiv (p. 21). Dante *De mon.* III. xvi (pp. 375–76). John of Paris *De pot. reg. et pap.* cap. ii (p. 110).

[137] I. xv. 10.

[138] II. viii. 9.

[139] II. xxi. 12.

own purposes but will, on the contrary, recognize both their autonomy and their superiority.[140] Marsilius, on the other hand, declares that the government must have the authority to grant or revoke teaching licenses, because men of letters have been "used" by church prelates as "instruments" for gaining and defending their usurpations against secular rulers. Consequently, the rulers are to employ their licensing power for the contrary purpose, to "acquire and preserve the favor of the learned and the wise," for such favor "outweighs all other outside aids for stabilizing and defending governments and constitutions."[141] The same procedure is used to give the government extensive control over all the benefices and other temporal goods of the priests. Where the papalists had declared that *omnia papae sunt,*[142] and where John of Paris had held in opposition that neither ruler nor pope has ownership or dispensation of the property which individuals acquire by their own labor,[143] Marsilius comes near the most drastic position of the Roman lawyers, asserting that *omnia principis esse possunt.*[144] Here again he counters the papalist extreme not by a

[140] Thomas *In Eth.* Lib. I. Lect. 2; Lib. VI. Lect. 6, 11, nn. 26–28, 1186, 1290–91 (pp. 9, 395, 422). Thomas' position is repeated in detail by John of Jandun *Quaest. in Metaphys.* Lib. I. qus. 21, 22 (fols. 18A-B, 19A-B). For the original basis of these restrictions, see Aristotle *N. Eth.* VI. 7. 1141a 20 ff.; VI. 13, 1145a 7 ff. See also Albert the Great *In Eth.* Lib. I. Tr. III. cap. xiii (pp. 46–47).

[141] II. xxi. 15. See Hobbes *Leviathan* ch. xviii (Everyman's ed., p. 95): "If he [the sovereign] give away the government of Doctrines, men will be frightened into rebellion with the fear of Spirits." See also *ibid.* ch. xlii (pp. 293–94).

[142] Egidius of Rome *De eccl. pot.* II. iv (p. 48): "omnia temporalia sub dominio et potestate ecclesiae et potissime summi pontificis collocantur." James of Viterbo *De reg. Christ.* II. vii (p. 240): "Spiritualis igitur potestas etiam super temporalia praeest. . . ." William of Cremona repeats Egidius' position in detail (*Reprobatio errorum* pp. 18–21), but combines it with a detailed opposition to the extreme Romanist doctrine (see below, n. 144) on the ground that the emperor is elected by the people and hence must be limited by its will (pp. 21–22).

[143] *De pot. reg. et pap.* cap. vii (p. 116).

[144] II. xxviii. 17: "Omnia enim quaecumque sint illa temporalia, possessio Caesaris sive fidelis sive infidelis esse possunt." Marsilius is here replying to the assertion of St. Ambrose that "jus Caesaris esse non potest Dei templum" (*Sermo contra Auxentium* cap. xxxv [PL 16, 1061], quoted II. xxvii. 5). But Marsilius' statement is directly evocative of the famous phrase of Justinian's Code that "omnia principis esse intelligantur" (*Corp. jur. civ., Codex* VII. xxxvii. 3). The medieval jurists differed in their interpretation of this phrase, some following Martinus who took it to mean that the emperor is owner of all the possessions of his subjects, while others held with Bulgarus that it meant only a "jurisdiction and protection" by the emperor, ownership remaining with the private individual possessors. On this point, see G. Meyer, *Das Recht der Expropriation* (Leipzig, 1868), pp. 86–94; O. von Gierke, *Political Theories of the Middle Age,* trans. F. W. Maitland (Cambridge, 1900), pp. 79, 178–79, n. 271; Carlyle, *op. cit.,* II, 72–74. The non-papalist philosopher who comes closest to Marsilius and even exceeds him on this point is John of Jandun, who, curiously enough, justifies it through Aristotle. See *Quaest. in Metaphys.* Lib. I. qu.18 (fol. 15M): *"omnia in civitate sunt principis,* quia politicus vir est in cuius potestate sunt omnia subiacentia, ut patet ex Ethicis, quia de voluntate sua et liberalitate nutrit infortunatos et colubatos." See Aristotle *N. Eth.* VIII. 10. 1060b 3, where, however, it is said only that a true king is "self-sufficient and excels in all goods; but such a man is lacking in nothing. . . ." That it is to this passage that John is referring is shown by his parallel statement in *Tractatus de laudibus Parisius* II. ix

moderate correction but by going to the opposite extreme. He not only recognizes the government's taxing power,[145] but declares that it can take over, even from priests and poor persons, all those ecclesiastic temporal goods which exceed the minimal needs. And where John of Paris had envisaged that only cases of extreme necessity bearing upon faith and morals will justify the pope in making common all the goods of individuals and dispensing them as needed,[146] Marsilius justifies such taking over by the government whenever "it necessarily needs such goods to defend *or otherwise sustain* the polity." [147]

3. THE UNITY OF THE STATE

The supremacy over the other parts of the state which the concept of peace gave to the government is completed by the concept of unity. Unity, in the scholastic metaphysics, is the "principle of indivision"; [1] and Marsilius uses it to show that the supreme governmental authority cannot be divided and still fulfill its function. Hence, just as the concept of peace had been used to prove an affirmative—that the government must have the highest political power of any part of the state—so the concept of unity is used to prove a negative—that no other part of the state except the government can have any political or governmental power. The Marsilian unity thus does away with all conceptions of dualistic or pluralistic authority; it is as much opposed to the plea of such moderates as John of Paris that the temporal and spiritual "powers" each be supreme in its own sphere, as it is to the papalists who insisted that plenitude of power belongs to the pope. Indeed, in its formal structure Marsilius' doctrine is far closer to the latter than to the former.

The concept of unity was as central to medieval thought as that of peace, and it received a similar universalized interpretation. The unity of God upon whom the world depends was the basis of an insistence that there must be corresponding unity in human society; analogies drawn from every conceivable source reinforced this emphasis.[2] With the entry of the Aristotelian philosophy into western Europe, the concept of political unity was given a more sober foundation. Aristotle had criticized Plato for

---

(p. 60): "*in perfectione regis continentur omnia bona suorum subditorum*, juxta illud Aristotelis Ethicorum libro 8°, 'Non enim est rex qui non per se sufficiens et in omnibus bonis superexcellens.' "

[145] II. xvii. 18. [146] *De pot. reg. et pap.* cap. vii (p. 116).

[147] II. xxi. 14. See II. xxv. 9.

[1] Thomas Aquinas *In Metaphys.* Lib. III. Lect. 12. n. 501 (p. 167): "nec aliquid addit unum supra ens nisi solam rationem indivisionis."

[2] See O. von Gierke, *Political Theories of the Middle Age,* trans. F. W. Maitland (Cambridge, 1900), pp. 9–10. See also above, pp. 14 ff.

reducing the state to the unity of the family and even of a single individual, pointing out that the state is a "multitude," a "composite thing." The Aristotelian state attains unity through education and through its "form" or "order," that is, through its constitution or government.[3] Marsilius and the other Aristotelians take over this correction, declaring that a state is not one by composition, colligation, continuity, mixture, or natural form. Rather, the "nominalist" position is upheld that the state is a multitude of men who are one by a "unity of order," and this because they are ordered to and by one government.[4]

That there should be such unity of government is argued by the Aristotelians not only through analogies drawn from organisms and from the governance of the universe (which Marsilius characteristically places last among his arguments),[5] but also through the central point that without unity of government there will be dissensions both among the rulers and among the people. According to Thomas Aquinas, in arguments repeated in almost the same words by Egidius of Rome, John of Paris, Alvarus Pelagius, and James of Viterbo, the rule of one man is better than the rule of many because the ruler's function is to preserve peace, and this peace is the unity of the multitude. But that which is itself one can better preserve unity than that which is multiple.[6] These references to "dissension" and "peace" evoke obvious reminders of the primary preoccupations of Marsilius. It must be remembered, however, that the peace which Thomas and his followers identify with unity is a moral bond of concord,[7] and the unity of government which they uphold is required for a unity of order leading to a single *end*. It is this unity of end or moral function which requires that the government be one in number.[8]

[3] *Pol.* II. 5. 1263b 31 ff.; III. 1. 1274b 38; 3. 1276b 2 ff.

[4] I. xvii. 9, 11. See Thomas Aquinas *In Eth.* Lib. I. Lect. I. n. 5 (p. 3); *In Sent.* Lib. IV. dist. 24. qu.3. a.2. quaestiunc. 3. Egidius of Rome *De reg. princ.* Lib. III. Pars. I. cap. viii. James of Viterbo *De reg. Christ.* I. iii (pp. 109, 111). Dante *De mon.* I. vi (p. 344). On the kinds of unity which are denied of the state, see Aristotle *Metaphysics* VIII. 6. 1045a 8 ff.; X. I. 1052a 18 ff. For restrictions on this nominalist view of the state, see below, pp. 210, 217 ff.

[5] I. xvii. 8, 9. See Thomas Aquinas *De reg. princ.* I. ii (p. 4). Ptolemy of Lucca *De reg. princ.* III. i (p. 46). Egidius of Rome *De reg. princ.* Lib. III. Pars II. cap. iii. John of Paris *De pot. reg. et pap.* cap. i (p. 110). Dante *De mon.* I. viii (pp. 344–45). James of Viterbo *De reg. Christ.* II. v (pp. 211–12).

[6] See texts of Aquinas, Egidius, John of Paris, James of Viterbo cited in preceding note. Also, Dante *De mon.* I. x, xv (pp. 345, 350). Alvarus Pelagius, *De planct. eccles.* I. xl (p. 64). William of Ockham *Octo quaestiones* III. i, v (pp. 101, 109–11).

[7] See above, pp. 95–96.

[8] See James of Viterbo *De reg. Christ.* II. v (p. 211): "Nam regimen sive gubernatio nichil est aliud quam directio gubernatorum ad finem, qui est aliquod bonum. Unitas autem pertinet ad rationem boni. . . Unde, illud ad quod tendit intentio multitudinem gubernantis, recte est unitas et pax multitudinis, in qua unitate consistit bonum et salus cuiuslibet societatis. Sed per se causa unitatis est unum natura. . . ."

This doctrine undergoes with Marsilius two decisive changes which give the whole conception of the unity of government a political specificity which it had not before received. In the first place, whereas such unity had always previously meant monarchy, a single person as ruler, Marsilius explicitly insists that governmental unity can be attained no matter how many "rulers" there may be in the government. An aristocracy or a polity can be a single government just as much as can a monarchy.[9] Marsilius is, indeed, the first medieval thinker to exhibit this thorough indifference toward monarchy. To be sure, he remarks at one point that royal monarchy is "perhaps" the best form of government,[10] and he bases some of his more detailed discussions upon factors peculiar to monarchy, on the ground of its being a form of government closely akin to that of the family.[11] But this does not enter at all into the question of governmental unity; and even this cautious, limited approval is offset by his explicit refusal to commit himself as to the relative merits of monarchy, aristocracy, and polity.[12] Indeed, he bases his entire doctrine upon a definition of *regnum* which makes it "something common to every species of temperate government," [13] as against the other Aristotelians, who restrict it to a monarchic kingdom.[14]

For this indifference to the numerical composition of the ruling body there appear to be several possible explanations. One is the changed relation of government to legislator in Marsilius' doctrine, for, as we shall see, the former is no longer identical with the latter.[15] Hence, the question of "kinds of government" loses the constitutional importance which it had for the other Aristotelians. Another factor is the composition of the "legislator" itself; since Marsilius insists that this must be the whole people,[16] the kind of apotheosis which the Aristotelian king had undergone, and by which kingship had been defended as the best governmental form, is no longer appropriate. Marsilius does, to be sure, set a high moral and intellectual standard for his "perfect ruler," [17] but he insists that not this, but election by the legislator, is the actual efficient cause of the governmental

[9] I. xvii. 2. [10] I. ix. 5. [11] I. ix. 4.

[12] I. ix. 9: "Quis vero principatuum temperatorum sit praestantior, an monarchia vel reliquae duae species, aristocratia vel politia . . . inquisitionem et dubitationem rationabilem habet. . . ." See I. viii. 4; and below, p. 172.

[13] I. ii. 2.

[14] E.g., John of Paris *De pot. reg. et pap.* cap. i (p. 109): "regnum proprie acceptum, sic potest diffiniri. 'Regnum est regimen multitudinis perfectae, ad commune bonum ordinatum ab uno.' . . . 'Ab uno' vero ponitur ad differentiam Aristocratiae, id est principatus optimorum, seu optimatum, ubi scilicet pauci dominantur secundum virtutem . . . ad differentiam Polycratiae, vel Politiae, ubi populus dominatur."

[15] See below, pp. 172 ff. [16] I. xii–xiii.

[17] I. xiv. See, however, below, pp. 243–44.

authority.[18] A third factor in Marsilius' indifference to the monarchic ideal was probably his own experience. The Italian city-states of his time frequently had non-monarchic governments; and despite his association with Ludwig of Bavaria and his enthusiasm for Henry VII and Philip the Fair,[19] he points out that different forms of government are suited to different peoples, places, and times.[20] This relativism is far removed from the single-minded emphasis of his predecessors upon monarchy.

The second change which Marsilius effects in the concept of unity of government is even more important than the first, and indeed provides its culminating explanation. The Marsilian unity is no longer a moral leadership to a single *end,* but solely a unity of governmental *function*—of coercive political *means.* Unity of government means that regardless of how many individual "rulers" are in the government, there must be a "numerical unity of every action, judgment, sentence, or command which is forthcoming from them." [21] All authorities in the state must thus be "reduced or ordered under one supreme government," [22] whether this consist in one man or in many.

This specification of the unity of government serves to distinguish it sharply from all interpretations with which it had long been identified. Like Marsilius' concept of order, it is strictly juridical, not personal, moral, or theological; like his concept of peace, it concerns solely transient acts, not immanent acts, and also, as we shall see, it involves only unity within a single state, not a universal unity as in Dante, Engelbert, and others.[23] The basic point is that if the state have two or more supreme governments, neither subordinated to the other, the resulting jurisdictional confusion will mean that "men's injuries will go unavenged," and this in turn will lead to "fighting, separation, and finally the destruction of the state." [24] Without governmental unity, therefore, the governmental function of judging disputes will itself be impossible. Hence, where Aquinas and his followers had said merely that for a state to have a single ruler is "better" and "more useful" than for it to have many rulers,[25] Marsilius declares that unity of government is "necessary," and its opposite "impossible," if the state is to endure at all.[26] Unity is a *necessary* attribute of government and of the state, and this not for moral or theological but for specifically political reasons. It is because Marsilius places such massive importance

[18] I. xv. 1, 2. [19] See I. xix. 10. [20] I. ix. 10.
[21] I. xvii. 2. [22] I. xvii. 3. [23] See below, pp. 126 ff.
[24] See I. xvii. 3, 5. Cf. Hobbes *Leviathan* ch. xxxix (pp. 252–53).
[25] See texts of Aquinas, John of Paris, Egidius, James of Viterbo cited above, p. 116 n. 5.
[26] I. xvii. 1, 3. Dante *De mon.* I. x (p. 345) also declares that monarchy is "necessary" in order to have a final judgment of disputes; but cf. below. Cf. *Disp. inter mil. et cler.* p. 14.

upon the bare preservation of the state and upon the supreme necessity thereto of the coercive govermental function, that his emphasis upon unity is so overwhelming. And it is because such unity can be had regardless of the number of men who rule, that Marsilius could afford to be so indifferent to the monarchic principle upon which his predecessors had insisted.

The full meaning of this doctrine of unity is found in the undivided scope it provides for the governmental authority. Marsilius' predecessors, as we have seen, had based the govermental unity upon a unity of order to a single moral end; hence the unified governmental authority reached only so far as that end itself. Thus Thomas Aquinas, Dante, and John of Paris, for all their praises of governmental unity, extend it only to temporal affairs and recognize an entirely separate authority, that of the pope, for spiritual affairs.[27] The papalists, on the other hand, do not betray the concept of unity in any such fashion. Like Marsilius, they insist upon a unity of order in which one "power" is entirely subordinate to the other.[28] But the order, far from being specifically political as in Marsilius, is of all kinds: moral, theological, psychological, and so on through their whole organic range of concepts. In Marsilius, consequently, the applications of the concept of governmental unity achieve an unparalleled political scope. All these applications bear upon the central point that the essential governmental authority must be one, so that whatever coercive power may be exercised in the state either belongs only to the government or is entirely subordinated to and derived from the government. "For two coercive dominions, neither subordinate to the other, and in respect of the same multitude, impede one another." [29]

The first application refers to the *acts* which fall under coercive political jurisdiction. It was an old tradition that sins against divine law came under the cognizance of the priest rather than of the secular judge, because the priest was the minister and preacher of divine law. But Marsilius points out that on this ground every "expert" would be coercive judge and ruler over those who "sinned" against his discipline: the physician over men who violated the rules of medicine, the goldsmith over those who falsified the gold in statues; and "there would be as many rulers as there are offices of the state against which one may sin. But the impossibility or superfluity of this has been shown above." [30] It will be noted that this applica-

[27] Dante *De mon.* III. xvi (pp. 376–77). John of Paris *De pot. reg. et pap.* cap. ii (p. 110). Thomas *De reg. princ.* I. xiv (p. 21).

[28] See Egidius of Rome *De eccl. pot.* III. ii (p. 152). James of Viterbo *De reg. Christ.* II. vii (pp. 238 ff.). Augustinus Triumphus *S. de eccl. pot.* qu.22. a.3. Alvarus Pelagius *De planctu eccl.* I. xl (p. 63).

[29] II. iv. 5.

[30] II. x. 8.

tion extends the concept of unity from the government to include the law which has binding force. No "discipline," whether the rules of Christ or of Hippocrates, is entitled to coercive sanctions, save the law by which the government acts. The authority of human, secular law is thus to be as undivided as is that of the government. It will be noted also how this application carries on Marsilius' levelling of ends or final causes. Marsilius places on the same level the values subserved by physicians, goldsmiths, and priests, so far as concerns the relation of acts opposing those values to their coercive regulation by government. The one and only relevant political category of acts and values becomes those acts which, by harming other men, require correction in order to preserve the state.

The second application of the governmental unity deals with the *persons* who come under coercive juridiction. The old system of clerical immunities had entailed separate "ecclesiastic" courts for all cases involving clergymen.[31] This was accepted even by John of Paris, striving to maintain the parallelism of the spiritual and temporal powers.[32] Hence Marsilius points out again that this practice would lead to the destruction of the state through an "unordered plurality of governments."[33] The fact that a transgressor of the law is a priest is just as "accidental" as the fact that he may be a farmer or carpenter; the only essential consideration is that he has transgressed the law. The relation of the secular judge or ruler to any transgressor of human law is that of an efficient cause or agent to its "proper or essential matter" on which it is its "nature" to act "for the end for which it is apt."[34] Hence to intrude into the operation of the ruler any factors other than the content of human law and the transgressor, as such, of

[31] See above, p. 26. For the papalist justification of the exemption of the clergy from secular jurisdiction, see especially Augustinus Triumphus *S. de eccl. pot.* qu.22. a.2. It was also traditionally held, to be sure, that divine law itself commands that "spiritual men" observe human laws: see *Corp. jur. can., Decret. Gratiani* Pars I. dist. 9. can. 1. § 1 and the gloss of Gratian; and Thomas Aquinas *S. theol.* II. 1. qu.96. a.5. ad 2. Marsilius repeats this position: II. ix. 11; see below, p. 162. But his primary argument, unlike his predecessors', is not from divine law but from the necessity of such observance for the preservation of the state itself; and even more importantly, his emphasis is that, contrary to the tradition, the judgment of clergymen who transgress human law pertains to the secular government.

[32] *De pot. reg. et pap.* cap. xiii (p. 127): "De privilegio a principibus indulto clerici nonnisi per suos episcopos iudicantur . . . Quidam tamen dicunt hos eis deberi iure divino et non privilegio principum. . . ." Cf. the complaints on this score by Averroes (*Paraphrasis . . . de Republica* Tr. III [fol. 514F]) and by Hobbes (*Leviathan* ch. xliv [p. 334]).

[33] II. viii. 9.

[34] II. viii. 7. It is significant of the extent to which Marsilius has assimilated the functioning of the political order to that of physical nature, that he supports this point by, and indeed derives his terminology in expressing it from, a citation of Aristotle's *Physics* II. 8. 199a 9. A similar point, but without the reference to "nature," was made by Peter of Auvergne *In Pol.* VII. Lect. 10 (p. 468): "Principans se habet ad subjectum sicut agens ad passum et movens ad motum: principantis enim est movere et dirigere subjectum, subjecti vero moveri et dirigi secundum quod huiusmodi."

that content is as irrelevant as to intrude accidental considerations into any art or natural science. "For that which is essential is not cancelled or varied by that which is accidental; otherwise there would be infinite species of judges." [35]

The third application refers to the control of entry into the other *functional groups* of the state. Should not such control be exercised by the experts in each group, as the best "judges" of the qualifications required? Marsilius opposes this decentralization on the same ground as in the other cases: the final coercive control must rest with the government, for otherwise "there would be in a single community as many supreme rulers as there are judges in the first sense of judgment [i.e., experts] concerning sufficiency or deficiency with regard to each of the offices of the state," [36] and Marsilius again adds that he has demonstrated the "impossibility" of this "if the state is to endure."

Marsilius' concepts of peace and unity, taken together, thus mean complete and unchallenged jurisdiction of the government over all individuals and groups in the state. Beginning with the plea that the state must be preserved, all acts, persons, and functions are subjected to strict governmental control. This outcome casts a revealing light on a central aspect of Marsilius' entire doctrine. His conception of the impulse which leads men to association in the state was, as we saw above, entirely an individualistic one. It is to satisfy their own individual needs, and not because they desire the friendly company of others for its own sake, that men are driven to associate with one another. But this individualism at the source eventuates in a broad governmentally controlled collectivism. Again, it was men's natural *desires* which led them to political association; but the governmental control over all the functional occupations of the state means a definite restriction of men's ability to follow their desires: men "must not and cannot turn *at will*" to whatever occupation they like.[37] The institutions of the Marisilan state thus appear as contrary to men's natural tendencies rather than as fulfillments of them; in this respect Marsilius is far closer to the Augustinian tradition than to the Aristotelian.

How far, then, does Marsilius go along the road to Hobbist absolutism?

[35] II. viii. 7. This point is similar to Aristotle's doctrine of rectificatory justice, where it is declared that the law treats the parties concerned in a suit as equals, considering not whether the men are morally "good" or "bad," but only the "distinctive character of the injury" (*N. Eth.* v. 4. 1132a 2).

[36] II. xvii. 14. On Marsilius' revision of the concept of "judgment," on which the arguments cited in the text also rest, see below, pp. 227 ff.

[37] I. xv. 10: "Propter quod non licitum est alicui *pro libito* sibi assumere officium in civitate, maxime advenis. Non enim debet nec rationabiliter potest *pro voto* quilibet se convertere ad militare vel sacerdotium exercendum. . . ." I. xvii. 7: there must be unified governmental control, for otherwise *"eliget* sibi quod quisque *volet* officium. . . ."

The plea that the state is in danger of destruction might be used to defend almost any degree of governmental power, and to deny its subjects all corrective recourse. Such quietistic indications are not lacking in the *Defensor*. There are fulminations against the papacy for stimulating the subjects to "sedition" and "rebellion" against the government.[38] The whole idea of "peace" as involving the performance by each part of the state of its own function "without impediment" betokens, like the idea of unity, an absolute power of government with no interference from the other "parts" of the state. For whoever "impedes" the governmental function is "the efficient cause of strife." [39] And the fact that Marsilius views the various parts of the state as being based upon "natural aptitudes" in men themselves—some being inclined to farming, others to soldiering, and still others to the "prudence" required for ruling the state [40]—would seem to indicate the same kind of rigid political and social stratification as Plato developed in the *Republic*. The same tendency is suggested by the use of the organic analogy to develop the idea of peace in such fashion that the ruler becomes the "heart" which establishes and activates the other parts of the state.[41]

There are, however, basic considerations which must be adduced on the other side if the import of Marsilius' doctrine is to be properly understood. In the first place, his unitary emphasis was in an important sense a liberating force. It meant the removal of the multiplicity of coercive jurisdictions to which men had been subjected through the development of feudalism and the several secular and ecclesiastic authorities: only one coercive jurisdiction was now to be valid. Consequently, apart from the commands of the human law as enforced by the secular authority, men were free to do completely as they wished. "For if human law did not prohibit anyone from becoming drunk, or making and selling shoes according to his means or desires, or practising medicine, or teaching, or working at other such functions as he pleased *(pro libito)*, then no one who became drunk, or who acted wrongly in any occupation, would be punished." [42] Marsilius' unity thus meant that, for perhaps the first time in medieval political thought, men were conceived to come under coercive jurisdiction not on moral or theological grounds but only on specifi-

[38] See II. xxi. 13; II. xxvi. 13–15.

[39] I. xix. 3. See above, pp. 59, 99.

[40] I. vii. 1. It is a significant incidental point that Marsilius attributes this diversification of aptitudes among men only to "nature," and not, like Thomas Aquinas, to divine providence. See *Quodib.* VII. qu.7. a.17. Resp.; also James of Viterbo *De reg. Christ.* I. iii (p. 115). However, Dante is similarly naturalistic; see *De mon.* II. vii (p. 357).

[41] I. xv. 1, 2.

[42] II. x. 3. See II. x. 8: "Si enim peccata huiusmodi non essent humana lege prohibita, ea committentes nequaquam punirentur."

cally legal-political ones, that is, for reasons deriving not from some authoritatively promulgated moral or religious code but only from the authority of the positive law and ruler concerned primarily with the adjudication of disputes and the regulation required for the preservation of the social fabric. Such a difference might, to be sure, be depicted as a change from the benevolent surveillance of objective and eternal values to the unhindered sway of arbitrary force. Yet when it is seen that one of its results was a sharp restriction in the severity and the mandatoriness of the sanctions imposed for heresy and similar violations of divine law, and even a complete removal of those sanctions,[43] the liberating aspect of Marsilius' doctrine becomes evident.

An internal difficulty might, to be sure, be found in this aspect of the doctrine as compared with the one examined earlier. According to the latter, the governmental regulation of the entry into and the performance of the various functions of the state was necessary to peace and hence to the preservation of the state.[44] But according to the considerations just presented, this regulation depends entirely upon what is commanded or prohibited by human law, so that, in the absence of a given law, complete freedom in the matter of entry into and performance of functions is assured. These two aspects thus might appear to be opposed as the "objective" necessary requirements of the constitution of any state as Marsilius sets it forth, and the "subjective" variabilities of the content of human law as posited by a particular human authority. It is, indeed, partly from this contrast that Marsilius' doctrine takes on the appearance now of absolutism, now of liberalism. But the contrast itself is readily explicable in the light of Marsilius' polemical purpose, for the appeal to the "objective" requirements of the preservation of the state brings the priesthood under the jurisdiction of the government, while the insistence upon the unity of the government and law, in the sense that only what the law commands is to have coercive force, removes such authority from the priesthood.

The further explanation of this contrast emerges when we turn to a second basic consideration affecting the seeming absolutism of the doctrines of peace and unity: that the government, despite the great authority which those doctrines give to it, is in the complete Marsilian doctrine itself subordinated to the whole people of which it is only a part. To begin with, despite his doctrine of "natural aptitudes," Marsilius insists that these give no natural right to rule; the ruler must in all cases derive his authority from election by the citizen-body.[45] Hence the rigidity of the hierarchic political structure of the Platonic ideal state is lacking in the

[43] See below, pp. 154 ff., 165–66. [44] See above, pp. 111–12, 121. [45] I. xv. 1, 2.

Marsilian "peace." Moreover, to see in its proper perspective Marsilius' obsession with the preservation of the state, it must be recognized that he conceives that preservation as requiring thoroughgoing control of the ruler by the whole people. Thus there is this significant difference between his organic analogy and that of his predecessors, that they give the dominant position, that of being the "soul" or "reason" or "heart" of the state or church-state, to either the ruler [46] or the priest.[47] Marsilius, on the other hand, gives this dominant position to the "soul of the whole body of citizens," which "forms" the government analogous to the heart, and gives it its internal "beat" or "power," that is, the law.[48] It follows, therefore, that just as the heart will not fulfill its function unless it is "ruled" by its power, so the government "must be regulated by the law" in all its functioning, "for otherwise the ruler would not act toward his due end, the conservation of the state." [49] Thus Marsilius emphatically ties even the preservation of the state to the ruler's subjection to the law made by the people.[50] The same preservation of the state, as has already been mentioned, is also invoked to prove that the law must be made by the people, and that the people must "correct" the ruler when he acts contrary to the law.[51] And Marsilius' doctrine of unity involves not only an "ordering" of men to one supreme government, but the ordering must be voluntary: "the men of one city or province are called one city or state because they *want* one government." [52]

This, then, is the central paradox of Marsilius' political doctrine, that in the name of the preservation of the state he insists upon the strict control both of the ruler by the people and of the people by the ruler. In the former respect, he is the ancestor of Locke; in the latter, of Hobbes. But more than any of his predecessors Marsilius emphasized the constitutional structure of the state as a continual two-way affair, involving the constant flow of authority first from the corporate people to the ruler and then from the ruler to the individuals and particular groups of the state. Neither of these two aspects can be omitted from the Marsilian doctrine without distorting its central basis. Both, indeed, are strongly reminiscent of the status of the *podestà* in the Italian communes, for the extensive authority of the *podestà* over all groups was limited by the "greater council" of the commune.

[46] Plato *Republic* IV. 428B ff., 441E ff. Aristotle *Pol.* I. 5. 1254a 34 ff.; IV. 4. 1291a 24 ff. Thomas Aquinas *De reg. princ.* I. xii, xiii (pp. 18–19). Egidius of Rome *De reg. princ.* Lib. I. Pars II. cap. xi.

[47] John of Salisbury *Policraticus* V. ii (I, 282). Ptolemy of Lucca *De reg. princ.* III. x (pp. 59). Augustinus Triumphus *S. de eccl. pot.* qu.I. a.I; qu.6. a.5.

[48] I. xv. 6.

[49] I. xv. 7.

[50] See also I. xi. 5.

[51] I. xii. 7; I. xviii. 4. See above, p. 107.

[52] I. xvii. 11.

Might it not be possible to urge, however, that the exigencies of preserving the state require an absolute government *without* popular control, because of the inevitable unwieldiness, uncertainty, and factious disunity involved in the reaching of decisions by the people? It was largely on this ground, indeed, that Marsilius' predecessors rejected the "rule by many" and considered it the worst of the "just" forms of government.[53] But it is very significant that Marsilius does not take this step. Whenever the popular and preservationist principles appear to clash, he chooses the former over the latter. Thus to the argument that rulers must attain their power by hereditary succession rather than by popular election because the latter method may involve disagreements which "lead the entire state into sedition," [54] Marsilius replies that although this danger of schism "must be heeded above all other objections," popular election is still preferable because the people's will is always for the common benefit.[55] He insists also that when the citizens see that they are perpetually deprived of the opportunity to wield governmental authority, "they will justly engage in sedition." [56]

As these answers make clear, there is no real opposition between the principles of the people's supremacy and the preservation of the state as Marsilius conceives them; for the will of the people is the best judge and indeed the guarantee of the preservation of the state. The broader significance of Marsilius' emphasis upon unity emerges, therefore, when it is seen to be a unity not merely of the government as such but also of the law and the people-legislator, that is, of the whole political authority of the Marsilian state. This is, indeed, entailed by the status of the government itself; for unity of government requires unity of the law by which the government rules, and this in turn requires unity of the legislator from which the law emanates. The doctrines of the law and the legislator must themselves be examined, consequently, before we can understand the full meaning of the unity of the Marsilian state in this broader sense.[57]

4. THE UNIVERSALITY OF THE STATE

Marsilius' doctrine of unity, setting forth a principle necessary for the preservation of any state, had been a reaction to the civil strife of the kind found between the burghers and clergy of Padua and other Italian cities and also between the *magnati* and *popolani*. Hence, while the doctrine marks

[53] See Thomas Aquinas *De reg. princ.* I. ii, iii, v(pp. 4–8). Dante *De mon.* I. v (p. 344). For other references, see texts cited above, p. 116, n. 4. See also William of Ockham *Octo quaestiones* III. v (pp. 109–11); and below, pp. 201–2.

[54] I. xvi. 5. See I. xvi. 7.

[55] I. xvi. 19.

[56] I. xvi. 21.

[57] See especially below, pp. 256 ff.

a specifically political termination of the theory of medieval feudalism, in a sense in which the traditional theologico-political *ordinatio ad unum* does not, the problems for which Marsilius invoked unity were not peculiar to him. His solution, however, was unique not only for the kind of unity he espoused but also for the kind of limitation he placed upon it. The Marsilian unity is a departure not only from medieval particularism but also from medieval universalism.

The concept of unity as Marsilius treats it raises insistently the problem of the quantitative political context within which unity may be achieved. If for the preservation of the state the unity of its government is so necessary, then should not such unity take the form of a universal state? Marsilius' predecessors and contemporaries, proceeding from their own premises, either gave a completely affirmative answer to this question or else took important steps toward such affirmation. Thus where Aristotle had listed three "communities," the family, the village, and the "city-state" (πόλις, translated *civitas* by William of Moerbeke),[1] the medieval Aristotelians add further units beyond the *civitas:* some only the "province" (*provincia*) or "state" (*regnum*),[2] but others also the universal "monarchy" (*monarchia*) or "empire" (*imperium*) or community of the "whole world."[3] And among the reasons given for the existence of such larger communities are some which appear close to Marsilius' preoccupation: the *provincia* or *regnum* is more secure in its peace than is the *civitas,* for since the former is a combination of several cities, it is better able to withstand attack by enemies;[4] moreover, its ruler, having greater power behind him, is better able to coerce and punish those who disturb the peace.[5] Closer still to Marsilius' orientation is one of the arguments for a universal state or *monarchia,* that unless there is one supreme government for the

[1] *Pol.* I. 2. 1252b 13 ff.

[2] Thomas Aquinas *De reg. princ.* I. i (p. 3). Egidius of Rome *De reg. princ.* Lib. II. Pars I. cap. ii–iv; Lib. III. Pars I. cap. i, v. John of Paris *De pot. reg. et pap.* cap. iv (p. 112). James of Viterbo *De reg. Christ.* I. i (p. 91); see *ibid.* II. v (p. 205) for the *communitas totius mundi.*

[3] Thomas Aquinas *S. theol.* Suppl. qu.40. a.6. Resp. Engelbert of Admont *De ortu* cap. xv (p. 370 G). Dante *De mon.* I. v (p. 344). Ptolemy of Lucca *De reg. princ.* III. xii, xiii (pp. 63 ff.). John of Jandun *Quaest. in Metaphys.* Lib. XII. qu.22 (fol. 144C). William of Ockham points out that Aristotle "solummodo loquitur de politiis quae in *civitatibus* custodiuntur" and not "in toto orbe": *Dialogus* Pars III. Tr. I. Lib. II. cap. xxx (p. 819). See also Augustinus Triumphus *S. de eccl. pot.* qu.1. a.6. Cf. O. von Gierke, *Political Theories of the Middle Age,* trans. F. W. Maitland (Cambridge, 1900), pp. 21, 96–97, 129, 193–94; C. N. S. Woolf, *Bartolus of Sassoferrato* (Cambridge, 1913), pp. 272 ff.

[4] Thomas Aquinas *De reg. princ.* I. i (p. 3). Egidius of Rome *De reg. princ.* Lib. II. Pars I. cap. iv; Lib. III. Pars I. cap. v. Dante *De mon.* I. v (p. 344). Engelbert *De ortu* cap. xiii (p. 369 G) puts the same point in terms of the distinction between *parva* and *magna regna.* This point is all the more significant in that it appears to contradict Aristotle's insistence that a mere "military alliance" for defense against attack does not constitute a state (*Pol.* III. 9. 1280a 34 ff.).

[5] Egidius *De reg. princ.* Lib. III. Pars I. cap. v.

whole world there will be no means of adjudicating disputes among the rulers of lesser units or among their inhabitants in relation to one another.[6]

Yet Marsilius does not fall in with this trend toward universality. He does not even insist upon the partial enlargement from *civitas* to *provincia* or *regnum* which all his predecessors had made. When he gives the Aristotelian listing of the three "communities," family, village, and *civitas,* he does not add any larger community.[7] In his initial nominal definitions of *regnum* he presents as one meaning "a number of *civitates* or *provinciae* contained under one government," pointing out that in this sense *regnum* differs from *civitas* "with respect to quantity"; but he refuses to restrict himself, as had the other Aristotelians, to this meaning of *regnum,* declaring instead that the meaning he will use throughout his treatise is "something common to every species of temperate government whether in a single *civitas* or in many *civitates.*" [8] Indeed, he sometimes uses *civitas sive regnum* interchangeably,[9] as also *provincia;* [10] but the single term which occurs most frequently, by far, is *civitas.*

From this it follows *a fortiori* that Marsilius does not look with favor upon a universal state or government. So thoroughly intra-state is his conception of the peace and unity for which he argues, that when the question arises as to whether the requirement of a single supreme government does not entail government for the whole world, he can reply that this question "deserves reasonable study, but is different from our present project." In his very statement of the question, moreover, he raises numerous objections: such a government would have to extend over widely separated parts of the world and to deal with persons speaking different languages and differing greatly in morals and customs; moreover, nature herself would seem to be against such world government, since she uses wars and epidemics to lessen the population in order that the earth may provide enough sustenance for all.[11] This from an exponent of "peace"!

What underlies this refusal to accept the idea of a universal state which men like Dante had propounded so earnestly, and to which Ludwig of Bavaria, whose cause Marsilius espoused, was dedicated as Holy Roman Emperor? In part, it may be a reflection of the striving of the Italian city-states for independence of the empire, an independence which the Lom-

[6] Dante *De mon.* I. x, xv (pp. 345, 350). Engelbert *De ortu* cap. xviii (p. 374 A). William of Ockham *Octo quaestiones* III. i (pp. 100–101); note the strong resemblance of this text to *Def. pac.* I. xvii. 3, 4.

[7] I. iii. 3–5.

[8] I. ii. 2.

[9] See I. ii. 3; I. xvii. 1–3, 7, 11–13; II. xxviii. 14.

[10] See I. xv. 2; I. xvi. 16, 17; I. xix. 8; II. viii. 7. See I. xvii. 11, where *civitas aut provincia* is used interchangeably with *civitas aut regnum* in the same sentence.

[11] I. xvii. 10.

bard cities, including Padua, had somewhat precariously enjoyed *de facto* if not *de jure* since 1183. Yet Marsilius' preoccupation is not confined to the city-states as such; he frequently adverts to the *Italicum regnum* as the example of a state whose "peace" has been lost,[12] and deplores the fact that it is "divided and lacerated in almost all of its parts." [13] Again, however, Marsilius' essential concern is neither with the *Italicae civitates* nor with the unification of the *Italicum regnum,* since he also expresses concern for the "Germans" [14] and the "French." [15] The central fact is that, as he himself declares, he is striving for the "peace" of the *"regnum and any other temperate civil community whatsoever."* [16] It is the temporal pretensions of the priesthood and papacy, wherever they may appear, that Marsilius is opposing as a threat to "peace"; and it is the generality of this aim which accounts for the generality and indifference of his quantitative specifications of political contexts. This generality forms the link between the struggle of the Padua burghers against their clergy and the struggle of kings and emperors against the papacy. And it is the pretensions of the papacy to universal plenitude of power that account, in particular, for Marsilius' hostility to the idea of a universal state.

Together with these considerations, the philosophic basis of Marsilius' whole doctrine helps to explain his opposition to a world government. He was not the first to point out the diversities among men which militate against world unity,[17] and others had also justified wars through "nature" or God.[18] But his conceptions of both "nature" and "peace" are especially apposite to such particularism, for neither is placed within the theological or rationalist context by which many of the papalists and imperialists sought to justify their universalist pretensions. Marsilius' "nature," being

[12] I. i. 2; I. xix. 4; II. xxiii. 11; II. xxvi. 19. See also Previté-Orton, "Marsilius," *Proc. Brit. Acad.,* XXI (1935), 139–40.

[13] I. xix. 11. Another similar passage, at II. xxvi. 20, is likened by Previté-Orton (his edition, p. 423, n. 1) to a passage of Machiavelli's *Il principe* cap. xxvi.

[14] See I. xix. 11; II. xxvi. 15.

[15] This emerges in references to Philip the Fair and other "Francorum reges"; see I. xix. 10; II. xvii. 17; II. xxi. 9. Cf. Lagarde, *Marsile,* p. 53.

[16] III. iii: "Hiis [i.e., the lessons of the *Defensor pacis*] comprehensis memoriterque retentis et diligenter custoditis sive servatis, salvabitur *regnum et quaevis altera quaecumque temperata civilis communitas* in esse pacifico seu tranquillo. . . ." This is Marsilius' final summation.

[17] See the objection which Engelbert of Admont raises against his doctrine of the universal state: *De ortu* cap. xvi (p. 372B). See also John of Paris *De pot. reg. et pap.* cap. iii, xxiii (pp. 111–12, 141). Dante *De mon.* I. xiv (p. 349). It is significant, in view of the universalist orientation of much of medieval thought, that both Engelbert and John appeal to Augustine as a source of anti-universalist arguments. See *De civ. Dei* IV. iii–xv.

[18] See Egidius of Rome *De reg. princ.* Lib. III. Pars III. cap. xxiii. Dante considers wars a means by which God's judgment is revealed to men: *De mon.* II. viii ff. (pp. 358 ff.). See William of Ockham's argument against world monarchy that wars are justified by the *jus gentium* (*Dialogus* Pars III. Tr. II. Lib. I. cap. ii [p. 874]), and his reply (*ibid.* cap. xi [p. 879]).

only physical and biological, cannot lead to a universal law of nature founded upon reason,[19] nor his "peace" to a similar universal order. He insists, in fact, that for men to live peacefully together it suffices to have "numerical unities of governments according to provinces," without going beyond these to a world government.[20]

A further factor underlying Marsilius' particularism is the republican framework which he holds to be necessary for political authority. The only valid legislator is the whole body of citizens *"in that community* over which the law is made"; [21] and the making of the laws requires direct participation of all the citizens in a general assembly.[22] This conception, based on the experience of the Italian communes, is obviously possible only in a relatively small community.[23] Moreover, the basic arguments for the doctrine involve the insistence that the common benefit can be attained and freedom secured only if men themselves control the laws under which they live.[24] This position was antithetical alike to the imperialist and papalist universalisms which regarded the emperor or the pope as the lawgiver for all peoples.

There are, nevertheless, traces of universalism in Marsilius' thought. Some are only peripheral, as in his references to the past hegemony of the *Italicum regnum* over the whole world.[25] But one factor especially compels Marsilius to admit a universalist political orientation: the conception of a universal church and faith, with which he deals in the second discourse. Yet even here he resists the idea for as long as possible, and makes only the least possible concessions. Thus while defining the church as the *universitas fidelium,* he hastens to add that the church exists also in "all the parts of this *universitas* in every community, even the family." [26] The universality of the church is hence distributive only, not collective in the sense in which Thomas Aquinas had insisted that despite the diversities of dioceses and cities there is one church, one Christian people, and hence there must be one head.[27] Thus Marsilius argues that the church is one only in the sense in which the faith is one in all believers; but since this is only a specific or generic, not a numerical unity, the church does not essentially require a numerically single head.[28] And just

[19] See above, p. 55. See also the positivist interpretation of *jus naturale* (II. xii. 7) and the statement that this is related only "equivocally" to *jus naturale* in the sense of "rectae rationis agibilium dictamen" (II. xii. 8). See below, pp. 149 ff.

[20] II. xxviii. 15.

[21] I. xii. 3.

[22] See below, pp. 169, 188.

[23] See also below, p. 254.

[24] I. xii–xiii. See below, pp. 205 ff.

[25] I. i. 2. See *Def. min.* XII. i, where the universal hegemony of the *Romanus populus* is viewed as contemporary.

[26] II. ii. 3.

[27] *Cont. gent.* IV. lxxvi.

[28] II. xxviii. 13. See below, pp. 274 ff.

as in the first discourse, he had declared that the human legislator is the *universitas civium "in that community* over which the law is made," [29] so he is similarly particularistic in the second discourse in dealing with such ecclesiastic questions as excommunication and ordination of ministers.[30]

It is only when Marsilius comes to the problem of determining the truth in matters of faith that he is unable to circumvent a universal approach. This might seem paradoxical in view of his insistence that a unified government is necessary only because of men's "contentious acts." [31] But the particularism which had been justified in the latter context breaks down when confronted with a universal faith, differences with respect to which would lead to eternal damnation. Whether or not Marsilius took such damnation seriously—and we have seen important reasons to doubt that he did—the circumstances of his time compelled him to deal with it. And his rejection of the traditional argument that the unity of the faith requires a single divinely appointed head of the church compelled him to propound other means of preserving such unity. John of Paris, with his separation of spiritual and temporal powers, had solved the problem by making the spiritual power universal but limited to spiritual affairs, and the temporal power localized to provinces and limited to temporal affairs.[32] But Marsilius has substituted for the complete jurisdiction claimed by the papal plenitude of power an even fuller jurisdiction to be wielded by his *legislator humanus fidelis,* the *universitas civium fidelium;* and because of the unity and universality of the faith, the *legislator* likewise becomes universal. Although his solution, the general council, does not explicitly involve a lessening of the supremacy of particular "legislators," there emerges nevertheless the gradually implied recognition of the world unity entailed by the world faith. Thus Marsilius writes that the members of the council are elected by "all the notable provinces or communities of the world in accordance with the determination of their human legislator, *whether one or more* . . ." [33] The need for universal unity in this sphere is aggravated by the fact that while each legislator can "compel" the attendance of its elected delegates,[34] there is no one to compel the legislators them-

[29] I. xii. 3.

[30] II. vi. 12: The power to excommunicate "pertinet ad fidelium universitatem *in communitate illa in qua debet aliquis tali judicio judicari,* vel ad ipsius superiorem, vel ad concilium generale." II. xvii. 8: In the appointment of priests in "communitatibus fidelium jam perfectis . . . causa factiva immediata sit seu debeat esse universa *ejus loci* fidelium multitudo. . . ." II. xvii. 9: "fidelium multitudinem *ejus loci,* super quam intendere debet promovendus minister. . . ." See also *Def. min.* xv. 8.

[31] II. xxviii. 14. See above, p. 118; below, p. 275. On the relation between faith and coercion, see below, pp. 155 ff.

[32] *De pot. reg. et pap.* cap. iii (pp. 111–12).

[33] II. xx. 2. See below, p. 286.

[34] II. xx. 3.

selves thus to elect or support the council,[35] despite the insistence that the determination of matters of faith by the council is necessary to avoid error and schism,[36] and that belief in the truth of its decisions is necessary to salvation.[37] Hence we now find Marsilius referring to the *humanus fidelis legislator superiore carens* which alone has the authority to convoke a general council, "by coercive force" if necessary,[38] to enforce its decisions by a "coercive command,"[39] and to appoint (with or without the general council) the head of all bishops and churches.[40] Even this *superiore carens,* however, is still only a "particular state without a suzerain,"[41] not a "supreme" state in the sense in which the empire was in some theories regarded as having universal hegemony. Yet the requirement of a universal legislator is obliquely recognized in references to the *humanus fidelis legislator* as *supremus,*[42] *universalis,*[43] *primus.*[44] This concept of a universal primacy refers to the *supremus Imperii Romani humanus legislator*[45] which in Marsilius' doctrine consists in the first instance of the *universitas civium* of the empire. It comes in the *Defensor minor* to represent Marsilius' concession to the imperialist theory as a consequence of his association with Ludwig of Bavaria.[46]

In these fluctuations with regard to the universality of the state, Marsilius reflects the internal stresses of his entire doctrine. The secular values and popular control of the state in his central conception of it involve smaller rather than larger units; but the problem of the papacy and the empire to which he is forced to apply his doctrine involve an enlargement which eventually becomes universal. Subsequent developments can be seen to be mirrored in this situation, for the conciliarist movement attempted to combine ecclesiastic universality with secular particularism, and the Protestant outcome of national churches is probably what Marsilius himself would have espoused could he have broken away from the idea of a universal faith determined and enforced by a single universal agency.

[35] II. xxii. 13. [36] II. xx. 1. [37] II. xix. 1–2.
[38] II. xviii. 8; II. xxi. 1. [39] II. xxi. 4. [40] II. xxii. 9.

[41] See Previté-Orton in his edition, p. 334, n. 1; O. von Gierke, *Political Theories of the Middle Age,* trans. F. W. Maitland (Cambridge, 1900), pp. 97, 195, nn. 338–39. This is also what is meant by Pierre Dubois *De recup. terre sancte* par. 12 (p. 11), when he refers to "civitates et multi principes superiores in terris non recognoscentes."

[42] II. xviii. 8; *Def. min.* III. vii; XI. iii; XII. i. Cf. Previté-Orton, "Marsilius," *Proc. Brit. Acad.,* XXI (1935), 178, n. 67.

[43] II. xviii. 8; II. xxi. 11.

[44] II. xxi. 8. This use of *primus* as referring to the *legislator* which authorizes and sanctions decisions of the general council indicates a more universal and absolute primacy than what is elsewhere referred to as merely the particular *legislator primus in communitate* (I. xii. 3) or *in provincia vel provinciis* (II. xxx. 8).

[45] II. xxx. 8. [46] See *Def. min.* XII. 1, 3. See also below, pp. 249 ff.

CHAPTER IV

LAW: HUMAN AND DIVINE

I. THE DEFINITION OF LAW

A THEORY OF LAW may stand in one of two general relations to a theory of the state: either the state is conceived in terms of law, or law in terms of the state. These relations, each of which may admit of many specific variations, involve important differences with respect to the nature and function of law. The traditional medieval theory of law, amid the many changes in detail which it underwent through the impact of the Roman and the Aristotelian conceptions, exhibited in all its main phases the fundamental influence of the Stoic and Augustinian metaphysics from which it was derived. According to that metaphysics, as we have already seen in several connections,[1] the universe was a rational and divine order of "peace" governed by law. Justice and right reason were hence immanent in the nature of things, and the state itself was based upon that universal law.

Marsilius' departure from the traditional theory of law results from the fact that he rejects this metaphysics of peace and order, and its concomitant emphasis on final causes. The naturalistic-biological context in which he centers his political philosophy has as consequence that, far from the state being based upon a subsistent moral law, law will rather be based upon the state, and will derive its essential characteristics from the attributes which that context had entailed for the state. Hence, just as there was an intelligible sense in which Marsilius' conceptions of the "perfection," the "peace," and the "unity" of the state could be regarded as specifically political, so too his conception of law involves a similar specificity in contrast to the moral and theological interpretation which the tradition had given to law. This contrast is pursued by Marsilius throughout his various analyses of the traditional divisions of law: human, natural, and divine. The very status of these divisions, moreover, exhibits marked differences from the tradition, involving at once a simplification of their relations and a new complexity in the theory of human law. Before treating these aspects, however, we must examine their initial bases in the general characteristics of law itself, as they are found in Marsilius' doctrine

[1] See above, pp. 14 ff., 37–38, 95 ff.

of the kinds of law, the essence of law, and the relation of law to justice.

(1) Like Thomas Aquinas, whose famous formulation sums up the antecedent tradition, Marsilius presents a classification of four different kinds or senses of law. But the only resemblance between the respective classifications is in the number. For Thomas, all four kinds of law, *qua* law, have the same essential characteristics, and there is an affirmative, consequential relation among them. They fall into an ordered hierarchy, with natural law derived by "participation" from the eternal law which is God's reason governing the universe,[2] while human law is derived from natural law by deduction and determination,[3] and divine law is derived partly from eternal law,[4] partly from natural law.[5] For Marsilius, on the other hand, the relation among his four kinds of law is entirely negative: they are related only by equivocation, as having the same name but no common content or source.[6] Thus the first two kinds which he lists are immediately discarded; at no point does either reappear.[7] The third kind, divine law, is similarly listed as a separate class, but without even a suggestion of any direct relation to the fourth kind, human law. For, as Marsilius had said at the outset, he was going to distinguish between the various meanings of "the *name* 'law' ";[8] these *nominal distinctions* are in no sense *derivations* of *concepts* or *things* one from another. Human law thus becomes entirely *sui generis,* requiring for its comprehension nothing outside the sphere of human society itself.

(2) For the antecedent tradition, since law is immanent in the rational order of the universe, the essence of law is reason.[9] Marsilius, on the other

[2] *S. theol.* II. I. qu.91. a.2.

[3] *Ibid.* II. I. qu.91. a.3; qu.95. a.2.

[4] *Ibid.* II. I. qu.91. a.4. ad I.

[5] *Ibid.* II. I. qu.98. a.5; qu.100. a.1; II. II. qu.57. a.2 ad 3.

[6] Thus Marsilius prefaces his list of the "kinds" of law as follows: "ne *propter nominis multiplicitatem* eveniat discolia, distinguere convenit intentiones seu significata huius nominis 'lex' " (I. x. 3).

[7] These first two kinds or meanings of "law" appear to be literal reinterpretations of Thomas' natural and eternal laws, with all their metaphysical aspects excluded. The first kind, "naturalis inclinatio sensitiva ad actionem aut passionem aliquam," reveals again Marsilius' interpretation of the "natural" as the primitive and non-rational. It corresponds not to Thomas' *lex naturalis* but to his "law of desire" (*lex fomitis*) or "sensuality" (*S. theol.* II. I. qu.91. a.6); thus both Marsilius and Thomas give the same illustration from St. Paul (Romans 7:23). The second kind of law bears a similar distant relation to Thomas' eternal law; whereas the latter refers to an *exemplar rerum artificiatarum* to illustrate analogically the *divine* creation and governance of the universe (*S. theol.* II. I. qu.93. a.1. Resp.), Marsilius uses the same phrase literally to indicate only a measure or pattern of objects made by *human* art: "forma rei operabilis existente in mente, a qua tamquam *exemplari* sive mensura formae *artificiatorum* proveniunt . . ." (I. x. 3).

[8] See above, n. 6.

[9] See Augustine *De libero arbitrio* I. vi (PL 32, 1229): "lex est ratio summa insita in natura." This definition is derived from Cicero *De legibus* I. vi. 18, from whom the tradition partly begins. Thomas Aquinas *S. theol.* II. I. qu.90. a.1. Resp.: "lex est aliquid pertinens ad rationem."

hand, distinguishes two aspects of law: "materially," it is the science or doctrine of civil justice and benefit; "formally," it is a coercive command. It is the latter aspect which constitutes the essence of law.[10] This applies to divine law as well as human law,[11] so that the two laws agree in their "form" although no specification is made, as with Aquinas, of any common "matter" or content. Thus, just as human law had been given a specifically human-social meaning, so law as such is given a specifically political definition, not a moral or a theological one.

(3) The medieval tradition, as a consequence of its equation of law with reason, is overwhelming in its insistence that there can be no law without justice, that an unjust law is not a law at all.[12] For Marsilius, on the other hand, since rationality is not essential to law, laws need not be just. Even unjust statutes—or, as he puts it, "false doctrines of matters of justice"—"become laws when there is given a command that they be observed, or when they are made by way of such a command."[13] For while every law, when viewed in itself (*secundum se*), as to its "matter" or content, must contain statements dealing with "what is just or unjust, beneficial or harmful" in relation to human acts,[14] those statements need not be "true" or "absolutely perfect." It is sufficient that they have the "proper form," that is, a coercive command, even if they lack a "proper condition," which would be "the proper and true ordering of matters of justice."[15]

Marsilius thus is a legal positivist, in contrast to the predominantly

[10] I. x. 4: "Alio modo considerari potest secundum quod de ipsius observatione datur praeceptum coactivum per poenam aut praemium in praesenti saeculo distribuenda, sive secundum quod per modum talis praecepti traditur, *et hoc modo considerata propriissime lex vocatur et est.*" See II. ix. 3. For the distinction of the "material" and "formal" aspects of law, see I. x. 5; I. xii. 2. Marsilius' use of the terms *materia* and *forma* in this connection is the opposite of the traditional Aristotelian view of their relations with respect to law; for justice was traditionally regarded as making good the claim of coercion to be "lawful," so that the normative factor provided the culminating "form" to the "matter" of coercion. See Thomas Aquinas *S. theol.* II. I. qu.95. a.3. Resp.; James of Viterbo *De reg. Christ.* II. vii (pp. 232–33).

[11] II. ix. 3.

[12] See Augustine *De libero arbitrio* I. v (PL 32, 1227): "non videtur esse lex quae justa non fuerit." Thomas Aquinas *S. theol.* II. I. qu.96. a.4. Resp.: "Injustae autem sunt leges dupliciter. . . Et hujusmodi magis sunt violentiae quam leges." See *ibid.* II. I. qu.90. a.I. ad 3; qu.92. a.I. ad 4; qu.95. a.2. Resp. Godfrey of Fontaines *Quodlib.* IV. qu.11 (II, 267): "Quod autem a lege naturali discordat est legis corruptela." Egidius of Rome *De reg. princ.* Lib. III. Pars II. cap. xxvi: "lex humana . . . debet esse justa, aliter non est lex sed corruptio legis." Dante *De mon.* II. v (p. 354): "si ad utilitatem eorum qui sunt sub lege leges directae non sunt, leges nomine solo sunt, re autem leges esse non possunt." James of Viterbo *De reg. Christ.* II. iv (p. 190): "Leges autem posite tales esse debent, ut per eas fiant homines boni et virtuosi; alias non sunt leges sed corruptiones legum." William of Ockham *Dialogus* Pars I. Lib. VI. cap. c (p. 630): "quaecumque lex civilis repugnat legi divinae vel rationi apertae, non est lex. . . ." This tradition also begins in good part from Cicero; cf. *De legibus* II. v. 11 ff.

[13] I. x. 5. [14] I. x. 4. [15] I. x. 5.

rationalist and normative tradition of the middle ages. It is here that his kinship is most manifest with that strand of Augustine's political philosophy which was neglected by most of the antecedent doctrines, the view that "true justice" is not essential to the state or its institutions.[16] This is a positivism, however, with respect not to justice but to law. Indeed, when Marsilius comes to consider the traditional normative concept of law as "the dictate of right reason in practical matters," he subsumes right reason under divine law and declares that in this meaning of the term "what is lawful (*licitum*) and what unlawful in the strict sense (*simpliciter*) must be determined according to divine law rather than human law."[17] Yet he also declares repeatedly that human law may "disagree" with divine law,[18] since it is not its rationality but its coerciveness which constitutes it a law. Thus only those acts which human law prohibits are punishable.[19] Indeed, it is precisely for this reason, as we shall see later, that divine law in this world is not a law at all.[20]

Marsilius' positivism thus consists not in a denial that there are objective norms of justice but rather in an insistence upon not confusing those norms with the precepts which effectively function as laws in the state. The criteria of such functioning are dependent not upon conformity to right reason or divine law but upon fulfillment of the conditions required for the adjudication of disputes and the regulation of other acts affecting the preservation of the state. And the assurance of this fulfillment is obtained by specifying not the content or matter of laws but rather their coercive form and the agency from which derive both that form and the matter on which it is imposed.

The effect of these differences from the tradition is found throughout Marsilius' discussion of law. A significant case in point is his definition of the fundamental operations of law: command, prohibition, permission.[21] Thomas Aquinas defines these operations by reference to the ethical quality of the acts which are their objects: a command is given for acts which are essentially good ("for law commands all the acts of

[16] See above, p. 38.

[17] II. xii. 8, 9. See II. xxiii. 3 *fin.* See below, pp. 149 ff. As an example of laws which are not just, Marsilius cites what occurs "in regionibus barbarorum," where it is decreed that "homicidam absolvi a culpa et poena civili, reale aliquod pretium exhibentem pro tali delicto" (I. x. 5). Similar instances had been used by other writers as examples of statutes contrary to natural law and hence not laws. See Thomas Aquinas *S. theol.* II. I. qu.94. a.4. Resp.: "apud Germanos olim latrocinium non reputabatur iniquum, cum tamen sit expresse contra legem naturae." Albert the Great *In Eth.* Lib. v. Tr. III. cap. ii (p. 368): "apud Trivallos fas est occidere parentes."

[18] II. x. 7; II. xii. 9; II. xiii. 2. On this point, see also below, p. 149, n. 16.

[19] See above, p. 122, n. 42.

[20] See below, pp. 154 ff.

[21] For a source of these concepts, see *Corp. jur. civ.*, *Digestum* I. iii. 7.

the virtues"), a prohibition for acts which are essentially bad, and a permission for those which are ethically indifferent. It is only as something additional that law also gives punishment: "that whereby law induces men to obey it is the fear of punishment; and in this respect punishment is posited as the effect of law."[22] As against these "material" definitions, Marsilius defines the operations of law "formally," that is, by the punishment they entail. A command is an "affirmative statute obliging its transgressor to punishment"; a prohibition is a negative statute similarly obliging; while a permission is an explicit or implicit ordinance "not obliging to punishment."[23] Thus Marsilius completely omits the "material" reference to the moral quality of the acts which are the objects of these operations.

2. HUMAN LAW

Although the ultimate basis of these departures from the normative legal orientation of the middle ages is to be found in Marsilius' withdrawal of the state from the moral-divine order under which it had traditionally been subsumed, their proximate basis consists in the function which he assigns to human law. As a consequence of that function and of its context in the whole state, the essential coerciveness of law does not mean that it is based upon arbitrary violence, nor does its non-essential relation to justice mean that there are no constitutional means to ensure that laws shall be just. On the contrary, Marsilius' distinction of law from justice involves in important respects a fuller guarantee that laws will be just than does his predecessors' insistence upon defining law by an essential derivation from justice. It is important for an understanding of Marsilius' political philosophy to grasp the motivation and the method of both the coercive and the just aspects of law.

Marsilius had derived his definition of law from Aristotle: "Law has coercive force, being discourse which proceeds from a kind of prudence and understanding."[1] This statement indicates, of course, the two aspects of coerciveness and rationality which Marsilius distinguishes as the "formal" and "material" aspects of law. But the interpretations it receives at the hands of Aristotle and Marsilius differ in important ways. For Aristotle, it is the rational aspect which both explains and justifies the coercive. His statement occurs in the last chapter of the *Nicomachean Ethics*, at the

[22] *S. theol.* II. I. qu.92. a.2. Resp. See *ibid.* II. I. qu.108. a.I. Resp., where the commands and prohibitions of divine law are similarly defined by reference to the theological quality of the acts which are their objects, i.e., by the acts' "necessary agreement or contrariety to interior grace." See below, p. 154.

[23] II. xii. 3, 4.

[1] *N. Eth.* x. 9. 1180a 21.

transition from ethics to politics; it concerns the means of carrying into effect the ethical precepts of that work. He has pointed out that "discourses" alone are insufficient to make men virtuous, for most men are amenable not to what is honorable but to fear and punishment.[2] Consequently, they must be habituated to virtue by a system based upon both prudence and coercion. The requisite coerciveness, however, is not possessed by parents or by any other private authority,[3] but only by public authority, whose instrument is the law. Aristotle's statement of the coerciveness of law, which occurs at this point, is thus pointed directly toward the moral end of habituating men to the virtues; and the same moral emphasis appears in the medieval Aristotelians and in the general ecclesiastic-political tradition.[4] The essence of law, consequently, will consist primarily in its moral, rational end and content; coercion is only a means to that end.

For Marsilius, on the other hand, as we have seen, political authority is directed not to "leading men to virtue" but rather to the adjudication of disputes and punishment of crimes; and this in order to preserve the state.[5] It is for this reason that the essence of law is its coerciveness, since it functions primarily as a punitive weapon, which is not attached to a content having a specifically moral end. Law, indeed, is correlative with government; it is the "form" of which the government is the "matter."[6] Hence, just as the doctrine of the unity of the government, which reserves all coercive authority in the state to the government, is a cardinal theme of the Marsilian politics, so the corresponding emphasis with regard to law is that it alone among "disciplines" or "standards" (*regulae*) of human acts has coercive authority. Thus the papalist view that divine and canon law are superior in political authority to human law because of their higher moral end undergoes the same refutation as was seen with respect to the relation between priesthood and government.[7]

As a consequence of these considerations, there is found throughout

[2] *Ibid.* 1179b 4 ff.

[3] *Ibid.* 1180a 19 ff.

[4] See Thomas Aquinas *S. theol.* II. I. qu.90. a.3. ad 2: "persona privata non potest inducere efficaciter ad virtutem; potest enim solum monere, sed si sua monitio non recipiatur, non habet vim coactivam, quam debet habere lex, ad hoc quod efficaciter inducat ad virtutem, ut Philosophus dicit." Augustinus Triumphus *S. de eccl. pot.* qu.44. a.1: "cum [lex] habet vim coactivam, ut Philosophus dicit, poenarum terrore et comminatione habet homines ad virtutem inducere et a malo retrahere." See also the much-cited dictum of Isidore of Seville *Sent.* Lib. III. a.51. n.4 (PL 83, 723): "Quod non praevalet sacerdos efficere per doctrinae sermonem, potestas hoc imperet per disciplinae terrorem." This statement is quoted by Hugh of Fleury *Tract. de regia pot. et sacerdotali dignitate* I. iv; II. v (MGH, *Libelli de lite,* II, 469, 493); Gregory of Catino *Orthodoxa defensio imperialis* cap. ii (*ibid.,* II, 536); Cardinal Humbert *Adversus simoniacos* III. 21 (*ibid.,* I, 226); Augustinus Triumphus *S. de eccl. pot.* qu.35. a.4.

[5] See above, pp. 106 ff.

[6] I. x. 1, 2; I. xiv. 10. See below, pp. 230, 237.

[7] See above, p. 108.

Marsilius' work an unprecedentedly sharp insistence upon the *coerciveness* of human law as against the non-coerciveness of all other "disciplines." This results in a lengthy list of specifications as to what the coerciveness involves, and from what it is distinguished. It is not the mere threat of punishment, but the ability to make good on the threat: human law alone "obligates" or "binds" its transgressors to punishment.[8] The punishment, moreover, must be "real or personal,"[9] and in the present world;[10] it is not the "spiritual" castigation or upbraiding which invokes punishment in the future world. Coercion is hence distinguished from correction by words,[11] and from power which is merely doctrinal, familial, theoretic, or practical.[12] It operates by material or corporeal means, not by spiritual or verbal ones;[13] it is by armed force, by dominating, by violent action or compulsion, by seizure or imprisonment, not merely by teaching, exhorting, arguing, correcting, or even frightening.[14]

Marsilius never tires of reiterating these distinctions, for it is by them that the operation of human law is distinguished from all pretenders which claim to be but are not such law. The principle of the distinctions is not, of course, new: it is found in the Aristotelian distinction between paternal and political power, and in the medieval distinction between the spiritual and material swords. What is new in Marsilius, however, is not only the exceptionally recurrent emphasis he gives to this coerciveness of human law and authority, but also the fact that it is at the same time

[8] II. xxv. 9: "Non enim Romano papae vel sibi cum clero tantummodo in communitate fidelium convenit leges aut decretales aliquas condere quemquam *obligantes ad poenam*." See II. v. 5.

[9] II. iv. 9: "cunctos subesse debere *realiter et personaliter* coactivo judicio. . . ." *Def. min.*, xv. 7: "praeceptum ad aliquem realiter vel personaliter compellendum." *Ibid.* i. 7: by the *Decretals* "compelli non potest aut debet quis ipsorum transgressorum poena vel supplicio reali vel personali."

[10] II. viii. 5.

[11] *Def. min.* iii. 2: "tales correctiones verborum sunt, *non coactivae,* arguendi videlicet seu increpandi delinquentes."

[12] *Ibid.* iv. 3: "Praefatarum autem potestatum sive auctoritatum *nulla coactiva* est, sed omnes sunt doctrinales vel oeconomicae, sive speculativae sive operativae." See *Def. pac.* II, viii. 4. Cf. the famous rejoinder which the French legist Pierre Flotte made to Pope Boniface VIII: "vestra potestas est verbalis, nostra autem realis" (quoted in J. Rivière, *Le Problème de l'église et de l'état au temps de Philippe le Bel* [Louvain, 1926], p. 121, n. 2). Cf. also John of Paris *De pot. reg. et pap.* cap. iii (p. 111); Hobbes *Leviathan* ch. xlvi (p. 373).

[13] *Def. min.* iii. 2: the "arma" of the priesthood "sunt spiritualia sive verbalia," but those of human law "carnalia sunt, quibus homines compelluntur, id est, materialia seu corporalia."

[14] *Def. pac.* II. xxviii. 17: "constat huiusmodi iuste compelli posse per iudicem coactivum et armatam potentiam secundum leges humanas." See II. v. 6. See the sharp contrasts which specify the "coercive" still more plainly; e.g., II. vii. 4: the priest, like the physician, cannot "compellere, sed solummodo exhortari et docere atque terrere per sui iudicium . . . prognosticum." II. ix. 4: "corrigendo, non tamen cogendo." II. ix. 5: "doceri . . . *cogi vero minime.*" II. x. 2: by the priest "docendus et exhortandus est homo in vita praesenti, arguendus, corripiendus peccator, atque terrendus iudicio seu prognostico futurae gloriae vel damnationis aeternae, *nequaquam cogendus.*" See also II. xxix. 12.

distinguished from moral and theological factors. The concept of the legal-political thus receives a specificity which it had previously attained only in such rare instances as Aristotle's book on revolutions and Augustine's positivist definition of the state.

Marsilius' theory of law is not, however, completely exhausted in this emphasis upon coerciveness. For he also insists upon the traditional Aristotelian doctrine of the rule of laws rather than of men. And he does so for reasons which reintroduce the concept of justice which he had distinguished from the essential definition of law. No man, not even the "best man," is completely lacking in perverted emotions and ignorance;[15] but "in the law is determined well-nigh perfectly what is just or unjust, beneficial or harmful, with respect to every human civil act."[16] Is this a contradiction to the admission made in the immediately preceding chapter that law may be unjust? So it has been held.[17] It is necessary, however, to look further into this whole conception of the rule of law by comparing Marsilius' position with that of Aristotle, for the same problems are to a large extent involved in both.

Despite the fact that Aristotle distinguishes between the rule of law and the rule of men, he does not, like the subsequent Ciceronian tradition, regard law as immanent in the universe or as a metaphysical standard based upon the nature of things.[18] The rule of law means that "laws rightly laid down must be dominant."[19] Aristotle recognizes the distinction between "unwritten law," or custom, and written law,[20] but he holds that both of these must be "laid down" or "posited" by men,[21] and he distinguishes, among the "parts of all constitutions," a "deliberative" which is "dominant . . . with regard to laws."[22] In this sense, then, all law is positive law for Aristotle.[23] The rule of law does not mean non-human agency: the laws which rule must be made by men.

Arist

Marsilius is even more insistent on this point. Law, as we have seen, is a coercive command; hence it must emanate from an efficient cause which has the authority or power to give such a command. When Marsilius considers the question of who is to make the laws, he brushes aside the agency of God as not relevant to his purpose: he intends to discuss "the establishment of only those laws and governments which emerge immediately from the decision of the human mind."[24] His interpretation

[15] I. xi. 6.

[16] I. xi. 3.

[17] Lagarde, *Marsile*, pp. 171–72.

[18] See Cicero *De legibus* I. xviii ff.

[19] *Pol.* III. 11. 1282b 2.

[20] *Ibid.* III. 16. 1287b 5.

[21] *Ibid.* VI. 5. 1319b 40. See *ibid.* III. 15. 1286a 23.

[22] *Ibid.* IV. 14. 1298a 4–5.

[23] No essential qualification needs to be made in this statement because of Aristotle's doctrine of natural justice; see below, pp. 147 ff.

[24] I. xii. 1.

of the rule of law, moreover, is accompanied by a literalness of emphasis which sharply separates his position from that of the "higher law" theorists. Thus when he quotes with approval Aristotle's statement that "laws rightly laid down must be dominant," he at once adds, "that is, rulers must govern in accordance with them."[25] The "rule of law" hence involves human efficient causality both in the making of law and in ruling in accordance with it.

What, then, can Aristotle and Marsilius hold to be the meaning of the distinction between the rule of laws and the rule of men? This problem is aggravated by the further fact that in not making justice essential to law Marsilius also follows Aristotle. For the latter holds that laws are made in function of constitutions;[26] but since some constitutions are unjust, so too are some laws.[27] Hence, Aristotle himself raises the question of what value there can be in the rule of law. His reply, which extends through many of the most fundamental passages of the *Politics,* may be summarized by means of two distinctions. By examining in turn Marsilius' position on each of these, we shall be able to find how in his Aristotelian doctrine of law he provides the analogue of Aristotle's own normative extension of the positive view of law sketched above.

(1) *Universality and particularity*. Law is a *universal* rule in the sense that it is posited to cover entire classes of situations. Hence it excludes, as such, the emotional vagaries which might lead a man, judging apart from such a universal rule, to apply different standards to those whom he likes or dislikes. In this sense, law is "reason without desire."[28] This distinction between the rule of law and the rule of men is equivalent to that between constitutional and non-constitutional states. For there is a constitution only when there are laws, which are universal regulations; but non-constitutional states rule only by special "decrees" (ψηφίσματα), and "it is impossible for a decree to be universal."[29] Thus even in oligarchy and democracy, which for Aristotle are "perverted" constitutions because in them rule is not exercised for the common benefit, there is the distinction between those species which are ruled by the law and those ruled by men, that is, by decree.[30]

Marsilius similarly makes universality essential to law. His generic definition of human law is the "*universal* judgment of civil justice and

[25] I. xi. 4. Note the three other similar interpolations made by Marsilius in this paragraph of the *Defensor pacis*.

[26] *Pol.* IV. I. 1289a 13.

[27] *Ibid.* III. 10. 1281a 22; 11. 1282b 8; IV. 8. 1294a 7. *N. Eth.* V. I. 1129b 25.

[28] *Pol.* III. 16. 1287a 28. See *ibid.* III. 15. 1286a 16.

[29] *Ibid.* IV. 4. 1292a 37.

[30] *Ibid.* IV. 4. 1292a 7–10, 1292a 28–1293a 34.

benefit";[31] it is of this definition that justice and coerciveness, "matter" and "form," are the two aspects.[32] Hence, while the coercive "form" is the essence of law, whereas the just "matter" is separable therefrom, the coerciveness must always be attached to a "universal judgment." Marsilius frequently insists upon this universality.[33] It is indeed entailed by his basic conception of the function of coercive law and government in the state. Thus he points out that in the original familial units out of which grew the village and the state the father was able to "punish domestic injuries *entirely according to his will and pleasure,*" because they affected his family alone. But in the village, partiality in the administration of justice "was not allowed," for it would have led to "the fighting and separation of the villagers."[34] This is still more true in the state: its very preservation requires a "standard of justice"[35] whereby the "excesses" of transient acts "are corrected and reduced to equality or due proportion."[36] The justice here involved is, of course, what Aristotle calls rectificatory justice:[37] it must be impartial but, as Marsilius has said, it need not be "absolutely just."[38]

(2) *Absolute and relative justice.* By this further distinction Aristotle separates the rule of law from the rule of men within constitutional states themselves. For while such states are all ruled by the application of impartial or universal standards, those standards may not be absolutely just. The justice here involved is distributive rather than rectificatory. Like so many of Aristotle's terms, "justice" involves a sliding scale. Every law is just "in some sense" (πως), relatively to the specific constitution under which it has been enacted.[39] Insofar as law is universal, it is impartial and preserves a mean between giving individuals in it more or less than they deserve. But this desert may itself be evaluated by different criteria or final causes, which in turn define different constitutions: freedom in democracies, wealth in oligarchies, virtue in kingdoms and aristocracies.[40] Of these criteria, virtue is the best; it defines the "common benefit," the final cause which distinguishes absolutely just constitutions from those which are only relatively just.[41] In this sense, the rule of law means not

[31] I. x. 3.

[32] I. x. 4.

[33] I. xi. 1: "lex . . . non enim facta est ad amicum aut inimicum utilem vel nocivum, sed *universaliter* ad agentem civiliter bene aut male." I. xiv. 7: "lex sub rigoris universalitate comprehendit. . . ."

[34] I. iii. 4.

[35] I. iv. 4: "oportuit in hac communicatione statuere iustorum regulam. . . ."

[36] I. v. 7.

[37] *N. Eth.* v. 4. 1131b 25 ff.

[38] I. x. 5.

[39] *N. Eth.* v. 1. 1129b 11–25.

[40] *Ibid.* v. 2. 1131a 25–31.

[41] *Pol.* III. 13. 1284a 2. See *ibid.* III. 9. 1281a 3–8; III. 13. 1284b 24; VII. 9. 1328b 38. See below, pp. 203–4.

merely impartiality or universality, but the various discriminations of distributive justice whereby political offices and rewards go to the most virtuous. Since such superiority in virtue exists objectively, and virtue, unlike other qualities, is essential to good government, it follows that laws which award political power on this ground are recognitions of a "natural order" rather than arbitrary enactments.[42] In this normative context, the rule of law means the observance of absolute justice, and no law can be unjust.[43]

This specification of law by final causes is closely matched by the medieval tradition's own interpretation of virtue and the highest good. And it is precisely on this point that Marsilius departs from Aristotle. To be sure, he takes over the position that "that law is best which is made for the common benefit of the citizens," [44] and it is with the common benefit that he equates justice.[45] But, as we have seen,[46] Marsilius does not introduce the discriminations by which Aristotle tied the common benefit to virtue conceived in the highest terms. For Marsilius, the common benefit remains rather at the general level of the "sufficient life" desired by all men. Hence, where Aristotle had specified the efficient cause of law and government by the final cause of the state, so that because virtue was the highest good aristocracy or kingship was the best possible constitution, Marsilius treats virtue only instrumentally, as an efficient cause toward a largely undifferentiated end. He does echo Aristotle's emphasis upon "proper proportion" in making democracy one of the "diseased" forms of government [47] and in his concept of the weightier part of the citizens as determined by quality as well as quantity.[48] But the differences here involved make themselves felt but little at the highest level of legislative authority,

[42] Such a rule of law may require either political equality among men or the supremacy of one or a few. See *Pol.* III. 16. 1287a 13: "for persons similar in nature, it is necessary that there be the same justice and the same value in accordance with nature. . . But *this is already law; for order is law.* Therefore it is preferable for the law to rule than some one of the citizens." At the other extreme, if there are outstanding persons who are like "God among men . . . with regard to such persons there is not law, for *they are themselves law*" (*ibid.* III. 13. 1284a 13). The same supremacy is found even in "perverted" states which are "lawful" in this sense; see *ibid.* IV. 4. 1292a 8: "in democracies which are in accordance with law, a demagogue does not arise, but the best of the citizens are in positions of preëminence."

[43] Thus in reference to the best possible state, Aristotle writes that "it is not lawful to rule not only justly but also unjustly" (*Pol.* VII. 2. 1324b 28).

[44] I. xii. 5; see *Pol.* III. 13. 1283b 40.

[45] See I. xii. 5, where Marsilius quotes Aristotle as follows: *"Rectum autem forte* (in legibus scilicet) *ad conferens civitatis et ad commune civium."* This, except for the interpolated phrase, is William of Moerbeke's translation of *Pol.* III. 13. 1283b 40; it is ambiguous because William rendered Aristotle's ἴσως, meaning "equally," as *forte,* meaning "perhaps." Marsilius regularly couples *justum* with *conferens commune* or *civile;* see I. v. 3; I. x. 3, 4, 5, 6; I. xi. 1, 3; I. xii. 2, 8, and *passim.*

[46] See above, p. 64.

[47] I. viii. 3.

[48] I. xii. 3. See below, pp. 190 ff.

for all the citizens constitute the legislator. At the secondary level, the ruler who executes the laws, Marsilius also stresses the importance of moral and intellectual virtue,[49] but even here virtue creates no "natural" right, for election by the people is insisted upon as the efficient cause of government as well as of law.[50]

If, then, he does not follow Aristotle in specifying the nature of law by its highest final cause, what addition besides impartiality must be made to Marsilius' initial definition of law in his defense of the rule of law? It is in keeping with the basic orientation of his political philosophy that the further specification in question is placed by Marsilius in the efficient cause of the law. When he puts the essence of law in its being a "coercive command," he indicates that this command "is given" by someone,[51] and that this giver is a human authority.[52] Law hence involves not mere coerciveness, even applied impartially; it must emanate from those who have the *authority* to coerce. And this authority, as he subsequently shows, can belong only to the people.[53] Hence his full definition of law provides that it is "the command of the *whole body of citizens.*"[54] Any statute which has emanated from someone who lacks such legislative authority is "completely null."[55] Consequently, the Decretals or *jura canonica* based upon the papal authority *"are not, as such, laws divine or human,"* for "inasmuch as they have been made by the Roman bishop, together with his college of clergymen, *without authorization by the faithful legislator or ruler* . . . such statutes bind no one to any guilt or punishment, especially temporal."[56] And as if to emphasize this separation of law from mere unauthorized coercion, Marsilius adds that the makers of these Decretals "induce everyone to observe them by means of crafty words, as it were *coercing* them by threatening their simple transgressors with eternal damnation."[57]

It is from the people as efficient cause of the law that Marsilius derives that justice which his predecessors had derived through the dependence

[49] I. xiv. See, however, below, p. 243.

[50] I. xv. 2. See I. xv. I.

[51] I. x. 4.

[52] I. x. 6: "Comprehenduntur autem sub hac legis acceptione omnes iustorum et conferentium civilium regulae *auctoritate humana* institutae. . . ."

[53] I. xii. 3. See I. xii. 2, where the making of law "secundum ultimam significationem et propriam," i.e., as coercive command, is distinguished from the mere *inquisitio* and *inventio* of law viewed *materialiter,* which can best be done by experts. See also below, pp. 168 ff.

[54] *Def. min.* i. 4: "Lex vero humana est praeceptum universitatis civium. . . ."

[55] II. xxv. 7.

[56] II. xxviii. 29 (p. 468). See *Def. min.* xiv. 2: "non sunt tamen nec dici debent *leges* ordinationes huiusmodi, sed potius documenta seu regulae. . . ." See II. v. 5; II. xxiii. 13. On the other hand, before he has identified the legislator as the people, Marsilius lists *decretales* together with "consuetudines, statuta, plebiscita" as examples of laws (I. x. 6).

[57] II. xxviii. 29.

of human law upon some higher law. Thus the arguments he presents for the people as legislator are almost exactly parallel to those he gives to show the final cause of law, i.e., the value of the "rule of law." In each case the same volitional and intellectual qualities are invoked: volitionally, both the people [58] and the law [59] aim impartially at the common benefit; intellectually, both the people [60] and the law [61] are best able to determine what is just, that is, what is for the common benefit. Moreover, the arguments against legislation by one or a few men, rather than by the whole people, are the same as those used against the rule of men without law: in each case stress is laid upon the inevitable perversion to private interests either of laws made by a limited group,[62] or of judgments made at the ruler's own discretion without law.[63] We shall examine these arguments for the people's possession of legislative authority in the following chapter. But it can be seen that the justice which justifies the rule of law thus emerges not from some higher law nor from the conditions embodied in ideal ends, but rather from the agency of the people which makes the law: it emerges from the efficient rather than from the final cause of the law.

If, then, the laws made by the people will embody such thoroughgoing justice, why does Marsilius refuse to make justice essential to law? It is not too difficult to surmise the considerations underlying this refusal, on the basis of the doctrinal and institutional developments of his time. Such essentiality would open the way to the consequences of papal interference and anarchy. For if the "lawfulness" of a law depends directly upon its justice, then agencies other than the whole people can proclaim themselves the "judges" of such justice. This was the papalist procedure through its theologizing and consequent papalizing of morality. Thus Augustinus Triumphus, declaring that "every just law depends upon divine law," at once concludes from this that human law "depends upon the authority of the pope." [64] The same inference from justice to papal

[58] I. xii. 8. "Volunt omnes aut plurimi legem convenientem communi civium conferenti." I. xii. 5: "Ex universa multitudine magis attenditur legis communis utilitas . . . quod non fieret si per unum aut paucos quosdam, proprium magis quam commune attendentes commodum, lex ipsa feratur. *Hanc quoque sententiam satis adjuvant quae de legum necessitate assignavimus in XI° hujus.*"

[59] I. xi. 1: "Lex omni caret affectione perversa; non enim facta est ad amicum aut inimicum utilem vel nocivum, sed universaliter ad agentem civiliter bene aut male."

[60] I. xiii. 6: "congregata multitudo discernere potest et velle amplius commune justum et conferens harum partium quacumque seorsum accepta quantumcumque prudentum."

[61] I. xi. 3: "in ipsa [lege] determinatum est quasi perfecte, quid justum aut injustum, conferens aut nocivum, secundum unumquemque humanum actum civilem."

[62] I. xii. 5, 8; I. xiii. 5.

[63] I. xi. 2, 6.

[64] *S. de eccl. pot.* qu.44. a.1: "Omnis ergo justa lex dependet a lege divina . . . *Illo ergo jure lex imperialis dependet ab auctoritate papae quo jure dependet a lege divina,* cujus ipse

control is also made by other papalists.[65] From this will also result all the divisions and disorder which the traditional conception of a "higher law" did in fact entail, since the very legality of laws may always be attacked by appealing to a justice above the laws.[66] The same result follows if, with Thomas Aquinas, one holds that "legal laws" must have not only the proper "author" or efficient cause but also the proper "end" and "form." [67] A specific case in point is that of the Roman law tradition, for here law was based both upon the people's authority and upon justice. Thus, on the one hand, *lex* is defined in the *Institutes* as that written *jus* "which the Roman people has enacted at the request of the senatorial magistrate, such as the consuls"; [68] and Isidore of Seville similarly declares that *lex* is "the enactment of the people." [69] But on the other hand, whereas Marsilius makes *lex* identical with *jus*,[70] these other writers make *lex* a species of *jus* [71] and hence dependent for its legality upon its justice. As a consequence, however, the Roman tradition was faced by the problem of the constancy of the conjunction of the two factors of the efficient and final causes, the "people's" will and justice, which were conjoined in the definition. Thus the pseudo-Irnerius, having defined *jus* as "enacted equity" or "authority together with equity," declares that an enactment by "authority" is sometimes found lacking in "equity." Nevertheless, such an inequitable decree is still called *jus,* although "improperly," for "it is enacted by him who ought to enact equity." [72] But it is contradictory to define law as equity and then to call even inequitable statutes laws; moreover, to say that such laws are "improperly" so called is to invite the further step that the statutes in question are not laws at all. By not making justice an essential part of the definition of law, therefore, Marsilius avoids these results. While laws to be laws must be made by the people, and will as a consequence be just, it is not their justice but rather their emanating from

papa est vicarius et minister potissime. . . Unde nulla lex populo Christiano est danda nisi ipsius papae auctoritate. . . ." See *ibid.* qu.44. a.4.

[65] See James of Viterbo *De reg. Christ.* II. viii (pp. 260–61); Egidius of Rome *De eccl. pot.* II. vi (pp. 69–70).

[66] See J. Dickinson, *The Statesman's Book of John of Salisbury* (New York, 1927), p. xxx; F. Kern, *Kingship and Law in the Middle Ages,* trans. S. B. Chrimes (Oxford, 1939), pp. 200–203.

[67] *S. theol.* II. I. qu.96. a.4. Resp.

[68] *Corp. jur. civ., Inst.* I. ii. 4.

[69] *Etymologiae* v. x. I (PL 82, 200).

[70] II. xii. 3. See *Def. min.* i. 2: "jus autem idem est quod lex."

[71] *Corp. jur. civ., Inst.* I. ii. 3. Isidore *Etymol.* v. ii. 3 (PL 82, 199). See also the repetition of Isidore's formula in *Corp. jur. can., Decretum Gratiani* Pars I. dist. I. can. 1–3; dist. 2. can. I; and in Thomas Aquinas *S. theol.* II. II. qu. 57. a. I. ad 2. The same essential dependence of law upon justice may also be propounded by making *lex* the basic term instead of *jus.* See Cicero *De legibus* I. vi. 19.

[72] *Quaestiones de juris subtilitatibus* I. ii (pp. 54–55). Cf. *Corp. jur. civ., Dig.* I. i. II.

the people's authority which constitutes them laws. On the other hand, many "standards of human acts" other than those emanating from the people may embody justice, but they are not thereby laws. Such are the papalist Decretals, some of which, Marsilius admits, "may contain many useful teachings and counsels." [73]

The same consideration serves to explain why Marsilius, despite his emphasis upon the preservation of the state, does not give an "objective" definition of law as that "proportion" among men whose preservation preserves society and whose destruction destroys it.[74] For the question would still remain of how this proportion is to be determined and enforced. What is necessary for the preservation of the state is that there be a uniform and binding method of settling disputes, and that this method emanate from the people. From Marsilius' point of view, therefore, the definition of law as that proportion which preserves the state gives not the proximate essence or efficient cause of law, but a consequent of it which is itself explained by the concept it is supposed to explain.

It is also the fact that the people is the efficient cause of the law which removes the apparent opposition between Marsilius' emphasis upon coercion and his voluntarism. The coercive is contrary to the voluntary; [75] coercive law and judgment will inflict punishment upon a transgressor of the law even against his will *(etiam non volentem);* [76] and yet it is from the "election or will" of the whole body of citizens that the law emanates.[77] Hence the source of the coercion is collectively the same as the individuals who severally undergo it. The situation here is precisely the same as in the case of government: there is a double flow of authority from the whole people to the law which they establish, and from the law to the individuals who violate it or whose disputes require settlement through it. It is only by ignoring the former aspect that Marsilius' definition of law as coercive command can be made to appear as mere violence.[78] In order

[73] II. xxviii. 29.

[74] See Dante *De mon.* II. v (p. 354): "Ius est realis et personalis hominis ad hominem proportio, quae servata hominum servat societatem, et corrupta corrumpit." See Aristotle *N. Eth.* v. I. 1129b 18.

[75] See II. xxviii. 19: "Spontanei, non coacti. . . ." II. xviii. 6: "Gratuite, non coacte. . . ." Marsilius does not examine the traditional scholastic doctrines of the kinds of coercion. See, e.g., the distinctions of Alexander of Hales (*Summa universae theologiae* Lib. II. Membrum I. cap. iv [III, 731]) between *coactio absoluta* and *conditionalis* (also in Augustinus Triumphus *S. de eccl. pot.* qu.24. a.1); of Thomas Aquinas between acts done *per metum* and *per vim* (*S. theol.* II. I. qu.6. a.6. ad 1); of Durand of St. Pourçain between *impeditio ab actu convenienti* and *compulsio ad actum repugnantem* (*In Sent.* Lib. III. dist. 25. qu.4. pars 3 [fol. 148*r*]). The first two distinctions are derived from Aristotle *N. Eth.* III. I. 1110a 1 ff.

[76] II. xxx. 4.

[77] I. xii. 3.

[78] See Lagarde, *Marsile,* p. 171: "La loi est ce que tu dois faire si tu ne veux pas être pendu. Inutile de continuer l'entretien."

to be efficacious, law must be coercive; [79] and it is by its coerciveness that law differs from all other "standards" of human acts; but this does not mean that men are always being coerced or that they obey only under coercion.

The significance of these basic aspects of law emerges further in the reorientations they give to the concepts of natural and divine law.

3. NATURAL LAW

Marsilius' discussion of natural law is brief but highly revealing of his whole philosophic attitude. As we have seen, he did not list natural law in his initial nominal distinctions of the meanings of "law." [1] Natural law thus does not constitute a separate kind of law, as in the antecedent tradition; it is merely positive human law with a certain qualification, or else it is not a law at all. Thus, while Marsilius purports to be simply restating the doctrine of natural justice which Aristotle presents in the *Nicomachean Ethics,* his restatement exhibits significant divergences from that doctrine, from the tradition of commentaries on it, and from the whole medieval conception of natural law.

Aristotle differentiates "natural" and "legal" justice as the two species of "political justice," which comprises all the virtues viewed as functioning in some state and as prescribed by its laws.[2] The distinction between natural and legal justice is in important respects the same as that which is expressed in the *Politics* between absolute and relative justice, or between the absolutely best constitution and other constitutions.[3] Natural justice is defined as "that which has the same validity (δύναμιν) everywhere, and does not depend upon men's thinking one way or another." [4] The universality expressed by the word "everywhere" (πανταχοῦ) is thus a universality not of opinions or beliefs, let alone of positive laws or enactments, but rather of objective validity.[5] Natural justice is that justice whose deserts are based upon virtue rather than upon such other criteria as wealth

[79] The same point is made by Thomas Aquinas *S. theol.* II. II. qu.67. a.1. Resp.: "sicut lex generalis . . . ita etiam sententia judicis debet habere vim coactivam, per quam constringatur utraque pars ad servandam sententiam judicis; *alioquin judicium non esset efficax.*"

[1] See above, p. 133.

[2] *N. Eth.* v. 7. 1134b 18 ff. Cf. *ibid.* v. 1. 1129b 12 ff.; v. 6 1134a 25 ff.

[3] *Pol.* III. 6. 1279a 19; III. 13. 1284b 24; IV. 8. 1294a 8; VII. 9. 1328b 38. See *N. Eth.* v. 7. 1135a 3: "the things which are just not by nature but by human enactment are not the same everywhere, since neither are the constitutions the same, but there is only one constitution which is everywhere in accordance with nature, the best." (It should be pointed out that the interpretation of this passage is made difficult by questions of punctuation as well as by other problems.) Thus natural justice will not be found in every state to the same degree.

[4] *N. Eth.* v. 7. 1134b 19. See also above, p. 54.

[5] See *Pol.* I. 6. 1255a 31. See above, pp. 141–42.

or freedom, which are the determinants of justice in states whose constitutions are not absolutely just. Now virtue itself is "determined by reason and as the prudent man would determine it." [6] Hence natural justice is the political embodiment of practical reason or prudence. As such, however, it is an ideal or limiting case; it is not determined by what all or most men think, for it "does not depend upon men's thinking one way or another."

The tradition of commentaries on this doctrine of natural justice was influenced more by Cicero than by Aristotle himself. For Cicero, all law is based upon nature and reason; [7] but these are now immanent in the entire universe, and reason is shared by all men. Hence natural right (*jus*) ceases to be an ideal limit, as with Aristotle, and becomes instead the moral principles recognized as just by all men.[8] The universality of natural law becomes a matter not of universal rational *validity,* as with Aristotle, but rather of universal rational *belief;* it is no longer specifically ethical but rather dialectical and rhetorical because based upon the common opinion of all.[9] And it is this psycho-sociological approach which predominates in the interpretations of commentators on Aristotle's text. Thus Heliodorus expounds natural justice as that which "is thought just by all"; [10] the anonymous Greek commentator says that it is what is believed "among most men," specifying these as men who are "normal and in accordance with nature"; [11] Albert the Great, after quoting Cicero, redefines Aristotle's natural justice as "that which reason, informed from the principles of reason alone . . . dictates to each person"; [12] and Thomas Aquinas, referring both to Cicero and to the Roman lawyers, renders Aristotle's concept as "that justice with which nature has endowed the human mind," comprising "principles naturally known," akin to the self-evident principles of theoretic sciences.[13]

[6] *N. Eth.* II. 6. 1107a 1. [7] *De legibus* I. vi. 19. [8] *Ibid.* I. vii. 23; I. xii. 33.

[9] It is significant that in the *Rhetoric* Aristotle gives definitions which are almost identical with those of Cicero: "common law" is "whatever unwritten things seem *agreed to by all*" (*Rhet.* I. 10. 1368b 9); "There is by nature a common justice and injustice *which all somewhat divine. . . .*" (I. 13. 1373b 6). The *Rhetoric,* however, presents not Aristotle's own philosophic doctrines but rather materials useful for persuasion. See *ibid.* I. 2. 1356a 30 ff.

[10] *In Ethica Nicomachea paraphrasis* v. x (*Commentaria in Aristotelem Graeca* [Berlin, 1889], XIX, 101): πᾶσι δίκαιον δοκεῖ.

[11] *In Eth. Nic. commentaria* v. x (*ibid.,* XX, 232). See, to similar effect, Michael of Ephesus *In Eth. Nic.* v. x (*ibid.,* XXII, 46–47).

[12] *In Eth.* Lib. v. Tr. III. cap. iii (p. 367).

[13] *In Eth.* Lib. v. Lect. 12. nn. 1017–23 (p. 340). This mode of interpretation has continued into modern discussions; see F. Pollock, "The History of the Law of Nature," in *Essays in the Law* (London, 1922), p. 33, where it is said that for Aristotle, "Rules of natural justice are those which are universally recognized among civilized peoples." See also John Buridan *Quaestiones super Ethic. Arist.* Lib. v. qu. 19–20 (Paris, 1518), fols. 104*v*–105*r*. For similar conceptions of natural justice or law in Aristotelians who were not commenting on the *Ethics,* see Egidius of Rome *De reg. princ.* Lib. III. Pars II. cap. xxiv; Duns Scotus *Op.*

Marsilius' interpretation of Aristotle's natural law or justice represents the furthest extreme of the orientation of the commentators. As was to be expected from his general approach to law, natural law is given a completely positivistic meaning. He takes over the commentators' aspect of universal acceptance, but this acceptance is now no longer based upon reason or final causes but rather upon explicit legislative enactment: "natural law (*jus naturale*), according to Aristotle in the fifth book of the *Ethics,* means *that statute of the legislator* with respect to which almost all men agree that it is honorable and should be observed."[14] Such statutes *"depend upon human enactment,"* but are called "natural" since, like the acts of irrational beings, they are believed lawful in the same way everywhere. Marsilius' exclusively physical view of the "natural" thus leads him to base the universality of natural law not upon universal rational apprehension, like his predecessors, but only upon universal occurrence in the manner of physical objects.

But Marsilius is also aware that his predecessors mean by "natural law" the moral dictates of "right reason," and he points out that natural law in this sense is usually placed under divine law.[15] What, however, is the relation of this view of natural law to the first one propounded by Marsilius? Obviously the two do not completely coalesce, for not all rules of right reason are human "laws" in the sense of having coercive sanctions attached to them by the legislative authority, and conversely not all human laws are rational, "for in some things they fall away from right reason."[16] This latter point is, of course, the reiteration of Marsilius' unique position that justice is not essential to law. But he now goes still further. Even apart from legislative enactment, if "natural law" be taken with the previous tradition as meaning self-evident rules of justice, then it is not the same

---

Oxon. III. dist. 37. qu. I. n. 2 (XV, 783–84); John of Jandun *Quaest. in Metaphys.* II. qu. 11 (fol. 34Q ff.). It is significant of the further influence of this "Ciceronian" interpretation of Aristotle, that when Father Mersenne in the seventeenth century wished to show that the idea of God is innate because universally held, he explicitly used the phrase whereby Aristotle (as translated by William of Moerbeke) had defined natural justice. Cf. Mersenne *Quaestiones celeberrimae in Genesim* cap. i. vers. I. art. 8 (Paris, 1623), col. 41.

[14] II. xii. 7.

[15] II. xii. 8. For the tradition here referred to, which subsumes natural law under divine law, see Cicero *De re publica* III. xxii. 33; *Corp. jur. civ., Institutes* I. ii. 11; Isidore of Seville *Etymologiae* v. ii. I (PL 82, 198); *Corp. jur. can., Decret. Gratiani* Pars I. dist. I, and the gloss of Gratian. The civilians and canonists continue this tradition. See Carlyle, *Hist. of Mediaeval Political Theory,* II, 29 ff., 102 ff. On the other hand, cf. Thomas Aquinas *S. theol.* II. I. qu.91. a.4.

[16] II. xii. 8: "in quibusdam a recta ratione deficiunt." Both from the context and from Marsilius' other discussions of law it is clear that the extent to which human law may thus *deficere* is far more extreme than the divergences from natural law which Thomas Aquinas allows to human law because of the latter's particularity. See *S. theol.* II. I. qu.94. a.4. Resp. and ad 2; II. II. qu.57. a.2. ad I; and compare *ibid.* II. I. qu.93. a.3. ad 2.

as natural law in the sense of the dictates of right reason; for "many" such dictates are not self-evident to all men, and consequently are not universally admitted or accepted. Hence Marsilius concludes that the term "natural" is used equivocally in these two interpretations of natural law.[17]

Now this general problem of the non-universality of natural law was a very old one. For Aristotle the problem was of the following kind: If natural justice is that which has the same validity everywhere, then why does no rule of justice have universal *validity* or *applicability?* For the subsequent Ciceronian tradition, on the other hand, the problem was: If all men are rational, and natural law consists in rational rules, then why do not all men *accept* or *believe* them? [18] Aristotle's answer was to point out that "the matter of practical affairs" is itself variable; it is this which makes equity necessary as a supplement to justice.[19] But the Ciceronian tradition's answer was to ascribe variability not to the subject matter of justice but rather to the men who evaluate that subject matter. Thus from Cicero to Thomas Aquinas it was pointed out that bad customs and pleasures corrupt men's reasons and prevent a universal acceptance of the rational rules of justice.[20]

The Ciceronian tradition, however, also emphasized, together with the vagaries of men, the common rationality of all the rules of natural law. Thus Thomas Aquinas distinguishes between the primary and the secondary precepts of natural law, the former being the "most common" principles of practical reason and self-evident to all men, while the latter are the "proper conclusions" deduced from the former and not equally known to all.[21] This distinction is equivalent to that between *jus naturale* and *jus gentium*.[22] But when Marsilius says that the word "natural" is used "equivocally" when it is viewed as referring both to what is self-evident and hence universally accepted, and to what is in accordance with right

[17] II. xii. 8: "Verum 'naturale' hic et supra aequivoce dicitur."

[18] In this "Ciceronian" form the argument against natural law goes back to the Greek sophists and skeptics. See the restatement of the arguments of Carneades in Cicero *De re pub.* III. viii ff. See also John Locke's arguments against innate ideas (*Essay concerning Human Understanding* I. ii–iii). It is significant that innateness is attributed to natural law by Cicero himself (*Rhetorici libri de inventione* II. xxii. 65); this is repeated by Albert the Great *In Eth.* Lib. v. Tr. III. cap. iii (p. 367) and by Thomas Aquinas *In Eth.* Lib. v. Lect. 12. n. 1017 (p. 340). See also Father Mersenne, above, n. 13.

[19] *N. Eth.* v. 10. 1137b 12 ff.; see *ibid.* I. 3. 1094b 12 ff. See above, p. 46.

[20] Cicero *De legibus* I. xii. 33. Michael of Ephesus *In Eth. Nic.* v. x (*Comm. in Arist. Graeca*, XXII, 46). Albert the Great *In Eth.* Lib. v. Tr. III. cap. iii (p. 369). Thomas Aquinas *S. theol.* II. I. qu.94. a.4. Resp.; a.6. Resp. Thomas also invokes here, however, the Aristotelian answer of the variability of practical affairs as such. See also Locke's *Second Treatise of Civil Government* viii. 111; ix. 128.

[21] *S. theol.* II. I. qu.94. a.4. Resp.

[22] *Ibid.* II. I. qu.95. a.4. Resp. See also Albert the Great *In Eth.* Lib. v. Tr. III, cap. iii (p. 370).

reason, he is refusing to recognize the implicative connection which Thomas had indicated between these. As he points out elsewhere, the fact that a practice is widespread has nothing to do with its value.[23] It is to be noted that whereas Aquinas views the "self-evident" in terms of the "practical reason," Marsilius views it simply in terms of universal belief, agreement, and enactment, without indicating in any way that such universality may have a rational basis. Consequently he is not forced to find a logical or rational relation between such self-evident, universally accepted beliefs and those "many" propositions which, while they "are in accordance with the dictate of right reason," are nevertheless "not self-evident to all men." His statement that these two senses of natural law are related only by equivocation is along precisely the same lines as his initial distinction of the four meanings of "law" as having only the name in common, without any common essence or content.[24] His method of literal definition confines the term "law" to coercive commands made by proper legislative authority. To be sure, he goes on to say that "what is lawful and what unlawful in the strict sense (*licitum et illicitum simpliciter*) must be viewed in accordance with divine law rather than human law." [25] But, as we have seen, this strict lawfulness, which is absolute justice, is both distinct from and not the necessary basis of the human "laws" which Marsilius accepts as genuine laws in the state.[26]

Marsilius' discussion of natural law is thus in keeping with his basic devaluation of reason and his separation of specifically political concepts from the moral connotations by which they had traditionally been interpreted. It brings out sharply the sense in which he is a positivist and a voluntarist. His discussion amounts, in fact, to a rejection of natural law in the traditional sense of a body of principles which, in virtue of their own rationality, are self-evident to all rational beings and are hence anterior to and conditions of the legality of all positive law. Marsilius' natural law simply *is* positive law; it is in no sense a norm to which positive law must correspond. Hence once again the "unity" of the state and of its political authority is preserved: natural law presents no challenge to the supremacy of the laws made by the people of the state.

It is, indeed, in the will of the people that Marsilius finds the equivalent of natural law in something corresponding to the traditional sense. Not only is the state itself based upon the "natural desire" of all men for a sufficient life and their consequent "natural impulse" to live in the state, but the desire of all or most men for good laws is itself guaranteed by the

[23] See I. xvi. 17, 23. [24] See above, p. 133. [25] II. xii. 9.
[26] See above, pp. 134–35; also I. x. 5, and below, pp. 162–64.

"nature" to which human desire belongs.[27] This "nature," however, is biological rather than moral and rational; it hence functions not as a moral limit above positive law but rather as the originative source below it. But its political consequence is that the explicit will of the whole people, and not rules of right reason supposedly apprehended by each person, is to be the check upon the legality of laws.[28]

4. DIVINE LAW

It will be recalled that in Marsilius' initial distinctions of the various senses of "law," the third meaning had referred to divine laws, or, as he also calls them, "religions" (*sectae*).[1] Now law in this sense has no essential connection with law in the fourth and "most proper" sense of coercive command, although the two may sometimes coalesce.[2] It is with the conditions which negate such coalescence in the present world that Marsilius' discussion of divine law is chiefly preoccupied.

From this point of view, Marsilius' rejection of the Old Testament or Mosaic law[3] takes on added significance. Does this law contain anything which is still binding upon Christians? Like Thomas Aquinas, Marsilius declares that the "legal" and "ceremonial" commands of the Old Testament were abrogated with the advent of Christ.[4] But Thomas contrasts with these the "moral" commands, which can be reduced to the ten commandments,[5] and which, since they all pertain to natural law and hence are essentially in conformity with reason,[6] cannot be abrogated or dispensed with, but always retain their validity.[7] Marsilius, on the other hand, completely ignores these moral commands belonging to natural law. To the legal and ceremonial commands which have been abrogated he contrasts not, like Thomas, the "natural" basis of these "positive" commands, but rather those ceremonial commands which bear upon the giving of sacrifices and hostages for the redemption of sins; and his point with regard to these is that "no one was compelled to fulfill them by pain or

[27] I. xiii. 2. See above, pp. 57 ff.; below, pp. 208 ff.

[28] For further aspects of Marsilius' conception of natural law, see above, pp. 144 ff., and below, pp. 211–12, 213–14.

[1] See above, p. 133.

[2] I. x. 7.

[3] See above, p. 72.

[4] II. ix. 10. See Thomas *S. theol.* II. I. qu.103. a.4. Resp.; qu.104. a.3. Resp. Thomas calls "judicial" commands what Marsilius means by "legal" commands. For Thomas the "legal" commands are part of the ceremonial commands, and include such acts as circumcision. See *ibid.* II. I. qu.104. a.4.

[5] *S. theol.* II. I. qu.100. a.3. Resp.

[6] *Ibid.* II. I. qu.99. a.2. Resp.; qu.100. a.I. Resp.

[7] *Ibid.* II. I. qu.98. a.5. Resp.; qu.100. a.8. Resp.; qu.108. a.3. ad 3. See, to the same effect, Duns Scotus *Op. Oxon.* Lib. III. dist. 37. qu. unic. (XV, 783 ff.).

punishment of the present world."[8] Marsilius' view of the Mosaic law thus reproduces faithfully his approach to law as a whole: what had traditionally been considered natural law is discarded, and attention is fixed upon the aspect of coercion and punishment.

Marsilius' discussion of divine law is thus effectively limited to what he calls variously the evangelic law,[9] the law of grace,[10] the new law,[11] and the law of eternal salvation.[12] His approach to it follows the same pattern as his positivistic view of law in general, and shows the same contrasts to the traditional orientation. For Thomas Aquinas, the new law is only in a secondary sense a written law; primarily it consists in the supernatural grace which is an "endowment" of the human heart, just as natural law is an "endowment" of human nature.[13] For Marsilius, on the other hand, the divine law consists simply in the writings contained in the New Testament; and as we have seen,[14] he insists upon a literal interpretation of these writings. Hence, whereas for Thomas the new law, as grace, is an immediate aid to its own fulfillment by men,[15] for Marsilius it is a body of regulations external to men, laying down requirements which men must meet in order to attain eternal life. There is, consequently, no inherent rationality in divine law, not even the palpable general relation of means to end which human law's coerciveness bore to the preservation of the state. For just as the fact of eternal life itself is neither self-evident nor demonstrable, so the means to it are similarly devoid of any rationality which the human mind can grasp.[16] To be sure, the divine procedure in leading men from the easier requirements of the old law to the more difficult ones of the new was like that of a "skilled physician";[17] and the new law contains the "truth."[18] But that truth as Marsilius describes it derives solely from the will of God, its "legislator." Apart from God's command, no reason is given for the contents of the new law being what they are.[19] Thus where Thomas distinguishes within divine law a "natural" and a "positive" part, the former containing what is just from the very nature of the case,[20] for Marsilius the whole of divine law appears

[8] II. ix. 11. According to Thomas, the giving of sacrifices to God is commanded by natural law (*S. theol.* II. II. qu.85. a.1. Resp.), although the kind of sacrifice is determined differently in the "old" and "new" laws (*ibid.* qu.85. a.4. Resp.).

[9] I. vi. 4, 7, 8; I. x. 3; II. ix. 3, 6, 9–12.

[10] I. vi. 4; II. ix. 10.

[11] II. xv. 1, 2.

[12] II. v. 4, 5.

[13] *S. theol.* II. I. qu.106. a.1. Resp. ad 2.

[14] See above, p. 76.

[15] *S. theol.* II. I. qu.106. a.1. ad 2.

[16] See above, pp. 69–70, 83–84.

[17] I. vi. 3, 6.

[18] See above, p. 84.

[19] See I. vi. 4; I. xix. 4; II. ix. 1. See also above, p. 69, on the impossibility of giving demonstrative reasons for God's acts and other religious matters.

[20] *S. theol.* II. II. qu.57. a.2. ad 3; II. I. qu.99. a.3. ad 2.

as a positive construction of God. His literal emphasis takes the form of insisting upon what Christ "willed" and "did in fact" (*de facto*), and this is only "such as we can prove through the words of Scripture, nothing else."[21]

This contrast extends to the attitudes to be taken toward the law by men themselves. For both Thomas and Marsilius, divine law contains commands, prohibitions, and counsels; but whereas Thomas specifies these by their inherent relation to grace and faith,[22] Marsilius stresses only the reward or punishment attached to their observance.[23] Whereas for Aquinas the old and new laws are distinguished by the contrasting motivations of fear and love,[24] for Marsilius the two laws both essentially involve fear of punishment, the only distinction being that the old law's punishments were given in this world, while the new law's will be inflicted in the next.[25]

Marsilius' primary concern in his discussion of divine law is to make clear the sense in which it is a "law." Like human law, it is a "standard" (*regula*) containing commands, prohibitions, and counsels bearing upon the performance of human acts in the present world. But whereas human law deals only with transient acts and only insofar as they affect the present life, divine law deals with both transient and immanent acts according as they affect the attainment of eternal life.[26] From this difference, however, derives what is for Marsilius the most significant feature of divine law: since it is coercive only in the future world, inasmuch as its rewards and punishments are given only in the future world, not in the present one, it is not properly speaking a "law" in this world at all.[27] Thus Marsilius' definition of law as coercive command attains one of its most far-reaching conclusions and destroys one of the main supports of the papalist position.

This conclusion is, of course, in perfect harmony with Marsilius' basic political doctrines, and he adduces them anew in support of it. The preservation of the state requires unity of government and hence of law: two

[21] II. iv. 2; II. vi. 1; II. xxix. 2. In this positivist and voluntarist conception of God's acts there is a general resemblance to the theological doctrines of Duns Scotus and William of Ockham, but it can equally well be attributed to Marsilius' Averroist view of the relation between reason and faith. See above, pp. 69–70, 79 ff.

[22] *S. theol.* II. I. qu.108. a.1. Resp.; a.2. Resp.

[23] II. xii. 3, 4. For the similar contrast in relation to human law, see above, pp. 135–36.

[24] *S. theol.* II. I. qu.107. a.1. ad 2. Thomas attributes the sanctions invoked in the new law to the fact that a relatively few "carnal" men have "not yet attained the perfection" in which it consists. See, however, below, pp. 164–66.

[25] II. ix. 9. See below, p. 156, for passages in which fear of punishment is invoked as a dominant motivation of the new law. Also above, p. 138, n. 14.

[26] II. viii. 5; II. xii. 3, 4.

[27] II. ix. 3: "Ideoque ad statum hominis in hoc et pro hoc saeculo comparata, dici debet doctrina, non lex. . . ."

coercive powers, neither subordinated to the other and in respect of the same multitude, would "impede" one another.[28] All coercive power in this world belongs only to human law and its legislator and ruler.[29] There are, however, two specific arguments which Marsilius presents for the non-coerciveness of divine law in the present world. Their bearing can be seen from his insistence that even if coercive sanctions were attached to divine law, as such, in the present world, they would contravene its very nature and purpose.[30] Non-coerciveness attaches to the very essence of divine law in this world. The arguments to this effect provide further insight into Marsilius' conception of the coerciveness of law and of political authority in general.

(1) *The argument from volition.* The purpose of divine law is to help men attain eternal salvation. But both the faith and the abstention from sin which are required for such attainment must be voluntary; for in the spiritual realm the immanent acts which underlie and motivate transient acts determine the value of the latter. Hence if men's faith and acts were moulded in accordance with divine law only through coercion and fear of punishment, they would not thereby be helped at all toward salvation.[31]

It will be noted that this argument is severely limited in its scope. Marsilius does not, like Locke, appeal to any natural right of religious freedom,[32] but solely to the contrariety between the coercive and the voluntary. The argument views the former as involving "violent action or compulsion . . . through armed force." [33] It hences raises anew a cardinal question of the Marsilian politics. Is there no other kind of coercion besides that here envisaged? Is the only coercion in the state that exercised by the police and the military acting under human law? It was upon precisely this point that Marsilius' sixteenth-century critics seized. Thus Albert Pighius writes:

> *There are various modes of coercion and of coercive authority,* which everyone to whom has been entrusted governance (*gubernatio*) over others has over his subjects. The same authority does not belong to all, but to each his own: to fathers over children, to masters over slaves, to teachers over pupils, to abbots over their monks, to civil magistrates over those subject to them, *to ecclesiastics (of whom we now speak) over those entrusted to their care and rule* . . . But not one and the same mode of coercing belongs to all . . . For to one belongs

[28] II. iv. 5. See above, pp. 59, 99, 118 ff.

[29] II. v. 6; II. ix. 4. Cf. Hobbes *Leviathan* ch. xlii (p. 283).

[30] See II. v. 6; II. ix. 2, 4.

[31] II. v. 6: "Nam *coactis* nihil tale proficeret ad aeternam salutem." See II. ix. 2, 4, 5. Cf. Hobbes *Leviathan* ch. xlii (p. 269).

[32] See John Locke *Letters Concerning Toleration* I (London, 1870), 32: "Liberty of conscience is every man's natural right, equally belonging to dissenters. . . ."

[33] II. ix. 5.

flogging, to another the ferule, to another scourges, foot-shackles, prisons, to another the sword.[34]

Similarly, Antonius Paulutius charges Marsilius with arguing

from the fact that the church does not have the means and methods by which the lay power coerces and avenges its subjects, therefore it has no jurisdiction at all, and if it did have, it would be entirely ineffective, unarmed, and devoid of all coercive force, *as if there were no power or coercive jurisdiction except that which proceeds through hanging, beheading, and torture;* but this conclusion is entirely fallacious.[35]

This criticism hits, of course, at the central point of the Marsilian doctrine. If instead of there being only one kind of coercion or power in the state, that exercised by human law and authority, there is a pluralistic sliding scale of coercions exercised by all those having any "governance" over others in all the groups within the state, then the argument for unity as involving a monopoly of coercive power by the government is refuted. Marsilius' critics would appear to be returning in part to the Platonic assimilation, criticized by Aristotle, of the authority of the political ruler over his subjects to that of parent over child and master over slaves.[36] But the situation is more complex, for Marsilius cannot be said to be upholding a simple Aristotelian position. The difference, together with the whole point of Marsilius' divorce of divine law from this-worldly coerciveness, emerges from the fact that, as we have seen, he has also divorced the coerciveness of human law and government from that kind of moral purpose which the antecedent tradition regarded as primary. Thus Thomas Aquinas can write, like Marsilius, that "in the society of men no one has coercion except through public power"; [37] but he can at once insist that rulers have such power only to do justice, and in the context of his entire doctrine this involves the positive inculcation of virtue.[38] But if Marsilius were to make such a purpose the justification of the application of coerciveness in the state, then he would have to grant that divine law as well as human may be coercive in this world.

This point emerges still more sharply from the fact that Marsilius, despite his insistence that faith to be meritorious must not be coerced, holds also that a valid motive of faith may be the threat of punishment in the future world.[39] It might well be argued that for a society which takes

[34] *Hierarchia eccles.* v. vi (p. 147). See *ibid.* v. ii, viii (pp. 129, 155).

[35] *Jurisprudentia sacra* I. vii (in *Bibliotheca maxima pontificia,* ed. J. T. Roccaberti [Rome, 1698], IV, 273).

[36] See Plato *Politicus* 258E ff., 294A ff.; Aristotle *Pol.* I. I. 1252a 7 ff.

[37] *S. theol.* II. II. qu.66. a.8. Resp.

[38] See above, pp. 103–4; below, pp. 228–29.

[39] Thus one of the functions of priests in relation to divine law is "corripere delinquentes seu transgressores illius, *ipsosque terrere judicio futurae sibi damnationis et poenae inflictionis*

seriously the existence of a future world, the latter threat constitutes coercion and removes the voluntariness and hence the meritoriousness of faith and works equally as much as does the threat of punishment to be applied in this world. Plainly Marsilius' argument holds only if the meaning of "coercion" is restricted to actual punishment as against the threat of it.[40] And indeed he does distinguish such threats and exhortations from coercion.[41]

(2) *The argument from mercy.* Marsilius' second essential argument for the non-coerciveness of divine law is based upon the consideration that mercy rather than immediate punishment should be the prime factor in dealing with sins. No man is to be judged irrevocably as a sinner in this world, for Christ mercifully allows sinners to repent and earn merit to the very end of their lives. Punishment for transgressions in this world would hence seem to close books which in fact remain open to the very last.[42] It will be noted that coercion is here viewed as a final punishment for sins, not as a temporary chastisement or threat to discourage future sinning.

A direct corollary of this argument is the position that men's final deserts cannot be known with certainty in this life. For men may sin against divine law by immanent acts just as they do by transient acts; but only God perceives immanent acts.[43]

The problem of the nature and purpose of coercion is raised again by this argument. May not coercion and punishment be viewed as medicinal and educational rather than as merely the avenging of wrongs? It is significant that in discussing the punitive function of rulers Marsilius does cite the Aristotelian analogy of punishments to medicines,[44] but he does not give it the ethical, educational interpretation stressed by Aristotle. Hence Marsilius' view of coercion once more operates to separate it from the spiritual goals of divine law; and by the same token it separates both that law and its maker from all this-worldly efficacy. The divine law is in the world with its "teachers," the priests, commissioned in their essential priesthood by God; but their moral mission, as such, entails no coercive means such as are used by the government. And God himself, having placed the divine law and the priesthood in this world, has left

per judicem coactivum, Christum scilicet, in saeculo venturo" (II. x. 2). See II. vii. 4. See, on the other hand, Augustine *De civ. Dei* XIV. x: "Neque enim nullum peccatum est ea quae lex Dei prohibet concupiscere atque ab his abstinere timore poenae, non amore justitiae."

[40] It should be noted that according to Aristotle an act done through fear of a worse alternative is not thereby rendered involuntary. See *N. Eth.* III. 1. 1110a 4 ff.; and also Thomas *S. theol.* II. 1. qu.6. a.6.

[41] See texts cited above, p. 138, n. 14.

[42] II. ix. 1: "Voluit enim ex sui misericordia Christus usque ad extremum cujusque periodum concedere mereri, et de commissis in ipsius legem poenitere posse. . . ." See II. x. 2; II. xxx. 1.

[43] I. v. 11; II. ix. 11. See above, p. 109.

[44] I. xv. 11. See Aristotle *N. Eth.* II. 2. 1104b 17.

them without further control on his part. Thus Marsilius' insistence that God punishes only in the future world is in strong contrast to the Augustinian doctrine of God's frequent intervention in human affairs by punishing the wicked.[45]

Thus far we have been examining Marsilius' clear general position that in the present world divine law is not coercive, and hence not a "law," but only a "doctrine." But the position is complicated when we examine its specific applications. For, to begin with, Marsilius accepts excommunication as a "punishment" which is "in accordance with evangelic law" and is effected by "coercive judgment," justifying it on the ground that it prevents other believers from being infected by the sinner.[46] To be sure, he also says that divine law "counsels" rather than "commands" the infliction of this punishment, since believers can be saved even if they tolerate the company of a man who has offended against divine law.[47] Consequently, divine law itself remains a "doctrine" rather than a "law" since it does not "command" its coercive enforcement in this world, that is, it does not provide that failure so to enforce be punished. Nevertheless, there is an obvious contradiction between even this position and the view upon which Marsilius insists at so many other points, that coercive enforcement in this world is against the very nature and purpose of divine law.

The various qualifications which Marsilius' position undergoes in the *Defensor minor* clarify the bases of this contradiction even if they do not remove it. He there attacks "spiritual" excommunication (separation from the sacraments) as not being in accord with divine law, on the same grounds as he denies coerciveness to divine law; in this he explicitly dis-

[45] See *De civ. Dei* I. ix: "Deo placet perditos mores etiam temporalium poenarum adflictione punire." See *ibid.* xx. ii, iii. However, Augustine also makes the same point as Marsilius, that bad men to the very end of their lives may change for the better and hence should be borne with by good men; see *ibid.* I. ix: "Si nollent esse socii, ferrentur et diligerentur inimici, *quia donec vivunt semper incertum est utrum voluntatem sint in melius mutaturi.*" In sharpest contrast, Thomas Aquinas brushes aside this argument, which had been repeated by the heretical Cathari, and declares that bad men may be killed; for the danger they present is greater and more certain than the good which might result from their correction. See *Cont. gent.* III. cxlvi. The argument which Marsilius was subsequently to urge is here presented by Thomas in almost the same words as Augustine had used: "Inducunt etiam quod homo, *quamdiu in mundo est, potest in melius transmutari.*" Thomas' reply: "Quod vero mali, quamdiu vivunt, emendari possunt, non prohibet quin juste possint occidi; quia periculum quod de eorum vita imminet est majus et certius quam bonum quod de eorum emendatione expectatur." See also *S. theol.* II. II. qu.11. a.3. arg.1 and ad 1, where a similar objection and reply are presented in specific reference to the excommunication of heretics and the church's "leaving" them to the secular power to be killed. Cf. *ibid.* Suppl. qu.21. a.2. arg.3 and ad 3, which gives a detailed justification of excommunication as punishment for sin; and also *ibid.* Suppl. qu.21. a.3. Resp.

[46] II. vi. 12.

[47] II. vi. 13.

sents from Peter Lombard and the whole tradition of commentators on his *Sentences*.[48] As for "civil excommunication," Marsilius there similarly denies its legitimacy according to divine law insofar as it is a mode of exile accompanied by real and personal punishment, so that there remains only the kind of social avoidance which is merely a "shame" and does not interfere with economic intercourse.[49] Yet he then goes on to admit that such economic excommunication is "perhaps" a counsel of divine law. He argues further that even if it is a command, its *enforcement* through compulsion and punishment is not a command; [50] and finally, that even if such compulsion were a command, the coercive authority to enforce it would belong not to the priesthood but to the local "church," which comprises all the believers, not only priests.[51] This *dénouement* is identical with that of the *Defensor pacis;* [52] and it shows that Marsilius' primary concern is not with safeguarding religious freedom or the non-coerciveness of divine law, but rather with removing coercive power even in religious matters from the priesthood. For it is always with the priesthood that he couples his denials of coerciveness to divine law,[53] while on the other hand he insists that the coercive power over excommunication belongs to the whole body of the faithful (*universitas fidelium*), that is, the local "church."

At this point the obvious question arises: if coercion in matters of faith is not in accord with divine law, why should coercion in such matters be any more legitimate when exercised by the *universitas* than by the priesthood alone? Now when Marsilius upholds the possession of such coercive authority by the *universitas* as against the priests, he does not advert to his arguments against the coerciveness of divine law,[54] but rather brings in an entirely different group of arguments designed to show that the whole body is more trustworthy than any of its "parts," including the priesthood. We shall examine these arguments in the following chapter.[55] But this merges into still another consideration. Since the *universitas*

[48] *Def. min.* x. 2. See Peter Lombard *Libri IV sententiarum* Lib. IV. dist. 18. cap. viii (PL 192, 888). St. Bonaventura *In Sent.* Lib. IV. dist. 18. pars 2. a.I. ad 1–2. Thomas Aquinas *S. theol.* Suppl. qu.23. a.I. Duns Scotus *Opus Oxon.* Lib. IV. dist. 19. qu. unic. (XVIII, 641–42).

[49] *Def. min.* xv. 6.

[50] *Ibid.* xv. 7.

[51] *Ibid.* xv. 8.

[52] II. vi. 12, 13.

[53] See texts cited above, p. 155, n. 31; p. 157, n. 42.

[54] At only one point, and that in the *Defensor minor,* does Marsilius interpret the non-coerciveness of divine law to preclude its coercive enforcement by the whole "church" as well as by the priests; but this refers only to the *traditio Satanae.* See xii. 2: "Unde cum dicitur quod possint sacerdotes sive pastores, *cum ecclesia sive sine ecclesia fidelium,* privare peccatores orationibus et suffragiis . . . sicut videtur Magister intendere, cum similiter opinantibus sibi, non videtur mihi scripturae consonum, sed dissonum manifeste. Unde ipsius et sic dicentium videtur sententia declinanda."

[55] See below, Ch. V, esp. Secs. 6 and 7. See also p. 283.

fidelium is in Christian countries largely or entirely identical with the *universitas civium*,[56] which is the "legislator" of human law, the authority to enforce divine law by coercion is now reserved to human law. The approach is entirely positivistic; after having insisted upon the non-coerciveness of divine law as such in the present world, Marsilius adds: "by these considerations, however, we do not mean that it is inappropriate that heretics or those who are otherwise infidel be coerced, but the authority for this, *if it be lawful to do this,* belongs only to the human legislator." [57] What human law commands is now the standard; but what it should command Marsilius does not say, although he frequently contemplates without protest the possibility that it *may* command the coercion of heretics.[58] Even more, he provides for the human legislator's coercive enforcement of the interpretations of divine law made by general councils.[59]

On what basis, however, does Marsilius sanction such coercion in matters of faith by the human legislator? To a certain extent, it is on the grounds not of faith or religion itself, but rather of its civil consequences. Since the "faithful human legislator" is numerically identical with the church, the unity of the latter is essential to the former, and schism in the latter would mean that very disruption of peace and destruction of the state to whose prevention Marsilius' work is addressed. But what this proves is that for Marsilius, as for his papalist opponents, no sharp distinction is ultimately possible between spiritual and temporal questions. As for the papalists every "temporal" question has its "spiritual" side and hence comes under ultimate papal control, so for Marsilius every "spiritual" question has its "temporal" side and consequently comes under the control of human law.[60]

Yet the Marsilian approach is even more inclusive; for the faithful human legislator controls spiritual concerns even *qua* spiritual, not merely *qua* temporal. Thus the general council, whose decisions the legislator may enforce by coercive power, is a necessary institution because without its determinations "the unity of faith would not be preserved, and error and schism would arise among the believers of Christ." These determinations are concerned with doubts and disagreements "regarding divine law. For diversities or contrarieties of opinions in this would lead to diverse

[56] See below, pp. 291 ff. [57] II. v. 7.

[58] See II. ix. 7; II. x. 3, 6, 8, 11; II. xxv. 7; II. xxviii. 15; III. ii. 30. In the *Defensor minor* (x. 5, 6 [p. 30]) Marsilius gives a highly qualified approval to human law's providing that heretics be separated from the company of believers "praesertim quantum ad convictum domesticum aut consortium, seu contubernium et collocutionem, de his quae pertinent ad ritum fidei conservandum . . ."; heretics "devitandi sunt, ne reliquos inficiant. . . ."

[59] II. xix. 3; II. xxi. 1, 4–9. See below, pp. 286, 296 ff.

[60] See above, pp. 107 ff.; below, pp. 294 ff.

sects, schisms, and errors."[61] Although these diversities may be regarded as leading in turn to "civil" disunities, Marsilius does not explicitly mention the latter in this connection; rather, he presents as an *additional* concern of the general council "defining other matters outside divine law which are related to the common utility and peace of the believers."[62] The coercion which Marsilius envisages hence attaches to matters of faith as such, not because of their civil consequences. The issue is rather as to who should be the agent of such coercion; thus Marsilius argues that "a universal ruler can conserve the believers in unity more than can a universal bishop. For in ancient times schismatics were coerced by rulers to keep the unity of the faith . . . they could not be coerced by bishops, because these lacked coercive authority, which does not belong to them as such."[63]

Human law and its governmental agent, therefore, may exercise that coercive enforcement in matters of faith which Marsilius has denied to the priesthood and divine law; and this enforcement is based upon the same end as had been the basis for the non-coerciveness of divine law. Yet surely if coercion is of no aid to the attainment of eternal salvation when exercised by the priesthood, it is no more so when exercised by authority of human law. In relation to the theological basis of his denial of coerciveness to divine law, Marsilius' position is thus clearly contradictory. On the other hand, in relation to his central political conceptions it is a completely logical consequence of that unity of government, and hence of law, which he insists is necessary for the preservation of the state.[64] For while Marsilius firmly holds in principle that coercion in matters of faith is contrary to divine law, his conception of the necessity of the unity of political authority makes it impossible to admit of such a limitation upon the authority to coerce; for this authority is identical with political authority, and hence such a limitation would produce that division of authority which leads inevitably to the state's destruction. The human law and government cannot be denied coercive authority over "spiritual" affairs any more than over "temporal" affairs.

Put in another way, the problem arises from the fact that Marsilius has asserted both a final cause—the moral and theological reasons which necessitate the limitation of coercive authority in matters of faith—and an efficient cause—the undivided, hence unlimited, authority of human law and its governmental agency whose functioning is necessary for the minimal end of preserving the state. When the two causes clash, such

61 II. xx. 1. 62 II. xx. 3. 63 II. xxviii. 15.
64 See above, pp. 118 ff.

is the basic position of the Marsilian philosophy that the final cause gives way and the efficient cause remains supreme. The arguments by which Marsilius upholds the whole people's right to be the legislator of human law provide further reinforcement of these considerations, for, as we shall see, the concept of the "whole" exerts the same absorptive force as does the concept of unity.[65]

From every point of view, then, the upshot is that while the priesthood may teach divine law and administer its sacraments, the ultimate control of all ways in which divine law may be made efficacious in this world belongs to the agents of human law. The completeness of this unifying absorption of divine law into human law may be grasped from Marsilius' explicit discussions of the relations between the two laws. These discussions are, in his own terms, entirely "formal"; that is, he does not, like his predecessors, examine the *contents* of divine law to determine their application to the conditions of secular life, but rather he presents a calculus of the possible agreements and disagreements between the sanctions of the two laws. Thus there is no question of bringing divine law any more than the traditional natural law to bear upon the moral contents of human laws and political institutions.

Marsilius begins by stressing the "diversity" of human and divine law: they have different ends and lead to them in different ways. Human law provides coercive regulation of transient acts for the sufficiency of the present life, whereas divine law provides only teaching and the sacraments for the attainment of eternal life.[66] Yet the two laws do touch to a large extent upon the same human acts in the present world, and in this case the laws may either agree or disagree. One important agreement is that divine law itself commands the observance of human law; hence, to violate human law is also to violate divine law, although the converse is not the case.[67] As we shall see, Marsilius is able to base a doctrine of the divine right of rulers upon this consideration.[68]

On the other hand, where the two laws disagree, divine law rather than human law is to be obeyed.[69] This would appear to mark a distinct limit upon the authority of human law. Does it not leave the way open for that intervention by the priesthood which Marsilius' whole doctrine opposes? To the contrary, he is careful to fix the precise limits of this very limitation of human by divine law. To begin with, divine law is not a source from which human law must be *derived,* as it is for the antecedent

[65] See below, pp. 212 ff., esp. 217–19. [66] II. ix. 12; see II. viii. 5.
[67] II. ix. 11. See *Def. min.* viii. 3. See also above, p. 120, n. 31.
[68] See below, pp. 250–51.
[69] II. v. 4, 5, 7; II. ix. 9; II. xii. 9; II. xxvi. 13; II. xxx. 4. *Def. min.* viii. 3; xiii. 6; xv. 3, 4.

tradition,[70] so that the limitation of human by divine law involves not an affirmative obligation to apply the provisions of divine law but only a negative obligation not to infringe them. Secondly, as we have seen, divine law as such is not coercive in this world; hence, the priest can in no way enforce that provision of divine law which is contradicted by human law.[71] Finally, and perhaps most decisive of all, the interpretations of divine law, which authoritatively determine what any of its doubtful articles mean, are to be made not by priests alone, nor by any individual believer or group, but by general councils composed of both laymen and priests and *elected by the human legislators*,[72] who also are alone entitled to give coercive enforcement to their interpretations.[73] Hence, the makers of human law are in final control over the determination of the meaning of divine law. The limitation of the former law by the latter is consequently all but devoid of practical efficacy, just as Marsilius' use of the distinction between reason and faith had similarly removed the theological realm from doctrinal influence over the political.

The outcome of Marsilius' discussion of law is thus to remove all coercive power from the priesthood and to extend even to matters of divine law that monopoly of coercive power by human law and government which the doctrine of the peace and unity of the state had established. The dialectic of the Marsilian unity pushes the argument to the point where, in the *Defensor minor*, he is forced to consider the objection that there is no difference between human and divine law.[74] He replies that they do differ in all four causes. But an earlier statement, which had evoked the objection, is far more revealing of the extent to which Marsilius has erased the boundaries between the two laws:

Although the commands, prohibitions, and counsels of divine law, taken actively, differ from those of human law, since they are established and ordained by different legislators, and for different ends, and under different punishments to be inflicted upon their transgressors at different times and in different ways, nevertheless *in almost all cases, or at least in most, the persons to whom each law gives commands, together with their voluntary acts and deeds, can be and are the same*. For example, both divine and human law command that theft

[70] See above, pp. 132, 144–45, 149 ff.

[71] See especially II. v. 4: "si praeceperit imperator aliquid faciendum contra legem salutis aeternae, quae Dei praeceptum est immediatum, in hoc imperatori non esse obtemperandum; in quo papae praecipienti secundum hanc legem, scilicet divinam, *quamvis in hoc saeculo neminem cogere potenti neque debenti secundum ipsam,* magis esset obtemperandum . . ." See also II. xxx. 6.

[72] II. xx. 2, 5. See below, p. 286. Cf. Hobbes *Leviathan* ch. xliii (p. 319).

[73] II. xix. 3; II. xxi. 4. See below, Ch. VII, Sec. 4.

[74] *Def. min.* xv. 5: "Sed dicet aliquis ex praedictis sequi legem divinam et humanam non differre. . . ."

must not be committed, nor homicide, nor robbery with violence, nor fraud, nor bearing false witness. Similarly with affirmative commands, as that one must return a loan. Again, the persons can be the same, and their acts similar, to whom and about which each law gives commands, *with regard both to temporals and to spirituals*.[75]

Thus from his initial emphasis upon the "diversity" of human and divine law, Marsilius concludes their practical identity; "the human legislator justly commands and can command . . . that nothing unlawful be done *with respect to spiritual things*." [76] His divisive method had operated to separate the priesthood from the government and the non-coerciveness of divine law from the coerciveness of human law. But once that separation has been attained, Marsilius' unificatory method absorbs the former into the latter.

In view of this *dénouement,* what are we to make of the frequent claim that Marsilius, because of his emphasis upon the non-coerciveness of divine law, is a pioneer of religious freedom and tolerance? [77] His provision that human law may exercise coercion in religious matters and even for religious reasons shows that the motive of his position is in many respects different from that of Locke. Moreover, while his emphasis upon the contrariety between coercion and the voluntariness which all faith must have if it is to be meritorious, is at one with Locke's view,[78] it was also the original doctrine of the church, as Marsilius' citations from Origen, Chrysostom, Ambrose, and Hilary make clear.[79] Nor was it at all unfamiliar to Marsilius' immediate predecessors and contemporaries.

Nevertheless, his position does present a marked change from that which was current in his time. Thomas Aquinas, for example, insists that the "new" divine law—that of the New Testament—differs from the "old" in that it induces observance of its commands not through fear of punishment but through love of virtue; [80] and that the attainment of eternal life requires voluntary action, not coercion.[81] But on the other hand, because of "carnal men" the incentives of fear and temporal promises are required in the new law as well as the old,[82] and punishment coercing men to make them observe the precepts of divine law is to be given even in the present world by those who execute God's providence.[83] Thomas recog-

[75] *Ibid.* xiii. 5–6.
[76] *Ibid.* xv. 4.
[77] See above, p. 4, n. 8.
[78] See Locke *Letters Concerning Toleration* I (*ed. cit.*, p. 6): "true and saving religion consists in the inward persuasion of the mind, without which nothing can be acceptable to God . . . And such is the nature of the understanding, that it cannot be compelled to the belief of any thing by outside force . . . though the rigor of laws and the force of penalties were capable to convince and change men's minds, yet would not that help at all to the salvation of their souls."
[79] See II. iv. 13; II. v. 6; II. ix. 3, 4, 5.
[80] *S. theol.* II. I. qu.107. a.I. ad 2.
[81] *Cont. gent.* III. cxlviii.
[82] *S. theol. loc. cit.; Cont. gent.* III. cxli ff.
[83] *Cont. gent.* III. cxlvi.

nizes the necessary connection of faith and volition, and their contrariety to coercion.[84] Yet this recognition is used, not only by Thomas but also by Alexander of Hales, Augustinus Triumphus, and Alvarus Pelagius, merely to state that while infidels as such are not to be compelled to take up the Christian faith, heretics and others who have already taken up the faith *"must* be even corporeally compelled" to retain their faith and thereby to fulfill their promise.[85] The penalty for such unbelievers ranges from excommunication [86] to death.[87]

It may, however, be argued that since Marsilius provides that human law may exercise the same coercive enforcement in matters of faith as the antecedent tradition had provided for divine law, there is no essential difference between the respective positions. But this overlooks a decisive point. For to remove coerciveness from divine law as such in this world is to remove at the same time the absolute sanction, the quality of "command" which such coercion had been regarded as having. And to assign coerciveness in matters of religion to human law is to endow it with all the relativity which the content of human law has for Marsilius. To be sure, this difference is itself in part a consequence of the relative importance attached to religious and secular matters by Marsilius and by his predecessors. Marsilius' emphasis upon the necessity of coercive enforcement of human law for the preservation of the state contrasts not only with his indifference as to the use of coercion by human law in religious matters, but also with the precisely reversed position of Thomas Aquinas, who insists that if the killing of counterfeiters and other malefactors is justified, then "much more" is the killing of heretics, because "it is much graver to corrupt the faith than to falsify money." [88] But whatever be the underlying evaluative motivations, there is a considerable difference between Thomas' emphatic statements that "heretics *must* be compelled to hold the faith," [89] and "can justly be killed," [90] and Marsilius' conditional state-

[84] He states as an argument against his own position that "voluntas cogi non potest. Ergo videtur quod infideles non sint ad fidem cogendi" (*S. theol.* II. II. qu.10. a.8. arg.3). In the body of the same article he writes that infidels who have never taken up the faith "nullo modo sunt ad fidem compellendi ut ipsi credant, *quia credere voluntatis est. . . .*"

[85] *Ibid.* Resp.: "Alii vero sunt infideles qui quandoque fidem susceperunt, et eam profitentur, sicut haeretici, et quicumque apostatae; et tales sunt *etiam corporaliter compellendi,* ut impleant quod promiserunt, et teneant quod semel susceperunt." *Ibid.* ad 3: "sicut vovere est voluntatis, reddere autem necessitatis: ita accipere fidem est voluntatis, sed tenere eam acceptam est necessitatis. Et ideo haeretici sunt compellendi ut fidem teneant." See *Corp. jur. can., Decret. Gratiani* Pars I. dist.45. can.5 (I, 162). Alexander of Hales *Summa universae theologiae* Lib. II. Tit. II. Membrum I. cap. iv (III, 731). Augustinus Triumphus *S. de eccl. pot.* qu.24. a.1; qu.59. a.4. Alvarus Pelagius *De planctu eccl.* I. xxxvii (pp. 45–6).

[86] *S. theol.* II. II. qu.10. a.9; qu.39. a.4.

[87] *Ibid.* II. II. qu.11. a.3. Resp.

[88] *Ibid.* II. II. qu.11. a.3. Resp.

[89] *Ibid.* II. II. qu.10. a.8. ad 3.

[90] *Ibid.* II. II. qu.11. a.3. Resp.

ment that "*if* it be lawful to coerce heretics, the authority for this belongs to the human legislator alone." [91] The difference is indicated strongly in Marsilius' statement that if punishment of heretics is not prescribed by human law, then "individuals must be permitted to teach what they wish concerning the faith." [92] Thus, by his position that human law may possibly not authorize coercion in matters of faith, thereby removing its only authorization in this world, Marsilius' doctrine directly opens the way, as that of his predecessors could not have done, for the further positions not only that human law does not authorize such coercion—and he accepts this as the existing fact in his time [93]—but also that it must not so authorize.

Religious indifference and concentration upon secular values, the aim of removing coercive power from the priesthood as the rival to the government's power, the conviction that religious faith and coercion are incompatible—all of these motivations entered into the Marsilian doctrine, as they were to enter into the later movements which culminated in the establishment of religious toleration. The combination formed by the capitalists, monarchists, libertarians, and others who were to share one or more of these motivations was as varied, as unstable, and in some respects as contradictory as was the combination of these ideas in Marsilius. His doctrine exhibits in clear detail the multiple rationale which historically underlay one of the most significant developments of modern times.

[91] II. v. 7. Note the similar conditional form in all the other texts cited above, p. 160, n. 58, where the possibility that human law may *not* command the punishment of heresy is stated.

[92] II. xxviii. 17: "Unde vel sic dicendum in communitatibus fidelium, *aut singulos permittendum de fide docere quod volunt. . . .*" It is hence a misinterpretation to say that for Marsilius "heresy . . . *must* be punished" (d'Entrèves, *Medieval Contribution,* p. 81; my italics). Lagarde's interpretation (*Marsile,* pp. 279–80) is similarly one-sided.

[93] See II. x. 3: "Si vero haereticum aut aliter infidelem commorari fidelibus in eadem provincia non fuerit prohibitum humana lege, *quemadmodum haereticis ac semini Iudaeorum iam humanis legibus permissum extitit,* etiam temporibus Christianorum populorum, principum, atque pontificum, dico cuipiam non licere haereticum aut aliter infidelem quemquam iudicare aut arcere poena vel supplicio, reali aut personali, pro statu vitae praesentis."

CHAPTER V

THE PEOPLE AS LEGISLATOR

I. THE CONCEPT OF THE LEGISLATOR

THE POLITICAL STRUCTURE of the Marsilian state differs from the traditional medieval conception in that the supreme authority rests not in some "higher law" embodying ultimate values or final causes, but rather in a positive human agency or efficient cause called the "legislator." It is from the legislator that the laws derive their authority, and it is the laws, in turn, which regulate the functioning of the government. Hence Marsilius recasts the standard debate as to whether, under the "higher law," the temporal government or the priesthood has the superior authority, by setting the legislator over both. And this legislator is the people.

Few doctrines in the history of political philosophy have occasioned so much disagreement among commentators as this theory of popular sovereignty. We have already noted the critical divergences ranging from those who acclaim it as a revolutionary forerunner of modern democracy to those who assert that it does not depart from traditional medieval conceptions and those who declare that it is a totalitarian doctrine.[1] Yet the position which is the subject of these contradictory interpretations is the central thesis of Marsilius' entire political philosophy. It, and the arguments supporting it, are invoked to establish not only that the people makes the laws,[2] but also that the people elects [3] and "corrects" [4] the government, establishes the other parts of the state,[5] including the priesthood,[6] controls excommunication,[7] defines articles of faith through its elected general council,[8] makes binding all the council's enactments,[9] and elects the head bishop or pope of the church.[10] Marsilius' popular sovereignty hence is not confined to the two chapters of Discourse I where it is initially presented in regard to the making of laws; it pervades the whole of the *Defensor pacis*. It therefore requires intensive analysis if the Marsilian political philosophy itself is to be understood. Yet his arguments received

[1] See above, pp. 4–6.
[2] I. xii–xiii.
[3] I. xv. 2.
[4] I. xviii. 3.
[5] I. xv. 4, 9.
[6] II. xvii. 9–12.
[7] II. vi. 13; II. xxi. 8, 9.
[8] II. xx. 2 ff.
[9] II. xxi. 1, 3, 4.
[10] II. xxii. 9–11.

their last detailed study at the hands of Albertus Pighius [11] in the sixteenth century, and then from an avowedly hostile point of view.

In this chapter we shall deal primarily with the legislative authority of the people, for it is this which underlies all the other powers attributed to the people by Marsilius. The fuller examination of these latter powers will be presented in the two following chapters. With regard to the former, two central questions must be considered: first, precisely what is the meaning of the doctrine that the legislator is the people; second, what are the arguments advanced to prove it?

Marsilius' initial statement of his position is as follows: "Let us say, in accordance with the truth and the counsel of Aristotle in the *Politics,* Book III, Chapter 6, that the legislator, or the primary and proper efficient cause of the law, is the people or the whole body of the citizens, or the weightier part thereof . . ." [12] Four concepts in this statement call for special examination: "legislator," "people," "citizen," "weightier part."

Marsilius' conception of the legislator and the legislative process can be best understood when it is viewed in the light of Aristotle's analysis of the mental acts involved in the solution of a practical problem, for the Marsilian doctrine is expressed in the terms used in that analysis. The first of these mental acts is "deliberation" (βουλεύεσθαι, translated *consiliari* by William of Moerbeke), which is divided into "inquiry" (ζητεῖν, *quaerere*) into the means of solution, and "discovery" (εὑρεῖν, *invenire*) of likely means.[13] Both these deliberative acts are assigned by Marsilius to elected "prudent experts" who inquire into and discover potential regulations dealing with the common benefit and the administration of justice.[14] But then, in a social or political context where these means must be proposed to others for their choice, there occurs "understanding" (ξυνιέναι, *syniene*), which is a "judgment" (κρίνειν, *judicare*) as to which proposal must be adopted,[15] followed by "choice" or "election" (προαιρεῖσθαι, *eligere*) of that proposal.[16] In Marsilius' doctrine, similarly, the experts must lay their recommendations before the whole people, which will then "discern" and "judge" the value of these proposals and

[11] *Hierarchia ecclesiastica* Lib. v (pp. 122 ff.).

[12] I. xii. 3.

[13] *N. Eth.* III. 3. 1112b 18 ff.; VI. 9. 1141a 32. Moerbeke's translation is found in Thomas Aquinas' commentary on the *Nicomachean Ethics;* see Bibliography, below, p. 322. For Marsilius, as for Aristotle, the "wish" (βούλησις, *voluntas*) for the end must precede the deliberative search for the means to the end (*N. Eth.* III. 4. 1113a 15 ff.). See, however, below, p. 220, on the relation between the common benefit and the allocation of legislative authority.

[14] I. xiii. 8: "futuras leges vel statuta *quaerendas* seu *inveniendas* et examinandas prudentibus et expertis per universitatem civium committi, conveniens et perutile est." See I. xii. 2.

[15] *N. Eth.* VI. 10. 1143a 10 ff.

[16] *Ibid.* III. 2. 1112a 15 ff.; III. 3. 1113a 10 ff.

"choose" the ones to be adopted.[17] Nor do this judgment and choice constitute an automatic ratification. They involve the right of each individual (*quilibet*) to object against any proposed law, and the right of the people to add to, subtract from, change, or completely reject the experts' recommendations. Marsilius conceives these alternate solutions as occurring after discussion in the general assembly of all the citizens,[18] which is on the model of the "greater council" of Padua and other cities.[19] And finally, when the citizens have made their decision, they give a coercive command (*coactivum praeceptum*) that the rules approved by them shall be laws; [20] this act corresponds in Aristotle's analysis to the act of "command" (*ἐπιτάττειν*, *praecipere*), which follows the "judgment" as to the best course of action, fixing that course as an imperative to be acted upon.[21]

The Marsilian legislator thus exercises a threefold control over the laws. It elects the deliberative experts who "discover" and propose rules of justice and civil benefit for possible enactment into law; [22] it discusses and judges the adequacy of these proposals; and finally by its vote of approval it affixes the coercive command which makes an actual law. These laws are not merely the fundamental constitutional principles of the state but also the specific regulations dealing with all the objects indicated in Marsilius' various discussions of law; although, as we have seen, their primary concern is with "disputes" requiring coercive regulation.[23] It is hence incorrect to say that Marsilius' legislator has a "constituent" rather than a "legislative" function; [24] it has both.

[17] I. xiii. 3: "Quamvis enim non quilibet aut maior multitudo civium sit legum *inventor*, potest tamen quilibet de inventis et ab alio propositis *judicare*, addendum vel minuendum aut mutandum discernere." See, to the same effect, I. xiii. 4, 7. This division among the "deliberation" of the experts and the "judgment" and "choice" of the people does not mean that the experts do not also "judge" and "choose" appropriate solutions to the problems they are investigating for legal regulation. But there is a distinction between judging the results of one's own deliberation and judging "what someone else says" about practical matters. For the former, see *N. Eth.* III. 3. 1112a 12; for the latter, which Aristotle ascribes to *σύνεσις*, see *ibid.* VI. 10. 1143a 15.

[18] I. xiii. 8. See the references to the citizens' right to "object" (*reclamare*) (I. xii. 5, 6; I. xiii. 8), "repel" (*repellere*) (i. xii. 7), "reject" (*spernendum*) (I. xiii. 7, 8). Lagarde is hence in error when he says (*Marsile*, p. 188) that Marsilius "accepte en définitive de réduire le rôle de la communauté à une approbation plus théorique que pratique."

[19] See above, p. 23.

[20] I. xiii. 8, *fin.*

[21] See *N. Eth.* VI. 10. 1143a 9. However, Marsilius departs from Aristotle on the further specification of this point; for Aristotle holds that the command issues from prudence, which would mean, in Marsilius' application of this virtue, that the laws are "made" by the experts who "discover" them. But for Marsilius, the command issues rather from those who "understand" the results of the discovery, and "judge" and "choose" among these. This is another aspect of Marsilius' republican distinction of expert knowledge from political authority. See also below, p. 176; p. 231, n. 34.

[22] I. xiii. 8.

[23] See above, pp. 106 ff., 137 ff.

[24] McIlwain, *op. cit.*, p. 305; Lagarde, *Marsile*, p. 180; d'Entrèves, *Medieval Contribution*, p. 59.

This conception of the legislator involves a fundamental change from the antecedent doctrines. In the medieval tradition, legislation meant not the independent enactment of laws, but rather the judicial interpretation of the principles of higher laws or customs by positive ordinances. Even the papal plenitude of power involved in this respect not a legislative authority *in radice* but rather a judicial authority subordinate to and limited by the fundamental laws of God and nature.[25] Marsilius' departure from the tradition is a consequence of his changes in the doctrine of law itself. Since the essence of law is not reason but coercive command,[26] the basic act of legislation similarly consists not in the rational interpretation or application of substantive rules of reason but rather in a command. This command, moreover, is not essentially an act of reason, as it is for Aquinas; [27] rather, in accordance with the basic voluntarism of Marsilius' doctrine, the command emanates from the "election or will" of the people, determining that some act be done or omitted, and providing temporal punishment for transgressors of that command.[28] To be sure, this command occurs after "deliberation" by the experts and "judgment" by the people. But the experts' deliberation could be dispensed with, and the people's coercive commands would no less be laws. Everything other than the people's elective-imperative act is required for the "well-being" of the laws, not for their "being": [29] that act is the necessary and sufficient condition of the validity of the laws, and everything else which may precede, accompany, or follow it may add to the value of the laws, but is, strictly speaking, not necessary to them. The people electing and commanding is hence the "primary and proper efficient cause of the law," while the deliberative experts "are not and cannot be the legislator in the strict sense

[25] For the judicial character of the legislative authority, see Thomas Aquinas *S. theol.* II. I. qu.95. a.1. ad 2; a.2. Resp.; II. II. qu.57. aa.2, 3. James of Viterbo, *De reg. Christ.* II. iv (pp. 189–90). Alvarus Pelagius *De planctu eccl.* I. liii (p. 130). For the limitation of the papal plenitude of power by divine and natural law, see Augustinus Triumphus *S. de eccl. pot.* qu.5. aa.1, 2; qu.22. a.1; qu.23. a.4. James of Viterbo *De reg. Christ.* II. iv, viii (pp. 190, 260–61). Alvarus Pelagius *De planctu eccl.* I. vii, xxxiv (pp. 28, 37). This limitation is also implied in Egidius of Rome's characterization of the laws with which the pope may dispense as *positiva jura* (*De eccl. pot.* III. vii, viii [pp. 181, 190]). See the important discussions of this whole subject in McIlwain, *op. cit.*, pp. 187–88, 217–18, 286–87.

[26] See above, p. 134.

[27] *S. theol.* II. I. qu.17. a.1. Resp.: "Imperare autem est quidem essentialiter actus rationis. . . ." See *ibid.* II. I. qu.90. a.1, *sed contra:* "ad legem pertinet praecipere et prohibere. Sed imperare est rationis. . . ." Contrast Duns Scotus *Opus Oxon.* Lib. IV. dist. 14. qu.1. n. 5 (XVIII, 52): "imperare non convenit nisi appetitui vel voluntati . . ."

[28] I. xii. 3: "per suam electionem seu voluntatem in generali civium congregatione per sermonem expressam, praecipientem seu determinantem aliquid fieri vel omitti circa civiles actus humanos sub poena vel supplicio temporali. . . ."

[29] I. xii. 3. See I. xii. 2; I. xiii. 8. This provision removes the papalist claim that laws, in order to be valid, require confirmation by the pope. See especially James of Viterbo *De reg. Christ.* II. v, vii (pp. 207, 232, 234), and also above, pp. 8, 144–45; below, p. 245, n. 61.

(*simpliciter*) but only in a relative sense (*ad aliquid*) and for a certain time and in accordance with the authority of the primary legislator." [30] The distinction between the primary legislator and the "discoverers" of the laws is thus parallel to that between the formal and the material aspects of law—the coercive command on the one hand, and the content to which that command is attached, on the other.[31] Since the essence of law consists in the former aspect, it is the authority to give a coercive command which transforms a proposed regulation into a law, and which hence constitutes the legislator.

The concept of the legislator thus brings out forcefully one of the most basic aspects of the Marsilian politics. The supreme act of political authority no longer consists in adhering to a supreme final cause, but rather in being the supreme efficient cause of the rules which govern the state. While those rules should at their best adhere to ethical ends of justice, there is nothing mandatory in such adherence; without it, complete legitimacy can still be attained. It is this point which constitutes the real political significance of the difference between Marsilius' voluntarism and the rationalism of the antecedent tradition: in the one case, political authority is limited by rationally apprehended ends, but in the other the will of the legislator is itself supreme.

The further significance of this concept of the legislator emerges when it is compared with its Aristotelian source. As we have seen, Marsilius refers to the sixth chapter of Book III of the *Politics* in support of his position that the legislator is the people. Now this chapter does not mention the "legislator" at all; it deals rather with the question "what must be the dominant authority (τὸ κύριον) of the state." [32] Nevertheless there is a fundamental agreement between the general orientations of Aristotle's and Marsilius' discussions. For Aristotle, the "dominant authority" of the state is the government (πολίτευμα),[33] and the government is equivalent to the constitution (πολιτεία).[34] From the constitution, in turn, derive the laws, which are the specific rules proceeding from the general order of the state, so that they "must be laid down in relation to the constitution." [35] Hence, to ask what must be the dominant authority of the state is to ask who shall control the constitution, and through it the laws; which is directly Marsilius' question.

[30] I. xii. 3.

[31] I. xii. 2.

[32] *Pol.* III. 10. 1281a 11. William of Moerbeke regularly translates Aristotle's κύριον by *dominans* or *dominativum*. (The fact that Marsilius uses longer chapter divisions of the *Politics* than those found in the Berlin and Oxford editions should be kept in mind in reading his references. Cf. Susemihl's ed. of Moerbeke.)

[33] *Ibid.* III. 6. 1278b 11.

[34] *Ibid.* 1278b 12.

[35] *Ibid.* IV. 1. 1289a 13; see III. 11. 1282b 11.

The Marsilian discussion of the "legislator" is thus equivalent to one of the central questions of Aristotle's *Politics,* and indeed of all political philosophies: what is the best kind of constitution or government.[36] Marsilius' insistence that only the whole people should be the legislator, accordingly, puts him in the camp of those who hold that a "democracy" or a "polity" is the answer to this question.[37] It is in this discussion, and not in his separate treatment of the various forms of "government" (*principatus*), that Marsilius' answer to this constitutional question is to be found. Hence, despite the agreement which we have seen between the general orientation of his discussion and that of Aristotle, there is an important difference both in their terms and in their interpretation of them. For Aristotle, the fundamental constitutional question is a question about *governments,* since the government is equivalent to the constitution and hence is the source of the laws. For Marsilius, on the other hand, the fundamental constitutional question deals with the *legislator.* And just as the legislator had been distinguished from the deliberative experts who discover and recommend possible laws, so too the legislator is distinct from and superior to the government, since the latter is simply the "executor" of the laws,[38] which it does not make.

In Marsilius, then, for perhaps the first time in political philosophy, the constitutional question is entirely separated from the question of kinds of government. The latter question is no longer important; he is quite indifferent as to the "species of temperate government" which the state may have.[39] The underlying reason for this divergence is that Marsilius makes a different approach to the fundamental question of kinds of constitution, a sequence whose middle term is found in Cicero. For Aristotle the question of kinds of constitution or government is essentially a question not of the *number* of those who rule the state but rather of the *moral values* which are both the *ends* envisaged by the governing class and hence also the *criteria* (ὅροι) by which governmental power is distributed.[40] It is because the government determines these values in the state by the constitution and the laws that the constitutional question is a question about governments. For Cicero, on the other hand, there is a body of natural

[36] On the different senses of "best" in relation to this question, and Marsilius' position toward them, see above, pp. 33 ff.; also below, pp. 203–5.

[37] On the distinction between democracy and polity, and Marsilius' choice, see below, pp. 181, 190–91.

[38] I. xv. 4. See below, pp. 229 ff.

[39] See his refusal to engage in the traditional discussion of the relative merits of monarchy, aristocracy, and polity, I. viii. 4: "Quis autem bene temperatorum principatuum sit optimus, aut quis vitiatorum pessimus, de reliquorum quoque ordine in bonitate vel malitia dicere, *non habet praesentem speculationem.*" See also I. ix. 9; I. xvii. 2; and above, p. 117. Typical discussions of the relative merits of kinds of government are found in Thomas Aquinas *De reg. princ.* I. ii–v. Egidius of Rome *De reg. princ.* Lib. III. Pars. II. cap. iii, iv. John of Paris *De pot. reg. et pap.* cap. i (pp. 109–10).

[40] See *Pol.* III. 5. 1279b 20 ff.

law above and prior to the state and its government; [41] this law determines the moral values of the state quite irrespective of the particular kind of government which the state may have. Hence Cicero reduces the governmental question to a merely numerical one, and decides it on grounds not of central moral values but solely of expediency: the sovereignty of natural law requires human determination and enforcement by government,[42] which consequently is a judicial rather than a legislative agency. The medieval Aristotelians follow Cicero rather than Aristotle on this point. Marsilius completes the sequence; for while he has no natural law setting the moral values of the state, he substitutes therefor the "legislator" from whom derives whatever morality or values the positive laws of the state may attain. It is the will or desire of the people which hence acts as a substitute for the natural law of Cicero.[43] But since Marsilius, in common with the medieval tradition, regards government as primarily a judicial function,[44] that by which the government "judges" can be only a positive law, and the maker of this law, accordingly, holds the same sovereign position as the higher law held in the antecedent tradition. The distinction between legislator and government was thus forced upon Marsilius by his failure to accept the doctrine of a higher law. But as a consequence, the question of forms of government does not have for Marsilius even the secondary importance which it has for Cicero and for the medieval tradition, since the locus of sovereignty is already a human agency—the legislator—and it is from this that government receives its authority and its limitations. Thus where Aristotle distinguishes good from bad governments on the criterion of their aiming at the common benefit, which he also calls "justice"; [45] and where Cicero declares that without law and justice there is no state at all; [46] Marsilius' fundamental insistence is not in terms of such final causes but rather of an efficient cause: that the people must be the legislator, the maker of the laws.

There was consequently nothing in the antecedent traditions of political philosophy which exactly corresponded to Marsilius' concept of the legislator. Aristotle's "law-giver" (νομοθέτης, translated *legislator* by William of Moerbeke) is primarily a deliberative law-discoverer,[47] but also he may be a ruler who "gives" the laws to his subjects.[48] Although in another connection Aristotle also distinguishes the governmental "part" of the consti-

[41] *De re publica* III. xxii. 33; *De legibus* I. vi. 18 ff.
[42] *De re publica* I. xxvi. 41 ff. Cicero here refers to the governmental function as *consilium*.
[43] See above, pp. 151–52.
[44] See I. v. 7. Also above, p. 170, n. 25; and below, pp. 229 ff.
[45] *Pol.* III. 7. 1279a 26 ff.
[46] *De re pub.* I. xxv. 39; xxxii. 49; xxxiii. 50; III. xxi. 43; xxiii. 45.
[47] See *Pol.* II. 7. 1266b 9; II. 12. 1273b 27–35; VII. 7. 1327b 36; 13. 1332b 9, and *passim*.
[48] See *ibid.* III. 13. 1283b 38; III. 15. 1286a 22.

tution from the deliberative, which controls the laws,[49] this still leaves the latter identical with the supreme government (πολίτευμα), for both are defined as the "dominant authority of the constitution."[50] Hence, while Aristotle, like Marsilius, views the act of "command" as the most characteristic function of political magistrates,[51] this command is limited by the antecedent deliberation and judgment of the supreme deliberative authority.[52] The medieval Aristotelians, like Aristotle, identify the legislator with the ruler-king,[53] although this legislator, as we have seen, is primarily a judicial agent applying higher laws in positive statutes. And while both Ptolemy of Lucca[54] and Egidius of Rome[55] distinguish the "deliberators" (*consiliarii*), who "discover" the laws, from the "rulers" (*principes*), who enforce them, they identify the latter with the "legislator."[56] For Ptolemy and Egidius, then, as for Marsilius, "legislation" essentially means not intellectual discovery of laws but control of what measures shall be laws; but this control is still conceived as judicial enforcement of higher laws rather than as original command of completely independent statutes. Thus Marsilius, by distinguishing the legislator from both the deliberators and the government, makes legislation, like law itself, completely *sui generis.*

The Marsilian concept of the legislator is of profound importance for its consequences in the basic structure of politics. The legislator, having the same independence of all "higher laws" as was seen in the Marsilian doctrine of human law, continues the reversal of the claims of the papalists based upon divine law, and marks the attainment of a kind of sovereignty without parallel in the tradition of medieval political philosophy, the complete independence of the secular state. Such independence had been approached only in Augustine's positivist conception of the *res publica* as not having to

[49] *Ibid.* IV. 14. 1297b 36 ff.

[50] *Ibid.* III. 6. 1278b 10; IV. 14. 1299a 1. See also the discussion of what kind of offices are to be called ἀρχαί (IV. 15. 1299a 15 ff.).

[51] *Ibid.* IV. 15. 1299a 28.

[52] The development which the medieval Aristotelians give to Aristotle's concept of "command" brings out clearly its dependence upon antecedent moral and intellectual values. See Thomas Aquinas *S. theol.* II. II. qu.47. a.8. Resp.: "est tertius actus ejus praecipere; qui quidem actus consistit in applicatione consiliatorum et judicatorum ad operandum." Also John of Jandun *Quaest. in Metaphys.* Lib. I. qu.18 (fol.14M): "proprius actus principis est praecipere, ex 40 *Politice* . . . Sed inter omnes actus hominis nobilissimus est cognoscere Deum, et in illo actu praecipiendi consistit felicitas politica in principe. . . ."

[53] Thomas Aquinas *S. theol.* II. II. qu.50. a.1, ad 3: "Philosophus denominat regnativam a principali actu regis, qui est leges ponere." See *ibid.* II. I. qu.92. a.1. Resp.; II. II. qu.47. a.12, *sed contra.* Egidius of Rome *De reg. princ.* Lib. III. Pars II. cap. xxi: "rex sive princeps est legislator." See *ibid.* III. Pars II. cap. xxii, xxiii. See also James of Viterbo *De reg. Christ.* II. iv (p. 190). Dante *De mon.* I. xii, xiii (pp. 347, 348). John of Paris *De pot. reg. et pap.* cap. xviii (p. 132). Ptolemy of Lucca *De reg. princ.* III. iii (p. 48). John of Jandun *Quaest. in Metaphys.* Lib. I. qu.1 (fol. 2A). Augustinus Triumphus *S. de eccl. pot.* qu.44. a.1. Alvarus Pelagius *De planctu eccl.* I. liii (p. 130).

[54] *De reg. princ.* IV. xxiv (p. 110).

[55] *De reg. princ.* Lib. III. Pars II. cap. i.

[56] See above, n. 53.

conform to true (i.e., Christian) justice, and perhaps in some of the Roman civilians and French legists; yet in the first two, divine and natural law remained in the background as the real bases of legitimacy, while in the legists no such systematic development and omnicompetence are found as in the Marsilian doctrine. Among the moderns, it is Hobbes and Austin rather than Bodin who carry on this conception of legislative sovereignty.

Yet it is no contradiction that Marsilius insists that this sovereignty belongs only to the whole people, and that he does so in part from considerations of that same "justice" which figured in antecedent doctrines of natural and divine law. In his doctrine, for the first time, such a relation is set up between the political concept of the nature of legislative sovereignty and the moral concept of the ends of sovereignty, that the two can be sharply distinguished in essential content even while they become united in the will of the people. Rousseau was later to effect the same relation, but with basic qualifications with which Marsilius was able to dispense.[57]

2. THE CONCEPT OF THE CITIZEN

Since the legislator consists in the "whole body of citizens," it is important to see what Marsilius means by a "citizen," and whom he admits to citizenship. He takes his definition of a "citizen" from Aristotle: "A *citizen* I define, in accordance with Aristotle in the *Politics,* Book III, Chapters 1, 3, and 7, as one who participates in the civil community, in the governmental, deliberative, or judicial function according to his rank." [1] It will be noted that citizenship is here an inclusive conception, involving "participation" in any of the political agencies of the state, not merely the legislative process. And just as Aristotle had pointed out that his definition applies directly to democracies,[2] so Marsilius' is most apposite to the "polity," which he defines as that species of government "in which each citizen participates in some way in the governmental or deliberative function in turn in accordance with his rank and ability or condition . . ." [3]

In the further development of this conception of citizenship, however, there emerge important divergencies between Marsilius and Aristotle, with respect to the "participation" of the citizens in political authority. For Aristotle, different kinds of constitutions have different criteria of citizenship. In the best possible state, every citizen can take his turn at actually exercising the ruler's function,[4] for to be a citizen in the fullest sense means "to have the knowledge and ability to rule as well as to be

[57] On the points here indicated, see also below, pp. 258–59.

[1] I. xii. 4; see *Pol.* III. I. 1275a 22, 1275b 19; 5. 1277b 33; 13. 1283b 42.

[2] *Pol.* III. I. 1275b 6. [3] I. viii. 3. [4] *Pol.* VII. 14. 1332b 26.

ruled." [5] But since in democracies all freemen are citizens, regardless of whether or not they have such knowledge and ability, Aristotle raises a sharp alternative: "Is it true that a citizen is one who has the authority to participate in government, or must artisans also be counted citizens?" [6] His reply is that since the best state is dedicated to the life of virtue, it will make the possession of virtue the criterion of citizenship; hence it "will not make the artisan a citizen." [7]

Marsilius, on the other hand, not only has a far more moderate view of the end of the state, but he separates the legislative from the governmental or executive function. Consequently, he is not affected by Aristotle's sharp alternative: there is a middle position between being a citizen-ruler and not being a citizen. To be a citizen, it is not necessary to have the degree or kind of prudence needed for ruling or for discovering the laws; it is sufficient to be able to judge the performance of one's rulers and the adequacy of proposed legislation.[8] In terms of Aristotle's division of the intellectual virtues, Marsilius is saying that to be a citizen it is sufficient to have the virtue of "understanding" (σύνεσις), even if one lack prudence or "deliberative excellence" (εὐβουλία).[9] Hence, the sense in which Marsilius' citizens "participate" in government is not, as with Aristotle, that they actually perform the various ruling or judicial functions, but rather that they control the legislative process in the sense indicated earlier.[10] To be sure, this distinction is itself partly derived from Aristotle's discussion of democratic constitutions; [11] but Marsilius makes it basic to his whole constitutional doctrine. The practical consequence of this difference between Aristotle and Marsilius can be seen in the fact that whereas the former excludes farmers and artisans from citizenship in his best state, insisting that they be made slaves,[12] for Marsilius all the functional groups of the state, including artisans and farmers, are citizens.[13]

Marsilius goes on, however, to exclude from citizenship "children, slaves, foreigners, and women." [14] These exclusions are all, of course, found in

[5] *Ibid.* III. 4. 1277b 13; see 1277a 27.

[6] *Ibid.* III. 5. 1277b 34. Thomas Aquinas states this alternative by a distinction between being a citizen *simpliciter* and *secundum quid* (*S. theol.* II. I. qu.105. a.3. ad 2).

[7] *Pol.* III. 5. 1278a 8. See *ibid.* VII. 9. 1328b 39.

[8] I. xiii. 3, 7.

[9] See *N. Eth.* VI. 9. 10. 1142a 31 ff. See also above, p. 168.

[10] See above, pp. 168 ff.

[11] See *Pol.* III. 11. 1281b 26, where Aristotle declares that the "multitude of the citizens" should not "participate in the highest governmental offices" (τῶν αρχῶν τῶν μεγίστων) but only in "deliberative and judicial functions." A similar distinction is found in William of Ockham *Dialogus* Pars III. Tr. I. Lib. II. cap. V (p. 794).

[12] *Pol.* VII. 9. 1329a 26; 10. 1330a 26–32.

[13] I. xiii. 3, 4.

[14] I. xii. 4.

Aristotle,[15] and are repeated in the tradition of Roman law [16] as well as in the other medieval Aristotelians.[17] Indeed, so ardent a defender of freedom as Spinoza, writing three and one-half centuries after Marsilius, could describe "democracy" as a form of government in which these same groups are excluded from citizenship.[18]

Marsilius' attitude toward women is on a par with that of his time.[19] In this respect some political writers were more advanced, such as Pierre Dubois in his provisions for the education of women; [20] William of Nogaret in his statement that in matters affecting all, "anyone of the people, even a woman," is to be allowed to speak; [21] and especially William of Ockham, who declares that women as well as men should be admitted to general councils.[22]

With regard to slavery, on the other hand, Marsilius effects subtle yet important departures from the Aristotelian tradition. According to Aristotle, there is a distinction between "natural" rulers and "natural" slaves, in that some men possess reason in superior degree whereas others lack reason to the extent needed to govern themselves.[23] Among the medieval Aristotelians there is a striking agreement on this doctrine. It is repeated in unmitigated form by Thomas Aquinas,[24] Ptolemy of Lucca,[25] Godfrey of Fontaines,[26] Egidius of Rome,[27] John of Jandun,[28] Augustinus Triumphus,[29] William of Ockham; [30] the same distinction is repeated, with the same Aristotelian terminology, by Dante to justify the supremacy of the Roman Empire,[31] by Egidius of Rome and others to support the papal

[15] *Pol.* III. I. 1275a 8, 14; 5. 1277b 39–1278a 6. See *ibid.* I. 12. 1259a 39 ff.

[16] Irnerius *Summa codicis* III. i (ed. H. Fitting [Berlin, 1894], p. 47); Rogerius *Summa codicis* III. i (*Bibl. jurid. med. aevi,* ed. A. Gaudentius [Bologna, 1888], I, 39).

[17] See Thomas *S. theol.* II. I. qu.98. a.6. ad 2; qu.105. a.3. Resp. ad I, and ad 2.

[18] *Tractatus politicus* xi. 3 (*Opera,* ed. Van Vloten-Land, 3d ed. [Hague, 1913], II, 81).

[19] See II. xvii. 12; II. xxvi. 7. For statements of the inferiority of women, see also Egidius *De renunciatione papae* cap. xvi (p. 41); Thomas *In Sent.* IV. d.19. qu.I. a.I. quaestiunc. 3. ad 4.

[20] *De recuperatione terre sancte* paras. 61, 74, 85-86 (pp. 51, 62, 70–71).

[21] *Requesta contra Bonifacium VIII* (in P. Dupuy, *Histoire du différend d'entre le Pape Boniface VIII et Philippe le Bel* [Paris, 1655], p. 75).

[22] *Dialogus* Pars I. Lib. VI. cap. lxxxv (p. 605); see *ibid.* Pars I. Lib. V. cap. xxxii (p. 503); Pars I. Lib. VI. cap. c (p. 631).

[23] *Pol.* I. 5. 1254b 15 ff.; see *ibid.* I. 2. 1252a 30.

[24] *S. cont. gent.* III. lxxxi. See *S. theol.* II. I. qu.94. a.5. ad 3; II. II. qu.57. a.3. ad 2, where the doctrine is qualified by the distinction of *jus naturale* and *jus gentium.*

[25] *De reg. princ.* II. x; IV. xviii. Elsewhere, Ptolemy follows the Augustinian position that slavery is not natural but rather the result of sin: see *ibid.* II. ix; III. vii, ix, xi.

[26] *Quodlib.* VIII. qu.16 (IV, 145).

[27] *De reg. princ.* Lib. I. Pars II. cap. vii; Lib. II. Pars III. cap. xiii–xiv.

[28] *Quaest. in Metaphys.* Lib. I. qu.22; Lib. XII. qu.22 (fol. 18J, 144D).

[29] *S. de eccl. pot.* qu.22. a.6; qu.23. a.3.

[30] *Dialogus* Pars III. Tr. I. Lib. II. cap. iii (p. 793).

[31] *De mon.* II. vii; see *ibid.* I. iii (*fin.*).

supremacy,[32] by Pierre Dubois to support the hegemony of the king of France,[33] by John of Jandun to justify the leadership of philosophers over other men and hence of metaphysics over other sciences,[34] and by Engelbert of Admont,[35] James of Viterbo,[36] and Duns Scotus[37] to justify government in general. Only John of Paris, among the Aristotelians prior to Marsilius, shows any distaste for the doctrine.[38]

There is an echo of the Aristotelian doctrine in Marsilius, when he writes that "those who live in a state do not only live, which beasts or slaves do, but live well, having leisure for the liberal functions . . ."[39] Moreover, he has a doctrine of natural aptitudes similar to that of the other Aristotelians. But where for them "reason" or "prudence" has an exalted status, and is differentiated sharply from the lack of it, Marsilius puts prudence on the same level as the other "habits" needed for the other "offices" of the state.[40] This levelling is but another aspect of his refusal to regard as had his predecessors the dualisms of soul-body, spiritual-temporal, reason-desire, on which the papal claim to supremacy had been based. He does indeed insist upon the importance of prudence for the "perfect ruler,"[41] but this gives no "natural right" of rulership: the "prudent" rulers or judges, so far from having an absolute political superiority because of their prudence, must rather be under the firm control of all the citizens of the state, including the farmers and artisans. Thus Marsilius' doctrine of natural differences does not, as with the other Aristotelians, lead to a doctrine of natural slavery. On the contrary, he declares that all the citizens "are of sound mind and reason,"[42] for although most of them

[32] *De eccl. pot.* II. ix (pp. 89–90). Konrad of Megenberg *De translatione Romani imperii* cap. x (pp. 282–83).

[33] *Summaria brevis,* p. 37.

[34] *Quaest. in Metaphys.* Lib. I. qu.21 (fol. 17N). John puts this role of leadership (*principalis*) directly in terms of Aristotle's distinction: "Illa scientia est maxime principalis secundum quam aliquis est maxime sciens . . . Unde Aristoteles dicit primo Politicae, 'Vigentes intellectu naturaliter sunt domini aliorum. Robusti autem corpore et deficientes intellectu naturaliter sunt servi aliorum.' Ideo ille est principalis qui habet illam scientiam et per consequens illa scientia est principalis. Sed secundum metaphysicam aliquis est maxime sciens. . . ."

[35] *De ortu* cap. i (p. 363).

[36] *De reg. Christ.* II. ii, x (pp. 165–66, 302–3).

[37] *Reportata Paris.* IV. d.36. qu.2 (XXIV, 458 f.). See *Opus Oxon.* IV. d.36. qu.1 (XIX, 447). Duns distinguishes this "natural or political" slavery from "despotic or tyrannical" slavery.

[38] See *De pot. reg. et pap.* cap. xi (p. 124), where the clergymen's superiority over laymen in reason is cited as an argument for their political superiority: "Item dicunt, quod clerici plus vigent ratione et intellectu, quam laici: et tales debeant regere in utrisque." John's reply is given in cap. xxi (p. 139): "Quod XL. opponitur de clericis, qui magis pollent ratione: respondeo, Si sic est, non ideo praecipue debent regere in omnibus, sed in maioribus et in melioribus, scilicet in spiritualibus."

[39] I. iv. I.

[40] I. vii. I. See above, pp. 60, 64 ff.

[41] I. xiv. 3–5.

[42] I. xiii. 3. Marsilius' statement that "omnes aut plurimi sanae mentis et rationis sunt et recti appetitus," seems directed specifically against such formulations as that of James of

may not be able to discover the laws (thus lacking what Aristotle calls "deliberative excellence"—εὐβουλία), yet they can "judge" well concerning possible laws which have been "discovered" and proposed to them by others, for they have the quality of "understanding" (which Aristotle calls σύνεσις).[43]

If Marsilius does not accept the Aristotelian doctrine of natural slavery, then what does he mean by the "slaves" whom he excludes from citizenship? We have seen above that he contrasts slaves with citizens because the latter "have leisure for liberal functions";[44] but the citizens include the artisans and farmers whom Aristotle makes slaves in his best state. Does Marsilius regard any slavery as *legitimate?* Two other passages in which he refers to slaves may provide a possible answer. Following Aristotle, he says that the inhabitants of Asia endure a hereditary tyranny "because of their barbaric and slavish nature."[45] At another point, after emphasizing the almost universal desire of men for social life, he writes that "those who do not wish the state to endure are counted among slaves, not among citizens."[46] These passages suggest that for Marsilius the criterion of deserved slavery is volitional and political rather than intellectual and individual: those men should be slaves who voluntarily accept tyranny, or who do not desire the basic conditions making possible men's social life. It is the fact that Marsilius has a less exalted view of the place of reason in the state, and a conception of human "nature" which stresses its biological uniformities rather than its intellectual culmination, that underlies his differences from his predecessors with respect to citizenship and slavery. The significance of these differences is brought out further in Marsilius' view of the "people," with which he equates the citizen-body.

Viterbo, who writes that in some men "regimen proprie rationis non sufficit," so that they must be ruled by others who are "intellectu prestantiores et appetitu rectiores" (*De reg. Christ.* I. ii [pp. 165–66]). Another sign of Marsilius' departure from the Aristotelian approach to slavery is found in his discussion of the family. The children, slaves, and women whom he excludes from citizenship are the "subject" members of the three groupings or "communities"—parent-child, master-slave, husband-wife—which according to Aristotle compose the family or household (*Pol.* I. I. 1252a 26 ff.; 2. 1253b 6–8). But Marsilius' chapter on the family mentions only the first and third of these groupings, completely omitting the master-slave relation (I. iii. 3, 4), whereas the other Aristotelians who discuss the family mention all three of these groupings. See Thomas *S. theol.* II. I. qu.104. a.4. Resp.; qu.105. a.4. Resp.; II. II. qu.57. a.4; qu.58. a.7. ad 3. Egidius of Rome *De reg. princ.* Lib. II. Pars I. cap. v. Engelbert of Admont *De ortu* cap vii, xii, xvii (pp. 365, 368, 373). James of Viterbo *De reg. Christ.* I. i (p. 90). William of Ockham *Dialogus* Pars III. Tr. I. Lib. II. cap. iii (pp. 792–93).

[43] I. xiii. 3, 7. For Aristotle's discussion of "deliberative excellence" and "understanding," see *N. Eth.* VI. 9, 10. 1142a 32 ff.

[44] I. iv. I. See, above, p. 64. Strictly speaking, all Marsilius' citizens should have such leisure, for he attributes it to "those who live a civil life (*viventes civiliter*)."

[45] I. ix. 4. See *Pol.* III. 14. 1285a 20. [46] I. xiii. 2.

3. THE CONCEPT OF THE PEOPLE

The concept of the "people" has traditionally had two different meanings in political thought. Among the Greeks, the δῆμος was a particular group of citizens, comprising not the entire citizen-body but only the "multitude," the mass of freemen "who neither are rich nor have any merit of virtue," [1] as distinct from the "notables." [2] Among the Romans, on the other hand, the *populus* included all of the citizens, not only the *plebs* who are roughly equivalent to the δῆμος,[3] but also the "patricians and senators" corresponding to the Greek "notables." [4] Now Marsilius, as we have seen, refers to Aristotle for corroboration of his position that the legislator is the "people" (*populus*). But Marsilius defines the people in the Roman sense, as the *universitas civium;* [5] he views it as comprising not only the *vulgus* (equivalent to the δῆμος or *plebs*),[6] that is, farmers, artisans, and the like; but also the *honorabilitas,* "who are few." [7] And belonging to the *honorabilitas,* and hence to the *populus,* is also the clergy.[8] Marsilius' position,

[1] *Pol.* III. 11. 1281b 16–26, 1282a 28.

[2] See *ibid.* IV. 4. 1291b 17 ff., where the δῆμος is shown to include the farmers, artisans, merchants, seamen, manual laborers, men with little property, and men not of free birth on both sides. Distinct from this group is the class of the "notables" (γνωρίμοι), comprising men of wealth, good birth, virtue, education, and other similar "upper-class" characteristics. A similarly restricted view of the δῆμος as a particular group is found in Plato *Republic* VIII. 565 A, and in Thucydides, VI. lxxxix. 4. Aristotle also uses δῆμος to refer to the "popular assembly" as distinct from the deliberative council (βουλή) and the court (δικαστήριον) (*Pol.* III. 11. 1282a 35, 39). McIlwain twice interprets Aristotle's δῆμος as "the whole body of citizens" (*op. cit.,* pp. 81, 86); but subsequently he renders it as "the free citizens . . . the poor who are in the majority" (*op. cit.,* p. 91).

[3] See Albert the Great *In Eth.* Lib. VIII. Tr. II. cap. ii (p. 541): "Δῆμος enim Graece, Latine *plebs* est."

[4] See *Corp. juris civilis, Institutiones* I. ii. 4: "Plebs autem a populo eo differt, quo species a genere. Nam appellatione populi universi cives significantur, connumeratis patriciis et senatoribus; plebis autem appellatione sine patriciis et senatoribus ceteri cives significantur." See also Isidore of Seville *Etymologiae* IX. iv (PL 82, 349): "Populus ergo tota civitas." This definition goes back to Cicero's equation of *res publica* with *res populi* (*De re publica* I. xxxix).

[5] I. xii. 3: "populum seu civium universitatem." See *Institutiones* I. ii. 4: "appellatione populi universi cives significantur." Isidore of Seville *Differentiae sive de proprietate sermonum* I. 445 (PL 83, 55): "populus est generalis universitas civium."

[6] See Isidore *Etymol.* IX. iv (PL 82, 349): "Vulgus vero plebs est."

[7] I. xiii. 4. See I. v. 1. Marsilius' use of the term *honorabilitas* is the result of a misinterpretation which he, together with the other Aristotelians, derived from William of Moerbeke's translation. William used *honorabilitas* to render Aristotle's τίμημα, meaning "property-qualification." (Cf. on this point M. Guggenheim, "Marsilius von Padua und die Staatslehre des Aristoteles," *Historische Vierteljahrschrift,* VII [1904], pp. 354–55, n. 2.) The Aristotelians, however, took it to mean "honor"; see Thomas Aquinas *In Pol.* Lib. III. Lect. 4 (p. 219); Peter of Auvergne *In Pol.* Lib. III. Lect. 9 (p. 240). Hence Marsilius' use of *honorabilitas* as meaning "the honorable class," a sense also found in Thomas *S. theol.* I. qu.108. a.2. Resp. On the other hand, in Padua *honorabilis* is used as an honorific adjective for *populus;* see *Stat. com. Pad.* n. 1152 (p. 351).

[8] For the inclusion of the priesthood in the *honorabilitas,* see I. v. 1. For the explicit inclusion of the clergy in the "people," see II. xxv. 9: "A quo siquidem populo non excluditur,

clergy

therefore, does not have the same meaning as the "democratic" view which Aristotle is defending in the chapter to which Marsilius appeals. For Aristotle's "democracy" is the rule of the δῆμος alone; and Marsilius similarly defines democracy as the government in which the *vulgus seu egenorum multitudo* "rules alone without the will or consent of the other citizens." [9] The Marsilian constitution is thus rather a "polity," in which "every citizen" shares in power.[10]

Marsilius' interpretation of the concept of the people has important bearings for his entire doctrine. The *clerus,* as part of the *populus,* must come under the same laws and political authority as the rest of the people; thus Marsilius turns aside the clericalist distribution of the *universitas fidelium* into *clerus* and *populus,* the former superior to the latter in its way of life and hence too in its way of government.[11] The very inclusiveness of the *populus,* moreover, is one of Marsilius' chief considerations in support of its having supreme authority. For the *populus* is the *universitas,* and "every whole is greater than any of its parts." [12] Hence the particularism whereby the clergy or the papacy would arrogate plenitude of power to itself is refuted by pointing out that however much virtue this group may have, it cannot be so great as that of the whole of which it is but a "part." [13]

By the same token, the Marsilian *populus* is distinct from the *populus* of the Italian cities, for the latter comprises only a part of the citizen-body.[14] To the incessant warfare of the *populares* against the *magnates* (equivalent in part to the *vulgus* and *honorabilitas* of his state) Marsilius seems to be saying that both have a right to share in political power, but neither group should try to arrogate all power to itself alone. His main arguments, how-

sed includitur clerus, cum pars sit illius." See also II. xvi. 14; II. xvii. 14; II. xxv. 6. 9. To similar effect William of Ockham *Breviloquium* VI. 2 (pp. 158, 159). For the source in Roman law see *Corp. jur. civ., Dig.* I. i. 2; repeated by Thomas Aquinas *S. theol.* II. I. qu.95. a.4. Resp.; see also *ibid.* II. II. qu.57. a.4. ad 3.

[9] I. viii. 3; see *Pol.* III. 7. 1279a 38 ff.

[10] See I. viii. 3.

[11] See Honorius of Autun *Summa gloria* cap. i (MGH, *Libelli de lite,* III, 64–5): "Cum universitas fidelium in *clerum* et *populum* distribuatur, et *clerus* quidem speculativae, *populus* autem negociativae vitae adscribatur . . . et ista sacerdotali, illa autem regali virga gubernetur, solet plerumque apud plerosque queri, utrum sacerdotium regno, an regnum sacerdotio jure debeat in dignitate preferri. Ad quod breviter possem respondere, quod sicut . . . clerus precellit populum ordine, sic sacerdotium transcenderet regnum dignitate." Jerome had distinguished "duo genera Christianorum," the *clerici* and the *laici.* "Λαὸς enim est populus" (in *Corp. jur. can., Decret. Gratiani* Pars II. can. 7. C. XII. qu.1 [II, 678]). Jerome's division is repeated by Alvarus Pelagius *De planctu eccl.* I. xliv (p. 78).

[12] I. xiii. 2.

[13] I. xiii. 4, 6.

[14] Cf. G. Salvemini, *Magnati e popolani in Firenze dal 1280 al 1295* (Florence, 1899), Ch. 2; *Il costituto . . . di Siena dell'anno 1262,* ed. Zdekauer, pp. xxxii ff., lxiii ff., lxxvii–lxxviii; *Le Statut des neuf gouverneurs . . . de Sienne, 1310,* ed. Luchaire, pp. 28 ff.; *Idem, Les Démocraties italiennes* (Paris, 1915), pp. 94 ff., 113 ff. In the Padua statutes, *populus* is similarly used in the restricted sense; see *Stat. com. Pad.* n. 101 (p. 38), where it is provided that the syndics shall include "unus judex, unus miles, et duo de populo."

ever, are directed against those who would deprive the *vulgus* of power, for it was here that the main controversy lay with the defenders both of monarchic constitutions and of the papal plenitude of power.

Although the Marsilian *populus* is thus like the Roman in being all-inclusive, it does not have a similar relation to law. For Cicero it is consent to law that makes a people,[15] for Marsilius it is the people that makes law. We thus find the same situation as in the concept of the "legislator": the Marsilian people is not limited by natural law as was the people of Cicero and the Roman lawyers, nor by an affirmative relation to divine law, as is the people of Augustine's normative definition of *res publica.*[16] The conception of Marsilius is far closer to the positive definition subsequently put forth by Augustine as a formulation which would include both Christian and pagan peoples: "a people is the assemblage of a rational multitude associated by a concordant communion in the things which it loves."[17] This definition, like Marsilius', is neutral with respect to specific values; but Marsilius' emphasis falls not primarily upon the people's "love," but rather upon its possession of sovereignty. In this respect, Marsilius' people combines the Augustinian positivism with the legalistic corporate character of the classic Roman doctrine.

4. THE CONCEPT OF THE WEIGHTIER PART

It will be recalled that in his initial statement that the legislator is "the people or the whole body of the citizens," Marsilius had added, "or the weightier part thereof" (*aut eius valentiorem partem*).[1] This concept of the *valentior pars* is used throughout the *Defensor pacis.* Most scholars used to interpret it simply as "the majority," until, quite recently, examination of the manuscripts[2] disclosed conclusively for the first time that Marsilius had specified the *pars valentior* by "quality" as well as by "quantity."[3] Hence, other terms than "majority" have been advanced as translations of *valentior:* "better"[4] "more influential,"[5] "more able,"[6] "ef-

[15] *De re pub.* I. xxv. 39.

[16] *De civ. Dei.* XIX. xxi. See above, p. 37.

[17] *De civ. Dei* XIX. xxiv.

[1] I. xii. 3.

[2] See Previté-Orton, "Marsiglio of Padua, Doctrines," *Eng. Hist. Rev.* XXXVIII (1923), 8; also his edition, p. 51 nn. g, 2; and Scholz's edition, p. 64, n. 1. See also the review of antecedent interpretations in Battaglia, *Marsilio,* pp. 81 ff.

[3] I. xii. 3: "valentiorem inquam partem considerata quantitate personarum et qualitate in communitate illa super quam lex fertur." The words "et qualitate" were omitted in a younger group of manuscripts and also in Goldast's edition (*Monarchia,* II, 169). See also II. xx. 2, where a similar qualitative criterion is added to the quantitative in the election of general councils; and I. viii. 3, where "democracy" is criticized as not being "according to proper proportion."

[4] P. Janet, *Histoire de la science politique dans ses rapports avec la morale* (Paris, 1887), I, 460: "la meilleure partie"; also E. Gebhart, in *Revue historique,* XXV (1884), 166.

[5] J. B. Schwab, *Johannes Gerson* (Würzburg, 1859), p. 31: "der einflussreichere Theil."

[6] Labanca, *Marsilio,* p. 141: "la parte più valente."

fective majority,"[7] "dominant,"[8] "prevailing,"[9] "worthier,"[10] "more numerous and estimable,"[11] "more notable,"[12] "élite,"[13] "more outstanding."[14] Most of these translations, however, err in one of two directions: either they overemphasize the qualitative aspect at the expense of the quantitative, or they express the consequential rather than the direct meaning of *valentior*. For what Marsilius is trying to prove is that the *valentior pars* of the people *should* be "dominant" or "prevailing" in the state; hence, if *valentior* initially had these latter meanings, his whole argument would be redundant.

The translation "weightier," originally suggested by Previté-Orton,[15] has here been adopted as perhaps the best term available in English to render the complex variety of qualitative and quantitative features embodied in Marsilius' term. But the ascertainment of the full significance of *valentior* requires a more thorough analysis of its sources and of Marsilius' interpretation of it than has yet been undertaken if the mystery still surrounding it is to be further dispelled.[16] Such an analysis is justified not only because of its bearing upon this concept itself but also because it should help clarify the concept of the "people" which for Marsilius is the source of all political power. In addition, it occupies an important place in the history of the ideas constituting the theory of republicanism and democracy.

The term *valentior* is obviously related to other similar terms which had been used to indicate some kind of political preponderance, such as *valere*[17] and *praevalere*.[18] The direct source of Marsilius' *valentior*, how-

[7] J. W. Allen, "Marsilio of Padua and Mediaeval Secularism," in F. J. C. Hearnshaw, ed., *The Social and Political Ideas of Some Great Mediaeval Thinkers* (London, 1923), p. 181. See A. Dempf, *Sacrum Imperium* (Munich, 1929), p. 435: "stärkerer Mehrheit."

[8] McIlwain, *op. cit.*, pp. 301–3.

[9] Sabine, *op. cit.*, p. 295.

[10] I. Edman and H. W. Schneider, *Fountainheads of Freedom* (New York, 1941), p. 269.

[11] J. MacKinnon, *The Origins of the Reformation* (London, 1939), p. 61.

[12] Valois, *op. cit.*, p. 575: "la plus notable partie"; also B. Landry, *L'Idée de chrétienté chez les scolastiques du xiii siècle* (Paris, 1929), p. 162. Piovano, *op. cit.*, p. 167: "la parte più notevole."

[13] M. de Wulf, *Histoire de la philosophie médiévale*, 5th ed. (Paris, 1925), II, 209.

[14] G. Mosca, *Storia delle dottrine politiche*, 3d ed. (Bari, 1939), p. 102: "la più cospicua."

[15] See his edition of the *Defensor*, p. xvi. This term has also been accepted by F. W. Coker, *Readings in Political Philosophy*, rev. ed. (New York, 1938), p. 246.

[16] See G. Capograssi, "Intorno a Marsilio da Padova," *Rivista internazionale di filosofia del diritto*, X (1930), 581: The concept of "*valentior pars* . . . è rimasto un enigma nella letteratura marsiliana."

[17] See Cicero *De re publica* II. xxii. 39: "semper in re publica tenendum est, ne *plurimum valeant* plurimi." The two words italicized mean "have the greatest power." See *ibid:* "maior multitudo . . . nec *valeret nimis*," i.e., "the greater number should not *have too much power*." See also *Corpus juris civilis, Institutiones* I. ii. 4: "plebiscita . . . non minus *valere* quam leges coeperunt."

[18] See Alexander of Hales *Summa theologiae* Lib. II. Tit. III. cap. x (III, 748). Thomas *S. theol.* II. I. qu.97. a.3. ad 3; *De reg. princ.* I. vi. Ptolemy of Lucca *De reg. princ.* III. x. Dante *De mon.* II. ix; III. xiv.

ever, appears unquestionably to be in Aristotle's *Politics*. William of Moerbeke uses *valentior pars* to translate Aristotle's expression κρεῖττον μέρος; and two passages in which this term appears are quoted from the *Politics* by Marsilius in the course of his arguments on behalf of the legislative authority of the people or of its *valentior pars*.[19] Apart from the commentaries on the *Politics* by Albert the Great, Thomas Aquinas, and Peter of Auvergne, *valentior* does not appear to have been used in medieval political philosophy prior to Marsilius; [20] it is not used very much after him, but wherever it does appear, there is an almost certain sign of Marsilian influence.[21] For Aristotle, however, κρεῖττον means simply "politically stronger," [22] whereas for Marsilius, as was pointed out above,[23] this is not the direct but rather the consequential meaning of *valentior*. To understand its direct meaning, we must now consider how Marsilius himself defines it.

Marsilius presents three distinct, although mutually coherent, specifications of the *valentior pars*. The first is by rational concepts: "By 'weightier part,' I mean to take into consideration *the quantity and the quality of the persons in that community over which the law is made*." [24] The second specification is by historical experience: "The weightier part of the citizens must be considered in accordance with *the honorable custom of polities*." [25] The third is by authority: the weightier part "must be determined in accordance with *the view of Aristotle in the Politics, Book VI, Chapter 2*." [26] Let us now examine each of these specifications in turn.

[19] I. xiii. 2, quoting *Pol.* IV. 12. 1296b 14: "oportet *valentiorem* esse *partem* civitatis volentem non-volente manere politiam" (δεῖ γὰρ κρεῖττον εἶναι τὸ βουλόμενον μέρος τῆς πόλεως τοῦ μὴ βουλομένου μένειν τὴν πολιτείαν). *Ibid.*, quoting *Pol.* VII. 14. 1332b 29: "totque multitudine esse eos in politeumate ut sint *valentiores* hiis omnibus, unum impossibilium est" (τοσούτους τε εἶναι τοὺς ἐν τῷ πολιτεύματι τὸ πλῆθος ὥστ' εἶναι κρείττους πάντων τούτων ἕν τι τῶν ἀδυνάτων ἐστίν).

[20] The only use I have found of *valentior* outside those mentioned is in a strange context: a report of the beliefs and practices of the heretical Cathari (*Protocols of the Inquisition in Languedoc*, in *Beiträge zur Sektengeschichte des Mittelalters*, ed. I. v. Döllinger [Munich, 1890], II, 175): "Dicebant, quod quasi omnes meliores et *valentiores* de Ax erant eorum amici et credentes. . . ." This statement, which occurs in the "confessio Sibiliae, uxoris Raymundi Petri de Archas, super crimine haeresis," was made about 1321 (see *ibid.* II, 147), some three years before Marsilius wrote. See also Godfrey of Fontaines *Quodlib.* XI. qu.17: "lex est quid *valentius* et firmius, cum ei non adsint passiones. . . ." This is based upon Aristotle-Moerbeke: "*valentius* (κρεῖττον) autem cui non adest quod passionale . . ." (*Pol.* III. 15. 1286a 18).

[21] See William of Ockham *Dialogus* Pars III. Tr. II. Lib. III. cap. xvii (p. 948). Cardinal Zabarella *De schismatibus auctoritate imperatoris tollendis* (ed. S. Schard, *De jurisdictione imperiali* [Basel, 1566]), p. 689; Comm. on Decretals I. vi. 6 (quoted in Carlyle, *op. cit.*, VI, 165, n. 1).

[22] The English translators Jowett, Welldon, Rackham, and Barker use "stronger" to translate Aristotle's κρεῖττον; Taylor uses "superior," but obviously to the same effect of political preponderance.

[23] See above, p. 183.

[24] I. xii. 3.

[25] I. xii. 4.

[26] *Ibid.*

Quantity and Quality

(1) *Quantity*. Marsilius' addition of a qualitative specification of *valentior* to the quantitative has so impressed recent commentators that they have tended to move to the opposite extreme from the egalitarian, democratic, majoritarian interpretation originally placed upon his position. As a result, it has been largely overlooked not only that Marsilius does mention quantity as well as quality, but also that almost all of his subsequent elucidations of *valentior* are quantitative. He begins with a statement implying unanimity: the laws must be made by "the whole body of citizens." But it is because unanimity is difficult or impossible to attain that he adds the *pars valentior* as an alternative: the laws must be made by "the whole body of citizens or the weightier part thereof, which represents the whole; for it is not easy, or not possible, for *all persons* to agree upon one decision, because *certain men* have a deformed nature, disagreeing with the common decision through singular malice or ignorance."[27] The *pars valentior* thus comprises "all persons" (*omnes personas*) except the "certain men" (*quorundam*) who "have a deformed nature." This exceptive concept of the "deformed" (*orbatam*) is the same restriction on universality which we saw in the case of Marsilius' first principle that "all men not deformed (*orbatos*) or otherwise impeded naturally desire a sufficient life."[28] The sequence from this principle to the legislative authority of the *pars valentior* is direct: the quantitative difference between the whole body of citizens and the weightier part thereof is these relatively few "deformed" persons. The *pars valentior* thus comprises the overwhelming majority of the citizens.

That this is the quantitative meaning of the *pars valentior* is also shown by the expressions which Marsilius uses as its synonyms. The *pars valentior* is "most" (*plurimi*,[29] *pluralitas*[30]) of the citizens; it is the citizen-body "in respect of most of its members" (*secundum eius plurimum*),[31] "for the most part" (*ut in pluribus*);[32] it is the "greater number" (*maior pluralitas*) of the citizens as against any smaller part thereof;[33] it is the "more ample part" (*pars amplior*)[34] of the citizens, the "number which exceeds" (*superflua pluralitas*),[35] as against one or a few. Thus Marsilius uses the terms *plures* and *plurimi* as quantitatively synonymous with *valentior*. At one point he explains that the term *plures* may be used to mean either the positive "many" or the comparative "more"; in the latter sense he

[27] I. xii. 5. [28] I. iv. 2. See above, pp. 58–59. [29] I. xii. 8; I. xiii. 3.
[30] I. xiii. 3. [31] I. xiii. 2. [32] *Ibid.*
[33] I. xii. 5. See I. xiii. 1: "pars maior." [34] I. xii. 6; see I. xiii. 4.
[35] I. xiii. 1.

assimilates it both to *major pars* and to *valentior*.[36] But the *valentior pars* as he conceives it comprises not merely a bare majority (*major pars*) but an overwhelming majority.

The same quantitative conclusion also emerges from Marsilius' use of the maxim "every whole is greater than its part." He interprets it not in the sense that "whole" means the *universitas civium* and "part" means the *pars valentior,* but rather in the sense that "whole" means the *universitas or* its *pars valentior,* "which must be taken for the same thing," while "part" means "any part thereof taken separately" (*quacumque sui parte seorsum*).[37] Quantitatively, then, Marsilius does not think of the *pars valentior* as being distinct from the *universitas;* rather, they are almost identical.

What, then, is the bearing of this quantitative view of the weightier part of the citizens as comprising all except the "deformed" few who refuse to agree to the common judgment? It does not involve forced agreement, for, as we have seen, Marsilius expressly reserves to the citizens the right to protest against the recommendations of the elected experts, and to revise or to reject them entirely.[38] Moreover, one of the objections which he considers against his own position is that "it is very difficult or impossible for the many depraved and unintelligent persons to agree in their judgments; which is not the case with regard to the few and virtuous. It is therefore more useful for the law to be made by the few than by the whole body of the citizens or the exceeding number of them."[39] Marsilius' reply admits that it is easier for the few to agree than for the many, but he insists that this is offset by the superiority in judgment of the whole body of citizens as against the few.[40] Agreement as such, then, is not the primary consideration in Marsilius' view, at least not in its initial bearings with regard to the legislative and other judgments of the whole body of the citizens. In this sense, it was rather the monarchists who emphasized the importance of agreement as such; the Marsilian conception of the whole people as having supreme authority is the target of their argument (which Marsilius has repeated as an *argumentum a contrario* against his own position) that "many" would disagree, therefore "one" must rule.[41]

[36] I. xiv. 8; see II. xxii. 6: "parte valentiori sive majori." [37] I. xiii. 2; see I. xii. 5.

[38] See above, p. 169. [39] I. xiii. 1. [40] I. xiii. 5.

[41] Thomas *De reg. princ.* I. ii: ". . . quinimmo multitudo *dissentiens* sibi ipsi sit onerosa . . . Amplius, manifestum est, quod plures multitudinem nullo modo conservarent, si omnino *dissentirent.* Requiritur in pluribus quaedam unio ad hoc, quod quoquo modo regere possint . . . Melius igitur regit unus . . . Nam provinciae vel civitates, quae non reguntur ab uno, *dissensionibus* laborant." See also Egidius *De reg. princ.* Lib. III. Pars II. cap. iii; John of Paris *De pot. reg. et pap.* cap. ix (p. 110). Subsequently (cap. xxii [p. 141]), John repeats the same

The burden of Marsilius' reference to the impossibility of unanimity as requiring recourse to the "weightier part" is rather that even after full discussion, revision, and the final voting, there still may remain some who refuse to accept the decision. Such stubbornness whereby "two or three men who are moved by contentiousness contradict the common consensus of all," had been a problem of episcopal elections as far back as the first Council of Nicaea.[42] William of Ockham mentions a similar problem in connection with the calling of general councils, and uses a phrase almost identical with that of Marsilius for its solution;[43] indeed, the problem existed in every sphere of medieval political life.[44] It is quite likely, however, that Marsilius was thinking specifically of the two groups who, as we saw in Padua, refused to accept the common jurisdiction and decisions of the city as a whole: the priesthood and the *magnates*. The expressions which were applied to these groups—*privilegiati* and *maleablati*[45]—indicate the same situation as the "unreasonable protest or contradiction" because of which Marsilius invokes the "weightier part" as an alternative to unanimity.

The relation of the *pars valentior* to the whole body of citizens is, therefore, quite different from that which a general council was conceived to have to all of Christendom, or the electoral princes or the Roman Senate to the Roman people. In each case, there is a relation of "representation"; moreover, there is a presumed similarity between Marsilius' reason for invoking the *pars valentior* and the reason given in Roman law for the invocation of the Senate. But this similarity is only apparent; it rests upon

---

argument as having been advanced by the proponents of universal monarchy; in this guise he rejects it. See also above, pp. 116–18; and below, pp. 201–2.

[42] *Nicaenum concilium* cap. vii, in *Corp. jur. can., Decret. Gratiani* Pars I. dist. 65. can. 1 (I, 249): "Sane, si communi omnium consensui rationabiliter probato secundum ecclesiasticam regulam, *duo vel tres animositate ducti per contentionem contradicant,* obtineat plurimorum sententia sacerdotum." See *Decretal. Greg. IX* Lib. 1. Tit. 6. cap. 19 (II, 60): ". . . semper id debeat praevalere, quod a pluribus et sanioribus fuerit ordinatum . . . . *non obstante contradictione vel appellatione paucorum* . . ." See A. Esmein, "L'Unanimité et la majorité dans les élections canoniques," *Mélanges Fitting* (Paris, 1906), I, 369; E. Ruffini-Avondo, *Il principio maggioritario, profilo storico* (Turin, 1927), p. 26.

[43] *Dialogus* Pars I. Lib. VI. cap. lxxxiv (p. 603): "*Disc.* Quod si aliqua parochia vel etiam diocesis nollet aliquos mittere ad concilium generale? *Magist.* Respondetur, quod propter *contradictionem* ipsorum non esset communis utilitas omittenda. . . ." See *Def. pac.* I. xii. 5: "propter quorum irrationabilem reclamationem seu contradictionem non debent communia conferentia impediri vel omitti." See also Konrad of Megenberg *De transl. Rom. Imp.* cap. xv (p. 302); and Ockham *Dialogus* Pars III. Tr. II. Lib. 1. cap. xxvii (p. 899).

[44] See Hugolinus *Dissensiones dominorum sive controversiae veterum juris Romani interpretum qui glossatores vocantur* par. 75 (ed. C. Haenel [Leipzig, 1834], p. 317): "Quomodo enim major pars universitatis jurabit, quum *per se consentire non possit?* Imo unus de universitate unam eliget sententiam, alius aliam!" (quoted in O. von Gierke, *Das deutsche Genossenschaftsrecht* III [Berlin 1881], 231, n. 140). Cf. other similar texts quoted in *ibid.*, pp. 218 ff.

[45] See above, pp. 27–29.

a misunderstanding of Marsilius' concept. Two texts of Roman law tell us that the Roman people had increased to such an extent that it was difficult for it to be assembled into one group; for this reason the making of laws devolved to the Senate.[46] The quantitative relation of the people to the Senate is thus that of *very many* persons to *very few,* and the primary consideration motivating the devolvement of legislative authority from the former to the latter is that of *physical assemblage* into one group. The quantitative relation of the Marsilian people to the *pars valentior,* on the other hand, is, as we have seen, that of *all* to *nearly all,* and the primary consideration in the devolvement of authority to the latter is that of *volitional agreement.*[47] This volitional emphasis is, of course, fully in keeping with the voluntarism of Marsilius' entire doctrine.[48] The difficulty of physical assemblage is not invoked by Marsilius at all in connection with the *pars valentior.* It is only in connection with the *discovery* of the laws by the relatively few *experts* that Marsilius invokes a consideration even slightly similar to the Roman. But this consideration is not that the multitude is too large to "come together"; it is rather that if all the citizens spent their time in the initial investigations of possible laws, the performance of the necessary functions of the community would be unduly disturbed.[49] But the "discovery" to which these investigations lead is not, as we have seen, the legislative enactment, nor are the experts what Marsilius means by the *valentior pars.* On the contrary, he expressly provides for the "assemblage" of the whole body of citizens to elect the "experts," to consider their recommendations, and to pass the final laws.[50]

For the same reason, it is necessary to distinguish the kinds of "representation" to which Marsilius refers. The experts who draw up proposed

[46] *Corp. jur. civ., Institutiones* I. ii. 5: "Nam quum auctus est populus Romanus in eum modum, ut difficile esset in unum eum convocari legis sanciendae causa, aequum visum est senatum vice populi consuli." *Digestum* I. Lib. I. Tit. II. 2. § 9: "Deinde, quia difficile plebs convenire coepit, populus certe multo difficilius in tanta turba hominum, necessitas ipsa curam reipublicae ad Senatum deduxit." The former text is cited by McIlwain, *op. cit.,* p. 304; the latter by O. von Gierke, *Political Theories of the Middle Age,* trans. F. W. Maitland (Cambridge, 1900), pp. 168–69, n. 236. Both authors regard the Marsilian position on this point as closely parallelling the Roman; Lagarde (*Marsile,* p. 196, n. 115) agrees.

[47] Thus the Roman law phrases "in unum eum convocari" and "convenire . . . in tanta turba hominum," adduced by McIlwain and Gierke, have a quite different meaning from Marsilius' phrase "in unam convenire *sententiam.*" The same misinterpretation is made by J. Lecler ("Les Théories démocratiques au moyen âge," *Etudes,* CCXXV [Oct.–Dec., 1935], 23) when he presents as the reason for Marsilius' "delegation" of power, "la réunion de tout le corps politique étant elle-meme une impossibilité"; and by McIlwain (*op. cit.,* p. 302), "because it is seldom possible or convenient for the entire body to meet together."

[48] See especially above, pp. 57–58.

[49] I. xiii. 8. See also below, pp. 235–36.

[50] I. xii. 3: "in generali civium congregatione." I. xiii. 6: "omnium congregata multitudo." I. xiii. 8: "ab omnibus simul congregatis civibus"; "in universitate civium congregata"; "per auditum et consensum universae multitudinis"; "in universali civium congregatione."

legislation "represent" the whole body of the citizens [51] (just as a general council which determines matters of faith "represents" the whole body of the faithful) [52] in the sense that they are elected by the whole body to perform a specific function; they thus "represent its place and authority." The weightier part of the citizens, on the other hand, "represents" the whole body of the citizens in the sense that the former comprises all but a few of the latter, and *"is taken for the same thing."* [53] In each case, that which "represents" can act for that which is "represented"; but the weightier part, far from being "elected" by the whole body of citizens, rather *is* almost that whole body in the literal numerical sense. And whereas the representative authority of both the legislative experts and the general council is severely limited, since their decisions must be ratified by the *universitas,* or legislator in the strict sense,[54] there is no limitation of any kind placed upon the weightier part in relation to the *universitas:* the authority of the former is completely co-extensive with that of the latter.

The quantitative aspect of the weightier part, as we have discussed it so far, emerges quite clearly from Marsilius' statements. His primary quantitative concern, as we have seen, is with the final situation when a "common decision" has already been carried in the citizen-assembly: then all but the "deformed" few will accept it. But if we now ask what, within this overwhelming majority, is the specific quantity of votes required, either alone or in conjunction with qualitative factors, to carry a decision in the first place, no explicit information is given by Marsilius. We shall find some indications of this specific quantitative factor when we turn to his two other specifications of the "weightier part"; but he presents none himself. The nearest he comes to such an indication is in his statement that the legislative experts will be elected "by each of the primary parts of the state . . . but according to the proportion of each." [55] That this "proportion" is not, however, merely quantitative, is shown by the fact that democracy is classed among the "diseased" forms of government because it is not "according to proper proportion." [56] But that it involves at least a numerical majority is also shown by each of the texts we have so far considered. Marsilius is primarily concerned with es-

[51] I. xiii. 8: "vicem et auctoritatem universitatis civium repraesentantes."

[52] II. xx. 2: "vicem universitatis fidelium repraesentantes." See below, pp. 286, 290.

[53] I. xii. 5: "pars valentior, quae totam universitatem repraesentat"; "hoc autem fieri optime per civium universitatem tantummodo, aut eius valentiorem partem *quod pro eodem de cetero supponatur.*"

[54] For the legislative experts, see I. xii. 2, 3; I. xiii. 8. For the general council, see II. xxi. 4: its decisions are, as such, non-coercive; only the legislator can make them coercive.

[55] I. xiii. 8.

[56] I. viii. 3.

tablishing the principle that the legislative authority rests with the whole people rather than with the one or a few of monarchic or oligarchic constitutions. He does not specify the precise method or proportions by which the people must arrive at its decisions, since these are variable factors. He insists only that the decisions be arrived at freely, and that they bear the sanction of either the whole citizen-body or of the all-but-a-few who, regardless of their initial position, accept and support the "common decision."

(2) *Quality.* By "quality" Marsilius means both the functional differentiations among the different parts of the state and the personal characteristics of the citizens. He uses the term in the former sense when he repeats Aristotle's warning against disproportionate growth of any part of the state "in quantity and in quality";[57] he uses the term in the latter sense when he mentions the early Christians' "weakness in quantity and in quality; for they were crude . . . and easily misled,"[58] and when he refers, usually disparagingly, to the "quality of the priests."[59] But despite the fact that he specifies the weightier part by the "quantity and quality of *persons,*"[60] the qualitative differentiations which he indicates in relation to such discriminations as would be involved in voting refer primarily to the differences between parts of the state. It is from this point of view that Marsilius divides the parts into *honorabilitas* and *vulgus,* which are parts "in the strict sense" (*simpliciter*) and "in the broad sense" (*large*), respectively, because the latter "are functions (*officia*) necessary to the state according to the view of Aristotle."[61] Thus Marsilius here echoes the aristocratic position of Aristotle's best possible state, although he does not follow Aristotle in denying these "necessary" parts citizenship and making them slaves. It is from a similar point of view, however, that he condemns "democracy" in the Aristotelian sense as the rule of the *vulgus* alone, and not "according to proper proportion."[62] The *vulgus* would numerically outweigh the *honorabilitas;* it is for this reason that qualitative considerations are invoked. Marsilius' underlying assumption is here the same as that of Aristotle; it is based also upon the actual experience of the Italian communes. This assumption is one of class warfare: the *vulgus* and the *honorabilitas* (substitute the various groups of the *popolani,* on the one hand, and *magnati* and clergy, on the other) will each act as

[57] I. xv. 10; cf. *Pol.* v. 3. 1302b 33 ff.

[58] II. xvii. 7.

[59] II. xv. 5; II. xvii. 12; II. xxi. 15; II. xxv. 5.

[60] I. xii. 3.

[61] I. v. 1. See Aristotle *Pol.* VII. 8–9. 1328a 22 ff. Failure to note this Aristotelian background of the distinction between parts *simpliciter* and *large* has led some commentators to misinterpret it as meaning, respectively, the "public" and "private" functions in the state. See Franck, *op. cit.*, p. 140; Labanca, *Marsilio,* p. 137; Vadala-Papale, *op. cit.*, p. 77.

[62] I. viii. 3.

a homogeneous political unit to advance its own economic and political power, and to reduce that of the other.[63] It is to avoid such particularism that Marsilius leavens quantity with quality. But this proportion operates as much against oligarchy or aristocracy as against the Aristotelian kind of democracy: Marsilius upholds rather the "polity" in which "each citizen participates . . . according to his rank and ability or condition."[64] The degree of participation in political power by each citizen will hence depend upon his "rank" (*gradus*),[65] and the rank, in turn, is determined by the functional group to which he belongs. In this mode of differentiating the state or the people into higher and lower ranks, or orders, or status, Marsilius is one with the other Aristotelians, and indeed with the whole orientation of medieval thought.[66]

The specific content of these qualitative differentiations as Marsilius views them would also appear to be derived at least in part from Aristotle. In the *Politics,* it is declared that "every state consists of quality and quantity. *By quality I mean freedom, wealth, education, good birth;* by quantity I mean the superior numbers of the multitude."[67] Now this sentence occurs directly after one which mentions the κρεῖττον μέρος (*valentior pars*) and which Marsilius quotes;[68] it would hence seem a plausible inference that he is referring directly to this passage in specifying his *valentior pars* by "quantity and quality." To be sure, he uses the specification to a different end from that of Aristotle; for the latter goes on to indicate which kinds of constitution are best suited to various states according to the proportions of the numbers and the qualitative characteristics of their inhabitants.[69] The constitution of the Marsilian state, as we have seen, does not have the variability which Aristotle here indicates; Marsilius explicitly refuses to allow, for example, any case where an oligarchic constitution would be "naturally" called for.[70]

The qualitative characteristics which Aristotle lists in this passage, however, all receive some attention from Marsilius. Freedom is used as a

[63] See Aristotle *Pol.* III. 7. 1279b 9; 10. 1281a 13; IV. 4. 1292a 19; 13. 1297a 14 ff.; V. 5. 1304b 22 ff.; VI. 3. 1318a 25. See also above, p. 28, n. 37.

[64] I. viii. 3.

[65] This is also specified in the definition of the "citizen" as "qui participat . . . secundum *gradum* suum" (I. xii. 4).

[66] See Thomas *S. theol.* I. qu.108. a.2: "Unde et in civitatibus triplex ordo hominum invenitur; quidam enim sunt supremi, ut optimates; quidam autem sunt infimi, ut vilis populus; quidam autem sunt medii, ut populus honorabilis." Peter of Auvergne *In Pol.* Lib. IV. Lect. 4 (p. 289): "Sunt autem tres gradus in ea civitate: infimus, medius, et supremus." Ptolemy of Lucca *De reg. princ.* IV. iii: "civitas quamdam causat harmoniam . . . ex summis videlicet, infimis, et mediis ordinibus, quibus moderatur." Egidius *De reg. princ.* Lib. III. Pars II. cap. ii: in "politia . . . intenditur bonum commune bonorum egenorum, mediarum personarum, et divitum, et omnium secundum suum statum. . . ."

[67] *Pol.* IV. 12. 1296b 17.

[68] I. xiii. 2; see above, p. 184, n. 19.

[69] *Pol.* IV. 12. 1296b 25 ff.

[70] I. xiii. 5, 6; see *Pol.* IV. 12. 1296b 31–35.

characterization of all the citizens.[71] Good birth is dealt with only negatively, for he argues against hereditary succession on the ground that virtuous qualities are not necessarily inherited.[72] The case is partly the same with regard to wealth, for he insists that "virtuous poor men" must have the opportunity of becoming rulers; [73] and a large part of his polemic against the papacy is based upon its concern with wealth.[74] Moreover, the "financial" (*pecuniativa*) part of the state is classed among the *vulgus*,[75] in contrast to Aristotle, who assigns its analogue, "an abundance of moneys," to the upper classes [76] in the same sextuple list of parts of the state which Marsilius adopts. In another sense, however, he accepts and applies the criterion of wealth through the concept of "leisure," which is invoked frequently. It is leisure for liberal functions which distinguishes the citizens from slaves; [77] but it is also leisure which distinguishes those citizens who participate in all the deliberative activities of the state from the "mechanics" who are so preoccupied with acquiring the necessities of life by their labor that they do not have the time for such activities.[78] Marsilius, like Aristotle, thus assumes the division of society into a small leisure class and a large body of men occupied in "mechanical" labor. His references to the remaining kind of quality listed by Aristotle, "education," follow similar lines in the guise of "prudence," which is conceived as being concomitant with leisure,[79] and which is one of the main "qualities" of the "perfect ruler." [80]

Yet Marsilius does not hold this position in the rigid manner of Aristotle's absolutely best state. Aristotle's attitude toward leisure had been ambivalent: he emphasized the importance of the "best citizens" being able to have leisure (σχολάζειν),[81] and on this ground he excluded the farmers and artisans from citizenship in his absolutely best state; [82] but on the other hand, in his less normative approaches it is precisely their lack of leisure which he upholds as the condition required for the success of the democratic state, since their preoccupation with obtaining the necessities of life forces them to govern through laws.[83] Marsilius' attitude is

[71] I. iv. I; I. xii. 4, 6. [72] I. xvi. 24; see I. xi. 7. [73] I. xiv. 8.
[74] See II. xi. 4. [75] I. v. I. [76] *Pol.* VII. 9. 1329a 18–20.
[77] I. iv. I: "viventes civiliter non solum vivunt, quod faciunt bestiae aut servi, sed bene vivunt, *vacantes* scilicet operibus liberalibus. . . ."
[78] I. xii. 2: ". . . licet inquisitio haec convenientius fieri possit et compleri melius ex observatione potentium *vacare* seniorum et expertorum in agibilibus quos prudentes appellant, quam ex mechanicorum consideratione, qui ad acquirenda vitae necessaria suis operibus habent intendere." For similar references to the *vacantes,* see I. xiii. 4; I. xvi. 21; I. xvii. 4. The men who are preoccupied by "necessary" labor are also referred to at I. xiii. 8; II. xx. 2.
[79] See references in preceding note. [80] I. xiv. 3–5.
[81] *Pol.* II. 11. 1273a 34. [82] *Ibid.* VII. 9. 1329a I.
[83] *Ibid.* IV. 6. 1292b 28 ff.; VI. 4. 1318b 12. See above, p. 97, n. 42.

different. He insists that "the less learned, or those who do not have leisure for liberal functions," should nevertheless share in political power, for they "participate in the understanding and judgment of practical affairs, although not equally with those who have leisure." [84] As we saw in the case of his concept of the citizen,[85] he does not have so strict a demarcation between the leisured and the unleisured in the exercise of political functions as have some of the other Aristotelians. It is, however, the combination of prudence with leisure which for Marsilius constitutes the qualitative criterion entering into the determination of the weightier part of the citizens.

(3) *Relation between quantity and quality*. Marsilius does not indicate the precise proportions in which the *vulgus* is to be weighed against the *honorabilitas,* or numbers against leisure and prudence. Such proportions had been set forth by Aristotle and by Cicero, among others; we shall recur to the former below.[86] The canonist doctrine of the *major et sanior pars* of a cathedral chapter as being decisive in episcopal elections was an important institutional procedure along these lines, and it has been regarded both as influential upon and as basically similar to the quantitative-qualitative *valentior pars* of Marsilius.[87] There are, indeed, important resemblances between the two concepts. Each began from the notion of unanimity, and was invoked because unanimity proved impossible of attainment; [88] each involves a combination of quantity and quality. Moreover, Marsilius himself refers to the *sanior pars* "of the priests" [89] and "of the faithful multitude," [90] although he does not identify this concept with the *valentior pars*. A further factor is that the *major et sanior pars* was invoked in the statutes of Padua itself as governing the election of the

[84] I. xiii. 4.

[85] See above, pp. 176 ff.

[86] See below, p. 198. For Cicero, see *De re publica* II. xxii. 39–40.

[87] See McIlwain, *op. cit.*, p. 305, n. 1; Lagarde, *Marsile*, p. 196. Both these writers, however, regard the Roman as the primary influence on Marsilius' concept (see above p. 188, n. 46). See also H. Rehm, *Geschichte der Staatsrechtswissenschaft* (Freiburg i. B. and Leipzig, 1896), pp. 190–91; Lecler, "Les Théories démocratiques au moyen âge," *Etudes*, CCXXV (Oct.–Dec., 1935), 23, n. 3; W. Ullmann, *The Origins of the Great Schism* (London, 1948), p. 198; H. J. Laski, "Political Theory in the Later Middle Ages," *Cambridge Medieval History,* VIII (1936), p. 628.

[88] See *Corp. jur. can., Decretal. Greg. IX* Lib. I. Tit. 6. cap. 2, 5, 6 ff. (II, 48 ff.). See A. von Wretschko, "Die *electio communis* bei den kirchlichen Wahlen im Mittelalter," *Deutsche Zeitschrift für Kirchenrecht,* XI (1902), 328 ff.; A. Esmein, "L'unanimité et la majorité dans les élections canoniques," *Mélanges Fitting* (Paris, 1906), I, 357–382; E. Ruffini-Avondo, "Il principio maggioritario nella storia del diritto canonico," *Archivio Giuridico,* XCIII (1925), fasc. 1, pp. 15–67.

[89] II. vi. 12: "stari debet judicio collegii sacerdotum aut *sanioris partis illius*." II. xx. 5: "Unde sacerdotibus invicem dissidentibus de credendis ad salutem aeternam, de ipsorum *saniori parte* fidelium pars valentior habet judicare."

[90] II. xvii. 15: "sacerdoti vel episcopo cum *saniori parte* fidelis multitudinis."

gastaldiones of the guild of notaries[91]—to which Bonmatteo dei Mainardini, Marsilius' father, probably belonged.[92]

Despite these points of contact, however, there is a fundamental difference in the interpretation of the two concepts. Not only did the *major et sanior pars* move from unanimity of priests and "people" to a vote restricted to the priesthood alone,[93] but even among the latter their "soundness," consisting in their "authority, zeal, and merit," was made to count for more than their numbers.[94] The relation between *majoritas* and *sanioritas* was conceived as being capable not only of agreement but also of opposition: it was denied that "where the number is greater, there the zeal is presumed better,"[95] and instead it was insisted that *sanioritas* may accompany "fewness" (*paucitas*).[96] To be sure, Pope Gregory X provided in 1274 that a two-thirds vote should carry an election, but even then the possibility of nullification was not ruled out on qualitative and legal grounds.[97]

Marsilius' interpretation of the *pars valentior,* on the other hand, views its quantitative and its qualitative aspects as being in complete agreement. This is brought out clearly by the use which he makes of the maxim "every whole is greater than its part": he holds that it "is true in respect both to magnitude or mass and to practical virtue and action."[98] Thus an increase in quantity will bring with it an increase in qualitative value, and by this means he answers the arguments to the effect that the many

[91] *Stat. com. Pad.* n. 398 (p. 129): "Si vero in capitulo aliquo constituto pro gastaldionibus electis vel eligendis, questio vel discordia fuerit, illi sint gastaldiones fratalie notariorum et a potestate Padue confirmentur, qui de voluntate *majoris et sanioris partis* notariorum in illo capitulo congregatorum fuerint electi." The statute is also printed in Roberti, "Le corporazioni padovane," pp. 169–70, with a few minor changes. The *major et sanior pars* is also invoked in the elections of officials by the Norman "nation" at the University of Paris; see *Chartularium Univ. Paris.,* ed. H. Denifle and A. Chatelain (Paris, 1891), II, 456.

[92] See above, p. 20.

[93] *Corp. jur. can., Decretal. Greg. IX* Lib. I. Tit. 6. cap. 56 (II, 95).

[94] See *ibid.* cap. 53, 57 (II, 93, 95).

[95] *Ibid.* cap. 57 (II, 95): "ubi major numerus est, zelus melior praesumatur." The ensuing discussion rejects this dictum.

[96] Gerhoh of Reichersberg *De investigatione Antichristi* I. liv (MGH, *Libelli de lite,* III, 363): "[Electores] quos etiam quamvis *pauciores* numero *saniorem* fatentur partem. . . ." *Dialogus de pontificatu sanctae Romanae ecclesiae* (MGH, *Libelli de lite,* III, 531): "*Paucitatem* eorum qui me elegerunt cardinalium mihi obicis. Sed ut taceam illud vulgare quo dicitur: *ea pars maior que sanior,* audi evangelium. . . ." Augustinus Triumphus *S. de eccl. pot.* qu.2. a.8: "populus sequendus non est in judicio sed doctores qui licet sint *pauciores* numero sunt tamen *sanioris* consili." See also O. von Gierke, *Das deutsche Genossenschaftsrecht,* III (Berlin, 1881), 322–30.

[97] *Corp. jur. can., Sext.* Lib. I. Tit. 6. cap. 9 (II, 951). See Egidius of Rome *De eccl. pot.* III. ix (p. 191): "electio episcopi dependet ab institutione Summi Pontificis, qualiter debeat fieri electio praelatorum, et quomodo eligentes debeant se habere et quantum ad zelum et quantum ad meritum et quantum ad numerum, ut *quantus* debeat esse numerus eligentium et *quales* debent eligentes ad hoc quod electus sit rite assumptus. . . ."

[98] I. xiii. 2.

who are less learned are not so good judges of legislation as the few who are more learned: "the *number* of the less learned could be *increased* to such an extent that they would judge about these things *equally as well as or better than* the few who are more learned."[99] The multitude of the whole people "is *more ample, and consequently* its judgment *is more secure,* than that of some part taken separately."[100]

It is not surprising, therefore, that the *valentior pars* should have been interpreted solely in quantitative terms for so many centuries before critical scholarship restored the words *et qualitate* to Marsilius' text. To be sure, this quantity is not that of equal individual units but rather that of groups; yet Marsilius conceives the qualitative equality or superiority of one group in relation to another as determinable by their respective quantities. He places two limitations upon this quantitative determination, which would otherwise lead logically to a complete acceptance of democracy as defined by the Aristotelian tradition. One is the particularism in his view of democracy which was discussed above.[101] The other is his developmental conception which finds that in primitive communities quality does not always accompany quantity.[102] But apart from these, the whole emphasis of his defense of the *valentior pars* of the citizens as legislator is along the same lines as defenders of democracy had upheld. Hence it is incorrect to infer from his introduction of quality that the *pars valentior* corresponds with the "anti-democratic ideas of Aristotle."[103] This is to overlook that the *pars valentior* includes the *vulgus* (Aristotle's δῆμος) and that the arguments in behalf of the *pars valentior* explicitly oppose the "anti-democratic" view that only the wise men, the experts, should be the legislator. It is the "few" who are the villains, and the "many" who are the heroes of Marsilius' drama.[104] As against the aristocratic doctrine that only the virtuous few should "legislate," Marsilius vindicates the rights of "the other citizens,"[105] the "men of humbler intellect,"[106] the "less learned,"[107] the "farmers, artisans, and such,"[108] who "must not be called undiscerning . . . but must rather be counted among the good":[109] "For most of the citizens are neither vicious nor undiscerning

[99] I. xiii. 4. [100] *Ibid.* [101] See above, pp. 190–91.

[102] See I. iii. 4; II. xvii. 7; II. xxviii 3. [103] McIlwain, *op. cit.,* p. 304.

[104] See I. xii. 6, 8; I. xiii. 5. With this should be contrasted the position of Cicero, who, despite his doctrine of the natural equality of all men (*De legibus* I. x. 29 ff.), disparages the *vulgus* and extols the *doctissimi viri* (*ibid.* I. vi. 18–19).

[105] I. xii. 6. [106] I. xiii. 7. [107] I. xiii. 4. [108] *Ibid.*

[109] I. xiii. 7. There is thus no such emphasis in Marsilius as is found in William Marshall's marginal note to his 1535 translation of the *Defensor* I. xii. 6: "In all this longe tale he speaketh not of the rascall multytude, but of the parlyament." Marshall renders Marsilius' *vulgus* by "the commune sorte or rascall" (*The Defence of Peace, translated out of Latin into English* I. v [London, 1535], fol. 14*v*) and by *"rascall communes"* (*ibid.* I. viii [fol. 20*r*]). See also below, p. 301, n. 47.

in most cases and most of the time; for all or most are of *sound* mind and reason . . ." [110] It is possible to see in this defense of the "soundness" of most of the citizens an indirect rebuttal of the canonist doctrine of the "greater and sounder part" of the priesthood as being the only appropriate elector of bishops. Far from corresponding with the "anti-democratic ideas of Aristotle," this defense of the *pars valentior* is in direct opposition to those ideas; it is based, instead, upon those brief passages of the *Politics* in which Aristotle tentatively defends the democracy which he elsewhere condemns. In terms of Aristotle's distinctions of constitutions, Marsilius' state is closer to democracy than to any other constitution except polity.

The Honorable Custom of Polities

When we turn to Marsilius' second specification of the "weightier part" —"according to the honorable custom of polities" [111]—we find, of course, a less definite indication of its meaning. It is by no means certain to which "polities" he is referring, nor even that he is using "polity" in its specific as opposed to its generic sense—as a certain kind of constitution or government rather than as a constitution or government in general.[112]

If we turn first to Padua, we can find illustrations of quantitative-qualitative combinations which are in general similar to those indicated by Marsilius. The term *valentior* does not occur in Gloria's collection of the Padua statutes,[113] but *valentia* does; and it is used consistently to refer to the "value" of the "immobile goods" which men must have in order to hold office.[114] In this sense, *valentior* would mean simply "wealthier," which, as we have seen, is far from Marsilius' meaning.[115] A closer analogue to the qualitative weights of leisure and prudence attached by Marsilius to the *pars valentior* is found in the procedure indicated by a Padua statute of 1266 for the composition of the "greater council" of six hundred members, which was the legislative body of the city. The *podestà,* himself elected directly or indirectly by the "greater council," [116] was to

[110] I. xiii. 3. Of this statement Emerton (*op. cit.,* p. 26) writes: "One is reminded of President Lincoln's immortal version of the same truth."

[111] I. xii. 4.

[112] See I. viii. 3; and Aristotle *Pol.* III. 7. 1279a 38.

[113] Although Labanca (*Marsilio,* p. 142) writes that "le parole *valentiores populi* erano religiosamente rispettate negli Statuti Patavini," it does not occur in Gloria's collection. However, Labanca refers elsewhere (*op. cit.,* p. 89, n. 1) to "Statuti del 1274 e del 1277, ms. della Bib. civica," which I have been unable to consult.

[114] *Stat. com. Pad.* n. 238 (p. 83): no one can hold office "nisi habuerit bona immobilia in Padua vel Paduano districtu *valentia* libras quingentas denariorum venetorum." *Ibid.* nn. 326–27 (p. 105): "nullus possit esse potestas citadellae . . . nisi tempore electionis habuerit bona immobilia *valentia* libras quingentas denariorum venetorum." See *ibid.* n. 416.I (p. 134).

[115] See above, p. 192, and I. xiv. 8.

[116] *Stat. com. Pad.* nn. 1, 1.I (pp. 5–6).

"reduce" the council to six hundred members by admitting only persons "whom he thought better" and by "removing others whom he found to be servants (*famulos*) or serfs (*servientes*) of someone." If the number remained still in excess of six hundred, "then let there be withdrawn all who are not cavalrymen (*milites*) and infantrymen (*pedites*) from all arms and . . . then those who are less useful (*minus utiles*)."[117] In 1277, when the greater council was increased to one thousand members, the additions were made by the *anziani* (literally, the "elders" of the commune) "from among other good citizens of Padua possessing immobile goods."[118] These references to "good," "better," "useful" are, of course, quite vague; but in their context they undoubtedly indicate both economic and political considerations, the latter ranging from lack of criminal record[119] to willingness to assume political responsibilities and sympathy with the party in power, whether the *grassa borghesia* or the *popolo minuto*.[120] It should be added, however, that the statutes also provide that every citizen paying a certain minimum tax is eligible to vote for the "captains and custodians of the Padua district,"[121] and that the "entire community" is to be assembled by the *anziani* at least once every four months.[122]

Other examples of the weighting to which Marsilius may have been referring as "the honorable custom of polities" are found in Siena[123] and Florence.[124] A similar weighting may be seen in the frequent references of the Padua statutes to "quality of person." These references deal with the fines which must be paid for doing bodily violence to someone, and the fines are graded "according to the quality of the person, the blow, and the place."[125] What is meant by "quality of person" is shown by the further provision that assault against a *miles* is to be fined twice as heavily

[117] *Ibid.* n. 16 (p. 13).

[118] *Ibid.* n. 16.I (p. 14). Within the greater council itself a bare majority (*major pars*) was generally required to pass an enactment (*ibid.* nn. 1, 31 [pp. 5, 18]), but a three-fourths vote was needed to make a statute (*ibid.* n. 1182.I [p. 361]).

[119] See the references to "omnes forbanniti pro maleficio" (*ibid.* n. 16. I [p. 14]).

[120] See Roberti, "Le corporazioni padovane," pp. 37 ff.,54 ff.

[121] *Stat. com. Pad.* n. 16.I (p. 14). [122] *Ibid.* n. 466 (p. 150).

[123] *Il costituto . . . di Siena dell' anno 1262* I. 385 (p. 146): the *podestà* must choose at least half the members of the "general council of the bell" from among those who are "abstricti et iurati universitati populi"—where *populus* means the opposite of *grandi* or nobles. See also *ibid.* I. 128, 131, 517 (pp. 57, 58, 189).

[124] "La pace del Cardinal Latino" IV (in G. Salvemini, *Magnati e popolani in Firenze dal 1280 al 1295* [Florence, 1899], p. 325): the "councils and offices" are to be divided among the Guelph and Ghibelline parties and the neutrals by proportional representation, i.e., "juxta numerum capitum que invenientur in singulis partibus."

[125] *Stat. com. Pad.* n. 67 (p. 30): "Et insuper de injuria satisfaciant injuriam passo secundum *qualitatem personae,* percussionis, et loci." See *ibid.* nn. 548, 765 (pp. 177, 255).

as that against a *pedes*.[126] This provision is similar to that of the nominal fine which, as we have seen, was the only penalty for killing a clergyman, according to a Padua statute of 1282.[127] Balancing this estimation of the relative value of *miles* and *pedes,* however, was the further provision that the former was to pay twice as heavy a fine as the latter for infringement of various statutes.[128]

The weighting of various groups of the community, then, was a sociological fact in the "polities" to which Marsilius was probably referring. While it is impossible to know the precise polities or proportions which he had in mind, his general meaning is the same as that of Egidius of Rome when he wrote in 1285 that "in the cities of Italy the many, as the whole people, commonly rule. . . . This is a polity, in which . . . what is aimed at is the common good of the good needy persons, the middle class, and the rich, *and of all according to their status,* and then it is right and fair." [129]

The View of Aristotle in the Politics

Marsilius' third specification of the *pars valentior* said that "it must be determined according to the view of Aristotle in the *Politics,* Book VI, Chapter 2." [130] This specification is in general consistent with the preceding, for in the chapter referred to, Aristotle recommends that mixture of democratic and oligarchic principles which he elsewhere calls "polity." [131] He rules out both numerical equality and weighting on the basis of assessed property (τίμημα) as just principles of suffrage when either is taken alone, recommending instead that they be combined in such manner that a majority of both the "rich" and the "poor" be required for the passing of an enactment. But if the two groups disagree, then those are to win "who are greater in number and whose assessed property is greater." [132] It is quite likely, however, that Marsilius did not interpret this provision

[126] *Ibid.* n. 67 (p. 30). See Roberti, *op. cit.,* p. 39: "Di più, le multe, comminate per le colpe degli anziani, non sono per tutti eguali . . . Il guidrigildo, come veniva raddoppiato per i nobili, *la cui persona valeva quasi il doppio di quella del popolano,* cosi veniva raddoppiato per gli anziani della comunanza."

[127] *Liber regiminum Paduae,* An. 1282 (p. 125); see above, p. 27.

[128] *Stat. com. Pad.* nn. I. I, 29 (pp. 6, 18). See *ibid.* n. 640 (p. 208) for the heavy fine to be paid "si aliquis de male ablatis vel aliquis de potencioribus qui non habentur de comunancia percussent aliquem de comunancia vel percuti fecerint pensate. . . ." See also "Gli ordinamenti di giustizia del 6 luglio 1295" in Florence, cap. vi: "De penis impositis et ordinatis contra magnates offendentes populares" (in Salvemini, *op. cit.,* pp. 394–400).

[129] *De reg. princ.* Lib. III. Pars II. cap. ii. See also below, p. 239.

[130] I. xii. 4.

[131] *Pol.* VI. 3. 1318a 27 ff. (It should be remembered that Marsilius uses the older chapter-divisions of the *Politics.* See above, p. 171, n. 32.) See also *Pol.* IV. 8. 1293b 32 ff.; IV. 9. 1294a 30 ff. Cf. Cicero *De re pub.* II. xxii. 39.

[132] *Pol.* VI. 3. 1318a 33: οἱ πλείους καὶ ὧν τὸ τίμημα πλεῖον . . .

in the same sense as Aristotle, for as was mentioned above, both Marsilius and other Aristotelians are misled by William of Moerbeke's translation of τίμημα as *honorabilitas* into thinking that the latter means the quality of being "honorable" rather than "assessed property." [133] Thus Peter of Auvergne interprets the passage just cited as meaning that the vote will be decided "according to some other excellence, either of virtue or of desire for the common good," [134] and Albert the Great similarly takes it to mean that "honorable persons" are to prevail, because they "deviate less from the truth." [135] Since Marsilius interprets *honorabilitas* as the three "upper" parts of the state, the passage of Aristotle to which he refers probably means for him the joint participation of the *honorabilitas* and the *vulgus* in political power; and its bearing upon the *pars valentior* is thus that balancing of the former's prudence and leisure with the latter's judgment and numbers which is the basis of his defense of the *populus* as legislator.

Marsilius' concept of the "people" as it emerges from these several aspects may be briefly summed up in the following characteristics. First, its basic units are not individuals but classes or functional groups. Second, none of these groups is to dominate the others, but all are to have a share in political authority. Third, the share accruing to each group is determined by both quantitative and qualitative standards, which prevent the domination of, respectively, the *honorabilitas* alone or the *vulgus* alone. Fourth, as a consequence, the people is the all-inclusive political body of the state; it is a corporate "whole," a *universitas,* which can act as "one."

5. THE OPPONENTS OF MARSILIUS

Such being the meaning of Marsilius' doctrine that the legislator is the people, the whole body of citizens or the weightier part thereof, we must now examine the arguments by which this doctrine is upheld. It is in these arguments that the full significance of his popular sovereignty emerges, both as doctrine and as polemic. For if, as recent commentators have held, Marsilius' republicanism departs in no essential way from the normal medieval position, it may well be wondered why he finds it necessary to devote two full chapters to its defense. To be sure, the statement

[133] See above, p. 180, n. 7.

[134] Peter of Auvergne *In Pol.* Lib. vi. Lect. 3 (p. 406): "tunc justum determinandum erit non secundum praedictum modum, sed secundum aliquam excellentiam aliam, vel virtutis, vel desiderii ad bonum commune. Et tunc illud quod videbitur parti, quae excellit secundum illud, collatione facta, justum erit."

[135] Albert the Great *In Pol.* vi. ii. (p. 571): "'et quorum honorabilitas amplior,' supple, hoc praevaleat in judiciis: quia semper probabile est quod *honorabiles personae* minus deviant a veritate . . . 'Quorumcumque igitur honorabilitas excedit,' supple, et maxime *ex virtute. . . .*"

of arguments *a contrario* and of replies thereto was a standard scholastic procedure. But the elaborateness and detail of Marsilius' discussion of the subject are strong indications that it was controversial, that he was not merely repeating an accepted doctrine. And indeed, it is quite possible to identify the opponents who may have furnished the arguments he cites against the popular sovereignty he is upholding, and against whom his own emphasis and arguments are directed, even though Marsilius, like most medieval writers, does not mention his opponents by name.

The writers whose statements are echoed in Marsilius' arguments *a contrario* fall into two somewhat related groups. The first comprised those philosophers who took over certain anti-democratic aspects of the doctrines of both Aristotle and Augustine. Such were Engelbert of Admont [1] and James of Viterbo,[2] who transformed Aristotle's distinction between natural rulers and natural slaves into a distinction between all rulers and their subjects. They thus made Aristotle's justification of "despotism" into a justification of government as such, on the ground that most men cannot govern themselves and need to be controlled by one who is "superior in intellect." Similarly opposed to Marsilius on this point were all the other writers who were mentioned earlier as having applied this distinction to justify the hegemony of some particular ruler.[3] Marsilius repeats their position in his arguments *a contrario,* which assert that "most men" (*homines ut in pluribus*) are "depraved," "stupid," "undiscerning," "unlearned," and "crude," as opposed to the "few" who are "virtuous," "learned," and "wise." [4]

Other Aristotelians made much of Aristotle's arguments directed specifically against the δῆμος on the ground of its lack of moral and intellectual virtue. In particular, Peter of Auvergne throughout his commentary frequently gives anti-democratic expositions of Aristotle's statements. Thus where Aristotle declares that "without rulers it is impossible for the city to exist," [5] Peter comments, "this is necessary, because the people is without reason, and hence it needs some directive, lest it be moved contrary to reason." [6] Moreover, whenever Aristotle is critical of democracy, Peter expands and supplements his statements, particularly with regard to the "tyranny" of the people.[7] One of Marsilius' arguments *a contrario,* about

[1] *De ortu et fine Rom. imp.* cap. i (p. 363).
[2] *De reg. Christ.* II ii, x (pp. 165–66, 302–3).
[3] See above, pp. 177–78. [4] I. xiii. 1. [5] *Pol.* IV. 3. 1291a 35.
[6] *In Pol.* Lib. IV. Lect. 3 (p. 290). See *ibid.* Lib. IV. Lects. 11, 13 (pp. 320, 333); Lib. VI. Lect. 5 (p. 412).
[7] See *ibid.* Lib. III. Lect. 8 (p. 234); Lib. IV. Lect. 4 (p. 295).

the viciousness of "most men," is found in almost the same words in both Peter and John of Jandun.[8]

Other writers made a similar distinction between kinds of "people" on the basis of the doctrine of St. Augustine. For Augustine had declared that whether or not a people should have self-government depends upon whether it is "well-moderated and grave" or is "depraved and prefers its private welfare to that of the public and has venal suffrage." [9] This distinction is repeated by Thomas Aquinas,[10] James of Viterbo,[11] and Ptolemy of Lucca.[12] The latter also declares against "political" (republican) rule on the ground of man's corrupted nature as a result of original sin; he cites in this connection a statement from Ecclesiastes (1:15) which was repeated by Marsilius in one of his arguments *a contrario:* "infinite is the number of the stupid." [13] For Ptolemy too, the people is an "unlearned multitude" [14] which "is moved more by sensible things than it is led by reason." [15]

A further combined Aristotelian-Augustinian source of anti-democratic arguments was that devoted to the question of agreement and harmony in the control of the state. Aristotle had mentioned as one argument against the rule of many that they would divide into factions, whereas "one man is without faction." [16] This argument is taken over and expounded by Thomas Aquinas,[17] Egidius of Rome,[18] James of Viterbo,[19] and John of Paris [20] by means of the Augustinian assimilation of peace and unity:

[8] *Def. pac.* I. xiii. 1: "homines enim, ut in pluribus, videntur pravi et stulti." Peter *In Pol.* Lib. VI. Lect. 5 (p. 413): "Homines enim ut in pluribus a recta ratione deficiunt." John of Jandun *Quaest. in Metaphys.* Lib. II. qu.4 (fol. 26B): "homines ut in pluribus sunt proni ad malum ex politica et plurima negocia hominum sunt mala 2° *Rhet.* et isti habent appetitum inordinatum." Cf. Aristotle *Rhetoric* II. 13. 1389b 16; also *Pol.* II. 5. 1263b 23; 7, 1267b 1; and William of Ockham *Breviloquium* II. vii (p. 87). Note the resemblance to Machiavelli *Discorsi sopra la prima deca di Tito Livio* I. iii, ix; *Il Principe cap.* xvii, xviii. Marsilius also expresses this view in one of the arguments *a contrario* which he adduces against his own electoral principle (I. xvi. 5).

[9] *De libero arbitrio* I. vi. 14 (PL 32, 1229).

[10] *S. theol.* II. I. qu.97. a.1.

[11] *De reg. Christ.* II. viii (p. 267).

[12] *De reg. princ.* III. vi (p. 63).

[13] *Ibid.* II. ix (pp. 34–35). See *Def. pac.* I. xiii. 1 (p. 54). The same statement is quoted by Albert the Great to show the necessity of coercive law for the enforcement of moral sermons (*In Eth.* Lib. X. Tr. III. cap. i [p. 634]), by Godfrey of Fontaines in connection with the obstacles to charity (*Quodlib.* X. qu.5 [IV, 317]), and by William of Ockham to explain the need for private property (*Breviloquium* III. vii [p. 87]).

[14] *De reg. princ.* II. ix (p. 35): "populus et indocta multitudo." See *Def. pac.* I. xiii. 1: "multitudinis indoctae. . . ." See also Albert the Great *In Eth.* Lib. X. Tr. II. cap. v (p. 632): "Interiora enim bona communis plebs ignorat, vilis et indocta existens. . . ."

[15] *De reg. princ.* II. xi (p. 37). See Egidius *De reg. princ.* Lib. I. Pars I. cap. vi: "vulgus communiter non percipit nisi delectationes sensibiles." See *ibid.* Lib. I. Pars I. cap. i (*Tertia via*); Lib. III. Pars II. cap. xxxvi.

[16] *Pol.* III. 10. 1286b 2.

[17] *De reg. princ.* I. ii (p. 4).

[18] *De reg. princ.* Lib. III. Pars II. cap. iii.

[19] *De. reg. Christ.* II. v (p. 212).

[20] *De pot. reg. et pap.* cap. i (p. 110).

the end of the state is peace, which requires the unity of the multitude, and this can be best secured by a single ruler, for many would fall into disagreement. The same argument that it is difficult or impossible for the many to agree appears among Marsilius' arguments *a contrario*.[21]

The second chief group of opponents of Marsilius' popular sovereignty were the writers who contributed to or commented upon the canon law. In a statement which reflects the Augustinian influence, Pope Nicholas II in the eleventh century declared that "the most religious men [i.e., the cardinals] must be the leaders in the election of a supreme pontiff, while the others must be followers," in order to avoid the "disease of venality"; and by "the others" he meant the *clerus et populus*.[22] This statement was based upon an earlier formula, "the people must be taught, not followed," which was repeated frequently thereafter.[23] The formula played its part in the increasing restrictions placed upon lay participation in episcopal elections and other branches of ecclesiastic government during the twelfth and thirteenth centuries; and in support of it were found anti-popular statements similar to those which Marsilius was to list as arguments against his own position. Thus Innocent III inveighed against the custom whereby "the statement of the people is regarded as decisive in ecclesiastic cases"; for this meant that *quid juris* was asked equally of "the lettered and the unlettered, the wise and the foolish."[24] With regard to the election of bishops it was declared that the "letters of the people" should not be accepted as final, because "it is manifest that many of them who do not have sincere faith could have been corrupted by bribery."[25] Augustinus Triumphus summed up the position in the statement that "the people quickly deviates in its judgment through persuasion or corruption . . . the people must not be followed in judgment but rather the teachers who, though fewer in number, are yet of sounder counsel."[26]

[21] I. xiii. I. See also above, pp. 116, 186.

[22] *Corp. jur. can., Decret. Gratiani* Pars I. dist. 23. can. 1 (I, 77).

[23] "Docendus est populus, non sequendus," attributed to Pope Celestine I (A.D. 422–432). Repeated, *ibid.* Pars I. dist. 62. can. 2; Pars I. dist. 63. can. 12 (I, 234, 238). Repeated also by Cardinal Humbert *Adversus simoniacos* III. xxi (MGH, *Lib. de lite,* I, 226). Deusdedit *Libellus contra invasores et simoniacos* viii (MGH, *ibid.,* II, 307). *Dialogus de pontificatu sanctae Rom. eccl.* (MGH, *ibid.,* III, 532). *Tractatus pro clericorum connubio* (MGH, *ibid.,* III, 594). Augustinus Triumphus *S. de eccl. pot.* qu.2. a.8. Alcuin's statement of the formula is given with *ducendus* instead of *docendus* (Epist. 166; PL 100, 458).

[24] *Corp. jur. can., Decretal. Greg. IX* Lib. I. Tit. 4. cap. 3: "a praesentibus literatis et illiteratis, sapientibus et insipientibus, quid juris sit quaeritur." See the argument *a contrario* in *Def. pac.* I. xiii. I: "per sapientes et doctos utilius lex feratur. . . ." See also Augustinus Triumphus *S. de eccl. pot.* qu.2. a.7: "magis credendum est literatis quam ydeotis et magis clericis quam laicis." William of Ockham *Dialogus* Pars I. Lib. VI. cap. c (p. 633): "Mirabile est, quod idiota de clerico, imperitus de perito, illiteratus de literato in his, quae ad sacras literas spectant, debeat et valeat judicare. . . ."

[25] *Corp. jur. can., Decretal. Greg. IX* Lib. I. Tit. 6. cap. 2 (II, 48).

[26] *S. de eccl. pot.* qu.2. a.8.

This canonist position, to be sure, was applied explicitly only with regard to ecclesiastic affairs, such as the election of prelates and the decision of law cases and dogma. But it was extremely difficult to draw the line between ecclesiastic and secular politics, and the doctrine of plenitude of power, with which the canonists were allied, was dedicated to eradicating the distinction in practice. It was thus inevitable that the arguments advanced in behalf of that doctrine should be anti-democratic, and that Marsilius, opposing it, should uphold a pro-popular position. The central orientation of both the papalists and the Aristotelians was that of the superiority of "experts," so that their arguments joined in distinguishing between the few wise and the many foolish. Marsilius, for his part, similarly applied his anti-"expert" arguments in the context of both secular and ecclesiastic politics.[27] His support of the people's sovereignty was thus a blow against absolute monarchy or the dominance of a few in both state and church.

6. THE ARGUMENT FROM WILL

Marsilius' arguments for the legislative supremacy of the people are presented first in four separate proofs, each propounded syllogistically with supporting prosyllogisms; and then in a group of four objections to which, after a fresh statement of principles, replies are given. The entire sequence of arguments, however, is centered in two basic considerations, the adequacy of the laws and the freedom of the citizens. The former consideration, in turn, has two different aspects, for its conclusion that the best laws are those made by the whole people is based on the double ground of the people's will and of its understanding. The principle of both these former arguments is Aristotle's doctrine of distributive justice, that political power belongs to those who contribute most to the end for which the power exists. And that end Marsilius also repeats from Aristotle: it is "the common benefit of the state and of the citizens."[1]

With respect to these arguments, however, two questions must be kept in mind. First, what is meant by the "common benefit"? Second, what is the relation between the achievement of the common benefit and the allocation of political power? On both these questions, Marsilius departs from the antecedent traditions. The latter will be considered prior to examination of his argument from freedom; but the former must be dealt with now.

For Aristotle and the Aristotelian tradition, the common benefit is an exclusive concept, not an inclusive one. The common benefit is not whatever any community happens to desire or regard as its benefit. On

[27] See especially II. xvii. 14.

[1] I. xii. 5. See Aristotle *Pol.* III. 13. 1283b 40.

the contrary, the definitory criteria (ὅροι) of common benefit which are usually put forth in justification of claims to governmental authority are in fact not correct.[2] The only criterion which is absolutely just is that which constitutes the end of the absolutely best state: the life of virtue,[3] defined in the normative terms with which Aristotle prefaces his analysis of that state.[4] Thus, while the common benefit is the benefit "of the whole state" and is "common" to all its "citizens," both "state" and "citizens" refer directly only to those men who are able to live in accordance with virtue, for only they should participate in government.[5] Consequently, the "common" benefit is in fact not "common" to all the members or inhabitants of the state.

This point is brought out clearly by John of Jandun's distinction between two senses of "common" good: a good may be common by causality or by inherence. Thus theoretic knowledge of God is man's common good in the sense that it is the final cause to which men are ordered; but that end does not inhere in all men because most are "deformed" in their nature and hence do not desire it and cannot attain it.[6] This interpretation by John is not, to be sure, faithful to Aristotle in all respects; yet it is on similar grounds that Aristotle can make aristocracy a just governmental form despite the fact that in it most men are disfranchised, while democracy, in which most men participate in government, is not just; for the former does, and the latter does not, aim at the common benefit conceived in this highly restricted manner.

For Marsilius, on the other hand, the common benefit is itself defined by the natural desire of all "non-deformed" men for a sufficient life. It is hence a moderate, not an ideal concept, an inclusive, not an exclusive one, since for Marsilius relatively few men are deformed.[7] Consequently when in his initial arguments he declares that the legislative authority belongs to those who can make the "best" laws, and that these are laws which are

[2] *Pol.* III. 13. 1283b 27.
[3] *Ibid.* III. 9. 1281a 3 ff.; III. 13. 1283a 23 ff.
[4] *Ibid.* VII. 1. 1323a 14 ff.
[5] *Ibid.* III. 13. 1283b 36 ff.; VII. 9. 1328b 34–1329a 3.
[6] *Quaest. in Metaphys.* Lib. II. qu.4 (fol. 25J): "Dicendum quod felicitatem esse commune bonum hominis potest intelligi dupliciter: vel quod sit commune communitate causalitatis vel communitate inherentiae. Modo non omnem felicitatem esse commune bonum secundum inherentiam ad multa supposita simul hominis, sed sufficit quod sit communis causalitate, quia cognitio dei est causa finalis omnium cognitionum sensibilium . . . et est communis hominibus non orbatis, quibus non deficit inclinatio naturalis ad felicitatem et speculationem, quia tales attingunt illum finem ut cognoscere deum in specie humana. Sed si sint orbati ex natura indivisibili, i.e., quod careant inclinatione naturali ad speculandum et virtutes, talibus non est communis felicitas." As this passage implies, John interprets the "deformed" (*orbati*) as frequent, not as relatively rare; he continues (*ibid.*, fol. 26B): "Illud bonum regimen [intellectus] deficit in multis, quia homines ut in pluribus sunt proni ad malum ex politica . . . et per consequens retrahuntur a speculatione abstractorum." See also above, p. 201.
[7] See above, pp. 58–59, 185 ff.

made "for the common benefit of the citizens," [8] he is referring to a goal which is both desired and attainable by practically all the men in the state. The generality and moderation of Marsilius' view of values lead to a concomitant generality in the allocation of the political authority which achieves those values. This generality is reinforced when it is remembered that the function of law in the Marsilian state is primarily the regulation of disputes by an impartial system of rectificatory justice, rather than the affirmative leading of men to a moral goal.

Let us first consider the argument from will.

As we have seen, one of the chief bases of the anti-democratic position had been the inevitable corruption and dissension of the people when entrusted with power. Accompanying this negative argument had been a positive espousal of the rule of one or a few virtuous men—the king and the aristocrats in the Aristotelian tradition, the pope and the cardinals in the canonist doctrine. Marsilius emphatically reverses both sides of this position. He argues, in effect, that the ideal of one or a few men ruling for the common benefit, either in the secular or in the ecclesiastic sphere, is impossible of attainment—that, in Aristotelian terms, not kingship or aristocracy but tyranny or oligarchy must result. And his reason, which he states repeatedly, is precisely that which the anti-democrats had upheld against the people: that if one or a few men were entrusted with supreme power, they would in all probability pervert it to their own selfish interests:

> For these few would not discern or will the common benefit equally as well as would the entire multitude of the citizens. Indeed, it would be insecure . . . to entrust the making of the law to the discretion of a few. For they would likely consult therein their own private benefit, as individuals or as a group, rather than the common benefit, as is quite apparent in those who have made the clerical Decretals, and as we shall also show sufficiently in Chapter 28 of Discourse II. For by this means the way would be opened to oligarchy, just as when power to make the laws is given to one man alone, a place is made for tyranny . . .[9]

Thus at one blow Marsilius sweeps aside the entire Aristotelian-papalist tradition upholding the political supremacy of one or a few virtuous men.

In this position of Marsilius there was, as such, nothing new. Aristotle, Cicero, and the medieval Aristotelians as well as other writers had warned

[8] I. xii. 5.

[9] I. xiii. 5. See *ibid.* I. xii. 5: "per unum aut paucos quosdam, proprium magis quam commune attendentes commodum. . . ." I. xii. 8: "Non ad solum unum . . . inspiciendo scilicet magis proprium conferens quam commune, unde tyrannica foret. Propter eandem vero causam non pertinet hoc ad pauciores. . . ." Marsilius' assimilation of clerical domination to oligarchy and tyranny, in the passage quoted in the text, is strikingly reminiscent of the position of Averroes. See *Paraphrasis in libros de Republica Platonis* Tr. III (fol. 513B).

that kingship may degenerate into tyranny, and aristocracy into oligarchy;[10] and various remedies had been suggested, including "mixed government," control by the papacy, and universal monarchy. In the papallist tradition, too, there had been warnings against the pope's abuse of his powers.[11] But Marsilius is the first to regard this degeneration and abuse as so very likely to occur that he will not even countenance the political supremacy of one or a few men (conceived as real supremacy, that is, in what he calls the legislative as opposed to the merely "secondary" governmental power). The popular sovereignty of Marsilius thus has a fixity, an absoluteness, which, as we shall see more fully below, is unparalleled in antecedent political philosophy. In contrast, some of the other Aristotelians follow rather that part of Aristotle's doctrine which holds that tyranny is more likely to result from the "rule of many" than from the rule of one man.[12]

What is the basis of this Marsilian reversal? It is his view, which he attributes to Aristotle but which follows from his own individualist interpretation of man's natural desire for a sufficient life,[13] that human nature is inevitably swayed by passion and selfish desire. Thus, for corroboration of his contention that one or a few men having legislative power would pervert it to their own interests, he refers to his chapter on the need for laws.[14] In that chapter he had insisted that "every soul sometimes has perverted emotion," refusing to recognize any exception even in the case of the "very best man."[15] Now this conception of the emotional factor in all men as rendering necessary government by laws was a commonplace among the Aristotelians.[16] But what distinguishes Marsilius is that he applies this same consideration to the question of the efficient cause of the law. Aristotle and the other Aristotlelians had concluded, from this neces-

[10] Aristotle *Pol.* v. 7. 1307a 23, 34 ff.; v. 10. 1313a 2 ff. Cicero *De re pub.* I. xxviii. 44. Thomas Aquinas *S. theol.* II. I. qu.105. a.I. ad 2. John of Paris *De pot. reg. et pap.* cap. xx (p. 137). Egidius of Rome *De reg. princ.* Lib. III. Pars II. cap. iv, vii. Dante *De mon.* I. xi (p. 346). James of Viterbo *De reg. Christ.* II. vii (p. 234).

[11] St. Bernard *De consideratione* I. vi; II. vi (PL 182, 735–36; 748). John of Salisbury *Policraticus* VIII. ii–iii (II, 409 ff.). William Durand, Jr. *De modo generalis concilii celebrandi* Lib. I. Rubr. 4 (fol. 155v).

[12] *Pol.* IV. 4. 1292a 15 ff.; v. 5. 1305a 7 ff. See Thomas *De reg. princ.* I. v (pp. 7, 8): "Nam fere omnium multorum regimen est in tyrannidem terminatum . . . tyrannis autem non minus, sed magis, contingere solet in regimine plurium, quam unius. . . ." Also Egidius of Rome *De reg. princ.* Lib. III. Pars II. cap. v. See above, pp. 116, 200–202; below, pp. 240 ff.

[13] See above, pp. 61–63.

[14] I. xii. 5: "Hanc quoque sententiam satis adiuvant quae de legum necessitate assignavimus in XI° huius."

[15] I. xi. 6; see I. xi. 2.

[16] See Aristotle *Pol.* III. 15. 1286a 17; *Rhet.* I. I. 1354b 8. Thomas Aquinas *S. theol.* II. I. qu.95. a.I. ad 2. Egidius of Rome *De reg. princ.* Lib. III. Pars II. cap. xx. Dante *De mon.* I. xi (p. 346).

sity for laws, that "the ruler must be a legislator." [17] But it is precisely this further power that Marsilius also insists upon withdrawing from one or a few men: not only must the ruler govern through laws, but he, whether one man or several, must not be the maker of those laws.

Underlying this position is the fact that Marsilius has done away with the natural law which was traditionally conceived as at once guiding and limiting political power. Whereas for the other Aristotelians the ruler-legislator makes only human laws, which are but determinations of natural law and are not laws at all if they go counter to it, for Marsilius the legislator is a true sovereign. Marsilius must hence find in the seat of the legislative authority itself that limitation upon government which the antecedent tradition had found in natural law. Moreover, his discarding of natural law compels him to view the question of the ruler's "virtue" in concretely personal terms, not as the abstract quality of general moral principles inherent in human reason. In this particularizing emphasis there is a resemblance to the nominalism which William of Ockham applied in other fields; [18] but it rests upon the same literalness of perspective as we have seen to characterize Marsilius' use of terms.[19]

At bottom, however, it is the whole context into which Marsilius fits his doctrine that explains this departure from the tradition. His entire political philosophy is based upon a conception of government viewed as dedicated, not, as in his predecessors, to ultimate values and virtues, but to the minimal end of preserving the state. In this context the paramount fact of human activity appears as strife, disputes among men requiring governmental regulation in order to prevent the dissolution of the entire social fabric. Hence, political power is no longer conceived in moralistic and intellectual terms, as educating men to the virtues, but rather in specifically political, coercive terms, as immersed in the everyday struggles of men to advance their interests.[20] It was only natural, therefore, that the traditional conception of the virtuous king as enlightened lawgiver should give way to a more realistic portrait when regarded from the standpoint of this function. By this concentration upon "contentious acts" Marsilius is also marked off from Aristotle himself as well as from the other medieval Aristotelians. For while Aristotle did not have a doctrine of natural law in the sense of the medieval tradition, his high conception of human excellence or virtue at its best led him to hold that outstandingly virtuous men

[17] *Pol.* III. 15. 1286a 22. For the Aristotelians who make the ruler a legislator, see above, p. 174, n. 53.

[18] On the relation between Marsilius and Ockham, see above, p. 22, n. 21.

[19] See above, pp. 46 ff.

[20] See above, pp. 61 ff., 80 ff., 106 ff.

"are themselves a law,"[21] so that they should be "kings for all time."[22] On the other hand, in Marsilius' emphasis that, regardless of men's cognitive expertness, their perversion of legislative power to their own private interests through passion is almost inevitable, it is possible to find a political application of Aristotle's opposition to the Platonic identification of knowledge and virtue, carried to an extreme.[23]

Marsilius does not confine himself, however, to this argument against the legislative power of one or a few men; he also propounds an argument for the people as repository of this power. The argument concludes that the will of the whole people, or of its weightier part, is necessarily for just laws—laws directed to the common benefit; thus it is precisely the opposite of the inevitability of that perversion to private benefit which he had insisted would occur in the case where the legislator is one or a few men. The basis of this argument has been discussed in an earlier chapter: it is his biological conception of human nature and of man's natural desire,[24] and the concomitant view of the strictly demonstrative method of the political philosophy which he erects upon that conception.[25] The combination of this biological conception and demonstrative method leads to an ascription of necessary non-pervertibility to the processes of the human will as rigorous as the necessities which Marsilius conceives to be involved in the processes of nature.

The argument contains four steps.[26] The first is Marsilius' principle that "all men desire sufficiency of life." The second is that, as a consequence, all men have a "natural impulse" to live in a state, since the state is necessary to the attainment of sufficiency of life. We see here already the determinist feature of Marsilius' doctrine. He does not content himself merely with the objective necessity that the state is required for the attainment of the sufficient life; he insists that the same necessity is found in human desire or impulse. Precisely because of the former necessity it is likewise necessary that all men have a natural impulse to live in a state. This necessity of desire is continued in the two following steps, which themselves "necessarily" follow in turn from the first two. Since the endurance of the state is necessary for men's living therein, "that part of the state which wishes the polity to endure *must* be weightier (*valentiorem*) than that part which does not wish it"; "it is *impossible* that those . . . who do not

[21] *Pol.* III. 13. 1284a 14.

[22] *Ibid.* 1284b 34. Aristotle also holds, however, that such "kingly" men do not "now" exist; cf. *Pol.* V. 8. 1313a 4 ff.; VII. 13. 1332b 23 ff. With this may be compared the similar recognition by Plato in the *Laws* IX. 875D. Cf. also William of Ockham *Dialogus* Pars III. Tr. I. Lib. II. cap. vi (p. 795).

[23] See *N. Eth.* VII. 2–3. 1145b 22 ff.

[24] See above, pp. 57 ff.

[25] See above, pp. 48 ff.

[26] I. xiii. 2.

care to live in a state be so many in number that they are weightier (*valentiores*) than . . . those who wish so to live." These two statements are quoted by Marsilius from the *Politics*.[27] It will be noted that the "all" of the first two steps has now given way to "weightier part"; for it is Marsilius' point that there *are* a few men—the papal party—who do not want the preservation of a state organized on natural principles. The "weightier part" thus figures again as quantitatively including all but a relatively small number of the citizen body. The ground upon which Marsilius asserts that this third step "necessarily follows" from the second invokes his concept of nature: "nothing is desired by the same specific nature in respect to most of its members (*secundum eius plurimum*) and immediately, at the same time as its destruction, for such a desire would be empty . . . this would mean that nature errs or is deficient in most cases (*ut in pluribus*)." In other words, it is impossible that, while all the members of the human species have a natural desire to live in the state, most of the members of that same species should at the same time desire the destruction of the state.

The fourth step, finally, is that since good laws are necessary to the endurance of the state, the "weightier multitude of the state desires" such laws. Again natural necessity is invoked in proof: if the weightier multitude did not so will, "there would occur deformity (*orbatio*) in *nature* and art in most cases (*secundum plurimum*); the impossibility of which is assumed from *natural science*." The will of the whole people, or of the weightier part thereof, cannot be perverted in the making of laws or in any other exercise of political power.

It need hardly be pointed out that this striking argument contains glaring misinterpretations of Aristotle, particularly in transforming the hypothetical moral necessities of the *Politics* into absolute physical necessities.[28] The argument is an excellent example of what Aristotle calls "dialectical syllogisms" dealing with "topics" common to physics, politics, and other disciplines,[29] although Marsilius would refuse to recognize any gulf between these at the ubiquitous level of the "nature" which he here invokes. The argument as he conceives it is a rigorous demonstration based upon the premise, which we have seen that he shares with other Averroists, that the human will is a part of "nature." There is, furthermore, a strong reminiscence here of another Averroist doctrine, the unity of the intellect. Marsilius is not, indeed, holding that the human will is one in number in all men. But in taking as the subject of his demonstration a "specific nature"

[27] *Pol.* IV. 12. 1296b 14; VII. 14. 1332b 29.

[28] On these misinterpretations see Appendix to my translation of the *Defensor pacis*.

[29] See *Rhet.* I. 2. 1358a 10 ff.

(*eandem naturam specie*) whose desires are necessarily had by "most of its members" (*secundum eius plurimum, ut in pluribus*), Marsilius is making the attributes of that nature so much one in kind in the individuals falling under it that he obtains for the will a unifying effect similar to that which the other Averroists had maintained for the intellect, particularly in view of his emphasis on the corporate character of the people's will.[30]

This point also raises, however, the question of the coherence of the argument with Marsilius' preceding insistence upon the inevitable perversion of the will of a few men entrusted with supreme legislative power. If "every human soul" necessarily has selfish passions, does not this mean that the "whole" people has these also? Can one consistently denigrate "each" while extolling "all"?

In answering this question, it should first be made clear what Marsilius' position does *not* mean. He is not, like Thomas Aquinas, saying that the "common benefit" to which just laws must be directed is something over and above the private benefits of each individual, differing from the latter not only in number but in kind.[31] On the contrary, the common benefit is simply the sum of these private benefits, either of all or at least of the "weightier multitude" of the citizens of the state.[32] Nor is Marsilius saying, like Aquinas, Remigio de' Girolami, and others, that the citizen loves the community, and the common good, more than he loves himself, or his private good.[33] On the contrary, in keeping with the individualist side of

[30] For a fuller discussion of the relations of Marsilius' argument both to the Averroist doctrine of the single intellect and to the scholastic theories of the non-futility of natural desire, see Appendix to my translation of the *Defensor pacis*.

[31] *S. theol.* II. II. qu.58. a.7. ad 2: "bonum commune civitatis et bonum singulare unius personae non differunt solum secundum multum et paucum, sed secundum formalem differentiam." See *ibid.* II. II. qu.47. a.11. Resp. See also Egidius of Rome *De reg. princ.* Lib. III. Pars III. cap. i. Compare Siger of Brabant *Quaestiones super libros Physicorum* (ed. P. Delhaye [Louvain, 1941]), Lib. II. qu.18.

[32] See I. xii. 5, 7, 8. See Thomas Aquinas *S. theol.* II. II. qu.58. a.9. ad 3: "bonum commune est finis singularium personarum in communitate existentium. . . ." Also *ibid.* II. II. qu.47. a.10 ad 2; and William of Ockham *Dialogus* Pars III. Tr. II. Lib. II. cap. xxviii. This point is also used to show that democracy is the best of the unjust forms of government. See Thomas Aquinas *De reg. princ.* I. iii (p. 5): "plus autem receditur a bono communi in oligarchia, in qua quaeritur bonum paucorum, quam in democratiis, in qua quaeritur bonum multorum. . . ." See to the same effect Peter of Auvergne *In Pol.* Lib. IV. Lect. 11; Egidius of Rome *De reg. princ.* Lib. III. Pars II. cap iv. On the relation between the two conceptions of the "common good," as simply the sum of individual goods and as something specifically different from these, see E. Lewis, "Organic Tendencies in Medieval Political Thought," *American Political Science Review,* XXXII (1938), 852 ff.; d'Entrèves, *Medieval Contribution,* pp. 27–29. Both writers seem to me to make too facile a reconciliation of these two conceptions in Thomas and other medieval thinkers. See also below, pp. 215 ff.

[33] Remigio de' Girolami *Tractatus de bono communi,* p. 85: "civis praeamat sibi commune suum. Utilitas enim partis dependet ab utilitate totius. . . ." *Ibid.,* p. 87: "civis praeamat civitatem sibi propter majorem similitudinem quam habet pars ad totum, quam habeat ad seipsam. . . ." See Thomas Aquinas *S. theol.* II. II. qu.26. a.3. Resp.: "unaquaeque

his interpretation of natural desire, it is because "no man knowingly harms or wishes injustice *to himself*" that "all or most of the citizens want a law conducive to the common benefit." [34]

What, then, is the basis of Marsilius' ascription of a necessary desire for the common benefit to the wills of all or most of the citizens, each of whom is an individual desiring his own benefit? An important part of his answer will be examined in the following section.[35] But here it is to be noted that in the Aristotelian physics which underlies Marsilius' doctrine, nature is the realm of necessary sequences, and these sequences occur "always or for the most part . . . if there is no impediment." [36] Since human desire is a part of that realm, it will undergo both the same necessity and the same generality. Hence, given the initial natural desire of "all men" for a sufficient life, the sequence upon this of other desires objectively necessary to it will similarly occur "always or for the most part . . . if there is no impediment" (for "always," read "in the whole body of citizens"; for "for the most part," read "the weightier part of the citizens"; for "impediment," read "deformity"). "Nature does not lack in necessaries"; [37] hence, just as she generates men with the various inclinations and aptitudes necessary to fulfill the needs required for the desired sufficient life, so she follows through with the desires themselves which are necessary to that basic initial desire. The alternative would be natural futility.

The meaning of this natural basis in the Marsilian doctrine emerges more fully when it is compared with the traditional doctrine of natural law. For Thomas Aquinas the first principle of practical reason is that "the good is that which all things desire," and upon this he bases an ordered series of "natural inclinations" similar in content to the objects of Marsilius' natural desires: for self-preservation, for commingling of male and female, for living in society.[38] But where Marsilius views these desires simply as physico-biological facts necessitated by nature, Thomas views them as effects of the rational ordering of the universe by God, an order-

---

pars naturaliter plus amat commune bonum totius quam particulare bonum proprium . . . Apparet etiam hoc in politicis virtutibus, secundum quas cives pro bono communi dispendia et propriarum rerum et personarum interdum sustinent." Durand of St. Pourçain *In Sent.* Lib. III. dist. 29. qu.2 (fol. 228v): "pars plus amat bonum totius quam suum bonum proprium, sicut patet in naturalibus et in politicis. . . ."

[34] I. xii. 8: "Quia enim lege debent omnes cives mensurari secundum proportionem debitam, et *nemo sibi scienter nocet aut vult injustum,* ideoque volunt omnes aut plurimi legem convenientem communi civium conferenti." See I. xii. 5: "Adhuc, ex universa multitudine magis attenditur legis communis utilitas, eo quod *nemo sibi nocet scienter.*" These statements are strikingly similar to Rousseau's justifications of popular sovereignty: "il est impossible que le corps veuille nuire à tous ses membres" (*Contrat Social* I. vii); "nul n'est injuste envers lui-même" (*ibid.* II. vi). Compare Aristotle *N. Eth.* V. 9. 1136b 6; 11, 1138a 15.

[35] See below, pp. 215 ff.

[36] Aristotle *Physics* II. 8. 199b 24. See above, p. 59.

[37] I. vii. 1. See Aristotle *De anima* III. 9. 432b 22.

[38] *S. theol.* II. I. qu.94. a.2.

ing which man recognizes through his rational participation therein.[39] Hence, whereas for Marsilius the just laws which are necessary to social life appear simply as effects of a natural desire necessarily had by all or most men, for Thomas they are desired by men only to the extent that men rationally apprehend their connection with the society to which they are ordered. This apprehension will be had by men "for the most part" (*ut in pluribus*), but not by all, because "some men have a depraved reason through passion, or bad custom, or bad natural condition." [40] Thus, while Thomas and Marsilius come to similar conclusions as to the prevalence of socially beneficial desires among men, for the former it is the use of reason, for the latter the ubiquity of natural necessity, which explains this prevalence. Hence, where the assertion of such prevalence can be only tentative and probable for Thomas, it is a dogmatic certainty for Marsilius; and where for Thomas its basis is a moral "ought," for Marsilius it is a biological "must." But for this reason, too, where Thomas can entrust the legislative authority to one fully and hence permanently rational man,[41] Marsilius is forced to rely rather upon the mass of men; for while one man's desire may always be exempted from the general necessity of nature, that of men "for the most part" cannot. It is this contrast between reason and desire, and between the general necessity and individual precariousness of men's desire for just law, which underlies Marsilius' position.

7. THE ARGUMENT FROM UNDERSTANDING

The argument from will is supplemented by another which emphasizes the people's understanding even more than its will. The need for this new argument is, of course, obvious, and had been emphasized by most of the anti-democratic arguments which were examined above. For even if all or most of the people desire the common benefit and laws embodying it, they may nevertheless be too stupid to know how to make or recognize such laws. To surmount this objection, Marsilius adduces a new principle, even more dialectical than the preceding. This is the "common conception of the mind," that "every whole is greater than its part." The interpretation he gives of this principle emphasizes that conformity of quantity and quality which was noted in our examination of the concept of the "weightier part"; for Marsilius at once adds that the principle "is true in respect both to magnitude or mass and to practical virtue and action." From this it "necessarily" follows that the whole body of citizens, or the weightier

[39] See above, p. 133.

[40] *S. theol.* II. I. qu.94. a.4.

[41] This is, of course, the theme of the *De regimine principum*. See I. ix, xii, xv (pp. 13–14, 18, 22–23), also *S. theol.* II. II. qu.47. a.12. Resp.; qu.50. a.1; *Cont. gent.* III. lxxxi.

part thereof, can discern what must be chosen and what rejected better than can any part of that whole body taken separately.[1]

This simple argument touches upon questions which had been long debated in medieval philosophy. Its assimilation of quantitative mass and qualitative virtue is opposed to the doctrine of Augustine, repeated by Thomas Aquinas and Egidius of Rome, that "to be greater is to be better" holds true only "in those things which are not great in mass." [2] The assimilation of physical and political part-whole relationships was opposed by Durand of St. Pourçain.[3] And, most directly, Aristotle had pointed out the incommensurability of various kinds of quality and quantity with one another, and had insisted that political authority must properly be based upon superiority in specifically "political virtue," which does not necessarily accompany quantitative superiority at all.[4]

If Marsilius' principle were taken literally it would mean that in every sphere, theoretic as well as practical, a larger group is more capable than a smaller one. But he restricts it to practical matters; and even within these he delimits its application more precisely by a distinction derived from Aristotle, who had used it to reply to Plato's allocation of political authority to the scientific expert [5] just as Marsilius was to use it against his anti-democratic opponents. This is the distinction between discovery and judgment, which has already been mentioned above: only a few men can discover a law, but all can judge it and discern what must be changed in it, because they must live under it and hence are sensitive to its effects.[6] It is by this consideration that Marsilius answers the objection that the experts could do a better job if left to themselves, that the addition to them of a mass of less well educated men, far from increasing their effectiveness, would rather be hindrance.[7] It is similarly by this consideration that Marsilius turns aside the anti-democratic allocation of "right reason" to the wise and mere "coercive force" to the people.[8]

This argument from understanding completes the analogy and contrast of Marsilius' position to the traditional doctrine of natural law. The anal-

[1] I. xiii. 2. See I. xii. 5; I. xiii. 4; II. xvii. 14.

[2] Augustine *De trinitate* VI. vii. 18 (PL 42, 929). Thomas Aquinas *S. theol.* I. qu.42. a.I. ad I. Egidius *De eccl. pot.* I. ix (p. 33).

[3] *In Sent.* Lib. III. dist. 29. qu.2 (fol. 228v): "non est simile de parte naturali et civili respectu totius naturalis et communitatis."

[4] *Pol.* III. 7. 1282b 23 ff.

[5] See Plato *Statesman* 292C ff.

[6] I. xiii. 3, 7. See *Pol.* III. 11. 1282a 18. See also above, pp. 168 ff., 176.

[7] I. xiii. I. See the reply: I. xiii. 7, 8.

[8] See Peter of Auvergne *In Pol.* Lib. III. Lect. 9 (p. 241): "duo exiguntur in regimine politiae. Unum est recta ratio; hoc autem habet ista multitudo per illos sapientes. Aliud est potentia, ut possit coercere et punire malos: hoc autem habet per populum." See *ibid.* Lect. 11 (p. 249).

ogy consists in the fact that both Marsilius and the tradition hold that all or most men have a natural desire for justice or the "common good" and can rationally understand what this is. For both positions, therefore, there is a basic sense in which justice is not the arbitrary creature of positive enactment but has a "natural" basis. The contrast between the two positions, however, rests upon the relation which is set up between reason or understanding and desire. For Marsilius, there is no question of a "practical reason" apprehending the principles of goodness as self-evident propositions, nor of a *synderesis* as a natural habit containing such principles.[9] Rather, reason and understanding are purely instrumental to the attainment of the sufficient life and common benefit which all men naturally desire; there is no ground, rational or otherwise, for the value of these objects other than the natural desire which all men have for them. Reason does not itself apprehend an order of values which subsists objectively and constitutes the valid ends of desire; justice, insofar as it is equivalent to the generalized sufficient life, the common benefit, is constituted simply by being the object of natural desire. But the means to the realization of this object will, as correct means, themselves be just; and it is justice in this instrumental sense which for Marsilius is the object of reason and understanding. This radical voluntarism with respect to the end also distinguishes his position from that of Aristotle. The "understanding" which Marsilius attributes to the people is, as we have seen, his application of the quality of σύνεσις,[10] which Aristotle defines as the use of opinion for judging well what someone else says concerning the practical matters with which prudence is concerned.[11] Now for Aristotle prudence can exist only when the end for which it deliberates is good, and this goodness is defined by the moral virtues.[12] But where the latter, in turn, involve for Aristotle the submission of desires to "right reason" (ὄρθος λόγος) [13] which is therefore the measure of the moral value of the desires, for Marsilius natural desire itself is the basis of all politically relevant values, while reason is its instrument. Consequently, Marsilius, unlike Aristotle, can make the desire for the common benefit a factor distinct from the deliberative excellence of the "most prudent" men, and can base his popular sovereignty on the strong likelihood of the divorce between such desire and prudence where the latter is unchecked by the will of the many.[14]

[9] See Thomas Aquinas *S. theol.* I. qu.79. a.12; II. I. qu.94. a.I. ad 2; a.2. Resp.

[10] See above, pp. 168, 176.

[11] *N. Eth.* VI. 10. 1143a 13.

[12] *Ibid.* VI. 9. 1142b 21; VI. 13. 1144b 31.

[13] *Ibid.* I. 13. 1102b 13 ff.; II. 6. 1106b 36; VI. I. 1138b 18 ff.

[14] Although at I. xiv. 2 Marsilius follows Aristotle in upholding the inseparability of prudence from the moral virtues (cf. *N. Eth.* VI. 13. 1144b 30), his distrust of the few, "however prudent," when unchecked by the many, is perhaps a sign of a different conception of prudence. See I. xiii. 5, 6; and *De translatione imperii* cap. iv (p. 149).

This argument from understanding also brings out the sense in which Marsilius has a doctrine of equality. He does not, as we have seen, hold that all individuals are equal in either ability or authority.[15] But by virtue of his quantitative interpretation of the part-whole principle, he can hold that the many who are less learned "can judge *equally* as well as or better than the few who are more learned."[16] Equality thus holds not between individuals but between classes; each of the *vulgus* is inferior to each of the *honorabilitas,* but the whole *vulgus* is equal or superior to the whole *honorabilitas.* It is significant of the egalitarian trend of Marsilius' doctrine, however, that Albertus Pighius in resuming his argument could attribute to him a doctrine of natural equality of all men.[17]

The part-whole argument furnishes a final answer to the question raised in the preceding section concerning the apparent incoherence between Marsilius' double insistence that each individual desires his private benefit and that the will of all or most men must necessarily be directed to the common benefit.[18] The most direct answer might appear to be that since the common benefit is simply the sum of the private benefits of each individual, the desires of the latter for their private benefits combine by arithmetic addition into a desire for the common benefit. But this answer raises questions of its own, since it is precisely the desires of each individual which result in harmful transient acts requiring legal regulation,[19] and which also make it impossible to entrust supreme authority to one or a few men. Yet Marsilius does not, like Rousseau, invoke an ideal "general will" which shall be different from the actual "will of all."[20] Rather, he distinguishes between the will of all together and the will of each separately. All or most taken together have characteristics which do not pertain to each taken alone; the fact that the whole is greater than its part means that "the as-

[15] The patristic doctrine of the natural equality of all men underlying their existing political inequality was standard in medieval thought until the reception of Aristotle's *Politics.* See Carlyle, *op. cit.,* I, 111 ff., 199 ff.; III, 88 ff. See also Thomas Aquinas *S. theol.* I. qu.96. a.3; and above, p. 191. Probably the first to return to the patristic conception thereafter was Nicholas of Cusa in the fifteenth century, and then only in a qualified sense. See *De concordantia catholica* II. xiv (p. 533). The original equality of all men had been an important theme of the *Roman de la rose,* and equality in freedom as consequence of original descent from Adam was used by John of Jandun to describe the claims of the democrats. See *Quaest. in Metaphys.* Lib. I. qu. 18 (fol. 14 L): "Ulterius egeni dominantur propter proprium bonum neglecto bono principis et divitum, unde ibi dominantur pauperes propter libertatem, quia dicunt quod unus est ita liber sicut alius, quia omnes filii Adae sumus, et talis dicitur democratia."

[16] I. xiii. 4. See I. xiii. 5: "hii pauciores non *aeque* bene discernerent neque vellent commune conferens, quemadmodum universa civium multitudo."

[17] *Hierarchia ecclesiastica* v. i (p. 123): "Vis demonstrationis maioris . . . in hoc consistit, quod aut divinitus, aut humanitus, necessario competat oportet uni hominum super alium superioritas, aut iurisdictionis auctoritas eiusmodi, *cum nativitatis, quantum ex se est, conditio, omnes pares, aut aequales faciat.*"

[18] See above, p. 210.

[19] See above, pp. 61 ff.

[20] *Contrat social* II. iii. See above, p. 58, n. 34.

sembled multitude of all can discern *and desire* the common justice and benefit to a greater degree than can any part of that multitude taken separately."[21] To argue that because each individual desires his private benefit, or makes erroneous judgments, therefore the whole community will similarly be split into desires regarding only private benefits, or will fall into error, is to commit the fallacy of composition.[22]

The qualitative change in ability or virtue effected by quantitative increase in persons had been a recurrent theme of medieval political thought; but in no case did the principle attain the force and application which it has in Marsilius. The superior excellence of a "multitude" over each individual was invoked primarily in connection with the power of excommunication;[23] when it was applied in connection with the state it was rather to show that the rule of one is better than that of many, since unity rather than multiplicity is the cause of effectiveness: for example, many men together can haul a barge which could not be hauled by each separately, only because the many are conjoined into one.[24] Subsequently, William of Ockham opposed Marsilius' argument on the nominalistic ground that those who are fallible separately are fallible together.[25] Although the primary source of Marsilius' part-whole argument is Aristotle's *Politics*,[26] Aristotle himself uses the principle in such fashion that virtue, not num-

[21] I. xiii. 6. See I. xii. 5; I. xiii. 5.

[22] See *Def. min.*, xii. 5, and Aristotle *Pol.* III. 15. 1286a 32–36. This point is relevant also to the seeming contradiction between Marsilius' defense of the intellectual superiority of the whole people over its parts, and his frequent complaint that one of the strongest obstacles against his enterprise arises from the "custom" that "most men" have of believing the papalists' falsehoods. See II. i. 1; II. xxi. 14; II. xxv. 20; II. xxvi. 18, 19. On the connection of this whole point with the Averroist doctrine of the unity of the intellect, see Appendix to my translation of the *Defensor pacis*.

[23] See Albert the Great *In Sent.* Lib. IV. dist. 19. A. a.6. ad 4 (XXIX, 808): "multitudo bene causat potentiam activam in excellentia, sed numquam defectum et impotentiam sive passionem. Exemplum autem hujus est quod multitudo potest trahere navem et trahit, et nullus per se de multitudine." The same principle and example are found in St. Bonaventura *In Sent.* Lib. IV. dist. 18. pars 2. a.1. qu.3; Thomas Aquinas *S. theol.* Suppl. qu.22. a.5. Resp. Marsilius also uses the principle in *Def. min.* xii. 5. See the related dictum, "Facilius invenitur quod a pluribus quaeritur," adapted from *Corp. jur. can., Decret. Gratiani* Pars I. dist. 20. can. 3 (I, 66), by *Oculus pastoralis* II. iii (col. 806); William Durand, Jr., *De modo generalis concilii celebrandi* I. Rubr. 4 (fol. 155v); and William of Ockham *Dialogus* Pars III. Tr. I. Lib. II. cap. ii (p. 791). The first two, however, make only a limited application of the dictum, while Ockham goes on to deny its universal truth (*op. cit.* cap. xix [p. 805]).

[24] Thomas Aquinas *De reg. princ.* I. ii, iii. Egidius of Rome *De reg. princ.* Lib. III. Pars II. cap. iii.

[25] *Dialogus* Pars I. Lib. V. cap. xxv, xxxv (pp. 495, 506). See G. de Lagarde, "L'Idée de représentation dans les oeuvres de Guillaume d'Ockham," *Bulletin of the International Committee of Historical Sciences*, IX (1937), 444.

[26] *Pol.* III. 11. 1281a 40 ff. Aristotle here, however, abstracts from the specific ends which he had declared in a preceding chapter (III. 9. 1280a 25 ff.) should constitute the criteria for the allocation of political power, so that the discussion is entirely aporematic and tentative; see *ibid.* 10. 1281a 11: Ἔχει δ' ἀπορίαν . . . See Egidius of Rome *De reg. princ.* Lib. III. Pars II. cap. iv, where this aporematic character is emphasized.

bers, constitutes the criterion of "part" and "whole";[27] and Peter of Auvergne, in conformity with this approach, introduces the Marsilian interpretation of the argument only to illustrate disparagingly the rhetorical devices of demagogues in the "extreme" democracy.[28] It is significant that very few of the other Aristotelians use or even mention the pro-popular chapter of the *Politics* which Marsilius makes basic to his own doctrine. Only Egidius of Rome and William of Ockham make extensive reference to its arguments, but merely to refute them,[29] on the ground, which Marsilius had listed among his arguments *a contrario*,[30] that where fewer men suffice, more should not be called upon. Marsilius himself accepts this "razor" argument in every other connection,[31] but not where the supreme legislative power is in question.

The most significant aspect of Marsilius' use of the part-whole argument, however, is the emphasis it places upon the "whole" in relation to the "part." Where his predecessors had adumbrated the argument, they had dealt not with the whole-part relation but rather with that of "more" and "less."[32] This had entailed the recognition in various ways that the majority also involves a minority outside it, whose views, desires, and authority are not absorbed into those of the larger group. For Marsilius, on the other hand, the whole is so completely superior to the part that there remain outside it no independent powers or "rights" such as those which the traditional doctrine of a "higher law," natural or divine, had excluded from political authority. Marsilius' "holistic" doctrine of political authority would appear to be similar to that suggested by Aristotle's statement that the state is prior in nature to the individual because "the whole is necessarily prior to the part,"[33] and by Remigio de' Girolami's amplification of this position by means of Aristotle's physical analysis: that "the whole *qua* whole exists actually, but the part *qua* part exists only potentially."[34] But

[27] *Pol.* III. 17. 1288a 27 ff. See Peter of Auvergne *In Pol.* Lib. III. Lect. 16 (p. 274): "pars non est nata excedere suum totum: sed iste *in virtute* excedit omnes alios: ergo *alii sunt pars respectu istius*. . . ."

[28] *In Pol.* Lib. IV. Lect. 4 (p. 295): "dicunt quod tota multitudo debet dominari et judicare quae fiunt per alios magistratus. Omnia enim debent referri ad populum; et *melius est totum principari quam partem*."

[29] Egidius *De reg. princ.* Lib. III. Pars II. cap. iv: "Quibus argumentis potest ostendi quod apparet melius esse civitatem vel regnum regi per plures quam per unum. *Et quomodo haec argumenta solvi possent*." Also William of Ockham *Dialogus* Pars III. Tr. I. Lib. II. cap. ii, xix (pp. 790–92, 804–6).

[30] I. xiii. I.

[31] See below, pp. 235–36.

[32] Egidius *loc. cit.*: "plura cognoscunt plures quam unus." Ockham *Dialogus* Pars III. Tr. I. Lib. II. cap. ii (p. 791): "plures melius et certius in talibus judicant et discernunt, ac plura talia perpendunt et vident, quam unus solus . . . plura et certius vident plures quam unus et optimus." See Augustinus Triumphus *S. de eccl. pol.* qu.2. a.2: "plura vident plures quam unus." See also texts cited above, p. 216, n. 23.

[33] *Pol.* I. 2. 1253a 19.

[34] *Tractatus de bono communi*, p. 83.

whereas these expressions suggest what in medieval terms might be called a "realistic" as opposed to a "nominalistic" view of the state, Marsilius' conception of the original "natural" basis of men's political association is nominalistic, that is, individualistic; [35] so too is his insistence that the state, as well as each of its functional "parts," is one only by a unity of order, not of number, since it is composed of persons who "are many in actuality and formally separate from one another in number." [36] Also, as we have seen, he does not regard the common benefit as anything distinct from the benefits of each individual.[37] The Marsilian doctrine thus involves a transition from original individualism to corporatism, from nominalism to realism, from the parts to the whole. Just as the preservation of the state had necessitated the subordination of all other parts of the state to the government, and just as "peace" had involved the contribution by each part of the state to the harmonious functioning of the whole, so the superiority of the whole to the part necessitates the complete monopolizing of power by the whole community, for which the government acts as executive. Thus, while Marsilius provides for the freely expressed opposition of individuals to proposed laws when they are being considered in the popular assembly,[38] once those laws have been enacted there is no further provision for individual or group opposition to the will of the "legislator." The people or *universitas* is assumed to contain a harmony of all the wills and interests of the various groups of the *vulgus* and *honorabilitas,* so that it is a corporate whole rather than simply a collection of individuals, in the drastic sense that men's belonging to the *universitas* is the complete expression of their political being.

The full meaning of Marsilius' corporate application of the whole-part principle can be seen in the manifold further applications which it undergoes throughout the *Defensor*. Negatively, as we have seen, its insistence upon the inferiority of the part to the whole is a complete denial of the political trustworthiness of individuals or partial groups when entrusted with supreme authority. Thus it does away with the Aristotelian apotheosis of the "one best man" and the papalist apotheosis of the "vicar of God," and cuts the ground from under the easy transitions which had been effected from God to the pope or priesthood on account of their divine mission.[39] Marsilius' repeated refrain is that "every priest"—and in this he includes the pope—"can sometimes err, or be moved by perverted emotion, or both." [40] On this ground, he contends that not the priest but God

[35] See above, pp. 90–91.

[36] I. xvii. 11. See above, p. 116.

[37] See above, pp. 210–11.

[38] See above, p. 169.

[39] See above, p. 16.

[40] II. vi. 9. See II. vi. 3, 13; II. vii. 3; II. viii. 7; II. xx. 6; II. xxi. 3, 9; II. xxv. 10, and *passim*.

alone has definitive power in such matters as absolution from sin, for "it is God alone who cannot be deceived about human thoughts and actions . . . and who alone has no perverted will." [41] On the other hand, in the positive application of his collective principle Marsilius comes near to the same apotheosis of the whole people which he has denied of the priesthood. "By the election of the legislator the common benefit is almost always, with rare exceptions, aimed at and achieved." [42] Thus, whereas the pope and his cardinals can fall into crime and heresy, "this cannot happen to the faithful legislator or the whole body of the faithful, because it or its weightier part cannot be thus misled, either in civil affairs . . . or in spiritual affairs." [43] For this reason, excommunication, election of priests, and all other ecclesiastic matters must be controlled by the whole body of the faithful, because its "judgment is made with greater certainty and freedom from suspicion than that made by the will of a single priest or group of priests, whose judgment would more readily be perverted by love or hate or consideration of private benefit than the judgment of the whole body of the faithful, to whom one comes always to appeal." [44] Hence while Marsilius does not explicitly repeat the maxim *vox populi, vox Dei,*[45] it emerges clearly from his statements.

8. THE ARGUMENT FROM FREEDOM

Both the arguments which have been examined thus far are centered in the consideration that the whole people must be the legislator because only then is there assurance that the laws will be made for the common benefit. These arguments thus raise the question whether the common benefit is the sole consideration in the allocation of political authority. If this be so, then such authority will belong to one or a few men if it can be proved that the laws will thereby more adequately attain or subserve the common benefit. It was on this ground that the antecedent tradition made the king, conceived as a wise and good man, the "legislator." For Marsilius, on the other hand, even such moderate final causes as he regards as the "common benefit" cannot be the ultimate criterion for the allocation of authority. His basic voluntarism makes the people's will the supreme efficient cause of laws because of a consideration entirely inde-

[41] II. vii. 4. See II. vi. 9; II. xvii. 5; and below, pp. 265 ff.

[42] I. xvi. 11. For similar statements, see above, pp. 57–58, and n. 34.

[43] II. xxi. 3.

[44] II. vi. 13. See II. xvii. 10, 14. See also II. xvii. 6, where the same majoritarian principle is applied to the apostles: "Verisimile enim est omnes aut plures apostolorum simul certius deliberasse ac minus errasse . . . quolibet ipsorum seorsum accepto."

[45] This maxim is stated, only to be denied, by Alcuin, Epist. 166 (PL 100, 458), and by Gerbert, Epist. 186 (PL 139, 252). See also Peter Damiani *Carmina sacra* c. 222 (PL 145, 975): "Potestas est in populo/A summo data Domino."

pendent of the ends they may achieve. This consideration is that self-legislation is essential to freedom.

The argument to this effect is initially stated with reference to the observance of the laws. "That law is better observed by every one of the citizens which each is seen to have imposed upon himself." But the reason for this is that every citizen must be "free"; and if one or a few men by their own authority made law over all the rest, the former would be "despots," and such a law, *"no matter how good it was,"* would be obeyed either unwillingly or not at all by the other citizens, comprising the "more ample part." On the other hand, when the law is made by the hearing or consent of the entire multitude, then *"even if it be less useful,"* it is readily obeyed by each citizen, "because each is seen to have imposed it upon himself." [1]

It will be noted that this consideration is along quite different lines from the preceding ones. The question of the adequacy of the laws is now explicitly brushed aside: a less adequate law made by all the citizens will be better observed than a very adequate law made by one or a few, and this because in the former case the citizens are "free," while in the latter they suffer "another's despotism, that is, slavish dominion." [2] What is of central importance is the conception of the nature of freedom to which this argument appeals. In support of his insistence that "each citizen must be free," Marsilius quotes Aristotle's dictum that "the state is a community of free men." [3] But the meaning of freedom as Aristotle here views it is quite different from that of Marsilius. For the former, men are politically free when they are governed for the common benefit; it is by this criterion that just constitutions are distinguished from unjust ones.[4] For Marsilius, on the other hand, political freedom consists in self-government, in the sense that the laws under which men live derive from their own wills or consent. The two conceptions thus differ in that they regard men as free when they are, respectively, the final causes and the efficient causes of the political power which is exercised over them.[5]

[1] I. xii. 6. A point somewhat similar to this argument, but without its exclusive insistence upon the necessity of "freedom" as here interpreted, is made by Thomas Aquinas *De reg. princ.* I. iv (pp. 6–7), and by Ptolemy of Lucca *De reg. princ.* IV. viii (pp. 90–91).

[2] I. xii. 6. It will be noted that in Aristotle's terminology which Marsilius is following, the "despot" is the correlative of the "slave." See *Pol.* I. 2. 1252a 33; 3. 1253b 7, 15 ff.

[3] *Pol.* III. 6. 1279a 21.

[4] See the entire discussion from *Pol.* III. 6. 1278b 31 through III. 7. 1279a 22. Cf. *ibid.* VII. 14. 1333a 2–5. Although in Aristotle's complete doctrine freedom requires the possession of prudence, which distinguishes those who are naturally able to rule themselves from natural slaves (*ibid.* I. 2. 1252a 31 ff.; 5. 1254a 18 ff.; see above, p. 177), it is significant that when he comes to distinguish just from unjust constitutions by the criterion that the former are over "freemen," the conception of freedom he invokes is that given in the text.

[5] This point is completely missed by Lagarde, who interprets as a reference to deception of the people Marsilius' statement that the people will readily obey without protest "even

This difference is a logical consequence of Marsilius' first principle of men's natural desire for a sufficient life; for since the state is the result of that desire, political power in the state must also derive its authority from the wills of those upon whom it is exercised. This means that Marsilius has again rejected the Aristotelian conception of kingship and aristocracy as ideally the best kinds of constitution, but for a different reason from the one previously indicated.[6] He is now saying that even if the laws made by one or a few men were of the very best, such supreme legislators would still be "despots,"[7] simply because they made the laws by their own authority and not by that of the citizens. In this conception, Marsilius would seem to be holding more consistently than Aristotle himself to the latter's definition of the citizen as one who has the authority to participate in government.[8] For it is difficult to see how there can be such "citizens" in the life-long kingship which Aristotle upholds for the exceptionally virtuous man,[9] who is both a law unto himself[10] and the legislator for the whole state.[11] The difference between Aristotle and Marsilius on this point is that the former, in his most normative doctrine, regards the state as a rational order of distributive justice dedicated to virtue, so that citizenship will consist in taking one's place in that order and recognizing the "natural" authority of those who are more virtuous.[12] In a similar way, Egidius of Rome's assimilation of politics to the divine order entailed a *dominium* of God and the pope over all men and a corresponding *servitus* of all men to God and hence to the pope.[13] Marsilius, on the other hand, has done away with the divine order, and has made reason and virtue not the constitutive order of the state, but rather the means by which the natural desires motivating men to live in the state may be satisfied. Hence the desires or wills of all the citizens must be the controlling authority.

---

a less useful" law made by itself, because "hanc quilibet sibi statuisse videtur." Thus Lagarde comments: "Peut-on exprimer avec plus de candeur la piperie que constitue la prétendue souveraineté populaire? Laissez croire au peuple que c'est lui qui a fait la loi, vous lui enlèverez tout droit de protester contre elle" (*Marsile*, p. 186, n. 96). This is a travesty of Marsilius' position.

[6] See above, pp. 205 ff.

[7] I. xii. 6: "sic enim legem ferentes aliorum *despotes* essent. . . ." See also I. xviii. 3, where a similar conception is applied to the ruler: if he were not corrigible for infractions of the law, "*despoticus* fieret quilibet principatus, et civium vita *servilis* et insufficiens."

[8] See above, p. 175.

[9] *Pol.* III. 13. 1284b 33; 17. 1288a 29.

[10] *Ibid.* III. 13. 1284a 14.

[11] *Ibid.* III. 17. 1288a 19.

[12] See above, p. 142. This does not mean that Aristotle's ideal ruler will govern *against* the will of his subjects; on the contrary, they obey him "joyfully" (*ibid.* III. 13. 1284b 32), and he abdicates as soon as they "do not wish" him to rule any longer (*ibid.* V. 10. 1313a 14). But Aristotle conceives such "will" of the subjects not as the whole ground of the ruler's authority, but rather as a recognition of its ground in superior virtue. See also below, p. 241.

[13] *De eccl. pot.* I. vi; II. x. (pp. 14, 195). Marsilius in turn accuses the popes of making themselves "legislators" and thereby "casting peoples into slavery." See II. xxv. 14, 17; II. xxvi. 7.

This conception of freedom was not, of course, new in Marsilius. It is found in Cicero [14] and also in Aristotle himself, although in caricature, when he comes to describe it as it is conceived by the democracies of his time; for freedom "to live as one wishes" without a corresponding basis of virtue is little better than anarchy.[15] Most of the medieval Aristotelians follow Aristotle in holding that political freedom and slavery depend upon whether government aims at the common benefit or at the ruler's private benefit.[16] This difference is a cardinal illustration of the political consequences which depend upon whether final causes or efficient causes, ends or means, are made the primary determinants of political authority. The different conceptions herein embodied of the political relevance of rational ends had also accounted for Marsilius' failure to follow the other Aristotelians in their related doctrine of natural slavery.[17]

Both these conceptions of freedom have obvious dangers. In the finalistic conception freedom may involve subjection to paternalistic rule, as may be seen in Aristotle's assimilation of the king to the father [18] and in the whole political spirit of medieval papalism (as the very name *papa* indicates). In the conception of freedom as self-legislation, on the other hand, even apart from the extreme of anarchy there is the danger which comes from the indeterminacy or absence of criteria for those who are fit to exercise power and for the ends to which power is to be directed. Marsilius' argument from freedom must thus be completed by his other arguments for the people's

[14] *De re publica* I. xxvii. 43; II. xxiii. 43. Cf. however *ibid.* I. xliii. 66–xliv. 68.

[15] *Pol.* VI. 2. 1317a 40 ff. See *ibid.* VI. 4. 1319b 29. Plato's view is similar; see *Republic* VIII. 562E ff. In Aristotle's review of Solon's constitution, however, he is more sympathetic to this view of freedom; commenting on Solon's bestowal on the δῆμος of the power to elect and correct the rulers, he says that "if the δῆμος were not in control of this *it would be a slave* and an enemy" (*Pol.* II. 12. 1274a 17).

[16] Thomas Aquinas *De reg. princ.* I. i; *S. theol.* I. qu.96. a.4. Egidius of Rome *De reg. princ.* Lib. III. Pars II. cap. ii. James of Viterbo *De reg. Christ.* II. ii. Dante *De mon.* I. xii. William of Ockham *Dialogus* Pars III. Tr. I. Lib. II. cap. vi (pp. 794–95); Pars III. Tr. II. Lib. II. cap. xx (p. 918). *Octo quaestiones* qu.3. cap. vi. See, however, Thomas *S. theol.* II. I. qu.97. a.3. ad 3. Peter of Auvergne consistently interprets freedom as requiring that men be both the final and the efficient causes of their acts, although he gives an intellectualistic interpretation of both causalities. See *In Pol.* Lib. VIII. Lect. 1 (p. 493): "homo liber est, qui est suiipsius causa et in ratione moventis et in ratione finis, sicut dictum est prius. In ratione quidem moventis, quando ab illo per quod est homo et quod est principale in eo, puta ab intellectu, movetur praejudicando et ordinando modum et rationem agendi. In ratione autem finis cum movetur ad bonum et finem ipsius secundum illud idem quod principale est in eo secundum intellectum. . . ." See *ibid.* Lib. V. Lect. 7; Lib. VI. Lect. 2; Lib. VII. Lect 2 (pp. 347, 402, 435). Ptolemy of Lucca first views freedom, like Marsilius, as consisting in men's being the efficient causes of their government, for he "reduces" despotic rule to kingly rule on the ground that the king, like the despot, rules by his own laws and is not corrigible or otherwise controlled by his subjects (*De reg. princ.* II. ix; III. xi [pp. 34, 63]). But Ptolemy also returns to Aristotle's conception, distinguishing the two kinds of rule by their final cause, since "ille legitimus est rex, qui principaliter bonum subditorum intendit" (*ibid.* III. xi [p. 61]).

[17] See above, pp. 55, 178.

[18] *N. Eth.* VIII. 10. 1160b 24 ff.; *Pol.* I. 12. 1259b 10 ff.

legislative authority. Yet in his insistence that "each citizen must be free" in the sense of sharing in legislative authority, even if less useful laws result therefrom, there may be seen the same political voluntarism which leads him to make the "consent of the subjects" rather than the "common benefit" the primary criterion of good government.[19] Both points present a noteworthy emphasis on the intrinsic value of the political self-determination of "each individual" (*quilibet*).[20]

This emphasis on freedom and individualism is not, then, contradictory to the naturalistic determinism and corporatism of Marsilius' other arguments. His reconciliation of these two poles is not, indeed, effected from the finalistic side, as in the doctrine of Rousseau, wherein men become truly free and attain their true individuality only as members of the political whole, through each man's recognition of and submission to the ideal common interest.[21] Rather, Marsilius' doctrine distinguishes simply between freedom for a few men and freedom for every man. Each of these freedoms involves the "unimpeded" pursuit of desires which have a natural origin; [22] but the latter freedom involves in addition the fitting of both the desires and the pursuits into an organized whole in which the entire sequence from desire to fulfillment is assured for each individual.

It is from this point of view that we may best consider Marsilius' use of the famous maxim that "what can affect the benefit or harm of all must be known and heard by all." [23] To be sure, he binds this principle to the adequacy of the laws, pointing out that the sufficiency of life for whose attainment men formed the state depends in large part upon good laws: if the laws are bad, there will result "slavery and unbearable oppression and misery of the citizens, and finally the destruction of the state." The concept of "slavery" is here invoked to indicate not only lack of control of the political power to which one is subject, as in the previous argument, but also the "unbearable" conditions which result from that lack. Fundamentally, however, Marsilius is saying the same thing in each argument. The citizens become slaves when the laws under which they live are beyond their control, and this because of both the nature of freedom and the consequences of its loss.

The maxim *quod omnes tangit ab omnibus approbetur* had a long his-

[19] I. ix. 5. See above, p. 60; below, p. 241.

[20] See the many invocations of this individualist theme in I. xii. 6: "lex illa melius observatur a *quocumque* civium, quam sibi *quilibet* imposuisse videtur;" "*quilibet* civis liber esse debet;" "Latam [legem] vero ex auditu seu consensu omnis multitudinis, etiam minus utilem, *quilibet* civium faciliter observaret et ferret, eo quod hanc *quilibet* sibi statuisse videtur . . ."

[21] *Contrat social* I. vii, viii. See also above, p. 58, n. 34; p. 215.

[22] See II. xii. 16; and also above, p. 59.

[23] I. xii. 7.

tory prior to its use by Marsilius.[24] The interpretation it received, however, was not in all cases the same as that which he gave to it. For, like the equality of man and other famous principles of political theory, the maxim is so sweeping and unqualified that it could be made to mean as little or as much as its particular exponent desired. What is the criterion of whether a matter "touches all"? Precisely what is the scope of the "approval" which "all" must give in such matters? And is this approval given by "all" who are thus "touched," or by some smaller group presuming to speak for "all"? When these questions are asked, it can be seen that many uses of the maxim are far from the democratic or republican orientation which it might initially appear to entail. Thus it could be interpreted in such fashion as to restrict the determination of matters of faith to the pope and prelates,[25] or to give general councils composed only of prelates a merely advisory role in such determination,[26] or to argue on behalf of the *magnati* of Florence against the monopoly of political power by the *popolani* of the guilds.[27] In the form "those who must obey the pontiff must elect him," the maxim was invoked on behalf of the emperor by Peter Damiani;[28] and the principle of the maxim—"in all things, to order toward an end pertains to him whose proper end it is"—was used by Thomas Aquinas to argue that laws must be made by "the whole multitude or the public person who has care of that multitude."[29] In this case, the maxim can be made as restrictive as such "public person," especially when the method by which that person attains his "care" is left indeterminate. It is only in conjunction with Marsilius' other arguments, then, that the maxim's full meaning for him is revealed.[30]

The emphases contained in Marsilius' arguments for the people's legislative sovereignty, despite their qualitative as well as quantitative interpretation of majoritarianism, are such as defenders of republicanism and

[24] For a succinct presentation of some important phases of this history, see P. S. Leicht, "Un principio politico medievale," *Rendiconti della R. accad. dei Lincei* (Classe di sci. mor., stor. e filol.), 5th series, XXIX (1920), 232–45. Through a strange oversight, Leicht declares (p. 242) that Marsilius does not cite the maxim. See also the excellent discussion in G. Post, "A Romano-Canonical Maxim, 'Quod Omnes Tangit,' in Bracton," *Traditio,* IV (1946), 197–251; and also McIlwain, *op. cit.,* p. 302, n. 3.

[25] Augustinus Triumphus *S. de eccl. pot.* qu.10. a.1.

[26] William Durand, Jr. *De modo generalis concilii celebrandi* Lib. I. Rubr. 4; Lib. II. Rubr. 41 (fols. 155v, 165v). See below, p. 287.

[27] Leicht, *op. cit.,* p. 242.

[28] *Disceptatio synodalis* (MGH, *Libelli de lite,* I, 78).

[29] See *S. theol.* II. I. qu.90. a.3. Resp.

[30] See also II. xvii. 11, where the principle of the maxim is invoked to prove that the "populus fidelis" must choose its own priest, "eo quod ex ipsius officio unicuique commodum aut incommodum atque periculum evenire potest. Cuius quidem discretionis aut cautelae populus fidelis habet et rationabiliter habere debet potestatem, *aliter namque inconveniens hoc evitare non posset.*"

democracy in all ages have invoked. The superior trustworthiness of the people's will, the greater intelligence of the whole than of the part, the necessity in any case that a free people control its own destiny—these principles receive at the hands of Marsilius a decisive affirmation such as political philosophy had seldom previously witnessed. To be sure, he does not invoke in connection with them any doctrine of "natural rights."[31] The language of "rights" (*jura*), like that of natural law, is all but absent from the *Defensor pacis*.[32] However, the issue between doctrines based on natural rights and those based on utility is at once more complex and less insoluble than may be gathered from the facile reductions and omissions which extreme partisans of each doctrine have worked on the other.[33] One need not point out that in Marsilius' arguments from will and from understanding, the "common benefit" to which they appeal, and which he equates with "justice" (following Aristotle),[34] may thereby also be equated with "right" (*jus*).[35] It suffices to emphasize that, even apart from his dogmatic insistence that the only assurance of laws being for the common benefit lies in the people's being the legislator, his argument that the citizens must be free erects political freedom into an absolute, non-"utilitarian" value, since there must be self-legislation even if the laws thereby made be "less useful."

[31] Cf. Previté-Orton, "Marsilius of Padua," *Proc. Brit. Acad.*, XXI (1935), p. 153: "It is characteristic of Marsilius that the reasons which he gives for this democratic institution are utilitarian—he is no inventor of the 'rights of man.'" Cf. also J. W. Allen, "Marsilio of Padua and Mediaeval Secularism," p. 182; Lagarde, *Marsile*, p. 186.

[32] See I. i. 4; I. xix. 13, for references to *jus* which Marsilius takes over from Cicero *De officiis* I. vii. 22, 23. See also the four definitions of *jus* which Marsilius presents introductory to his arguments for evangelical poverty.

[33] For an excellent discussion of this point, see F. Pollock, *History of the Science of Politics* (London, 1885), pp. 43–46. Cf. also E. Lewis, "Natural Law and Expediency in Medieval Political Theory," *Ethics*, L (1939), 144 ff.

[34] See above, p. 142.

[35] Cf. Thomas Aquinas *S. theol.* II. II. qu.57. a.1: "Jus est objectum justitiae." Also Edmund Burke *Reflections on the Revolution in France* (*Works* [London, 1894], II, 331): "If civil society be made for the advantage of man, all the advantages for which it is made become his right."

CHAPTER VI

THE GOVERNMENT

I. THE FUNCTIONS OF GOVERNMENT

ALTHOUGH Marsilius' conception of the general function of government has been discussed in an earlier chapter,[1] that conception has important additional aspects which must now be considered. They bear both upon the fundamental revisions which he effects in the doctrines of the papalists and upon the nature, kinds, and separation of the powers involved in civil government.

The primary function of the government of Marsilius' state is the judgment of disputes. It was because of the necessity of this function to the preservation of the state that the government had been regarded as possessing coercive authority over all the other parts of the state, including the priesthood, and as being the "first part." This concept of judgment, however, is not simple. The elucidation of precisely what it involves, and the discrimination of it from a host of other meanings with which it had become confused, constitute one of the major contributions of Marsilius to the development of political theory.

The concept of "judgment" played an important part in the doctrine and arguments of the exponents of the papal plenitude of power. The basis of its use was the traditional view of the priestly power of "jurisdiction" as including the administration of the sacrament of penance, in which the priest heard confessions, imposed satisfactions, pardoned sins, and employed the "power of the keys" to open or to lock the gates both of heaven and of the church communion. Now all of these functions came to be viewed in political terms. For the papalists, the hearing of confessions and the determination of sentences are acts of "judiciary power," and since *"to judge properly pertains to the office of a king,"* it follows that every priest having the power of jurisdiction is a "king," just as the church is a "kingdom" (*regnum*).[2] But as between spiritual and temporal kings, the former are superior, for "just as the science of the holy scripture *judges* any physical science, so does the spiritual power *judge* the temporal";[3] and just as "the *judgment* of a sense, when it is defective, is

[1] See above, Ch. III, pp. 106 ff.

[2] James of Viterbo *De reg. Christ.* II. iii, iv (pp. 180, 192, 195). On the church as *regnum*, see above, pp. 93–94, and below, pp. 261 ff.

[3] *Ibid.* II. vii (p. 234).

corrected by the *judgment* of the understanding," so too the spiritual power "has to *judge* the temporal power."[4] One of the principles of this expansion of the concept of judgment is stated explicitly by Egidius of Rome: "Just as we see in the judgment concerned with wisdom and theory (*in judicio sapientiali et speculativo*), so must we consider in the judgment concerned with power and government (*in judicio potestativo et gubernativo*)."[5] Thus the political conclusion that the spiritual power has judicial authority over the temporal can be established by finding analogous axiological relations of "judgment" in every sphere of science, art, and morals.[6]

When Marsilius sets out, then, to insist upon careful distinctions of the different senses of "judgment," it is quite clear against whom his endeavor is directed. It is necessary, he writes, "to distinguish the meanings of these terms 'judge' and 'judgment' . . . For they are among the terms which have many meanings, and that multiplicity introduces ambiguity which impedes the determination of questions."[7] His distinctions fall against the central lines of the papalist assimilations. In one sense, a "judge" means a "knower or discerner"; and as illustrations of this Marsilius mentions experts in the various theoretic and practical spheres—mathematics, medicine, morals, architecture—whose "judgments" had previously been assimilated to the political. In a second sense, a "judge" means a lawyer, "one who has the science of political or civil law." And in a third sense, distinct from both the preceding, a "judge" means the "ruler" (*principans*), and "judgment" means the "sentence of the ruler," a "ruler" being "one who has the authority to judge concerning matters of justice and benefit in accordance with the laws and customs, and to command and execute through coercive force the sentences made by him."[8]

The basis of these distinctions is the same as that in the case of "law."[9] It is between the coercive and the non-coercive, and this not in the sense of what men are and are not *actually* exercising coercion, but rather in the legal-political sense of what "judges" have and do not have the *authority* to coerce. Similarly, the distinction between the first and the third senses of "judgment" means not that the ruler lacks knowledge, but that knowledge is not essential to him as such,[10] as it is to the "judge" in the first sense. The third sense of judgment, then, like the "proper" sense of law,

[4] *Ibid.*

[5] *De eccl. pot.* II. x. (p. 90).

[6] See *ibid.* I. ii. (p. 6). James of Viterbo *De reg. Christ.* II. iii (p. 182). Augustinus Triumphus *Tractatus brevis de duplici potestate,* pp. 499–500.

[7] II. ii. 8.

[8] *Ibid.* Cf. the same distinctions in *Def. min.* xiii. 7, where, however, the second sense of "judge" is omitted.

[9] See above, pp. 134, 138.

[10] See I. xv. 1; II. xxx. 4.

is specifically political, distinguished from all the irrelevant concepts with which it had been confused.

By means of this distinction between the judgment of experts and the judgment of political authority, Marsilius breaks the analogical arguments of the papalists. Since the exercise of coercive judgment is determined only by possession of governmental authority, not by moral or intellectual dignity, there is no validity in the argument that the spiritual power must "judge" the temporal because he who "judges" the nobler and more perfect must also "judge" the less perfect. For the fact that the soul is nobler than the body, and the future life than the present life, means only that he who teaches concerning the former may also teach about the latter; but if it involved coercive authority, then the mathematician would be the coercive judge of the physician, and the astronomer of the zoologist.[11] By the same token, the claim of the priest to control excommunication, because he is the best "judge" of what sins require this penalty, cannot stand, for to judge in the sense of having knowledge does not entail judgment in the sense of exercising coercive authority. If these were not distinguished, then the physician could coerce and expel the sick, the goldsmith could do the same to counterfeiters, and, in short, "there would be as many rulers as there are functions against which it is possible to sin."[12] The specificity of the coercive judgment involved in rulership undergoes manifold further applications throughout the *Defensor pacis*,[13] and their upshot is to confirm what the peace and unity of the state had made necessary, the removal of the priesthood from political power and its subjection to the government.

Marsilius was not, to be sure, the first to present such specifications of the nature of legal-political judgment. Thomas Aquinas had distinguished the practical from the theoretic judgment, on the ground that the former, unlike the latter, can affect its objects for good or ill,[14] and can involve external compulsion toward its acceptance;[15] within practical judgments he had also distinguished the private and paternal from the public or political judgment, on the ground that the former kind of judgment cannot give so complete a punishment as can the latter, because the "community" over which the father or some other private person presides is a lesser one.[16] But Marsilius' distinction throws into much sharper relief

[11] II. xxx. 1, 2. A similar point is adumbrated, but with less explicitness, by John of Paris *De pot. reg. et pap.* cap. v, xviii. (pp. 113, 131, 132).

[12] II. x. 8.

[13] For other applications of the distinction of kinds of *judicium*, see II. vi. 12; II. vii. 4, 5; II. viii. 9; II. ix. 2, 3, 7; II. x. 2- 5, 9, 11, 12, 13; II. xvii. 14; II. xx. 2; II. xxi. 4, 6; II. xxviii. 19; II. xxx. 3, 4.

[14] *S. theol.* II. II. qu.60. a.4. ad 2. See *ibid.* II. I. qu.93. a.1. ad 3.

[15] *Ibid.* II. II. qu.60. a.6. ad 1.

[16] *Ibid.* II. II. qu.65. a.2. ad 2.

the specifically political judgment, for it separates from this all other kinds of judgment, both theoretic and practical. Thomas' distinctions are gradual, indicating not only the physical, though limited, coerciveness found in private practical judgments, but even a kind of intellectual "coerciveness" in theoretic judgments: "It cannot be called a judgment unless it has *coercive force,* because a judgment involves a decision upon one side; that decision is made in theoretic matters by virtue of the first principles, which cannot be resisted, and in practical matters through the *imperative force* (*vim imperativam*) residing in the judge . . . the ecclesiastic judge through the key admits the worthy and excludes the unworthy."[17] This conception thus admits coerciveness for the ecclesiastic judgment of the priest in the administration of penance. Marsilius' distinctions, on the other hand, simply consign all coerciveness to the third—the ruler's—kind of judgment, so that no other judgment can be coercive without usurping the ruler's function. The specificity of the political judgment thus involves the same monopoly of coercive authority for the government and its laws as had the doctrine of unity and the non-coerciveness of divine law.[18]

Apart from this sharp specification of the nature of the political judgment, Marsilius' conception of the governmental function has many aspects in common with the antecedent tradition. The governmental act is basically a judicial act, and this is conceived as little more than the application of a major premise—a statement of the law—to a minor premise—a particular case.[19] It is only in comparatively recent years that this "mechanistic" view of the judge's function has begun to be challenged. Yet Marsilius' doctrine is based upon precisely the factors which have been most prominent in the challenge: the inevitable emotional bias and intellectual limitations of men. In common with the whole tradition, he holds that it is possible so to circumscribe the judge by the law that these factors will be rendered largely inoperative.

However, Marsilius also distinguishes the judicial from the legislative function as his predecessors had not. Whereas the judicial application of the law was traditionally conceived to involve the making of positive laws which were interpretations of a higher law, natural or divine,[20] for Mar-

[17] Thomas Aquinas *S. theol.* Suppl. qu.17. a. 3. On the coerciveness of theoretic principles here referred to, see also Augustinus Triumphus *S. de eccl. pot.* qu.59. a.4: "In assensu principiorum scientiae humanitus inventae est coactio propter evidentiam speculationis. . . ." The emphasis upon the intellectual coerciveness of "clear and distinct ideas" in judgment carried over into the modern Augustinian tradition. See Descartes *Meditationes* V (*Oeuvres de Descartes,* ed. C. Adam and P. Tannery [Paris, 1905], VII, 65); and cf. A. Gewirth, "The Cartesian Circle," *Philosophical Review,* L (1941), 368–95, esp. at 371–72.

[18] See especially above, pp. 154 ff.

[19] See I. xi. 1; II. x. 4–6. See also Thomas Aquinas *S. theol.* II. I. qu.95. a.1. ad 2; II. II. qu.60. a.6. Resp. Egidius of Rome *De reg. princ.* Lib. III. Pars II. cap. xx. Dante *De mon.* I. xiv (p. 349).

[20] See above, pp. 170 ff.

silius the ruler judges according to the positive laws made and interpreted by the people.[21] Hence the traditional formula that the ruler must judge according to the laws has a far more restrictive meaning in Marsilius.[22] The ruler is to the law as "matter" to "form,"[23] so that in his functioning he must be regulated by the law:[24] his function is simply to regulate (*regulare*) the civil acts of all men in the state in accordance with a standard (*regula*) which is the law,[25] by giving punishments and rewards as this standard directs.[26]

For Marsilius, moreover, the ruler is so closely bound by the laws that his judicial application of the law does not involve the "interpretation" of the law, apart from those exceptional cases in which "equity" is required.[27] It is rather the legislator who interprets the laws, in the sense of determining what they mean.[28] To be sure, in this coalescence of legislation and interpretation Marsilius was in line with the medieval tradition.[29] But the tradition also assigned judgment to the legislative authority; indeed, legislation, interpretation, judgment, and government were all viewed as pertaining to the same authority and necessarily entailing one another.[30] It remained for William of Ockham to point out that the maker of the law need not be its interpreter.[31]

[21] This point also separates Marsilius' position from that of Egidius of Rome. Egidius, following Aristotle (*Pol.* IV. 14. 1298a 1 ff.; 16. 1300b 13 ff.), distinguishes the *legislator* from the *praetorium* which judges according to the laws (*De reg. princ.* Lib. III. Pars II. cap. i), which is like Marsilius' distinction of the *legislator* from the ruler-judge. However, for Egidius it is the ruler (*princeps*) who is the *legislator* (*ibid.* Lib. III. Pars II. cap. xxi–xxiii) as well as the *custos legis* (*ibid.* Lib. III. Pars II. cap. i). See also above, p. 174.

[22] On this point, see also below, pp. 242 ff.

[23] I. x. 1, 2; I. xiv. 10.

[24] I. xv. 7.

[25] I. x. 1.

[26] I. xv. 11.

[27] See I. xiv. 7.

[28] I. xii. 3: "ab eadem auctoritate debent leges, et alia quae per electionem statuuntur, suscipere . . . interpretationem. . . ." I. xii. 9: "Convincitur legum approbationem, interpretationem . . . ad solius legislatoris auctoritatem tantummodo pertinere."

[29] See *Corp. jur. can., Decret. Gratiani* Pars II. can. 30. C. XI. qu.1, and the gloss of Gratian (I, 635): "ille solus habet ius interpretandi canones, qui habet potestatem condendi eos. . . ." See also *Corp. jur. civ., Codex* I. xiv. 12.

[30] Thomas Aquinas *S. theol.* II. II. qu.60. a.6: "ille qui judicium fert, legis dictum quodammodo interpretatur, applicando ipsum ad particulare negotium. Cum autem ejusdem auctoritatis sit legem interpretari, et legem condere; sicut lex condi non potest nisi publica auctoritate, ita nec judicium ferri potest nisi publica auctoritate; quae quidem se extendit ad eos qui communitati subduntur." Egidius of Rome *De eccl. pot.* III. viii (pp. 186–87): "Ex qua plenitudine potestatis ista ecclesia tripliciter se habet ad leges et ad jura; primo quia ejus est leges condere, secundo quia ad eam spectat leges conditas populis fidelibus dare, tercio quia ad eam pertinet leges primo conditas et postea gentibus datas exponere et interpretari . . . cujus est leges condere, ejus est leges dare et ejus est leges datas interpretari. . . ." The French legists are no less sweeping; see *Disputatio inter militem et clericum,* p. 14: "Manifestum est ergo, illum debere secundum leges iudicare, et secundum easdem de iusto et iniusto cognoscere, cuius est leges condere, et habere interpretari, exponere et custodire, facere et gravare et mollire, cum videbitur expedire."

[31] *Dialogus* Pars I. Lib. VI. cap. c (p. 628): "non illius solius est interpretari legem, cujus est condere. . . ." Ockham's point here is that interpretation is simply a clarification of meaning, and a law may require such clarification not only because it contains equivocal

Having thus been separated from both legislation and interpretation, the Marsilian ruler's judicial function includes only those further acts which are entailed by the coercive judgment itself. Marsilius' analysis of these acts is expressed in terminology taken from Aristotle's discussion of the steps involved in prudential action. We have already examined those steps as they are repeated in Marsilius' account of the legislative process: the "deliberation" (*consiliari*) of the experts, the people's "judgment" (*judicare*) of the experts' recommendations, and finally the "command" (*praecipere*) which the people affixes to those recommendations it judges worthy, and which makes them laws.[32] Now Marsilius' statements of the acts of the ruler are simply sequential upon these steps. He regularly expresses those acts in a three-fold sequence: "judgment" (*judicare*), "command" (*praecipere*), and "execution" (*exequi*), in that order.[33] The identity of the first two of these acts with the last two steps of the legislative process is owing to the fact that Marsilius has separated the ruler from the legislator, whereas Aristotle not only identifies these but also does not distinguish the deliberative experts from the "legislator" as such.[34] The "judgment" of Marsilius' ruler is, therefore, different from

---

terms (in which case alone it must be interpreted by its *conditor*), but also because its most recent meaning, as determined by other positive laws or exceptions, may not be known (in which case it must be interpreted by reference to "custom, which is the best interpreter of laws," and by judges and lawyers), or because the law's relation to divine or natural law or to natural reason may not be known (in which case it must be interpreted by theologians and moral philosophers).

[32] See above, pp. 168–69.

[33] For statements of this triad, see I. xv. 6: "auctoritas judicandi, praecipiendi, et exequendi"; I. xv. 7: "potestatem agendi secundum illam [legem] judicia civilia, praecipiendi, et exequendi"; *ibid.*: "judicando, praecipiendo, et exequendo"; I. xv. 8: "judicium, praeceptum, et executionem"; I. xvii. 2: "judicii, seu sententiae, vel praecepti"; I. xvii. 3: "judicium, praeceptum, et executio"; I. xviii. 3: the same; II. ii. 8: "auctoritas est judicare . . . praecipiendi et exequendi"; II. vi. 12: "fieri debet executio talis sententiae praecepto judicis"; II. viii. 6: "praecipiat, regulet, seu judicet, ac etiam exequatur." In some contexts the intermediate step is omitted, only *judicare* and *exequi* being given: I. xiv. 3; I. xviii. 1; II. iv. 7; II. viii. 6. It is hence difficult to see the point of McIlwain's statement (*op. cit.*, p. 307) that the Marsilian ruler "is usually called *pars iudicialis seu consiliativa,* rarely *pars executiva.*" See following note.

[34] See above, pp. 172–74. It is significant that whereas Marsilius assigns "deliberation" to the law-discovering experts, and "judgment" and "command" to the people-legislator and the ruler, although in different ways, Aristotle applies the entire triad to the governmental function (*Pol.* IV. 15. 1299a 26). In his early chapters Marsilius repeats the terminology of Aristotle, referring to the government as "judicialis seu principans *et consiliativa*" (I. v. 7; see I. vii. 1; I. viii. 2). However, no reference to the governmental function as *consiliativa* occurs after the last passage cited; when Marsilius subsequently refers to the ruler's "prudence," it is only as required for dealing with cases *"not determined by law"* (I. xiv. 3–4). The ruler's "deliberation" would hence not be identical with that of the deliberative experts who discover the laws. In this, Marsilius parallels Aristotle, who distinguishes three "parts of all constitutions": deliberative, governmental, judicial (*Pol.* IV. 14. 1298a 1 ff.): for whereas the deliberative is "dominant *with respect to the laws*" (*ibid.* IV. 14. 1298a 1 ff.), the governmental "deliberates *about some matters*" (*ibid.* IV. 15. 1299a 26).

the "judgment" of the legislator. The latter is an estimation of the appropriateness of proposed means to a projected end, whereas the ruler's judgment is an application of the law to a particular case.[35] This judgment is followed by a "command" that the punishments, rewards, or other decisions contained in the judgment be carried out. It is the authority to give such a command which differentiates the ruler's judgment (the "third sense") from all non-coercive judgments (the "first sense"). And finally, the ruler "executes" through the coercive force of the "military part" of the state[36] the judgments which he has handed down in the first step and commanded in the second. Since these judgments must be in accordance with the law, the ruler is the "executive" of the legislator or law.[37]

Because of this conception of the ruler's "executive" function as distinct from the people's "legislative" function, Marsilius has been acclaimed as the founder of the doctrine of "separation of powers,"[38] although that he propounds such a doctrine has more recently been denied.[39] There were, indeed, sources to which his emphasis upon the distinction between legislative and executive functions can be traced, although none of them is identical with his own position.[40] The concept of the "executive" has clear roots in the Aristotelian tradition. In Aristotle's analysis of prudential action, from which, as we have seen, Marsilius' other concepts of the ruler's functions are derived, after deliberation, judgment, and command there comes "action" (πράττειν),[41] whereby one carries out the command. And appropriately enough, in the *Politics* where Aristotle writes of the "actions" (πράξεις) whereby verdicts of law courts are carried out,[42] William of Moerbeke consistently translates πράξεις by *executiones*.[43] Here, however, the "executive" is not a ruler carrying out the enactments of the legislative, but rather an official responsible for the penal enforcement of judicial sentences; he is hence equivalent to the "military part"

[35] Whereas the Latin and English have one word—*judicium*, "judgment"—for the two operations here indicated, the Greek has the common term κρίσις and the special terms σύνεσις for what Marsilius regards as the legislator's act and δίκη for the ruler's. See *N. Eth.* vi. 10. 1143a 10 for σύνεσις, and *ibid.* v. 6. 1134a 31 for δίκη.

[36] See I. v. 8; I. xiv. 8.

[37] I. xv. 4; II. viii. 6.

[38] See above, p. 4, n. 9.

[39] See Battaglia, *Marsilio*, p. 104; McIlwain, *op. cit.*, p. 307; Lagarde, *Marsile*, pp. 177 ff.; d'Entrèves, *Medieval Contribution*, p. 58.

[40] In Aristotle's division of the "parts of all constitutions" into "deliberative," "ruling," and "judicial" (*Pol.* IV. 11. 1297b 37 ff.), since the deliberative is the supreme power of the constitution (*ibid.* 1299a 2), it is identical with the government (πολίτευμα) (see *ibid.* III. 4. 1278b 11); whereas for Marsilius government and legislator must be distinct unless the government is a polity. Moreover, there is no indication that what Aristotle here calls the ruling "part" is restricted, as is Marsilius' ruler, to executing the laws made by the legislative or deliberative part.

[41] *N. Eth.* VI. 10. 1143a 9.

[42] *Pol.* VI. 8. 1322a 16.

[43] In *Thomae Aquinatis opera*, ed. Fretté, XXVI, 419; also ed. Susemihl, p. 489.

which subserves the "ruling part" in the Marsilian state.[44] But there is a further point in the Aristotelian doctrine where the distinction is explicitly between legislative and executive. Aristotle distinguishes between two aspects of political prudence, the "legislative," which is architectonic, and the "political," whereby men "act" (πράττουσι),[45] that is, carry out the provisions of the law. Thomas Aquinas interprets the latter as *executiva,* so that for him there is a real distinction between "legislative" and "executive."[46] It is not the ruler, however, but rather the subject who is the "executive" for Thomas; thus he writes that the ruler's function is to "command," the subject's is to "execute."[47] This is precisely the terminology of Marsilius; but where for Thomas the ruler both makes the law and commands its observance, while the subject executes that command, for Marsilius the people makes the law while the ruler both commands and executes it.

An additional factor in Marsilius' specific emphasis upon the ruler as "executive" may be found in the use which the papalists made of the concept of execution. They held that the ruler has temporal power not *secundum auctoritatem* but only *secundum executionem,* thus, that the primary authority even in temporal affairs belongs to the pope, while the ruler is only the "executive" of that authority.[48] In this papalist "division of powers" Marsilius simply substitutes the people-legislator for the pope.

It is, indeed, through Marsilius' unique emphasis upon the people as sole legislator that his distinction between the legislative and the executive involves a departure from the antecedent traditions. In the normal medieval

[44] I. v. 8.

[45] *N. Eth.* VI. 8. 1141b 24.

[46] *In Eth.* Lib. VI. Lect. 7. nn. 1197–99 (pp. 399–400): "ejus habitus qui est circa totam civitatem, una pars est quasi prudentia architectonica, quae dicitur *legis positiva* . . . Alia autem pars politicae communi nomine vocatur politica, quae scilicet consistit circa singularia operabilia . . . ad ejusmodi politicam *executivam* pertinet sententia . . . ista *executiva* legis positivae retinet sibi commune nomen politicae. . . ." Of the parts of *prudentia,* "quaedam vero dicitur *legis positio,* idest prudentia *ponendi leges;* quaedam vero est politica, idest prudentia *exequendi leges.*"

[47] *S. theol.* II. II. qu.60. a.1. ad 4: "justitia in principe quidem est sicut virtus architectonica, quasi imperans et praecipiens quod justum est; in subditis autem est tanquam virtus *executiva* et ministrans." See *ibid.* II. II. qu.50. a.1. ad 1; qu.58. a.1. ad 5.

[48] Egidius of Rome *De eccl. pot.* III. v (p. 173). Also James of Viterbo *De reg. Christ.* II. viii, x (pp. 250–51, 289–90). Augustinus Triumphus *S. de eccl. pot.* qu.1. aa.1, 7. Alvarus Pelagius *De planctu eccl.* I. xiii. This distinction between *auctoritas* and *executio* is derived by way of interpretation from St. Bernard's distinction between having a sword *nutu* and *manu* (*De consideratione* IV. iii [PL 182, 776]). See Egidius *De eccl. pot.* I. viii, ix; II. xiv; III. vii, x (pp. 28–34, 133, 181, 197); James of Viterbo *De reg. Christ.* II. x (p. 289). See also J. Rivière, *Le Problème de l'église et de l'état au temps de Philippe le Bel* (Louvain, 1926), Appendice III: "Place de Saint Bernard dans la controverse," pp. 405 ff. Marsilius himself refers to this source; see *Def. pac.* II. xxviii. 24: "Sed dicet Bernardus aut ejus interpres . . . quod quamvis *auctoritas* jam dicta ad sacerdotem pertineat, tamen *executio* per ipsum fieri non debet."

doctrine the ruler is both "legislator" and "executive"[49] in relation to the positive law. When John of Salisbury writes that the ruler "obeys the law and rules the people by its dictates,"[50] he is referring to the "higher law," not to a positive law explicitly made by an agency other than the ruler himself. On the other hand, in the "polity" or republic, as opposed to the kingdom, the laws are regarded as being "made" or "enacted" by the people, while the ruler is restricted to executing those laws.[51] Marsilius' distinction between the legislative and the executive simply systematizes a situation found in the republics of his time and adumbrated in those of his predecessors who described that situation as part of their constitutional analysis. But, as we shall see more fully in the next section, none of his predecessors based their doctrine so completely upon republicanism as he did.

Nevertheless, entirely apart from the fact that Marsilius does not distinguish between the "executive" and the "judicial" powers (since both pertain to the ruler), his distinction between the legislative and the executive is not such a "separation of powers" as Montesquieu made famous in modern times. For Marsilius, political authority is unilinear: it moves in a straight line from the legislator, to the ruler who judges by authority of the legislator and thereby "executes" the law, to the military or police which exercises compulsion ultimately through the legislator's authority but immediately through the ruler's, and thereby itself "executes" the ruler's judgments. For Montesquieu, on the other hand, political authority moves in a circular direction, for each power—legislative, executive, judicial—is checked by the others, and no one is ultimate in the sense of controlling the others while not being controlled by them.[52] The practical difficulties of this conception have frequently been pointed out; indeed, Marsilius' own arguments for the unity of the state and its government, invoking the dangers which the lack of a supreme governmental

[49] See Egidius of Rome *De reg. princ.* Lib. III. Pars II. cap. i, xx: the *rex* is both *legislator* and *custos legis.* Dante *De mon.* I. xiii (p. 348) refers to the monarch as "legislator et legis executor." Augustinus Triumphus *S. de eccl. pot.* qu.44. a.1: "legem condere et executioni tradere non pertinet nisi ad personam publicam." See also above, p. 174, n. 53.

[50] John of Salisbury *Policraticus* IV. i.

[51] *Stat. com. Pad.* n. 52 (p. 25): "Potestas Padue teneatur et debeat omnes refformationes maioris conscilii observare et eas *executioni mandare. . . .*" See Egidius *De reg. princ.* Lib. III. Pars II. cap. ii: "totius [populi] est condere statuta quae non licet dominum transgredi." John of Paris *De pot. reg. et. pap.* cap. xviii (p. 133): "praeest . . . secundum leges quas cives vel alii instituerunt." Ptolemy of Lucca *De reg. princ.* IV. 8: "judicant secundum leges eis traditas . . . tales leges ab ipsa multitudine sunt institutae." See also O. von Gierke, *Political Theories of the Middle Age,* trans. F. W. Maitland (Cambridge, 1900), p. 177, n. 268.

[52] *De l'esprit des lois* XI. vi.

authority would bring,[53] themselves constitute a critique of the basic presuppositions of such a separation of powers.

Marsilius' differentiation of the legislative and executive functions is not, then, a separation *in radice* but rather a utilitarian device of economy, a division of labor for the sake of greater efficiency. "The execution of the law is done more conveniently by the ruler than by the entire multitude of citizens, since in this function one or a few rulers suffice, while the entire community would needlessly be occupied therein, and would be distracted from the other necessary functions." [54] The principle here invoked may be called "Marsilius' razor," for it applies to politics the same conception with which the phrase "Ockham's razor" is associated in logic and metaphysics: more persons must not be used in some political function where fewer would suffice; or, in other words, officials must not be multiplied beyond necessity. With Marsilius as with Ockham, this is only a methodological principle, and is not given the status of an absolutely necessary condition of political freedom such as Montesquieu makes of his separation of powers. Yet Marsilius does invoke a real harm as the consequence of non-observance of the principle, for the other functions necessary to the state would be hindered if governmental functions were attended to by all indiscriminately, or by more than are required to perform them. Indeed, this is but a consequence of his concept of "peace" as involving the performance by each part of the state of its own proper function. Thus the "razor" principle receives a wide application throughout Marsilius' doctrine. It is used to show that the inquiry for the discovering of good proposed laws must be carried on by a relatively small number of experts,[55] that there must not be more than one supreme government in the state,[56] that the general council must consist of a relatively small number of men,[57] and that the church should have only one head bishop.[58]

Yet even more significant than these applications of the principle is the one context in which Marsilius resolutely refuses to accept it. For the principle, and the Marsilian concept of "peace," are, as we have seen above, close analogues of the Platonic concept of "justice" whereby supreme political power must itself be marked off from other functions of the state and given over to the one or a few who are wisest. It was, indeed, by appealing to the same "razor" that Dante, Egidius, and William of Ockham withdrew political power from the many (*plures*) and assigned

[53] I. xvii. 3. See above, pp. 118 ff.
[54] I. xv. 4.
[55] I. xiii. 8.
[56] I. xvii. 6.
[57] II. xx. 2.
[58] II. xxii. 7.

it instead to one ruler.[59] Marsilius himself lists the same principle among his arguments against the legislative power of the people: the few wise men would suffice to make the laws.[60] But here, as we have seen, he flatly rejects it, because it is not safe to entrust this power to a few, and because the less well educated multitude is of indispensable aid in the legislative process.[61]

2. THE NATURE OF REPUBLICAN GOVERNMENT

The specific theory of government which Marsilius develops in some detail is that which the other Aristotelians called "political," in contradistinction from "kingly." The term "political" as designating a particular species of government or constitution is derived from Aristotle's *πολιτεία*, which, as he explains, means both "constitution" in general, and a specific kind of constitution, that is, one in which "the multitude" rules for the common benefit.[1] The terms "republican" and "constitutional" are hence the Latin and English synonyms for "political" in this specific sense,[2] although the former includes a connotation of "popular" absent from the Greek, because of the derivation of *publica* from *populus*. Now Marsilius does not apply the term "political" to the kind of government which he upholds, for by his distinction between the legislator and the government, the difference between kingly and political government has become en-

[59] Dante *De mon.* I. xiv: "Et quod potest fieri per unum, melius est per unum fieri quam per plura." William of Ockham *Dialogus* Pars III. Tr. I. Lib. II. cap. xix (p. 804): "quando tamen ad alicujus inventionem sufficit unus solus, qui tunc non indiget favore vel auxilio, aut consilio plurium, melius est quod queratur et inveniatur ab uno quam a pluribus . . . Quando autem pauci sufficiunt ad videndum perfecte, quid est agendum et quid omittendum, non expedit multitudinem convenire ad tractandum, sed melius est quod conveniant pauci, sufficientes tamen. Et ideo quando unus sufficit, non oportet convenire multos." Ockham also says, however, that where many are needed, then the "multitude" must come together; and also that even when one rules alone, he is corrigible by the "multitude." See also Egidius *De reg. princ.* Lib. III. Pars II. cap. iv.

[60] I. xiii. 1: "Adhuc, frustra fit per plures, quod per pauciores fieri contingit. Cum ergo per sapientes (qui pauci sunt) lex ferri possit, ut dictum est, frustra occuparetur in hoc universa multitudo aut ipsius pars major."

[61] I. xiii. 7. See above, pp. 205 ff.

[1] *Pol.* III. 5. 1279a 39.

[2] The transition from "political" to "republican" is partly owing to Cicero: where Aristotle writes of three kinds of *πολιτεία*, Cicero writes "de tribus generibus *rerum publicarum*" (*De re pub.* I. xxviii. 44), although he uses *res publica* only in the generic sense, not also for the specific *civitas popularis*. Thomas Aquinas, on the other hand, uses *res publica* as synonymous with *politia* in both senses; thus where William of Moerbeke's translation runs "Est autem *politia* ordo civitatis," Thomas comments: "Ostendit quod sit *res publica;* et dicit quod *respublica* nihil est aliud quam ordinatio civitatis. . . ." (*In Pol.* Lib. III. Lect. 5 [p. 220–21]). Again, where Moerbeke has "Quando autem multitudo ad commune conferens vivit, vocatur communi nomine omnium politiarum *politia,*" Thomas' paraphrase has, "vocatur *respublica* quod est nomen commune omnibus politiis" (*ibid.* Lib. III. Lect. 6 [p. 225]). The two passages of the *Politics* here rendered are III. 6. 1278b 9; 7. 1279a 37. Moerbeke's translation of these two passages is also found on pp. 173 and 179 of Susemihl's edition.

tirely one of the number of those who rule,[3] not of the source, extent, and limitation of their power. Although, therefore, he assumes kingly monarchy as the kind of government existing in his state,[4] it is precisely of the kind which his predecessors called "political." It is worth examining his analysis of this government with some care, because of the central place which it occupies in his doctrine, because of its integral connection with his theory of the people as legislator, because of the controversy which has raged over its "novelty," and because it presents a conception of government whose basic features are still of vital concern.

The source of this conception of "political" government is in Aristotle's *Politics;* but it is not a mere copy. For Marsilius' republicanism has a dogmatic singleness of emphasis which is lacking in the encyclopedic analysis of Aristotle himself, where the "polity," like other constitutions, undergoes successive qualitative redefinitions.[5] The conception of political or republican government developed by Marsilius comprises four basic features: (*a*) the people makes the laws; (*b*) the ruler must govern in accordance with the laws; (*c*) the people elects the ruler; (*d*) the people can correct, depose, and punish the ruler if he infringes the laws. Let us consider each of these in turn.

(*a*) This has been examined in the preceding chapter.

(*b*) This has been examined in the first section of this chapter.[6]

(*c*) The people's election of the ruler follows in the first instance from the fact that the people makes the law. For law and ruler are correlative, since the law is to the ruler as form to matter; and those who generate a form determine also the matter of that form.[7] Hence all the arguments

[3] See I. viii. 3. [4] See I. ix. 4, 5.

[5] The "polity" means now the rule of those men who bear arms (*Pol.* III. 7. 1279b 2; see *ibid.* II. 6. 1265b 28; III. 17. 1288a 13; IV. 13. 1297b 1); now the rule of both the poor and the rich in a "mixture" of democracy and oligarchy (*ibid.* IV. 8. 1293b 34 ff.; IV. 13. 1297a 39 ff.; V. 7. 1307a 7 ff.); now the rule of the middle class (*ibid.* IV. 10. 1295a 34 ff.; IV. 12. 1296b 38); now the rule of those who meet a certain property qualification (τίμημα), so that in this last sense it is called "timocracy" (*N. Eth.* VIII. 10. 1160a 34 ff.; see *Pol.* IV. 9. 1294b 5). William of Ockham sums up some of these senses of "polity" as follows: "Tertia species politiae temperatae et rectae ac justae diversis nominibus appellatur. Uno nomine vocatur communi nomine *politia,* quod in una significatione est commune ad omnem politiam rectam et non rectam. In alia significatione signat solummodo quandam speciem politiae, quae alio nomine *timocratia* nominatur, de qua sunt diversae opiniones. Una est, quod timocratia sive politia communi nomine dicta est illa, in qua principantur multi propter bonum commune, sive sint optimi sive non optimi, sive sint divites sive pauperes, ita quod politia per se per multitudinem distinguitur ab aristocratia. Alia est, quod politia est illa, in qua principantur aliqui egeni virtuosi propter bonum commune. Alia est, quod politia est illa, in qua principantur aliqui neque optimi neque mali, sed mediocres propter virtutem et bonum commune, ita quod per defectum virtutis et bonitatis distinguitur ab aristocratia" (*Dialogus* Pars III. Tr. I. Lib. II. cap. viii [p. 796]).

[6] See especially above, p. 230; also below, pp. 242–44.

[7] I. xv. 3.

for the people as legislator apply equally to the people as alone entitled to the authority to elect the ruler.[8]

(*d*) The people's power to correct, depose, and punish the ruler is a clear consequence of the preceding limitations upon the ruler. For since the "form" of the ruler's functioning is the law, by which he is "the standard and measure of every civil act," it follows that if he transgresses the law, he becomes himself subject to being "measured and regulated" by someone else who has the authority so to act.[9] Although this authority may be exercised by various persons, its primary control, just as that of the law itself and of the ruler's election, belongs to the legislator alone.[10] Hence, just as each of the citizens is subject to the government which must correct any of his "excesses," transgressions of the law, so if the ruler in thus functioning, or in any other action, himself commits an "excess," he must in turn be himself corrected by all the citizens. This limitation of the ruler, like the control of the law itself by the people, is essential to freedom as Marsilius conceives it: any government not subject to correction by its citizens becomes despotic, and the life of the citizens themselves becomes slavish.[11]

The precise circumstances of such correction of the ruler by the people are presented by reference to three factors, bearing upon the gravity, frequency, and legal determination of the ruler's excess. Any grave excess of the ruler must be punished, regardless of the other two factors; for otherwise the people would become outraged, and the resulting disturbances might lead to the destruction of the state. If the law does not explicitly determine the penalty for such excess, it must be dealt with by a "sentence" of the legislator specifically directed toward it; it should, however, be determined by law to the fullest possible extent.[12] On the other hand, a slight excess, if it is infrequently committed by the ruler, must be overlooked, since the advantages accruing from its correction would be outweighed by the harm arising from disturbance of the normal functioning of the government, from the disrespect in which the ruler would be placed, and from the possibility of scandal and disruption of the habitual obedience of the citizens to the government and the laws.[13] But frequent commission of excesses by the ruler, even if each be slight, requires corrective action and punishment, and this should be determined by law; failure so to punish "would be of notable harm to the polity."[14]

[8] I. xv. 2. [9] I. xviii. 2. [10] I. xviii. 3.

[11] *Ibid.* "alioquin despoticus fieret quilibet principatus, et civium vita servilis et insufficiens." See I. xii. 6; and above, pp. 220 ff.

[12] I. xviii. 4. [13] I. xviii. 5–6. [14] I. xviii. 7.

Such, then, in brief outline, is Marsilius' doctrine of the "political" or republican constitution or government which he prescribes for the state. It can be seen that its primary emphasis is upon the limitation of the ruler by the people and its laws. This limitation is the counterpoise to the broad powers which Marsilius' doctrines of peace and unity assigned to the ruler over all the other parts of the state. Yet they follow from the same principles of the biological interpretation of individual and collective desires, and the concentration upon efficient causes.

The full meaning of Marsilius' republicanism emerges only when it is compared with the doctrines of his predecessors and contemporaries. That the idea of such a republican government is by no means original with Marsilius is obvious from both institutional and doctrinal history. To seek no further, such governments were found in the Italy of Marsilius' time, and their lineaments were discussed by most of the Aristotelians, taking their point of departure from Aristotle himself. Both these aspects are brought out clearly in an excellent brief description of the Italian "polities" by Egidius of Rome, in the *De regimine principum,* part of which we have cited previously.[15] It will be noted how this description contains the four basic features of the Marsilian republic:

In the cities of Italy the many, as the whole people, commonly rule (*dominantur*). The consent of the whole people is sought in establishing statutes, in electing the *podesti* (*potestatibus*), and even in correcting the *podesti*. For although there is always found some *podestà* or lord (*dominus*) who governs the city, nevertheless the whole people rules more than does the aforesaid lord, because it pertains to the whole people to elect him, to correct him if he acts badly, and to establish statutes which the lord is not allowed to transgress. This is a polity, in which the many, as the whole people, rule, or what is aimed at is the common good of the good needy persons, the middle class, and the rich, and of all according to their status, and then it is right and fair.[16]

Similarly, Ptolemy of Lucca presents analyses of "political" government as differing from kingly government in that the former involves the people's election of the ruler,[17] the ruler's restriction by laws[18] made by the people,[19] and examination and punishment of the ruler if he transgresses these laws.[20] Other Aristotelians who mention the *politicus principatus,* although they do not give so full statements as these, still maintain its central feature of a constitutional limitation of the ruler by the laws

[15] See above, p. 198.

[16] Egidius *De reg. princ.* Lib. III. Pars II. cap. ii. See *ibid.* Lib. II. Pars I. cap. xiv.

[17] Ptolemy of Lucca *De reg. princ.* III. xx; IV. i, xviii (pp. 74, 79, 103).

[18] *Ibid.* II. viii; III. xxi; IV. i, viii, xxvi (pp. 34, 75, 79, 91, 101, 110).

[19] *Ibid.* IV. viii (p. 91).

[20] *Ibid.* IV. i (p. 80).

and the people.[21] And some familiar features are embodied in the "mixed" constitution.[22]

In expounding his republican doctrine, therefore, Marsilius is not presenting a new principle; its sources can, indeed, be found much earlier than these Aristotelians. Nevertheless, it would be a mistake to conclude the absence of novelty in the Marsilian doctrine. For, to begin with, there is this decided difference between Marsilius' position and that of his predecessors: that for Marsilius such constitutionally limited government is the *only legitimate kind*. For Egidius, political rule is merely one of three "just" species, and in fact is held to be far inferior to kingship;[23] it is to the latter that he devotes almost his entire discussion. For Ptolemy, similarly, there are priestly-kingly and kingly-imperial governments as well as political government; not only does he regard each of these as legitimate, but the first is by far preëminent over the others,[24] and the second is preferable to the political in many ways.[25] And although Thomas Aquinas and John of Paris call the "mixed" government the "best" kind,[26] they are far from considering its principle of popular election the *sine qua non* of legitimate government. On the contrary, they both consider kingship, where such election is not requisite, the best of the "pure" or unmixed forms,[27] and base most of their discussions upon it.

For Marsilius, on the other hand, no other kind of government is even to be considered legitimate. He flatly rejects any ruler or government which is not under the law[28] or not subject to correction by the people for transgressing the law,[29] as well as any law which is not made by the people.[30] Moreover, amid all the relativities which he admits as possible with regard to forms of government, owing to the diversities of peoples, places,

[21] Thomas Aquinas *In Pol.* Lib. I. Lects. 1, 10 (pp. 93, 133). Engelbert of Admont *De ortu* cap. xvi (p. 372B). John of Paris *De pot. reg. et pap.* cap. xviii (p. 133). The fact that all these writers here cite Aristotle for their definitions not only of "political" government but also of kingly government, the latter involving the king's ruling "according to his own laws" or "by his own will," shows that Carlyle is in error when he declares that the Roman law is the source of Ptolemy's and Egidius' conception of the legislative authority of the ruler (*op. cit.*, V, 468). Aristotle himself defines the "absolute king" (παμβασιλεύς) as one who rules all men according to his own will (*Pol.* III. 16. 1287a 9). See also William of Ockham *Dialogus* Pars III. Tr. I. Lib. II. cap. vi (p. 794): "sunt enim ipsius modi plures, secundum ipsum [i.e., Aristotelem] 3 *Poli.* c. 16 sed potissimus ipsius modus videtur, quando aliquis regnat et principatur in regno, non secundum legem, sed secundum voluntatem suam."

[22] See Thomas Aquinas *S. theol.* II. I. qu.95. a.4. Resp.; qu.105. a.1. Resp. John of Paris *De pot. reg. et pap.* cap. xx (p. 137).

[23] Egidius *De reg. princ.* Lib. III. Pars II. cap iii.

[24] Ptolemy *De reg. princ.* III. x (p. 59).

[25] *Ibid.* II. ix; III. vii, xi; IV. viii (pp. 34–35, 54, 63, 90).

[26] See texts cited above, n. 22.

[27] See Thomas *De reg. princ.* I. ii (p. 4); *S. theol.* II. II. qu.50. a.1. ad 2. John of Paris cap. i, xx (pp. 110, 137).

[28] I. x. 1; I. xi. *passim*, esp. 6; I. xv. 7.

[29] I. xviii. 3.

[30] I. xii. 3.

and times,[31] he insists that the ruler be elected, and that, while the method of election may vary, yet *"in whatever way it may be diversified, this must be observed in each case,* that such election or establishment *always be made by authority of the legislator,* whom we have frequently said to be the whole body of citizens or the weightier part thereof." [32] Thus he dogmatically insists upon all four of the basic traits of his republicanism, and on the same ground as all his other dogmatisms: these republican controls are absolute conditions of the state's existence and preservation.[33]

There is, consequently, a sharp difference between Marsilius and his Aristotelian predecessors. His single-minded emphasis upon government limited by law and the people means that only popular, constitutional government is henceforth to be considered legitimate, and that the criteria of legitimacy, hitherto centered in final causes—normative considerations of justice, natural law, God—are now tied to efficient causes—positive institutional controls established and maintained by the people. Thus where Aristotle, followed by most of the medieval Aristotelians, classifies governments as just or unjust depending upon whether or not they aim at the "common benefit," [34] Marsilius makes the primary criterion the will and consent of the subjects,[35] which he subsequently specifies as requiring that the government be elected by the people.[36] This does not mean that Aristotle does not also hold that a just government will have the consent of its subjects,[37] nor that Marsilius does not also hold that a just government will aim at the common benefit. It is rather a question of which is the primary or essential criterion: Aristotle places it in the final cause, Marsilius in the efficient cause. For Marsilius, ends are less important than means, not only because the attainment of ends will best be assured

[31] I. ix. 10.

[32] I. xv. 2.

[33] See also above, p. 107, nn. 97, 98, 101, 102.

[34] *Pol.* III. 6–7. 1279a 17 ff. See Thomas Aquinas *De reg. princ.* I. i (p. 3). Egidius of Rome *De reg. princ.* Lib. III. Pars II. cap. 2. John of Paris *De pot. reg. et pap.* cap. i (p. 109). Dante *De mon.* I. xii (p. 347). James of Viterbo *De reg. Christ.* II. ii (p. 166). John of Jandun *Quaest. in Metaphys.* Lib. I. qu.18 (fol. 14K). William of Ockham *Dialogus* Pars III. Tr. I. Lib. II. cap. vi (p. 794); *Octo quaest.* qu.3. cap. iv (pp. 105–6).

[35] I. ix. 5. In his initial classification, Marsilius makes both ruling for the common benefit and the will of the subjects the joint differentiae between "well-tempered" and "diseased" governments (I. viii. 2–3). But subsequently the latter becomes the primary differentia: "Haec igitur duo praedicta [i.e., consensus subditorum et commune conferens] principatum temperatum et vitiosum separant . . . *simpliciter autem aut magis subditorum consensus*" (I. ix. 5). See I. ix. 6, 7, 9.

[36] I. ix. 7.

[37] Aristotle sometimes distinguishes "kingly" from "tyrannical" governments by the consideration that the former is always over voluntary subjects while the latter is not; see *Pol.* III. 14. 1285a 27; IV. 10. 1295a 16; V. 10. 1313a 6–16. For the very minor way, however, in which this volitional difference figures in the Aristotelian tradition, see Egidius of Rome's chapter on how the king differs from the tyrant: *De reg. princ.* Lib. III. Pars II. cap. vi. See also above, p. 221, text and n. 12.

by centering attention upon means, but also because the control of political means is itself the essence of political freedom.

The consequences of these differences are of such importance for an understanding of Marsilius' doctrine, and have been subject to so frequent misinterpretation, that it is worth examining their various aspects in further detail by comparison with the positions of his predecessors. The most convenient approach will be to consider in turn each of the four rubrics of Marsilius' republicanism.

(*a*) To begin with, what of the doctrine that the legislator must be the people? For most of Marsilius' predecessors, it is rather the king who is the legislator.[38] Even allowing for the difference between Marsilius' concept of the legislator and that of his predecessors,[39] the fundamental idea of decisive control of positive human laws is common to all. When popular control of laws is provided for, moreover, it is accompanied by various qualifications which seriously restrict its decisiveness. Thus Thomas Aquinas declares that the laws are made by the "multitude" *or* by its ruler, without indicating which of these is primary, or what is the precise source or control of the ruler's legislative authority.[40] At other points Ptolemy of Lucca and John of Paris describe as equal alternatives, without indicating any choice between them, "kingly" and "political" governments, wherein the laws are made by the ruling king or by the people, respectively.[41] At still other points, Thomas and Ptolemy make the choice between these alternatives to depend upon the "quality" or "condition" of the people.[42] In no case, then, do we find Marsilius' uncompromising insistence that the people must be the legislator.

(*b*) That the ruler must govern in accordance with law and must himself be "under the law" was a standard medieval doctrine.[43] But the "law" in question was usually custom or some higher law rather than a positive law made by the people, or it was a law made by the ruler himself. This last is the position taken by Aristotle in his discussion of kingship; [44] in this, as we have seen, he is followed by most of the medieval Aristotelians. When the law was specified as a higher law, the ruler could nonetheless be declared to be above positive law,[45] or to be subject to it only volun-

[38] See above, p. 174, n. 53. [39] See above, p. 170.

[40] *S. theol.* II. I. qu.90. a.3. Resp., and ad 2; qu.97. a.3. ad 3; qu.104. a.3 ad 2; II. II. qu.57. a.2. Resp.

[41] Ptolemy of Lucca *De reg. princ.* II. viii; III. xx; IV. i, viii, xvi, xxv (pp. 34, 75, 79, 91, 101, 110). John of Paris *De pot. reg. et pap.* cap. xviii (p. 133).

[42] Thomas *S. theol.* II. I. qu.97. a.1. Resp. Ptolemy of Lucca *De reg. princ.* II. ix; III. xi; IV. viii (pp. 35, 63, 90). Above, p. 201. [43] See Carlyle, *op. cit.*, III, 30 ff., 52 ff., 125 ff.

[44] *Pol.* III. 10. 1286a 22.

[45] Egidius *De reg. princ.* Lib. III. Pars II. cap. xxix; *De eccl. pot.* III. vii, xi (pp. 181, 195). James of Viterbo *De reg. Christ.* II. ix (p. 273). Augustinus Triumphus *S. de eccl. pot.* qu.22. a.1.

tarily or "directively," not "coercively" in the same way as his subjects.[46]

The difference between Marsilius and the entire antecedent tradition on this point is well illustrated by the respective doctrines of the qualities of the "perfect ruler." On this subject, standard in political treatises not only throughout the middle ages but also in early modern times (including such a work as Machiavelli's *Prince*), Marsilius presents notable departures which are consequences of his own reorientation of the powers of government. When the ruler is conceived as being subject only to the higher law, his personal virtues become of first importance, for they are the only insurance of his conformity to that law. Thus John of Salisbury, Egidius of Rome, and the entire tradition present long lists of virtues incumbent upon the ruler: chastity, charity, humility, generosity, affability, and many others.[47] No distinction is made between "private" and "public" virtues precisely because no such distinction is relevant; *all* the qualities of the ruler, limited as he is by no positive law, become invested with public significance. When the ruler is conceived as himself the legislator, as in the Aristotelian tradition of the king, he requires "legislative prudence," [48] and indeed he is not a "true king" unless he excels his subjects in all the virtues.[49] When the ruler is conceived as subserving the attainment of eternal life, he requires the theological virtues.[50]

In contrast to all of these, Marsilius' list of the virtues of the "perfect ruler" is specifically political, and fits precisely into the legally limited power he has prescribed for government. There is no mention of theological virtues at all, nor of personal, non-political virtues, for both are irrelevant to the ruler's function as he conceives it. And although the virtues he does list are taken from Aristotle,[51] there is no mention of "legislative" prudence among them. On the contrary, all the ruler's virtues—prudence, justice, equity—are required *only for those relatively few cases which are impossible to determine by law* because of their variation from the univer-

[46] Thomas Aquinas *S. theol.* II. I. qu.96. a.5. ad 3. This distinction goes back to John of Salisbury *Policraticus* IV. ii.

[47] See John of Salisbury *Policraticus, passim;* and also J. Dickinson's introduction to his translation, pp. l–li. Also Thomas Aquinas *De reg. princ.* I. ix (pp. 13–14). Ptolemy of Lucca *De reg. princ.* III. xi (pp. 62–63). Egidius of Rome *De reg. princ.* Lib. I, *passim.* See L. K. Born, "The Perfect Prince," *Speculum,* III (1928), 470–504.

[48] See Thomas Aquinas *S. theol.* II. II. qu.50. a.1. ad 3. Egidius of Rome *De reg. princ.* Lib. I. Pars II. cap. vii. The source of this conception is Aristotle *N. Eth.* VI. 8. 1141b 25 ff.; *Pol.* III. 4. 1277a 15; 1277b 25.

[49] Aristotle *N. Eth.* VIII. 4. 1160b 4; *Pol.* III. 17. 1288a 16. Egidius of Rome *De reg. princ.* Lib. I. Pars II. cap. vii. James of Viterbo *De reg. Christ.* II. viii (p. 258). John of Jandun *Quaest. in Metaphys.* Lib. I. qu.18 (fol. 14M). Alexander of St. Elpidius *Tract. de eccl. pot.* II. ix (p. 27).

[50] See Augustine *De civ. Dei* V. xxiv. Thomas Aquinas *De reg. princ.* I. viii, ix. Ptolemy of Lucca *De reg. princ.* II. xv, xvi; III. iii (pp. 42–44, 48–49). Egidius of Rome *De reg. princ.* I. Pars I. cap. xii. Francis of Mayron *Tract de princ. temp.* IV (p. 65). Durand of St. Pourçain *De orig. jurisdict.* II (pp. 129G–130A).

[51] See *Pol.* V. 9. 1309a 33.

sal norm.[52] The assumption is, indeed, that if, *per impossibile,* complete determination by the laws were possible, the ruler would not require any virtues at all! At any rate, Marsilius conceives the legal limitation of the ruler as so thorough that his need for virtue is of secondary rather than primary importance to the state.

Moreover, it is not virtue but authority derived from election by the people which makes a ruler.[53] To be sure, a ruler *should* be virtuous;[54] but even if a man has all the virtues, this at most makes him only "potentially" a ruler, not "actually."[55] And on the other hand, a man, if he has been duly elected, is a ruler even if he is lacking in virtue or is inferior to his subjects.[56] The only criterion of the legitimacy of government is thus its emanating from the proper efficient cause, not its embodiment or attainment of final causes.

(*c*) The doctrine that the ruler must be elected by the people was upheld by many of Marsilius' predecessors with various restrictions. Some held that only a "good" people should have this elective power; if a people is corrupt, it should not.[57] For Marsilius, on the other hand, the consideration that there was a lesser number of prudent men at the time when states were first arising is an argument for continued election of rulers as against a single election followed by hereditary succession; for the latter would perpetuate an error made by that primitive electorate.[58] Other in-

[52] Prudence is needed only when a case "non determinatur a lege" (I. xiv. 3–5). Justice is needed only because it is "non facile aut non possibile simul omnia determinare legibus, sed *aliqua* committi oportere principantis arbitrio, *in quibus* laedere potest politiam si fuerit affectionis perversae" (I. xiv. 6). Equity is needed only for those cases "in quibus lex deficit" because of its universality (I. xiv. 7). No account has hitherto been taken of the striking divergence of Marsilius from the tradition on this point. See, e.g., L. K. Born, "The Perfect Prince" (above, n. 47); A. H. Gilbert, *Machiavelli's Prince and Its Forerunners* (Durham, N.C., 1938); F. Gilbert, "The Humanist Concept of the Prince and the *Prince* of Machiavelli," *Journal of Modern History,* XI (1939), 449 ff.

[53] I. xv. 1, 2.

[54] I. ix. 7; I. xiv; I. xv. 7; I. xvi. 24.

[55] I. xv. 1.

[56] See II. xxii. 13; II. xxx. 4. A similar distinction between personal virtue and official authority had, however, been adumbrated in one segment of the medieval tradition. See the distinction between "power" and "person" or "use of power," as stated by Augustine in a gloss quoted by Marsilius (II. v. 4). See also Thomas Aquinas *S. theol.* II. II. qu.60. a.6. ad 4. A similar distinction is applied to the priesthood by Egidius of Rome *De eccl. pot.* I. ii; II. x, xii (pp. 7, 89, 101), and by James of Viterbo *De reg. Christ.* II. vi (pp. 226–27). In none of these cases, however, is the distinction accompanied by the insistence that only the people is the efficient cause of the ruler's authority.

[57] See above, p. 201.

[58] I. xvi. 19. Marsilius' opposition to hereditary succession follows, of course, from his insistence upon popular election as the only basis of political authority. Hereditary succession was upheld in the latter years of the thirteenth century and the early years of the fourteenth by partisans of the French king and by papalists: by the former in order to remove the monarchy from papal control, and by the latter in order to assert such control on the basis of the papacy's jurisdiction over inheritances. The arguments which Marsilius adduces in favor of hereditary monarchy (I. xvi. 1–10), to which he subsequently replies, are found in such treatises as Egidius of Rome *De reg. princ.* Lib. III. Pars II. cap. v; Peter of Auvergne

terpretations of election regarded it as the "best" but not the only legitimate method;[59] or as being performed not by the people but by some partial group of nobles or prelates;[60] or as incomplete until approved and ratified by the spiritual power.[61] For the papalists, of course, every *regnum* which is not "established" by the priesthood is "usurped."[62]

(*d*) It is in connection with the "correction" of the ruler that there emerges the full significance of all the other factors in Marsilius' republicanism. His emphasis upon efficient causes has the result that the criteria rendering the ruler corrigible, and the agency of such correction, are both explicitly formulated in the positive law itself, and the control of both rests with the people. The antecedent tradition's emphasis upon final causes, on the other hand, had the result that the criteria rendering the ruler corrigible were formulated in terms of "injustice" or "tyranny," but these in turn referred not to explicit provisions of positive law but rather to a "higher law." As a consequence, in Marsilius there is no question as to when the ruler is subject to correction for transgressing the law, or as to the people's authority to correct him and punish him by intra-legal means. But in the antecedent tradition there is much room for disagreement as to whether the ruler has become a tyrant. Apart from the papal claims, there is no positive agency, independent of the ruler, from which law and ruler derive their authority, and which can unambiguously judge the "lawfulness" of the ruler's actions, and regulate and correct him for lapses therefrom. The only form which can be taken by corrective action

---

In Pol. Lects. 11, 13, 14 (pp. 247, 258, 265); Pierre Dubois *De recup. terre sancte* par. 13 (p. 12); Francis of Mayron *Tract. de princ. temp.* III (pp. 61–62). Augustinus Triumphus uses the same arguments for hereditary succession of the emperor (*S. de eccl. pot.* qu.35. aa.6–7), but he refuses to accept them with respect to hereditary succession of the pope (*ibid.* qu.2. aa.2–3).

[59] Thomas *S. theol.* II. I. qu.105. a.1. Resp. John of Paris *De pot. reg. et pap.* cap. xx (p. 137).

[60] See John of Paris *De pot. reg. et pap.* cap vii, xi, xvi, xx (pp 116, 120, 130, 137): the ruler is elected by the people; but, *ibid.* cap. xiv, xvi (pp. 127, 130): the ruler is elected and corrected by the "barons." Ptolemy of Lucca *De reg. princ.* III. xix, xx (pp. 72, 74): the imperial ruler is "elected" by seven German princes, or by the army or senators. Augustinus Triumphus *S. de eccl. pot.* qu.35. aa.1, 2: the emperor is "elected" by German princes, but these elect only by authority of the pope.

[61] See James of Viterbo *De reg. Christ.* II. iii (p. 186): "Regiam quoque potestatem terrenam quidam recte adepti sunt, sive per electionem et communem consensum multitudinis, sive per divinam ordinationem; quidam autem indebite per violentiam." See *ibid.* II. iii, x (pp. 179, 303). On the other hand, see *ibid.* II. viii (p. 232): "Imperfecta quidem et informis est omnis humana potestas, nisi per spiritualem formetur et perficiatur. Haec autem formatio est approbatio et ratificatio." See to the same effect Ptolemy of Lucca *Determinatio compendiosa* cap. iii–iv. Henry of Cremona *De potestate papae,* p. 466. It is against this position that Marsilius directs his emphatic statement that "ceremonies and solemnities" are not essential to the validity of an election (I. xii. 3).

[62] Egidius of Rome *De eccl. pot.* I. v; II. v, vii. James of Viterbo *De reg. Christ.* II. vii (pp. 242–43). Augustinus Triumphus *S. de eccl. pot.* qu.36. a.1. Alvarus Pelagius *De planctu eccl.* I. xxxviii (p. 44). See also above, pp. 8, 15–16, 144–45.

against the tyrant is hence outside the positive legal and governmental framework of the state: the only alternative to submission is tyrannicide [63] or revolution.[64]

These central differences are brought out clearly in the doctrine of Thomas Aquinas. Although, as we have seen, he declares that the "best" government is that "mixed" form in which the whole people both makes the positive human law [65] and elects the ruler,[66] it is not the people's causal efficacy which is the source of the legitimacy of law and government but rather the ideal norm of justice and natural law. Hence Thomas, unlike Marsilius, can contemplate with equanimity, and consider as admissible alternatives, those cases where the human law is made and the ruler is chosen not by the people but by some "superior power" or ruler.[67] Consequently, while the ruler ought to act in accordance with the human law,[68] and is guilty of unfaithfulness or imprudence if he dispenses with the law without reason,[69] nevertheless in the cases just mentioned there is no one who can effectively correct the ruler if he acts contrary to the law.[70] Moreover, as against Marsilius' triple set of alternatives with regard to such correction,[71] Thomas distinguishes merely between "intolerable excess" and "non-excess" of tyranny; in the former case, if the people do not have the right of deposing the ruler, then all that remains is to appeal to the "superior" who has such right. If this is of no avail, recourse must be had to God.[72] Similar considerations with respect to criteria and methods of corrigibility apply to Manegold of Lautenbach's discussion of the ruler's breaking of the "pact" which obligates him to "do justice," [73] and to John of Paris' provisions for the correction of the ruler who has "sinned in temporal things." [74]

It is consequently not true to Marsilius' basic intent to say that his

[63] See John of Salisbury *Policraticus* III. xvii; VIII. xvii, xx.

[64] See Thomas Aquinas *S. theol.* II. II. qu.42. a.2. ad 3; qu.104. a.6. ad 3. These differences between Marsilius and his predecessors are completely missed by Lagarde, who disparages Marsilius' provisions for the correction of the ruler on the ground of their "caution" and "modération, remarquable pour l'époque" (*Marsile,* pp. 51, 176, 187, 198), presumably as opposed to his predecessors' justification of revolution. A more correct interpretation is given by McIlwain, *op. cit.,* p. 330.

[65] *S. theol.* II. I. qu.95. a.4. Resp.

[66] *Ibid.* II. I. qu.105. a.I. Resp.

[67] See *ibid.* II. I. qu.97. a.3. ad 3: "Si vero multitudo non habeat liberam potestatem condendi sibi legem, vel legem a superiori potestate positam removendi. . . ." *De reg. princ.* I. vi (p. 9): "Si vero ad jus superioris pertineat multitudini providere de rege. . . ."

[68] *S. theol.* II. I. qu.95. a.I. ad 2.

[69] *Ibid.* II. I. qu.97. a.4. Resp.

[70] *Ibid.* II. I. qu.96. a.5. ad 3: "Sic igitur princeps dicitur esse solutus a lege, *quia nullus in ipsum potest judicium condemnationis ferre, si contra legem agat.*"

[71] See above, p. 238.

[72] Thomas *De reg. princ.* I. vi (p. 9). See Locke *Second Treatise of Civil Government* xiv. 168.

[73] *Ad Gebehardum* cap. xxx, xlii, xlviii (MGH, *Libelli de lite,* I, 365, 391–94).

[74] *De pot. reg. et pap.* cap. xiv (p. 127).

"voluntarism" marks a "subjective" orientation as against the "objective" approach of his predecessors.[75] On the contrary, his emphasis upon will and consent is motivated by the aim of placing government under palpable, positive controls. For to define the criterion of just government by its end still leaves open the question of who shall guarantee that a government actually aims at that end. From Marsilius' point of view, the moral controls or final causes of his predecessors, expressed as virtue, justice, natural law, are in fact "subjective" despite their appeal to objective principles, because they do not indicate the precise means or efficient causes by which they are to be enforced. Consent or election, on the other hand, is an objective criterion because it indicates precisely the basis and means by which the performance of government is to be adjudged and controlled.

This point also throws further light on the question of the relation between morals and politics in the Marsilian doctrine.[76] It is not in "divorcing" politics from morals that Marsilius departs from the antecedent tradition, but in providing a positive, legal method of assuring the morality of the political order. Rather than defining law and government so that they are determined by moral and theological criteria, Marsilius insists upon strictly political definitions of such concepts and then indicates the specific efficient cause which controls them, so that there is no basis upon which laws and rulers may claim inherent justice apart from popular election.

The difference between Marsilius and his predecessors may be summed up in terms either of general principles or of specific methods of applying those principles. As we have seen, no aspect of his republicanism, as such, is really new. What is new is his insistence upon all these aspects to the exclusion of alternative positions; but underlying this insistence are real differences in principle. Indeed, the central doctrinal sources of Marsilius' emphatic republicanism are to be found in all the principles which were examined in our second chapter. Of particular importance is his biological voluntarism, which views the wills of individuals or partial groups as always directed to their own private advantage while only the will of the whole community is for the common benefit. Together with this is his change from the restricted values of his predecessors to the broad inclusive values of the sufficient life viewed as both attainable and controllable by all. And finally, where the antecedent tradition insists upon certain final causes, but does not specify the people as the unique efficient cause for their attainment, Marsilius leaves final causes relatively undifferentiated

[75] See Lagarde, *Marsile*, p. 92.

[76] On this relation, see also above, pp. 34–36; below, p. 306.

and places all his emphasis upon that specific efficient cause. Thus he replaces the traditional reliance upon ideal norms by a reliance upon the people and its own will.

3. REPUBLICANISM AND ABSOLUTISM

Thus far we have been considering Marsilius' republican doctrine primarily as it is developed in Discourse I of the *Defensor pacis*. But we must now examine the further development of these ideas throughout the remainder of Marsilius' writings, i.e., Discourse II of the *Defensor pacis* and the *Defensor minor*.

One segment of the medieval tradition has been intentionally omitted from the various comparisons traced above between Marsilius and his predecessors. That segment is the Roman, as found in the law books of Justinian and their various commentators, as well as in the whole institutional development of the republic and the empire. Some students of Marsilius have held that the primary source of his republican doctrines of the legislator and the government is this Roman tradition.[1] There are indeed significant similarities between them. Marsilius' theory that the law is to be made by the people has direct analogues in the Roman law books. In the *Digest* laws are said to derive their binding force only from their approval by the people; [2] and in the *Institutes* law is itself defined as that which the people has established.[3] Similarly, the medieval civilians, such as Irnerius and Bulgarus, explicitly declare that "the *universitas,* that is, the *populus,*" establishes or states the law.[4]

The analogy between Marsilius and the Roman tradition goes still further. According to the famous Roman *lex regia,* "what has pleased the ruler has the force of law," because "the people has granted to him all its command and power." [5] This statement indicates both that the original legislative power is, or was, in the people, and that the ruler possesses and exercises it by grant of the people. Out of this text grew a continuing de-

[1] See Piovano, *op. cit.,* pp. 170–71; McIlwain, *op. cit.,* pp. 304–5; Lagarde, *Marsile,* pp. 193–94; Carlyle, *op. cit.,* VI, 10.

[2] *Corp. jur. civ., Digest* I. iii. 32: "Nam cum ipsae leges nulla alia ex causa nos teneant, quam quod judicio populi receptae sunt, merito et ea, quae sine ullo scripto populus probavit tenebunt omnes. . . ." Marsilius' *populus,* as we have seen, is the Roman *universitas civium,* not the particularistic Greek δῆμος. See above, p. 180.

[3] *Corp. jur. civ., Institutes* I. ii. 4: "Lex est quod populus Romanus senatorio magistratu interrogante, veluti tribuno, constituebat."

[4] Irnerius (?) *De aequitate* cap. ii: "Universitas, id est populus, hoc habet officium singulis scilicet hominibus quasi membris providere. Hinc descendit hoc ut legem condat." This passage and a parallel one from Bulgarus are quoted by Carlyle, *op. cit.,* VI, 10, to show that "Marsilius is restating the doctrine of the ancient Roman law and of the medieval Civilians." Two similar passages from Irnerius and Bulgarus are quoted to the same end by Lagarde, *Marsile,* p. 194.

[5] *Corp. jur. civ., Dig.* I. iv. 1; *Inst.* I. ii. 6.

bate as to whether the people had completely surrendered its power or whether it could resume it.[6] But even apart from this question, the Roman emperors in fact exercised supreme and absolute power, and yet they preserved the republican forms whereby their power was derived from and limited by the people. The Roman imperial tradition thus rested upon a "fiction," a "difference between law and fact." [7]

Important signs of the same fundamental situation can be found in the relation beween the Marsilian people-legislator and the ruler. Discourse I, as we have seen, had proclaimed in explicit and uncompromising terms the supremacy of the people over the ruler as to his election, his limitation by the laws, and his correction and deposition for infringing them. But as was also seen above, the ruler acting according to the laws is the representative agent, the executive of the people: when he acts, the entire community act through him.[8] Hence in Discourse II this normal relation of ruler and people is taken for granted, and as a result the ruler becomes practically synonymous with the legislator. The basic formula to describe the repository of authority is now "the human legislator *or the ruler by its authority.*" [9] But even more, the ruler is described as himself the source of the laws. Thus Marsilius refers to "the laws of the Roman rulers," [10] and to "the laws and customs of secular rulers"; [11] the priests did not claim that they were "not subject to the laws and edicts of the rulers, but pressingly beseeched the rulers to make such laws." [12] Moreover, "laws were and have been established by the same rulers about the definite number of priests in respect of provinces." [13] The ruler is even several times characterized explicitly as the "legislator." [14] Other functions of the legislator are also assigned seemingly exclusively to the ruler.[15]

The similarity of this coalescence to the Roman tradition is augmented by the fact that Marsilius at several points echoes the *lex regia*. In the *Defensor minor,* it is stated that the "supreme legislator . . . was and is and ought to be the *universitas hominum*" in each province; but they "transferred" this legislative power to the Roman people; "and if this people has transferred to its ruler the authority to make laws, it must be said similarly that the ruler has such power." [16] That Marsilius holds that

[6] See O. von Gierke, *Political Theories of the Middle Age,* trans. F. W. Maitland (Cambridge, 1900), pp. 43 ff., 150, nn. 158–59.

[7] See McIlwain, *op. cit.,* pp. 133–36.

[8] I. xv. 4: "Nam et hoc facientibus hiis, id facit communitas universa, quoniam secundum communitatis determinationem, legalem scilicet, id faciunt principantes. . . ."

[9] See II. xvii. 9, 15–18; II. xxi. 5–8, and *passim.*

[10] II. ii. 7; II. xvii. 17.

[11] II. xvii. 17. See II. xxv. 6.

[12] II. xxv. 4. See II. xxi. 6.

[13] II. xxv. 5.

[14] II. xxi. 2; II. xxii. 10.

[15] See II. xvii. 17.

[16] *Def. min.* xiii. 1. See *Def. pac.* II. xxv. 9.

the power was indeed transferred is shown when he says that the power to relax or dispense with a human law "belongs only to the Roman ruler *qua* human legislator." [17]

This Roman absolutism of Marsilius goes still further, for he echoes the fiction of the medieval empire whereby the seven German princes who elect the emperor do so as representatives of the "Roman people." We read of the "prince electors" by whom the election "is celebrated and made": "three solemn Christian archbishops" and "four faithful secular rulers." [18] And the cycle is completed when it is seen that Marsilius removes from the people not only its legislative authority and its election of the ruler, but also its correction of the ruler for infringing human laws. For the ruler now governs by divine right. In Discourse I, God had been declared to be the "remote cause" of all governments; [19] and in Discourse II, accordingly, we read that secular rulers "are to be established by authority of the human legislator" but that "God has sent them." [20] Marsilius was not, to be sure, the first to combine popular election with divine ordainment of the ruler.[21] The latter circumvents the claim of some papalists that the spiritual power has greater dignity than the temporal because the former is established by God, the latter by men or by the spiritual power.[22] But Marsilius uses such divine ordainment to endow the ruler with an absolute power far removed from the limitations of his previous republicanism. In Discourse I the insistence had been that the ruler must govern in accordance with *human* law, and is corrigible by the people for transgressing it. But now, on the basis of literal interpretations of such texts as that "the powers that be are ordained of God," [23] it is declared that the ruler must be obeyed so long as he does not contravene *divine* law. "All men . . . must be subject in coercive judgment to the secular judges or rulers, nor must these be resisted unless they have commanded that something be done against the law of eternal salvation."[24] "Subjects must obey even infidel lords (*dominis*) *regardless of how bad*

[17] *Def. min.* i. 7. See also William Ockham *Breviloquium* III. xiv; VI. xi (pp. 96, 157).

[18] II. xxvi. 9.

[19] I. ix. 2.

[20] II. v. 8. See II. xxx. 4: "princeps iudex existens in hoc saeculo Dei ordinatione (quamvis immediate humani legislatoris aut alterius cuiusvis humanae voluntatis institutione). . . ." See also II. xxiv. 17.

[21] See John of Paris *De pot. reg. et pap.* cap. xi (p. 120): "potestas regia nec secundum se, nec quantum ad executionem, est a Papa: sed *est a Deo et a populo regem eligente* in persona vel in domo. . . ." Also see James of Viterbo *De reg. Christ.* II. iii (p. 179). Alexander of St. Elpidius *Tract. de eccl. pot.* II. viii (p. 24). William of Ockham (*Breviloquium* IV. iii [pp. 107–8]) attributes this position to expositors of both civil and canon law.

[22] See Egidius of Rome *De eccl. pot.* I. v (pp. 14–15). James of Viterbo *De reg. Christ.* II. iii (pp. 176–77). Augustinus Triumphus *S. de eccl. pot.* qu.1. a.1. Francis of Mayron *Quaestio de subjectione* II. 2 (p. 88).

[23] Rom. 13:1; quoted II. v. 4.

[24] II. v. 4.

they may be; with this sound understanding, however, that the obedience does not apply to those things which are opposed to divine law in word or deed." [25]

That the two requirements of the ruler's non-transgression of human and of divine law are not identical is apparent from the fact that the two laws sometimes disagree.[26] But even apart from such disagreement, human law is silent on points covered in divine law, and vice versa.[27] It appears, then, that the ruler must be obeyed if he gives a command which contravenes human law, so long as it does not contravene divine law. To be sure, divine law itself commands the observance of human law; [28] and at one point Marsilius writes that men "must obey secular rulers in all things which do not contradict the law of eternal salvation, *especially in those things which are in accordance with human laws or honorable and approved customs.*" [29] But the "especially" shows that the conformity to human law which had been a rigid requirement of governmental legitimacy in Discourse I has now become only a strong recommendation. The positive necessity of the ruler's obeying human laws has given way to the negative necessity of his not infringing divine laws.

It is clear, then, that the republicanism of Discourse I of the *Defensor pacis* undergoes serious absolutistic divergences in Discourse II and in the *Defensor minor.* To a certain extent, the divergences had been foreshadowed in the first discourse: in the definition of law as coercive command without the requirement of conformity to justice or natural law; in the concepts of peace and unity which gave the government supreme and unrivalled coercive authority over the other parts of the state. But these had been combined in Discourse I with the insistence that the law must be made by the people and that the ruler must act in accordance with the law; thus the absolutist chapter on the unity of the government had been followed immediately by the one setting forth careful positive controls to be exercised by the people over the ruler, involving his correction, deposition, and punishment for transgressions of the human law.

What, then, can be the basis of Marsilius' departures from such popular control of the ruler? It is possible to answer this question by assuming a single and all-consuming motivation in the Marsilian enterprise: opposition to the papal plenitude of power. In the light of this motivation, Marsilius' popular sovereignty would be simply a device to remove the papal sovereignty: the apotheosis of the people as against the inevitable

[25] II. xxvi. 13. For a list of other similar passages, see above, p. 162, n. 69.

[26] II. xii. 8, 9; II. xiii. 2.

[27] II. ix. 9–13.

[28] II. ix. 11; *Def. min.* viii. 3.

[29] II. v. 5.

perversion of one or a few men is an effective counter against the apotheosis of the pope; the people's making of the laws and its election and correction of the ruler are counters against the papal claims to these powers. Then, all powers having been consigned to the people, Marsilius can transfer them to the ruler as the people's "executive"; the Roman fiction will thus have been completely reenacted.[30]

This answer to the problem, however, is too simple. If Marsilius' aim from the very outset was to take the "regal," "imperialist" side in the "church-state" controversy without any reservations, then why should all the popular and legal limitations upon the government have been developed so painstakingly in the first discourse? It may be replied that otherwise the way would have been left open for the papacy to invoke and control those limitations. But if Marsilius was a Roman imperialist, why should he have insisted upon such limitations at all? Many of the Roman civilians did not.[31] Why did he not declare from the very outset, like Egidius of Rome, that the king is above all positive human laws? [32] And why did he not make the king the "legislator," like so many of the other Aristotelians, and apotheosize him in the manner of Aristotle, or at least accord him the broad powers, uncontrolled by positive human means, which were standard for so many of the other Aristotelians? The question is not merely whether Marsilius' popular sovereignty could lend itself to the secular ruler's sovereignty, but rather whether the former was *necessary* to the latter. Obviously, this was not the case. Why, then, did Marsilius insist upon rigorous subjection of the ruler to the law, upon the inevitable perversion to private benefit of any ruler's will uncontrolled by law and by the people-legislator, upon the exaltation of the "many" or "all" and the disparagement of the "few"? To say that all this was subtly aiming at a subsequent release of the ruler from control by law and the legislator is to stretch credulity and plausibility too far.

The Romanist interpretation of Marsilius is cast under further doubt by the sharp contrast between the manner in which the legislative authority of the people is expounded by the law books and civilians, on the one hand, and by Marsilius on the other. The Roman popular legislator is only a

[30] Valois, *op. cit.*, p. 587: "théorie purement démocratique, mais déjà toute prête à se transformer, grâce à une série de fictions et de sous-entendus, en doctrine impérialiste. . . ." See Piovano, *op. cit.*, pp. 170–71; Rivière, "Marsile de Padoue," *Dict. de théol. cath.*, X, 160; Lagarde, *Marsile*, pp. 193, 198; F. Battaglia, review of Lagarde's *Marsile*, in *Rivista di storia del diritto italiano*, VIII (1935), p. 156; B. de Jouvenel, *Power* (London, 1948), p. 39.

[31] See O. von Gierke, *Political Theories of the Middle Age*, trans. F. W. Maitland (Cambridge, 1900), pp. 43, 150, n. 158. Carlyle, *op. cit.*, II, 59 ff. It should be noted that even in the *Defensor minor* xii. 1 Marsilius follows that wing of Romanists who hold that the delegation of authority to the emperor is revocable. Cf. Battaglia, *Marsilio*, p. 247.

[32] *De reg. princ.* Lib. III. Pars II. cap. xxix.

formula. It is neither analyzed nor defended; it is simply stated and left unmentioned thereafter. Even the glosses on the *lex regia* discuss only the theoretic question of whether the "Roman people" *could* at some time in the future take back its power from the ruler; the assumption is not, as in Marsilius' first discourse, that of the active, continuing control of the laws and the ruler by the people. Nor does the Roman tradition find it necessary to justify or demonstrate that the people must be the legislator. To be sure, it might be held that the tradition regarded this point as beyond argument, as a first principle; but if so, it was only a legal principle or a fiction. It is not the burning polemical issue which leads Marsilius into two chapters of arguments and rebuttals. If, then, he took over from the Roman tradition the people's legislative authority, why does he regard such defense of it as necessary? And the defense itself is far removed from the abstract Roman legalism; whatever may be thought of the adequacy of his arguments, they are based upon biological and dialectical premises which no Romanist, despite the introductory statements concerning natural law, could have presented.

The fuller explanation of the shift from the republicanism of the first discourse to the absolutism of the second is to be found in the doctrinal relation of the two discourses themselves. Aspects of this relation were briefly indicated in our opening chapter in the contrast between the two chief political milieux of Marsilius' life prior to the *Defensor:* republican Padua and Paris, which was the capitol of an absolutistic French kingdom;[33] and in the further contrast between the political Aristotelianism on which he bases the first discourse and the political Augustinianism of the second.[34] The *pars principans* of the first discourse is the republican *podestà* of Padua and the ruler of the Aristotelian polity; but in the second discourse he is frequently the king of France or the Holy Roman emperor, and the *imperator, dominus, Caesar* of Augustine and other glossators on the New Testament. This shift was necessitated by the requirements of Marsilius' program itself. The second discourse "confirms" by revelation and its "saintly interpreters" the rational demonstrations of the first.[35] Hence whereas the doctrinal milieu of the first discourse is a state established by reason in response to natural desire, that of the second is the kind of supernatural political environment found in the writings of the apostles and the early church fathers. Moreover, the project of the second discourse involves the tracing of the historical development of the papal power from primitive times to Marsilius' own day.[36] Most of

[33] See above, pp. 30–31.
[34] See above, p. 39.
[35] I. i. 8. See above, pp. 12–13, 42, 70 ff.
[36] II. xviii. 1 ff.

the salient points of this development took place in the empire in which the emperor was in fact the "legislator."

The polemical opposition to the papacy runs through both discourses, although it is far less apparent in the first. But the approach to that problem is different in the two discourses. In the first it appears in much the same guise as in Padua and other north Italian cities, as the opposition of the *borghesia* to a priesthood inimical to its earthly interests, both economic and political. But in the second it appears as the traditional large-scale opposition between the "emperor" and the "pope," the *regnum* and the *sacerdotium*. Hence where the former case could involve the *popolani* in a passionate defense of their interests, the latter had no such directly popular basis but was rather a conflict between "powers." Consequently, when Marsilius transfers his concern from the one canvas to the other, the political ramifications of the relations among people, ruler, and priesthood undergo corresponding changes. Yet this transfer was necessary precisely because Marsilius intended to deal with the problem as a general one, at all political levels from city-state to empire, in the "*regnum* and any other temperate civil community whatsoever." [37]

The quantitative shift itself forces a change in the conception of the people's legislative authority. In the first discourse, as we have seen, the assumption is that the *universitas civium* will function as a citizen-assembly in considering, approving, or rejecting laws; it is akin to the "greater council" of Padua and even more to the "town meeting" of all the citizens held three times yearly.[38] But in the second discourse, where the units are frequently "France" or "Germany" or the *Italicum regnum* as a whole,[39] such direct participation of the citizens is obviously an impossibility, as Albertus Pighius pointed out in his critique of Marsilius.[40] It is here that Marsilius should have invoked the Roman law statement of the reason why the legislative authority devolved from the people to the Senate; [41] but he does not do so. It is hence inevitable that the conception of the legislative control by the *universitas civium*, applied literally in the second discourse, should take on a fictional quality.

Yet it must also be noted that despite all these factors leading to the frequent coalescence of legislator and ruler in the second discourse, at

[37] III. iii. See above, p. 128.

[38] See above, p. 188; cf. pp. 23, 197.

[39] See above, pp. 30–31, 128 ff.

[40] Albertus Pighius *Hierarchia eccles.* v. ii (p. 129): "Accipe, ut sunt, immensam aliquam communitatem civilem, quale est Galliarum, aut Hispaniarum regnum, aut Romanum, quale adhuc est imperium, quo pacto universitas alicuius ex his civilis multitudinis, optimis legibus ferendis erit idonea? *Nam quomodo in unum conveniet*, ut de lege ferenda in commune deliberet? ut inveniat, ac statuat quod optimum?"

[41] *Corp. jur. civ., Instit.* I. ii. 5. See above, p. 188.

crucial points where the relation of their respective authorities arises Marsilius is careful to distinguish them and to insist upon the subordination of the ruler. Thus he reiterates that the "human legislator" alone has the authority to correct and punish the ruler for infractions of human law; [42] and in the last chapter of the book he emphasizes that the "subject multitude" must watch that the ruler does not act contrary to the laws, since "in its expressed will consists the power and authority of government." [43] He also points out in at least two other connections that the ruler as such, "according to his own will alone," does not have the authority to appoint men to priestly office; he has such authority only "by the authority of the legislator," [44] "by the authority of the whole body of believers." [45] Marsilius' popular sovereignty is thus maintained throughout his work. This fact can be recognized even if it is accepted, as is undoubtedly the case, that his chief aim is to destroy the temporal power of the papacy. For he regards his popular sovereignty not only as compatible with but as indispensable to that aim. Having established the ruler's subordination to the people in Discourse I, as well as the subordination of every other "part" of the state to the "whole" people, he can take the former subordination for granted throughout most of Discourse II and use the latter to carry on his primary polemical aim. But to take it for granted that the ruler acts "by authority of the legislator" is not to deny his subordination.

A further factor in the interpretation of this question is the positive rather than normative modality which is found throughout Marsilius' work.[46] The "necessities" he demonstrates are presented primarily as facts which are and must be, rather than as values which should be. Thus, he writes that the people "is" (*esse*) the legislator [47] and that legislative authority "belongs" (*pertinere*) to the people.[48] To be sure, he also writes that this authority "should" (*debet*) belong to the people; [49] but in a basic sense Marsilius considers that what should be, is and must be, for since his politics is a theoretic science allied with biology rather than a practical science allied with ethics, it follows the physical necessities of nature rather than the moral urgencies of the human reason; it is impossible, therefore, that its propositions not be realized in the existing world. Specifically, Marsilius has demonstrated that unless his basic doctrines were carried out, no state could endure; but since states have been enduring and do now endure, short of "impediments" such as those deriving from the papal

[42] II. xxx. 8. See also *Def. min.* ii. 7; and *De transl. imp.* cap. vi (p. 150).
[43] III. iii.
[44] II. xxv. 8.
[45] II. xxviii. 17.
[46] See above, pp. 48 ff., 211–12.
[47] I. xii. 3.
[48] I. xii. 5.
[49] I. xii. 7.

ambitions,[50] his doctrines must in fact have been realized. Consequently, on the basis of his demonstrations that the people is and ought to be the legislator, Marsilius seemingly gives *carte blanche* to all political authorities during the entire Christian era: "the supreme human legislator, especially from the time of Christ to the present time, and perhaps during some earlier times, was and is and ought to be (*fuit et est et esse debet*) the entirety of the men who must (*debent*) be under the coercive commands of the law." [51]

In another direction, even more profound problems concerning political authority are raised by the absolutist aspects of Marsilius' republicanism. For if the principle of the sovereignty of the people is always maintained by Marsilius, he does not set any effective limits, even in theory, to that sovereignty itself. This point emerges clearly from his doctrine of unity; for while, as was seen above, his insistence upon the undivided authority of the government did not lessen the supremacy of the people over the government,[52] the same concept of unity as undivided authority applies also to the law (since law and government are correlative) and *a fortiori* to the people-legislator which makes the law and elects the ruler.[53] There is no natural law above positive law; [54] and although laws opposed to divine law are not to be obeyed, this, as we have seen, is not an effective limitation.[55] The human legislator, therefore, is a real sovereign; and Marsilius' doctrines of peace and unity, when viewed in broader perspective as applying not only to the government but to the legislator which controls the government, are seen to entail a completely unlimited political power. The Marsilian legislative power involves fuller sovereignty than either the papalist plenitude of power or the *majestas* of Jean Bodin, for unlike the former it is a legislative power *in radice,* not merely a judicial power to interpret higher laws by positive ordinances; [56] and unlike both other conceptions, it is not limited by natural law, while the limitation of divine law, which the other conceptions also admit,[57] is as slight for it as for the papalist plenitude.[58] There was, indeed, no medieval precedent for

[50] See above, p. 59.

[51] *Def. min.* xii. 1. On the other hand, cf. *Def. pac.* II. xxv. 12.

[52] See above, pp. 123 ff.

[53] See *Def. min.* ii. 5, where the requirement of unity is explicitly applied to the legislator as well as the government: "sic contingeret plures esse *legislatores* humanos et principantes coactivos super eandem multitudinem, non subinvicem positos in hoc saeculo, praesertim importabile est cuilibet politiae. . . ."

[54] See above, pp. 149 ff.

[55] See above, pp. 162–63.

[56] See above, p. 170.

[57] For the limitation of the papal plenitude of power by natural and divine law, see above, p. 170, n. 25. For Bodin's *majestas,* see *De republica* (Frankfurt, 1641), I. viii: the sovereign is limited by divine and natural law (pp. 134–35, 152 ff.), the "common law of all nations" (p. 158), the property rights of individuals (p. 157).

[58] For the limits of divine law's limitation of the papal power, see below, pp. 284–85.

the completeness of the Marsilian legislator's authority. In the Roman law conceptions the emperor and the *lex* were limited at least by natural law; and the claims represented by the famous phrase of the French publicists *Rex est imperator in regno suo* envisaged only an authority in the kingdom equal to that of the emperor in his "empire."[59] It is rather to the modern period that one must look for analogues: Marsilius' insistence on the unity of the legislative-governmental authority is directly in line with Bodin's and Hobbes' rejections of the very possibility of mixed or divided sovereignty.[60]

The same point emerges still more clearly from Marsilius' extensive use of the part-whole principle.[61] For the "whole," by virtue of its superiority in discernment and in volition over all of its parts, comes to absorb all power over every aspect of human life, religious as well as secular. It is here that what has been called the "totalitarianism" of Marsilius' "whole" people or *universitas* joins hands with that of the papalists, whose doctrine of plenitude of power similarly meant that the pope is a "whole" whose power is "total."[62] Marsilius' polemic against the papalists is revelatory in this respect: he opposes plenitude of power for the papacy, but he is not opposed to such power in itself. Of the eight possible meanings of plenitude of power which he lists, we may disregard the first two, which are superhuman. The third, which is the most extensive possible to man, comprises "supreme coercive jurisdiction over all the governments, peoples, communities, groups, and individuals in the world; or again over some of these, yet following every impulse of the will," and "limited by no law."[63] But, if we change the term "world" to "state," is not this precisely the power which belongs to the human legislator within each state? Thus Marsilius declares in one of his conclusions that "no ruler . . . has plenitude of control or power *apart from the determination of the mortal legislator.*"[64] The legislator possesses, and hence can grant, such plenitude;[65] so that Marsilius' republicanism as to the source of power is

[59] On this formula, see C. N. S. Woolf, *Bartolus of Sassoferrato* (Cambridge, 1913), pp. 380 ff.; F. Ercole, *Da Bartolo all' Althusio* (Florence, 1932), pp. 86 ff., 184 ff.; J. Rivière, *Le Problème de l'église et de l'état au temps de Philippe le Bel* (Louvain, 1926), pp. 424–30.

[60] See Bodin *De republica* I. viii; Thomas Hobbes *Leviathan* ch. xviii (Everyman's ed., p. 95).

[61] See above, pp. 212 ff., esp. 217–18.

[62] See Egidius *De eccl. pot.* III. ix (p. 193): "*totum* posse, quod est in ecclesia, reservatur in summo pontifice" (it should be remembered that by *ecclesia* Egidius here means the whole of Christendom). See *ibid.* III. x (p. 197): "summus pontifex *totus* est plenus potestate. . . ."

[63] II. xxiii. 3.

[64] III. ii. 13.

[65] See II. xxiii. 4: "Utrum autem humana lege sit clerico cuiquam, episcopo vel sacerdoti aut non-sacerdoti, talis potestatis plenitudo concessa, secundum aliquem modum possibilis quidem concedi, et ex causa rationabili legislatoris humani iudicio revocari, certificandum est ex humanis legibus et rescriptis seu privilegiis legislatoris eiusdem." It is important, in interpreting this passage, to keep in mind that Marsilius is here referring to the third meaning of

coupled with an absolutism as to the extent of power. In the terms which we have been using in this study, this outcome is a consequence of his placing supreme emphasis upon the efficient causes of power, rather than, like his predecessors, upon the final causes.

The philosopher who is the antithesis of Marsilius on this basic point is William of Ockham. The one theme which emerges most prominently from his writings is the limitation, in principle, of *all* political power. Where Marsilius had defined plenitude of power as power limited *by no law,*[66] Ockham defines it as power limited *only by natural and divine law:*[67] thus even the furthest extreme of power which he is willing to consider, and of course to refute, is limited to an extent not envisaged by Marsilius. Where Marsilius had set no limits to the power of the people or its *valentior pars,* Ockham declares that the decision of a majority or a plurality must not always be decisive.[68] Hence Ockham's doctrine provides no place, as does Marsilius', for absolute power, no matter by whom held or exercised. The former opposes plenitude of power as such; the latter, only plenitude of power not held by the people.

The contrast between these two conceptions of political authority emerged in modern times in the theories of Locke and Rousseau, the descendants on this general point of Ockham and Marsilius, respectively.[69] And the debate is far from being ended today. But underlying Marsilius' own position in the debate is that aspect of his doctrine which represents at once his closest liaison with the medieval tradition and one of his main departures from it. For the inevitable justice of the people's will, which we saw to be one of the grounds of his ascription of absolute authority to the people, means that the laws which it makes must also necessarily be just. The Marsilian doctrine thus eventuates in a perfectly just state, parallel in this respect to the apotheosized kingdoms of the papalists and the monarchists. To be sure, this justice, and hence too the idealization of the people which is its basis, are far more modest in scope than that

"plenitude of power," which is defined in the text above. Other writers had used the phrase *plenitudo potestatis* in a more restricted sense than had Marsilius' direct papalist opponents. E.g., St. Bernard *De consideratione* II. viii (PL 182, 752); and Thomas Aquinas, who ascribes *plenitudo potestatis* both to kings and to popes, but to each in his own sphere. For the ascription to kings, see *S. theol.* II. II. qu.67. a.1. ad 2; a.4. Resp.; *In Eth.* Lib. VIII. Lect. 10. n. 1674 (p. 450); *In Sent.* Lib. IV. dist. 24. qu.2. a.1. quaestiunc. 1. ad 3. For the ascription to popes, see *S. theol.* II. II. qu.89. a.9. ad 3; III. qu.72. a.11. ad 1; *In Sent.* Lib. IV. dist. 20. qu.1. a.4. quaestiunc. 3; Lib. IV. dist. 25. qu.1. a.1. ad 3.

[66] II. xxiii. 3. See I. xi. 8.

[67] *Dialogus* Pars III. Tr. II. Lib. II. cap. xxvi (pp. 922–23). Cf. *Breviloquium* II. i (p. 17).

[68] *Dialogus* Pars III. Tr. I. Lib. II. cap. xxvii (p. 816): "non semper est standum maiori parti, nec pluralitati."

[69] The relation between Marsilius and Rousseau is, however, more complex than is indicated by this general similarity. See above, p. 58, n. 34; p. 215; also text below. For Locke, see especially *Second Treatise of Civil Government* xi. 135.

which is found in the perfect states of his predecessors, for justice as Marsilius conceives it concerns not the whole range of moral, intellectual, and religious values to which they had dedicated the political community but rather the more moderate and generalized "sufficient life" or "common benefit" which is the final cause of his state. And even within this, the primary emphasis of his conception of justice, as also of law and government, falls upon that impartial regulation of disputes which is necessary for the state's preservation. On the other hand, the inevitability of this perfect justice of the state and its law is more rigid in Marsilius than in the doctrine of such an Aristotelian as Thomas Aquinas, for Marsilius lacks the latter's recognition of the contingency of the practical.[70] The doctrine that no law can be unjust is itself attended with a corresponding diversity of meaning. For the medieval tradition this doctrine is not a description of what positive laws in fact are but a precept of what they should be: conformity, or at least non-contradiction, to the principles of justice contained in natural law is a necessary condition of the validity of positive law. But for Marsilius, no positive law can be unjust because the will which establishes the law aims at and establishes the common benefit with the same necessity as is found in the processes of nature. This is a statement of fact, not merely a prescription of right; it is mitigated only by the condition that no statute is a "law" unless it emanates from the authority of the people as legislator.

Each of these conceptions of the relation of law, and hence of political authority, to justice has obvious dangers. Each may lead to the inference that all existing "laws," since they are accepted as or function in some minimal sense as laws, are by that very fact just, either through conformity to natural law or through derivation from the people's will. However, as against the tradition's failure to provide intra-constitutional means of judging whether laws conformed to natural law, Marsilius' explicit provision for the people's making and correcting the laws does present a positive method for checking the continuing conformity of the laws to the requirement which in his doctrine assures that they will be just. And, apart from the metaphysical context into which he puts the people's will, his doctrine has the effect, which may well be considered a merit, of making the degree of justice attained in the state depend upon the efforts of the people alone.

[70] See above, pp. 46 ff., 255–56.

CHAPTER VII

THE PEOPLE'S CHURCH

I. THE NATURE OF THE CHURCH

MARSILIUS' DOCTRINE of the people's sovereignty, and his conception of the peace and unity of the state, entail decisive consequences for the church. Those consequences may be considered in two ways: with respect to the internal structure of the church, and with respect to the relation between church and state. Many aspects of the latter question have already been discussed in earlier chapters, for the peace and unity of the state had meant that the priesthood must be subordinate to the government, which, as agent of the people, controls all matters affecting the preservation of the state; and the non-coerciveness insisted upon for divine law had meant that the priests have no coercive authority and that human law is left unchallenged. But to understand more fully how the church itself is related to the priesthood, and hence how the restrictions upon the priesthood and divine law affect the relation between church and state, we must first examine the nature and internal structure of the church itself.

Marsilius' conception of the church exhibits both basic similarities to and basic differences from his conception of the state. The ground of each of these is found in his definition of the church. In its truest and most proper sense, he insists, the name "church" means not the clergy or the priesthood alone, but "the whole body of the faithful, who believe in and invoke the name of Christ, and all the parts of this whole body in every community, even the family."[1] This definition, as such, was not new. In support of its truth and propriety, Marsilius appeals to the Scriptures; but the same definition is found in many of his direct predecessors and contemporaries, including some of the strongest upholders of the papal plenitude of power.[2] Similarly, the corollary which Marsilius at once

[1] II. ii. 3.

[2] See Hugh of St. Victor *De sacramentis* II. ii. 2 (PL 176, 417): "Ecclesia Sancta, id est universitas fidelium corpus Christi vocatur." Thomas Aquinas *Sent.* Lib. IV. dist. 20. quaestiunc. I. a.4. qu.I: "Sed cum Ecclesia sit congregatio fidelium. . . ." James of Viterbo *De reg. Christ.* I. i (p. 89): "Ecclesia communitas quaedam est, cum sit congregatio vel adunatio, vel convocatio multorum fidelium." Augustinus Triumphus *S. de eccl. pot.* qu.7. a.3: "Per *ecclesiam* potest intelligi praelatus vel ipsa congregatio fidelium quae locum praelati tenet in causa fidei. . . ." Alvarus Pelagius *De planctu eccl.* I. xxxvi (p. 37): "ecclesia enim accipitur

draws, that all believers, non-priests as well as priests, are "churchmen" (*viri ecclesiastici*),[3] is paralleled by the frequent assertion of both papal and anti-papal writers that all the believers, not merely those who are formally members of the clergy, are priests.[4] Behind these verbal similarities, however, there is an essential doctrinal difference. It rests upon one point which may be expressed by either of two questions: In what sense is the church a "whole body," an *universitas?* In what sense is it "of" the faithful? It is because Marsilius' answers to these questions are diametrically opposed to those of the antecedent tradition that his doctrine of the church entails such revolutionary consequences.

Whatever their differences regarding the precise relation of the state to the church, Marsilius' direct predecessors and contemporaries conceive the church on the model of the state, as a *regnum,*[5] a *congregatio politica,*[6] a *politia Christiana,*[7] a *monarchia clericalis et spiritualis.*[8] That the church must have a government to control at least the "spiritual" acts of its members, and that this government must be monarchic in order to preserve the unity of the church—these propositions are upheld not only by the papalists but also by such opponents of the papal plenitude of power as John of Paris [9] and William of Ockham.[10] Concomitant with the unity of the church is its order: a hierarchic structure of "preachers and hearers, rulers and

---

pro congregatione fidelium"; *ibid.* I. xxxvii (p. 42): ". . . de congregatione fidelium, quae est ecclesia. . . ." See *ibid.* I. xxxviii (p. 58).

[3] II. ii. 3.

[4] Thomas Aquinas *De reg. princ.* I. xiv: "Omnes Christi fideles, inquantum sunt membra ejus, reges et sacerdotes dicuntur." John of Paris *De pot. reg. et pap.* cap. viii (p. 116): "Omnes fideles inquantum sunt membra Christi qua homo Deus quasi unum cum capite Christo, vocantur per fidem et charitatem reges et sacerdotes." See *ibid.* cap. xix (p. 133). James of Viterbo *De reg. Christ.* II. iii: "quisque fidelis dicitur sacerdos dum pro se offerat Deo spirituale sacrificium." (Repeated by Alvarus Pelagius *De planctu eccl.* I. li [p. 125].) Alexander of St. Elpidius *Tract. de eccl. pot.* Tr. I. cap. i (p. 2): "bonus homo dicitur Sacerdos mistice, quia sacrificium mysticum offert Deo. . . ."

[5] James of Viterbo *De reg. Christ.* I. i (p. 89 ff.). Cf. *ibid.* I. iv (p. 128) on *res publica.*

[6] Thomas Aquinas *In Sent.* Lib. IV. dist. 20. qu.I. a.4. quaestiunc. I (X, 579).

[7] Alvarus Pelagius *De planctu eccl.* I. xl (p. 60).

[8] Alexander of St. Elpidius *Tract. de eccl. pot.* I. vii (p. 8).

[9] John of Paris *De pot. reg. et pap.* cap. iii (pp. 111–12). See also *Quaestio in utramque partem* a.5 (p. 103).

[10] Although Ockham presents arguments against as well as for unity of church headship in the *Dialogus* Pars III. Tr. I. Lib. II (pp. 788–819), he discusses the government of the church from the same standpoint as secular government. Indeed, his basic discussion of forms of government is contained in that book of his *Dialogus* which treats the question "an expediat toti communitati *fidelium* uni capiti, principi et praelato *fideli* sub Christo subjici et subesse" (*loc. cit.* cap. i [p. 788]). He comments on his argument in support of monarchic government of the *church* as follows: "Ex ista ratione conjicio, quod ex his quae potero invenire in secundo tractatu istius tertiae partis Dialogi primi libri: ubi tractatur an expediat toti mundo, uni principi *seculari* subesse: potest perpendi faciliter, qualiter pro utraque parte hoc valeat allegari. *Omnia enim illa vel plura possunt ad istam materiam applicari*" (*loc. cit.* cap. ii [p. 790]).

subjects."[11] In this order, deriving directly from the pope who rules or heads (*praeest*) the church in the whole world, jurisdiction is exercised by successively lesser prelates over correspondingly lesser communities. From the standpoint of the lay believers, then, the church is "of" the faithful in the sense that they are the recipients of the sacraments from the priesthood and are willingly subjected to the "judiciary power" of the hierarchy;[12] but no one can be a member of the church unless he acknowledges the pope as his head.[13] And just as the pope is vicar of God, so the entire hierarchic differentiation from laity through the various orders of ministers to the pope is itself the result of divine ordainment. As a consequence the church comes to be identified with the pope himself.[14]

Marsilius' doctrine of the church subverts this entire hierarchic structure. He weakens the continuum between priesthood and God, reverses the superiority of clergy over laymen, and equalizes priests, bishops, and pope in that respect in which their authority had been considered essentially unequal. This revolution is accomplished by the different interpre-

[11] James of Viterbo *De reg. Christ.* I. iii (p. 116). This whole chapter of James' treatise is a superlative account of the unity and order of the church: "Quod regnum est unum et quomodo et per quid" (pp. 106–121).

[12] See Augustinus Triumphus *S. de eccl. pot.* qu.23. a.1: " 'Esse de ecclesia' potest intelligi tripliciter: Primo, judiciaria potestate, et sic omnes sunt de ecclesia, boni et mali, fideles et infideles. Quia sicut omnes habent unum Deum, sic omnes de jure debent habere unum pastorem, qui vicem ejus gerat. Secundo, imitatione et voluntate, et sic omnes fideles et boni sunt de ecclesia. Tercio, occasionaliter, fructuosa utilitate, et sic omnes pagani et infideles possunt dici esse de ecclesia." James of Viterbo *De reg. Christ.* II. ix (p. 273): "potentia summi pontificis et Christi vicarii plena dicitur, primo quia ab hac potentia nullus ad ecclesiam militantem qualitercumque pertinens, exciptur; sed omnis homo in praesenti ecclesia existens ei subicitur." Egidius *De eccl. pot.* II. vi (p. 65) indicates clearly this different conception of the universality of the church: "Ecclesia ergo est sancta et catholica, id est universalis; vere autem universalis non esset, nisi omnibus universaliter *praeesset.*" See Durand of St. Pourçain De *origine et usu jurisdictionum* qu.3 (p. 131E).

[13] See Alvarus *De planctu eccl.* I. xxiv (p. 33): "Qui non habet Papam pro capite, non habet caput Christum, nec est vivum membrum de cornore ejus mystico, Ecclesia scilicet Catholica militante. . . ." Cf. above, p. 16.

[14] See Egidius *De eccl. pot.* III. xii (p. 209): "Ecclesia quidem est timenda et mandata ejus sunt observanda, sive summus pontifex, qui tenet apicem ecclesiae *et qui potest dici ecclesia,* est timendus et sua mandata sunt observanda. . . ." Alvarus *De planctu eccl.* I. xxxi (p. 35): "Ubicumque est papa, ibi est ecclesia Romana . . . nam Petrus Ecclesiam significat." Earlier, the canonist Huguccio had emphasized the difficulty of denouncing an heretical pope to the "church": "cui ecclesiae fieret denuntiatio, *cum ipse* [*Papa*] *sit ecclesia?*" (in J. F. von Schulte, *Die Stellung der Concilien, Päpste, und Bischöfe* [Prague, 1871], Anhang, p. 263). See William of Cremona *Reprobatio errorum,* p. 17; also J. N. Figgis, *Churches in the Modern State* (London, 1914), p. 84: "In common parlance the Church in the Middle Ages meant not the *congregatio fidelium*—though, of course, no one would have denied this to be the right meaning—not the whole body of baptized Christians as distinct from those who were not, but rather the active governing section of the Church—the hierarchy and, I suppose, the religious orders . . . the Church is used to distinguish the spirituality from the laity. . . ."

tation which he places upon the definition of the church as the *universitas fidelium*. The phrase "of the faithful" no longer means that the laity are the subjects of a ruling hierarchy. Instead, it means not only that the church exists for all the faithful,[15] but even more important, that the church is controlled by all the faithful, not merely by the clergy or the pope. Thus the same arguments which had been used to demonstrate that the *universitas civium* must be the legislator [16] and elect the ruler [17] are now explicitly invoked to demonstrate that the *universitas fidelium* must control excommunication,[18] elect the priesthood to its posts,[19] define articles of faith through the general council,[20] elect the council,[21] make binding all its decisions,[22] and elect the pope or "head bishop." [23] The standard formula used for this purpose is that these propositions "can be proved by the same or similar demonstrations whereby we showed in Chapters 12, 13, and 15 of the first discourse that the making of laws and the establishment of governments pertain to the whole body of citizens, only the minor term of the demonstration being changed."

Now these powers thus given to the whole body of the faithful had all, in the antecedent tradition, belonged to the pope or the bishops. It might seem, then, that Marsilius differs from that tradition only regarding the locus of power within the church, but not regarding the status of the church itself as a political organization or society. There has, however, been a difference of interpretations on this point.[24] The difference arises from the double fact that the Marsilian church resembles the state in consisting in an *universitas,* but differs from it in that this *universitas* comprises not *cives* but *fideles*. For to be a "citizen" is to control or to participate in legislative and governmental coercive power whose end is civil peace in this world. But to be a "faithful" is to believe in Christ for the sake of eternal happiness.[25] Hence, insofar as state and church

[15] II. ii. 3; II. xxiv. 7; II. xxvi. 2. [16] I. xii–xiii. [17] I. xv. 2.
[18] II. vi. 12–13. [19] II. xvii. 11. [20] II. xx. 4.
[21] II. xxi. 1, 3. [22] II. xxi. 9. [23] II. xxii. 11.

[24] See on the one hand McIlwain (*op. cit.,* p. 309): "Marsiglio recognizes as fully as James of Viterbo that this *Ecclesia* or Church is a true *regnum,* and that its government is monarchical and regal; he even admits that the Bishop of Rome is in a limited sense supreme within it in the matters within its lawful competence. It is a Christian commonwealth. But it is none the less a commonwealth. . . ." On the other hand, Lagarde writes (*Marsile,* p. 238): "La vérité c'est que, selon Marsile, la communauté spirituelle, réduite à elle-meme, n'a rien qui puisse constituer une véritable société."

[25] Cf. the definition of *civis,* I. xii. 4, with the definition of *fidelis,* II. ii. 3. See also *Def. min.* xv. 5, where Marsilius indicates this difference by relation to divine and human law. The "material cause" of divine law is "homines inquantum susceptibiles suae felicitatis aeternae, dispositi videlicet per fidem Christi, charitatem et spem et similia reliqua." The material cause of human law, on the other hand, is "homines . . . dispositi et affecti ad hujus saeculi tranquillitatem et potestatem et alia plura."

both comprise *universitates,* both will be controlled by their respective members. But insofar as those members are defined by temporal civil power and by spiritual faith, respectively, the nature of this control will correspondingly differ. We have already seen this difference in the comparison of human and divine law:[26] it means that since faith must not undergo coercion, coercive power may be exercised only in the state, but not in the church, as such. There is consequently nothing in the church exactly corresponding to the government in the state. But since it had been the exercise of coercive power by the government which had been the focus of such unity and order as the state possessed, it follows that the church does not have a corresponding structure. In the church as in the state, authority flows from all the members to the head; but the church does not, like the state, have the reverse flow of authority from the head to the individual members.[27] Marsilius' sharp distinction between coercive and non-coercive law and judgment means that the priesthood is only a teacher of the faith and a dispenser of the sacraments, and that these functions do not carry with them any power of enforcement over those upon whom they are exercised.

We must therefore expect to find two different aspects in the Marsilian church. On the one hand, it is a political institution in which power is exercised by the collectivity of the faithful on the same grounds, although not in precisely the same way, as power is exercised by the whole citizen-body in the state. On the other hand, it is a discrete collection of individuals in each of whom faith in Christ rather than membership in a visible institution is the defining feature. The former aspect emphasizes transient acts and corporate, "public" power; the latter emphasizes immanent acts and individual, private conduct and belief. The corporate view of the church merges readily both with Marsilius' view of the state and with the papalist tradition, since it simply substitutes the whole body of the faithful for the pope or the priestly hierarchy in the powers which the tradition had assigned to these latter. The individualist view, on the other hand, is related rather to some of the mystical and heretical sects which denied the institutional aspects of the church, and emphasized the directness of the believer's relation to God. In reference to Protestantism, the former view is a forerunner of Calvin, the latter of Luther. But each approach serves in its own way to deëmphasize the power of the priesthood. The political approach is used wherever it is possible to turn over

[26] See above, pp. 154 ff.

[27] Compare the controlling function of the government as the "heart" of the state establishing and regulating the other members (I. xv. 6), with the purely advisory function of the pope as "head" of the church (II. xxii. 6; II. xxiv. 12–13).

to the whole body of the faithful institutional powers traditionally assigned to the priesthood. It is in such a context that excommunication, appointment of priests, and the other powers listed above are admitted as ecclesiastic functions but removed from the priest, or the bishop, or the pope by whom they had formerly been exercised. On the other hand, wherever traditional priestly powers cannot be simply assigned to the *universitas fidelium,* an internal, religious, or individualist approach is adopted. It is through such an approach that Marsilius makes God the sole cause of pardon of sins,[28] insists upon the essential equality of all priests,[29] and extols poverty and humility as the virtues which they should all maintain.[30] The direct argument employed in the former approach is the moral and intellectual superiority of the whole body of the faithful to the priest or priests taken alone; the direct argument employed in the latter approach is the moral and intellectual superiority of God to mere men. Thus the priesthood loses its political or institutional authority to the whole body of the faithful, and its religious or sacramental authority to God.

Marsilius was not the first, to be sure, to employ this double approach in ecclesiastic doctrine. In one form or another such ambivalence is inevitable in any doctrine which sets up a criterion of moral or religious values in terms of internal factors of faith, will, or love, and then erects an external institution to embody, regulate, and foster those values. The problems of such a doctrine are clearly apparent in the debates which have been held over whether St. Augustine means by the *civitas Dei* the visible church or only those believers who conform to the standards of love which he sets up for that *civitas*. We shall best be able to understand how Marsilius meets these problems if we examine the successive applications of his approach to the church in the various relations subsisting among God, priesthood, and laity.

2. THE PRIESTHOOD AND THE SACRAMENTS

Like the entire tradition, Marsilius holds that the sacraments, as well as the articles of faith and the whole law of the gospels, were established by God. He also affirms that the priestly power to administer the sacraments is divine in origin, and that participation in them is necessary for salvation.[1] Since his interest is not in theological questions as such but in the relation of the priestly powers to those of the state, he deals in detail with only two sacraments, penance [2] and order, although he refers to the

[28] II. vi. 9.
[29] II. xv. 4.
[30] II. xiii–xiv.

[1] I. vi. 4; I. xix. 4–5; II. vi. 2–3; II. xv. 2.
[2] II. vi. 3 ff.

latter not as a sacrament but only as the "bestowal of orders."[3] In connection with each of these, however, a double question emerges: With regard to the direct effectuation of the sacrament, what are the respective relations to God of the priest who administers the sacrament and of the individual believer who receives it? With regard to the external, institutional operations which follow upon the sacrament, what is the relation between the priests and the whole body of believers?

Marsilius' answer to the first of these questions places the individual believer in a more direct relation to God than his predecessors had allowed, and thereby undermines the traditional view of the priest as an essential "middleman" (*medius*) between God and man. This result emerges most clearly in his discussion of penance. He takes his point of departure from the section on penance in the *Sentences* of Peter Lombard;[4] considered in the context of the many other commentaries on that standard work, his position appears as a radical departure from the traditional interpretations. Where Peter had declared that the priest's function in penance is that of "showing" to the church which men have been loosed from sins and which not,[5] the later theologians undertake to present such a definition of "showing" as will assure for the priest more than a merely passive, *ex post facto* role. Thus St. Bonaventura distinguishes between showing by mere demonstration, as in pointing to something with the finger; and showing by exhibition, as an artist exhibits a portrait when he has painted it. The priest shows in the first way that the sinner has been absolved of guilt; but he shows in the second way, "not only by manifesting to the sense, but also *by perfecting and exhibiting,*" that the sinner has been absolved of punishment.[6] Thomas Aquinas[7] and Duns Scotus[8] draw similar distinctions between kinds of "showing." The conclusion in each case is that the priest plays a positive, active, essential role in the dismissal of sins. God is the prime agent in the process, but the priest also has in some sense an indispensable causal function.

Marsilius, on the other hand, reduces the priest's role to a completely

[3] II. xv. 2 ff. Of the other sacraments, Marsilius mentions baptism (II. vi. 2; II. xvii. 12, 15) and eucharist (I. xix. 5; II. vi. 14; II. xv. 2, 4; II. xvi. 2). Marriage is treated as a sacrament only in the *Defensor minor* (xv. 10).

[4] *Sent.* Lib. IV. dist. 18 (PL 192, 885–89).

[5] *Sent.* Lib. IV. dist. 18. cap. v–vi (PL 192, 887).

[6] Bonaventura *In Sent.* Lib. IV. dist. 18. pars 1. a.2. qu.2. ad 1. See also Albert the Great *In Sent.* Lib. IV. dist. 18. a.13.

[7] Thomas *In Sent.* Lib. IV. dist. 18. qu.1. a.3. quaestiunc. 1. ad 1. See *S. theol.* III. qu.84. a.3. ad 5: ". . . ista expositio: 'Ego te absolvo,' id est, 'absolutum ostendo,' quantum ad aliquid quidem vera est, non tamen est perfecta. Sacramenta enim novae legis non solum significant, sed etiam faciunt quod significant. . . Esset autem perfectior expositio: 'Ego te absolvo,' id est, 'sacramentum absolutionis tibi impendo.' "

[8] Duns Scotus *Op. Oxon.* Lib. IV. dist. 19. qu.1.

passive, external relation. The sinner's pardon by God is completely without an intermediary. All that is required for true and effective penance is that the sinner be contrite and have the firm intention of confessing his sin to a priest at the earliest opportunity. As soon as there is such contrition and intention, "God alone"—"before any action by the priest"—expels the sinner's guilt, restores his grace, and relieves him from eternal punishment.[9] But if God does all this alone, then what is the function of the priest in the process, and why is actual confession to him necessary? Marsilius' answer repeats the position of Peter Lombard with complete literalness, and without the distinctions of the other commentators. The priest has in this respect merely a social role; he is the church's informant as to what God has done, "showing" it to the church but contributing nothing to it.[10] The power of the keys is hence not a judiciary power.

The drastic curtailment which this position produces in the efficacy of the priestly function in penance emerges fully only from the "infallible demonstration" of it which Marsilius presents. For it might still be thought that, even if the priest contributes nothing directly to the absolution of sins, at least his action is a sure guide to what action has been taken with regard to the absolution by God. Thus the antecedent tradition had held that one reason why confession to a priest is necessary for salvation is that the sinner cannot otherwise be *certain* that his contrition is sufficient for forgiveness.[11] From the side of the priest, concomitantly, it was held that he proceeds with *certainty* in his ministerial task of absolution, because of God's revelation made to him through Peter.[12] To be sure, this revelation is only "general"; in dealing with particular cases, it was admitted, the priest may err in using his "key of knowledge" (*clavis scientiae*); [13] and in such cases his binding and loosing does not take effect with God.[14] This fallibility of the priest was not, however, applied against the fundamental efficacy of his role as confessor, judge, and mediator between God and man. But it is precisely on this ground of the priest's fallibility that

[9] II. vi. 6.

[10] II. vi. 7. See the analogies of God and the priest to the judge and the turnkey (II. vii. 3), and to nature and the physician (II. vii. 4–5).

[11] Thomas *In Sent.* Lib. IV. dist. 17. qu.2. a.1. quaestiunc. 1. ad 8: "quamvis tota poena possit per contritionem dimitti, tamen adhuc necessaria est confessio et satisfactio: tum quia homo non potest esse *certus* de sua contritione, quod fuerit ad totum tollendum sufficiens. . . ." See *ibid.* Lib. IV. dist. 17. qu.2. a.5. quaestiunc. 2. ad 1.

[12] Thomas *S. theol.* III. qu.84. a.3. ad 5: "cum [sacerdos] dicit 'Ego te absolvo,' ostendit hominem absolutum non solum significative sed etiam effective. *Nec tamen loquitur quasi de re incerta. . . .*"

[13] Thomas *In Sent.* Lib. IV. dist. 18. qu.1. a.1. quaestiunc. 3. ad 2; Duns Scotus *Op. Oxon.* Lib. IV. dist.19. qu.1 (XVIII, 610).

[14] Thomas *In Sent.* Lib. IV. dist. 18. qu.1. a.3. quaestiunc. 4 (X, 531); Duns Scotus *Op. Oxon.* Lib. IV. dist. 19. qu.1 (XVIII, 651–2).

Marsilius discards him in the causal sequence. For every priest, "even the Roman bishop . . . can sometimes err, or be inclined by perverted emotion, or both." Hence, if forgiveness of sins depended upon the priest, Christ's promise to reward the good and punish the bad in the future world would "very frequently" remain unfulfilled. Since, therefore, God alone cannot err, it is he who alone forgives or retains sins through his own direct insight into the acts and intentions of the sinner.[15] Thus even the priest's "showing" of whose sins have been forgiven or retained need not be regarded as absolutely certain: the priest has been reduced entirely to the level of human fallibility. Despite the divine source of the priestly "character," in the actual operation of the sacrament of penance a veritable chasm has been hacked out between God and the priesthood.

On Marsilius' view of the purpose of confession, it is of course difficult to understand why even the intention to confess to a priest should be regarded as essential to forgiveness. The way is clear to the further step, which the Cathari in fact had taken, that it is sufficient to have internal contrition for one's sins and to confess them to God alone,[16] and that the priest's only function in the forgiveness of sins is that of spiritual guide or instructor.[17]

The same effect is found in Marsilius' account of the bestowal of the priestly character, traditionally called the sacrament of order, although he does not so name it. According to Thomas, the bishop alone bestows this sacrament,[18] and while its source is God, its efficacy resides principally in the bishop rather than in its "matter" (i.e., the "things" used in the sacrament) which in the other sacraments signifies the divine virtue.[19] The bishop's benediction and laying on of hands, which precede the actual

[15] II. vi. 9. See II. vii. 4. Cf. the same point in Hobbes *Leviathan* cap. xlii (pp. 273–74).

[16] See Alan of Lille *De fide catholica contra haereticos* I. lii (PL 210, 356): "Sunt alii haeretici qui dicunt sufficere soli Deo confiteri." See Moneta *Adversus Catharos et Valdenses*, ed. T. A. Ricchinius (Rome, 1743), IV. iv. 4; Etienne de Bourbon *Anecdotes historiques*, ed. A. Lecoy de la Marche (Paris, 1877), p. 305.

[17] In the *Defensor minor* (v. 14), Marsilius raises the objection that, if the priest's only function in binding and loosing is that of "divulging to the church" what persons have been bound or loosed, then even non-priests, especially those who are learned in Scripture, can bind and loose. His reply (v. 16) distinguishes between personal knowledge and official authority: a non-priest learned in Scripture may indeed know who has been bound and loosed, and may also know how to "promulgate it to the church," yet because he lacks the priestly character given by Christ, "hoc neque debet neque facere potest . . . quoniam licet noverint, non tamen habent a Christo, qui dator est hujus auctoritatis, potestatem talia exercendi." He analogizes this situation to that of men who have medical knowledge but cannot practice medicine because they have no license (v. 17).

[18] *S. theol.* Suppl. qu.38. a.1.

[19] *Ibid.* Suppl. qu.34. a.5. Resp.: "efficacia aliorum sacramentorum principaliter consistit in materia, quae virtutem divinam et significat, et continet, ex sanctificatione per ministrum adhibita; sed efficacia hujus sacramenti principaliter residet penes eum qui sacramentum dispensat."

giving of the priestly power, are essential preparatory steps, for the former binds the recipient to divine services, and the latter gives the fullness of grace which renders him suitable for great functions.[20] According to Marsilius, on the other hand, the priestly character is bestowed directly by God.[21] The laying on of hands and the "uttering of the proper words" (which is Marsilius' version of "benediction") are preliminary steps "which perhaps effect nothing toward this bestowal, but are thus made to precede it by some divine pact or ordinance."[22] All the efficacy of holy orders hence derives from God, not from the minister who laid his hands on the recipient.[23] As in the case of forgiveness of sins, the intermediation of the priest is made external and non-efficacious.

Despite this deëmphasis of the role of the priesthood in connection with the sacraments, Marsilius is not prepared to abandon it completely. The sacraments are necessary for salvation, and the priests are in some sense necessary to the sacraments. The latter point is intimated in Marsilius' insistence that priests who are unwilling to administer the sacraments may be forced to do so by the legislator or ruler, "lest by their perversity someone incur the peril of eternal death, through lack of baptism or of some other sacrament."[24] Hence, either Marsilius contradicts himself in describing the priestly function as extrinsic to the efficacy of the sacraments, or else he does not intend that extrinsicity to be so complete as to render the function entirely inefficacious. Probably his position is closest to what has been described as the doctrine of "occasional causality."[25] But whereas for St. Bonaventura and Duns Scotus this was a doctrine concerning the efficacy of the sacraments themselves, for Marsilius it is a doctrine concerning the efficacy of the priesthood in relation to the sacraments. His divisive technique operates here as elsewhere to separate, at least in part, what his predecessors had held together.

3. THE STRUCTURE OF THE CHURCH

When Marsilius turns from the question of the source and efficacy of the sacraments as such to the question of their external or institutional effectuation, the priesthood suffers a similar loss of power. In the traditional doctrine a distinction was drawn between the priestly powers of "order" and of "jurisdiction." The power of order is both sacramental and official. In the former sense, it derives directly from the "character" essential to the priest as such, whereby he can administer the sacrament

[20] *Ibid.* Suppl. qu.37. a.5. Resp.
[21] II. xv. 2.
[22] II. xv. 10.
[23] II. xvi. 13.
[24] II. xvii. 15. See II. xvii. 8, 12.
[25] See P. Pourrat, *Theory of the Sacraments* (St. Louis, 1914), pp. 167–69.

of the eucharist, having to do with the "true body" of Christ. But as an "office" order is concerned with certain other sacred functions in respect to the "mystic body" of Christ, the external church.[1] The power of jurisdiction, on the other hand, gives the "use" or "execution" of the sacramental power of order, with respect to the external church; that is, it gives coercive headship or "command" (*imperium*) over a "subject multitude" upon which the power of order can be exercised.[2] Consequently, although all priests are equal in order,[3] the bishop has the power of order to "perfection," because he can bestow it upon others; [4] with respect to jurisdiction there is also inequality, for the bishop has powers in the church superior to those of the *presbyter,* and the pope is likewise superior to the bishop.[5] Both order and jurisdiction are from God, but the former directly, the latter by mediation of the pope.[6] Hence the hierarchic differences within the priesthood are not merely human in origin, but have a divine sanction. Thus such sacraments as confirmation and order, which involve consummatory powers over other persons, whether laymen or priests, can be bestowed only by bishops, not by simple priests; [7] similarly, according to Thomas Aquinas, only bishops and greater prelates can excommunicate,[8] although opinions differed on this point.[9]

The position of Marsilius begins from these traditional distinctions, but soon leaves them far behind. He divides the powers of the priesthood into "essential" or "intrinsic" or "inseparable," on the one hand, and "accidental" or "extrinsic" or "separable," on the other. It is clear that he intends these to correspond to the traditional powers of order and of jurisdiction, at least in their initial bearings; [10] for the essential power, like the power

[1] Thomas *In Sent.* Lib. IV. dist. 24. qu.I. a.I. quaestiunc. 2. Augustinus Triumphus *Tractatus brevis de duplici potestate prelatorum et laicorum,* p. 490.

[2] Thomas *In Sent.* Lib. IV. dist. 17. qu.3. a.3. quaestiunc. 4; Lib. IV. dist. 24. qu.I. a.3. quaestiunc. 2. ad I. St. Bonaventura *In Sent.* Lib. IV. dist. 18. pars 2. a.I. qu.3; Lib. IV. dist. 25. a.I. qu.2. ad 4.

[3] Thomas *In Sent.* Lib. IV. dist. 19. qu.I. a.3. quaestiunc. I. ad I: "ad absolutionem a peccato requiritur duplex potestas; scilicet potestas ordinis, et potestas jurisdictionis. Prima quidem potestas est aequaliter in omnibus sacerdotibus, non autem secunda. . . ." Augustinus Triumphus *De duplic. pot.,* pp. 491–92. Bonaventura *In Sent.* Lib. IV. dist. 25. a.I. qu.2. ad 4.

[4] Augustinus Triumphus *De duplic. pot.,* pp. 490–91. Thomas *In Sent.* Lib. IV. dist. 24. qu.3. a.2. quaestiunc. 2. John of Paris *De pot. reg. et pap.* cap. xxiv (p. 146). Bonaventura *In Sent.* Lib. IV. dist. 24. pars 2. a.2. qu.3. c.

[5] Thomas *S. theol.* III. qu.82. a.I. ad 4.

[6] Augustinus Triumphus *De duplic. pot.,* pp. 491–92). Thomas *In Sent.* Lib. IV. dist. 24. qu.3. a.2. quaestiunc. I. Alexander of St. Elpidius *Tract. de eccl. pot.* I. iii–viii.

[7] Thomas *S. theol.* III. qu.72. a.II. Resp.; *In Sent.* Lib. IV. dist. 25. qu.I. a.I. Bonaventura *In Sent.* Lib. IV. dist. 25. a.I. qu.I.

[8] Thomas *In sent.* Lib. IV. dist. 18. qu.2. a.2. quaestiunc. I.

[9] See St. Bonaventura *In Sent.* Lib. IV. dist. 18. pars 2. a.I. qu.3. Resp.

[10] See II. XXV. 4: ". . . officia ecclesiastica, tam inseparabilia, quae vocant *ordines,* quam separabilia, quae vocant *praelationes* sive curas animarum. . . ."

of order, derives directly from the priestly character [11] and is equal in all priests,[12] while the accidental power, like the power of jurisdiction, is the power to apply the essential power to a determinate group of people,[13] and is unequal in various priests according to their rank in the hierarchy.[14] Moreover, the essential power is directly from God,[15] while the accidental power is not.[16]

At this point, however, begin Marsilius' differences from the tradition. They were already foreshadowed in his terminological changes. For the "essential" power is indeed so completely essential to and hence equal in every priest, that there is no place for grades of perfection; where the tradition had reserved some sacraments for the bishop, Marsilius insists that by the essential power every priest has the authority to administer "*all* the sacraments" without qualification, including holy orders as well as the power of the keys or penance.[17] The deacon, to be sure, stands below the priest in essential authority,[18] since only the priestly (*sacerdotalis*) order has the "character" whereby it can perform the sacraments; but within the priesthood (*sacerdotium*) itself there is no distinction whatsoever between *presbyteri,* bishops, archbishops, patriarchs, and pope. Even more, the substitution of "accidental" power for "jurisdiction" indicates Marsilius' conviction that the claim of the priesthood to jurisdiction rests upon a confusion of various meanings of the terms *jus* and *jus dicere;* [19] in most of its senses, "jurisdiction" does not rightfully belong to priests as such, for they lack all coercive power.[20] Most significantly of all, the term "accidental" brings out the crux of Marsilius' doctrine: that all the hierarchic inequalities ranging from bishop to pope, far from having been established by God directly or indirectly, are solely human in origin; and far from being necessary to the divine mission of the priesthood, are extrinsic to that mission. What this means is that the traditional ecclesiastic hierarchy from bishop to pope is solely a human contrivance, having no divine sanction whatsoever. The human is thus once again separated from the divine.[21]

There were, of course, precedents for this drastic reversal of the traditional doctrine. St. Jerome, as well as heretics from the early years of the

[11] II. xv. 2, 4. [12] II. xv. 4. [13] II. xv. 9. [14] II. xv. 6.
[15] II. xv. 2, 10. [16] II. xv. 6, 10. [17] II. xv. 4. [18] See II. xv. 3, 7.
[19] See *Def. min.* i. 1: "Quoniam autem in prioribus recitavimus, juxta Magistri Sententiarum intentionem, potestatem quamdam ligandi atque solvendi sacerdotes habere . . . *quam quidem jurisdictionem appellant,* convenienter utique inquirendum videtur, quid sit jurisdictio et quot modis dicatur, et utrum secundum modum aliquem imperatoris episcopis sive sacerdotibus jurisdictio debeatur." The reference is to *Def. pac.* II. vi. 11, where Peter Lombard is quoted: *Sent.* Lib. IV. dist. 18. cap. viii (PL 192, 889).
[20] *Def. min.* i. 6–7. [21] See above, pp. 68 ff., 73 ff.

church to Marsilius' own day, had held that the distinction between priests (*presbyteri*) and bishops derived only from man, not from God;[22] and the *York Tracts* had made the same assertion concerning the primacy of the Church of Rome over the other churches.[23] Indeed, the "Pseudo-Apostles," followers of Gerard Segarelli, went even further and declared that the whole distinction of orders was a detriment to the faith.[24] And the Cathari, within their own "church," likewise rejected the distinction between bishops and *presbyteri,* retaining only bishops and deacons from the traditional hierarchy,[25] and emphasizing equality even between these.[26]

It is, however, in the arguments which Marsilius adduces for this reversal, and their connection with his general doctrine of political authority, that his position advances far beyond that of the heretical sects. The traditional doctrine of the divinely ordained superiority of bishops to priests, and of pope to bishops, was based upon the conception of the unity and order of the church. This conception, as we have seen, invoked direct analogies to the state. The church would not be ordered unless it had a hierarchy of superiors and inferiors: above the priests there must be a bishop as

[22] Jerome *Commentariorum in epistolam ad Titum liber unus* I. ver. 5 (PL 26, 597–98): "Idem est ergo presbyter qui et episcopus . . . ita episcopi noverint se magis consuetudine quam dispositionis dominicae veritate presbyteris esse majores, et in communi debere Ecclesiam regere." See also Jerome's *Epistola 146 ad Evangelum* (PL 22, 1192 ff.); cited by Marsilius II. xv. 5, 8. Augustine *De haeresibus* liii (PL 42, 40) writes of Aerianus: "Dicebat etiam presbyterum ab episcopo nulla differentia debere discerni." Bernard Gui reports that the Waldensians "ordines sacros Romanae Ecclesiae non reputant esse a Deo, sed a traditione hominum" (*Practica inquisitionis hereticae pravitatis,* ed. C. Douais [Paris, 1886], p. 248). See also *Errores haereticorum Waldensium* (in I. v. Döllinger, *Beiträge zur Sektengeschichte des Mittelalters* [Munich, 1890], II, 337): "Sexto dicunt, quod Papa, archiepiscopi, episcopi non habeant majorem auctoritatem, quam sacerdotes."

[23] *Tract. Eborac.* III (p. 659): "Romana ecclesia ab hominibus, non a Christo vel apostolis ei prelata est."

[24] "Item, quod omnes ordines religiosorum et sacerdotum et dyachonorum et subdyachonorum et prelatorum sunt ad fidei catholicae detrimentum" (Bernard Gui, *op. cit.,* pp. 259, 337–38). It need hardly be pointed out that great caution is required in interpreting statements attributed to heretics by their inquisitors and other enemies.

[25] Salvi Burce *Supra Stella:* "Vestrum vocabulum est episcoporum et filii majoris et filii minoris et diaconum; ponamus, quod filius major et filius minor non contradicatur vobis, ubi est vocabulum presbyteri?" (Döllinger, *op. cit.,* II, 82). See C. Schmidt, *Histoire et doctrine de la secte des Cathares ou Albigeois* (Paris, 1849), II, 141 ff. It should be noted that the Waldensians, in the hierarchy of their own "church," differ from Marsilius on this point, for they regard bishops as being an order separate from *presbyteri:* "Inter nos non esset perfectus ordo, qui consistit in tribus ordinibus, episcopatu, presbyteratu et diaconatu, sive eo, qui debet habere ordinem majoralem, qui ordo est gradus perfectionalis" (Döllinger, *op. cit.,* II, 98. See *ibid.,* II, 128, 143–44; Bernard Gui, *op. cit.,* pp. 136 ff., 247). Marsilius, on the other hand, refuses to regard bishops as a separate order; his standard phrase is "presbyteros *seu* episcopos atque diaconos" (II. ii. 2); "episcopi *seu* presbyteri et diaconi" (II. ii. 3; see Emerton, *op. cit.,* p. 33, n. 1; and Previté-Orton's introduction to his edition, p. xxi, n. 1). Lagarde (*Marsile,* p. 131–32) is hence mistaken in seeing here an identity or resemblance between Marsilius and the Waldensians.

[26] See Döllinger, *op. cit.,* II, 227.

princeps sacerdotum, for, as in an army, order requires that there be some officials who control and direct others.[27] But above the bishops there must be one supreme power, that of the pope, as a universal government (*regimen*) aiming at the common good above particular governments aiming at special goods. Without such a single head, the church would not be preserved in unity, nor would it achieve the one end to which all its parts are ordered.[28] This argument from church unity to monarchy is hence exactly parallel to the arguments for monarchy in secular government. There are the same references to imitation of the divine governance of the world, to the connection between unity and peace, to the expeditious and authoritative settlement of disputes,[29] except that in the church the disputes bear upon the interpretation of the faith.[30] It was to indicate this unity of headship of the church that Christ said to Peter alone, "Thou art Peter, and upon this rock (*petram*) I shall build my church";[31] just as it was to indicate the divinely ordained distinction of bishops from priests that Christ first had his twelve apostles and then chose seventy-two disciples as a lower order.[32] And finally, these arguments and texts are completed by the tradition that the popes at Rome are the official successors of Peter.

We have already discussed above the methodological bases of Marsilius' replies to the arguments based upon Scripture.[33] His literal approach achieves its most decisive result in his examination of the Roman-papal succession from Peter. The *York Tracts* had anticipated him in denying the historical basis of the Roman primacy conceived as ordained by Christ, and had declared that on true historical grounds Jerusalem, not Rome, was "the mother of all churches,"[34] just as Marsilius declares that the true historical successor of Peter is the bishop of Antioch, not of Rome.[35] The Cathari and Waldensians had even anticipated him in declaring that there

[27] Thomas *In Sent.* Lib. IV. dist. 24. qu.3. a.2. quaestiunc. 1; Lib. IV. dist. 25. qu.1. a.1. See James of Viterbo *De reg. Christ.* I. iii (p. 116).

[28] Thomas *In Sent.* Lib. IV. dist. 24. qu.3. a.2. quaestiunc. 3. See *Cont. gent.* IV. lxxvi, where this argument is presented in greater detail. See also James of Viterbo *De reg. Christ.* I. iii (p. 117).

[29] Compare Thomas on monarchy in the state: *De reg. princ.* I. ii; and in the church: *Cont. gent.* IV. lxxvi.

[30] See below, p. 284.

[31] Matt. 16:18.

[32] Luke 10:1. The standard interpretation of this text was given in the gloss of Bede: "Sicut in apostolis forma est episcoporum, sic in septuaginta duobus discipulis forma est presbyterorum secundi ordinis" (*Glossa ordinaria;* in Thomas Aquinas *Catena aurea;* quoted by Marsilius, II. xxvii. 1). It will be noted that Bede's use of the term *forma* brings out the analogical character of his interpretation. The same text, with Bede's gloss, is cited to the same effect in *Corp. jur. can., Decret. Gratiani* Pars I. dist. 21. 1 Pars. can. 3 (Gratian) (I, 67); Thomas *S. theol.* II. II. qu.184. a.6. ad 1; Alexander of St. Elpidius *Tract. de eccl. pot.* I. x (pp. 12–13).

[33] See above, pp. 76–77.

[34] *Tract. Eborac.* III (p. 659).

[35] II. xvi. 15 ff.

was no scriptural evidence for Peter's ever having been in Rome.[36] But Marsilius advances beyond mere assertion to a meticulous critical analysis of the scriptural evidence bearing on the question; and he concludes "that it must indubitably be held through the holy Scripture" that the Roman bishops are successors of Paul rather than of Peter, and that the successors of Peter are rather the bishops of Antioch.[37] That this analysis wreaks havoc upon the historical basis traditionally ascribed to the Roman papacy goes without saying. Philosophically, however, it is in his replies to the arguments taken from the political structure of the church, that his most important doctrinal alteration is found. For his position is parallel to the tradition at least in this respect, that in each case the rational arguments on the structure of the church are held to be supported by scriptural texts: reason and revelation are in complete agreement.

Marsilius' reply to the argument from unity to monarchy in the church is both similar to and different from his reply to the argument for monarchy in the government of the state. Just as he had insisted that monarchy is not necessary to the unity of the secular government or of the state, so he now replies that monarchy is not necessary to the unity of the church. But the reasons he gives for these respective denials are quite different, and they bring out clearly the difference between state and church as he conceives them. The necessity of monarchy in the state's government had been rejected because the unity of *coercive authority* required by the state could be attained through the government of a few or of many persons as well as through that of one.[38] But the necessity of monarchy in the church is rejected because, since the church is the whole body of the *faithful,* it is one only in the sense *faith* is one in all the faithful. But this latter unity is only specific or generic, not numerical, so that it does not require the numerical unity of a single head.[39] Thomas Aquinas had also held

[36] Moneta of Cremona *Adversus Catharos et Valdenses* v. ii. 1 (p. 411): "Praeterea dicunt, Petrum numquam fuisse Romae, unde arguunt nos de inquisitione ossium ejus Romae, cum in novo Testamento, nullum testimonium habeatur, quod Petrus fuerit Romae." See *Def. pac.* II. xvi. 16: "De beato vero Petro . . . dico per Scripturam Sacram convinci non posse, ipsum fuisse Romanum episcopum specialiter, et quod amplius est, ipsum umquam Romae fuisse." Moneta was writing in 1244.

[37] II. xvi. 18.

[38] See above, pp. 117–18.

[39] II. xxviii. 13: "sumendo *ecclesiam* in propria significatione pro fidelium multitudine, sic esse unam ecclesiam, sicut fides est una. Et quoniam fides non est una numero in omnibus fidelibus, sed specie vel genere, idcirco non concludit argumentum, ecclesiam aliter unam. Et cum additur, ecclesiam non esse unam nisi per unitatem numeralem alicujus episcopi ceteris superiorem, hanc nego. . . ." See II. xxviii. 15, and the argument to which it is a reply: II. xxvii. 4. arg. 14; also II. xxviii. 16: "Ecce qualiter ovile fit unum, quoniam in fidei unitate." This argument has overtones of opposition to the Averroist doctrine of the unity of the intellect; see Siger of Brabant *Quaestiones de anima intellectiva* cap. vii (pp. 164–69) and Thomas Aquinas *Cont. gent.* II. lxxii.

that the unity of the faith in the believers is only specific, not numerical; [40] but he had insisted that the preservation even of this unity requires a numerically single head of the church.[41] Marsilius, on the other hand, while similarly admitting that there must be authoritative determinations of the true content of the faith, because "without these the unity of the faith would not be preserved," entrusts them to a general council composed of many men rather than one.[42]

But Marsilius' rejection goes much further. For might not the church be deemed to require at least a unified headship under its general council in the same non-numerically personal sense as the state under its government? Here emerges the consequence both of Marsilius' specifically political interpretation of social unity and of his fideistic view of the church. Narrowly restricted as social unity is to the coercive functions of government, it can no longer serve as the basis for those analogical generalizations whereby the tradition had proved the necessity of the unification of the church by the pope. And the church, in turn, as a congregation of believers, requires only such unity as the common faith can give. Thus when Marsilius considers the argument that "just as temporal things are reduced to one principle, that is, the government, so too must spiritual things be reduced to one first principle, that is, the bishopric," [43] his reply is that "the comparison can be denied, for the numerical unity of the primary ruler or government is necessary *because of the contentious acts of men,* as was demonstrated in Chapter 17 of Discourse I. But this unity is not necessary in any of the other offices of the city or state." [44] Here, it will be noted, it is the unity of the priesthood as a part of the state that is being considered, not the unity of the church. But a similar contrast exists between the state and the church itself on this point. For since the church is based upon faith, which is voluntary, it cannot have the kind of unity which the coercive judgment of contentious acts had necessitated for the state. Thus the general council's definitions of articles of faith amount only to "judgments in the first sense," non-coercive counsels rather than commands.[45] And although in ancient times when the church first arose the believers

[40] *S. theol.* II. II. qu.4. a.6. Resp.: "si fides sumatur pro habitu quo credimus, sic fides est una specie, et differens numero in diversis." Compare *Def. pac.* II. xxviii. 13: "fides non est una numero in omnibus fidelibus, sed specie vel genere. . . ."

[41] *Cont. gent.* IV. lxxvi.

[42] II. XX. 2 ff. See II. xviii. 8 init.

[43] II. xxvii. 4.

[44] II. xxviii. 14.

[45] See II. XX. 2: The members of the general council act "tanquam judices *secundum judicis significationem primam.*" II. xxi. 4: "Quod vero diffinitorum seu judicatorum et reliquorum ordinatorum *primae significationis judicio* per generale concilium. . . ." On the transformation which this non-coerciveness undergoes in the *Defensor minor,* see below, p. 297.

were "preserved in unity" by the bishops of Rome through their regulations with respect to church ritual and other "lawful and honorable" matters, this unification did not and could not extend to "contentious acts," because the Apostle did not wish that these be judged by priests.[46] Thus the contrast of faith and coercion is used to deny to the church the kind of coercively enforced unity which had been required in the state.

A final step follows closely from this contrast. For since Christ is founder of the faith on which the church is based, it is he who is, and who has always remained, the real head of the church. For it is not a question here of a visible political society, so that Marsilius can reject outright the arguments of his predecessors that Christ would not have left the church ordered in the best possible way if he had not left some head in his place.[47]

The same view of the opposed natures of the political and the religious society is also applied within the priesthood itself in a manner which serves to annul the basis of the episcopal as well as the papal authority. For such authority, to be effective, would involve the aggrandizement or "domination" of some over others, and hence would be contrary to that self-effacement and equality which Christ enjoined upon the apostles. Thus the same scriptural texts which had been invoked against the coerciveness of divine law, and hence of priests over laymen, are now used against any kind of divinely based authority for pope or bishops over other priests: "The rulers of the gentiles lord it (*dominantur*) over them; but you not so." [48] This point shows clearly the effect of Marsilius' reduction of all political authority to coercive power. Hence where Thomas Aquinas had placed hierarchic political authority in a setting which emphasized its continuity in all orders, including the cosmological, Marsilius sharply separates political from ecclesiastic authority by emphasizing the specifi-

[46] II. xxii. 16–17. Note the striking contrast expressed by the phrase "*in licitis et honestis* . . . circa ecclesiarum ritum," on the one hand, and "*de contentiosis autem actibus* altera quidem ratio est."

[47] II. xxviii. 27; see II. xxii. 5: "Caput enim ecclesiae simpliciter et fidei fundamentum Dei ordinatione immediata, secundum Scripturam sive veritatem, unicum est Christus ipse, non aliquis apostolus, episcopus, aut sacerdos. . . ." See also II. xvii. 2; II. xxviii. 5. The same position is taken in *Quaestio in utramque partem* a.5 (p. 103): "totius Ecclesiae unum solum esse caput, sicut una est columba Ecclesiae. Sed istud caput dicimus esse Christum, qui solus est proprie caput Ecclesiae. . . ." See also John of Paris *De pot. reg. et pap.* cap. xix (p. 134). Both these authors, however, apply this headship of Christ not to the internal structure of the church (for each grants that Peter, and from him the pope, was made head of the church by Christ, as their subsequent statements show), but rather to the relation between spiritual and temporal powers. Each is denying that the pope is head of both powers: thus both the passages just quoted are immediately continued by the words "a quo derivata [in *Quaestio;* 'distributa' in John] est utraque potestas. . . ." For the position which Marsilius is denying, see Thomas *Cont. gent.* IV. lxxvi. The same position is taken by John of Paris *De pot. reg. et pap.* cap. iii (p. 111).

[48] Matt. 20:25–26; Luke 22:25–26; quoted II. iv. 13; II. xvi. 10, 11. See also Matt. 18:8; quoted II. xvi. 6, 10.

cally coercive quality which he has assigned to the former. Christ wanted the apostles to maintain equality with one another; hence the episcopal and papal claims to superior jurisdiction have no divine foundation.

The divine basis of the papal authority is further denied by another sharp distinction, this time not between coercive domination and priestly equality or fideistic communion, but between divine perfection and human imperfection. For all human beings, unlike God, are subject to malice and ignorance, so that Christ would not have made a mere man head of the church; even "Peter, so long as he was a wayfarer, could err and sin through his freedom of will." [49] Again, therefore, only Christ can be head of the church; and the papalists' apotheosis of the pope [50] is halted.

This emphasis upon human fallibility undergoes a further application in which the distinction is no longer between the divine and the human but between one and many humans. For if one man is fallible, at least many men are less so than one. Thus the same majoritarian argument employed to prove that the whole people, as against one or a few men, is rightful possessor of supreme authority in the state, is now used to prove that no one priest should have supreme control over others. For "all or most of the apostles deliberated with greater certainty and erred less . . . than any one of them taken separately"; [51] hence "the congregation of the apostles had greater authority than Peter or any other apostle alone." [52] Between Marsilius' alternate invocations of the absolute infallibility of God and the lesser fallibility of the whole group, as well as of the distinction between faith and coercion, the traditional arguments for the supremacy of one man in the church are lost.

As a consequence of these considerations, the Marsilian church emerges as a purely spiritual congregation of believers, connected by no ties but their common faith and participation in the sacraments. The priesthood which teaches the faith and ministers the sacraments consists of ministers exercising no coercive authority over the believers and maintaining complete equality with one another. Such equality, in the sense of absence of all jurisdictional superiority, is the direct result of Christ's ordainment, which extends only to the essential power, traditionally called the power of order.

Marsilius does not, however, remain with this conception of the church. He reinstates the inequalities of authority which the tradition had viewed as degrees of superiority within the priestly power both of order and of jurisdiction; but he treats them as having only a human, institutional, utilitarian, and historical basis. Thus he recognizes that the equality of

[49] II. xxviii. 5. [50] See above, p. 16. [51] II. xvii. 6. [52] II. xvi. 6.

both apostles and priests in their essential authority does not annul either the fact that some may be superior to others in zeal and ability,[53] or the need for some organizational control of the work of the priesthood. It is on this basis that he explains the development of a distinction between priests and bishops, where there had been no such distinction in the days of the apostles themselves.[54] It is on this basis, too, that he grants the desirability of a visible, mortal "head bishop" of the church in addition to its "immortal" head.[55] Indeed, the grounds for such distinctions among priests take on much of the color of the reasons previously assigned for the necessity of secular government and of its unity: to avoid "scandal and schism," [56] superfluous effort,[57] confusion and quarrelling in deliberative assemblies,[58] and the disturbance of the public welfare which would result therefrom.[59] Moreover, Marsilius goes on to prescribe for the church the same formal organization as is required for the state: as in a well-formed body the head is not directly connected to the hands, fingers, and all the other members, but there must be an ordered articulation of parts, so too *"this form and manner must be observed in the ecclesiastic as well as in every civil régime."* [60] The universal pastor or ruler must direct the functioning of provincial officials only through progressively subordinate officials: archbishops through patriarchs, bishops through archbishops, chapters through bishops.

Despite these resemblances, the authority of Marsilius' head bishop is not a political power or "domination"; there are attached to it, as such, no coercive sanctions.[61] The head bishop cannot appoint or remove priests or bishops, or make binding definitions on matters of faith. Although he can judge "spiritual" disputes and questions of church ritual between bishops and churches, even this is hemmed in with restrictions: his judgment must be approved by a majority (*parte valentiori sive majori*) of the college of priests established as his aides by the legislator; the bishops or

[53] II. xvi. 10, 14, 19.

[54] II. xv. 5, 6. In pointing out that *presbyter* and *episcopus* originally denoted the same persons, and that the terms differed only analytically, the former indicating age, the latter care over others, Marsilius is following an old tradition. See Jerome *Epist. 146 ad Evangelum* (PL 22, 1192), which is cited, II. xv. 5; Isidore of Seville *Etymologiae* VII. xii; *Corp. jur. can., Decret. Gratiani* Pars I. dist. 21. can. 1, 12, where Isidore is quoted; Thomas *S. theol.* II. II. qu.184. a.6. ad 1.

[55] II. xxii. 7.

[56] II. xv. 6: "ad scandalum et schisma evitandum"; see I. xix. 6; II. xvii. 4; II. xxii. 7. Thomas Aquinas similarly says that bishops were distinguished from priests "ad schisma vitandum" (*S. theol.* II. II. qu.184. a.6. ad 1).

[57] II. xxii. 7; cf. I. xvii. 6. See above, p. 235.

[58] II. xxii. 7; cf. I. xvii. 4.

[59] II. xxii. 7: "ne propter talium diversitatem et quandoque contrarietatem publica fidelium turbetur aut differatur utilitas." Cf. I. xvii. 4: "talium pluralitate supposita, omnis communis utilitas turbaretur."

[60] II. xxiv. 12.

[61] II. xxii. 6: ". . . nequaquam vero potestate aliqua coactiva poenae realis aut personalis inflictiva pro statu et in statu praesentis saeculi."

churches for whom he is judging must not be subordinate one to the other (he must respect the "jurisdiction" of other bishops); he must judge according to rules made not by himself alone but by a general council; and finally, an appeal can always be made from his decisions.[62] He is hence a purely advisory and executive official: he carries out policies which he does not make. Indeed, his primary function is to serve as a moral example.[63]

Since, then, Marsilius holds that the best arrangement of the church is for it to have such a non-coercive head bishop, and under him a hierarchized structure of progressively subordinated officials, on what score does he refuse to grant that it was thus ordered by God, who "does not lack in necessaries"? [64] Marsilius provides two answers to this question, one direct, the other indirect. We shall recur to the latter subsequently.[65] The direct answer, as indicated by the arguments discussed above, is that these arrangements of authority are no *necessary* conditions, but only expedient aids, to the fulfillment of the essential priestly mission. Thus to have one bishop at the head of the church "is not commanded by divine law, since even without this the unity of the faith would be preserved, although not so easily." [66] It is for this reason that Marsilius calls all such arrangements "accidental," "separable," and "extrinsic" powers of the priesthood. What is essential to the priest is his power to minister the sacraments; this power derives from the "character" or "habit of soul" impressed upon him immediately by God, and is equal in every priest as such. Everything else which supervenes upon this power, all the external arrangements made for the regulation of the priests' relations with one another, for the distribution to them of economic goods, for their assignment to particular places—all these are accidental to the priests as such, and hence the inequalities among priests which are consequent upon these arrangements are likewise accidental. Their efficient cause, consequently, is not God but man. The essential, intrinsic church, as Marsilius conceives it, remains a purely spiritual, sacramental community.

[62] *Ibid.*

[63] Thus whereas Thomas Aquinas holds that the bishop's primary qualifications should be political rather than moral, Marsilius insists solely upon moral and intellectual virtues for his head bishop. See *S. theol.* II. II. qu.185. a.3. Resp.: "Et ideo ille qui debet aliquem eligere in episcopum, vel de eo providere, non tenetur assumere meliorem simpliciter, quod est secundum charitatem; sed meliorem *quoad regimen Ecclesiae,* qui scilicet possit Ecclesiam et instruere, et defendere, et pacifice gubernare." Compare *Def. pac.* II. xxii. 8: "Quem vero episcopum et qualem . . . sic caput aliarum instituere magis conveniat, qualem primum assignantes, dicamus secundum veritatem eum qui ceteris vita et sacra doctrina cunctis praepollet, in quo tamen est bonae vitae potius attendendus excessus." See II. xvi. 14.

[64] See I. vi. 3: "Deus . . . numquam facit frustra quicquam neque deficit in necessariis. . . ."

[65] See below, p. 282.

[66] II. xxii. 6.

This point emphasizes further that divorce of the divine and the human which was seen to be fundamental to Marsilius' view of the history and traditions of the Christian era,[67] and which was also implied in the other considerations examined above. The rigid separation between the "essential" priestly powers established by Christ and the "accidental" powers deriving from man indicates that there is no essential connection or continuity between what has historically been done by God and by man. The emergence of the institutions of the visible church, including the hierarchy, was in no sense a consequence of a divine plan; the influence of God upon human institutions, including even the church, appears to have ceased in ancient times. It is only in certain minimal aspects of faith and the sacraments which are required for the functioning of the Christian religion as such, and which involve no institutional or political arrangements whatsoever, that God's cooperation with man is still maintained. This discontinuity of the divine and the human in the ecclesiastic sphere is in striking contrast not only to the antecedent tradition but also to the continuity between the human will and biological nature which underlies Marsilius' political doctrine.

From this point of view, it is also instructive to compare the essential and accidental powers of the priest with those of the ruler. For with the ruler, as well as with the priest, and indeed with every functional "part" of the state, there is the distinction between the mental quality or "habit" which renders a man apt for the exercise of a given function, and the actual authority to exercise that function in the state.[68] But it is revealing of Marsilius' doctrine that for the priesthood this distinction is turned in precisely the opposite direction to that applied in the case of the ruler. For the ruler's mental qualities of prudence and justice make him only "potentially" a ruler; to be "actually" a ruler he must have external coercive authority given to him by the proper efficient cause. It is such authority which constitutes the essence of rulership.[69] To the priest, on the other hand, it is his mental, inner quality or "character" which is essential; the external authority which supervenes upon this is only accidental. The "essential" realm of the priest, therefore, is the inner spiritual life of faith and the sacraments, whereas the "actual" realm of the ruler is the outer temporal life of the coercive regulation of transient acts. What is essential for each is thus accidental for the other.

Since the priest's essential power, as such, carries with it no accidental power, no appointment to any particular congregation upon which the

[67] See above, Ch. II, Sec. 4, pp. 71 ff., esp. p. 75; also pp. 157–58. See also below, p. 293.
[68] See I. vi. 9; I. vii. 1–3; II. xv. 2.
[69] I. xv. 1.

former power is to be exercised, it is a question of first importance who gives this accidental power. In the tradition, the priest receives his jurisdiction from the bishop, by virtue of the latter's hierarchic superiority.[70] As for the bishops themselves, their appointment had undergone many fluctuations in bitter contests throughout a large part of the middle ages; but by the middle of the thirteenth century, it devolved to the pope, who in turn was elected by the cardinals. These jurisdictional arrangements were defended by Marsilius' immediate predecessors and contemporaries on the same hierarchic grounds as were basic to their view of the church itself.[71] The exclusion of laymen from electoral authority was also upheld by anti-democratic arguments similar in orientation to those by which the political tradition from Plato and Aristotle on had deprecated popular power in the state; we have examined some of these in an earlier chapter.[72]

For Marsilius, on the other hand, it is the whole body of the faithful which controls all the "secondary establishments" of the priesthood: all appointments of priests to pastoral or "accidental" authority,[73] including that of the "head bishop."[74] In the former case, it is the faithful of the particular community who elect their priests, while in the latter it is the whole of Christendom. This position follows from Marsilius' own premises; all the arguments which had been invoked to prove that the whole body of citizens should be the legislator are here explicitly re-invoked.[75]

[70] Thomas *In Sent.* Lib. IV. dist. 20. qu.1. a.4. quaestiunc. 1; dist. 24. qu.3. a.2. quaestiunc. 1. Bonaventura *In Sent.* Lib. IV. dist. 18. pars 2. a.1. qu.3; dist. 25. a.1. qu.2. ad 3. John of Paris *De pot. reg. et pap.* cap. xiii (p. 125).

[71] See Thomas *In Sent.* Lib. IV. dist. 24. a.2. Egidius *De eccl. pot.* III. ix (p. 191). Augustinus Triumphus *S. de eccl. pot.* qu.2. a.8. James of Viterbo *De reg. Christ.* I. iii (p. 116).

[72] See above, pp. 202–3.

[73] II. xvii. 8.

[74] II. xxii. 9. A similar position had already been upheld by John of Paris, who declares himself in favor of a "mixed government" for the church as well as for the state: the bishops and priests are to be elected by the believers of each province rather than by the pope (*De pot. reg. et pap.* cap. xx [p. 137]), and the pope himself is to be elected, as well as deposed, by the people (*ibid.* cap. xxiv [pp. 144, 145, 147]). Although James of Viterbo indicates that temporal "kings" are at least partly elected by the people (*De reg. Christ.* II. iii; III. x [pp. 179, 186, 303]), he says of spiritual "kings" (by which he refers to the jurisdictional powers of the priesthood) merely that their power is from God through Peter (*ibid.* II. iii, vi, vii [pp. 180, 225, 230]) and "secundum ordinationem ecclesiae" (*ibid.* II. iii [p. 186]). Egidius of Rome, in his work defending the validity of the resignation of Pope Celestine V, frequently assimilates the papal headship to all kinds of political authority over a *multitudo,* and says that while it has a natural basis, "oportet tamen quod hoc compleatur *per consensum hominum*" (*De renunciatione papae* cap. xvi [p. 41]; see also cap. v, xi, xxiv [pp. 9, 34, 58, 61]). But despite this reference to consent, and the many references to *assensus eligentium* in the other passages cited, it is clear that by the electors of the pope Egidius means the cardinals: "in electione autem Summi Pontificis . . . *duabus partibus Cardinalium* consentientibus" (*ibid.* cap. xxiii [p. 58]). There is hence no justification for interpreting the phrase *per consensum hominum* to mean that for Egidius "the authority of the ruler was derived from the consent of the *people*" (Carlyle, *op. cit.,* V, 469; my italics).

[75] II. xvii. 11, 14; II. xxii. 11.

The priests themselves are to serve only as non-coercive "experts" or advisors on the qualifications of candidates for appointments,[76] analogously to the experts who drew up recommendations for enactment into laws by the whole body of citizens.[77] On the other hand, the priests are also a "part" of the "whole" people or multitude, and in this respect they also share in electoral power, but only to a proportionate extent. "For every whole is greater than any part of it taken separately." [78] Marsilius' holistic view of the people thus achieves one of its most decisive results.[79]

This electoral power of the people, moreover, has the divine sanction denied to the sacerdotal hierarchy itself. It will be recalled that one reason which Marsilius gave for this denial was that the hierarchy, including the unification afforded to the church by having one head bishop, is only expedient but not necessary to the church.[80] He also gives another reason whose bearing the present context of discussion makes clear. The best condition of the church is for it to have a mortal head in addition to its immortal head; moreover, Christ left the church in the best condition. Did Christ, then, himself appoint such a mortal head? No, replies Marsilius, this does not follow. For it would have been better for this head to be elected by the whole body of the faithful; and "this was the best disposition given by Christ to the church militant . . . Hence in leaving to the faithful the establishment of such a head of the church . . . Christ left it in the best disposition appropriate to human society." [81]

It will have been noted that this reply puts the headship of the church upon a new basis. It no longer holds that the headship, and the hierarchy, have no divine origin or recognition at all, and are purely conventional and human in origin; instead, it holds that the desirability of hierarchy among priests was recognized and indeed provided for by Christ himself. The only difference from the orthodox position, apart from the different powers assigned to the head and other bishops, is that Christ provided that they be chosen by the people rather than by a pope. But for that matter, Marsilius holds that the temporal ruler, although also elected directly by the people, is "ordained of God." [82] Still, the distinction remains for Marsilius between the absolute necessity that there be government in the state, and the mere high desirability that there be a head bishop in the church. The former is an object of divine command both as to its existence and its be-

[76] II. xvii. 14. [77] See above, p. 168. [78] II. xvii. 14.

[79] See above, p. 181. On the other hand, with respect to the specifically political authority of the "people" in the state, Marsilius tends to separate the priesthood from the people. See above, pp. 80 ff., and especially below, pp. 298 ff. [80] See above, p. 279.

[81] II. xxviii. 27. For the divine sanction of popular sovereignty in the state, see above, p. 250.

[82] See above, p. 250.

ing obeyed; the latter is an object of counsel alone, whose effectuation is left to the discretion of the faithful.

Marsilius' discussion of the power of excommunication follows the same lines as his discussion of the election of priests. In the traditional doctrine, it was held that the power to excommunicate was given to Peter not *qua* priest but *qua* prelate, and only bishops and major prelates have this power. However, since it requires only jurisdiction, not the priestly order, it may be entrusted by prelates even to non-priests, such as archdeacons and chapters.[83] For Marsilius, on the other hand, the power of excommunication belongs only to the *universitas fidelium* of the community in which it is to occur,[84] just as does the election of priests to their accidental authority. Thus once again the people takes the place of the bishop, and through the same argument: that the judgment of the whole body of the faithful is "more certain and more free from suspicion" than that of the priests alone.[85] The latter must, indeed, serve as advisory "judges in the first sense," discerning from divine law what are the crimes for which one should be excommunicated, just as they serve as experts on the qualifications of candidates for pastorates; but the coercive judgment which acquits or condemns to excommunication pertains to the whole ecclesiastic community, laymen as well as priests.[86]

4. THE GENERAL COUNCIL

Marsilius' reform of the church is completed by his doctrine of the general council. The central problem for which he invokes the council is that of determining articles of faith. Although he had defined the church as the whole body of the faithful, and had declared that faith is not subject to

[83] See St. Bonaventura *In Sent.* Lib. IV. dist. 18. pars 2. a.I. qu.3. Thomas *In Sent.* Lib. IV. dist. 18. qu.2. a.2. quaestiunc. I; dist. 19. qu.I. a.I. quaestiunc. 3. See also *Corp. jur. can., Decret. Gratiani* Pars II. C. XI. qu.3, *passim* (I, 642 ff.); *Sext.* Lib. V. Tit. 39, *passim* (II, 889 ff.).

[84] II. vi. 12. As holder of this power, alternatively to the *universitas fidelium,* Marsilius adds: "vel ad ipsius superiorem vel ad concilium generale." His subsequent elucidations of the point, however, all attribute the primary power to the *universitas fidelium,* "ad quam semper appellare contingit" (II. vi. 13).

[85] II. vi. 13. Some of the commentators on the *Sentences* had upheld the right of a "multitude" to excommunicate, and had even argued that the "multitude" has advantages not possessed by its individual members, and lacks their disadvantages. But the multitude referred to is a *capitulum* or *congregatio;* it does not comprise all the members of the *universitas fidelium* of the community, as with Marsilius. Thus it is significant that they assimilate this multitude to an aristocracy rather than to a polity. See Albert the Great *In Sent.* Lib. IV. dist. 19. a.6. St. Bonaventura *In Sent.* Lib. IV. dist. 18. pars 2. a.I. qu.3. *ad ultim.* Thomas *In Sent.* Lib. IV. dist. 19. qu.I. a.I. quaestiunc. 3. ad 3; see *ibid.* qu.2. a.3. quaestiunc. 2.

[86] On this point, as on so many others in ecclesiastic as well as general politics, the doctrine of Hobbes is strikingly similar to that of Marsilius, even as to mode of expression—to such an extent as to suggest a direct influence. Cf. *Leviathan* ch. xlii (p. 274) and *Def. pac.* II. vi. 12.

coercion, this does not mean that he is prepared to leave to each individual the content of the faith in which he will believe. He insists upon the necessity for interpretation of the Scriptures, especially on the articles of faith, since doubts concerning their true meaning may arise; and even more, he holds that these interpretations must be made by some official agency, for a reason which is the reverse of individualism: "diversities and contrarieties of opinions with respect to divine law would lead to diverse sects, schisms, and errors." [1] Hence, although he has decentralized the church by making its hierarchy of bishops headed by a single pope a matter of human convenience rather than of divine necessity, and has withdrawn from it all coercive power, Marsilius nevertheless halts the decentralization at the point where it affects that unity of the faith on which he has said that the unity of the church depends. On this point, then, as to both the fact and the reason of the necessity for authoritative determinations of the faith, Marsilius is in agreement with the tradition.[2] The issue arises over the locus of this authority.

In the tradition, this authority to define the content of faith is assigned to the pope on both rational and scriptural grounds. The central position is that unity of the faith requires personal unity of the agency determining the true meaning of the faith, and that Christ himself therefore instituted a unified headship of the church in the person of Peter.[3] This position, akin to the arguments for monarchic unity both in the secular sphere and in church-state controversies, was upheld in specific application to the church and the faith not only by partisans of the papal plenitude of power [4] but also by such opponents of the papacy's temporal jurisdiction as John of Paris.[5] The Scriptures, moreover, were held to support the inference that the papal determinations are guided by the Holy Spirit and are infallible, for it was to Peter's and the popes' interpretations of articles of faith that Christ was referring when he said to his disciples that "I am with you always, even unto the end of the world." [6]

Various qualifications, to be sure, had been attached to this doctrine

[1] II. xx. I.

[2] With the paragraph cited in note 1, compare Thomas *Cont. gent.* IV. lxxvi.

[3] *Ibid.* See *S. theol.* II. II. qu.1. a.10. Resp.; qu.11. a.2. ad 3.

[4] Egidius *De eccl. pot.* I. i. James of Viterbo *De reg. Christ.* I. iii (pp. 111–12, 117). Alexander of St. Elpidius *Tract. de eccl. pot.* I. iv. Augustinus Triumphus *S. de eccl. pot.* qu.10. a.1.

[5] John of Paris *De pot. reg. et pap.* cap. iii (p. 111).

[6] Matt. 28:20; see Luke 22:32. See Thomas *Quodlib.* IX. qu.7. a.16; *In Sent.* Lib. IV. dist. 20. qu.1. a.3. quaestiunc. 1; *Cont. gent.* IV. lxxvi. Alexander of St. Elpidius *Tract. de eccl. pot.* III. x. Guido Terreni *Quaestio de magisterio infallibili Romani pontificis,* ed. P. M. Xiberta (Monastery, 1926). Augustinus Triumphus *S. de eccl. pot.* qu.6. a.1: "Sententia igitur papae et sententia Dei una sententia est. . . ." See P. Viollet, *L'Infaillibilité du pape et le syllabus* (Paris, 1904); E. Dublanchy, "Infaillibilité du pape," *Dict. de théol. cath.,* VII, 1638 ff.

before Marsilius. Infallibility pertains to the office of the pope, not to his person;[7] the pope may fall into heresy, in which case he ceases to be head of the church,[8] and is to be regarded as dead.[9] A pope accused of heresy is to be judged by a general council.[10] The councils, however, were normally regarded as depending upon the papal authority for their validity: their decisions must be ratified by the pope, who alone has power to convoke them,[11] except when he falls into heresy.[12] Only John of Paris before Marsilius declared that "the council is greater than the pope" with respect to matters of faith.[13] But since John also upholds the monarchic principle in the church as being by divine ordainment,[14] the superiority of the council is by no means unambiguous.

It is in Marsilius that the antecedent conciliar tendencies reach their culmination, for he completely reverses the traditional doctrine of the relation between pope and general council. It is the latter, not the former, which is referred to in Christ's promise that he would be with his disciples until the end of the world;[15] it is the council, therefore, which is guided by the Holy Spirit;[16] which, under that guidance, defines articles of faith;[17] whose decisions are therefore infallible,[18] and belief in them necessary for salvation.[19] It is the council, and behind it the "faithful human legislator," which elects the pope,[20] gives him whatever authority

[7] Thomas *Quodlib.* IX. qu.17. a.6. James of Viterbo *De reg. Christ.* II. vii (p. 230). Egidius *De eccl. pot.* I. ii. Augustinus Triumphus *De duplic. pot.*, p. 499. Guido Terreni *Quaest. de magist.*, pp. 27–28.

[8] John Teutonicus (in J. F. von Schulte, *Die Stellung der Concilien, Päpste, und Bischöfe* [Prague, 1871], Anhang, p. 265): "desinit esse caput ecclesiae."

[9] John of Paris *De pot. reg. et pap.* cap. xxxiv (p. 146). Augustinus Triumphus *S. de eccl. pot.* qu.5. a.1: "Si ergo papa deprehendatur devius a fide, mortuus est ipsa vita spirituali, et per consequens aliis influere vitam non potest."

[10] For an excellent discussion of the whole background of the conciliar doctrine, see V. Martin, "Comment s'est formée la doctrine de la superiorité du concile au pape," I, *Revue des sciences religieuses,* XVII (1937), 121–43. For the development at the end of the thirteenth century and the beginning of the fourteenth, see also H. X. Arquillière, "L'Appel au concile sous Philippe le Bel et la génèse des théories conciliaires," *Revue des questions historiques,* LXXXIX (1911), 23–55; and Arquillière, "L'Origine des théories conciliaires," *Académie des Sciences morales et politiques, Séances et travaux,* CLXXV (1911), 573–86.

[11] *Corp. jur. can., Decret. Gratiani* Pars I. dist. 16. can. 8; dist. 17. can. 2, 5. Thomas Aquinas *S. theol.* II. II. qu.1. a.10. ad 1; see *ibid.* I. qu.36. a.2. ad 2. Egidius *De eccl. pot.* I. i. Augustinus Triumphus *S. de eccl. pot.* qu.3. a.2; qu.6. a.6; qu.10. a.1.

[12] Augustinus Triumphus *S. de eccl. pot.* qu.5. a.6. See *ibid.* qu.3. a.2. For a discussion of Augustinus' conciliar doctrine, see K. Hirsch, *Die Ausbildung der konziliaren Theorie im XIV. Jahrhundert* (Vienna, 1903), pp. 3–9.

[13] *De pot. reg. et pap.* cap xxi (p. 139): "concilium est majus Papa solo." Cf. cap. xxiv (p. 146): "Quod ergo dicitur in principali argumento, quod Papatus est summa virtus creata, et sic non potest auferri. Respondeo: Licet sit summa virtus in persona, tamen *est ei aequalis vel major in collegio, sive in tota ecclesia.*"

[14] See above, 284.

[15] II. xix. 2.

[16] *Ibid.;* also II. xxi. 9.

[17] II. xx. 2.

[18] II. xix. 2–4.

[19] II. xix. 1.

[20] II. xxii. 9.

he possesses, and deposes him for cause.[21] And, although the council does not have numerical unity, it is the council, not the pope, which preserves the unity of the faith.[22]

This reversal of authority is sufficiently drastic in itself; but its full scope is understood only when it is recognized as a far more fundamental change than the mere substitution of the council for the pope. It is not merely a numerical change from one prelate to several. Marsilius is the founder of conciliarism because he provides for the dependence not only of the pope upon the general council, but also of the council upon the laity and hence upon the whole "church." This dependence emerges, first, in the fact that the council is elected by all the believers of the several states. This election follows the same pattern as the making of laws in every state, for the several legislators are here weighted, as had been the legislative citizen-body, "according to their proportion in quantity and quality of persons." [23] Secondly, it is the "faithful legislator," not the pope, which calls and assembles the council and gives coercive enforcement to its decisions.[24] In the third place, the council is composed of laymen as well as priests; [25] both groups are to take part in the deliberations, and although unanimous decisions of the priests at the council are to be accepted as definitive, if the priests disagree the *valentior pars* of the believers must judge which *pars* of the priests is *sanior*.[26] Thus where for Pope Gregory IX the criteria of *sanioritas* had been "merit, zeal, and authority," with the last counting most heavily and the pope himself as final arbiter,[27] for Marsilius the criterion rests in the judgment of the "weightier part" of the believers themselves. Hence, just as in the traditional doctrine the bishops or the cardinals represent the apostles,[28] so Marsilius adjusts his own version to provide that the general council "truly represents by succession" the assembly of the apostles, the elders, and the other believers of that time,[29] all of whom, as he points out, deliberated together on questions regarding the faith.[30] But in addition, the council also "represents" the whole body of believers, the church which has elected it.[31]

[21] II. xxii. 6.
[22] II. xx. 1.
[23] II. xx. 2. Cf. I. xii. 3; and above, pp. 182 ff.
[24] II. xxi. 1 ff.
[25] II. xx. 2.
[26] II. xx. 5: "Unde sacerdotibus invicem dissidentibus de credendis ad salutem alternam, de ipsorum saniori parte fidelium pars valentior habet iudicare. . . ." Note Marsilius' further emphasis in this paragraph that the priests will have been appointed "ad ordines quemadmodum diximus xvii° huius," i.e., by the "faithful multitude."
[27] *Corp. jur. can., Decretal. Greg. IX* Lib. I. Tit. 6. cap. 57 (II, 95).
[28] See Thomas Aquinas *S. theol.* III. qu.72. a.11. Resp.: "in primitiva Ecclesia per impositionem manus *apostolorum,* quorum vicem *gerunt episcopi,* plenitudo Spiritus sancti dabatur." See *ibid.* II. II. qu.184. a.6. ad 1. Augustinus Triumphus *S. de eccl. pot.* qu.6. a.5: "Unde salvator Jo. XIII dixit *discipulis, quorum personas cardinales representant. . . .*"
[29] II. xix. 2.
[30] II. xvi. 5; II. xx. 5.
[31] II. xx. 2.

This inclusion of laymen in the general council marks a decided change from the antecedent doctrine, in which the council was composed only of bishops.[32] The exclusively episcopal composition had been maintained even by William Durand, Jr.,[33] despite his use of the maxim "what affects all must be approved by all" to justify the calling of a general council when articles of faith are to be determined or new ecclesiastic laws enacted.[34] Marsilius' inclusiveness follows from the same principles as all his other republican changes in the church. The priesthood alone is less competent morally and intellectually than when aided by laymen.[35] And that "which can benefit or harm all the faithful" requires even more than other matters the full concentration of effort by laymen as well as priests.[36]

This conciliarist doctrine raises obvious problems, some of which have already been examined above. There is the contrast between the generality of the council and the particularity of individual states.[37] Since each state is independent, who will guarantee that its "legislator" will elect representatives to the council and support its decisions? If it be held that such support, like faith itself, is to be entirely voluntary, there is the further contrast between the non-coerciveness of faith and the coercive sanctions which the several legislators are to attach to the council's decisions.[38]

Most directly of all, however, there is the contrast between the infallibility of the general council's decisions and the fallibility which Marsilius ascribes to all human utterances.[39] A similar contrast was noted above between the latter and the certainty attributed by Marsilius to his own demonstrations.[40] Moreover, since the general council is elected by the whole body of the faithful, it corresponds in the legislative process not to the whole body of citizens or its weightier part, but rather to the elected "experts" who prepare proposed bills for enactment into law by the *universitas.* Yet Marsilius had insisted that the experts taken alone cannot be trusted to be the final arbiters, for their wills might be perverted by selfish class interests. To be sure, the council is elected, and its decisions are made coercively binding, only by the several legislators. But Marsilius claims infallibility for the council's decisions themselves; and he invokes for the council's authority to make such decisions the same arguments as he had previously invoked for the entire *universitas civium* in the making of laws and for the *universitas fidelium* in the election of priests.

[32] See *Corp. jur. can., Decret. Gratiani* Pars I. dist. 17, 18 *passim* (I, 50 ff.).

[33] See *De modo generalis concilii celebrandi* Lib. II. Rubr. 11 (fol. 160*r*).

[34] *Ibid.* Lib. I. Rubr. 4 (fol. 155*v*); Lib. II. Rubr. 41 (fol. 165*v*). See above, p. 224.

[35] See II. xx. 5 ff.; II. xxi. 3.

[36] II. xx. 4. Cf. above, pp. 223 ff.

[37] See above, Ch. III, Sec. 4, esp. pp. 130–31.

[38] See above, Ch. IV, Sec. 4, esp. pp. 155 ff.

[39] See above, pp. 73 ff.

[40] See above, p. 74.

What is undoubtedly at work in this context is Marsilius' realization of the practical problems involved in the matter. For the whole of Christendom cannot, because of obvious practical difficulties, be brought together to define articles of faith—and he gives exactly the same explanation for this as for the inadvisability of assembling the whole body of citizens of a single state to "discover" (although not to *enact*) the laws [41]—so that the best practical substitute is a general council composed of both laymen and clergy elected by the whole. But then, feeling the need to give this expedient the same footing as the papal definitions had enjoyed, he invokes for it an infallibility grounded upon the Scriptures.

This question also involves, however, some of the central principles of Marsilius' conception of political authority. Directly, the issue is: Who are the persons referred to in Christ's promise that he would "be with *you* always until the end of the world"? The papalists, with their monarchic view of theologico-political authority, interpreted the "you" to mean primarily the pope, and only through him the other believers. Marsilius, on the other hand, with his corporate-majoritarian doctrine of the locus of authority, interprets the "you" as meaning the *universitas fidelium,* or the majority (*pluralitas*) of them, or the general council elected by them: Christ would not have "allowed the *majority* of believers to err concerning the true meaning of the faith." [42] There was, however, a third alternative, that of the individualism embodied in Marsilius' view of the sacraments and other theologico-religious aspects of the church. As we have seen, he himself illustrates such individualism in his own practice,[43] but not in his conciliar theory. William of Ockham, on the other hand, consistently opposes an individualist interpretation to the corporate position of Marsilius, devoting an entire book of the *Dialogus* to a criticism of the Marsilian theory of conciliar infallibility.[44] Thus Ockham's interpretation of Christ's

[41] II. xx. 2; compare I. xiii. 8. See above, p. 188. It should be noted that even with respect to assembling the entire "multitude of believers" Marsilius adduces the consideration not that their number is too large (as had the Roman lawbooks to explain the devolution of legislative authority from the "people" to the Senate), but rather that the multitude "turbaretur ab operibus necessariis ad vitae corporalis sustentationem; quod onerosum ei esset aut importabile forte."

[42] II. xix. 3. See II. xix. 2.

[43] See above, p. 75.

[44] *Dialogus* Pars III. Tr. I. Lib. III: *In quo pertractatur, quibus scripturis de necessitate salutis credere tenemur.* See *ibid.* Pars I. Lib. V. cap. xxv–xxviii. The relation between the conciliarist positions of Marsilius and Ockham is discussed in Emerton, *op. cit.*, pp. 55–58; Martin, *op. cit.*, IIme Partie: "Les Idées répandues par Marsile de Padoue et Occam touchant l'église," *Revue des sciences religieuses,* XVII (1937), 261–89; and two excellent articles by G. de Lagarde, "L'Idée de représentation dans les oeuvres de Guillaume d'Ockham," *Bulletin of the International Committee of Historical Sciences,* IX (1937), 425–51; and "Marsile de Padoue et Guillaume d'Ockham," *Revue des sciences religieuses,* XVII (1937), 168–85, 428–54. The latter article brings out some hitherto unknown historical relations between Marsilius and Ockham.

promise insists that it would be fulfilled even if all the believers save one were in error,[45] and even if the true faith remained only as a "habit" in baptized infants.[46] Similarly, where Marsilius attributes infallibility to the general council because it is the official, elected "representative" of the whole church, Ockham holds that a representative does not always enjoy all the prerogatives of that which it represents,[47] and that the general council, if it is truly to represent the whole church, must have the tacit or express consent of all Catholics both as to its meeting and as to its acts, with "no one contradicting or attacking it."[48]

From these divergences there emerge two further differences between Marsilius and Ockham with respect to the relation of the general council to the church and to the pope. In the first place, Ockham uniformly characterizes the general council as a "particular or special congregation,"[49] a "partial congregation,"[50] for since it does not numerically contain all the believers it is "only a part" of the whole church.[51] Hence he puts it on a par with "provincial councils and other congregations of Christians."[52] Marsilius, on the other hand, *distinguishes* the general council from "partial groups"[53] or "particular groups."[54] The point of the distinction is not that the general council contains more members, but that it is elected by, and hence "represents," the entire church; but even more, it is that the council includes laymen as well as clergy. As such, not only is it "representative" in the sense that an elected council consisting only of priests is not, but it embodies the central corrective effect which we have already seen applied in Marsilius' corporate interpretation of the part-whole principle in the case of the legislator: while the truth cannot be found by one individual or group acting alone, when each aids the other their several deficiencies are overcome. Quantitative increase results in qualitative improvement.[55] Thus the ignorance and selfishness of some of the priests are both checked and offset by the moral and intellectual qualities of the laymen who are elected with them to serve in the council.

[45] *Dialogus* Pars III. Tr. I. Lib. III. cap. xi, xiii (pp. 828, 830). See the same position in Augustinus Triumphus *S. de eccl. pot.* qu.20. a.6: "Ecclesia non potest errare, quia si unus solus catholicus remaneret, ille esset ecclesia."

[46] *Dialogus* Pars I. Lib. v. cap. xxxv (p. 506). See *ibid.* cap. xxv (p. 495).

[47] *Ibid.* Pars. I. Lib. v. cap. xxv (p. 494): "non omni praerogativa gaudet persona vel collegium, quae vel quod gerit vices alterius, qua gaudet communitas, cujus vices gerit. Ergo ex hoc quod ecclesia universalis non potest contra fidem errare, inferri non potest quod concilium generale non potest contra fidem errare licet gerat vices universalis ecclesiae."

[48] *Ibid.* Pars III. Tr. I. Lib. III. cap. xiii (pp. 830–31).

[49] *Ibid.* Pars I. Lib. VI. cap. xxii (p. 517).

[50] *Ibid.* Pars III. Tr. I. Lib. III. cap. v (p. 822).

[51] *Ibid.*

[52] *Ibid.* cap. viii (p. 825).

[53] II. xix. 4.

[54] II. xx. 4; II. xxi. 10.

[55] See *Def. min.* xii. 5. See above, pp. 215 ff.

So important does Marsilius consider this principle that he applies it to the apostles: they too, in their deliberations on matters of faith, had with them "other more learned believers." [56] It is for this reason that neither the pope alone nor any group of priests alone can be given supreme authority in matters of faith. By virtue of this corrective inclusiveness, therefore, the council elected by the entire church is a general, not a particular, group.

The second difference between the conciliarisms of Marsilius and Ockham follows directly from the first. According to Ockham, there is no essential difference between the ways in which the church is "represented" by the general council and by the pope, since the latter is a "public person" representing the entire community.[57] Hence he declares that the council will normally be called together by the pope, and that just as a heretical pope comes under the jurisdiction of the council, so if a council errs against the faith it becomes subject to the pope.[58] For Marsilius, on the other hand, the general council always remains superior to the pope or "head bishop." It, or the *universitas fidelium*, elects him and can also depose him; [59] and so limited is his authority that Marsilius never characterizes him, like the general council in relation to the church or the ruler in relation to the legislator, as "representing" the church.[60] The council is infallible, but not the pope; hence it is out of the question for the pope to "correct" the council.

Marsilius' position, however, also raises the same problem of positive as against normative interpretation which was seen in his doctrine of the legislator.[61] Indeed, he himself explicitly broaches it: the universal church is infallible on matters of faith; but since it has always believed in the papal primacy as being by divine ordainment, does it not follow that Marsilius' doctrine of the purely human basis of that primacy is in error? [62] The general problem here arises from the conflict between the assertion both of certain positions and of the infallibility of an agency which may contradict those positions; thus it confronts all those who uphold both popular sovereignty and the inviolability of certain political rights or institutions.[63]

[56] II. xvi. 5.

[57] See *Dialogus* Pars I. Lib. v. cap. xxv (p. 494): "sicut concilium generale repraesentat ecclesiam universalem, et ejus vices gerit; ita etiam Papa repraesentat ecclesiam universalem et ejus vices gerit: quia est persona publica totius communitatis gerens vices et curam." See *ibid.* Pars III. Tr. I. Lib. III. cap. ix (pp. 826–27).

[58] *Ibid.* Pars I. Lib. VI. cap. lxiv (p. 571).

[59] II. xxii. 9, 11.

[60] See above, pp. 188–89, 249.

[61] See above, pp. 255–56.

[62] *Def. min.* xi. 3.

[63] The same conflict was latent in Marsilius' principle of the superiority of the whole to the part; for what if the whole had voted for such an arrangement as a plurality of supreme governments, which he had declared "impossible" if the state is to endure? See above, p. 123; and below, p. 314.

But while in the political sphere Marsilius' reply had been to accept the medieval empire as the embodiment of his ideas, thus giving his norms a positive interpretation, his reply now is to distinguish between two ways in which the universal church may state a proposition: as mere customary belief, or as a conclusion propounded by a duly assembled general council. In the latter case, moreover, the conclusion may deal merely with institutional arrangements of the church, or with interpretations of Scripture on matters of faith, belief in which is necessary for salvation. Only, therefore, if each of the second alternatives is fulfilled—conciliar pronouncement as necessary for salvation—is the divine origin of the papal primacy to be accepted. But Marsilius holds that such origin has not been and cannot be established from Scripture, so that the primacy is solely of human origin.[64] The dependence of the pope upon the general council and the whole church remains unshaken. That Marsilius had not interposed similar conditions and distinctions prior to his qualified acceptance of the hegemony of the empire, however, is owing not only to his specific polemical position but also to his widely different conceptions with respect to the importance for society of unified political authority as against the papal headship.

Marsilius' conciliarist position, like that of Ockham, thus reflects his general doctrine of political power. Ockham's embodies the principle of limited circular power: the power of the council is limited by that of the pope, as well as *vice versa*. Marsilius' conciliarism, on the other hand, involves unlimited, unilinear authority: the pope is subject to the council, which is subject only to the whole body of the faithful, which in turn is subject to no one in spiritual matters; and these relations are not reversible.

5. THE CHURCH AND THE STATE

Thus far in this chapter we have been considering the Marsilian church from the standpoint of its internal structure and functioning. This internal concentration, however, has been made only for the sake of convenience; it actually involved an abstraction from the full context of Marsilius' own discussion. That abstraction can now be removed by a single statement: since in "fully developed" (*iam perfectae*) communities the *universitas fidelium* is largely or entirely identical with the *universitas civium,* the church is identical with the legislator, and consequently the supreme authorities in the church and in the state are likewise identical. Hence, in all the phases of ecclesiastic control discussed above—excommunication,

[64] *Def. min.* xi. 3.

election of priests and head bishop, election of general councils and enforcement of their decisions—where the supreme authority over each of these had been assigned to the *universitas fidelium* or "church," this authority belongs by the same token to the legislator.[1]

This, then, is the ultimate unification of the Marsilian politics. We have, indeed, seen its basic background in preceding chapters, where human law coalesced with divine law,[2] and where the "whole" people was the repository of all political power.[3] It now remains only to distinguish more directly its specific elements and consequences. Distinctions are particularly important here, precisely because Marsilius has established from so many different points of view the subordination of the priesthood, the quondam "spiritual power," to the government, the quondam "temporal" or "secular power." If the differences among those points of view are ignored, then one may conclude, as have so many students, that Marsilius "regards the Church as a department of the State,"[4] that for him "the Church is only a function of the State."[5] Yet this conclusion is not entirely correct when it is remembered that he means by "church" the whole body of the faithful, not merely the priests; and that he means by "state" the whole political community of citizens, not merely the government. In Marsilius' own terms, then, it would be far truer to say that the church *is* the state, and vice versa, at least "in perfect communities"; for since the *universitas fidelium* is also the *universitas civium,* both state and church consist in, and are controlled by, the same *populus fidelis* or *legislator fidelis* or *universitas civium fidelium.* It is rather the priesthood which is made a department and a function of the state; but it holds a similar relation to the church.

What, however, is the basis of this unification of citizens (*cives*) and believers (*fideles*)? It is, in the Aristotelian terms recognized by Marsilius, an accidental conjunction. He does, to be sure, apply to it the same Aristotelian notion of "perfection" in the sense of completed development as had papalists like James of Viterbo;[6] for when he distinguishes between those communities which existed "before the conversion of the people," when "the legislator was infidel," and those where the legislator is *fidelis,*

[1] This identification is first made explicitly in connection with the election of priests, which is declared to pertain "in communitatibus fidelium iam perfectis *ad legislatorem humanum solummodo seu fidelium multitudinem* eius loci, super quam intendere debet promovendus minister . . ." (II. xvii. 9). The identification is maintained consistently thereafter.

[2] See above, pp. 163–64.

[3] See above, pp. 217–19.

[4] McIlwain, *op. cit.,* p. 313.

[5] Lagarde, *Marsile,* p. 296. Throughout his book, Lagarde uses "church" in the restricted sense which Marsilius had denied.

[6] See James of Viterbo *De reg. Christ.* I. i(pp. 89 ff.). Augustinus Triumphus *S. de eccl. pot.* qu.I. a.6. Alvarus Pelagius *De planctu eccl.* I. xl (pp. 60–61).

he calls the former communities "less perfect" and the latter "perfect."[7] But this way of putting the distinction has for Marsilius none of the implications which it had for his predecessors. The concept of the "perfect community of believers" involves a kind of "perfection" which is specifically relevant only to the fact that the number of Christians in any given community was at one time too few to allow them to become the legislator. But this does not affect the general "perfection" of any state as such, whether Christian or infidel. Thus Marsilius, unlike the papalist Aristotelians, can refer even to infidel communities as being "perfect,"[8] for such perfection essentially involves only the differentiation of functions for the attainment of the sufficient life, and especially the presence of full-fledged government and law;[9] but none of these—sufficient life, government, law—need be Christian in order to possess their essential characteristics. Moreover, there is no divine plan of history which has led to the Christianization of society, and which requires the political hegemony of the pope; nor is the fact that some "perfect" communities are Christian a consequence of any such necessities as Marsilius finds in "nature," and which he invokes in his own politics. It is rather the "fraudulent" acquisition of temporal power by the papacy which Marsilius makes the object of careful historical analyses exhibiting a striking sensitiveness to the fact and the human agency of change.[10] Here he finds the dominant cause to have been a "wrong opinion and with it perhaps a perverted desire for rulership."[11] But the coincidence of citizens and believers is simply a historical fact and must be recognized as such, nothing more. Hence, to be a citizen is not necessarily to be a Christian; citizenship involves no moral obligations whose satisfaction necessarily entails theological commitments. Thus, while the *fideles* and *cives* are the same in person, they differ in the attributes whereby they have these respective designations;

[7] See II. xvii. 10, where the distinction is between "multitudini minus perfectae" and "in communitate fidelium perfecta." See also II. xvii. 8, 9, 11, 15, 17.

[8] See above, p. 18. Marsilius' view of the "perfect community" as not requiring Christianity is found not only throughout Discourse I, but also in Discourse II; see II. xxii. 15.

[9] See above, pp. 86 ff.

[10] See II. xvi. 14: "Unde tamen et propter quid principalitas pervenerit. . . ." II. xvii. 17: "Unde vero tanta pervenerit *alietas*. . . ." II. xviii. 1: "manifestare ortum et initium. . . ." II. xxii. 16: "Unde vero ad ipsum, et secundum quem modum pervenerit auctoritas haec. . . ." II. xxii. 20: "Quod cur tam *varie* contigerit. . . ." II. xxiii. 1: "ipsiusque initii atque processus, adhuc autem de illis in disconvenientem sibi prioritatis formam et speciem latenti transitu atque serpigine. . . ." II. xxv. 1: "eiusque processus a suo principio. . . ." II. xxv. 8: "hujus rei ortum et mysterium. . . ." II. xxvi. 18: "Sunt igitur quae jam narravimus quaesitorum initia vera, et quae etiam tam debite quam indebite processerunt post haec vel ab hiis. . . ." II. xxvi. 20: "De plenitudine quidem igitur potestatis et modis ipsius, adhuc autem *de illius origine atque progressu*. . . ."

[11] I. xix. 12, 13; II. i. 1; II. xxiii. 6.

in the terms recognized by Marsilius, they are the same in number (*numero*), but differ in essence (*ratione*).[12]

The question still remains, then, as to the relation between the respective grounds of the controls exercised by the believers in their church and by the citizens in their state. Here the answer is of a different kind. For matters of ecclesiastic authority affect the interests of the people not only as Christians interested in eternal life but also as citizens interested in this-worldly goods. So thoroughly do these interests coincide, that in the arguments supporting the control of various ecclesiastic functions by the whole body of believers (apart from the general arguments in behalf of any *universitas* as such, which are uniform for state and church), the civil, secular consequences of those functions are invoked even more frequently than their spiritual ones. We have already noted many examples of how the general consequence of the threatened destruction of the state had been advanced as the ground for control by the legislator and government over many ecclesiastic matters.[13] But specific secular consequences, apposite to each kind of function, are also invoked. The reason why excommunication must be controlled by the whole body of believers is that, while an unjust sentence of excommunication made by a priest would be of no harm to the accused in the future world (since God would not follow such an unjust judgment), the accused "would be harmed most gravely for the status of the present life, because he is defamed and deprived of civil association. And *for this reason* (*propterea*)," excommunication must be controlled by the whole body of the faithful.[14] The expostulatory emphasis upon this secular reason is in striking contrast to the comparative nonchalance with which Bonaventura, Thomas Aquinas, and other commentators on the *Sentences* contemplate the deleterious temporal effects of an unjust excommunication, while concentrating all their attention upon its spiritual effect—as to whether it is "ratified" by God.[15] Similarly,

[12] See above, pp. 263–64 incl. n. 25. The same point was subsequently made by Hooker: "Albeit properties and actions of one kind do cause the name of a commonwealth, qualities and functions of another sort the name of a church to be given unto a multitude, yet one and the selfsame multitude may in such sort be both, and is so with us, that no person appertaining to the one can be denied to be also of the other." *Laws of Ecclesiastical Polity* VIII. i. 3 (*Works* [Oxford, 1875], II, 486). See also Hobbes *Leviathan* chap. XXXIX (p. 252).

[13] See above, pp. 107 ff.

[14] II. vi. 12.

[15] Bonaventura *In Sent.* Lib. IV. dist. 18. pars 2. dub. 2: An unjust sentence of excommunication made by one who has canonic jurisdiction "tenenda est et timenda, quia non est subditorum discutere sententias majorum; et si contemnat, graviter peccat." Albert the Great *In Sent.* Lib. IV. dist. 17. a.63 (XXIX, 758): "Unde licet erret Ecclesia, tamen Deus approbat, quod iste se gerat pro excommunicato, et alii vitent eum. Et qui non vult vitare, vinculum Ecclesiae contemnit, et ideo peccat." See Thomas Aquinas *In Sent.* Lib. IV. dist. 18. qu.2. a.1. quaestiunc. 4 (X, 535); Duns Scotus *Opus Oxon.* Lib. IV. dist. 19. qu. 1 (XIX, 651–52). See also *Corp. jur. can., Decret. Gratiani* Pars II. can. 1. C. XI. qu.3.

if excommunication and the definition of articles of faith are controlled by the priesthood or pope alone rather than by all the believers, then governments can be broken up, removed from their rightful incumbents, and subjected to the power of the pope.[16] Again, one of the reasons why all the believers must control the election of priests to particular pastorates and offices is the "great *civil* harm" which vicious priests can do by seducing women in the confessional.[17]

Concomitantly with these temporal effects of the dispositions of authority in the church, spiritual effects bearing upon the future life are also invoked. A priest elected by other priests alone might teach his flock falsehoods about the means to salvation, and hence lead his flock to their "eternal death"; [18] a pope who had sole power to define articles of faith might similarly erect his own vicious predilections into binding dogma, so that "the whole body of the faithful will be under peril of shipwreck with regard to the faith." [19] Indeed, these "spiritual" consequences are declared to be even more important reasons for their control by the *universitas fidelium* than the temporal ones.[20]

These coalescences of spiritual and secular interests all refer to the political or institutional aspects of the church, to matters of external authority and control. But with respect to the fundamental attitudes, the *ethos,* underlying the respective interests, as we have already seen, there is a flat opposition.[21] Expanding on the ideas of the Spiritual Franciscans, the Cathari, the Waldensians, and other heretical sects, Marsilius conceives Christianity as involving an ascetic negation of all secular values. But the implications of this conception are developed with regard to the priesthood alone, not the other believers. At no point does Marsilius examine what would happen to the secular state, with its basis in biological desires and conflicts for the this-worldly "sufficient life," if all or most of the believers took seriously that "contempt for the world" which he says it is the duty of the priests to "inculcate in others." [22] He assumes, indeed, that most of the "citizen believers" are primarily citizens rather than Christians, that secular rather than religious values are their chief concern. Thus, while he is emphatic regarding the secular consequences of ecclesiastic functions as requiring the control of those functions by the "faithful legislator," he is very moderate with respect to the religious consequences of civil or secular-political functions. As we have seen, if human law or government contradicts divine law, then the latter, not the

[16] II. vi. 13; II. xx. 8.
[17] II. xvii. 12. See above, p. 26, n. 24.
[18] II. xvii. 11.
[19] II. xx. 7.
[20] II. xvii. 12; II. xx. 4.
[21] See above, pp. 79 ff.
[22] II. xi. 3.

former, must be obeyed.[23] But the inference drawn from this is not, as with the papalists, that the pope or priests must control human law because of its possible religious consequences, but rather that the *universitas* is the best guardian of both secular and spiritual interests. Since, however, the *universitas* is also the maker of human law, and the elector of general councils which determine the meaning of disputed articles of divine law, and the only coercive enforcer of those determinations, there is no means for independent control of the religious consequences of secular authority in either state or church.

Is there any way, then, of breaking this complete monopoly of power over ecclesiastic matters by the people-legislator? Marsilius deals with this question only obliquely, by referring to cases where "the legislator and the ruler are infidel." When the Christians are in a minority, who is then to control the designation of priests and the determination of matters of faith? It is still to be all the believers, or at least the "sounder part" (*pars sanior*) of the believers, not the priests alone, although the priests should properly take the lead in such matters.[24] In these cases, the legislator "would prohibit" the appointment of priests and the spreading of Christian doctrine, so that these activities must be carried on "without the ruler's knowledge or consent." [25] To this limited extent, then, Marsilius provides for the autonomy of religion and the church. He does not, however, raise the question of the relation of such an autonomous "sect" to the entire political community of which it is part. What if the legislator should conceive that the preaching of Christian doctrines is inimical to its secular interests, that the divided allegiance of Christians is antithetical to that unity of political authority which is necessary to the preservation of the state? No explicit answer is provided by Marsilius, but the implications of his central emphases are clear.

Marsilius' main position, in any case, is found in his dispositions of authority where the legislator is Christian. Here the legislator brings all its political authority to bear upon the control of ecclesiastic functions: it forces recalcitrant priests to administer the sacraments and perform their other duties,[26] it provides coercive enforcement of the general councils' decisions on matters of faith,[27] and Marsilius also notes that "in ancient times schismatics were compelled by rulers to preserve the unity of the faith." [28] Indeed, so complete is the Marsilian tendency toward coalescence of the church and the state, that whereas in the *Defensor pacis*

[23] See above, p. 162.
[24] II. xvii. 15; II. xxii. 12–15.
[25] II. xvii. 15.
[26] II. xvii. 8, 12, 15.
[27] II. xix. 3; II. xxi. 4.
[28] II. xxviii. 15.

the decisions of general councils are conceived only as non-coercive "judgments in the first sense" requiring ratification by the legislator before they may be coercively binding,[29] in the *Defensor minor* those same decisions are now themselves called "human laws."[30]

We have already examined the relation between this exercise of coercion in religious matters and Marsilius' insistence upon the non-coerciveness of divine law.[31] Its upshot is that the entire corporate political structure of the state is introduced into the church as well, with, however, the important difference that while coercive authority is necessary to the state, it is exercised in the church only at the discretion of the people-legislator. Hence, the people willing, complete freedom of religion may be established,[32] since divine law itself definitely does not command that non-conformists or heretics be punished. On the other hand, the same people's will may act to "establish" religion as a state-controlled institution. On this basic question of coercive enforcement, the relativities of the people's will take the place of the absolute sanctions which the antecedent tradition had derived from God.

There remains another aspect of this question which mitigates still further the sense in which the numerical identity of the state and the church entails control of the latter by an exclusively secular authority. For the priesthood is itself a "part" of the people,[33] and hence too of the church. Consequently, while the priests do not by themselves possess full authority over ecclesiastic matters, they do share in such authority, proportionately not only to their numbers—they will of course be in a minority in the church as a whole—but also to their moral and intellectual qualities, especially since they are the "experts" who have the greatest knowledge of divine law, the specific priestly "character" imprinted by God, and the authority which the community has given them to exercise this authority upon its members. Accordingly, the priests' exercise of their essential sacramental functions is accompanied by their participation in all the institutional authorities examined above—excommunication, definition of articles of faith, and "secondary" appointment of priests to hierarchic positions, to pastorates in particular communities, and to the dispensing of benefices. In all these modes of authority the priests function not only as non-coercive experts or "judges in the first sense"[34] but also

[29] II. xx. 2; II. xxi. 4.

[30] *Def. min.* v. 20: "obligantur Christi fideles ad hujusmodi praecepta et humana statuta per concilium generale quamdiu revocata non fuerint, *propterea quod humanae leges sunt. . . .*"

[31] See above, pp. 158 ff.

[32] See above, pp. 165–66.

[33] See texts cited above, p. 180, n. 8.

[34] See II. vi. 12; II. x. 5, 6; II. xvii. 14; II. xx. 2, 3, 5.

as full-fledged co-holders of the decisive authority with the rest of the "faithful people" or "whole body of faithful citizens." [35]

The holistic side of Marsilius' doctrine—his emphasis that the whole is greater than any of its parts—thus involves not only the subordination of the priesthood to the whole people-church but also its integral inclusion within that whole. Scope is provided, moreover, for the priests' employment of all the devices of persuasion whereby their views may be made to prevail.[36]

While this participation of the priests in ecclesiastic authority is thus made quite clear by Marsilius, their participation in the political authority of the state is left ambiguous. In Discourse I, indeed, the priesthood is explicitly listed as one of the parts of the *honorabilitas*,[37] and hence too of the *universitas civium*.[38] Thus the priesthood would be part of the legislator, which is the supreme authority of the state. But in Discourse II basic restrictions upon such priestly participation are introduced, drawn from considerations similar to those whereby the non-coerciveness of divine law had been established. Christ's subjection to Caesar, his refusal to exercise secular rulership, and his distinction of his "kingdom" from that of this world are adduced to prove that Christ prohibited the priests from having any part in coercive jurisdiction.[39] This point is made explicitly with regard to the priests' exercise of governmental authority; but since the whole body of citizens is the maker of coercive law and the elector of the government which exercises coercive jurisdiction, Christ's prohibition would apply to the priests' participation in legislative authority as well. Particular force is lent to this consideration by the interpretation which Marsilius gives of such texts as St. Paul's "no soldier on service to God entangleth himself in the affairs of this life," [40] as well as by the "contempt for the world" and evangelical poverty which Marsilius holds to pertain to the priestly function.[41]

There is, then, an important ambiguity in Marsilius' doctrine, whereby the priesthood is a part of the state dedicated to the sufficient life in both worlds, participating in the coercive authority required for the state's functioning, and at the same time is prohibited from such participation and inculcates values contrary to the this-worldly sufficient life.[42] This

[35] See II. vi. 12, 13; II. xvii. 14; II. xxi. 9 ff.

[36] See texts cited above, notes 34 and 35.

[37] I. v. I.

[38] I. xiii. 4.

[39] II. iv, *passim*, esp. 13: "Non igitur Christus . . . eis potestatem exercendi saecularia principum iudicia tradidit, neque in quemquam potestatem coactivam, sed hanc ipsis aperte *prohibuit*. . . ."

[40] II Timothy 2:4; quoted II. v. I.

[41] See II. xi–xiv, *passim*. See above, pp. 80 ff.

[42] A particularly important aspect of this ambiguity is found in the discussion of the power of the priesthood with respect to the correction and deposition of the ruler. On the one hand,

ambiguity is indeed only a further manifestation of the unresolved contrariety of the religious and secular spheres which we have seen to be characteristic of Marsilius' Averroist conception of values. It has a further political aspect which reveals a source directly related to the axiological one. For on the one hand, Marsilius emphasizes in many ways the necessary exclusion of the priests from all coercive authority; and indeed he declares that "by Christ's counsel and example, *they must refuse such rulership,* especially in communities of believers, if it is offered to them or bestowed on them by him who has the authority therefor."[43] But on the other hand, Marsilius also makes an exception to this exclusion of the priests from coercive authority: they are to have or exercise no such authority or jurisdiction "unless that jurisdiction shall have been granted to them by the human legislator, in whose power it always is to revoke this jurisdiction from them for a reasonable cause, *the full determination of which* is known to pertain to the same legislator, especially in communities of believers."[44] Thus Marsilius insists both that Christ made it a duty for the priests to refuse coercive jurisdiction even when it is offered to them by the legislator, and that the legislator has the authority of "full determination" as to whether or not the priests shall exercise coercive jurisdiction. This conflict in Marsilius' position, then, is between the complete authority which his secular politics bestows upon the legislator, and the complete credence which his explicit acceptance of the Christian faith makes him give to the words of Christ. Put in other terms, the contradiction is between Marsilius' Aristotelianism of efficient causality, which results in supremacy for the legislator as decisive agent of the state's institutions, and that aspect of his Augustinianism which derives ultimate justification of the state from God.[45] In respect of most questions, as we have seen, he is able to make the latter orientation support the former; but their latent opposition inevitably emerges in such contexts as the one just

---

Marsilius insists that the coercive authority to correct and depose the ruler for any "wrongdoing" belongs only to the human legislator, while the priesthood is "forbidden by sacred Scripture" to have any such authority (*Def. min.* ii. 7). But on the other hand, he declares that "the priests as such, collectively or individually, are not human legislators, *sed fortasse secundum quod pars aliqua civitatis existunt*" (*ibid.* xiii. 9; xvi. 4). The *fortasse* indicates Marsilius' hesitation between the two poles of popular sovereignty (which would admit the priests to a share in coercive authority) and a completely non-coercive, non-political priesthood. Contrast the provision for the pope's participation in correcting and deposing the ruler for both spiritual and temporal offenses, in John of Paris *De pot. reg. et pap.* cap. xiv, xvi (pp. 127, 130–31), and in William of Ockham *Breviloquium* VI. ii (pp. 157–59).

[43] II. iv. title.

[44] II. v. 9. See II. i. 4. See also *Def. min.* xiii. 9: "Non igitur a divina sed ab humana lege convenit cuiquam in hoc saeculo auctoritas et coactiva potestas, praecipue episcopo sive presbytero."

[45] For the similar basis of the conflict in Marsilius with respect to the coercive enforcement of divine law, see above, pp. 161–62.

considered. And it is because the former orientation is ultimately controlling in his doctrine that Marsilius finally gives to the legislator the decisive authority even over the priests' participation in coercive authority: the legislator's authority must be limited by nothing.

What, then, in final summation, is Marsilius' solution of the conflict between the "church" and the "state"? Keeping in mind not only the literal meanings he assigns to the terms involved in the question, but also the fact that the conflict itself was directly over relative "power" or "authority," we may divide his solution into two parts: (1) The priesthood (*not* the "church") must be subject to the coercive authority of the government (*not* the "state") in all *temporal* affairs, both on the temporal grounds centering in the preservation of the state and on the spiritual grounds of divine command. This, however, might be regarded, at least in principle, as part of the traditional Gelasian parallelism, although drastically extended by the large scope assigned to the "temporal grounds." (2) The *universitas* must have supreme authority in any social questions affecting it, *whether temporal or spiritual.* It is here that the *universitas civium,* the "legislator" of the Marsilian state, since it is numerically identical with the *universitas fidelium,* the "church," comes to control the church and the priesthood even in spiritual affairs and on spiritual grounds. To be sure, this control extends only to the institutional aspects of spiritual affairs, not to the "essential" priestly powers as such. But it is an inevitable consequence of the basic orientation and principles of the Marsilian political philosophy [46] that this distinction, like all the others in which the "internal" is compared with the "external," the immanent with the transient, has no political significance even for ecclesiastic or "spiritual" politics. For the effective authority to put the essential priestly powers into institutional operation, throughout the whole range from the sacraments of penance and bestowal of orders to the determination of articles of faith, belongs only to the *universitas civium fidelium,* not to the priests as such. We have already noted the contradictions involved in the relation of this point to Marsilius' complete denial of coercive authority to the priesthood. These contradictions reflect the double dialectic, alternately dualistic and monistic, whereby with respect to priesthood's active possession of authority Marsilius insists upon the difference between spiritual and temporal concerns, while with respect to the authority of the *universitas civium fidelium* he unites these concerns. Thus, side by side with this political unification of spirituals and temporals, as falling under a single omnicompetent authority, Marsilius maintains an ethical separation and even contrariety between them, and in-

[46] See above, pp. 104, 109 ff.

deed a *de facto* superiority of temporal or secular concerns over spiritual or religious ones. The earthly city, the "state" of Discourse I of the *Defensor pacis,* while given all institutional authority over spiritual affairs in Discourse II, loses thereby none of its essential earthliness even while becoming a "church."

The universal republicanism of Marsilius' doctrine is, therefore, integrally related to the superiority he effects for the "temporal power" over the spiritual. For the government always acts as the executive agent of the legislator, which is the *universitas civium;* and wherever this *universitas* is also *fidelis,* the government exercises *within the church* (in the Marsilian sense) the powers lodged in the *universitas fidelium.* It is essential, however, to note this sequence whereby the Marsilian government, the medieval "temporal power" or *regnum,* the modern "state," comes in the Marsilian doctrine to exercise coercive control over the "spiritual power" or *sacerdotium,* the modern "church," even in spiritual affairs. Initially, indeed, the mediation here insisted upon may seem only of verbal importance: the power of Ludwig of Bavaria over the "pope" whose installation he effected at Rome was no less real and complete for the theoretic derivation of the former's power from the people, as is also suggested by the fact that Marsilius' doctrine could be readily adapted to support the dominance of King Henry VIII over the church of England. Yet to see in Marsilius only the precursor of such royal absolutisms is to ignore the insistent republican phase of his doctrine which was continued by Hooker and, through him, by Locke and others.[47] The Marsilian church-state is far more "congregationalist" than royalist, in that it is the local congregation, the *universitas fidelium eius loci,* which on both spiritual and temporal grounds controls such matters as the excommunication of its members, the designation of its priests, and the election of members to the general council, just as it makes the laws and elects the ruler. Indeed, if the congregation so wills, by making "human laws" concerning such matters, it can depose the ruler for heresy and other sins against divine law![48] In any case, it is important to note that there is no trace in Marsilius of that Byzantinism which regarded the king as *Christus domini* and made him head of the church.[49] Moreover, the

[47] See below, p. 304, n. 9. It is also pertinent to note here, especially in connection with the use of Marsilian ideas by absolute monarchs, that the translation of the *Defensor pacis* which William Marshall made for King Henry VIII in 1535 omitted the various sections bearing on the people's election and correction of the ruler (I. ix. 6–11; xv. 1–5; xvi. 11–25; xviii. 1–7). See Previté-Orton's edition, p. 34, n. 1; p. 66, n. 4; p. 75, n. 1; p. 79, n. 4; p. 96, n. 2. See also above, p. 195, n. 109.

[48] See II. xxx. 6.

[49] Cf. *Tract. Eborac.* IV (pp. 665 ff.); Gregory of Catino *Orthodoxa defensio imperialis* cap. ii ff. (pp. 536 ff.). Cf. also F. W. Maitland, *English Law and the Renaissance* (Cam-

Marsilian system, viewed in its totality, provides the considerations which in modern times were to lead to the disestablished church and freedom of religion as well as to the established church and politically enforced religion. For when "legislators" came to see the injustice, or the inexpediency, or at least the needlessness of coercion in religious matters—and essential arguments for all three of these are presented in the *Defensor*—the sole ground of such coercion, according to the *Defensor,* was removed.[50] The Marsilian doctrine of the relation of church and state thus propounds the bases of all the solutions which modern secular states were to follow. Common to all these solutions, and the invariant aspect of Marsilianism, was the complete subordination in temporal affairs of the "church" to the "state," the removal of all temporal power from the priesthood. But it is an oversimplification of Marsilius' position to ignore the various considerations presented in it which promote the multiplicity of solutions by which this outcome was effected.

---

bridge, 1901), p. 14. A similar difference separates Marsilius from Hobbes' position that the "civil sovereign" is "the one chief pastor" of the church and therefore has the authority to administer all the sacraments (*Leviathan* chaps. xxxix, xlii [pp. 253, 295 ff.]).

[50] Cf. above, pp. 165–66.

CHAPTER VIII

THE SIGNIFICANCE OF MARSILIUS

THE IMPACT of Marsilius on the political developments of the two centuries following his composition of the *Defensor pacis* can be traced with some degree of precision.[1] Undoubtedly many further signs of that impact remain to be uncovered in the voluminous writings and documents of the period which are still unedited; but that he was being read and that his ideas were having their effect is shown by the violent denunciation, enthusiastic espousal, literal quotation, and other explicit mention of Marsilius which can be found in many of the major figures from Pope John XXII in 1327 [2] through Dietrich of Niem [3] and Nicholas of Cusa [4] among the conciliarists of the fifteenth century, to the period of the Reformation,[5] especially among the henchmen of Henry VIII of England.[6] He was cited by Hooker [7] and, at the beginning of the seventeenth century, by

[1] For references to and uses of Marsilius during these centuries, including editions of the *Defensor,* see especially James Sullivan, "Marsiglio of Padua and William of Ockham," *American Historical Review,* II (1904), 593–604. For the history of the manuscripts, see Sullivan, "The Manuscripts and Date of Marsiglio of Padua's *Defensor Pacis,*" *English Historical Review,* XX (1905), 293 ff.; R. Scholz, "Zur Datierung und Uberlieferung des *Defensor Pacis* von Marsilius von Padua," *Neues Archiv.* XLVI (1927), 490 ff.; Scholz's edition of the *Defensor,* pp. v ff.; Previté-Orton's edition, pp. xxvi ff.

[2] See the bulls of John in MGH, *Constitutiones,* Vol. VI, Part I, nn. 274, 361 (pp. 185 ff., 265 ff.). See also the tracts written at John's instigation by Sybert von Beek, William of Cremona, Peter of Lutra, Andreas de Perusio, and others, collected in R. Scholz, *Unbekannte kirchenpolitische Streitschriften aus der Zeit Ludwigs des Bayern, 1327–1354* (Rome, 1914), Vol. II. Also Alvarus Pelagius *De planctu ecclesiae* I. lxviii (p. 274).

[3] Dietrich incorporated many passages from the *Defensor* in an untitled work on the calling of general councils edited for the first time by H. Heimpel in *Sitzungsberichte der Heidelberger Akad. der Wissenschaften,* Phil.-hist. Klasse, Vol. XX, Abhandlung I (Heidelberg, 1929). On Dietrich's borrowings in the *De modis uniendi et reformandi ecclesia in concilio universali* (1410) see J. Haller, *Papsttum und Kirchenreform* (Berlin, 1903), p. 508.

[4] See *De concordantia catholica* II. xxxiv (p. 596).

[5] During the sixteenth century many defenders of the papacy accused Luther of having derived his doctrines from Marsilius, and undertook to refute the latter. In addition to Albertus Pighius *Hierarchia ecclesiastica* Lib. v, see especially Antonius Floribellus *De auctoritate ecclesiae* (in *Bibliotheca maxima pontificia,* ed. J. T. Roccaberti [Rome, 1698], IV, 245 ff.); Antonius Paulutius *Jurisprudentia sacra* I. vii (*ibid.,* IV, 272–73); Christianus Lupus *Dictatus S. Gregorii VII Pontificis* (*ibid.,* VI, 437–38); John of Turrecremata *Summa de potestate papali* II. xlv-xlvii (*ibid.,* XIII, 333–36); Dominicus Gravina *Liber praescriptionum adversus haereses* (*ibid.,* VIII, 374); Dominicus Jacobatius *Tractatus de concilio* (*ibid.,* IX, 512); Franciscus Suarez *De summo pontifice* (*ibid.,* XII, 594).

[6] See works cited above, p. 4, n. 5; also d'Entrèves, "La fortuna di Marsilio da Padova in Inghilterra."

[7] *Laws of Ecclesiastical Polity* VII. xi. 8, note (*Works* [Oxford, 1865], II, 385).

Althusius.[8] There is a strong presumption, but no conclusive evidence, that he was read by Machiavelli and Hobbes; and if Hooker actually derived from Marsilius all or part of the ideas which the parallels between their statements would seem to indicate, then an influence of Marsilius on Locke would be by no means impossible.[9]

The significance of Marsilius, however, as of any writer who deserves to be called a political philosopher, extends far beyond these items of literal influence, actual or conjectured. The questions with which Marsilius dealt, and the answers he gave, are of profound importance for the understanding of the modern world. They involve the basis, content, and validity of a secular morality and politics, and the nature and justification of popular sovereignty; issues whose contemporaneity is continuous, as indeed the shifting interpretations and evaluations of Marsilius have made clear. For his renewed popularity in the past century was in no small part the result of the heritage of the modern Enlightenment, which found a praiseworthy rationalism and humanism in the fact that he, like the other Averroists and like Hume, was skeptical of the rational foundations of revealed religion and critical of its upholders. Even more, the sequence whereby Marsilius has passed from being a "democrat" to being a "totalitarian" has largely been the result of the reëstimation which the ideas of Rousseau and the French Revolution have undergone in recent decades. When those ideas were regarded as fully valid, Marsilius' assertion of unlimited popular sovereignty classified him as a liberal democrat; but as various developments in the twentieth century led to the resurrection of the conviction that giving political power to the people would not of itself guarantee the solution of social problems, and especially as régimes arose which made manifest once again the evils of unlimited power, his doctrine has stood convicted as being similarly totalitarian; and this latter is the current fashion in Marsilian commentary. Indeed, the completion of the circle is shown by the fact that the guarantee of democracy and freedom is now in many quarters held to depend upon adherence to the very doctrines and authorities the liberation from which earlier made Mar-

[8] *Politica methodice digesta* xxviii. 32 (ed. C. J. Friedrich [Cambridge, Mass., 1932], p. 265).

[9] In addition to the parallels cited by Previté-Orton from Book VIII of *Laws of Ecclesiastical Polity* (see above, p. 4, n. 5), there are some striking similarities in expression as well as in doctrine between the *Defensor* and Book I, Chapter x of the *Laws*—the chapter from which Locke quotes frequently in the *Second Treatise on Civil Government*. For other aspects of Marsilius' influence on Hooker and his time, see A. P. d'Entrèves, *Riccardo Hooker* (Turin, 1932), pp. 57 ff.; F. J. Shirley, *Richard Hooker and Contemporary Political Ideas* (London, 1949), *passim*.

silius the exponent of rationalism and freedom. Nor is he the only important political thinker the interpretation of whom has undergone such shifts.[10]

Despite these difficulties of interpretation in which commentators on Marsilius appear to be involved because of the very contemporaneity of his ideas, a fair estimate of the significance of his doctrine and of its place in the history of political thought is not impossible if the character of his leading concepts and arguments, and their relation to those of his immediate predecessors and contemporaries, are kept in view.

The basis of Marsilius' departure from the medieval tradition consists initially in the fact that he dropped that tradition's emphasis upon ultimate normative values as the justification of the state and as the central concern of political philosophy. The referral of all political institutions to God for their legitimacy—a referral which was matched in other ages by an appeal to the Idea of the Good, or to an Eternal Law of Right Reason—was standard in the middle ages until the translation of Aristotle's *Politics* in the middle of the thirteenth century. In taking over the naturalistic basis which Aristotle had established for the state, philosophers substituted in varying degrees a this-worldly end for the supernatural end of union with God, but the former was still conceived as being ordered toward the latter and as itself consisting in the maximal development of the moral and intellectual virtues. In contradistinction from both these positions, Marsilius, while also treating the state, at least in part, as being justified by certain values whose attainment it renders possible, conceived them as being based essentially upon natural (in the sense of biological, not rational) desire, not upon theological love or rational apprehension. Hence, far from emphasizing the heights of moral, intellectual, or theological virtue, those values consist in the "proper proportioning" of men's actions and passions, with no attempt to elevate some of these above others, and in general socio-economic goods.[11]

Compared with the medieval tradition, then, Marsilius' values were much more moderate. They effected a sharp reversal of the distinctions among values which had been central to his predecessors' positions. The human as against the animal, reason as against desire, the noble as against the necessary, the theoretic as against the practical, the theological as against

[10] Not to mention the well-known phases in the interpretation of Machiavelli, reference may be made to recent discussions of Locke which hold that his doctrine is "collectivist in the extreme" (W. Kendall, *John Locke and the Doctrine of Majority-Rule* [Urbana, Ill., 1941], pp. 53, 66, 72), and "potentially totalitarian" (H. Johnston, "Locke's Leviathan," *The Modern Schoolman,* XXVI [1948–49], p. 210).

[11] I. v. 3, 4; I. xix. 2.

the secular—in these and other distinctions Marsilius gave either controlling or at least equal importance to the latter half.[12] His values were hence inclusive, not exclusive or hierarchic; they constituted the "*common* benefit" in a far more direct sense than was the case for many other Aristotelians who made the common benefit the end of government.[13] As a consequence, Marsilius' values were within both the reach and the control of all men, not only of a few who (as in the case of the intellectual virtues) could alone attain them or (as in the case of the theological virtues) could alone give the authoritative direction required for them. The motivation of Marsilius' axiological reversal is to be found, indeed, not only in his views as to values themselves but also in this shift which it makes possible in the locus of political authority.

This reversal meant, however, that from the standpoint of the medieval tradition Marsilius had removed the controlling position of moral and religious norms, of natural and divine law. These were no longer placed above the state as conditions of its legitimacy; rather, it was only insofar as such values were objects of natural desire, or means to such objects, that they entered into politics. The political consequence of this shift was to take away the foundation of the claims of the papalists, who derived from the objective absoluteness of these norms the justification of the papal hegemony. Yet the frequent inference that the failure to base the state on these norms condemns the Marsilian politics to amoralism or worse would appear to be overhasty. His concern with justice and the common benefit is no less genuine because he conceives these as being defined initially, so far as the state is concerned, by men's natural desires rather than by rational or theological criteria; for, once thus defined, the means to the attainment of the common benefit, and thus of justice, are objective and susceptible of rational inquiry. Hence it would seem far more correct to say that his reversal of the traditional norms effected a change from one conception of the content of morals in relation to politics, to a different conception of that content. From the standpoint of the latter conception, indeed, it would be easy to reverse the charge of immoralism, for the fact that one segment of the medieval tradition could erect a doctrine of plenitude of power while retaining the limitations set by natural and divine law made it quite clear that the doctrine of "higher laws" did not constitute as much of a moral restriction on political power—in the sense of "moral" indicated by the Marsilian view of the common benefit—as is commonly supposed. Further point is lent to this consideration by the manner in which Marsilius, despite his removal of the limitations set by the higher

[12] See above, pp. 60–66, 78 ff.

[13] See above, pp. 203–5.

laws, could espouse a popular sovereignty and an important lessening of the punitive sanctions which had been imposed on heretics and others in the name of the very values included under those laws.

The moderation which Marsilius introduced into the values basic to politics differentiates his doctrine from that of Machiavelli in the *Prince* as much as from that of his medieval predecessors. Since those values are initially defined by the natural desires common to "all men," they are distinct from the egocentric power-drive which is the primary axiological orientation of Machiavelli's prince, just as the republican framework of political authority which Marsilius sees to be necessary for the achievement of those values prevents that concentration upon methods of self-aggrandizement which is possible to an autocratic ruler, and which is the hallmark of Machiavellianism. The relation between Marsilius and Ludwig of Bavaria, therefore, cannot be too closely assimilated to that between Machiavelli and Cesare Borgia or Lorenzo de' Medici. The *pars principans* of Marsilius is not a "prince" in the modern sense in which the Florentine distinguished "principates" from "republics,"[14] nor are the "virtues" of Marsilius' "perfect ruler"[15] the *virtù* exalted for the "prince" by Machiavelli.[16]

The same axiological orientation which removes Marsilius' position both from his medieval predecessors and from Machiavellianism operates, however, to assimilate it closely to the less spectacular but more pervasive non-Machiavellian secular bourgeois values of the modern era, as expressed in some of the most characteristic phases of its political philosophy. Indeed, the Marsilian doctrine in this respect provides important clues to the manner in which the medieval political conceptions gave way to the orientation of modern republicanism. The theory of the modern republican state, like that elaborated by Marsilius, is marked not only by its secularism but also by its distinction of political ends—the goods which living in a state enables men to achieve—from the maximal moral and intellectual values with which the medieval Aristotelians had equated them. On this point, there is a remarkably familiar ring in Marsilius' conception of the benefits of civil peace as consisting in such values as the mutual aid and association of the citizens, their exchanges of their products and services, their "freedom," their "power, unimpeded from without, of exercising their proper and common functions."[17] These were the goods which motivated the *popolani* of Padua rather than the clergy or the *magnati* or

[14] *Il principe* cap. i, ii; *Discorsi sopra la prima deca di Tito Livio* I. ii.
[15] See *Def. pac.* I. xiv; and above, pp. 243–44.
[16] See *Il principe* cap. viii, xvii, xviii.
[17] I. xix. 2. See I. xii. 6, 7. See above, pp. 59, 64–65, 220 ff.

those latter-day descendants of the *signori* who were exemplified in Machiavelli's *Prince*. But the modern bourgeoisie took to the political arena largely for the defense of these same values. It is thus in Marsilius that the bourgeois state finds its first thorough spokesman. Hence, despite underlying differences, there is a distinct similarity between the Marsilian values just enumerated and the goods which Machiavelli regarded as the "common utility" (*comune utilità*) deriving to men living in a republic—"the power freely to enjoy their property without any worry, to have no fear for the honor of one's wife, one's daughters, or oneself" [18]—and which Locke regarded as the end for which men form a political society—"their comfortable, safe, and peaceful living, one amongst another, in a secure enjoyment of their properties, and a greater security against any that are not of it." [19] This emphasis on security had indeed been found in some of the medieval Aristotelians as well,[20] but they had regarded it only as a means to the achievement of heights of personal excellence, for which the state properly exists. Like Marsilius, then, the moderns have dropped this latter goal, at least so far as politics is concerned: the typical citizen is no longer the theologically or aristocratically virtuous man but rather the bourgeois merchant or artisan desiring above all else to be secure in what he has, and requiring for this security that he be free in the sense of controlling the laws and government under which he lives. Indeed, it is this moderateness in aspiration which largely underlies the shift espoused by republicanism in the locus of political authority from the pope or the supremely virtuous king to the whole body of citizens.[21]

There was, however, a second respect in which Marsilius departed from the axiological position of the medieval tradition, and which crossed his republicanism with a seemingly opposed political orientation. Just as the emphasis on security could be combined, as in Hobbes, with the reverse of freedom in the sense of self-government, so Marsilius' doctrine, in some of its most pervasive phases, is marked not, as before, by a shift from one set of ends to another but rather by a comparative lack of concern with any ends at all, other than the unimpeded functioning of government and law and the preservation of the state. This preoccupation is closely related to the preceding point; for since his generalized values were not differentiated on moral, intellectual, or religious grounds from a multiplicity of other, merely apparent values, Marsilius did not find it necessary, as had his

[18] *Discorsi sopra la prima deca di Tito Livio* I. xvi.

[19] *Second Treatise on Civil Government* viii. 95.

[20] See above, pp. 110, 126–27.

[21] See above, p. 66 and n. 89.

predecessors, to engage in lengthy arguments over comparative values;[22] the whole axiological question lost the central urgency which it occupied in past political philosophies. This change in orientation was in good part a reaction against the axiological emphasis by which the papalists had supported their claims, and against the resulting jurisdictional confusion which had brought many parts of Europe close to anarchy. The questions which now became paramount were concerned with the specifically political functions of the state, and especially with the necessary conditions of its preservation; hence they were applicable to any state, regardless of whether or not its people controlled the laws and the government. Abstraction was thus made from even the generalized moral values to which Marsilius had previously dedicated the state: morals and politics were distinguished in greater detail and degree than ever before in the middle ages.

The effect of this new orientation was to define with exceptional sharpness the conditions of the functioning of political authority as such, separated from the intrusions which the papalists had introduced into them. First, political authority means coercive authority; it is in terms of coerciveness that law, government, and the entire political structure of the state are to be defined. Thus the unity of the state is determined by the necessary requirements of the functioning of coercive authority, and the order of the state is determined by the control of such authority. Secondly, therefore, the basic questions of politics are questions not of final causes—"to what ultimate ends must political institutions conform to be legitimate?"—but rather of efficient causes—"by what agency must those institutions be controlled, that is, from whom must coercive authority be derived?" Thirdly, since the functioning of political authority is not determined by antecedent objective norms which must be rationally apprehended, but consists essentially in the giving of coercive commands, will rather than reason becomes the supreme political agency. Political *science,* to be sure, is ultra-rational, for the necessary conditions of the functioning of political agencies can be known and set forth in a demonstrative system. But the *subject matter* of political science is volitional rather than rational, since both the agents and the patients of political authority are defined by their respective wills. The basic political acts, consequently, are those of legislative command deriving from will or election, and of coercive judg-

[22] See Thomas Aquinas *De reg. princ.* I. vii–xv. Egidius of Rome *De reg. princ.* Lib. I. Pars. I. cap. iv-xii; Lib. III. Pars I. cap. ii; and *passim*. Dante *De mon.* I. iii (pp. 342–43). See also the discussion of the "argument from ends," above, pp. 104 ff.

ment deriving from that command; they are no longer the interpretive judgment which is an application of the rational principles of some higher law. Fourthly, politics is concerned with transient acts rather than immanent acts. It deals only with the external interrelations among men, since only these are capable of affecting the preservation of the state or of being controlled by political authority. This point is not contradictory to the voluntarist orientation just expounded, for it is the overt acts deriving from the will, rather than the internal acts of the will itself, that are relevant to politics. Thus Marsilius dropped completely the antecedent concern of politics with the inculcation of the virtues conceived as habits of character involving desire and knowledge. Politics aims not to make men "good" in this internal sense, but only to regulate their external acts when they affect other men. The personification of political authority is now no longer the teacher, the priest, or the philosopher, but solely the coercive judge. The internalism of Aristotle's finalistic orientation and of the Christian tradition gives way to an externalist emphasis similar to the legalism of the Roman tradition, but without the latter's "natural" law.

These determinations of the necessary conditions of the functioning of political authority, elaborated by Marsilius in opposition to the theologism with which the papalists had identified politics, comprise a calculus of power which is an important contribution to the development of the theory of sovereignty. Whether or not Marsilius was read by Machiavelli, Bodin, or Hobbes, as he was by Althusius, there can be no doubt that he is their forerunner in this respect. His doctrine clearly marks, in a way in which the morally and theologically oriented medieval theories of the universal church and empire do not, the point where the multiplicity of feudal and ecclesiastic jurisdictions, and the dualism of the traditional church-state allocation, gave way to the monism of authority in which the modern conception of the sovereign state consists.

Yet this aspect of Marsilius' doctrine, while it contains some of his most striking emphases, is not the whole of it. It must be combined with the aspect previously examined, which directly underlies his republicanism, if it is to be true to his entire doctrine. Thus each of the four points enumerated above requires an addition: first, political authority as Marsilius conceives it will be not only coercive but also just, that is, in accordance with the common benefit; for, secondly, it is ultimately dedicated to the end of assuring at least the minimal conditions for men's attainment of the sufficient life; hence, thirdly, the will which controls political authority must be that of the whole people; just as, fourthly, it is men's desire for the sufficient life and for freedom which motivates the entire process. What emerges from this recombination of the two separated aspects of Marsilius' doctrine is thus a popular sovereignty in which the will of the whole people, possessed of complete coercive authority, necessarily aims at and attains the common benefit. Hence the people's authority becomes absolutely unlimited; no appeal can be made to any ends or values outside it.

It would seem to be on this ground that recent commentators have taken to calling Marsilius a totalitarian.[23] If totalitarianism means unlimited political power, then this charge is indeed justified by his use and interpretation of the concepts of "unity" and "the whole," and his removal of the limitations which the antecedent tradition had imposed on positive law through natural and divine law. But if the the term "totalitarianism" be taken as meaning that the unlimited power in question is held by a relatively small ruling group, which exercises it over the people with no opposition permitted—and this is the usual connotation of the term—then the explicit doctrine of Marsilius is emphatically not totalitarian, for he insists that the unlimited authority can belong only to the whole people, from which alone both the laws and the government must derive their authority. The issue is not, however, so clear-cut as this explicit doctrine might seem to make it: the twentieth century, like other epochs, including that of the Roman Empire, has presented many instances in which the sovereignty explicitly claimed to belong to the people has been largely fictional, with actual sovereignty being held by one man or a small clique; and Marsilius' willingness to accept the possibility that the people "transferred" its legislative authority to the emperor [24] may seem similar to the manner in which some modern dictatorships have claimed an original "democratic" basis for their power. Yet, as we have seen,[25] this interpretation of his doctrine of the people as legislator is not supported by the central arguments and explications which he gives to it, such as his insistence that the citizens must be "free" in the sense of making their own laws,[26] and his repeated provision for freedom of dissent during the process of debating proposed legislation.[27] But the complexities inherent both in Marsilius' position and in the more general problem at issue are such that even this espousal of freedom does not settle the question. For his combination with it of an emphasis upon the unity and wholeness of political authority, such that there remain no private "rights" exempt from the authority of the whole people, makes the whole absolutely omnicompetent, whether the matter concern property, religion, functional occupation, or anything else.

[23] See above, p. 6, n. 17.

[24] See above, pp. 249–50.

[25] See above, pp. 252 ff.

[26] I. xii. 5. See above, pp. 220 ff.

[27] See above, p. 169 and n. 18.

The full understanding of Marsilius' position in this respect, however, requires that it be viewed in the context of his own time and the preoccupations engendered thereby. We have seen that many aspects of his "totalitarianism" are common to other political thinkers of his period.[28] More specifically, his work is a graphic illustration of the political truth that extremes give rise to the contrary extremes. The doctrine of the papal plenitude of power, which was the specific object of his polemic, had many of the characteristics now considered totalitarian.[29] Thus the Marsilian and the papal doctrines are remarkably isomorphic: the legislative sovereignty of the people and the plenitude of power of the pope are both absolute. If the submission of the papacy to natural and divine law, despite the fact that it largely controlled the interpretation of such law,[30] be regarded as mitigating its absoluteness, the derivation of the Marsilian people's sovereignty from that natural desire for the sufficient life which necessarily aims at and attains the common benefit is a similar mitigation. In either case, there is an instructive lesson in the structural similarity of outcome of the two doctrines starting from seemingly opposed termini of the axiological scale. Indeed, the extent to which Marsilius separates politics from morals can also be explained in large part by the fact that the papalists had so interpreted all moral values that any invocation of them led inevitably to the papal hegemony.

Yet the basic intent and scope of Marsilius' doctrine are not understood if it is viewed merely as the substitution of one absolutism for another. The fact that the sovereignty he espoused pertained to the people and not to the pope is highly important. It meant, for Marsilius, the difference between freedom and slavery in the sense of control by an authority not deriving from oneself; and it meant also the difference between authority which would work for the common benefit and that which, despite its invocation of the highest norms, would pervert authority to its private interest. These differences, which are obscured when attention is centered solely on the extent of authority, were crucial for Marsilius, as they were to be in most of the developments in the modern democratic tradition.

This popular control of political authority also led to a relativism which distinguishes his doctrine further from the papal absolutism. For it meant that coercive authority, far from having its objects fixed by absolute norms beyond the people's control, was to be applied only as the people willed. The significance of this point can be seen if one remembers such of its results as the declaration that whether or not heresy is to be punished

[28] See above, p. 112, n. 134.

[29] See above, pp. 8, 18, 102, 114, 119, 257.

[30] See above, pp. 284–85.

depends solely upon what human law prescribes, as against the mandatory compulsions on which most of Marsilius' predecessors had insisted.[31] Thus the basis was removed from the priestly threats and applications of this-worldly punishment for sinning against divine law, which were so pervasive a phase of medieval life. An important part of Marsilius' doctrine is hence the assertion that law and government are to be conceived in terms not primarily of some specific content but rather of their form—coerciveness—and their source—the people. The general consequence of this assertion is the familiar one that the area of freedom is defined by the silence of the laws. But since it is the people which controls the laws, the objects coming under coercive control similarly depend upon the people. In view of this dependence, Marsilius' position may indeed be considered a popular absolutism. But this must then be regarded as a potential absolutism, not necessarily as one which is actually put into operation. The extent to which it becomes actual is itself relative to the people's will. The potentially liberating import of this relativism may be further grasped by considering such a statement as that "if human law did not prohibit anyone from becoming drunk, or making and selling shoes according to his means or desires, or practising medicine, or teaching, or working at other such functions as he pleased, then no one who became drunk, or who acted wrongly in any occupation, would be punished."[32] When it is remembered that the priesthood is one of the "functions" exercised in the state, it can be seen that Marsilius' relativistic conception of the content of coercive authority can eventuate in freedom of the priesthood from all control by the legislator and government, as well as in the reverse. Moreover, the fact that the controls whose exercise he specified for political authority were justified primarily by their being necessary conditions required for the preservation of the state meant that, given different historical circumstances, the content of those controls would itself be altered. But with the papalists' grounding of the claim to absolute control on the unchanging values embodied in their divine mission, such relativity and mitigation of authority would not be possible.

The contrast of this relativism with the absolutism wherein Marsilius positively asserts the necessity for control of the membership and performance of all the functional parts of the state,[33] may be used to sum up the complexities of his entire doctrine. It involves the concomitant assertion of the following five propositions: (1) The essence of political authority is its coerciveness. (2) Political authority must be unified: there must ul-

[31] See above, pp. 122–23, 165–66, 302.

[32] II. x. 3. See II. x. 8; and above, p. 122.

[33] See above, pp. 111 ff.

timately be only one source of coercion in the state. (3) This source must be the people, acting as legislator, and electing the government of the state. (4) For the preservation of the state it is necessary that the last two propositions be fulfilled, and that, in addition, the membership of all the functional parts of the state be determined, and their performance controlled, by the government acting as coercive agent of the people. (5) Men "who live a civil life" (*viventes civiliter*) attain a "sufficient life."

It is from the relations among these five propositions that arise the difficulties in the interpretation of Marsilius' doctrine. The contrast between his absolutism and his libertarian relativism, for example, stems from the relation of Proposition 4 to Propositions 1 and 3; for from these latter it follows that in the absence of the people's legislative enactment, membership in and performance of any of the functional parts of the state are entirely free from any coercive control. Yet Proposition 4 asserts that if such control is lacking the state will not be preserved. It follows, then, that the people cannot in fact do as it will in making the laws; and yet it is ultimately the sole judge of what is required for the preservation of the state. The general point here at issue derives from the parallel assertion both of unlimited authority and of a definite content to which that authority must conform; for the latter constitutes a limit upon the former. A similar unbalance is to be found in the relation of Propositions 1 and 2 to Proposition 5; for unified coercive authority does not, as such, guarantee that the common benefit will be aimed at, let alone attained. Indeed, none of the five propositions, viewed in isolation from the rest, is necessarily connected with the others. Yet if the intent of Marsilius is to be grasped, the integral interconnection of all of these propositions in his complete doctrine must be recognized. It is through Proposition 3, and through the relation of that proposition to the first principles of his entire system, that this interconnection is effected. For Marsilius the whole people, and it alone, can be trusted with supreme political authority, for while any partial group, including the priesthood, may pervert power to its own selfish interests, or may be otherwise unable to discern what is required for the common benefit, the people "cannot be thus misled, either in civil affairs . . . or in spiritual affairs." [34] The doctrine thus returns to its starting point.

The strength of Marsilius' political philosophy lies in its concentrated analysis of the specifically political conditions of the functioning and preservation of a state conceived in terms of values and controls derived from the will of the people. Its weakness, correlatively, lies in the shallowness of

[34] II. xxi. 3.

its treatment of the moral values which must underlie political authority. These features, as we have seen, were themselves the well-nigh inevitable consequences of the kind of project he set for himself. The outcome of that project—viewed in the sense not so much of direct causal influence as of the conception of man and society which it exhibited—was the modern world. That the Marsilian doctrine is thus prophetic and, what is more important, illuminative of basic aspects of the ideas and institutions we call "modern" can be accepted even amid the recognition of the great complexity of the components of both the "medieval" and the "modern" periods of western history, and also amid the further recognition that Marsilius' doctrine, like that of all great revolutionary doctrinaires, combines aspects of the old with the new. Thus it is no accident that Marsilianism can be described by the same epithets customarily assigned to the modern era: naturalism, secularism, movement away from hierarchic controls and toward a libertarian individualism mingled with egalitarian collectivism. Any final judgment of Marsilius' achievement, therefore, must reflect one's attitude toward some of the most pervasive aspects of modern times. The opposition of judgments is an intelligible consequence of this fact: he was the herald of the faceless mass man uprooted from traditional ideas and practices, and also of the free-thinking, independent democrat; of immoral, irreligious politics and also of a politics rescued from the obscurantist appeals which masked the power-drives of vested interests. It requires no wholehearted acceptance of every aspect of the modern world, however, to recognize the sense in which the Marsilian doctrine represented an important force for human enlightenment, not only through its negative attack on the theologico-political authoritarianism of the middle ages but also through the confidence in the people's own abilities which it substituted for that authoritarianism. In this confidence, indeed, lies the crucial feature of the Marsilian system.

The problems of popular sovereignty raised by Marsilius' political philosophy have persisted to the present day, and his solution was one which many modern democratic theories were to imitate. Any doctrine which entrusts complete power to a single agency, even if that be the whole people, is confronted by these problems, just as complementary problems arise for any doctrine which indicates the limits of power but not the agency which shall enforce them. It may be granted that Marsilius' doctrine was a liberating one in the sense that it made the people's own will the sole source of coercion in the state, as against the external controls on whose imposition the papalists insisted. The unlimited authority he gave to the whole people thus meant not merely, or even primarily, the subjection of the priests to the civil authority, but rather that the people could pursue its interests as it conceived them and control its destiny through its own laws and government, free from the constant coercion and interference of the priests invoking divine law. It may also be allowed that his refusal to permit the division of political authority was designed to rectify the abuses of his own time as found in its jurisdictional confusion and in the exemption of the priesthood from the common standards of justice and the other common obligations of citizenship. Finally, it may even be admitted that any invocation, against Marsilius' position, of the need for limitations upon political power is confronted by the concomitant need for some human agency to fix and control those limitations; and any espousal of an agency other than, ultimately, the people for the authority over such control is confronted by the dangers which he indicated. When it is remembered that in the United States the control even over the Constitution and the Bill of Rights rests ultimately, as a matter of constitutional provision, with the people, and that in the democracy of Great Britain the people's control over the legislative body is not limited even by a written constitution, the arguments against the Marsilian popular sovereignty are seen to be less facile than they might at first appear.

Yet with all due allowance for these factors, it is still possible to recognize a solution of the problems raised by Marsilius which will avoid not only the dangers and errors against which he was striving, but also the clear dangers found in his own doctrine. In the first place, it is possible to assign supreme and undivided authority to the people, and yet to set up constitutional limitations with respect to the exercise of that authority by the people or its representatives—limitations which, while ultimately deriving from the people itself, embody long-range conditions and criteria of the just exercise of power to which the people is committed. Thus Marsilius' emphasis upon the supreme efficient causality of the people could be compatible with an explicit indication of the people's own limitation of its authority, so that the area of freedom from coercion, as well as the conditions of the exercise of coercion, would be defined in clear terms, as against being made relative to whatever might happen to be omitted from the laws. In the second place, while one may agree both that the "whole" people must have supreme authority and that ultimately, in such matters as affect the preservation of the society, the "common benefit" is the same for all the parts of this whole, it is yet possible to recognize that the whole people comprises many different parts having many particular interests and values which are not identical with nor simply reducible to the dimension of association falling under the political authority. It may be granted that Marsilius accepted the legitimate existence of such diversity in the specifically political sphere by providing for the free expression of different opinions during the law-making process. Nevertheless, in interpreting the Aristotelian conception of the state as the complete community to mean that the government acting for the whole could control all aspects of social life, he enunciated a doctrine which, to a greater degree than in any of the other non-papalist Aristotelians, could lead to a monolithic suppression of all diversity. It is undoubtedly true that his absorption of all matters bearing on religion and learning into the competence of the state's political authority was motivated largely by the similar absorption claimed by the papalists. But if he had countered their monistic subjection of all values to the theological, not by a similar monism centering in the preservation of the state, the "wholeness" of the people, and the "unity" of its authority, but by a recognition of the normal autonomy of other values in relation to the political, the dangers presented by his doctrine could have been avoided. It was by the development of the practices and institutions implicit in such constitutionalist and pluralist emphases that some of the most important phases of modern democracy were to advance beyond the Marsilian doctrine, which exhibits in so many other respects the genesis and the rationale of the modern state.

BIBLIOGRAPHY

1. WORKS BY MARSILIUS OF PADUA

Defensor minor. Ed. C. K. Brampton. Birmingham, 1922.
Defensor pacis. Ed. C. W. Previté-Orton. Cambridge, 1928.
—— Ed. R. Scholz. Hanover, 1932.
Tractatus de iurisdictione imperatoris in causis matrimonialibus. In *Monarchia s. Romani imperii,* ed. M. Goldast (Frankfort, 1611–14), II, 1386–90.
Tractatus de translatione imperii. In *Monarchia s. Romani imperii,* ed. M. Goldast (Frankfort, 1611–14), II, 147–53.

2. SOURCES [1]

A. Doctrinal Works

Albert the Great. Commentarii in libros Sententiarum. In *Opera omnia,* ed. A. Borgnet (Paris, 1890–99).
—— In Ethicorum libros. In *Opera omnia,* ed. A. Borgnet (Paris, 1890–99), Vol. VII.
—— In Politicorum libros. In *Opera omnia,* ed. A. Borgnet (Paris, 1890–99), Vol. VIII.
Albertus Pighius. Hierarchia ecclesiastica, Lib. v. In *Bibliotheca maxima pontificia,* ed. J. T. Roccaberti (Rome, 1698–99), Vol. II.
Alexander of Hales. Summa universae theologiae. Quaracchi, 1924–30.
Alexander of St. Elpidius. Tractatus de ecclesiastica potestate. In *Bibliotheca maxima pontificia,* ed. J. T. Roccaberti (Rome, 1698–99), Vol. II.
Alvarus Pelagius. De planctu ecclesiae. In *Bibliotheca maxima pontificia,* ed. J. T. Roccaberti (Rome, 1698–99), Vol. III.
Antequam essent clerici. In *Histoire du différend d'entre le pape Boniface VIII et Philippe le Bel,* "Preuves," ed. P. Dupuy (Paris, 1655), pp. 21–23.
Aristotle. Opera. Ed. I. Bekker. Berlin, 1831–70.
Augustine, St. De civitate Dei. Ed. B. Dombart. Leipzig, 1877.
—— De libero arbitrio. In J. P. Migne, ed., *Patrologia Latina,* Vol. XXXII.
Augustinus Triumphus. Summa de ecclesiastica potestate. Augsburg, 1473.
—— Tractatus brevis de duplici potestate prelatorum et laicorum. In R. Scholz, *Die Publizistik zur Zeit Philipps des Schönen und Bonifaz' VIII* (Stuttgart, 1903), pp. 486–501.
Averroes. Paraphrasis in libros de Republica Platonis speculativos. In *Aristotelis opera* (Venice, 1552–60), Vol. III.
—— Traité décisif sur l'accord de la religion et de la philosophie. Trans. L. Gauthier. Algiers, 1942.
Bodin, Jean. De republica libri sex. Frankfort, 1641.

[1] Only sources cited in more than one section of this study are listed here.

Boethius of Dacia. De summo bono sive De vita philosophie. In M. Grabmann, *Mittelalterliches Geistesleben* (Munich, 1936), II, 209–16.

Bonaventura, St. In libros Sententiarum. In *Opera omnia*. Quaracchi, 1882–1902.

Cicero. De re publica. De legibus. Ed. C. W. Keyes. London, 1928.

Dante Alighieri. De monarchia. In E. Moore, ed., *Le opere di Dante Alighieri* (Oxford, 1924), pp. 339–76.

Disputatio inter militem et clericum. In *Monarchia s. Romani imperii,* ed. M. Goldast (Frankfort, 1611–14), I, 13–18.

Duns Scotus. Opus Oxoniense. In *Opera omnia,* editio nova juxta ed. Waddingii. Paris, 1891–95.

Durand of St. Pourçain. De origine et usu jurisdictionum. In *Maxima bibliotheca veterum patrum* (Lyons, 1677), XXVI, 127–35. (Falsely attributed to Peter Bertrand.)

—— In Sententias theologicas Petri Lombardi commentariorum libri quatuor. Lyons, 1563.

Egidius Colonna of Rome. De ecclesiastica potestate. Ed. R. Scholz. Weimar, 1929.

—— De regimine principum. Venice, 1498.

—— De renuntiatione papae. In *Bibliotheca maxima pontificia,* ed. J. T. Roccaberti (Rome, 1698–99), Vol. II.

Engelbert of Admont. Liber de ortu, progressu, et fine Romani imperii. In *Maxima bibliotheca veterum patrum* (Lyons, 1677), Vol. XXV, pp. 363–78.

Francis of Mayron. Tractatus de principatu temporali. Quaestio de subjectione. Tractatus de principatu regni Siciliae. Ed. P. de Lapparent, in *Archives d'histoire doctrinale et littéraire du moyen âge,* XV–XVII (1940–42), 58–116.

Godfrey of Fontaines. Quodlibeta. In *Les Philosophes belges* (Louvain, 1904–), Vols. II–V.

Gregory of Catino. Orthodoxa defensio imperialis. In *Monumenta Germaniae historica, Libelli de lite,* II, 534–42.

Guido Vernani. De reprobatione Monarchiae compositae a Dante. Ed. T. Käppeli, in *Quellen und Forschungen aus italienischen Archiven und Bibliotheken herausg. vom Deutschen Inst. in Rom,* XXVII (1937–38), 123–46.

Henry of Cremona. De potestate papae. In R. Scholz, *Die Publizistik zur Zeit Philipps des Schönen und Bonifaz' VIII* (Stuttgart, 1903), pp. 459–71.

Hobbes, Thomas. Leviathan. "Everyman's Library." London, 1934.

Hooker, Richard. Of the Laws of Ecclesiastical Polity. In *Works,* ed. I. Walton, 2 vols. Oxford, 1875.

Hugh of St. Victor. De sacramentis. In J. P. Migne, ed., *Patrologia Latina,* Vol. CLXXVI.

Irnerius (?). Quaestiones de juris subtilitatibus. De aequitate. Ed. H. Fitting. Halle and Wittenberg, 1894.

Isidore of Seville. Etymologiae. In J. P. Migne, ed., *Patrologia Latina,* Vol. LXXXII.

James of Viterbo. De regimine Christiano. Ed. H. X. Arquillière. Paris, 1926.

John of Jandun. Quaestiones in duodecim libros Metaphysicae. Venice, 1525.

—— Super libros Aristotelis de Anima subtilissimae quaestiones. Venice, 1519.

—— Tractatus de laudibus Parisius. Ed. Le Roux de Lincy and L. M. Tisserand, in *Paris et ses historiens aux 14e et 15e siècles* (Paris, 1867), pp. 32–78.

John of Paris. De potestate regia et papali. In *Monarchia,* ed. M. Goldast (Frankfort, 1611–14), II, 108–47.

John of Salisbury. Policraticus sive De nugis curialium et vestigiis philosophorum. Ed. C. C. I. Webb. Oxford, 1909.

Konrad of Megenberg. De translatione Romani imperii. In R. Scholz, *Unbekannte kirchenpolitische Streitschriften aus der Zeit Ludwigs des Bayern, 1327–1354,* (Rome, 1911–14), II, 249–345.

Landulphus of Colonna. De translatione imperii. In *Monarchia s. Romani imperii,* ed. M. Goldast (Frankfort, 1611–14), II, 88–95.

Locke, John. Second Treatise on Civil Government. London, 1936.

Machiavelli, Niccolò. Il principe. Discorsi sopra la prima deca di Tito Livio. Florence, 1946.

Moneta of Cremona. Adversus Catharos et Valdenses. Ed. T. A. Ricchinius. Rome, 1743.

Nicholas of Cusa. De concordantia catholica. In S. Schard, ed., *De jurisdictione, auctoritate, et praeeminentia imperiali* (Basel, 1566), pp. 465 ff.

Oculus pastoralis. In L. A. Muratori, *Antiquitates Italicae medii aevi* (Arezzo, 1776), Vol. IX, cols. 791–856.

Quaestio de potestate papae ("Rex pacificus"). In *Histoire du différend d'entre le pape Boniface VIII et Philippe le Bel,* ed. P. Dupuy (Paris, 1655), pp. 663–83.

Quaestio in utramque partem. In *Monarchia s. Romani imperii,* ed. M. Goldast (Frankfort, 1611–14), II, 95–107.

Peter of Abano. Conciliator differentiarum philosophorum et medicorum. Venice, 1565.

Peter of Auvergne. In Politicorum Aristotelis libros commentarium. In *Thomae Aquinatis opera omnia,* ed. S. E. Fretté (Paris, 1875), XXVI, 226–513.

Pierre Dubois. De recuperatione terre sancte. Ed. Ch. V. Langlois. Paris, 1891.

—— Summaria brevis et compendiosa doctrina felicis expedicionis et abbreviacionis guerrarum ac litium regni Francorum. Ed. H. Kämpf. Leipzig and Berlin, 1936.

Plato. Republic. 2 vols. Ed. P. Shorey. London, 1930–35.

Ptolemy of Lucca. Determinatio compendiosa de iurisdictione imperii. Ed. M. Krammer. Hanover and Leipzig, 1909.

—— De regimine principum. Ed. J. Mathis. Turin, 1924. (Completion of Thomas Aquinas' work of same name.)

Remigio de' Girolami. Tractatus de bono communi. Extracts ed. R. Egenter in *Scholastik,* IX (1934), 79–92.

Rex pacificus. *See* Quaestio de potestate papae.

Rousseau, Jean Jacques. Du contrat social. Ed. C. E. Vaughan. Manchester, 1947.

Siger of Brabant. Quaestiones de anima intellectiva. In P. Mandonnet, *Siger de Brabant et l'averroïsme latin au XIIIe siècle,* 2d ed. (Louvain, 1911), Vol. II.

Siger of Brabant. Quaestiones morales. Ed. F. Stegmüller, in *Recherches de théologie ancienne et médiévale,* III (1931), 172–77.

Thomas Aquinas. De regimine principum. Ed. J. Mathis. Turin, 1924.

—— In decem libros Ethicorum Aristotelis ad Nicomachum expositio. Ed. A. M. Pirotta. Turin, 1934.

—— In libros Sententiarum. In *Opera Omnia,* ed. S. E. Fretté. Paris, 1874–89.

—— In Politicorum Aristotelis libros commentarium. In *Opera omnia,* ed. S. E. Fretté (Paris, 1874–89), XXVI, 89–226.

—— Summa contra Gentiles. Turin, 1938.

—— Summa theologica. Turin, 1938.

Tractatus Eboracenses. In *Monumenta Germaniae historica, Libelli de lite,* III, 645–87.

William Amidani of Cremona. Reprobatio errorum. In R. Scholz, *Unbekannte kirchenpolitische Streitschriften aus der Zeit Ludwigs des Bayern, 1327–1354* (Rome, 1911–14), II, 16–28.

William Durand, Jr. De modo generalis concilii celebrandi. In *Tractatus universi juris* (Venice, 1584), Vol. XIII, Part 2, fols. 154–82.

William of Moerbeke. Translations of Aristotle. *See* Thomas Aquinas *In decem libros Ethicorum* and *In Politicorum Aristotelis libros.* Also consulted for the translation of the *Politics:* Aristotelis Politicorum libri octo cum vetusta translatione Guilelmi de Moerbeke. Ed. F. Susemihl. Leipzig, 1872.

William of Ockham. Breviloquium de potestate papae. Ed. L. Baudry. Paris, 1937.

—— Dialogus. In *Monarchia s. Romani imperii,* ed. M. Goldast (Frankfort, 1611–14), II, 398–976.

—— Octo quaestiones de potestate papae. In *Guillelmi de Ockham opera politica,* ed. J. G. Sikes, I (Manchester, 1940), 13–221.

B. Institutional Documents

Corpus juris canonici. Ed. E. Friedberg. Leipzig, 1879–81.

Corpus juris civilis. Ed. P. Kruger *et al.* Berlin, 1908.

Costituto del comune di Siena dell' anno 1262. Ed. L. Zdekauer. Milan, 1897.

Liber regiminum Paduae. Ed. A. Bonardi, in *Miscellanea di storia Veneta,* 2d series, Vol. VI.

Monumenti della Università di Padova, 1222–1318. Ed. A. Gloria, in *Memorie del R. istituto veneto di scienze, lettere, ed arti* (Venice, 1882), Vol. XXII.

Roberti, M. Le corporazioni padovane d'arti e mestieri; studio storico-giuridico con documenti e statuti inediti. In *Memorie del R. istituto veneto di scienze, lettere, ed arti* (Venice, 1902), Vol. XXVI, No. 8.

Statut des neuf gouverneurs et défenseurs de la commune de Sienne (1310). Ed. J. Luchaire. Paris, 1901.

Statuti del comune di Padova dal secolo XII all' anno 1285. Ed. A. Gloria. Padua, 1873.

3. STUDIES OF MARSILIUS [1]

Allen, J. W. "Marsilio of Padua and Mediaeval Secularism." In *The Social and Political Ideas of Some Great Mediaeval Thinkers,* ed. F. J. C. Hearnshaw (London, 1923), pp. 167–91.

Atger, F. Essai sur l'histoire des doctrines du Contrat social. Nîmes, 1906. Pp. 70–82.

Battaglia, F. "Marsilio da Padova e il *Defensor Pacis," Rivista internazionale di filosofia del diritto,* IV (1924), 398 ff.

—— Marsilio da Padova e la filosofia politica del medio evo. Florence, 1928.

—— Review of G. de Lagarde, *Marsile de Padoue, Rivista di storia del diritto italiano* VIII (1935), 151–68.

—— "Sul *Defensor pacis* di Marsilio da Padova," *Nuovi studi di diritto, economia e politica,* II (1929), 128–46.

Baudrillart, A. "Des idées qu'on se faisait au XIVe siècle sur le droit d'intervention du souverain pontife en matière politique," *Revue d'histoire et de littérature religieuses,* III (1898), 193–224, 309–38.

Baumer, F. L. "Thomas Starkey and Marsilius of Padua," *Politica,* II (1936), 188–205.

Bigongiari, D. "Notes on the Text of the *Defensor Pacis," Speculum,* VII (1932), 36–49.

Bornhak, O. Staatskirchliche Anschauungen und Handlungen am Hofe Kaiser Ludwigs des Bayern. Weimar, 1933.

Brampton, C. K. "Marsiglio of Padua, Life," *English Historical Review,* XXXVII (1922), 501 ff.

Capograssi, A. "Intorno a Marsilio da Padova," *Rivista internazionale di filosofia del diritto,* X (1930), 579–90.

Cappa-Legora, A. La politica di Dante e di Marsilio da Padova. Rome and Turin, 1906.

Carlyle, R. W. and A. J. A History of Mediaeval Political Theory in the West. Vol. VI (Edinburgh, 1936), pp. 9–12, 40–44.

Castellotti, G. de. "La dottrina dello stato in Marsilio da Padova." In *Saggi di etica e di diritto* (Ascoli Piceno, 1903), II, 1–38.

Checchini, A., and Bobbio, N., eds. Marsilio da Padova: Studi raccolti nel VI centenario della morte. *Pubblicazioni della facolta di giurisprudenza della R. università di Padova* (Padua, 1942), Vol. III.

Dempf, A. Sacrum imperium. Munich and Berlin, 1929. Pp. 430–40.

Emerton, E. The *Defensor Pacis* of Marsiglio of Padua. Cambridge, Mass., 1920.

Entrèves, A. P. d'. "La fortuna di Marsilio da Padova in Inghilterra," *Giornale degli economisti e annali di economia,* n.s., II (1940), 135–52.

—— The Medieval Contribution to Political Thought. Oxford, 1939. Chs. 3, 4; pp. 44–87.

[1] A list of over 150 titles is presented in the excellent Bibliography appended to Battaglia, *Marsilio.* Many of these titles, however, contain merely incidental references to Marsilius of one page or less. The present list comprises only those studies in which there is some substantial discussion of Marsilius' work, and adds those which have been published since 1928.

Entrèves, A. P. d'. "Rileggendo il *Defensor Pacis*," *Rivista storica italiana*, LI (1934), 1–37.

Franck, A. Réformateurs et publicistes de l'Europe: moyen âge, renaissance. Paris, 1864. Pp. 135–51.

Friedberg, E. Die mittelalterlichen Lehren über das Verhältnis von Staat und Kirche. Leipzig, 1874.

Geissel, B. Die kirchenpolitische Lehre des Marsilius von Padua. Diss. Cologne, 1926.

Gentile, G. "La filosofia," in *Storia dei generi letterarii italiani*, ed. A. Albertazzi et al. (Milan, n.d.), Fasc. 41, pp. 150–63.

Gewirth, A. "John of Jandun and the *Defensor Pacis*," *Speculum*, XXIII (1948), 267–72.

Grabmann, M. "Studien über den Einfluss der aristotelischen Philosophie auf die mittelalterlichen Theorien über das Verhältnis von Kirche und Staat," *Sitzungsberichte der bayerischen Akademie der Wissenschaften*, Phil.-hist. Abt. (1934), Heft 2, pp. 41–60.

Guggenheim, M. "Marsilius von Padua und die Staatslehre des Aristoteles," *Historische Vierteljahrschrift*, VII (1904), 343–62.

Haller, J. "Zur Lebensgeschichte des Marsilius von Padua," *Zeitschrift für Kirchengeschichte*, XLVIII (1929), 166–99.

Hull, R. Medieval Theories of the Papacy. London, 1934. Pp. 73–104.

Huraut, A. Marsile de Padoue. Diss. Paris, 1892.

Jourdan, L. Etude sur Marsile de Padoue. Diss. Montauban, 1892.

Kates, P. The Two Swords; a Study of the Union of Church and State. Washington, D.C., 1928.

Labanca, B. "Marsilio da Padova e Martino Lutero," *Nuova antologia*, 2d series, XLI (1883), 210–27.

—— Marsilio da Padova, riformatore politico e religioso del secolo XIV. Padua, 1882.

Lagarde, G. de. "Marsile de Padoue et Guillaume de Nogaret," *Revue historique de droit français et étranger*, 4th series, XI (1932), 463–90.

—— "Marsile de Padoue et Guillaume d' Ockham," *Revue des sciences religieuses*, XVII (1937), 168–85, 428–54.

—— Marsile de Padoue ou le premier théoricien de l'état laïque. Saint-Paul-Trois-Châteaux, 1934.

—— "Une Adaptation de la politique d'Aristote au XIVe siècle," *Revue historique de droit français et étranger*, 4th series, XI (1932), 227–69.

Landry, B. L'Idée de Chrétienté chez les scolastiques du XIIIe siècle. Paris, 1929. Pp. 159–78.

Littlejohn, J. M. The Political Theory of the Schoolmen and Grotius, N.p., 1895. Pp. 228–36.

Martin, V. "Les Idées répandues par Marsile de Padoue et Occam touchant l'église," *Revue des sciences religieuses*, XVII (1937), 261–89.

McIlwain, C. H. The Growth of Political Thought in the West. New York, 1932. Pp. 297–313.

Meyer, P. E. Etude sur Marsile de Padoue. Strasbourg, 1870.

Miglio, G. "Questioni Marsiliane," *Rivista di filosofia neo-scolastica*, XXXVIII (1946), 26–37.

Müller, K. Der Kampf Ludwigs des Baiern mit der römischen Kurie. Tübingen, 1879–80. Vol. I, pp. 161 ff.; Vol. II, pp. 160 ff.

Nimis, A. Marsilius' von Padua republikanische Staatslehre. Mannheim, 1897.

Otto, H. "Marsilius von Padua und der *Defensor Pacis*," *Historisches Jahrbuch*, XLV (1925), 189–218.

Piovano, G. "Il *Defensor Pacis* di Marsilio Patavino," *Scuola cattolica*, 5th series, XXII (1922), 161–78, 342–59.

Poole, R. L. Illustrations of the History of Mediaeval Thought. 2d ed., revised. London, 1920. Pp. 230–45.

Preger, W. Die kirchenpolitische Kampf unter Ludwig dem Bayern und sein Einfluss auf die öffentliche Meinung in Deutschland. Munich, 1877.

Previté-Orton, C. W. "Marsiglio of Padua, Doctrines," *English Historical Review*, XXXVIII (1923), 1–21.

—— "Marsilius of Padua," *Proceedings of the British Academy*, XXI (1935), 137–83.

—— "The Authors Cited in the *Defensor Pacis*," in *Essays in History Presented to R. L. Poole* (Oxford, 1927), pp. 407 ff.

Riezler, S. Die literarischen Widersacher der Päpste zur Zeit Ludwigs des Baiern. Leipzig, 1874.

Rivière, J. "Marsile de Padoue," *Dictionnaire de théologie catholique*, Vol. X, cols. 153–77.

Ruffini-Avondo, E. "Il *Defensor Pacis* di Marsilio da Padova," *Rivista storica italiana*, XLI (1924), 113–66.

Sabine, G. H. A History of Political Theory. New York, 1937. Pp. 287–304.

Scaduto, F. Stato e chiesa negli scritti politici dalla fine della Lotta per le Investiture sino alla morte di Ludovico il Bavaro. Florence, 1882. Pp. 112 ff.

Schneider-Windmüller, V. Staat und Kirche im *Defensor Pacis* des Marsilius von Padua. Diss. Bonn, 1934.

Scholz, R. "Marsilius von Padua und die Genesis des modernen Staatsbewusstseins," *Historische Zeitschrift*, CLVI (1936), 88–103.

—— "Marsilius von Padua und die Idee der Demokratie," *Zeitschrift für Politik*, I (1907), 61–94.

—— "Zur Datierung und Uberlieferung des *Defensor Pacis* von Marsilius von Padua," *Neues Archiv der Gesellschaft für ältere deutsche Geschichtskunde*, XLVI (1927), 490 ff.

Schreiber, W. Die politischen und religiösen Doktrinen unter Ludwig dem Baiern. Landshut, 1858. Pp. 24–50.

Sikes, J. G. "A Possible Marsilian Source in Ockham," *English Historical Review*, XLI (1936), 496–504.

Stieglitz, L. Die Staatslehre des Marsilius von Padua. Leipzig, 1914.

Sullivan, J. "The Manuscripts and Date of Marsiglio of Padua's *Defensor Pacis*," *English Historical Review*, XX (1905), 293–307.

—— "Marsiglio of Padua and William of Ockham," *American Historical Review*, II (1896/97), 409–26, 593–610.

Tooley, M. J. "The Authorship of the *Defensor Pacis*," *Transactions of the Royal Historical Society*, 4th series, IX (1926), 85–106.

Vadala-Papale, G. "Le leggi nella dottrina di Dante Alighieri e di Marsilio da Padova," in *Studi giuridici a F. Schupfer* (Turin, 1898), II, 41 ff.

Valois, N. "Jean de Jandun et Marsile de Padoue, auteurs du *Defensor Pacis,*" *Histoire littéraire de la France,* XXXIII (1906), 528–623.

Vento, S. La filosofia politica di Dante nel *De Monarchia* studiata in se stessa e in relazione alla pubblicistica medievale da San Tommaso a Marsilio da Padova. Turin, 1921.

Villari, P. "Marsilio da Padova e il *Defensor Pacis,*" *Nuova antologia,* 5th series, CLXIV (1913), 369–79.

INDEX